Lecture Notes in Computer Science 3261

Commenced Publication in 1973
Founding and Former Series Editors:
Gerhard Goos, Juris Hartmanis, and Jan van Leeuwen

Tatyana Yakhno (Ed.)

Advances in Information Systems

Third International Conference, ADVIS 2004
Izmir, Turkey, October 20-22, 2004
Proceedings

 Springer

Volume Editor

Tatyana Yakhno
Dokuz Eylul University
Computer Engineering Department
Bornova, 35100 Izmir, Turkey
E-mail: yakhno@cs.deu.edu.tr

Library of Congress Control Number: 2004113292

CR Subject Classification (1998): H.2, H.3, H.4, I.2, C.2, H.5

ISSN 0302-9743
ISBN 3-540-23478-0 Springer Berlin Heidelberg New York

Springer is a part of Springer Science+Business Media

springeronline.com

© Springer-Verlag Berlin Heidelberg 2004
Printed in Germany

Typesetting: Camera-ready by author, data conversion by Scientific Publishing Services, Chennai, India
Printed on acid-free paper   SPIN: 11333784   06/3142   5 4 3 2 1 0

Preface

This volume contains the proceedings of the 3rd International Conference on Advances in Information Systems (ADVIS) held in Izmir, Turkey, 20–22 October, 2004. This was the third conference dedicated to the memory of Prof. Esen Ozkarahan. We are very proud to continue this tradition and keep the memory of this outstanding scientist.

The third conference covered many of the topics of the second one: databases and data warehouses, information systems development and management, information retrieval, distributed and parallel data processing, and evolutionary algorithms. Besides them some of the hot topics related to information systems were included in the scope of this conference, such as data mining and knowledge discovery, Web information systems development, information privacy and security, multimedia information systems, and network management.

This year we received 203 submissions from which the Program Committee selected 61 papers for presentation at the conference.

The success of the conference was dependent upon the hard work of a large number of people. We gratefully acknowledge the contribution of the members of the Program Committee who did their best to review all submitted papers. We also thank all the specialists who helped us in reviewing the papers.

We appreciated the constant support and help from the Rector of Dokuz Eylul University, Prof. Dr. Emin Alici.

I would like to express my personal gratitude to Natalya Cheremnykh and Olga Drobyshevich for their help in producing the camera-ready version of these proceedings.

August 2004   Tatyana Yakhno

Honorary Chair

Irem Ozkarahan, Dokuz Eylul University, Turkey

Program Committee Chair

Tatyana Yakhno, Dokuz Eylul University, Turkey

Program Committee

Sibel Adali, USA
Adil Alpkocak, Turkey
Farhad Arbab, Netherlands
Frederic Benhamou, France
Cem Bozsahin, Turkey
Fazli Can, USA
Yalcin Cebi, Turkey
Paolo Ciaccia, Italy
Cihan Dagli, USA
Mehmet E. Dalkilic, Turkey
Dursun Delen, USA
Oguz Dikenelli, Turkey
Yakov Fet, Russia
Victor Ganzha, Germany
Fabio Grandi, Italy
Ugur Gudukbay, Turkey
Cuneyt Guzelis, Turkey

Malcolm Heywood, Canada
Alp Kut, Turkey
Victor Malyshkin, Russia
Eric Monfroy, France
Erich Neuhold, Germany
Selmin Nurcan, France
Irem Ozkarahan, Turkey
Gultekin Ozsoyoglu, USA
Marcin Paprzycki, USA
Torben Bach Pedersen, Denmark
Dana Petcu, Romania
Ilias Petronias, UK
Malcolm Rigg, UK
Ozgur Ulusoy, Turkey
Krzysztof Wecel, Poland
Adnan Yazici, Turkey
Nur Zincir-Heywood, Canada

Conference Secretary

Emine Ekin, Turkey

Local Organizing Committee

Sedat Yilmaz
Serife Sungun
Berna Simsek

Tolga Berber
Mustafa Kasap
Gokhan Dalkilic

Sponsors

Support from the following institutions is gratefully acknowledged:

- Scientific and Technical Research Council of Turkey (TUBITAK)
- Dokuz Eylul University President's Office, Izmir, Turkey
- Microsoft

Additional Referees

Ismail Sengör Altingövde
Pascal André
Christian Attiogbé
Ceyhun Araz
Bilge Bilgen
Lucas Bordeaux
Sebastian Brand
Ali Cakmak
Ben Carterette
Dave Clarke
David Costa
Valerie Cross
Martine Ceberio
Marc Christie
Panagiotis Chountas
Gokhan Dalkilic
Nikolay Diakov
Allan G. Jost
Ozgur Eski
Kayhan Erciyes
Riza Cenk Erdur

Marc Gelgon
Gyozo Gidofalvi
Laurent Granvilliers
Ernst W. Grundke
Juan Guillen-Scholten
Nazlı İkizler
Joost Jacob
Mustafa Kasap
Ozcan Kilincci
Mustafa Kirac
Predrag Knezevic
Patrick Lehti
Valentina Markova
Pavel Mankevich
José Martinez
Pinar Mizrak
Efendi Nasibov
Rabia Nuray
Brice Pajot
Evgueni Petrov
Christophe Ringeissen

Stefano Rizzi
Gwen Salaün
Frédéric Saubion
Albrecht Schmidt
Onur Tolga Sehitoglu
Anton Selikhov
Hasan Selim
Malik Kemal Sis
Martin Steinebach
Bent Thomsen
Yasemin Topaloglu
Kristian Torp
Leon van der Torre
Irina Virbitskaite
Osman Unalir
Sedat Yilmaz
Meltem Turhan Yondem
Yury Zagorulko
Pedrito Maynard-Zhang
Peter Zoeteweij

Table of Contents

Databases and Data Warehouses

Data Mining and Knowledge Discovery

Web Information Systems Development

Information Systems Development and Management

Information Retrieval

Parallel and Distributed Data Processing

Multimedia Information Systems

Information Privacy and Security

Evolutionary and Knowledge-Based Systems

Software Engineering and Business Process Models

Network Management

Temporality in Databases

Invited Talk

Abdullah Uz Tansel

Department of Computer Engineering,
Bilkent University,
Ankara, Turkey

Temporality, or the time dimension is an essential aspect of the reality databases attempt to model and keep data about. However, in many database applications temporal data is treated in a rather ad hoc manner in spite of the fact that temporality should be an integral part of any data model. In this presentation we will address issues peculiar to temporal data and explore how we can add a temporal dimension to databases. We will specifically focus our attention on the relational data model and the object relational systems for managing temporal data since these systems are widely available and they are also widely used [1].

A database maintains data about an enterprise and its activities. It addresses organizational information requirements by maintaining accurate, complete, and consistent data from which information is extracted for various applications. Conventional databases are designed to capture the most recent data since they are built to process the transactions efficiently and effectively. As new data values become available through organizational transactions the existing data values are removed from the database and they are discarded or archived. Such databases capture a snapshot of reality, mostly the current snapshot of the reality. Although conventional databases serve many applications well, they are insufficient for those in which past and/or future data are also required. Such a need is very obvious in datawarehouses and OLAP applications for decision support. Thus there is an obvious need for a database that fully supports the storage and querying of data that varies over time. In the broadest sense, a database that maintains past, present, and future data is called a *temporal database*.

There are two common views of time, continuous and discrete time though the time is continuous in nature. Continuous time is considered to be isomorphic to real numbers whereas discrete time is considered to be isomorphic to natural numbers or integers. Both views assume that time is linearly ordered; for the two different time points t1 and t2, either t1 is before t2 or t2 is before t1. Discrete interpretation of time has commonly been adopted by the research community in temporal databases because of its simplicity and relative ease of implementation. Hence, we will interpret time as a set of equally spaced and ordered time points and denote it by T where $T = 0, 1, 2, ...now...$. The symbol 0 is the relative beginning, and *now* is a special variable to represent current time. The value of *now* advances as the clock ticks. Any point beyond *now* is future time. We do not specify any time units and time granularities for the sake of simplicity. Note that between two consecutive time points there is a time

T. Yakhno (Ed.): ADVIS 2004, LNCS 3261, pp. 1–3, 2004.

duration that is invisible unless a smaller time granularity is used. An interval or a time period is any consecutive set of time points and is designated by its boundary points. The closed interval [b, e] contains all the time points including b and e, whereas the half-open interval [b, e) does not include e. Any subset of T is called a *temporalelement*[1], that can also be considered as a disjoint union of time intervals. Any interval or temporal element that includes the special variable *now* expands as the value of *now* advances. Time points, intervals, and temporal elements are essential constructs for modeling and querying temporal data.

Snodgrass developed taxonomy of time in databases [2]. *Valid time* denotes the time when a fact becomes effective in reality. *Transaction time*, on the other hand, refers to the time when a new value is posted to the database. These two times are orthogonal and can be supported separately, or both can be supported in concert. The third variety, user-defined time, is an un-interpreted time domain managed by the user. User-defined time is the easiest to support and many conventional database management systems, as well as the SQL2 standard, include such support.

These kinds of time induce different types of databases. A traditional database supporting neither valid nor transaction time is termed a *snapshot database*. A *valid-time database* contains the entire history of the enterprise, as best known now. A *transaction-time database* supports transaction time and hence allows rolling back the database to a previous state. This database records all errors and provides a complete audit trail. As such, it is append-only. A *bitemporal database* records both valid time and transaction time and combines the features of the previous two types. It allows retroactive as well as post active changes; the complete history of these changes and the original values they replaced are all available.

We believe that any temporal database should meet the following fundamental requirements [4]. Let DB_t denote the database state at time t:

1. The data model should be capable of modeling and querying the database at any instance of time, i.e., D_t. The data model should at least provide the modeling and querying power of a 1NF relational data model. Note that when t is *now*, D_t corresponds to traditional database.
2. The data model should be capable of modeling and querying the database at two different time points, i.e., D_{t1} and D_{t2} where $t1 \neq t2$. This should be the case for the time intervals and temporal sets as well.
3. The data model should allow different periods of existence in attributes within a tuple, i.e., non-homogenous (heterogeneous) tuples should be allowed.
4. The data model should handle multi-valued attributes at any time point, i.e., in D_t.
5. A temporal query language should have the capability to return the same type of objects it operates on.
6. A temporal query language should have the capability to regroup the temporal data according to a different temporal attribute.

7. The data model should be capable of expressing set-theoretic operations, as well as set comparison tests, on the timestamps, be it time points, time intervals, or temporal elements.

We will discuss fundamental issues and their implications with respect to the desired features of temporal databases listed above [3, 5, 6]. These issues include temporal data modeling, adding times stamps to tuples or attributes, gluing or not gluing time to values (tuples), temporal integrity constraints, designing temporal relational databases, operations and expressive power of temporal query languages, and adding temporal support to SQL3. We expect the presentation will be beneficial to the researchers as well as the practitioners.

References

1. S.K. Gadia, *A homogeneous relational model and query languages for temporal databases*, ACM Transactions on Database Systems, 13 (4), pp. 418-448, 1988.
2. R. Snodgrass, *The temporal query language TQUEL"*, *ACM Transactions on Database Systems* 12 (2), pp. 247 - 298, 1987.
3. A.U. Tansel, *Adding time dimension to relational model and extending relational algebra*, Information Systems 11 (4), pp. 343 - 355, 1986.
4. A.U. Tansel and E. Tin, *Expressive power of temporal relational query languages*, IEEE Transactions on Knowledge and Database Engineering, 9 (1), pp. 120 - 134, 1997.
5. A. U. Tansel, *Temporal Relational Data Model*, IEEE Transactions on Knowledge and Database Engineering, Vol. 9, No. 3, May 1997, pp. 464 - 479.
6. A. U. Tansel, *On Handling Time-Varying Data in the Relational Data Model*, Journal of Information and Software Technology, Vol. 46, No. 2, February 2004, pp. 119 - 126.

On Uncertainty and Data-Warehouse Design

Panagiotis Chountas[1], Ilias Petrounias[2], Christos Vasilakis[1], Andy Tseng[2],
Elia El-Darzi[1], Krassimir T. Atanassov[3], and Vassilis Kodogiannis[1]

[1] Health Care Computing Group, School of Computer Science, University of Westminster
Watford Road, Northwick Park, London, HA1 3TP, UK
[2] Department of Computation, UMIST PO Box 88, Manchester M60 1QD, UK
[3] CLBME – Bulgarian Academy of Sciences, Bl. 105, Sofia-1113, Bulgaria
chountp@wmin.ac.uk

Abstract. In this paper we informally and formally defined what we mean by uncertain- ignorant information in relational databases and data warehouses. We classify proposed extensions to the relational data model that can represent and retrieve incomplete information. There are many different kinds of temporal ignorant information including information that is fuzzy, imprecise, indeterminate, indefinite, missing, partial, possible, probabilistic, unknown, uncertain, or vague. We will explore each variety of temporal ignorant information in detail with reference to database and data-warehouse design.

1   Introduction

Data warehouse is an amalgamated view on the data within an enterprise and a first step in integrating enterprise systems. Typically time is one of the dimensions we find in data warehouses allowing comparisons of different periods. The instances of dimensions, however, change over time, organisations unite and separate, and organisational structures emerge and vanish, or evolve. In current data warehouse architectures these changes cannot be represented adequately since all dimensions are considered as orthogonal, putting restrictions on the validity of queries defined over several eras. In this paper we propose an architecture for temporal data warehouse systems, which allows the accommodation of the temporal dimension of data belonged to evolving hierarchical structures. This paper concentrates on the temporal aspects of data warehouses (DWH) and their effects on On-Line Analytical Processing OLAP environments. We suggest a temporal model for multidimensional DWH-OLAP, motivated by the observation that ignoring temporal issues leads to questionable expressive power and query semantics in many real life scenarios. Our suggested model will allow the expression of temporal OLAP queries in an elegant and intuitive fashion. We introduce multidimensional modelling for demonstrating the conventional OLAP architecture, and introduce the term temporal OLAP, TOLAP. A TOLAP environment is an extended OLAP environment that is able to handle temporal data and semantics.

The rest of the paper is organised as follows: in section two we define the impact of time dimension in the design of data repositories i.e. warehouses or relational

T. Yakhno (Ed.): ADVIS 2004, LNCS 3261, pp. 4–13, 2004.
© Springer-Verlag Berlin Heidelberg 2004

databases. In section three we determine temporal ignorance with respect to time dimension. In section four the impact of temporal ignorance in the architecture of a relational database is discussed. In section five the representation of ignorant temporal data as part of a TOLAP environment is defined, with the emphasis in delivering a model for defining OLAP operators over changing hierarchies. Section six delivers a query model for defining evolving hierarchies with either implicit or explicit temporal semantics, based on similarity empowerment. Finally, we conclude and provide an outlook on future research.

2   Time and Data Repositories

Temporal data repositories should describe the evolving history of an enterprise. In the case of patient record data, it is frequently very important to enable *the monitoring* of data changes, i.e. to retain a complete history of past states. Correcting errors could be possible by posting compensating transactions with different timestamps to the data warehouse. In health informatics applications, keeping track of the diagnosis on which decisions where made may guard against wrongful, misconduct claims. When considering temporal DWH's we need to understand how time is mirrored in a temporal database and how this relates to the structure of the data. Temporal DWH's usually have to accommodate the following type of data;

Regular Data. Once a record is added to a database, it is never physically deleted, nor is its content ever modified. Rather, new records are always added to reflect transactions on data. Regular data thus offers a complete history of the changes occurred in the data. Temporal DWH's contain regular data.

Snapshot Data. A data snapshot is a stable view of data, as it exists at some point in time. It is a special kind of regular data. Snapshots usually represent the data at some time in the past, and a series of snapshots can provide a view of the history of an enterprise.

The focus of existing research [2] in temporal data warehouses is on storing "regular" data with the aid of time stamped status and event records. The intuition behind this stream of research is that a query needs to access current data. In a single timestamp scheme, the only way to identify current records is to find the latest timestamp of the regular set, which is an inefficient process. It has been proposed [1] time to be treated as a dimension and also to be considered as an intrinsic element of the fact table, see Fig.1.

Eventually what is proposed is an extension of the bi-temporal database model [4], with the inclusion of the load timestamp. The load timestamp is basically addressing the need of knowing when a piece of information was integrated in the data warehouse, while the revelation time is indicating when a piece of information was recorded as part of a particular source.

This paper is focused on the impact of the valid time dimension in multidimensional analysis. More specifically we advocate that:

- The assortment of a particular hierarchy may be variable through the valid time dimension. For example considering the disease assortment, a new disease may appear, or a disease may move from one group to another.

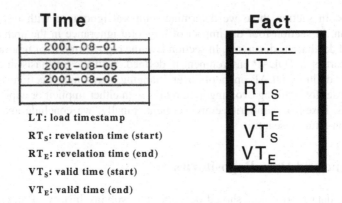

Fig. 1. Temporal fact table

- It may be possible to know for how long a piece of information is valid i.e. the length of the time interval is known, though the starting or the ending point may not be defined with precision. To put it differently the time dimension itself may be evolving.

In the next section the modeling concept of time as a geometric metaphor is defined. We also determine the different types of temporal information that can be encoded with the aid of time dimension.

3   The Dimension of Time

Time has a standard geometric metaphor. In this metaphor, time itself is a line; a point on the time-line is called a *time point*; and the time between two *time points* is known as a *time interval*.

Time Point: Our model of time does not mandate a specific time point size or (*minimum*) *granularity*; a time point may be of any duration. Time points are consecutively labeled with the integers in the set $T = \{0,...,N\}$ where N is the number of different values that a timestamp can represent. The set of time points is linearly ordered.

Time Line: is the geometric metaphor of the time. Conceptually, time is linear and consists of a set of time points. The time line is represented with the aid of the linear equation:

$$KX + B: (K, B, X) \in N \wedge C \leq B \leq C', (C, C') \in N \qquad (1)$$

Time Interval: A time interval is an instantiation of a time line and is bounded between two-time points of a specific duration. For example, assume the following triple values for the variables (K, B, X) respectively $(K=0, X=0, 3 \leq B \leq 5)$.

Time Hierarchy-Calendar: A *linear hierarchy of time units*, denoted H_r, is a finite collection of distinct time units with a linear order $|\subseteq|$ among those time units. H_r is a finite collection of distinct time units, with linear order among those units.

Conceptually, time may be extended to infinite $(\perp, \top)$ past or future.

Duration (l): is the length of a time interval. To prevent having ill-formed temporal intervals the specified length is not the distance between the n and n-1 projections over the set of time points T. The following functions define formally the starting point of a time interval $\vdash$ (t), the ending time point of a time interval $\dashv$ (t) and its length with respect to an arbitrary calendar, $|\bullet|$ (t).

$$\vdash (C, C', l) \rightarrow C \tag{2}$$

$$\dashv (C, C', l) \rightarrow C' \tag{3}$$

$$|\bullet| (C, C', l) \rightarrow l \tag{4}$$

It is now possible to extend the set of temporal intervals with the inclusion of null values {?}. To make the three functions given above work correctly we must extend them to include null values (?):

$$\vdash (C, C', l)_? \rightarrow \{C, \vee (C'-l)\} \tag{5}$$

$$\dashv (C, C', l)_? \rightarrow \{C' \vee (C + l)\} \tag{6}$$

$$|\bullet| (C, C', l)_? \rightarrow \{l \vee (C'-C)\} \tag{7}$$

The proposed time representation for the valid time dimension can be used for encoding two different types [3] of temporal information:

Definite Temporal Information: is defined over the interval $T_1=[C, C']$ when the time points C, C' are defined with precision over the time line. Using our time model definite temporal information can be utilised with the aid of equations (2), (3), (4).

Indefinite Temporal Information: is defined over the interval $T_1=[C, C']_?$, when the time points C, C' are not defined with precision over the time line but are bounded. Thus the time dimension itself is evolving. Indefinite temporal information in the context of our time reorientation can be utilised with the aid of equations (5), (6), (7).

Furthermore, the inclusion of "null" in the set of time intervals allow us to encode implicit temporal information that cannot be represented [5, 6] with the use of an explicit–strict temporal representation

We then classify firstly, temporal ignorance in databases with respect to the definitions of definite and indefinite temporal information.

4   Definition of Temporal Ignorance in Databases

The definition of ignorant is, perhaps, too concise; it is defined as "not complete". The definition of complete is of more help; complete means *entire* or *whole*. An object, then, is ignorant as opposed to an object that is entire or whole. It is very important to note that information is ignorant only with respect to more complete information (which in turn could be ignorant with respect to still other information).

We will assume that a *fact* is a *relation*. Each *fact instance (tuple)* corresponds to a *multiset* of values. A database, *D*, is a set of facts, $\{F_1,...,F_n\}$. The meaning of a database is a set of facts, where the meaning of each fact depends on the population fact instances, $\{f_1,...,f_n\}$, but in general is a multiset. Each fact in the database models everything that is known about the modelled world.

Each fact instance in the database has two potential interpretations: a *definite* interpretation and a *possible* interpretation. The definite interpretation is all the information that that fact definitely represents, while the possible interpretation is everything that the fact possibly represents.

Definition 1.1.1 The definite information in a fact instance $[f] = \{f_1,..., f_n\}$, written def_f, is

$$def_f \equiv \cap \{f_1,...,f_n\} \text{ where } \cap \text{ is set intersection}$$

Definition 1.1.2 The possible information in a fact instance $[f] = \{f_1,..., f_n\}$, written $poss_f$, is

$$poss_f \equiv \cup \{f_1,...,f_n\} - def_f \text{ where } \cup \text{ is set union}$$

Temporal ignorance-uncertainty is a kind of domain uncertainty. Temporal uncertainty models the situation where exactly one member of a set of times is the actual time, but we do not know which member. Another way to express this is simply "do not know when". In terms of relational databases this can be expressed as follows "A situation represented by *data tuple d, is in relation R at some point of time in the interval $[t_l, t_R]$*. Practically temporal uncertainty is generated due to the following cause: It is known that a situation *S*, did in fact occur once but is not known exactly when. This implies that if situation *S* occurs, between the bounds the of time interval $T_1 = [t_1...t_2]$, then situation *S* holds at some point *t*, in interval T_1.

The introduction of the causes related to temporal uncertainty, are indicating the main data representation issues. Since temporal uncertainty is a kind of domain uncertainty all representations issues related to domain uncertainty like the use of weights, to express possibilities or alternatives are still valid.

The temporal-alternative-unweighted-unrestricted school was first introduced by [9] with the proposition of a model based on three-valued logic. The temporal-alternative-unweighted-restricted school is represented from the model introduced by [13, 14] which proposes the use of constraints for representing event occurrences. His framework allows stating the facts that event *e1* occurred between 8 and 10 am, and that event *e2* occurred after 12 pm. From this, we may conclude that event *e2* occurred after *e1* and can explicitly encode in his tuples. A similar approach is followed by [10] who developed a system called LaTeR with the emphasis on query performance. The temporal-alternative school is represented by [11, 12] and the main objective is to model the situation where exactly one member of a set of times is the actual time, but we do not know which member. In addition, each member of the set of times has a weight. The weight is interpreted as the probability that the time is the actual time.

The main difference between [11] and [12] apart from the obvious difference of intervallic probabilistic weights used by [12], is that [11] philosophically adds probabilities to temporal databases on the contrary [12] is adding time to probabilistic databases. All approaches presented by the temporal alternative school are dealing with the representation of indefinite temporal information.

The temporal-possible, school was introduced by [15] and [16] later used a fuzzy logic-based approach to handle *generalized temporal events* — events that may occur multiple times. Both approaches belong to temporal-possible-weighted branch. A generalized temporal event is a single event that has multiple occurrences. For example the event "Mary's salary is high" may occur at various times as Mary's salary fluctuates to reflect promotions and demotions. The meaning of "high" is incomplete. "High" is not a crisp predicate. In [16] model all the possibilities for "high" are represented in a *generalized* event and the user selects some subset according to his or her interpretation of "high."

In the next section we distinguish the problem of temporal ignorance with respect to data-warehouse design. Then the temporal concepts that will allow the development of a temporal data warehouse as well as the formulation of TOLAP queries are defined.

5   Temporal Data and DWH-OLAP

Data warehouses (DWH) have been established as the core of decision support systems. On top of a DWH, different applications can be realised with regard to conventional reporting. On line Analytical Processing (OLAP) has reached the maturity as an interactive and explorative way of analysing DWH data. However DWH are mostly organised as snapshot databases with evolving dimensions defined over the dimension of time. Thus the number of members for a particular dimension is not certain with reference to distinct time points. Current approaches [7, 8] assume that cube facts have an implicit timestamp assigned by their time dimension. In contrast, the dimensional elements are considered as snapshots. However, this kind of treatment does not take into account the fact that hierarchical structures may change over time (Fig.2). Therefore the population of each hierarchy tree is not with precision at any time moment T. In this case, a typical requirement analysis could be to compare the new grouping with the old one. This type of uncertainty is unique and distinguishable from the common type of uncertainty defined in temporal database bibliography.

Factual data are stored in temporal fact tables. We will assume that given a set of dimensions M, a temporal fact table has a column for each dimension in M, a column for a distinguished dimension "Measure", and a column for the Time dimension. A temporal base fact table is a temporal fact table such that its levels are the bottom levels of each one of the dimensions in M (plus Time). As these bottom levels may vary during the lifespan of the data warehouse, the schema of a base fact table can change. Keeping track of the different versions of the fact tables is called, like in temporal database literature schema versioning. Note, however, that the attributes in any column of a fact table always belong to the same dimension. In temporal databases, in general, instances are represented using valid time; this is, the time when the fact being recorded became valid. A database schema holds within a time interval that can be different from the one within which this schema was valid in reality. Changes in the real world are not presented in the database until the database schema is updated.

On the contrary in the temporal data-warehouse model we are describing, things are different than above. An update to a dimension schema modifies the structure as well as the instance of the dimension. The associated rollups must correspond to the instants in which they actually hold "Fig.2." thus; we consider that temporal dimensions are represented by valid time.

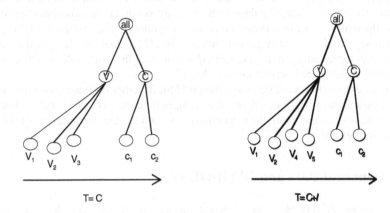

Fig. 2. Evolving groups—hierarchies

In solving this problem, we can annotate the edges of a hierarchy tree with valid time intervals. In this matrix, the parent nodes are the rows while children nodes are considered as columns; every cell takes a set of valid time intervals. This meta-information can be defined for every hierarchy tree in the data warehouse schema. Fig.3. represents the corresponding valid matrix of an arbitrary hierarchy tree for the arbitrary time interval $[C, (C+l)]$ where $\{C, (C+l)\} \in H_r(t)$. The corresponding valid matrix is also presented. For illustrative purpose we assume that $\{V_1, V_2, V_3, V_4, V_5, C_1, C_2\} \in N$. We use $\perp$ to present infinite past and $\top$ to present infinite future

	V_1	V_2	V_3	V_4	V_5	C_1	C_2	V	C
V	$\perp\top$	$\perp\top$	$\perp,C$	C+l, $\top$	C+l, $\top$				
C						$\perp\top$	$\perp\top$		
All								$\perp\top$	$\perp\top$

Fig. 3. Hierarchy trees & corresponding valid time matrix

The assumption is that the defined hierarchy trees and valid time matrix depict a possible temporal analysis trace. Such analysis can be performed with the aid of a TOLAP query. The formulation of such a query requires the setting of a valid time for each dimension. Therefore, a query language can be extended by a "WITH TIME INTERVAL <Hr> On DIMENSION <DIMENSION>" clause. For each dimension the user is required to select an explicit or implicit time interval-valid time.

Such a query is capable of defining for example, the ROLL-UP effect with respect to distinct time points C, (C+l) as well as with respect the time interval $[C, (C+l)]$. In the next section the temporal concepts that will allow the development of a temporal data warehouse as well as the formulation of TOLAP queries are defined.

6   The Query Model

In this section we put forward a proposal to provide representation for handling changing-evolving hierarchies and retrieving intentional answers at the query level through case based reasoning mechanisms (CBR).

The motivation behind this extension is based on the argument that in order to build TOLAP queries with their own information bases out of the existing ones, we need to raise the abstraction of operations on the metadata level. In this context, the case-based querying-technology can be focused on an alternative mechanism for designing intelligent TOLAP querying systems. It can be employed either at the conceptual level or at the instance level (metadata level) for matching a current query description (a query case) to a specially organised database of indexed previous situations, called a case base (info-base). Therefore, a TOLAP querying system searches for case histories (response cases) that fully or partially match this description. The CBR strong features arise from its emphasis on similarity matching.

Empowered similarity requires a model that elegantly combines into a single formula both hierarchy similarities and object dissimilarities with respect to distinct time points C, (C+l). A simple model to capture similarities and dissimilarities between objects was proposed by [17], that could be summarised as follows:

$$\text{sim}(H_A, \ H_B) = S(H_A \cap H_B) - S(H_A - H_B) - S(H_B - H_A) \tag{8}$$

In the context of a temporal environment this can be interpreted as follows: given two sample hierarchy trees H_A, H_B defined in the time interval [C, (C+l)], estimate the ROLL-UP effect with respect to distinct time points C, (C+l) as well as for the time interval [C, (C+l)].

H_{AB} should contain all Trevsky's components, $(S(H_A \cap H_B)$, $S(H_A - H_B)$, $S(H_B - H_A))$, respectively. The intuition is that the temporal ROLL-UP result, must express equally well the similarities $(S(H_A \cap H_B))$ and dissimilarities $(S(H_A - H_B)$, $S(H_B - H_A))$ between the evolving hierarchies (H_A, H_B).

The important issue in constructing Trevsky's components is the estimation of the $S(H_A \cap H_B) - S(H_A - H_B) - S(H_B - H_A)$ parameters for the distinct time interval [C, (C+l)].

With reference to "Fig.3." Trevsky's components for the time interval [C, (C+l)], are estimated as follows:

$$S(H_A \cap H_B)_{[C, (C+l)]} = \{\{V_1, V_2, \} \{C_1, C_2\}\} \text{ items} \tag{9}$$

$$S(H_A - H_B)_{[C, (C+l)]} = \{\{V_3\}\} \text{ items} \tag{10}$$

$$S(H_B - H_A)_{[C, (C+l)]} = \{\{V_4, V_5\}\} \text{ items} \tag{11}$$

With reference to the distinct time points C or (C+*l*) an extended ROLL-UP operator should reflect the effects occurring by the time query:

- Items not valid at a particular time point
- Groupings with same name but different elements
- Residual items excluded from the chosen time point

While drilling down can solve the first and second issues, the last issue requires an explanation of the instances hidden below the grouping "Residual".

The OLAP architecture has to be modified as follows: information about valid time has to be stored in the meta-data repository and the OLAP server must be able to receive queries with valid time clauses. The repository itself has to be extended for storing versioned meta-information.

7   Conclusions

Traditionally, there is no real-time connection between a DWH and its data sources. This is mainly because the write-once read-many decision support characteristics would conflict with the continuous update workload of operational systems resulting in poor response times. Consequently, up until recently, *timeliness* requirements were restricted to mid-term or long-term time windows. However ignoring these temporal issues leads to diminished expressive flexibility and questionable query semantics in many real-life scenarios.

We review the issue of time in data warehouses and meaning of time as part of a conventional OLAP architecture. We propose an extension of the conventional OLAP architecture in order to handle temporal uncertainty.

Important future research directions in this field will be the maintenance of data warehouses based on dynamically changing information systems (data updates, schema changes), and enhancements to the active behaviour in the field of active data warehouses and workflows.

References

1. S. Anahory, D. Murray. Data warehousing in the real world: A Practical Approach for Building Decision Support Systems, *Addison-Wesley* 1997.
2. M. Böhlen et al. Point-versus Interval-Based Temporal Data Models. *In Proceedings of 14th ICDE*, IEEE Computer Society Press, pp. 192-201, 1998.
3. P. Chountas, I. Petrounias, K. Atanassov, V. Kodogiannis, E. El-Darzi. Representation & Querying of Temporal Conflict. *FQAS 2002, LNAI, Springer-Verlag*, pp.112-123, 2002.
4. O. Etzion, S. Jajodia, S. Sripada. Temporal Databases: Research and Practice. *LNCS, Springer-Verlag*, 1998.
5. W. Inmon. Building the Data Warehouse. Second Edition, *John Wiley & Sons*, New York, 1996.
6. C. Jensen, R. Snodgrass. Temporal Data Management. *IEEE Transactions on Knowledge and Data Engineering*, Vol. 11(1): pp. 36-44, 1999.
7. R. Kimball. The Data Warehouse Toolkit. *John Wiley & Sons*, New York, 1996.

8. T. Pedersen, C. Jensen. Multidimensional Data Modeling for Complex Data. *In Proceedings of 15th ICDE*, IEEE Computer Society, pp. 336-345, 1999.

9. R. Snodgrass. Monitoring Distributed Systems: A Relational Approach, Ph.D. Dissertation. *Carnegie Mellon University*, 1982.

10. V. Brusoni, L. Console, P. Terenziani, B. Pernici. Extending Temporal Relational Databases to deal with Imprecise and Qualitative Temporal Information. *Proceedings of the International Workshop on Recent Advances in Temporal Databases, Springer-Verlag*, pp 3–22, 1995.

11. C. Dyreson, R. Snodgrass. Supporting Valid-time Indeterminacy. *ACM Trans. Database Systems*. Vol. 23, No1, pp 1–57, 1998.

12. Dekhtyar, R. Ross, V. Subrahmanian. Probabilistic Temporal Databases, I: Algebra", *ACM Trans. on Database Systems*. Vol. 26, No. 1, pp. 41-95, 2001.

13. M. Koubarakis. Database Models for Infinite and Indefinite Temporal Information. *Inf. Systems*. Vol. *19*, No. 2, pp. 141–173, 1994.

14. M. Koubarakis. Representation and Querying in Temporal databases: The power of temporal constraints. *Proceedings of the International Conference on Data Engineering*, pp 327–334, 1993.

15. D. Dubois, H. Prade. Processing Fuzzy Temporal Knowledge. *IEEE Trans. Systems Man Cybernetics*. Vol.19, No.4, pp 729–744, 1989.

16. S. Dutta. Generalized Events in Temporal Databases. *Proceedings of the 5th International Conference on Data Engineering*", IEEE Computer Society, pp118–126, 1989.

17. Trevsky, I. Gati. Studies of Similarity, Cognition and Categorization. *Hillsdale, NJ: Erlbaum*, 1978.

A Data Warehouse Engineering Process

Sergio Luján-Mora and Juan Trujillo

D. of Software and Computing Systems, University of Alicante
Carretera de San Vicente s/n, Alicante, Spain
{slujan,jtrujillo}@dlsi.ua.es

Abstract. Developing a data warehouse (DW) is a complex, time consuming and prone to fail task. Different DW models and methods have
been presented during the last few years. However, none of them addresses the whole development process in an integrated manner. In this
paper, we present a DW development method, based on the Unified Modeling Language (UML) and the Unified Process (UP), which addresses
the design and development of both the DW back-stage and front-end.
We extend the UML in order to accurately represent the different parts
of a DW. Our proposal provides a seamless method for developing DWs.

Keywords: data warehouse, UML, Unified Process, software engineering.

1 Introduction

In the early nineties, Inmon [1] coined the term "data warehouse" (DW): "*A data
warehouse is a subject-oriented, integrated, time-variant, nonvolatile collection
of data in support of management's decisions*". Building a DW is a challenging
and complex task because a DW concerns many organizational units and can
often involve many people. Although various methods and approaches have been
presented for designing different parts of DWs, no general and standard method
exists to date for dealing with the whole design of a DW.

In the light of this situation, the goal of our work is to develop a DW engineering process to make the developing process of DWs more efficient. Our proposal
is an object oriented (OO) method, based on the Unified Modeling Language
(UML) [2] and the Unified Process (UP) [3], which allows the user to tackle all
DW design stages, from the operational data sources to the final implementation and including the definition of the ETL (Extraction, Transformation, and
Loading) processes and the final users' requirements.

The rest of the paper is structured as follows. In Section 2, we briefly present
some of the most important related work and point out the main shortcomings.
In Section 3, we summarize our DW engineering process: first, we present the
diagrams we propose to model a DW (the results achieved so far), and then we
describe the different workflows that make up our process. Finally, we present
the main contributions and the future work in Section 4.

T. Yakhno (Ed.): ADVIS 2004, LNCS 3261, pp. 14–23, 2004.
© Springer-Verlag Berlin Heidelberg 2004

2   Related Work

During the last few years, different approaches for the DW design have been presented. On the one hand, different data models [4–8], both conceptual and logical, have been proposed. These approaches are based on their own visual modeling languages or make use of a well-known graphical notation, such as the Entity-Relationship (ER) model or the UML. However, none of these approaches has been widely accepted as a standard DW model, because they present some important lacks. Due to space constraints, we refer the reader to [9] for a detailed comparison and discussion about most of these models.

On the other hand, different DW methods [10–13], have also been proposed. However, all of them present some of these problems: they do not address the whole DW process, they do not include a visual modeling language, they do not propose a clear set of steps or phases, or they are based on a specific implementation (e.g., the star schema in relational databases).

A key approach is Kimball's *Data Warehouse Bus Architecture* [14], which addresses planning, designing, developing, deploying, and growing DWs. However, this approach also lacks a modeling language that comprises the different tasks.

In conclusion, no general and standard method exists to date for dealing with the whole design of a DW.

3   Data Warehouse Development

The goal of our work is to develop a DW engineering process to make the developing process of DWs more efficient. In order to achieve this goal, we consider the following premises:

- Our method should be based on a standard visual modeling language.
- Our method should provide a clear and seamless method for developing a DW.
- Our method should tackle all DW design stages in an integrated manner, from the operational data sources to the final implementation and including the definition of the ETL processes and the final users' requirements.
- Our method should provide different levels of detail.

Therefore, we have selected the UML as the visual modeling language, our method is based on the well-accepted UP, we have extended the UML in order to accurately represent the different parts of a DW, and we extensively use the UML packages with the aim of providing different levels of detail.

The rest of the section is divided into two clear parts: in Section 3.1 we present the results achieved so far, and in Section 3.2 we outline our current and future lines of work.

3.1   Data Warehouse Diagrams

The architecture of a DW is usually depicted as various layers of data in which data from one layer is derived from data of the previous layer [15]. Following this consideration, we consider that the development of a DW can be structured into an integrated framework with five stages and three levels that define different diagrams for the DW model, as shown in Fig. 1 and summarized in Table 1.

Table 1. Data warehouse design framework

- **Stages**: we distinguish five stages in the definition of a DW:
  - Source, that defines the data sources of the DW, such as OLTP systems, external data sources (syndicated data, census data), etc.
  - Integration, that defines the mapping between the data sources and the DW.
  - Data Warehouse, that defines the structure of the DW.
  - Customization, that defines the mapping between the DW and the clients' structures.
  - Client, that defines special structures that are used by the clients to access the DW, such as data marts (DM) or OLAP applications.
- **Levels**: each stage can be analyzed at three levels or perspectives:
  - Conceptual: it defines the DW from a conceptual point of view.
  - Logical: it addresses logical aspects of the DW design, such as the definition of the ETL processes.
  - Physical: it defines physical aspects of the DW, such as the storage of the logical structures in different disks, or the configuration of the database servers that support the DW.
- **Diagrams**: each stage or level require different modeling formalisms. Therefore, our approach is composed of 15 diagrams, but the DW designer does not need to define all the diagrams in each DW project: for example, if there is a straightforward mapping between the Source Conceptual Schema (SCS) and the Data Warehouse Conceptual Schema (DWCS), the designer may not need to define the corresponding Data Mapping (DM). In our approach, we use the UML [2] as the modeling language, because it provides enough expressiveness power to address all the diagrams. As the UML is a general modeling language, we can use the UML extension mechanisms (stereotypes, tag definitions, and constraints) to adapt the UML to specific domains. In Fig. 1, we provide the following information for each diagram:
  - Name (**in bold face**): the name we have coined for this diagram.
  - UML diagram: the UML diagram we use to model this DW diagram. Currently, we use class, deployment, and component diagrams.
  - Profile (*in italic face*): the dashed boxes show the diagrams where we propose a new profile; in the other boxes, we use a standard UML diagram or a profile from other authors.

The different diagrams of the same DW are not independent but overlapping: they depend on each other in many ways. For example, changes in one diagram may imply changes in another, and a large portion of one diagram may be created on the basis of another diagram. For example, the DM is created by importing elements from the SCS and the DWCS.

In previous works, we have presented some of the diagrams and the corresponding profiles shown in white dashed boxes in Fig. 1: *Multidimensional Profile* [16, 17] for the Client Conceptual Schema (CCS) and the *ETL Profile* [18] for the ETL Process and the Exporting Process. In light gray dashed boxes, we show our last contribution (submitted to review process), the *Data Mapping Profile* for

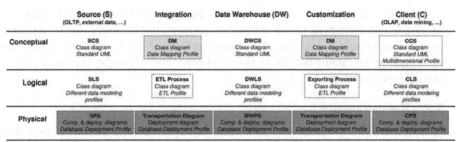

	Source (S) (OLTP, external data, ...)	Integration	Data Warehouse (DW)	Customization	Client (C) (OLAP, data mining, ...)
Conceptual	SCS Class diagram Standard UML	DM Class diagram Data Mapping Profile	DWCS Class diagram Standard UML	DM Class diagram Data Mapping Profile	CCS Class diagram Standard UML Multidimensional Profile
Logical	SLS Class diagram Different data modeling profiles	ETL Process Class diagram ETL Profile	DWLS Class diagram Different data modeling profiles	Exporting Process Class diagram ETL Profile	CLS Class diagram Different data modeling profiles
Physical	SPS Comp. & deploy. diagrams Database Deployment Profile	Transportation Diagram Deployment diagram Database Deployment Profile	DWPS Comp. & deploy. diagrams Database Deployment Profile	Transportation Diagram Deployment diagram Database Deployment Profile	CPS Comp. & deploy. diagrams Database Deployment Profile

LEGEND: CS: Conceptual Schema, LS: Logical Schema, PS: Physical Schema, Comp. & deploy: Component and deployment

Fig. 1. Data warehouse design framework

the Data Mapping (DM) between the Source Conceptual Schema (SCS) and the Data Warehouse Conceptual Schema (DWCS), and between the DWCS and the CCS. Finally, in dark gray dashed boxes, we show the profile we are currently working on, the *Database Deployment Profile*, for modeling a DW at a physical level.

On the other hand, the Common Warehouse Metamodel (CWM) [19] is an open industry standard of the Object Management Group (OMG) for integrating data warehousing and business analysis tools, based on the use of shared metadata. This standard is based on three key industry standard: Meta Object Facility (MOF), UML, and XML Metadata Interchange (XMI). We use the CWM when we need to interchange any DW information among different applications.

3.2 Data Warehouse Engineering Process

Our method, called *Data Warehouse Engineering Process* (DWEP), is based on the Unified Software Development Process, also known as Unified Process or simply UP [3]. The UP is an industry standard Software Engineering Process (SEP) from the authors of the UML. Whereas the UML defines a visual modeling language, the UP specifies how to develop software using the UML.

The UP is a generic SEP that has to be instantiated for an organization, project or domain. DWEP is our instantiation of the UP for the development of DWs. Some characteristics of our DWEP inherited from UP are: use case (requirement) driven, architecture centric, iterative and incremental.

According to the UP, the project lifecycle is divided into four phases (Inception, Elaboration, Construction, and Transition) and five core workflows (Requirements, Analysis, Design, Implementation, and Test). We have added two more workflows to the UP workflows: *Maintenance* and *Post-development review*. During the developing of a project, the emphasis shifts over the iterations, from requirements and analysis towards design, implementation, testing, and finally, maintenance and post-development review, but different workflows can coexist in the same iteration.

For each one of the workflows, we use different UML diagrams (techniques) to model and document the development process, but a model can be modified in different phases because models evolve over time. In the following sections, we comment the main details of the workflows and highlight the diagrams we use in each workflow.

3.3 Requirements

During this workflow, what the final users expect to do with the DW is captured: the final users should specify the most interesting measures and aggregations, the analysis dimensions, the queries used to generate periodical reports, the update frequency of the data, etc. As proposed in [20], we model the requirements with use cases. The rationale of use cases is that focusing *"on what the users need to do with the system is much more powerful that other traditional elicitation approaches of asking users what they want the system to do"* [20]. Once the requirements have been defined, the DW project is established and the different roles are designated.

The UML provides the use case diagram for visual modeling of uses cases. Nevertheless, there is no UML standard for a use case specification. However, we follow the common template defined in [21], which specifies for every use case a name, a unique identifier, the actor involved in the use case, the system state before the use can begin, the actual steps of the use case, and the system state when the use case is over.

3.4 Analysis

The goal of this workflow is to refine and structure the requirements output in the previous workflow. Moreover, the pre-existing operational systems that will feed the DW are also documented: the different candidate data sources are identified, the data content is revised, etc.

We use the Source Conceptual (Logical, Physical) Schema (SCS, SLC, and SPS) (Fig. 1) to model the data sources at different levels of detail. To get quality data in the DW, the different data sources must be well identified.

For example, in Fig. 2 we show the Source Logical Schema of a transactional system that manages the sales of a company. This system will feed with data the DW that will be defined in the following step of the design process.

3.5 Design

At the end of this workflow, the structure of the DW is defined. The main output of this workflow is the conceptual model of the DW. Moreover, the source to target data map is also developed at a conceptual level.

In this workflow, the main diagrams are the Data Warehouse Conceptual Schema (DWCS), the Client Conceptual Schema (CCS), and the Data Mapping (DM). The DM shows the relationships between the SCS and the DWCS and between the DWCS and the CCS.

For the CCS, we have previously presented [16] an extension of the Unified Modeling Language (UML) by means of a UML profile. This profile is defined by

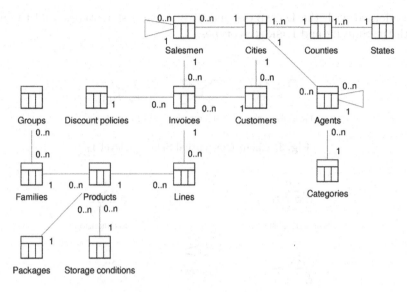

Fig. 2. Source Logical Schema

a set of stereotypes and tagged values to elegantly represent main multidimensional properties at the conceptual level. We make use of the Object Constraint Language (OCL) to specify the constraints attached to the defined stereotypes, thereby avoiding an arbitrary use of these stereotypes. The main advantage of our proposal is that it is based on a well-known standard modeling language, thereby designers can avoid learning a new specific notation or language for multidimensional systems.

For example, in Fig. 3 we show level 1 of a Client Conceptual Schema, composed of three schemas (Production schema, Sales schema, and Salesmen schema). In Fig. 4 we show level 2 of the Sales schema from level 1, composed of one fact (Sales fact) and four dimensions (Stores dimension, Times dimension, Products dimension, and Customers dimension). Finally, in Fig. 5, the definition of the Customers dimension with the different hierarchy levels is showed.

3.6 Implementation

During this workflow, the DW is built: the physical DW structures are built, the DW is populated with data, the DW is tuned for an optimized running, etc. Different implementation diagrams can be created to help this workflow.

The main diagrams in this workflow are the Data Warehouse Logical (Physical) Schema, the Client Logical (Physical) Schema, the ETL Process, the Exportation Process, and the Transportation Diagram. In the ETL Process, the cleansing and quality control activities are modeled.

For example, in Fig. 6 we show part of a Client Physical Schema. In this example, both the components and the nodes are stereotyped: the components

are adorned with the DATABASE and TABLESPACE stereotypes, and the nodes
with the SERVER and DISK stereotypes.

Production schema   Sales schema   Salesmen schema

Fig. 3. Client Conceptual Schema (level 1)

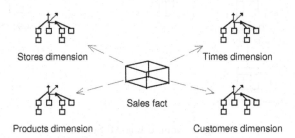

Stores dimension   Times dimension

Sales fact

Products dimension   Customers dimension

Fig. 4. Client Conceptual Schema (level 2)

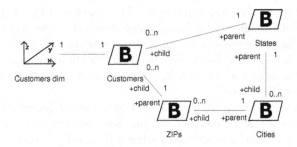

Fig. 5. Client Conceptual Schema (level 3)

3.7 Test

The goal of this workflow is to verify that the implementation works as desired.
No new diagrams are created, but previous diagrams (mainly design and implementation diagrams) may be modified according the corrective actions that are
taken.

3.8 Maintenance

Unlike most systems, the DW is never done. The goal of this workflow is to
define the refresh and loading processes needed for keeping the DW up to date.
This workflow starts when the DW is built and delivered to the final users, but
it does not have an end date (it lasts during the life of the DW).

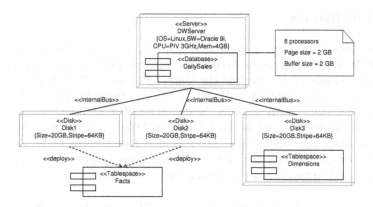

Fig. 6. Client Physical Schema

During this workflow, the final users can state new requirements, such as new queries, which triggers the beginning of a new iteration (UP is an iterative process) with the Requirements workflow.

3.9   Post-Development Review

This is not a workflow of the development effort, but a review process for improving future projects. We look back at the development of the DW, revise the documentation created, and try to identify both opportunities for improvement and major successes that should be taken into account. If we keep track of the time and effort spent on each phase, this information can be useful in estimating time and staff requirements for future projects.

3.10   Top-Down or Bottom-Up?

Nowadays, there are two basic strategies in the building of a DW: the top-down and bottom-up approaches. The top-down approach recommends the construction of a DW first and then the construcion of DMs from the parent DW. The bottom-up approach uses a series of incremental DMs that are finally integrated to build the goal of the DW. However, in almost all projects, the DMs are built rather independently without the construction of an integrated DW, which is indeed viewed no more as a monolithic repository but rather as a collection of DMs.

Our method also allows both approaches. In the top-down approach, the DW is built first and the data sources are the transactional systems; then, each DM is built independently by using our method, and the DW becomes the only data source for all of them. In the bottom-up approach, the DMs are built first from the transactional systems; then, the DW is built and the data sources are the DMs.

4   Conclusions

In this paper, we have presented the Data Warehouse Engineering Process (DWEP), a data warehouse (DW) development process based on the Unified Modeling Language (UML) and the Unified Process (UP). UP is a generic and stable process that we have instantiated to cover the development of data warehouses. Our main contribution is the definition of several diagrams (techniques) and UML profiles [16–18] in order to model DWs more properly. Whereas the different diagrams provide different views or perspectives of a DW, the engineering process specifies how to develop a DW and ties up all the diagrams together. The main advantages of our approach are:

– The use of a development process, the UP, which is the outcome of more than 20 years of experience.
– The use of the UML, a widely accepted visual modeling language, for designing the different DW diagrams and the corresponding transformations.
– The use of the UML as the modeling language provides much better tool support than using an own modeling language.
– The proposal of a DW development process that addresses both the back-end and the front-end of DWs in an integrated manner.

Currently, we are working on the *Database Deployment Profile*, for modeling a DW (and databases in general) at a physical level, we are concluding the definition of the different workflows that the process comprises, and we also plan to include new UML diagrams (sequence, collaboration, statechart, and activity diagrams) to model dynamic properties of DWs. Moreover, we plan to carry out an empirical evaluation of our proposal, in order to validate the correctness and usefulness of our approach.

References

1. Inmon, W.: Building the Data Warehouse. QED Press/John Wiley (1992) (Last edition: 3rd edition, John Wiley & Sons, 2002).
2. Object Management Group (OMG): Unified Modeling Language Specification 1.5. Internet: http://www.omg.org/cgi-bin/doc?formal/03-03-01 (2003)
3. Jacobson, I., Booch, G., Rumbaugh, J.: The Unified Software Development Process. Object Technology Series. Addison-Wesley (1999)
4. Golfarelli, M., Rizzi, S.: A Methodological Framework for Data Warehouse Design. In: Proc. of the ACM 1st Intl. Workshop on Data Warehousing and OLAP (DOLAP'98), Bethesda, USA (1998) 3–9
5. Cabibbo, L., Torlone, R.: A Logical Approach to Multidimensional Databases. In: Proc. of the 6th Intl. Conf. on Extending Database Technology (EDBT'98). Volume 1377 of LNCS., Valencia, Spain (1998) 183–197
6. Tryfona, N., Busborg, F., Christiansen, J.: starER: A Conceptual Model for Data Warehouse Design. In: Proc. of the ACM 2nd Intl. Workshop on Data Warehousing and OLAP (DOLAP'99), Kansas City, USA (1999)

7. Husemann, B., Lechtenborger, J., Vossen, G.: Conceptual Data Warehouse Design. In: Proc. of the 2nd Intl. Workshop on Design and Management of Data Warehouses (DMDW'00), Stockholm, Sweden (2000) 3–9

8. Trujillo, J., Palomar, M., Gómez, J., Song, I.: Designing Data Warehouses with OO Conceptual Models. IEEE Computer, special issue on Data Warehouses **34** (2001) 66–75

9. Abell, A., Samos, J., Saltor, F.: A Framework for the Classification and Description of Multidimensional Data Models. In: Proc. of the 12th Intl. Conf. on Database and Expert Systems Applications (DEXA'01), Munich, Germany (2001) 668–677

10. Kimball, R.: The Data Warehouse Toolkit. John Wiley & Sons (1996) (Last edition: 2nd edition, John Wiley & Sons, 2002).

11. Giovinazzo, W.: Object-Oriented Data Warehouse Design. Building a star schema. Prentice-Hall, New Jersey, USA (2000)

12. Cavero, J., Piattini, M., Marcos, E.: MIDEA: A Multidimensional Data Warehouse Methodology. In: Proc. of the 3rd Intl. Conf. on Enterprise Information Systems (ICEIS'01), Setubal, Portugal (2001) 138–144

13. Moody, D., Kortink, M.: From Enterprise Models to Dimensional Models: A Methodology for Data Warehouse and Data Mart Design. In: Proc. of the 3rd Intl. Workshop on Design and Management of Data Warehouses (DMDW'01), Interlaken, Switzerland (2001) 1–10

14. Kimball, R., Reeves, L., Ross, M., Thornthwaite, W.: The data warehouse lifecycle toolkit. John Wiley & Sons (1998)

15. Jarke, M., Lenzerini, M., Vassiliou, Y., Vassiliadis, P.: Fundamentals of Data Warehouses. 2 edn. Springer-Verlag (2003)

16. Lujn-Mora, S., Trujillo, J., Song, I.: Extending UML for Multidimensional Modeling. In: Proc. of the 5th Intl. Conf. on the Unified Modeling Language (UML'02). Volume 2460 of LNCS., Dresden, Germany (2002) 290–304

17. Lujn-Mora, S., Trujillo, J., Song, I.: Multidimensional Modeling with UML Package Diagrams. In: Proc. of the 21st Intl. Conf. on Conceptual Modeling (ER'02). Volume 2503 of LNCS., Tampere, Finland (2002) 199–213

18. Trujillo, J., Lujn-Mora, S.: A UML Based Approach for Modeling ETL Processes in Data Warehouses. In: Proc. of the 22nd Intl. Conf. on Conceptual Modeling (ER'03). Volume 2813 of LNCS., Chicago, USA (2003) 307–320

19. Object Management Group (OMG): Common Warehouse Metamodel (CWM) Specification 1.0. Internet: http://www.omg.org/cgi-bin/doc?ad/2001-02-01 (2001)

20. Bruckner, R., List, B., Schiefer, J.: Developing Requirements for Data Warehouse Systems with Use Cases. In: Proc. of the 7th Americas Conf. on Information Systems (AMCIS'01), Boston, USA (2001) 329–335

21. Arlow, J., Neustadt, I.: UML and the Unified Process. Object Technology Series. Addison-Wesley (2002)

Aggregation and Analysis of Spatial Data by Means of Materialized Aggregation Tree

Marcin Gorawski and Rafal Malczok

Silesian University of Technology, Institute of Computer Science,
Akademicka 16 street, 44-101 Gliwice, Poland
{Marcin.Gorawski, Rafal.Malczok}@polsl.pl

Abstract. In this paper we present a system of spatial data warehouse designed for aggregating and analyzing a wide range of spatial information. The data is generated by media meters working in a telemetric system. The data warehouse is based on a new model called the cascaded star model. The cascaded star is the spatial development of a standard star schema. We decided to use an indexing structure called aggregation tree. The aggregation tree materialization and integrated mechanism of available memory estimation highly improve the efficiency of the system. The theoretical aspects are confirmed by the presented tests results.

1 Introduction

The new situation on the markets for utilities such as electrical energy, natural gas and water, allows customers to choose a utilities deliverer. The most crucial issue in this regard is the metering of utilities customers' usage and the analysis of huge amounts of relevant data. In the case of electrical energy providers, meter reading, analysis, and decision making is highly time sensitive. For example, in order to take stock of energy consumption meter data should be read and analyzed every thirty minutes [3]. The requirement can be met by use of the data warehouse-based decision supporting systems [5] and GSM/GPRS technology.

A data warehouse is a repository of data integrated from various source systems. Its purpose is to provide an efficient analytical on-line processing useful for analysts and decision makers. Relational analytical on-line processing (RO-LAP) for spatial data is performed in data warehouses based on the cascaded star model [1]. The model is a spatial extension of a standard star schema. Such data warehouses are called Spatial Data Warehouses (SDW) [4].

In order to provide sufficient efficiency of SDW system, it is necessary to use appropriate indexing and pre-aggregating methods. In the traditional approach, ROLAP application contains hierarchies for individual dimensions. In order to reduce query answer time, the data is aggregated (materialized) on various levels of those hierarchies. With spatial hierarchies we do not know in advance all the hierarchies – defining the query, a user can choose any piece of the region in the map. Traditional range queries executing first classifies spatial objects and then aggregates their attributes. Such an approach, however, is very time consuming,

T. Yakhno (Ed.): ADVIS 2004, LNCS 3261, pp. 24–33, 2004.

the goal being to obtain only a single value without classifying every object. We propose an approach based on an aggregates index that supplements the traditional method with an additional summary information in the intermediate positions. The most popular aggregates index is R-Tree [2, 7] and aR-Tree (aggregation R-Tree) [6, 8]. Therefore, in order to increase the efficiency of SDW system we used the technique of materialized views in the form of aggregation trees.

The aggregation tree is a dynamic structure stored in the computer's memory; thus, we had to provide a mechanism to protect the system from memory overflows. We designed a special memory capacity evaluating mechanism discussed later in this paper. The aggregation tree contains huge amounts of data, calling for the use of the materialization of the indexing structure.

2 Basic System Description

The source of data for a SDW is a telemetric system of integrated meter readings. It sends the data using the GSM mobile phone net utilizing GPRS technology. The readings of utility meters located within a huge geographical region are sent to the data warehouse. One of the telemetric system's elements are collection nodes communicating directly with the headquarters housing the data warehouse. The nodes are the intermediate point of communication between the meters and the data warehouse. The nodes and meters are located in the same region. A single node is a collection point for a specified set of meters. The meters and nodes communicate via radio wave. Thus it features some restrictions – a single collective node can serve but a limited number of meters, and the distance between a node and a meter is limited. Those limits determine that the radio wave communication structure is akin to a set of circles, whose centers are collective nodes surrounded by meters (Fig. 1).

The system presented in this paper is real; it is a working system used for reading and storing data from media meters. The interactive system task is to provide user information about utilities consumption in regions encompassed by

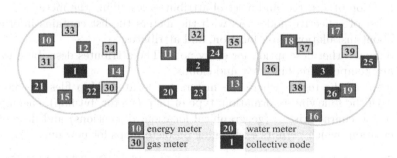

Fig. 1. The schema of radio wave-based communication structure: nodes and meters. Circles indicate the scope of nodes radio communication

the telemetric system. A user's interface relies on maps of the regions where the meters are located. The interface is very similar to that presented in [4]. A user, using a "rubber rectangle", defines an aggregation window – a piece of a region from which the aggregates are to be collected. The aggregation results are presented in form of both tables and graphs; the latter are generated by means of *JFreeChart* package.

3   Cascaded Star

Each data warehouse model consists of facts oriented in set of dimensions, which in turn are organized in hierarchical aggregates levels. The models are adapted to relational data base environment. The most popular are star and snowflake models. However, in order to efficiently represent a wide range of spatial data, a new model has to be introduced. The model called cascaded star allows integrating dimensions describing various aspects of the same issue. The model is a spatial improvement of a standard star schema. The cascaded star used for the first time by the authors of [1] for storing spatial data turned out to be useful in the SDW described in [4]. The cascaded star contains a central fact table; its main dimensions form smaller star schemas. The cascaded star allows convenient modeling of a wide range of spatial data. The necessity of cascaded star usage results from the fact that traditional schemas are not appropriate for storing spatial data.

A cascaded star schema used in the presented system is illustrated in Figure 2. Each meter communicates with its collective node in an appropriate frequency. This frequency differs according to type of meter. For example, electricity meters are read every thirty minutes, gas meters somewhat less frequently (every two hours), and water meters least frequently (every five hours). A single reading contains the following information: a precise timestamp, a meter identifier, and the reading values. The reading values vary depending on the type of meter. There are values of two zones for energy and water counters; gas counters have value of one zone. The system also collects the following data:

- a list of meters containing the meter installation date; three-dimensional location of a meter; and a set of attributes describing the meter,
- a list of collective nodes. As with the meters the list contains information about installation date, location, and attributes,
- daily weather description for every node. The attributes describing weather are: temperature, humidity and clouds,
- maps of the region where the meters are located. Map files are described with the following information: type of map (vector, bitmap), encompassed region characteristics (geographical location, dimensions) and date of map creation, which permits exchanging obsolete maps for new ones.

The cascaded star contains a central fact table – INSTALLATION, which interconnects the main dimensions – MAP, NODE and READING. The NODE dimension contains information about collective nodes in the installation. There is a reference in the INSTALLATION table – each collective node serves a few types of meters. These types are described by the table GROUP_OF_READING, which contains two columns. The first column ID_GROUP identifies a group of readings and a second column ID_READING defines a concrete reading. Thanks to this solution, it is possible to identify the group of readings to which a given reading belongs, in other words, from which collective node it comes and which medium it concerns. Another benefit is that there is no data redundancy. The MAP dimension is a star containing information about installation region maps.

Next to the above described data, we also store weather information. Spatial granularity for this information is node, because as far as the weather is concerned the distances between a node and surrounding meters are short enough to assume that the weather in the node's neighborhood is the same for all meters. The weather information can later be used in the analysis of weather influence on utilities consumption.

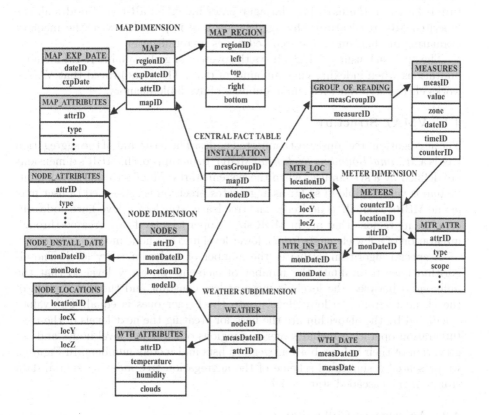

Fig. 2. A schema of used data model – cascaded star

4 Aggregation Tree

A user, after setting the lists of aggregation windows, selects those windows which are to be evaluated, and a process of evaluating aggregation windows list value begins. A special algorithm splits the overlapping windows and transfers them to an algorithm which evaluates the aggregates. This algorithm is performed separately for every aggregation window. A user expects that a data warehouse is provided with sufficient efficiency to be considered interactive. This can be accomplished by means of appropriate indexing and pre-aggregation. In our paper we present an aggregating spatial index called aggregation tree. The aggregation tree is a dynamic structure containing aggregates of spatial data. The index structure, tightly integrated with the applied cascaded star model as well as the innovative idea of partial aggregates materialization, makes the aggregation tree an efficient and natural way of indexing huge amounts of spatial data. We called the index *Virtual Memory Aggregation Tree* (VMAT), because the aggregation tree intensively uses a disk to store the aggregates. Its structure is based on the most popular aggregates index, an aR-tree. Besides all the inherited aR-Tree features the aggregation tree is provided with the memory evaluating mechanism and automated nodes materialization.

The approach using VMAT allows the overcoming of available RAM memory limitations when indexing huge amounts of data. The tests proved that VMAT works effectively even with small amounts of available memory.

4.1 VMAT Structure

The aggregation tree consists of connected nodes. The basic unit of the aggregation tree is a *Minimal Bounding Rectangle* (MBR). In our approach, MBR's dimensions are defined by a system user when the system starts. Thanks to this solution our system is very flexible in so far as aggregates precision is concerned (a user may define MBRs as small as desired). The tree leaves (the lowest level) are nodes encompassing regions that are in MBR size. Upper tree levels are created through integration of a few elements from a lower level into one node in the upper level.

A special algorithm evaluates the number of nodes on every level. The algorithm tries to evaluate the number of elements on every level so that the differential between the levels is more or less constant and the distribution of the elements from the lower levels onto the higher ones is equal. The values calculated by the algorithm are the base for creating the next levels of the tree. Integration operation includes merging regions of the lower level nodes and aggregation of their values; both aggregates lists and meters numbers. In Figure 3 we presented a simplified scheme of the aggregation tree indexing spatial data stored in the cascaded star model.

4.2 Aggregates Collection

Aggregates collecting operations are performed separately for each aggregation window. In the first place, by applying a recursive aggregation tree exploring

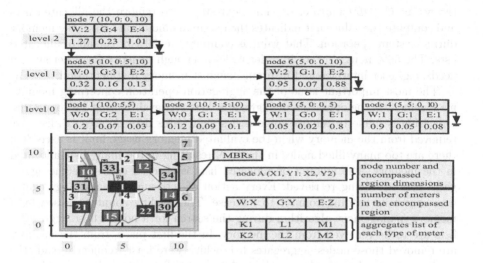

Fig. 3. A simplified scheme of aggregation tree

algorithm, the function marks those tree nodes from which the aggregates lists will be retrieved to preclude the removal from the memory of those nodes' aggregates lists due to be collected in the next step.

The aggregates collection algorithm starts from the tree root and proceed towards the tree leaves. For each node the algorithm checks whether the node's region has a common part with the aggregation window's region and, based on the result, the algorithm determines the proper action. If the regions share no part, the node is skipped. In case the regions overlap a bit, the algorithm proceeds recursively to the lower tree level (but only if the level in consideration is not the lowest level) as a window region assuming the overlapping part. In case the regions entirely overlap, then the algorithm aggregates the given node's aggregates lists. The aggregation operation consists of retrieving the node's aggregates lists and aggregates them to the lists of a global collecting element.

4.3   Materialization and Memory Management

Usage of an aggregation tree is intimately connected with the necessity of finding a solution to the problems of aggregates lists materialization and preventing the memory overflows. What lists should be materialized and when is determined by a memory management algorithm described below.

During the system start an empty tree structure (i.e., nodes not containing aggregates lists) is created. In order to estimate the amount of available memory the tree's nodes are filled (without accessing the data base or hard drive) with artificially generated aggregates lists. Each allocated aggregates list is counted. The action is continued as long as there is no more free memory and JVM throws an *OutOfMemory* error. The next step is to remove the allocated lists and compute the value that indicates the maximal amount of lists in the memory during system operation. That value is computed as 50% of the all of allocated lists. The 50% margin is set in order to leave enough memory for other system needs, e.g. user interface and insurance against memory fragmentation.

The most important issue of the aggregation operation concerning memory management is the operation of aggregates lists retrieval. During this operation a decision is made to remove some nodes aggregates lists. Aggregates lists are removed from the memory when the evaluated memory usage limit is exceeded; there are too many filled nodes in the tree, resulting in too many lists allocated in the memory. The amount of allocated lists is checked each time the aggregates lists are being retrieved. Every action of retrieving a node's aggregates lists causes its reading counter to increase. The reading counter is used by a memory management algorithm during the search for a node whose aggregates lists are to be removed from the memory. In the first place, from the memory are removed those nodes' aggregates lists which were least frequently read (the reading counter has the least value). Aggregates lists removal is preceded by materialization if the lists had not yet been stored in the data base.

After start, the system checks the availability of the *MatNode* table which contains materialized nodes data. The table consists of two columns, the first being NUMBER storing node's identifier, and the second being BLOB, storing materialized binary data of a given node's aggregates lists. The operation of materialization aggregates lists is initialized by the aggregation tree. The given tree node retrieves a handle to an input binary stream of a BLOB column from a row identified by its identification number. The handle is then transferred to all aggregates objects, which store their values to the stream. All the values (aggregates, timestamps) are stored in form of simple types (like *long* or *double*), not objects (we avoid standard Java serialization). We had to work out a simple data storing protocol; however, we avoided the redundancy resulting from storing the class identifiers and other unnecessary data. Thanks to this solution, the materialization and restoring data is very fast (in comparison with the raw data processing) and the demand on the disk space is reasonable.

5   Tests

We tested our spatial data warehouse on a computer equipped with AMD Athlon 2GHz processor and 1GB RAM. The data base was Oracle 9i; the runtime environment was Java Sun 1.4. The data gathered in the data base concerned weather information and meters readings over four months (from the 1st of January to the 1st of May of 1995). The data size exceeded 0,5 GB; the table with meters readings contained approximately 10 million rows.

In the tested system a single collection node served about 50 meters of various kinds. We performed the tests for a few sets of meters: 5, 20, 40, 80 and 160. We also used a few aggregation periods: one and two weeks, and one, two, three and four months.

The tests were performed for various percentages of materialized aggregates. First, we were executing queries with empty *MatNode* table (no materialized information). Then, we executed the same queries with a full set of materialized data. In the next steps we removed 75%, 50% and 25% of materialized aggregates lists. In so doing we were imitating the normal system operation, when the number of materialized aggregates lists increases with the number of executed queries.

The measured values were: query execution time (time of evaluating the value of a list of aggregation windows) and the number of lists which were materialized during query execution. In Figure 4 there are two graphs illustrating the relation between the aggregation query execution time and the length of aggregation period for various amount of materialized aggregates lists. The graphs show the relation for 80 (approximately two collection nodes) and 160 (approximately four collection nodes) meters. Both graphs show significant system efficiency growth when using the materialized information. The graphs show also that, thanks to the aggregates lists materialization, the time of evaluating aggregates for long aggregation periods does not increase as fast as for operations without any materialized information. The curve for 0% of materialized information is very steep; for 50% and more it is almost flat.

The test results show that thanks to the aggregates lists materialization it is possible to increase the system's efficiency approximately 15 times. The efficiency growth is evaluated as a ratio of the time required for evaluating an aggregation query without any materialized information, and the time of evaluating the same query with the use of a full set of materialized information. In the most extreme cases the growth is as big as 30 − 35 times.

A second analyzed value was the number of aggregates list materialized during aggregation query execution. Those values are the result of the memory management algorithm operation. In figure 5 we presented a graph showing the relation between the number of materialized aggregates lists and the number of meters located in the region encompassed by the query for various lengths of the aggregation period. The graph shows that the number of materialized (and also removed from memory) aggregates lists strongly increases with the growth of encompassed meters number. Very similar growth is observed for all tested lengths of aggregation period. We have to stress that aggregates list materialization and its subsequent reading from the data base is an operation of short duration and in comparison with the raw data processing, the materialization costs almost no extra time.

6   Conclusions and Future Work Plans

In this paper we presented a spatial data warehouse system designed for storing and analyzing a wide range of spatial data. The data is generated by media meters working in a radio wave based measurement system. The SDW works with the new data model called cascaded star model. The cascaded star model allows efficient storing and analyzing huge amounts of spatial data. We used a special in-

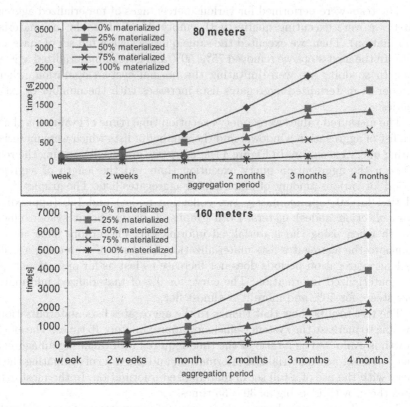

Fig. 4. Relation between the aggregation query execution time and the length of aggregation period for various amount of materialized aggregates lists

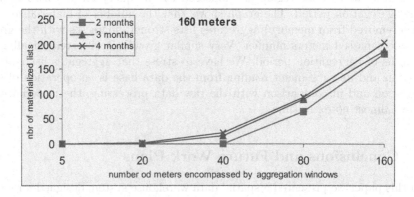

Fig. 5. Relation between the number of materialized aggregates lists and the number of meters encompassed by the query for various lengths of aggregation period

dexing structure called an aggregation tree. Its structure and operation is tightly integrated with the spatial character of the data. Thanks to an available memory evaluating mechanism the system is very flexible in the field of aggregates accuracy. A final selective materialization of indexing structure fragments performed by combining the Java streams and the Oracle BLOB table column strongly increases the system's efficiency. The approach using VMAT allows the overcoming of available RAM memory limitations when indexing huge amounts of data.

Tests results show that by means of aggregation tree materialization the system's efficiency can be greatly increased. Another positive outcome of materialization is, the more aggregation actions were performed, the faster the system works because more nodes were materialized. Moreover, the tests show that VMAT works effectively even with small amount of available memory and is a well-scalable solution appropriate for applying in data warehousing.

The future work plans involve SDW distribution and aspects of load balancing. We also plan to use lazy aggregates and UB-Tree indices.

References

1. Adam, N., Atluri, V., Yesha, Y., Yu, S.: Efficient Storage and Management of Environmental Information. IEEE Symposium on Mass Storage Systems, April 2002.
2. Beckmann, B., Kriegel, H., Schneider, R., Seeger, B.: The R*-tree: An Efficient and Robust Access Method. SIGMOD, 1990.
3. Gorawski, M.: Modeling the intelligent systems for strategic management. 4th Conf. MSK, Cracow 2003.
4. Gorawski, M., Malczok, R.: Distributed Spatial Data Warehouse. 5th Int. Conf. on Parallel Processing and Applied Mathematics, PPAM2003, Czestochowa, Spinger Verlag, LNCS3019.
5. Han, J., Stefanovic, N., Koperski, K.: Selective Materialization: An Efficient Method for Spatial Data Cube Construction. In Research and Development in Knowledge Discovery and Data Mining, Second Pacific-Asia Conference, PAKDD'98, 1998.
6. Papadias, D., Kalnis, P., Zhang, J., Tao, Y.: Efficient OLAP Operations in Spatial Data Warehouses. SSTD, Spinger Verlag, LNCS 2001.
7. Rao, F., Zhang, L., Yu, X., Li, Y., Chen, Y.: Spatial Hierarchy and OLAP - Favored Search in Spatial Data Warehouse. DOLAP, Louisiana,2003.
8. Tao, Y., Papadias, D.: Range Aggregate Processing in Spatial Databases. IEEE Transactions on Knowledge and Data Engineering (TKDE, 2004).

An Object-Oriented Framework for Reconciliation and Extraction in Heterogeneous Data Federations

Herman Balsters and Engbert O. de Brock

University of Groningen,
Faculty of Management and Organization,
P.O. Box 800,
9700 AV Groningen,
The Netherlands
{h.balsters,e.o.de.brock}@bdk.rug.nl

Abstract. Two major problems in constructing database federations concern achieving and maintaining consistency and a uniform representation of the data on the global level of the federation. The process of creation of uniform representations of data is known as data extraction, whereas data reconciliation is concerned with resolving data inconsistencies. Our approach to constructing a global, integrated system from a collection of (semantically) heterogeneous component databases is based on the concept of exact view. We will show that a global database constructed by exact views integrates component schemas without loss of constraint information. We shall describe a semantic framework for specification of database federations based on the UML/OCL data model. In particular, we will show that we can represent exact views by so-called derived classes in UML/OCL, providing the means to resolve in a combined setting data extraction and reconciliation problems on the global level of the federation.

1   Introduction

Information integration is a very complex problem, and is relevant in several fields, such as data re-engineering, data warehousing, Web information systems, E-commerce, scientific databases, and B2B applications. Information systems involving integration of cooperating component systems are called federated information systems; if the component systems are all databases then we speak of a federated database system ([20]). In this paper we will address the situation where the component systems are so-called legacy systems; i.e. systems that are given beforehand and which are to interoperate in an integrated single framework in which the legacy systems are to maintain as much as possible their respective autonomy.

Data integration systems are characterized by an architecture based on a global schema and a set of local schemas. There are generally three situations in which the data integration problem occurs. The first is known as global-as-view (GAV) in which the global schema is defined directly in terms of the source schemas. GAV systems

T. Yakhno (Ed.): ADVIS 2004, LNCS 3261, pp. 34–46, 2004.

typically arise in the context where the source schemas are given, and the global schema is derived from the local schemas. The second situation is known local-as-view (LAV) in which the relation between the global schema and the sources is established by defining every source as a view over the global schema. LAV systems typically arise in the context where the global schema is given beforehand and the local schemas are derived in terms of the global schema. The third situation is known as data exchange, characterized by the situation that the local source schemas, as well as the global schema are given beforehand; the data integration problem then exists in trying to find a suitable mapping between the given global schema and the given set of local schemas (cf. [18]). An overview of data integration concentrating on LAV and GAV can be found in [17]; papers [1,14,15] concentrate on LAV, and [11,21,22] concentrate on GAV. Our paper focuses on legacy problems in database federations in the context of GAV.

A major problem that we will address in this paper is that of so-called semantic heterogeneity (cf. [9,16,22]). Semantic heterogeneity refers to disagreement on (and differences in) meaning, interpretation, or intended use of related data. The process of creation of uniform representations of data is known as data extraction, whereas data reconciliation is concerned with resolving data inconsistencies. GAV as a means to tackle semantic heterogeneity in database federations is described in [4,5,11,21,22]. These papers concern the following topics: [11] treats data integration under global integrity constraints; [21] concerns integration of local integrity constraints; [22] abstracts from the relational model, as we do in this paper, by offering a solution based on an object-oriented data model (cf. [7,8]). Our paper differs from these papers in the following aspects. In contrast to [11], we also take local integrity constraints into account; furthermore, [11] adopts an approach restricted to so-called sound views instead of exact ones. Paper [21] abstracts from problems concerning data extraction by assuming that these problems have been resolved beforehand (i.e. before the actual mapping from local to global is investigated), and concentrates solely on integrating integrity constraints. Our paper, in contrast, treats data extraction and reconciliation in a combined setting and as an integral part of the mapping from local to global. Finally, paper [22] refrains from a structural approach (based on the concept of class, as we do, rather than instance) to solve problems concerning constraint integration.

We will focus on the UML/OCL data model to tackle the problem of semantic heterogeneity in data integration. The Object Constraint Language OCL ([19,23]) offers a textual means to enhance UML diagrams, offering formal precision in combination with high expressiveness. In particular [3] has shown that OCL has a query facility that is at least as expressive as SQL. Also, UML is the de facto standard language for analysis and design in object-oriented frameworks, and is being employed more and more for analysis and design of information systems, in particular information systems based on databases and their applications. By abstracting from the typical restrictions imposed by standard database models (such as the relational model), we can now concentrate on the actual modeling issues. Subsequently, papers [10,12,13] offer descriptions of methods and tools in which a transformation from our model to the relational data model could take place.

One of the central notions in database modeling is the notion of a database view, which closely corresponds to the notion of derived class in UML. In [3] it is demonstrated that in the context of UML/OCL the notion of derived class can be given a formal basis, and that derived classes in OCL have the expressive power of the relational algebra. We will employ OCL and the notion of derived class as a means to treat database constraints and database views in a federated context. In this paper we will demonstrate that our particular mediating system integrates component schemas without loss of constraint information; i.e., no loss of constraint information available at the component level will take place as the result of integrating on the level of the virtual federated database. Key to this result is the construction of a so-called homogenizing function mapping schemas of component databases to the schema of the integrated database. Using the concept of exact view (cf. [2,11]), we will establish that only when we construct a specific isomorphic mapping from the sources to the global schema, that we will obtain this result of no information loss. In this respect, we deviate from the approach adopted in [11].

2   Basic Principles: Databases and Views in UML/OCL

Let's consider the case that we have a class called Emp1 with attributes nm1 and sal1, indicating the name and salary (in euros) of an employee object belonging to class Emp1. Now consider the case where we want to add a class, say Emp2, which is defined as a class whose objects are completely derivable from objects coming from class Emp1, but with the salaries expressed in cents. The calculation is performed in the following manner. Assume that the attributes of Emp2 are nm2 and sal2, respectively (indicating name and salary attributes for Emp2 objects), and assume that for each object e1:Emp1 we can obtain an object e2:Emp2 by stipulating that e2.nm2=e1.nm1 and e2.sal2=(100 * e1.sal1). By definition the total set of instances of Emp2 is the set obtained from the total set of instances from Emp1 by applying the calculation rules as described above. Hence, class Emp2 is a view of class Emp1, in accordance with the concept of a view as known from the relational database literature. In UML terminology [3,10,23], we can say that Emp2 is a derived class, since it is completely derivable from other already existing class elements in the model description containing model type Emp1.

We will now show how to faithfully describe Emp2 as a derived class in UML/OCL ([3,23]) in such a way that it satisfies the requirements of a (relational) view. First of all, we must satisfy the requirement that the set of instances of class Emp2 is the result of a calculation applied to the set of instances of class Emp1. The basic idea is that we introduce a class called DB that has an association to class Emp1, and that we define within the context of the database DB an attribute called Emp2. A database object will reflect the actual state of the database, and the system class DB will only consist of one object in any of its states. Hence the variable self in the context of the class DB will always denote the actual state of the database that we are considering. In the context of this database class we can then define the calculation obtaining the set of instances of Emp2 by taking the set of instances of Emp1 as input.

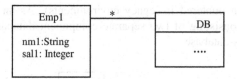

```
context  DB
def: Emp2: Set(Tupletype{nm2:String, sal2: Integer}) =
        (self.emp1 -> collect(e:Emp1 |
        Tuple{nm2=e.nm1, sal2=(100*e.sal1)}))-> asSet
```

In this way, we specify Emp2 as the result of a calculation performed on base class Emp1. Graphically, we could represent Emp2 as follows

DB
/Emp2:   Set(Tupletype{nm2:String,   sal2:

(1)

where the slash-prefix of Emp2 indicates that Emp2 is a derived attribute. Since in practice such a graphical representation could give rise to rather large box diagrams (due to lengthy type definitions), we will use the following (slightly abused) graphical notation (2) to indicate this derived class

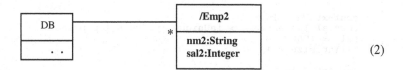

(2)

The intention is that these two graphical representations are to be considered equivalent; i.e., graphical representation (2) is offered as a diagrammatical convention with the sole purpose that it be formally equivalent (translatable) to graphical representation (1). Note that we have introduced a root class DB as an aid to represent the derived class Emp2. Since in OCL, we only have the possibility to define attributes and operations within the context of a certain class, and class Emp1 is clearly not sufficient to offer the right context for the definition of such a derived construct as derived class Emp2, we had to move up one level in abstraction towards a class such as DB. A derived class then becomes a derived attribute on the level of the class DB. We refer to [3,23] for more details on derived classes in UML/OCL.

In sections 5, 6 and 7 we will show how to model a database federation in the UML/OCL-framework as a certain view on component databases.

3   Component Frames

We can also consider a complete collection of databases by looking at so-called component frames, where each (labelled) component is an autonomous database system (typically encountered in legacy environments). As an example consider a component frame consisting of two separate component database systems: a CRM-database and a Sales-database

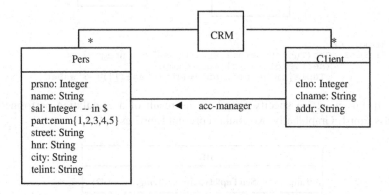

We offer a short explanation of some of the less self-explanatory aspects of CRM: `Pers` is the class of employees responsible for management of client resources; `part` indicates the number of days that employees are allowed to work part time; `hnr` indicates house number; `telint` indicates internal telephone number; `acc-manager` indicates the employee (account manager) that is responsible for some client's account. We furthermore assume that database CRM has the following constraints

```
context Pers inv:
Pers.allInstances --> isUnique (p: Pers | p.prsno)
sal <= 1500
telint.size = 4

context Client inv:
Client.allInstances --> isUnique (c: Client | c.clno)
```

The second database is the so-called Sales-database SALES

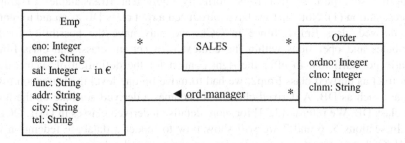

We offer a short explanation of some of the less self-explanatory aspects of SALES: `Emp` is the class of employees responsible for management of client orders; `func` indicates the function an employee has within the organization; `ord-manager` indicates the employee (order manager) that is responsible for some client's order. We assume, furthermore, that this second database has the following constraints

```
context Emp inv:
Emp.allInstances --> isUnique (p: Emp | p.eno)
sal >= 1000
tel.size <= 16

context Order inv:
Order.allInstances --> isUnique (c: Order | c.ordno)
ord-manager.func = `Sales'
```

We can now place the two databases CRM and SALES without confusion into one component frame CF as seen in the following diagram

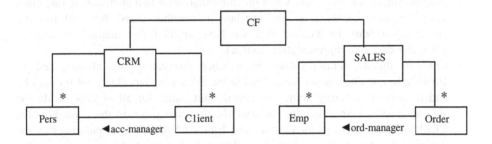

The two databases CRM and SALES are, in the case of this example, assumed to be related, in the sense that an order-object residing in class Order in SALES is associated to a certain client-object in the class Client in CRM.

4   Semantic Heterogeneity

The problems we are facing when trying to integrate the data found in legacy component frames are well-known and are extensively documented (cf. [20]). We will focus on one of the large categories of integration problems coined as semantic heterogeneity (cf. [9,16,22]). Semantic heterogeneity refers to disagreement on (and differences in) meaning, interpretation, or intended use of related data. Examples of problems in semantic heterogeneity are data extraction and data reconciliation. The process of creation of uniform representations of data is known as data extraction, whereas data reconciliation is concerned with resolving data inconsistencies. Integration of the source database schemas into one encompassing schema can be a tricky business due to: homonyms and synonyms, data conversion, default values, missing attributes, and subclassing. These five categories form the main problems in integrating data. We will now shortly describe in informal terms how these problems can be tackled. In sections 5, 6, and 7 we will show how these problems can be treated in the UML/OCL-framework.

– Conflicts due to homonyms are resolved by mapping two same name occurrences (but with different semantics) to different names in the integrated model. Synonyms are treated analogously, by mapping two different names (with the same semantics) to one common name. In the sequel, we will use the abbreviations **hom (syn)** to indicate that we have applied this method to solve a particular case of homonym (synonym) conflicts.

- Conflicts due to conversion arise when two attributes have the same meaning, but that their domain values are differently represented. For example, the two attributes sal in the Pers and the Emp class of databases CRM and SALES, respectively, both indicate the salary of an employee, but in the first case the salary is represented in the currency dollars ($), while in the latter case the currency is given in euros (€). One of the things we can do, is to convert the two currencies to a common value (e.g. $, invoking a function convertTo$). Another kind of conversion can occur when the combination of two attributes in one class have the same meaning as one attribute in another class. We will use the abbreviation **conv** to indicate that we have applied this method to solve a particular case of a representation conflict.

- Conflicts due to default values occur when integrating two classes, and an attribute in one class is not mentioned in the other (similar) class, but it could be added there by offering some suitable default value for all objects inside the second class. As an example, consider the attribute part in the class Pers (in CRM): it could also be added to the class Emp (in SALES) by stipulating that the default value for all objects in Emp will be 5 (indicating full-time employment). We will use the abbreviation **def** to indicate that we have applied this method to solve a particular case of a default conflict.

- Conflicts due to differentiation occur when the integration of two classes calls for the introduction of some additional attribute in order to discriminate between objects originally coming from these two classes., e.g. in the case of conflicting constraints. Consider as an example the classes Pers (in CRM) and Emp (in SALES). Class Pers has as a constraint that salaries are less than 1500 (in $), while class Emp has as a constraint that salaries are at least 1000 (in €). These two constraints seemingly conflict with each other, obstructing integration of the Pers and the Emp class to a common class, say PERS. However, by adding a discriminating attribute dep to PERS indicating whether the object comes from the CRM or from the SALES department, one can differentiate between two kinds of employees and state the constraint on the integrated level in a suitable way. We will use the abbreviation **diff** to indicate that we have applied this method to solve a particular case of a differentiation conflict.

- Discriminating attributes usually go hand in hand with the introduction of appropriate subclasses. For example, introduction of the discriminating attribute dep (as described above), entails introduction of two subclasses, say CRM and SALES of the common superclass PERS, by listing the attributes, operations and constraints that are specific to CRM- or SALES-objects inside these two newly introduced subclasses. Applying the principle of adding new subclasses in the integration process, is indicated by **sub**.

In the next section we will show how to apply **hom, syn, conv, def, diff** and **sub** in the UML/OCL-framework.

5   An Integrated Database

We now offer our construction of a virtual database DBINT, represented in terms of a derived class in UML/OCL. The database we describe below, intends to capture the integrated meaning of the features found in the component frame described earlier.

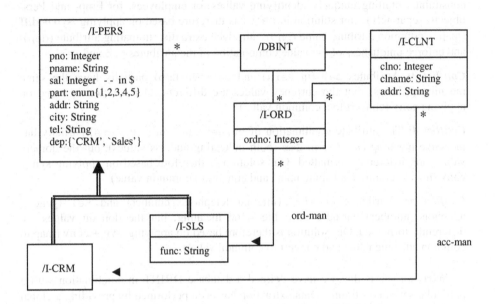

This database has the following constraints:

```
context I-PERS inv:
I-PERS.allInstances ->
  forall(p1, p2: I-PERS | (p1.dep=p2.dep and p1.pno=p2.pno) implies
p1=p2)
I-PERS.allInstances ->
  forall(p:I-PERS |
  (p.oclIsTypeOf(SLS)    implies    (p.sal    >=    1000.convertTo$    and
tel.size<=16 and part=5)) and
  (p.oclIsTypeOf(CRM) implies (p.sal <= 1500 and tel.size=4)))

context I-CLNT inv:
I-CLNT.allInstances --> isUnique (c: I-CLNT | c.clno)

context I-ORD inv:
I-ORD.allInstances --> isUnique (o: I-ORD | o.ordno)
ord-man.func = `Sales'
```

We shall now carefully analyze the specification of this (integrated) database DBINT, and see if it captures the intended meaning of integrating the classes in the component frame CF and resolves potential integration conflicts.

Conflict 1: Classes Emp and Pers in CF have partially overlapping attributes, but Emp has no attribute part yet, and one still needs to discriminate between the two kinds of class objects (due to specific constraints pertaining to the classes Emp and Pers). Our solution in DBINT is based on applying **syn + def + diff + sub** (map to common class name (I-PERS); add a default value (to the attribute part); add an extra discriminating attribute (dep); introduce suitable subclasses (I-CRM and I-SLS).

Conflict 2: Attributes prsno and eno intend to have the same meaning (a key constraint, entailing uniquely identifying values for employees, for Emp- and Pers-objects, separately). Our solution in DBINT is therefore based on applying **syn + diff** (map to common attribute name (pno); introduce extra discriminating attribute (dep)) and enforce uniqueness of the value combination of the attributes pno and dep.

Conflict 3: Attributes sal (in Pers) and sal (in Emp) partially have the same meaning (salaries), but the currency values are different. Our solution is based on applying **conv** (convert to a common value).

Conflict 4: The attribute combination of street and hnr (in Pers) partially has the same meaning as addr in Emp (both indicating address values), but the domain values are differently formatted. Our solution is therefore based on applying **syn + conv** (map to common attribute name and convert to common value).

Conflict 5: Attributes telint (internal telephone number) and tel (general telephone number) partially have the same meaning, but the domain values are differently formatted. Our solution is therefore based on applying **syn + conv** (map to common attribute name and convert to common value).

What we see is that we have defined a database DBINT in combination with a particular set of constraints. Data extraction has been performed by providing a global schema in which the local data coming from CRM and SALES can be uniformly represented, while data reconciliation has been performed by resolving constraint conflicts by suitable use of differentiation on the global level. Our argumentation is given in terms of an example, but the method we use in moving from local to global can easily be given in more general terms. Due to space limitations, we refer the interested reader to [6] for details on the general case.

In the following sections we will show how to explicitly map the local database schemas to the global schema.

6   Integrating by Isomorphism

Our strategy to integrate a collection of legacy databases -given in some component frame CF- into an integrated database DBINT is based on the following principle: An integrated database DBINT is intended to hold (and maintain to hold!) exactly the "union" of the data in the source databases in the component frame CF. In particular, this means that a given arbitrary update offered to the global database should correspond to a unique specific update on a (collection of) base table(s) in the component frame (and vice versa). We have to keep in mind that any update, say τ, on the global level is an update on a virtual (non-materialized) view; hence it has to correspond to some concrete update, say μ, implementing τ on the local level of the component frame. This is the existence requirement. There is also a uniqueness requirement that has to be met. Suppose, for example, that some update τ on the global level corresponds to two different updates, say μ and μ', on the local level. This would lead to an undesirable situation, related to the fact that in a database federation, existing legacy components remain to exist after integration, and also are assumed to respect existing applications   (i.e., those applications running on the legacy databases irrespective of the fact that such a legacy database happens to also participate in some global encompassing federation). Such an existing application could involve a query on a legacy database, which could give two different query results, depending on which of the two concrete updates μ and μ' is performed on the local level. A database view, such as DBINT, satisfying both the existence and uniqueness criterium as described above, is called an exact view. In our setting in which we wish to construct DBINT as an exact view over the component databases, the results offered in [2] entail that the universe of discourse of component frame CF and the universe of discourse of the integrated database DBINT are, in a mathematical sense, *isomorphic*. Only in this way will we not lose any information when mapping the legacy components to the integrated database (and vice versa). We can depict the situation as follows

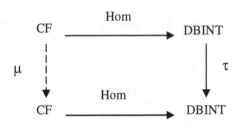

where, given a CF-state s and a transformation τ from $\text{Hom}(s)$ to some other state in DBINT, one is to find a unique mapping μ from CF-states to CF-states such that the diagram commutes; i.e. $\tau(\text{Hom}(s)) = \text{Hom}(\mu(s))$, for arbitrary s.

It is easily shown that, for a given (but arbitrary) transformation τ, such a mapping μ always and uniquely exists, when the homogenizing function Hom constitutes a bijection.

In the following section, we will construct such a bijective homogenizing function. This will be achieved by introducing suitable conversion operations, which will serve as basic building blocks for the eventual construction of our mapping Hom.

7   Mapping the Component Frame to the Integrated Database

In this section we will describe how to (implicitly) define a homogenizing function Hom inside CF satisfying the requirements as listed in Section 6 above. The idea is that we define a derived attribute /DBINT in the class CF satisfying the requirement that each CF-state is associated to one and exactly one value of DBINT. Hence, Hom applied to CF.self results in the value of CF.self.DBINT. We will show how to define such a derived attribute /DBINT. We proceed as follows. We introduce the following type abbreviations

```
PERSTYPE = TupleType(pno: Integer, pname: String, sal: Integer, part:
enum{1,2,3,4,5}, addr: String, city: String, tel: String, dep:
enum{`CRM', `Sales'})

SLSTYPE = TupleType(pno: Integer, pname: String, sal: Integer, part:
enum{1,2,3,4,5}, addr: String, city: String, tel: String, dep:
enum{`CRM', `Sales'}, bonus: Integer, func: String)

CLNTTYPE = TupleType(clno: Integer, clname: String, addr: String, acc-
man: PERSTYPE)

ORDTYPE = TupleType(ordno: Integer, ord-man: SLSTYPE)
```

Furthermore, we introduce a conversion function convertToI-CLNT within the class Client (of CRM) with the following definition

```
context   Client
def: convertToI-CLNT( ): CLNTTYPE =
Tuple{clno = self.clno, clname = self.clname, addr =self.addr, acc-man =
self.acc-manager.convertToI-CRM}
```

In the Pers-class we postulate the existence of a conversion function convertToI-CRM

```
context   Pers
def:  convertToI-CRM( ): PERSTYPE =
Tuple{pno=self.prsn, pname = self.name, sal = self.sal, part =
self.part, addr = self.street ->concat((`  ') ->concat(self.hnr)), city
= self.city, tel= `+31-50-363'->concat(self.telint), dep = `CRM'}
```

Notice that the function convertToI-CRM is injective! (We have assumed that the attribute hnr does not contain two consecutive spaces.) We also define two functions converting the objects in the Emp-class to corresponding objects in the I-SLS and I-PERS class of DBINT, by the conversion functions convertToI-SLS and convertToI-PERS within the class Emp with the following (rather trivial) definition

```
context   Emp
def:  convertToI-SLS( ): SLSTYPE =
Tuple{pno = self.eno, pname = self.name, sal = self.sal.convertTo$, part
= 5, addr = self.addr, city = self.city, tel = self.tel, dep = `SLS',
bonus = self.bonus, func = self.func}

def:  convertToI-PERS( ): PERSTYPE =
Tuple{pno = self.eno, pname = self.name, sal = self.sal.convertTo$, part
=5, addr = self.addr, city = self.city, tel = self.tel, dep = `SLS'}
```

A bit more difficult is the definition of a function converting the objects in the Order-class to corresponding objects in the I-ORD class of DBINT. We do this by employing a conversion function convertToI-ORD within the class Order with the following definition

```
context   Order
def:   convertToI-ORD( ):ORD =
Tuple{ordno = self.ordno,  ord-man = (self.ord-manager).convertToSLS,
Clnt = (self.linkToClient).convertToClnt}
```

where we assume an operation linkToClient to provide a unique link to the Client-object associated with a given Order-object. We are now in the position to relate the component frame CF to the integrated database, coined DBINT. We shall proceed by first defining a basic type DBINTTYPE, and showing how we can define a homogenizing function Hom inside the class CF, mapping elements of the component frame to the integrated database.

```
DBINTTYPE = TupleType(I-CRM: Set(PERSTYPE), I-SLS: Set(SLSTYPE),
I-CLNT: Set(CLNTTYPE), I-ORD: Set(ORDTYPE), I-PERS: Set(PERSTYPE))
```

We now introduce the definition of DBINT as a derived attribute within the context of the component frame class CF:

```
context   CF
def:  DBINT : DBINTTYPE =
Tuple{I-CRM=(self.CRM.Pers.allInstances ->
collect(p| p.convertToI-CRM))-> asSet,
      I-SLS=(self.SALES.Emp.allInstances ->
collect(e| e.convertToI-SLS))-> asSet,
      I-CLNT=(self.CRM.Client.allInstances ->
collect(c| c.convertToI-CLNT))-> asSet,
      I-ORD= (self.Sales.Order.allInstances ->
collect(o| o.convertToI-ORD)) -> asSet,
      I-PERS= ((self.CRM.Pers.allInstances ->
collect(p| p.convertToI-CRM))-> union(self.SALES.Emp.allInstances
                -> collect(e | e.convertToI-PERS)) -> asSet}
```

Since all of the conversion functions involved in the definition of DBINT are injective, we have established that each CF.self is not only associated to a value CF.self.DBINT, but also that each value CF.self.DBINT is associated to a unique state CF.self! We have thus implicitly constructed a homogenizing function Hom mapping a CF-state to a unique DBINT-state, as depicted below

```
(CRM(Pers-table, Client-table), SALES(Emp-table, Order-table))

                Hom

 (I-PERS-table, I-CRM-table, I-SLS-table, I-CLNT-table, I-ORD-table)
```

It is now easily verified that this definition of the homogenizing function indeed results in an integration isomorphism linking the component frame CF to the integrated database DBINT. Our definition of DBINT also captures the desired constraints specified in Section 5.

References

1. Abiteboul, S., Douschka, O.; Complexity of answering queries using materialized views; ACM PODS'98, ACM Press (1998)
2. Abiteboul, S., Hull, R., Vianu, V.; Foundations of Databases; Addison Wesley (1995)

3.   Balsters, H. ; Modeling Database Views with Derived Classes in the   UML/OCL-framework; «UML» 2003 6th Int. Conf.; LNCS 2863, Springer (2003)
4.   Balsters, H., de Brock, E.O.; An object-oriented framework for managing cooperating legacy databases; 9th Int. Conf. Object- Oriented Information Systems; LNCS 2817, Springer (2003)
5.   Balsters, H.; de Brock, E.O.; Integration of Integrity Constraints in Database Federations; 6th IFIP TC-11 WG 11.5 Conference on Integrity and Internal Control in Information Systems, Kluwer Academic Press (2003)
6.   Balsters, H.; de Brock, E.O.; Integration of Data Semantics and Integrity Constraints in Heterogeneous Database Federations, SOM Report, University of Groningen (2004)
7.   Balsters, H., de By, R.A., Zicari, R.; Sets and constraints in an object-oriented data model; Proc. 7th ECOOP, LNCS 707, Springer (1993)
8.   Balsters, H., Spelt, D.; Automatic verification of transactions on an object-oriented database, 6th Int. Workshop on Database Programming Languages, LNCS 1369, Springer (1998)
9.   Bouzeghoub, M., Lenzerini, M; Introduction to: data extraction, cleaning, and reconciliation, Special issue; Information Systems (26); Elsevier Science, 2001
10. Blaha, M., Premerlani, W.; Object-oriented modeling and design for database applications; Prentice Hall (1998)
11. Cali, A., Calvanese, D., De Giacomo, G., Lenzerini, M.; Data integration under intergrity constraints; CAISE 2002, LNCS 2348, Springer (2002)
12. Demuth, B., Hussmann, H.; Using UML/OCL constraints for relational database design; «UML»'99: 2nd Int. Conf., LNCS 1723, Springer (1999)
13. Demuth, B., Hussmann, H., Loecher, S.; OCL as a specification language for business rules in database applications; «UML» 2001, 4th Int. Conf., LNCS 2185, Springer (2001)
14. Grahne, G., Mendelzon, A.O.; Tableau techniques for querying information sources through global schemas; ICDT'99, LNCS 1540, Springer (1999)
15. Halevy, A.Y.; Answering queries using views: A survey; VLDB Journal (10) (2001)
16. Hull, R.; Managing Semantic Heterogeneity in Databases; ACM PODS'97, ACM Press (1997)
17. 17. Lenzerini, M.; Data integration: a theoretical perspective; ACM   PODS'02, ACM Press (2002)
18. Miller, R.J., Haas, L.M., Hernandez, M.A.; Schema mapping as query discovery; Proc. 26th VLDB Conf.; Morgan Kaufmann (2000)
19. Response to the UML 2.0 OCL RfP, Revised Submission, Version 1.6 (2003)
20. Sheth, A.P., Larson, J.A.; Federated database systems for managing distributed, heterogeneous and autonomous databases; ACM Computing Surveys 22 (1990)
21. Türker, C., Saake, G.; Global extensional assertions and local integrity constraints in federated schemata; Information Systems (25) 8 (2001)[
22. Vermeer, M., Apers, P.G.M.; The role of integrity constraints in database interoperation; Proc. 22nd VLDB Conf.; Morgan Kaufmann (1996)
23. Warmer, J.B., Kleppe, A.G.; The object constraint language (2nd ed.); Addison Wesley (2003)

On Optimising Data Access Via Materialised Methods in Object-Oriented Systems

Juliusz Jezierski, Mariusz Masewicz, and Robert Wrembel

Poznań University of Technology,
Institute of Computing Science,
Poznań, Poland
{jjezierski, mmasewicz, rwrembel}@cs.put.poznan.pl

Abstract. Optimising access to data returned by methods is an important issue in object–oriented programs, databases, and distributed object environments. Since methods are written in a high–level programming language, optimising their executions is a serious problem. In this paper we present our technique of reducing access time to data returned by methods by means of the *hierarchical materialization* that we developed. In this technique, the materialisation of method m results also in the materialisation of intermediate results of methods called from m. Moreover, we present data structures and evaluation of two optimisation techniques that allow to query results returned by methods.

1 Introduction

Object–oriented applications usually take advantage of methods as a mean of accessing objects [2]. A method can be a very complex program, whose computation may last long and therefore an efficient execution of a method has a great impact on an application response time. Optimising access to data returned by methods is difficult as methods are written in a high–level programming language.

A promising technique, called method precomputation or materialisation may be used in order to reduce access time to data. The *materialisation of a method* consists in computing the result of a method once, store it persistently in a database and then use the persistent value when the method is invoked next time. On the one hand, the materialisation of a method reduces time necessary to access the method's result, especially when its execution takes long time. But on the other hand, materialised results have to be kept up to date when data used to compute the results change.

Example 1. Let us consider a simplified CAD design of a personal digital assistant (PDA), as shown in Fig.1. Each of these classes has method power() that computes and returns power consumption of a certain object. A collaboration diagram between the instances of the above classes is shown in Fig.2. The value of power() for object m515 (the instance of *PDA*) is computed as follows: mb100->power()+sc100->power()+dsp100->power(), whereas mb100->power()

T. Yakhno (Ed.): ADVIS 2004, LNCS 3261, pp. 47–56, 2004.
© Springer-Verlag Berlin Heidelberg 2004

is computed as follows: `self->power_cons+cpu33->power(int v_frequency)`, where `power_cons` is an attribute that stores power consumption of a main board itself. The values of `sc100->power()` and `dsp100->power()` are computed similarly as for a main board.

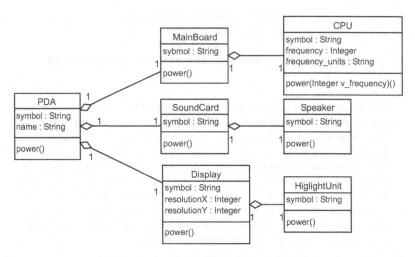

Fig. 1. An example CAD design of a PDA

A user can search the PDA designs mainly in two following ways: (1) querying various features of a given object as well as (2) searching for an object that fulfils certain criteria.

Querying Features of a Certain Object. Let us consider a user interested in getting power consumption of object `m515`. To this end, method `m515->power()` is executed. For any subsequent user interested in power consumption of `m515` the same method is executed every time it is invoked. In order to reduce access time to data computed by methods, their results can be persistently stored, i.e. materialised. Having materialised the result of a method computed for an object, any subsequent invocation of the same method, for the same object can then use the already materialised value.

Searching for an Object Fulfilling Certain Criteria. Let us assume that a user is interested in finding all PDAs whose power consumption is less than 1W. To this end, the system has to browse through all designed PDAs and for every PDA, method `power()` has to be executed. If this method is computationally complex, a user will observe high time overhead. In order to reduce this overhead an index defined on precomputed method results can be used.

This **paper contribution** includes the extension of our previous work on materialisation of methods (cf. [8, 9]) with the following: (1) the development and implementation of an index defined on method results; (2) the development

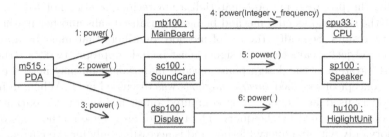

Fig. 2. An example collaboration diagram between class instances of a PDA design

and experimental evaluation of object searching technique using materialised methods and the index defined on method results.

This paper is organised as follows: Section 2 discusses related approaches to method materialisation. Sections 3 and 4 overview our technique of method materialisation and storage structures that support this technique, respectively. Their experimental evaluation is presented in Section 5. Section 6 summarises the paper.

2 Related Work

Method materialisation was proposed in [7, 1, 10, 11] in the context of indexing techniques and query optimisation. The work of [7] sets up the analytical framework for estimating costs of caching complex objects. Two data representations are considered, i.e. procedural representation and object identity based representation. In the analysis, the author has not considered the dependencies between calling and called procedures. Moreover, the maintenance of cached values has not been taken into account either.

In the approach of [1], the results of materialised methods are stored in an index structure based on B-tree, called *method–index*. While executing queries that use method M, the system checks the method–index for M before executing the method. If the appropriate entry is found, the already precomputed value is returned. Otherwise, method M is executed for an object. The application of method materialisation proposed in [1] is limited to methods that: (1) do not have input arguments, (2) use only atomic type attributes to compute their values, and (3) do not modify values of objects. Otherwise, a method is left non–materialised.

The concept of [10, 11] uses the so called *Reverse Reference Relation*, which stores information on: an object used to materialise method M, the name of a materialised method, and the set of objects passed as arguments to M. Furthermore, this approach maintains also the information about the attributes, called *relevant attributes*, whose values were used for the materialisation of M. For the purpose of methods invalidation, every object has appended the set of those method identifiers that used the object. The limitations of this approach are as follows.

Firstly, the proposed method materialisation technique does not take into account the scenario when a method being materialised calls another method and uses its results. Secondly, the set of method identifiers that must be appended to every object means that a designer must include appropriate data structures into the system at the design phase, even if materialisation may never be used.

A concept of so called *inverse methods* was discussed in [4]. When an inverse method is used in a query, it is computed once, instead of computing it for each object returned by the query. The result of an inverse method is stored in memory only within a query lifetime and is accessible only for the current query.

3   Hierarchical Materialisation of Methods — Overview

In [8] we proposed a novel technique of method materialisation, called *hierarchical materialisation*. When hierarchical materialisation is applied to method m_i, then the result of m_i is stored persistently and additionally, the results of methods called from m_i are also stored persistently. Selecting method m_i for the materialisation, causes that the result of the first invocation of m_i for a given object o_i is stored persistently. Every subsequent invocation of m_i for the same object o_i uses the already materialised value. When object o_i, used to materialise the result of method m_i, is updated or deleted, then m_i has to be recomputed. This recomputation can use unaffected intermediate materialised results, thus reducing the recomputation time overhead.

Example 2. In order to illustrate the idea behind the *hierarchical materialisation* let us consider a simple database of PDA designs, as discussed in Section 1. Let us assume that the power() method was invoked for instance m515 of the *PDA* class and was materialised hierarchically. In our example, the hierarchical materialisation results in materialising also mb100->power(), sc100->power(), and dsp100->power().

Having materialised the methods discussed above, let us assume that the component object cpu33 was replaced with another central processing unit using 133MHz clock, instead of 33MHz. This change results in higher power consumption of main board mb100, furthermore, a power consumption of the whole PDA m515 increases. The materialised values of m515->power() and mb100->power() have to be invalidated and recomputed during next invocation. However, during the recomputation of m515->power(), the unaffected materialised results of sc100->power() and dsp100->power() can be used.

Methods may have various numbers of input arguments, that can be of various types. Generally, methods that have input arguments are not good candidates for the materialisation. Moreover, hierarchical materialisation of methods is efficient in systems were data are read much more frequently than modified, i.e. materialised values change rarely. Thus, the main application area include object–relational data warehouses [5, 6, 3] where materialized object–oriented views are used for implementing such warehouses. While materialising an object–oriented view one has to consider the materialisation of objects structure as well as methods.

4 Data Structures

In order to materialise methods, maintain the materialised results, and use materialised values, we developed five data structures whose contents are stored in a database. These structures, which are described below, are called *Materialised Methods Dictionary*, *Materialised Method Results Structure*, *Graph of Method Calls*, *Inverse References Index*, and *Method Value Index*.

4.1 Materialised Methods Dictionary

Materialised Methods Dictionary (**MMD**) makes available the following data dictionary information about every defined method: (1) the name of a method, (2) the name of a class a method was defined in, (3) the type of a value returned by a method, (4) the implementation of a method, (5) a flag (set by a database administrator) indicating whether a method was set as materialised or not, and (6) the array of formal input arguments of a method.

4.2 Materialised Method Results Structure

Materialised Method Results Structure (**MMRS**) stores the following information about every materialised method: (1) the identifier of a method, (2) an object identifier of the object which a method was invoked for, (3) the array of input argument values a method was invoked with, (4) the value returned by a method while executed for a given object and for a given array of input argument values.

When method m_i is invoked for a given object o_i and this method has been previously set as materialised, then **MMRS** is searched in order to get the result of m_i invoked for o_i. If it is not found then, m_i is computed for o_i and the result is stored in **MMRS**. Otherwise, the materialised result of m_i is fetched from **MMRS** instead of executing m_i. When an object used to compute the materialised value of m_i is updated or deleted, then the materialised value becomes invalid and is removed from **MMRS**.

4.3 Graph of Method Calls

A method defined in one class can invoke other methods defined in other classes. The chain of method dependencies, where one method calls another one, is called *Graph of Method Calls* (**GMC**). **GMC** is used by the procedure that maintains the materialised results of methods. When materialised method m_j becomes invalid all the materialised methods that use the value of m_j also become invalid. In order to invalidate those methods the content of **GMC** is used. **GMC** stores pairs of values: the identifier of a calling method and the identifier of a method being called.

4.4 Inverse References Index

When materialised method m_j becomes invalid all the materialised methods that use the value of m_j have to be invalidated. In order to invalidate dependent methods the system must be able to find inverse references in object composition hierarchy. In order to ease the traversal of a composition hierarchy in an inverse direction we use so called *inverse references* for each object. An inverse reference for object o_j is the reference from o_j to an object that is referencing o_j. The references are maintained in a data structure called *Inverse References Index* (***IRI***). For example, an inverse reference for object cpu33 (cf. Fig.2) contains one reference to object mb100. At the implementation level, a separated ***IRI*** is created for every, but a root class in a composition hierarchy.

4.5 Method Value Index

Method Value Index (***MVI***) is an index defined on results of methods. Every method of a class has its own ***MVI***. The index stores the following: (1) the value of a method actual input argument, (2) the value returned by a method, and (3) an object identifier of an object a method was invoked for. By using this index, the system is able to quickly find answers to queries that use methods, e.g. show all PDAs with power consumption lower than 1W.

4.6 Optimising Data Access by Means of *MMRS* and *MVI*

Users most frequently interact with objects by querying their content in two following ways (as mentioned in Section 1):

- A user can query various features of a given object by means of calling methods of this object. Querying a particular object can be optimised by means of materialising methods results. In order to get the value of a method invoked with a certain set of input argument values and for a certain object, the content of ***MMRS*** is searched.
- A user can search for an object that fulfils given criteria. This requires reading many object and for each of them invoke methods of interest. This type of a query can be optimised by means of indexing method results. In order to find the set of objects that have a certain value of a given method with a given set of input argument values, the content of ***MVI*** is searched.

We propose two following algorithms for searching objects having a given value v of a given method m_i.

The "*MVI+FS*" algorithm. The algorithm is executed in the following steps.

1. Firstly, the content of ***MVI*** is searched. Objects whose method m_i returns value v are returned to a user immediately. Since the ***MVI*** might not contain all the objects, our algorithm has to scan all other objects in a database, in the second step.
2. While scanning the rest of a database, objects already returned to a user are skipped (to this end a hash table is used), whereas for all other objects method m_i is executed and if the condition is fulfilled, an object is returned to a user.

The "*MVI+SINDX*" algorithm. The algorithm is executed in the following steps.

1. Firstly, the content of **MVI** is searched. Objects whose method m_i returns value v are returned to a user immediately, as in previous algorithm.
2. Secondly, the difference between **MVI** and a standard index on an object identifier (OID), which is maintained by the system and which references every object in a database, is computed. Objects from the difference set are then accessed by the standard index on OID. For every object from this set method m_i is executed and if the condition is fulfilled, an object is returned to a user.

4.7   Maintaining Materialised Results of Methods

A materialised method becomes out of date when the values used to compute the method change. When the materialised value of m_i becomes obsolete it is removed from **MMRS**. The removal of the result of method m_j causes that the results of methods that called m_j also become invalid and have to be removed from **MMRS**. The removal of materialised results from **MMRS** is recursively executed up to the root of **GMC** by the procedure that traverses **GMC** and aggregation relationships in an inverse direction, i.e. from bottom to top. The procedure has two following input arguments: an identifier of a method being invalidated and an object identifier the method was materialized for.

5   Experimental Evaluation

The proposed hierarchical materialisation technique has been implemented as a prototype system (cf. [9] for details) in Java, on top of the *FastObjects t7* (ver. 9.0) object–oriented database system. The current implementation of hierarchical materialisation has a few following limitations: (1) selection of a method for the materialisation is explicitly made by a database administrator/designer during the system tuning activity; (2) the body of a method being materialised may not contain SQL commands as it would cause difficulties in registering the used object identifiers and values of the method in **MMRS**; (3) it does not contain a method access optimisation module.

This section presents experimental results that measure profits gained from using the hierarchical materialisation technique combined with using the *Method Value Index*. The structure of our *Graph of Method Calls* used in the experiments is shown in Fig.3. Every method from an upper level calls 5 different methods (of 5 different objects) at the lower level, except levels 8, 9, and 10 where every method calls 4 methods from a lower level. The number of levels in **GMC** equals to 10. Object composition hierarchy follows the structure of **GMC**, thus every root complex object is composed of 1332030 component objects. Our test database was composed of 10 root complex objects of parameterised size that ranged from 10B to 1kB, yielding in the latter case a database of over 13GB.

In our experiments we evaluated two algorithms described in Section 4.6. The algorithms were evaluated for objects of 10B (Fig.4) as well as 1kB (Fig. 5)

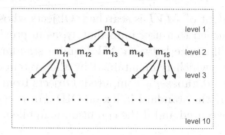

Fig. 3. A test *GMC*

of size. The number of materialised branches in *GMC* was parameterised and ranged from 0% (meaning no materialisation of branches in a direct lower level) to 100% (full materialisation of branches in a direct lower level). The results of applying the *"MVI+FS"* algorithm are shown in Fig.4 and 5, marked as "MVI+FS". Whereas the results of applying *"MVI+SINDX"* are shown in Fig.4 and 5, marked as "MVI+SINDX".

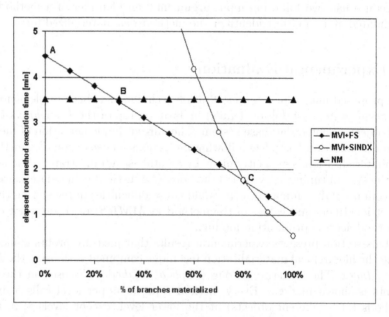

Fig. 4. Elapsed execution time of root methods executed on 10 root complex objects (object size=10B)

Point *A* in Fig.4 and 5 for the *"MVI+FS"* algorithm represents situation where no methods were materialised. Thus the time difference between point *A* and the value of "NM" represents time overhead for method materialisation.

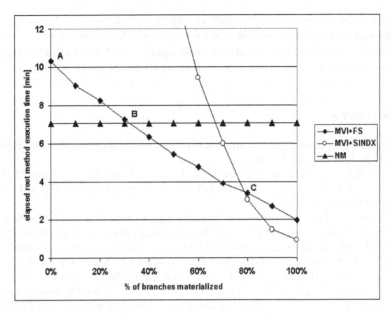

Fig. 5. Elapsed execution time of root methods executed on 10 root complex objects (object size=1kB)

The execution time of a non-materialised method (marked as **"NM"**) is constant, which is obvious. The materialisation of approximately 30% of branches compensates time overhead for searching the *MMRS*, cf. point *B* on the charts. When the number of materialised branches exceeds 30%, the hierarchical materialisation and the *"MVI+FS"* algorithm reduce access time to method results. When the number of materialised results grow, it is less efficient to scan the whole database with the *"MVI+FS"* algorithm. At point *C*, i.e. 80% of materialised branches, the *"MVI+SINDX"* algorithm gives better results as it uses a standard index on OID to fetch approximately 20% of database objects for method execution. This behaviour is independent on object sizes.

6   Summary, Conclusions, and Future Work

Materialisation of methods in object–oriented systems (databases, data warehouses, and distributed computing environments) is a promising technique increasing system performance. In this paper we refined our hierarchical materialisation technique [8], with: (1) the development and implementation of an index defined on method results, i.e. *MVI*, and (2) the development and experimental evaluation of two algorithms for object searching using materialised methods and *MVI*. As our results show, the *"MVI+FS"* algorithm is better for lower number of materialised branches in *GMC*, whereas the *"MVI+SINDX"* algorithm gives better results for larger number of materialised branches - 80% in our experiments. This observation leads us to a conclusion, that a method optimiser should dynamically apply an appropriate algorithm depending on the number of materialised branches and a cost of method execution.

Future work will concentrate on developing a cost model for methods and adding support for automatic selection of methods for materialisation.

References

1. Bertino E.: Method precomputation in object–oriented databases. SIGOS Bulletin, 12 (2, 3), 1991, pp. 199-212
2. Cattell R., G., G., Barry D., Berler M., Eastman J., Jordan D., Russel C., Shadow O., Stanienda T., Velez F.: Object Database Standard: ODMG 3.0, Morgan Kaufmann Publishers, 2000
3. Czejdo B., Eder J., Morzy T., Wrembel R.: Design of a Data Warehouse over Object–Oriented and Dynamically Evolving Data Sources. Proc. of the DEXA'01 Workshop Parallel and Distributed Databases, Munich, Germany, September, 2001
4. Eder J., Frank H., Liebhart W.: Optimization of Object–Oriented Queries by Inverse Methods. Proc. of East/West Database Workshop, Austria, 1994
5. Gopalkrishnan V., Li Q., Karlapalem K.: Efficient Query Processing with Associated Horizontal Class Partitioning in an Object Relational Data Warehousing Environment. In Proc. of DMDW'2000, Sweden, 2000
6. Huynh T.N., Mangisengi O., Tjoa A.M.: Metadata for Object–Relational Data Warehouse. In Proc. of DMDW'2000, Sweden, 2000
7. Jhingran A.: Precomputation in a Complex Object Environment. Proc of the IEEE Data Engineering Conference, Japan, 1991, pp. 652-659
8. Jezierski J., Masewicz M., Wrembel R., Czejdo B.: Designing Storage Structures for Management of Materialised Methods in Object-Oriented Databases. Proc. of the 9th Int. Conf. on Object-Oriented Information Systems (OOIS 2003), Geneva, Switzerland, September, 2003, LNCS 2817, pp. 202-213
9. Jezierski J., Masewicz M., Wrembel R.: Prototype System for Method Materialisation and Maintenance in Object-Oriented Databases. Proc. of the ACM Symposium on Applied Computing (SAC), Nicosia, Cyprus, March, 2004
10. Kemper A., Kilger C., Moerkotte G.: Function Materialization in Object Bases. Proc. of the SIGMOD Conference, 1991, pp. 258-267
11. Kemper A., Kilger C., Moerkotte G.: Function Materialization in Object Bases: Design, Realization, and Evaluation. IEEE Transactions on Knowledge and Data Engineering, Vol. 6, No. 4, 1994

Some Modifications of Bucket-Based Algorithms for Query Rewriting Using Views

Qingyuan Bai[1], Jun Hong[2], and Michael F. McTear[1]

[1] School of Computing and Mathematics, University of Ulster,
Newtownabbey, Co.Antrim BT37 0QB, UK
{q.bai, mf.mctear}@ulster.ac.uk
[2] School of Computer Science, Queen's University Belfast, Belfast BT7 1NN, UK
j.hong@qub.ac.uk

Abstract. Query rewriting using views is an important topic in data integration. A number of rewriting algorithms, such as the SVB algorithm, the MiniCon algorithm and the inverse rules algorithm, have been developed. All the algorithms can generate a maximally-contained rewriting of a given query, which is the union of a set of conjunctive rewritings contained in the given query. In this paper, we first argue that the condition for forming a shared-variable bucket in the SVB algorithm can be modified in the case where a shared variable in a query is mapped to a distinguished variable that is also a join attribute in a view. Under the modified condition, we may create more shared-variable buckets so that fewer rewritings can be generated than the SVB algorithm. Second, the SVB algorithm does not handle a constant in a view properly in the case where a shared variable of a query is mapped to a constant of a view. We propose to use a pseudo shared-variable bucket to address this issue. The only difference between the SVB algorithm and the MiniCon algorithm is that the latter considers a head homomorphism on a view. However, the head homomorphism on a view is not related to the condition we intend to modify in this paper. The modifications we present are also applicable to the MiniCon algorithm.

1 Introduction

In a mediator-based data integration system, a mediated schema is used to make queries and describe the contents of data sources. Because the actual data is stored in the data sources, we need to reformulate user queries over the mediated schema into new queries over the data source schemas. This process is called query rewriting using views. In general, there are two main approaches to query rewriting using views, i.e., Global As View (GAV) and Local As View (LAV). As stated in [3], the LAV approach is more suitable for a data integration system in a dynamic environment.

So far, there have been a number of rewriting algorithms. These algorithms can be divided into two categories, bucket-based algorithms and inverse rule-based algorithms. Both the SVB algorithm [5] and the MiniCon algorithm [6] are bucket-based algorithms. They can generate all the possible rewritings of a given query, whose union is a maximally-contained rewriting of the query. However, the condition for

T. Yakhno (Ed.): ADVIS 2004, LNCS 3261, pp. 57–67, 2004.
© Springer-Verlag Berlin Heidelberg 2004

forming a shared-variable bucket in the SVB algorithm or for forming a MCD containing multiple subgoals in the MiniCon algorithm can be modified in the case where a shared variable in a given query is mapped to a distinguished variable that is also a join attribute in a view. The following example shows that both algorithms generate a maximally-contained rewriting of the given query Q in a less efficient way.

Example 1 We use Datalog language to represent views and queries throughout this paper. A rule defines a query or a view. The left-hand side and right-hand side of a rule are called the head and the body of the rule respectively. The body of a rule consists of conjunctions of a set of subgoals. Suppose that there are two views:

$V_1(X, Z, Y)$:- parents(X, Z), parents(Z, Y).
$V_2(X, Y)$:- parents(X, Y).
The relation, parents(X, Y), is defined in a mediated schema, describing that X is a parent of Y.

A query is posed as follows:

$Q(X, Y)$:- parents(X, K), parents(K, J), parents(J, Y).

All the bucket-based algorithms are based on containment mappings from the variables of a query to those of a view. There are two types of variables in a query/view. A variable is a distinguished variable if it appears in the head of a query/view. Otherwise it is an existential variable. An existential variable is a shared variable if it appears in more than one subgoal in the body of a query/view. In order to proceed with the above example, we first have a brief look at the SVB algorithm.

The SVB algorithm creates two types of buckets, single-subgoal buckets (SSB for short) and shared-variable buckets (SVB for short). The algorithm creates a SSB for a subgoal R of a given query Q over a view V if R appears in V and the variable mappings from Q to V satisfy the following condition, i.e., for each variable in R of Q, if it is a distinguished variable then it should be mapped to a distinguished variable of V. The algorithm creates a SVB for a set of subgoals G of a given query Q over a view V only if G contains shared variables that are mapped to the existential variables of V. In this example, because the shared variables K and J are mapped to distinguished variables rather than existential variables, in V_1 and V_2, the SVB algorithm creates only SSBs rather than SVBs, as shown in Table 1.

Table 1. The buckets for every subgoal for the query in Example 1

parents(X,K)	parents(K,J)	parents(J,Y)
$V_1(X,K,Y_1)$	$V_1(K,J,Y_2)$	$V_1(J,Y,Y_3)$
$V_1(X_1,X,K)$	$V_1(X_2,K,J)$	$V_1(X_3,J,Y)$
$V_2(X,K)$	$V_2(K,J)$	$V_2(J,Y)$

There are up to 3*3*3=27 rewritings generated by combining a view from each of the buckets. For example, one rewriting of Q is:

$Q'(X, Y)$:- $V_1(X,K,Y_1)$, $V_1(K,J,Y_2)$, $V_1(J,Y,Y_3)$.

The union of these 27 rewritings is a maximally-contained rewriting of Q. However, the following rewriting that contains only two subgoals is a valid rewriting of Q.

$Q_1(X,Y) :- V_1(X,K,J), V_1(J,Y,Y3)$.

We can show that Q' and Q_1 are equivalent, but Q_1 can not be directly obtained by the SVB algorithm. In this paper, we present a new algorithm that can generate a smaller set of rewritings, some of which with fewer subgoals than the SVB algorithm.

In addition, the SVB algorithm does not handle constants properly. Usually, it treats constants as distinguished variables. As shown in the following example [8], this leads to the generation of an invalid rewriting.

Example 2 Suppose that a given query and two views are defined as follows:

$Q(X) :- P_1(U,X), P_2(X,U)$.

$V_1(Y) :- P_1(1, Y)$.

$V_2(X) :- P_2(X, 2)$.

We see that there exist mappings φ_1 and φ_2 from a shared variable U in Q to a constant in V_1 and V_2, i.e., $\varphi_1(U)=1$ and $\varphi_2(U)=2$. If a constant is treated as a distinguished variable, we would generate a rewriting using the SVB algorithm as follows.

$Q'(X) :- V_1(X), V_2(X)$.

However, this rewriting is incorrect because $1 \neq 2$.

These examples motivate us to modify the process of forming a SVB in the SVB algorithm. Though we focus only on the SVB algorithm, the modifications we make also hold for the MiniCon algorithm because the only difference between the SVB algorithm and the MiniCon algorithm is that latter considers head homomorphism [6] on a view, which does not affect our modifications.

The rest of the paper is organized as follows. In the next section preliminaries of query rewriting using views are given. In Section 3 we have a brief overview of the related work. In Section 4 we first present a modification of the condition for forming a SVB in the SVB algorithm. We then describe how to use a pseudo SSB and pseudo SVB to handle the case where a shared variable is mapped to a constant. In Section 5 we conclude the paper.

2   Preliminaries

2.1   Queries, Views and Query Containment

A conjunctive query without arithmetic comparisons has the form:

$$Q(\bar{X}) :- R_1(\bar{X}_1),...,R_k(\bar{X}_k)$$

where $R_1(\bar{X}_1),...,R_k(\bar{X}_k)$ are subgoals. The tuples $\bar{X}, \bar{X}_1,...,\bar{X}_k$ contain either variables or constants. We require that the query be safe, i.e., $\bar{X} \subseteq \bar{X}_1 \cup ... \cup \bar{X}_k$. The variables in $\bar{X}$ are distinguished variables, and the others are existential variables. We use Vars(Q) to refer to all the variables in Q and Q(D) refer to the evaluation of Q over a database instance D. A view is a named query.

A query Q_1 is contained in another query Q_2, denoted by $Q_1 \subseteq Q_2$, if the answers to Q_1 are a subset of the answers to Q_2 for any database instance. Containment mappings provide a necessary and sufficient condition for testing query containment. A mapping φ from $\text{Vars}(Q_2)$ to $\text{Vars}(Q_1)$ is a containment mapping if

(1) φ maps every subgoal in the body of Q_2 to a subgoal in the body of Q_1, and
(2) φ maps the head of Q_2 to the head of Q_1.

The query Q_2 contains Q_1 if and only if there is a containment mapping from Q_2 to Q_1. Q_1 is equivalent to Q_2 if and only if $Q_1 \subseteq Q_2$ and $Q_2 \subseteq Q_1$.

2.2   Query Rewriting Using Views

Given a query Q and a set of view definitions $\mathbf{V}=V_1,...,V_n$, a rewriting of Q using the views is a query expression Q' whose body predicates are only from $V_1,...,V_n$.

Note that the views are not assumed to contain all the tuples in their definitions since the data sources are managed autonomously. Thus, finding an equivalent rewriting for a given query is not often possible in data integration. Instead, we consider the problem of finding maximally-contained rewritings [6].

Definition 1 (Maximally-Contained Rewriting): Q' is a maximally-contained rewriting of a query Q using views V with respect to a query language **L** if

(1) for any database D, $Q'(D) \subseteq Q(D)$, and
(2) there is no other query rewriting Q'' in the language **L**, such that for every database D, $Q''(D) \subseteq Q(D)$, and $Q'(D) \subseteq Q''(D)$.

We need the concept of equivalence as rewritings to compare different rewritings.

Definition 2 (Equivalence as Rewritings): Let Q' and Q'' be two rewritings of a query Q, Q' and Q'' are equivalence as rewritings if Q'^{EXP} is equivalent to Q''^{EXP}, where Q'^{EXP} and Q''^{EXP} are the expansions of Q' and Q'' respectively, which are obtained from Q' and Q'' respectively by replacing all the views in Q' and Q'' with their corresponding base relations.

3   Related Work

As stated in Section 1, there are two categories of query rewriting algorithms, i.e., bucket-based rewriting algorithms and inverse rule-based rewriting algorithms. The key idea underlying the inverse rule-based algorithms is to first construct a set of rules called inverse rules that invert the view definitions, and then replace existential variables in the view definitions with Skolem functions in the heads of the inverse rules. The rewriting of a query Q using a set **V** of views is simply the composition of Q and the inverse rules for **V** using either transformation method [1], or u-join method [7], or resolution method [2].

A bucket-based algorithm consists of two stages. The first stage called view selection selects the views relevant to a given query and puts them into the corresponding buckets. The second stage generates all the possible rewritings by combining a view from each bucket. View selection is based on containment mapping from a query to views. The SVB algorithm and the MiniCon algorithm are the best among the bucket-based algorithms.

SVB Algorithm [5]:

In the SVB algorithm, given a query Q, two types of buckets, SSB and SVB are created. The SVB algorithm creates a SSB for a subgoal R of Q over a view V if the variable mappings from Q to V satisfy a containment condition shown in Example 1. The SVB algorithm creates a SVB for a set of subgoals G of Q over a view V only if G contains shared variables that are mapped to the existential variables of V. Once all the buckets are created, the algorithm generates rewritings by combining views from buckets which contain disjoint sets of subgoals of Q.

MiniCon Algorithm [6]:

In the first phase of the MiniCon algorithm, a MiniCon Description (MCD for short, like a bucket but contains homomorphism on a view and variable mappings) for a query Q over a view V is formed. The MCDs containing a single subgoal and the MCDs containing multiple subgoals correspond to the SSBs and the SVBs in the SVB algorithm respectively, because the conditions for forming the MCDs in the MiniCon algorithm are the same as ones for forming the buckets in the SVB algorithm. In the second phase, the MiniCon algorithm combines the views in the MCDs to generate query rewritings.

4   Some Modifications of Bucket-Based Algorithms

4.1   Modification of Condition for Forming a Shared Variable Bucket

In order to ensure that the unification procedure is successful, the following conditions should be satisfied:

(C_1) a distinguished variable of Q should be mapped to a distinguished variable or constant of a view;

(C_2) an existential variable B_Q of Q could be mapped to an existential variable B_V of a view. If B_Q is a shared variable, then there should exist a containment mapping from the variables in a set of subgoals CG_Q of Q containing B_Q to the variables in a set of subgoals CG_V of the view containing B_V, i.e., $CG_V \subseteq CG_Q$.

The condition (C_1) is used for forming a SSB, while the condition (C_2) is used for forming a SVB. Especially, (C_1) shows that if a shared variable B_Q in Q is mapped to a distinguished variable of a view, then a SSB rather than a SVB would be created. Only if B_Q is mapped to an existential variable in a view, then a SVB is considered. However, this will result in fewer SVBs. For example, continuing with Example 1, when unifying parents(X,K) in Q with parents(X,Z) in V_1, we have the mapping {X→X, K→Z}, where X and K are a distinguished variable and an existential variable in Q, respectively. According to (C_1), a SSB is created for subgoal *parents(X,K)* and V_1 is put into the bucket. Similarly, other two SSBs are created and V_1 is put into each of these buckets. This results in (1) no SVBs are created, and (2) there are always three subgoals in any of the rewritings generated. However, Q_1 in Section 1 is a valid rewriting of Q. Hence, the condition for forming a SVB should be modified.

Without losing generality, we suppose that B_Q is a shared variable in query Q and B_Q appears in the subgoals R_1 and R_2 of Q, i.e., there is a join, $R_1(X,B_Q) \wedge R_2(B_Q,Y)$ in Q ($\wedge$ means a conjunction between two subgoals throughout this paper.).

If there exists a variable mapping φ from Q to a view V such that $\varphi(B_Q)=B_V$, where B_V is a distinguished variable in V, then we need to check the following two cases:

Case 1: B_V is not a join attribute in V. Then a SSB can be created according to the condition (C_1).

Case 2: B_V is a join attribute of the subgoals R_1, R_2 in V. Under the case there would be a join $R_1(A,B_V) \wedge R_2(B_V,B)$ in V. We then create a SVB, not two SSBs, if the mappings from X to A and from Y to B satisfy the conditions (C_1) and (C_2). This new condition is denoted by (C'_2).

The following algorithm is for forming buckets. The process for generating query rewritings is the same as in [5], but omitted here.

Algorithm: Forming the buckets based on unification
Input: A given query Q, a set **V** of views V_i (i=1,2,....,n)
Output: A set of the buckets containing views V_j (j=1,2,....,t, t $\leq$ n).
Methods:
For each view V$\in$ **V**
  S=subgoals(Q) // The set of subgoals of Q.
  For each subgoal g $\in$ S
    For each subgoal g' $\in$ V
    Let φ be a mapping from g to g' such that $\varphi(g)=g'$.
    For each variable $B_Q \in$ Vars(g),
      (1) If B_Q is not a join attribute, create a SSB according to (C_1), S=S – {g}.
      (2) If B_Q is a join attribute, then
        (a) If $\varphi(B_Q)$ is a shared variable, create a SVB according to (C_2).
        (b) If $\varphi(B_Q)$ is a join attribute as well as being a distinguished variable,
          create a SVB according to (C'_2), S=S–{g_1, g_2}, where B_Q is a join
          attribute between the subgoal g_1 and g_2.
    Endfor.
    V is put into the bucket being created.
  Endfor.
  Endfor.
Endfor.

Example 3 Continue with Example 1. When unifying the first subgoal of Q with V_1, we create a SVB according to (C'_2), which is shown in Table 2 (2nd row, 4th column). Then we unify the rest of subgoals in Q with V_1 and create a SSB according to (C_1), which is shown in Table 2 (2nd row, 3rd column). The unification of the subgoals of Q with V_2 is the same as Table 1. We now get all the buckets as follows:

Table 2. The buckets for V_1, V_2, where g_i, i=1,2,3, is the ith subgoal of Q

g_1	g_2	g_3	$g_1\,g_2$
$V_2(X,K)$	$V_2(K,J)$	$V_1(J,Y,Y_3)$	$V_1(X,K,J)$
		$V_2(J,Y)$	

Then, we can generate 4 rewritings only rather than 27 rewritings as before. Each of these four rewritings is equivalent to some rewriting in the previous 27 rewritings.

4.2   Computational Complexity and Correctness of the Algorithm

It is obvious that the computational complexity of our algorithm is the same as the procedure of forming all the buckets in the SVB algorithm.

Now we compare our algorithm with the SVB algorithm. Suppose that there exists a mapping φ from Q to a view V such that $\varphi(B_Q)=B_V$, where B_Q is a shared variable in Q and B_V is a join attribute in V. As stated above, the difference between (C_2) and (C'_2) is that when B_V is a distinguished variable as well as being a join attribute, we create a SVB instead of two SSBs. In this case, due to forming an additional SVB, we will generate different rewritings of Q. Now we need to prove that any rewriting Q'' generated by our algorithm is equivalent to a rewriting Q' generated by the SVB algorithm as rewritings. In fact, we need only to consider the differences caused by using (C'_2) between Q' and Q''.

Without loss of generality, we first consider the case where Q contains $R_1(X,B_Q) \wedge R_2(B_Q,Y)$ only, i.e.,

$$Q(X,Y):- R_1(X,B_Q), R_2(B_Q,Y)$$

where, X and Y are the sets of distinguished variables, B_Q is a shared variable.

Correspondingly, we suppose that there is a view containing the join, $R_1(A,B_V) \wedge R_2(B_V,B)$ as follows,

$$V(A,B_V,B):-R_1(A,B_V), R_2(B_V,B)$$

where, A and B are the sets of distinguished variables, B_V is a distinguished variable also being a join attribute. Note that B_V is a distinguished variable in V, so the mapping $\{B_Q \rightarrow B_V\}$ always satisfies (C_1). Moreover, the mappings $\{X \rightarrow A, Y \rightarrow B\}$ satisfy (C_1) and (C_2) (otherwise no bucket can be created). Hence, the mappings $\{X \rightarrow A, B_Q \rightarrow B_V, Y \rightarrow B\}$ satisfy (C_1) and (C_2).

Let Q' be one of the rewritings of Q generated by the SVB algorithm and Q'' be one of the rewritings of Q generated by our algorithm. From the SVB algorithm, V appears twice in Q' because V must cover the subgoals R_1 and R_2 respectively, but in Q'', V appears only once because V can cover the conjunction of R_1 and R_2, i.e.,

Q'(X,Y):- $V(X,B_Q,Y_1)$, $V(X_1,B_Q,Y)$ // From (C_1) and (C_2)
Q''(X,Y):- $V(X,B_Q,Y)$ // From (C'_2)

We need to prove that Q' is equivalent to Q'' as rewritings, i.e., (1) $Q'^{EXP} \subseteq Q''^{EXP}$ and (2) $Q''^{EXP} \subseteq Q'^{EXP}$. We expand Q' and Q'' as follows.

$Q'^{EXP}(X,Y):- R_1(X,B_Q), R_2(B_Q,Y_1), R_1(X_1,B_Q), R_2(B_Q,Y)$
$Q''^{EXP}(X,Y):- R_1(X,B_Q), R_2(B_Q,Y)$

Both (1) and (2) hold because there exist a containment mapping $\{X{\to}X, X_1{\to}X, B_Q{\to}B_Q, Y_1{\to}Y, Y{\to}Y\}$ from Q'^{EXP} to Q''^{EXP} and another containment mapping $\{X{\to}X, B_Q{\to}B_Q, Y{\to}Y\}$ from Q''^{EXP} to Q'^{EXP}.

Second, we consider the case where there is another view U that can also be applied by (C'_2) over the subgoals R_1 and R_2, i.e., we have the buckets in Table 3.

Table 3. The buckets for R_1 and R_2 over V and U, where the first two columns are formed by (C_1) and (C_2) while the third column is formed by (C'_2)

R_1	R_2	$R_1 R_2$
$V(X,B_Q,Y_1)$	$V(X_1,B_Q,Y)$	$V(X,B_Q,Y)$
$U(X,B_Q,Y_2)$	$U(X_2,B_Q,Y)$	$U(X,B_Q,Y)$

We need to compare the following rewritings.

$Q'''(X,Y):- V(X,B_Q,Y_1), U(X_2,B_Q,Y)$ // From (C_1) and (C_2)
$Q''(X,Y):- V(X,B_Q,Y)$ // From (C'_2)

We expand Q''' as follows.

$Q'''^{EXP}(X,Y):- R_1(X,B_Q), R_2(B_Q,Y_1), R_1(X_2,B_Q), R_2(B_Q,Y)$

Similarly, Q''' is equivalent to Q'' as rewritings.

Hence, any rewriting generated by our algorithm is equivalent to some rewriting generated by the SVB algorithm as rewritings.

4.3 Modification of Treatment of Constants When Unifying

Now we consider the treatment of constants when unifying. Recall that in Example 2, if we treat a constant as a distinguished variable, we would form a bucket for subgoal $P_1(U,X)$ over $V_1(X)$ using the SVB algorithm. The reason that a constant is treated as a distinguished variable is that even though the value of a distinguished variable varies, we can enforce a specific value upon it if needed. Unlike a distinguished variable, an existential variable cannot be enforced by a specific value. However, as shown in Example 2, we have to carefully handle the case where a shared variable of a given query Q is mapped to a constant in a view.

Suppose that K is a shared variable among the relations $R_1,...,R_t$ in Q, denoted by $R_1.K=R_2.K=...=R_t.K,$. If there exists a mapping φ from Vars(Q) to Vars(V) such that $\varphi(K)=a$, where a is a constant, we apply the new condition (C'_2) described in Section 4.2 to create a pseudo SVB. We need to consider two cases as follows:

Case 1: Suppose that there exists a view V_i that contains subgoals $\{R_1, R_2, ..., R_t\}$ such that there exists a mapping φ from Vars(Q) to Vars(V_i) such that $\varphi(K)=a$, where a is a constant, then we create a SVB according to the condition (C'_2).

Case 2: Suppose that V_i contains subgoals $\{R_1, R_2, ..., R_s, s<t\}$ only, and there exists a mapping φ from Vars(Q) to Vars(Vi) such that $\varphi(K)=a$, where a is a constant, then we create a pseudo SVB according to the condition (C'_2) as follows (note that φ should satisfy (C_1) and (C_2) for the rest of variables. Otherwise no bucket is created.).

Table 4. A pseudo SVB for $\{R_1, R_2, ..., R_s\}$ over V_i

Subgoals of Q containing K	h(mapping)	View
$R_1, R_2, ..., R_s$	$\varphi(K)=a$	V_i

This SVB is called a pseudo SVB (p-SVB for short) because V_i can cover subgoals $\{R_1, R_2, ..., R_s\}$ only. If s=1, a pseudo SVB is called a pseudo SSB (p-SSB for short). Whether V_i can cover $\{R_1, R_2, ..., R_t\}$ depends on the consistency of constants appearing in the mappings in different p-SVBs (or p-SSBs). Then a p-SVB/p-SSB can be used to generate rewritings as follows:

(1) A p-SVB/p-SSB can be combined with SSBs or SVBs.

(2) A p-SVB/p-SSB can be combined with other p-SVBs/p-SSBs if their corresponding constants are the same.

Note that a p-SVB/p-SSB is considered only when a shared variable of Q is mapped to a constant in a view, and would be formed by (C'_2). When a p-SVB/p-SSB is combined with SSBs or SVBs, the obtained rewritings, if exist, are contained in Q because all the conditions (C_1), (C_2) and (C'_2) are satisfied. When a p-SVB/p-SSB is combined with other p-SVBs/p-SSBs, the obtained rewritings, if exist, are also contained in Q because the consistencies of the corresponding constants are required. It is not necessary for our approach to make a containment test after generating rewritings.

We end this section by the following example.

Example 4 Suppose that a query and a set of views are defined as follows:

Q(X):- R(X,K), S(K,J), W(K,U)
V_1(X):- R(X,a), S(a, X_1)
V_2(X):- W(X, X_2)
V_3(Y):- W(b, Y)
V_4(X,K):- R(X,K), S(K,X_3)

where a and b are constants and a≠b.

We create SSB, SVB, p-SVB and p-SSB as follows:

Table 5. All the possible buckets in Example 4, where g_i is the ith subgoal of Q, i=1,2,3

SVB	g_1,g_2	$V_4(X,K)$	
SSB	g_3	$V_2(K)$	
p-SVB	g_1,g_2	$K \rightarrow a$	$V_1(X)$
p-SSB	g_3	$K \rightarrow b$	$V_3(U)$

We can generate three rewritings as follows:

$Q_1(X){:}\text{-} V_2(K), V_4(X,K).$
$Q_2(X){:}\text{-} V_1(X), V_2(K).$
$Q_3(X){:}\text{-} V_3(U), V_4(X,K).$

When combining these two pseudo SVBs, due to the inconsistency of constants, i.e., a≠b, the conjunction of $V_1(X)$ and $V_3(U)$ is not a valid rewriting of Q.

5   Conclusions

In this paper, we have first modified the condition for forming a shared-variable bucket in the SVB algorithm so that we can create fewer buckets and reduce the number of query rewritings. We have shown that in the case where a shared variable in a query is mapped to a distinguished variable that also is a join attribute in a view, we could create new shared-variable buckets, instead of single-subgoal buckets. All the rewritings obtained by our algorithm are equivalent to some of the rewritings generated by the SVB algorithm as rewritings. Thus, the union of the rewritings generated by our algorithm is still a maximally-contained rewriting. Second, we have presented a pseudo SVB to handle the case where a shared variable of a query is mapped to a constant in a view. A pseudo SVB can be combined with any SSBs or SVBs to generate rewritings. However, when two or more pseudo SVBs are combined to generate rewritings, the consistency of the corresponding constants is required. Thus, our approach can guarantee that the obtained rewritings are valid. Because the main difference between the SVB algorithm and the MiniCon algorithm is only on the head homomorphism on views, our approach can also be applied to the MiniCon algorithm.

References

1. Duschka, O.M., Genesereth, M.R., Levy, A.Y.: Recursive Query Plans for Data Integration. Journal of Logic Programming, 2000, 43(1), 49-73.
2. Grant, J., Minker., J.: A logic-based approach to data integration. TLP, 2002, 2(3):323-368.
3. Levy, A.Y.:. Answering Queries Using Views: A Survey. The VLDB Journal, 2001, 10(4), 270-294.
4. Levy, A.Y., Rajaraman, A., Ordille, J.J.: Querying Heterogeneous Information Sources Using Source Descriptions. Proceedings of the 22nd VLDB Conference, 1996, 251--262.

5. Mitra, P.: An Algorithm for Answering Queries Efficiently Using Views. Proceedings of the 12th Australasian Database Conference, 2001, 99-106.

6. Pottinger, R., Levy, A.Y.: A Scalable Algorithm for Answering Queries Using Views. Proceedings of VLDB, 2000, 484-495.

7. Qian, X.: Query folding. Proceedings of the 12th IEEE International Conference on Data Engineering (ICDE'96), 1996, 48-55.

8. Wang, J., Maher, M., and Topor, R.: Rewriting General Conjunctive Queries Using Views. Proceedings of the 13th Australasian Conference on Database Technologies, Melbourne, Australia, 2002, 197-206.

A Data Mining Application on
Air Temperature Database

T. Tugay Bilgin[1] and A. Yılmaz Çamurcu[2]

[1]Maltepe University Faculty of Engineering,
Buyukbakkalkoy Campus,
Maltepe, Istanbul, Turkey
ttbilgin@maltepe.edu.tr
[2]Marmara University Faculty of Technical Education, Goztepe Campus,
Kadıköy, Istanbul, Turkey
camurcu@marmara.edu.tr

Abstract. In this study, a data mining application based on DBSCAN (Density Based Spatial Clustering of Applications with Noise) was carried out on air temperature database which contains daily temperature data from country wide meteorology stations in Turkey. At the end of data mining process, we obtained clusters that have similar temperature trends. These clusters have been used to categorize Turkey into regions according to climatic characteristics. Statistical methods are widely used in meteorology; however they need extreme computing power. Data mining methods provide more performance and reliability than statistical methods.

1 Introduction

Data mining (DM) is a multidisciplinary area. It is a combination of artificial intelligence, computer sciences, machine learning, database management, data observation, mathematical algorithms, and statistics fields [1,2,4]. DM is used for knowledge discovery on very large databases. Data mining technology provides various methods for decision support, problem solving, analysis, planning, diagnosis, integrity, prevention, learning and discovery [1-7]. Data mining discovers patterns, communities, anomalies and various structures on large databases with a semi automatic system [1,4].

Clustering discovers natural groups in data space. Each of these groups are called cluster. Clustering process should discover clusters that have high intra cluster similarity and low inter cluster similarity [1-7]. This is the rule that determines the quality of a clustering method. Choosing appropriate clustering method depends on data type and purpose of application.

The purpose of this study is to determine regions in Turkey that have similar air temperature characteristics. A density based clustering algorithm called DBSCAN (Density Based Spatial Clustering of Applications with Noise) is applied to the meteorology database that contains air temperature data of Turkey.

T. Yakhno (Ed.): ADVIS 2004, LNCS 3261, pp. 68–76, 2004.

2 Application

2.1 Algorithm

DBSCAN algorithm was announced by Ester, Kriegel, Sander and Xu in KDD'96 (Knowledge discovery and Data mining) [9]. It finds the number of neighbors with respect to a neighborhood parameter. If an object has neighbors more than it has a constant parameter, then it is marked as a cluster. DBSCAN algorithm presents a new approach to the data mining researches.

2.2 Dataset

Dataset contains daily maximum and minimum temperature records of Turkey, measured between the years 1930 and 1996. The dataset has been provided by State Meteorological Service of Turkey (SMST). It is 82 megabytes in size and it has 2,628,035 rows of records. The number of measurement stations increased along the years. In 1996, the records were gathered from 258 stations. However there were only 30 stations in 1930.

Dataset is stored on Microsoft SQL Server database management software. It has following columns: Station code, year of record, month of record, day of record, maximum temperature, minimum temperature.

Dataset does not provide information about station names and coordinates. These items have an important role on data visualization. We needed them in order to sketch clustering results on Turkish Map. We obtained the necessary information from SMST [10].

2.3 Application Software

Application software has been developed by MATLAB scripting Language on Windows platform. Due to having many built-in functions for graphics and arithmetic calculations, MATLAB has been preferred.

Data mining algorithm has been coded in the form of MATLAB m-files for modularity and convenience. M-files are interpreted as standard MATLAB functions when they are stored in the MATLAB workspace directory.

The software has been developed as a standalone application instead of a traditional client-server architecture.

The purpose of the study is to test the performance and effectiveness of the algorithm. It is not intended to develop commercial data mining software. Consequently, it has been designed as a standalone application instead of client server architecture.

2.4 Data Mining Steps

Data mining is the general name of knowledge discovery process and also the name of a step on knowledge discovery process. Knowledge discovery has four steps. These are *data preprocessing, data selection and transformation, data mining, pattern evaluation and data presentation*. These steps and our actions on each step are described below.

2.4.1   Data Preprocessing

On this step, we merged the air temperature database and meteorology stations position coordinates database in order to find the exact position of each measurement record. We executed a query that merges two tables, which have one-to-many primary key – foreign key relationship. These tables are shown in Figure 1. The arrow symbolizes the relationship.

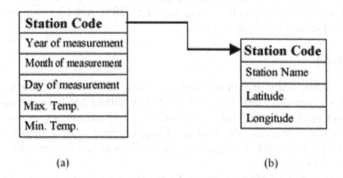

(a)   (b)

Fig. 1. (a) Air temperature database, (b) station position coordinates database

The merged table contains station code, station name, latitude, longitude, and year of measurement, month of measurement, day of measurement, maximum temperature, and minimum temperature. This table has enough information to sketch the results on the map of Turkey.

2.4.2   Data Selection and Transformation

Data mining is a time consuming and costly process. In order to achieve goals as quick as possible, only relevant data should be analyzed. On this step, we have retrieved task relevant fields of the dataset and built a new table. Task relevant data for our case is maximum temperature, minimum temperature, latitude field and longitude field.

Mining large databases requires faster hardware and effective software. We could not use whole dataset due to software and hardware limitations. Using whole dataset would require excessive amount of time. Consequently, we decided to take a sample slice from dataset. This has improved the computing time. Sample slice contains temperature data gathered from 248 stations in July 1996. The slice has 5454 rows and its computing time requirement is reasonable.

2.4.3   Data Mining

Consisting of four fields, air temperature database is four dimensions. It is not easy for a human being to imagine a four dimensions space. Due to this fact, database can be thought as two planes with two dimensions.

The first plane has temperature values and the second one has position coordinates. These planes can be seen in figures 2 and 3. On the first plane x axis shows the maximum temperature. Y-axis shows the minimum temperature values of a measurement point.

The second plane is constituted on MATLAB by using Map toolbox. Coordinate values of each station are gathered from State Meteorological Service Web site and sketched on the map of Turkey.

In fact there is no first plane or second plane. The database has four dimensions and DBSCAN algorithm can mine multidimensional databases. Consequently, it uses entire database without dividing it into two dimensional planes.

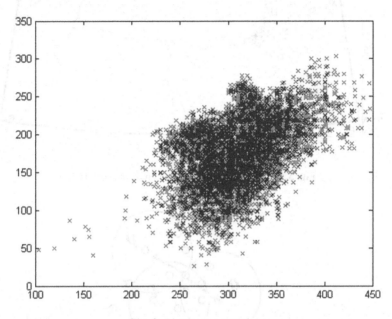

Fig. 2. Air temperature plane

As seen on the map, some of the stations are placed outside the Turkish border. This could be due to the map projection method of the MATLAB.

DBSCAN Algorithm:

If a data object has more neighbors than it has a constant value at its ε-neighborhood, then it is called a core object. ε-neighborhood is the distance between the data object and its neighbors, therefore it is called Eps. If a region is dense, then it should contain more points than a constant value named MinPts.

An object "p" is direct density reachable from object "q" if "p" is within the ε-neighborhood of "q", and "q" is a core object. As seen in figure 4, an object is density reachable from object "q" with respect to Eps and MinPts, if there is a chain of objects $p_1, p_2, p_3, \ldots p_n$, $p_1 = p$ and $p_n = q$ such that p_{i+1} is directly density reachable from p_1, with respect to ε and MinPts. An object "p" is density connected to object "q" with respect to ε and MinPts, if there is an object "o" such that both "p" and "q" are density reachable from "o" with respect to ε and MinPts.

MinPts and Eps parameters should be initially declared DBSCAN algorithm. The algorithm starts by choosing a random "p" point. If the ε-neighborhood of a point "p" contains more than MinPts, a new cluster with "p" as core object is created. DBSCAN

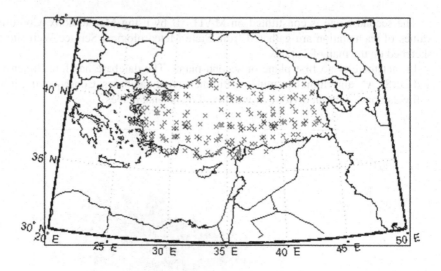

Fig. 3. Position coordinates plane on the map of Turkey

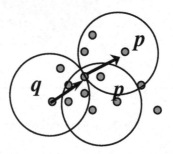

Fig. 4. Density reachable points [10]

then iteratively collects directly density reachable objects from these core objects which may involve the merge of a few density reachable clusters. The process terminates when no new point that can be added to any cluster. The algorithm repeats the same procedure by choosing a new random point. If the random point does not meet the core object requirements, it is marked as noise or outlier. Figure 5 illustrates these concepts.

Euclidian distance is used to find neighbors of a core object. The software code is rearranged in such a way that Euclidian distance formula is expanded in order to calculate four dimensional space distances. If A(x,y,z,t) and B(a,b,c,d) are points in four dimensional space, Euclidian distance is calculated as the following identity.

$$\text{Eps} = \sqrt{(x-a)^2 + (y-b)^2 + (z-c)^2 + (t-d)^2} \tag{1}$$

By using four dimensions not only the maximum and minimum temperature data but also longitude and latitude data of the points have been taken into consideration.

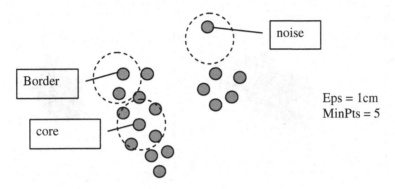

Fig. 5. Fundamental concepts of DBSCAN algorithm [1]

2.4.4   Pattern Evaluation and Data Presentation

DBSCAN algorithm is applied to the meteorological dataset repeatedly with different Eps and MinPts parameters.

We encountered two problems in data mining process:

- The dataset has four dimensions. The former two column values are represented in temperature degrees and the latter two column values are represented in latitude and longitude position degrees. Although all these values are in degrees, they are actually in different scales. Due to this fact, only one Eps value is insufficient.
- Clusters found on the dataset have different average density values. This caused problems in identifying clusters. We could not distinguish the clusters clearly.

There are two methods to solve the first problem:

a) *Data Standardization:* All different value scales on dataset could be converted to common standart scale. Then data mining could be realized on this standart scale. This process is called "data standartization" [1].
b) *Two Different Eps Values:* Determining two different Eps values for temperature degrees and position coordinates degrees. This method has an important advantage. There is no need to convert different scales to a common scale.

In this application we have chosen the first method explained in (a). Eps1 is chosen to determine neighborhood parameter for temperature degrees and Eps2 is chosen to determine neighborhood parameter in position coordinates degrees.

In order to solve the second problem, data mining process is applied in two stages as described below.

First Stage: On the first stage, we applied the algorithm with Eps1=7.9, Eps2=2, MinPts=20 parameters and obtained the clusters as seen on figure 6a. Outliers are not shown to see the clusters clearly. Outliers have been removed in figure 6b.

The results obtained on the first stage can be seen in figure 7. Marmara, Aegean, West Mediterranean and Interior Anatolia regions form a great single cluster. The clusters are marked and numbered in figure 7. Cluster number 1 covers the Eastern blacksea region. On number 2 there are two clusters. Due to the mountainous structure of this region, two clusters are placed in the same region at one within the other position. These two clusters were marked as one cluster because they could not

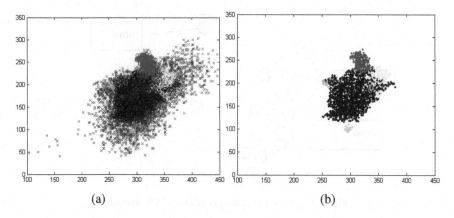

(a)   (b)

Fig. 6. (a) Clustering result with Eps=7.9, Eps2=2, MinPts=20 parameters. (b) Clustering result with Eps=7.9, Eps2=2, MinPts=20 parameters (outliers removed)

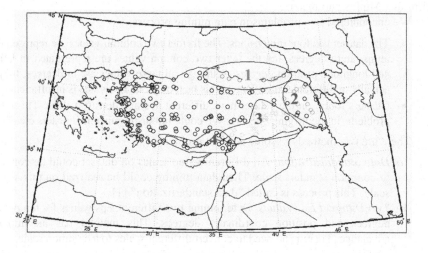

Fig. 7. Clusters obtained in the first stage

well distinguished. Cluster number 3 covers Southeast Anatolia region. Cluster number 4 covers East of Mediterranean.

Second Stage: The first stage could discover only four clusters as shown in figure 6.a. In order to find other clusters except those shown in figure 6.b, DBSCAN algorithm is applied again with different parameters. Figure 8.a shows results for Eps=5.2, MinPts=22, Eps2=2 values. In figure 8.b, outliers are removed to improve perception.

We obtained the results shown in figure 9 on the second stage. In figure 7, a single large cluster covering the remaining area from cluster number 1,2,3 and 4. This large cluster is separated into four clusters on the second stage. This could be seen in figure 9. Cluster number 1, 2 and 3 disappear in figure 9, since they are not dense enough to be discovered on the second stage. The clusters obtained in the second stage are enumerated as shown in figure 9.

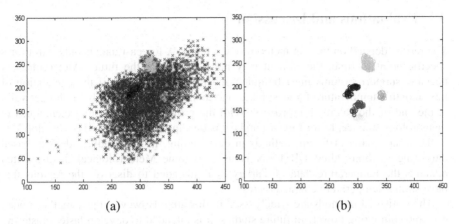

(a)   (b)

Fig. 8. (a) Clustering result for Eps=5.2 MinPts=22 Eps2=2 parameters. (b) Clustering result for Eps=5.2 MinPts=22 Eps2=2 parameters (outliers removed)

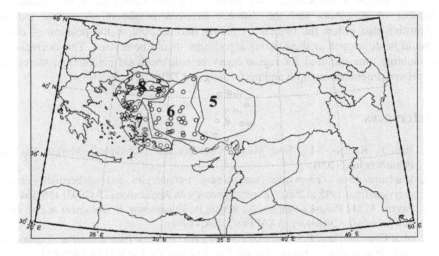

Fig. 9. Clusters obtained on the second stage (clusters enumerated)

In figure 9, cluster number 5 covers the middle and the east parts of the interior Anatolia region, cluster number 6 covers the east of the Aegean and the west of the Black sea regions, cluster number 7 covers the west of the Aegean and the west of the Mediterranean, and cluster number 8 covers the Marmara region.

Although they have similarities in shape, the clusters obtained at the end of the clustering process actually have many differences. The Mediterranean and the Black sea regions do not exactly match the clusters discovered in data mining process. Eastern part of the Black sea region forms a cluster. The western part of Black sea and eastern Aegean merge and form a cluster. Similar behavior is also valid for Mediterranean region. Eastern Mediterranean forms a cluster. However, the west Mediterranean and West Aegean parts become a cluster. Aegean region is divided into two parts. West part is cluster number 7 and east part is cluster number 6.

3   Evaluations and Discussion

The results depend on time in meteorology science. A forecast data is only valid for a specific point of time; therefore it may not be valid for the future. Meteorological decision support systems must be quick and fast. For example, if the calculation of next month's temperature forecast takes one month, the result will be no longer valid at the end of the calculation process. With the growth of data mining techniques in meteorology science, faster forecast and decision support systems will be developed.

There are many different methods in data mining. In this study, a density based clustering method called DBSCAN is used to mine Meteorological database that contains the temperature data of Turkey. It is intended to discover the regions that have similar temperature characteristics.

The statistical methods are widely used in this area. However, these methods need extreme computing power. In future studies, it is intended to develop faster clustering algorithms or to improve the performance of an existing algorithm to mine very large spatial databases.

The main bottleneck of density based clustering algorithms is to calculate the number of neighbors and the distance between neighbors. A spatial indexing algorithm that orders the objects by taking into account of the position of objects should be developed or the existing algorithms should be revised. This decreases the computing time required for region query or neighborhood calculation; therefore it improves general throughput and performance of DBSCAN algorithm.

References

1. Han, J.; Kamber, M.: "Data Mining Concepts and Techniques", Morgan Kaufmann Publishers Inc., (2001)
2. Shu-hsien Liao, "Knowledge management technologies and applications—literature overview from 1995 to 2002", Expert Systems with Applications 25 (2003) 155–164
3. Fayyad, U.M.; Piatesky-Shapiro, G.; Smyth, P.; Uthurusamy, R.; *Advances in data mining and Knowledge Discovery*. AAAI Pres, USA. (1994)
4. M.S. Chen.; J. Han.; P.S. Yu.: "Data Mining An Overview from a Database Perspective", IEEE Transactions on Knowledge and Data Engineering, Vol 8. (1996) 866-883
5. Michalski, R.S.; Step, R.E.: "Learning from Observation Conceptual Clustering", Machine Learning An Artificial Intelligence Approach, Palo Alto, California USA. (1983) 331-363
6. Fukunaga, K.: "Introduction to Statistical Pattern Recognition", Academic press, Inc., Boston, USA, 2 edition. (1990)
7. R. Grossman.; C. Kamath.; V.Kumar,: "Data mining for scientific and engineering Approach", Kluwer Academic Publishers, Inc., Section 1, (2001).
8. Berkhin, Pavel.: "Survey of Clustering Data Mining Techniques", Accrue Software Inc., San Jose, California, USA. (2002)
9. Ester, M.; Kriegel, H. P.; Sander, J.; Xu, X.: "A density based algorithm for discovering clusters in large spatial databases." *Int. Conference of Knowledge Discovery and Data Mining (KDD'96)*, Portland, USA (1996) 226-23
10. State Meteorology Service Web Site, station codes page. http://www.meteor.gov.tr/2003/doner/istasyonbilgi.htm. (Access date: February 2003)

Incremental Association Rule Mining Using Materialized Data Mining Views

Mikołaj Morzy, Tadeusz Morzy, and Zbyszko Królikowski

Institute of Computing Science,
Poznań University of Technology, Piotrowo 3A, 60-965 Poznań, Poland
{Mikolaj.Morzy,Tadeusz.Morzy,Zbyszko.Krolikowski}@cs.put.poznan.pl

Abstract. Data mining is an interactive and iterative process. Users issue series of similar queries until they receive satisfying results, yet currently available data mining systems do not support iterative processing of data mining queries and do not allow to re-use the results of previous queries. Consequently, mining algorithms suffer from long processing times, which are unacceptable from the point of view of interactive data mining. On the other hand, the results of consecutive data mining queries are usually very similar. This observation leads to the idea of reusing materialized results of previous data mining queries. We present the notion of a materialized data mining view and we propose two novel algorithms which aim at efficient discovery of association rules in the presence of materialized results of previous data mining queries.

1 Overview of Data Mining Processing

Data mining, also referred to as knowledge discovery in databases, is a nontrivial process of identifying valid, novel, potentially useful, and ultimately understandable patterns in data [4]. Data mining systems are evolving from systems dedicated to and specialized in particular tasks or domains to general-purpose systems, which are tightly coupled with the existing relational database technology. Most data mining queries are expensive in terms of processing cost and differ significantly from typical database queries. Hence, novel methods of query processing and optimization need to be developed in order to achieve satisfying data mining query performance.

From a user's point of view the execution of a data mining algorithm and the discovery of a set of patterns is an answer to a sophisticated database query. A user limits the mined dataset and determines the values of parameters that control a given algorithm. In return, the system discovers relevant patterns and presents them to the user. When the process starts, a user does not know the exact goal of the exploration. Rather, they achieve satisfying results in several consecutive steps. In each step the user verifies discovered patterns and, suitably to the needs, expectations, and experience modifies either the mined dataset, or algorithm parameters, or both. Mining practice shows that the vast majority of data mining queries are only minor modifications of former queries. Given these

T. Yakhno (Ed.): ADVIS 2004, LNCS 3261, pp. 77–87, 2004.

circumstances it is necessary to be able to exploit the results of previous queries in order to be able to answer a given query efficiently. A data mining system should be capable of answering a query in an incremental manner where the results of previous queries are maintained and tested against the current data set and parameter set and the base algorithm should be run only on the difference set. This principle applies also to the situation when the mining algorithm is run after a data warehouse refresh to discover new patterns. Usually, the volume of new or changed data after the data warehouse refresh is significantly smaller when compared to the size of the original data warehouse.

The basic problem in data mining is the processing time of data mining queries. In addition, the size of the result can easily surpass the size of the queried database. Such properties of mining process make it unsuitable for interactive and iterative pattern discovery. One possible solution is to use materialized views. Data mining query results can be materialized automatically or at a user's request. Materialized views have been thoroughly examined and successfully applied in traditional database systems. We propose to follow this path and introduce materialized views to data mining systems.

In this paper we present the concept of materialized data mining views. Section 2 contains definitions of basic terms used throughout the paper. The notion of a data mining query is presented in Sec. 3. Data mining views and materialized data mining views are presented in Sec. 4. We demonstrate the use of materialized views in association rule discovery in Sec. 5. Section 6 presents novel algorithms of complementary association rule mining using materialized data mining views. The paper concludes with the presentation of experimental results in Sec. 7.

2   Basic Definitions

Let $L = \{l_1, \ldots, l_n\}$ be a set of literals called items. Let D be a set of variable length transactions and $\forall T \in D : T \subseteq L$. A transaction T supports an item x if $x \in T$. The transaction T supports an itemset X if it supports every element $x \in X$. The *support* of an itemset is the number of transactions supporting the itemset. The problem of discovering frequent itemsets consists in finding all itemsets with the support higher than user-defined minimum support threshold denoted as *minsup*. An itemset with the support higher than minsup is called a *frequent itemset*.

An association rule is an implication of the form $X \rightarrow Y$ where $X \subset L, Y \subset L$ and $X \cap Y = \emptyset$. X is called the *head* of a rule whilst Y is called the *body* of a rule. Two measures represent statistical significance and strength of a rule. The *support* of a rule is the number of transactions that support $X \cup Y$. The *confidence* of a rule is the ratio of the number of transactions that support the rule to the number of transactions that support the head of the rule.

The problem of discovering association rules consists in finding all rules with support and confidence higher than the user-specified thresholds of minimum support and confidence, called *minsup* and *minconf* respectively. The problem of association rule mining was first introduced in [1]. The paper identified the discovery of frequent itemsets as a key step in association rule mining. In [2] the authors presented basic algorithm called Apriori which quickly became the seed of several other data mining algorithms.

3 Data Mining Queries

3.1 MineSQL

Several declarative data mining query languages have been proposed so far [7, 8, 9]. In this paper we use a multi-purpose data mining query language called MineSQL [11] to formulate example queries. MineSQL employs the concept of a data mining query to express data mining tasks. MineSQL syntax mimics that of standard SQL and allows to issue commands that discover frequent itemsets, association rules and sequential patterns. The following data mining query discovers all association rules with support higher than 10%, condfidence higher than 30%, and containing the item 'butter' in the consequent of the rule. Mining takes place in the part of the database that contains transactional data for the 4th quarter of 2003.

```
MINE RULE r, HEAD(r), BODY(r)
FOR items FROM (
  SELECT SET(item) AS items FROM Purchases
  WHERE t_date >= '01.10.2003' AND t_date <= '31.12.2003'
  GROUP BY t_id )
WHERE SUPPORT(r) > 0.1 AND CONFIDENCE(r) > 0.3
  AND HEAD(r) CONTAINS TO_SET('butter');
```

3.2 Relationships Between Data Mining Queries

Three relationships have been identified which occur between data mining queries Q_1 and Q_2.

- Two data mining queries are *equal* if for every database the result sets of patterns returned by both queries are identical and for every pair of patterns the values of statistical coefficients (e.g. support and confidence) are equal.
- A data mining query Q_2 *contains* a query Q_1 if for every database each pattern returned by Q_1 is also returned by Q_2 and the values of statistical coefficients are equal in both result sets.
- A data mining query Q_2 *dominates* a query Q_1 if for every database each pattern returned by Q_1 is also returned by Q_2 and the values of statistical coefficients determined by Q_1 are greater or equal to the values of respective coefficients determined by Q_2.

Equality of data mining queries is a special case of containment relation, and containment is a special case of more general dominance relation. Relations described above occur between the results of data mining queries and can be used to identify the situations in which a query Q_1 can be efficiently answered using the materialized results of another query Q_2. If for a given query Q_1 exist materialized results of another query Q_2 equal to Q_1 then no processing is required and Q_1 can be answered entirely from the results of Q_2. If materialized results are available from the query Q_2 containing the original query Q_1 then a full result set scan is required to filter out those patterns from Q_2 that do not satisfy constraints imposed on Q_1. If materialized results are available from the query Q_2 dominating the original query Q_1 then a full database scan is required to determine the values of statistical coefficients of patterns present in Q_2. Additionally, a scan of the result set is required to filter out patterns from Q_2 that do not satisfy the constraints imposed on Q_1.

4   Data Mining Views

A view is a derived relation defined in terms of base relations. Formally, a view defines a function from the set of base relations to the derived relation. This function is usually computed upon each reference to the view. A view can be materialized by storing tuples in the database. All data available in a materialized view are stored in the database, which shortens the time needed to access data. In a way, a materialized view resembles cache memory – it is a copy of the data that can be quickly accessed. The contents of a materialized view becomes invalid after any modification to base relations. View maintenance techniques are necessary to reflect changes that occur in base relations of a materialized view.

The work on materialized views started in the 1980s. The basic concept was to use materialized views as a tool to speed up queries and serve older copies of data. Multiple algorithms for view maintenance were developed [12]. Further research led to the creation of cost models for materialized view maintenance and determining the impact of materialized views on query processing performance. A summary of view maintenance techniques can be found in [5, 6].

Materialized data mining views were first proposed in [10]. A materialized data mining view is a database object storing patterns (frequent sets, association rules) discovered during data mining queries. Every pattern in a materialized view has a timestamp representing its creation time and validity period. With every materialized view the time period can be associated, after which the contents of the view is automatically refreshed. Below is a MineSQL statement that creates a materialized data mining view `mv_assoc_rules`.

```
CREATE MATERIALIZED VIEW mv_assoc_rules REFRESH 7 AS
MINE RULE r, SUPPORT(r), CONFIDENCE(r)
FOR items FROM (
  SELECT SET(item) AS items FROM Purchases
  WHERE item_group = 'beverages'
  GROUP BY t_id )
WHERE SUPPORT(r) > 0.3 AND CONFIDENCE(r) > 0.5;
```

Two classes of constraints can be identified in the above example. *Database constraints* are placed within the WHERE clause in the SELECT subquery. Database constraints define the source dataset, i.e. the subset of the original database in which data mining is performed. *Mining constraints* are placed within the WHERE clause in the MINE statement. Mining constraints define the conditions that must be met by discovered patterns.

5 Data Mining Query Optimization

In many cases contents of the materialized view can be used to answer a query that is similar to the query defining the view. In order to use the contents of a materialized view for data mining query optimization it is necessary to define the conditions that must be met by an answer using materialized patterns in order to be correct. Those conditions are based on relations occurring between data mining queries. Given materialized view based on query Q_v and a data mining query Q we say that:

- query Q *extends database constraints* of Q_v if
  - Q adds WHERE or HAVING clauses to the database constraints of Q_v
  - Q adds an ANDed condition to the database constraints of Q_v in the WHERE or HAVING clauses
  - Q removes an ORed condition from the database constraints of Q_v in the WHERE or HAVING clauses
- query Q *reduces database constraints* of Q_v if
  - Q removes WHERE or HAVING clauses from the database constraints of Q_v
  - Q removes an ANDed condition from the database constraints of Q_v in the WHERE or HAVING clauses
  - Q adds an ORed condition to the database constraints of Q_v in the WHERE or HAVING clauses
- query Q *extends mining constraints* of Q_v if
  - Q adds WHERE or HAVING clauses to the mining constraints of Q_v
  - Q adds an ANDed condition to the mining constraints of Q_v in the WHERE or HAVING clauses
  - Q removes an ORed condition from the mining constraints of Q_v in the WHERE or HAVING clauses
  - Q replaces mining constraint present in Q_v with a more restrictive constraint (e.g. higher *minsup* value)
- query Q *reduces mining constraints* of Q_v if
  - Q removes WHERE or HAVING clauses from the mining constraints of Q_v
  - Q removes an ANDed condition from the mining constraints of Q_v in the WHERE or HAVING clauses
  - Q adds an ORed condition to the mining constraints of Q_v in the WHERE or HAVING clauses
  - Q replaces mining constraint present in Q_v with a less restrictive constraint (e.g. lower *minsup* value)

Depending on circumstances several mining methods are available. *Full mining* (FM) refers to the situation when the contents of the view cannot be used to answer the query and the mining algorithm must be run from scratch. This situation occurs when the query Q extends database constraints of the query Q_v defining the materialized view. *Incremental mining* (IM) refers to the situation when one of incremental discovery algorithms is executed on the extended data view. This method is used when the query Q reduces database constraints of Q_v. Another possibility is *complementary mining* (CM). Patterns are discovered based on previously discovered patterns. This method can be utilized when the query Q reduces mining constraints of Q_v (all patterns available in the view will be present in the answer to the query Q). Finally, *verifying mining* (VM) consists in reading materialized view and pruning those patterns that do not satisfy extended mining constraints of Q. Knowing the relationship between the query Q and the definition of the materialized view Q_v the appropriate mining method can be determined using Table 1 (where DC denotes database constraints and MC denotes mining constraints).

Table 1. Possible mining methods

	reduce DC	extend DC	keep DC
reduce MC	CM, IM	CM	CM
extend MC	VM, IM	FM	VM
keep MC	IM	FM	—

6   New Algorithms for Complementary Mining

In this section we propose two new algorithms for complementary mining. The first algorithm deals with the situation in which mining is performed on a database view that extends database constraints of the view defining the materialized data mining view. Until now, most methods assumed a simple insertion or deletion of tuples from the source table [3, 13]. We acknowledge that in many situations mining is performed on the same (or similar) set of tuples, but the tuples are different. For example, let us assume that the original mining was performed on the data from the Purchase table, and grouping of items into itemsets was done based on the customer identifier, where all purchases made by a single customer in the year 2003 form a single set. After materializing the results of this mining in a materialized data mining view defined by query Q_v, the user issues a new query Q' that discovers all association rules describing customer purchase patterns, but limiting the analysis to the purchases made during working days (excluding weekends). This is an example of a query that extends database constraints of the query Q_v underlying the materialized view because it adds a new condition to the WHERE clause. Let D denote the source data set from which the patterns have been discovered. Let D' denote the new data set against which the query Q' is executing. Let t denote any transaction such that $t \in D$ and let t' denote any transaction such that $t' \in D'$. Let Δt denote the set difference between t and t', $\Delta t = t - t'$. Let L_k denote the set of frequent k-itemsets discovered by the traditional Apriori algorithm and let L'_k denote the set of frequent k-itemsets discovered by the modified version of the Apriori algorithm. The modified algorithm is presented below.

Algorithm 1 Apriori algorithm with extended database constraints

---

Require: L, the set of all frequent itemsets
 1: **for all** transactions $t \in D$ or $t' \in D'$ **do**
 2:　　$\Delta t = t - t'$;
 3:　　**for all** $L_k \in L$ **do**
 4:　　　**for all** $l \in L_k$ **do**
 5:　　　　**if** $\exists e : e \in l \land e \in \Delta t$ **then**
 6:　　　　　l.support --;
 7:　　　　**end if**
 8:　　　**end for**
 9:　　**end for**
10: **end for**
11: $L'_k = \{l \in L_k \mid \text{l.support} \geq minsup\}$
12: Answer $= \bigcup_{k=1}^{n} L'_k$;

Algorithm 1 performs a single scan of the source database. For each frequent itemset discovered by the traditional Apriori our algorithm checks whether the elements consisting the frequent itemset are not contained in the difference of the two source sets. If this is the case, the algorithm decreases the support count for this itemset. The main advantage of Algorithm 1 is a significant improvement of the execution time over the traditional approach. Instead of making k full passes over the source data set, our algorithm determines the support counts of all frequent k-itemsets in a single pass.

　　The second algorithm deals with the situation where the user's query reduces database constraints of the query defining the materialized data mining view. The user issues a data mining query Q' which aims at the discovery of association rules within entire customer purchases made in the years 2002 and 2003, including weekends. This is an example of a query that reduces database constraints of the query Q_v underlying the materialized view because it broadens a condition from the WHERE clause of the query Q_v. Let NB_k denote the set of k-itemsets belonging to the negative border of the set of frequent itemsets. The negative border of the set of frequent itemsets consists of the sets that are not frequent, but whose all proper subsets are frequent. Let NB denote the entire negative border of the set of frequent itemsets. Let LNB_k denote the set of k-itemsets from NB_k which become frequent in the extended database D'. Let $LNB = \bigcup_{k=1}^{n} LNB_k$. Let CL_k denote the set of candidate k-itemsets generated by joining L_1 and LNB_{k-1}. Algotithm 2 discovers frequent itemsets based on the materialized results of previous mining queries in the situation where the user's query Q' reduces database constraints of the query Q_v underlying the materialized view.

Algorithm 2 Apriori algorithm with reduced database constraints

---

Require: L, the set of all frequent itemsets
1: **for all** transactions $t \in D$ or $t' \in D'$ **do**
2:     $\Delta t = t - t'$;
3:     **for all** $L_k \in L$ **do**
4:         **for all** $l \in L_k$ **do**
5:             **if** $\exists e : e \in l \wedge e \in \Delta t \wedge l \subseteq t'$ **then**
6:                 l.support $++$;
7:             **end if**
8:         **end for**
9:     **end for**
10:    **for all** $NB_k \in NB$ **do**
11:        **for all** $n \in NB_k$ **do**
12:            **if** $\exists e : e \notin n \wedge e \in \Delta t$ **then**
13:                e.support $++$;
14:                $NB_1 + = \{e\}$;
15:            **end if**
16:            **if** $\exists e : e \in n \wedge e \in \Delta t \wedge n \subseteq t'$ **then**
17:                n.support $++$;
18:            **end if**
19:        **end for**
20:        $LNB_k = \{n \in NB_k \mid n.\text{support} \geq minsup\}$;
21:    **end for**
22: **end for**
23: $LNB = \bigcup_{k=1}^{n} LNB_k$;
24: $CL = generate(LNB, L_1)$;
25: $CL+ = generate(L, LNB_1)$;
26: $CL = subset\_new(CL)$;
27: Answer $= L \cup LNB \cup CL$;

Algorithm 2 uses both itemsets from the negative border NB and itemsets generated by the traditional Apriori algorithm and stored in L. Because of the reduction of database constraints, the mined data set is larger than the original data set. Consequently, the support of some itemsets from the negative border NB can increase above the *minsup* threshold, which means that these itemsets move from NB to LNB (they become frequent itemsets). After moving from NB to LNB the newly discovered frequent itemsets can produce additional, previously unknown candidate itemsets. New candidate itemsets are appended to the set CL. These candidate itemsets are created by joining LNB with L_1 (extending every new frequent itemset with a frequent 1-itemset) and by joining L with LNB_1 (extending every frequent itemset with a frequent new 1-itemset). The support of candidate itemsets contained in CL is computed by the function $subset\_new(CL)$ which requires an additional database scan.

The main advantage of Algorithm 2 is a significant improvement in the execution time as compared to the traditional Apriori algorithm. Algorithm 2 uses at most two full database scans to determine the support counts for all frequent itemsets in the database. The improvement is especially visible when the differences Δt within transactions are not large.

7   Experimental Results

All experiments were conducted on Pentium 333 Mhz with 256 MB of RAM memory running Windows 2000 and Oracle 8*i* RDBMS. The first experiment verifies the efficiency of the modified Apriori algorithm in the case of extended database constraints. Fig. 1 presents the results for a small data source (1000 transactions), while Fig. 2 presents the results for a larger data source (10 000 transactions). We performed the experiment subsequently removing random elements from transactions. This is how the improvement of the traditional Apriori observed on the plot can be explained. In practical applications the difference between original transactions and the transactions processed by a data mining query are not random. Rather, they tend to be skewed by the absence of certain groups of elements (e.g. perform data mining on the same data set but exclude el-

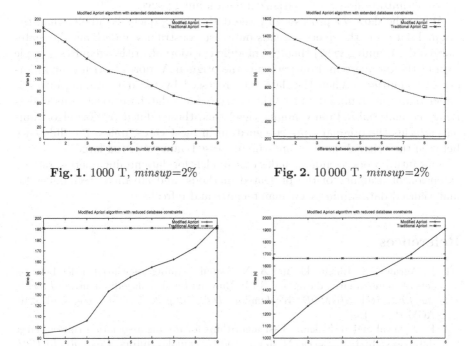

Fig. 1. 1000 T, *minsup*=2%   **Fig. 2.** 10 000 T, *minsup*=2%

Fig. 3. 1000 T, *minsup*=2%   **Fig. 4.** 10 000 T, *minsup*=2%

ements belonging to the category '*bakery*'). Nevertheless, our modified algorithm performs better than the traditional Apriori algorithm by an order of magnitude.

Fig(s). 3 and 4 present the execution times of our modified Apriori algorithm in the case of reduced database constraints. Fig. 3 presents the results obtained for a small data source (1000 transactions), while Fig. 4 presents the results obtained for a larger data source (10 000 transactions). As can be clearly seen, our algorithm outperforms the original Apriori in most cases. The original Apriori algorithm becomes better only when the difference between original transactions and processed transactions becomes too large. Also, it can be noticed that the algorithm for reduced database constraints performs worse than the algorithm for extended database constraints. This can be easily explained by the fact, that the algorithm for reduced database constraints has to process the negative border of the set of frequent itemsets and requires an additional database scan to determine the support counts for newly discovered candidate itemsets.

8   Conclusions

In this paper we have introduced the notion of a data mining query. We have presented the idea of a data mining view and we have illustrated how this idea can be employed to materialize the results of previous mining queries in a materialized data mining view. We have investigated the possibilities of data mining query optimization using materialized data mining views.

When the data set processed by the data mining query is smaller than the original data set (the query extends database constraints underlying the materialized data mining view) then the modified Apriori algorithm requires a single scan of the database and outperforms the original Apriori algorithm by an order of magnitude. When the data set processed by the data mining query is larger than the original data set (the query reduces database constraints underlying the materialized data mining view) then the modified Apriori algorithms outperforms the original Apriori algorithm in most cases, unless the difference between the original data set and the processed data set is too large.

Our future work agenda includes cost models for data mining queries, further extension of usability of the presented methods, and advanced techniques for materialized data mining view maintenance and refresh.

References

[1] R. Agrawal, T. Imielinski, and A. N. Swami. Mining association rules between sets of items in large databases. In P. Buneman and S. Jajodia, editors, *Proc. of the 1993 ACM SIGMOD, Washington, D.C., May 26-28, 1993*, pages 207–216. ACM Press, 1993.

[2] R. Agrawal and R. Srikant. Fast algorithms for mining association rules in large databases. In J. B. Bocca, M. Jarke, and C. Zaniolo, editors, *Proc. of VLDB'94, September 12-15, 1994, Santiago de Chile, Chile*, pages 487–499. Morgan Kaufmann, 1994.

[3] D. W.-L. Cheung, J. Han, V. Ng, and C. Y. Wong. Maintenance of discovered association rules in large databases: An incremental updating technique. In S. Y. W. Su, editor, *Proc. of ICDE'96, February 26 - March 1, 1996, New Orleans, Louisiana*, pages 106–114. IEEE Computer Society, 1996.

[4] U. M. Fayyad, G. Piatetsky-Shapiro, P. Smyth, and R. Uthurusamy. *Advances in Knowledge Discovery and Data Mining*. AAAI/MIT Press, 1996.

[5] A. Gupta and I. S. Mummick. Maintenance of materialized views: Problems, techniques, and applications. *IEEE Data Engineering Bulletin, Special Issue on Materialized View and Data Warehousing*, 2(18), Jun 1995.

[6] A. Gupta and I. S. Mummick. *Materialized Views: Techniques, Implementations, and Applications*. The MIT Press, 1999.

[7] T. Imielinski and A. Virmani. Msql: A query language for database mining. *Data Mining and Knowledge Discovery*, 3(4):373–408, 1999.

[8] Y. Kambayashi, W. Winiwarter, and M. Arikawa, editors. *A Comparison between Query Languages for the Extraction of Association Rules*, volume 2454 of *Lecture Notes in Computer Science*. Springer, 2002.

[9] R. Meo, G. Psaila, and S. Ceri. A new sql-like operator for mining association rules. In T. M. Vijayaraman, A. P. Buchmann, C. Mohan, and N. L. Sarda, editors, *Proc. of VLDB'96, September 3-6, 1996, Mumbai (Bombay), India*, pages 122–133. Morgan Kaufmann, 1996.

[10] T. Morzy, M. Wojciechowski, and M. Zakrzewicz. Materialized data mining views. In D. A. Zighed, H. J. Komorowski, and J. M. Zytkow, editors, *Proc. of PKDD'00, Lyon, France, September 13-16, 2000, Proceedings*, volume 1910 of *Lecture Notes in Computer Science*, pages 65–74. Springer, 2000.

[11] T. Morzy and M. Zakrzewicz. Sql-like language for database mining. In *Proc. of ADBIS'97, St.Petersburg, Russia, September , 1997, Proceedings*, 1997.

[12] N. Roussopoulos. Materialized views and data warehouses. *SIGMOD Record*, 27(1), 1998.

[13] S. Thomas, S. Bodagala, K. Alsabti, and S. Ranka. An efficient algorithm for the incremental updation of association rules in large databases. In D. Heckerman, H. Mannila, and D. Pregibon, editors, *Proc. of KDD'97, Newport Beach, California, USA, August 14-17, 1997*, pages 263–266. AAAI Press, 1997.

Outlier Effects on Databases

Ahmet Kaya

Ege University Tire Kutsan Post Secondary Vocational School,
35900, Tire, İzmir, Turkey
ahmetkaya_63@hotmail.com

Abstract. Real data and databases always contain some kind of heterogenity or contamination, which is called "outliers". Outliers are defined as the few observations or records which appear to be inconsistent with the remainder group of the sample and more effective on prediction values. Isolated outliers may also have positive impact on the results of data analysis and data mining. In this study, we are concerned with outliers in time series which have two special cases, innovational outlier (IO) and additive outlier (AO). The occurence of AO indicates that action is required, possibly to adjust the measuring instrument or at least to print an error message on the database. However, if IO occurs, no adjustment of the measurement operation is required. At the end of the study, the results of the simulation and variance analysis on the produced data sets are emphasized.

Keywords: ARMA, Outliers in Time Series, AO, IO, Outlier in Databases, Data Quality, Data Mining.

1 Introduction

The problem of outliers is one of the oldest in statistics, and during the last century and half, interest in it has waxed and waned several times. Currently it is once again an active research area after some years relative neglect, and recent work has solved a number of old problems in outlier theory, and identified new ones [11].

In practice, observed values are sometimes influenced by outliers, that may be the result of gross errors. Special promotions, strikes, certain system changes, and so forth. Some suspected outliers may have large residuals but may not affect the parameter estimates whereas others may not only have large residuals but may also affect model specification and parameter estimation. This may lead to misspecified models, biased estimates, and biased forecasts. Thus it is very important in practice to detect outliers and to have a procedure for model building (specification, estimation and checking) in the presence of outliers [1].

The outliers are values which seem either too large or too small as compared to rest of the observations [9]. An outlying observation, or outlier, is one that appears to deviate markedly from other members of the sample in which it occurs [8].

The detection of influential subsets or multiple outliers is more difficult, owing to masking and swamping problems. Masking occurs when one outlier is not detected

T. Yakhno (Ed.): ADVIS 2004, LNCS 3261, pp. 88–95, 2004.
© Springer-Verlag Berlin Heidelberg 2004

because of the presence of others, while swamping occurs when a non-outlier is wrongly identified owing to the effect of some hidden outliers [16].

1.1 Data Quality

The first concerns are then with the quality of the data and with what can be broadly called its structure. In this part discussing data quality may be important. Data quality analysis typically includes:

- Visual or automatic inspection of the data for values that are logically inconsistent or conflict with prior information about ranges likely to arise for the various variables.
- Examination of frequency distributions of the main variables to look for small group of discrepant observations.
- Examination of scatter plots of pairs of variables likely to be highly related, this detects discrepant observations more sensitively .
- A check of methods of data collection to discover the sources, if any, of biases in measurements which may be necessary to allow for in analysis, and to assess the approximate measurements and recording errors for the variables.
- A search for missing observations, including observations that have been omitted because of their highly suspicious character.

Concern that data quality should be high without extensive effort being spent on. Achieving unrealistically high precision is of great importance. In particular, recording of data to a large number of digits can be wasteful; on the other hand, excessive rounding sacrifices information. The extent to which poor quality can be set right by more elaborate analysis is very limited, particularly when appreciable systematic errors are likely to be present and cannot be investigated and removed. By and large such poor-quality data will not merit very detailed analysis [5].

1.2 Data Structure and Quantity

Most, although not all, data have the following broad form. There are number of individuals and on each individual, a number of types of observations are recorded. Individuals are thought to be in some senses independent of one another.

The following questions then arise :

- What is to be regarded as an individual ?
- Are the individuals grouped or associated in ways that must be taken into account of in analysis ?
- What are the variables measured on each individual ?
- Are any observations missing, and if so, what can be done to replace those values ?

Data structure is thus a question partly of the number and nature of the variables measured on each individual, and partly of the classification and groupings of individuals. The quantity of data is best thought of as having two aspects, the number of individuals and the number of variables per individual [5].

1.3   Why Outliers Should be Isolated?

The main reason for isolating outliers is associated with data quality assurance. The main exceptional values are more likely to be incorrect. According to the definition given by Wand and Wang [18], unreliable data represents an unconformity between the state of the database and the state of the real world. For a variety of database applications, the amount of erroneous data may reach to ten percent and even more.

For that reason, removal of outliers effect can improve the quality of data used for statistical inferences. Isolated outliers may also have positive impact on the results of data analysis and data mining [13].

Simple statistical estimates, like sample mean and standard deviation can be significantly biased by individual outliers that are far away from the middle of the distribution [13].

1.4   Outlier Detection

Detection methods are divided into two parts: univariate and multivariate methods. In univariate methods, observations are examined individually and in multivariate methods, associations between variables in the same data dataset are taken into account.

Classical outlier detection methods are powerful when the data contain only one outlier. However, these methods decrease drastically if more than one outliers are present in the data [10].

Before we address the issue of identifying these outliers, we must emphasize that not all are wrong numbers. They may justifiably be part of the group and may lead to better understanding of the phenomena being studied. When an outlier is detected, the analyst is faced with number of questions [6] :

- Is the measurement process out of control ?
- Is the model wrong ?
- Is some transformation required ?
- Is there an identifiable subset of observations that is important in its different behavior ?

2   Outlier Models

Consider a stationary autoregressive moving average (ARMA) process of order (p, q)

$$\phi(B)z_t = \theta(B)e_t \tag{2.1}$$

$$\phi(B) = 1 - \phi_1 B - \ldots - \phi_p B^p,$$

$$\theta(B) = 1 - \theta_1 B - \ldots - \theta_q B^q, \quad B^k z_t = z_{t-k} \tag{2.2}$$

e_t is a sequence of independent and identically distributed random variables with mean zero and variance σ^2.

Model (2.1) can also be written as

$$\pi(B)z_t = e_t \tag{2.3}$$

where $\pi(B) = \phi(B)/\theta(B) = 1 - \pi_1 B - \pi_2 B^2 - \dots$.

When estimating the impact of an AO (2.4) and of an IO (2.5), respectively, in a hypothetical situation in which all of time series parameters are known. Two types of outliers in time series introduced by Fox (1972), are additive and innovational.

The Additive Outlier-AO Model :
It is the type of outliers that effects a single observation and occurs as a result of a mistake made in observation or record. This model, defined as "additive outlier" in the literature, is shown as follows :

$$y_t = z_t + \delta x_t \tag{2.4}$$

where y_t is the observed value, δ is the magnitude of outlier and

$$x_t = \begin{cases} 1 & t = T \\ 0 & Otherwise \end{cases}$$

Innovational Outlier-IO Model :
It is the type of outliers that also affects the subsequent observations starting from its position, in other words that occurs as a result of natural randomness. This model, defined as "randomness outlier" in the literature, is shown as follows :

$$y_t = \frac{\theta(B)}{\phi(B)}(e_t + \delta x_t) \tag{2.5}$$

Thus the AO case may be called a gross error model, since only the level of the T'th observation is affected. On the other hand, an IO represents an extraordinary shock at time point T influencing $z_T, z_{T+1}, \dots$ through the dynamic system described by $\psi(B) = \phi(B)/\phi(B)$ [2].

The occurence of AO indicates that action is required, possibly to adjust the measuring instrument or at least to print an error massage on the database. However, if IO occurs no adjustment of the measurement operation is required [15].

The existence of AO can seriously bias the estimates of the ARMA coefficients and variance, whereas IO in general has much smaller effect [3].

2.1   Outlier Detection Stages

Stage-1. From the estimated model, compute the residuals $\hat{e}_t$, and let $\hat{\sigma}_a^2 = n^{-1}\sum_{t=1}^{n}\hat{e}_t^2$ be the estimate of σ_a^2.

Stage-2. Compute $\hat{\lambda}_{1,T} = \dfrac{e_T}{\sigma_a}$ and $\hat{\lambda}_{2,T} = \dfrac{\rho^2 \pi(F)e_T}{\rho\sigma_a}$, $\eta_t = \max\left\{\left|\hat{\lambda}_{1,T}\right|, \left|\hat{\lambda}_{2,T}\right|\right\}$

$\rho^2 = (1 + \pi_1 F + \pi_2 F^2 + ... + \pi_{n-T} F^{n-T})^{-1}$, F is forward shift operator such that $Fe_t = e_{t+1}$ If $\max \eta_t = |\hat{\lambda}_{1,T}| > C$, where C is a predetermined positive constant, then there is possibility of an IO at T. If $\max \eta_t = |\hat{\lambda}_{2,T}| > C$ there is possibility of an AO at T.

Stage-3. If an IO or an AO is identified in step 2, recompute $\hat{\lambda}_{1,T}$ and $\hat{\lambda}_{2,T}$ based on the same initial estimates of the time series parameters, but using the modified residuals and the estimate modified $\hat{\sigma}_a^2$ and repeat stage 2.

Stage-4. Continue to repeat stages 2 and 3 until no further outlier candidates can be identified [2].

This method was proposed [2] and named "iterative procedure" [3]. The power of it in detecting outliers was investigated [19]. Simulation results [2] were reorganized and remodeled under a suitable experimental design. The result of analysis of variance performed for this design indicated that iterative method implemented to the computer program [19] is effective.

2.2   Outlier Detection Algorithm

- Read observations from defined file.
- Read estimated ARMA parameters, using statistical package programs.
- Read calculated π_j's from the estimated model.
- Read $\hat{e}_t$'s to use $\hat{\sigma}_a^2$ and find outliers.
- Read critical values C which can be 3.00, 3.50 and 4.00.
- Do
  1. Calculate the $\hat{\sigma}_a^2$ from the $\hat{e}_t$'s .
  2. Increase   the index of the current value by one
  3. Calculate λ_{1T} , λ_{2T} .
  4. If $\lambda_{1T} > C$ then   display T, IO.
  5. If $\lambda_{2T} > C$ then   display T, AO.
            otherwise no outlier&stop
  6. Calculate   effect of IO or AO and update on new value in file.
  7. Reallocate new $\hat{e}_T$'s
- End Do.
- Go Reading   new observations from updated file and perform   algoritm again.

3   Some Important Results

A simulation study was conducted to obtain some inferences about the different AR(1) coefficients, series size, outlier types, and   sensitivity coefficients. Table 1, shows the probability of finding Additive Outlier-AO, and Innovational Outlier-IO, based on 10000 realizations of the AR(1) with $\phi = 0.5, 0.7, 0.9$ and the critical values are $C = 3.00,$ $C = 3.50,$ $C = 4.00$. For size $n = 50, 100, 200, 500$. The fact that critical value $C = 3.00$ is close to the $\%$ 1, $C = 3.50$ to the $\%5$ and $C = 4.00$ to the $\%$ 10 significance level. The location of outliers is set in the middle of the observational period, spesifically $T = 26$ when $n = 50$, $T = 51$ when $n = 100$, $T = 101$ when $n = 200$, and $T = 251$ when $n = 500$.

Table 1. Finding AO and IO probability based on 10000 replications of an AR(1) process

ϕ	n	C=3.0		C=3.5		C=4.0	
		AO	IO	AO	IO	AO	IO
	50	0.341	0.382	0.334	0.370	0.322	0.354
	100	0.442	0.482	0.428	0.466	0.431	0.464
0.5	200	0.577	0.610	0.559	0.596	0.540	0.579
	500	0.622	0.662	0.614	0.650	0.609	0.641
	50	0.529	0.562	0.525	0.555	0.512	0.551
	100	0.622	0.660	0.619	0.653	0.607	0.643
0.7	200	0.651	0.688	0.639	0.668	0.622	0.656
	500	0.750	0.787	0.743	0.776	0.723	0.757
	50	0.642	0.676	0.638	0.672	0.621	0.661
	100	0.691	0.728	0.688	0.721	0.681	0.715
0.9	200	0.795	0.836	0.791	0.830	0.782	0.815
	500	0.901	0.945	0.892	0.932	0.875	0.907

Table 2. Analysis of variance for Table 1

SOURCE	DF	Sum of Squares	Mean Square	F	P
AR(1)	2	0.84431	0.42216	819.86	0.000
Series Size	3	0.63409	0.21136	410.20	0.000
Critical Value	2	0.00549	0.00275	5.33	0.007
Outlier Type	1	0.02311	0.02311	44.85	0.000
Error	63	0.03246	0.00052		
Total	71	1.53948			

The data used in this study were obtained from the simulation experiments. Simulation results were reorganized and remodeled under a suitable experimental design. The type of factorial design was $(3^2 4\ 2)$ that is 2 factors each at 3 levels and two factors each at 1 level. Different AR(1) (0.5, 0.7, 0.9), sensitivity coefficients (3.00, 3.50, 4.00), series size n (50, 100, 200, 500), and outlier types (AO-IO) were statistically significant.

4   Concluding Remarks

- Although manual inspection of scatter plots is the most common approach to outlier detection, this is not the most effective method. Because the multidimensionality of databases provides a significant advantage to automated perceptions of outliers over the manual analysis of visualized data. Unlike the case of human decision-making, the parameters of the automated detection of outliers can be completely controlled, making it an objective tool for data analysis. Outlier detection in a database is to enhance the performance of data mining algorithms [13].
- The presence of AO in data causes loss of autocorrelation in outlier position. For that reason, finding IO is easier than finding AO.
- Since different AR(1) coefficients are evaluated as the measure of the relations among data, it is concluded that detecting the possible error on non-relational database is difficult.
- For the sample lengths of n =50, 100, 200 and 500, the probability of detecting error is considered important. So data analysis being easier for large databases is detained as a result.
- The proposed procedure is demonstrated to be useful for estimating time series parameters when there is the possibility of outliers. It can be applied to all invertible models. Moreover, it is flexible and easy to interpret, and it can be implemented with very few modifications to existing software packages capable of dealing with ARMA and transfer function models. In practice, we suggest that this procedure can be used in conjuction with other diagnostic tools for time series analysis to produce even better results [2].

References

1. Abraham, B. Chuang, A.: Outlier Detection and Time Series Modelling, American Statistical Association and the American Society for Quality Control (1989).
2. Chang, I., Tiao, G.C., and Chen C.: Estimation of Time Series Parameters in the Presence of Outliers, American Statistical Association and American Society for Quality Control. (Technometrics) Vol. 30, No.2. (1988).
3. Chang, I. and Tiao, G.C.: Estimation of Time Series Parameters in the Presence of Outliers. Technical Report 8. Statistics Research Center, University of Chicago, Chicago (1983).
4. Collett, D. and Lewis, T.: The Subjective Nature of Outliers Rejection Procedures, Applied Statist. 25, No.3, (1976) 228.

5. Cox, D.R. and Snell, E.J.: Applied Statistics-Principles and Examples, Great Britain (1980).
6. David, F. Andrews and Pregibon.: Finding the Outliers that Matter, J.R. Statist. Soc. B, 40, No 1. (1978) 85-93.
7. Elashoff, J.D. (1972).: A model for Quadratic Outliers in Linear Regression, Journal of American Statistical Association, 67, (1972) 478-485.
8. Grubbs, F.E.: Procedures for Detecting Outlying Observations in Samples, Technometrics, 11, (1969) 1-21.
9. Gumbel, E.J.: Discussion on Rejection of Outliers by Anscombe, F. J. Technometrics , 2, (1960) 165-166.
10. Hadi, A.S.: Identifying Multiple Outliers in Multivariate Data, J.R. Statist. Soc. B. 54, No.3, (1992) 761-771.
11. Hawkins, D.W. : Identification of Outliers, Chapman and Hall, Great Britain (1980).
12. Johnson, R.A and Wichern, D.W.: Applied Multivariate Statistical Analysis, Prentice Hall, New Jersey, ABD (1988).
13. Last, M., and Kandel, A.: Automated Detection of Outliers in Real World Data, www.ise.bgu.ac.il/faculty/mlast/papers.
14. Ljung, G.M.: On Outlier Detection in Time Series, J.R. Statist. Soc. B, 55, No. 2, (1993) 559-567.
15. Muirhead, C.R.: Distinguishing Outlier Types in Time Series, J.R. Statist.. Soc. B, 48, (1986) 39-47.
16. Pena, D. and Yohai, V.J.: The Detection of Influential Subsets in Linear Regression by Using an Influential Matrix, J.R. Statist. Soc. (1995) B 57, No. 1, (1995) 145-156.
17. Prescott, P.: An Approximate Test for Outliers in Linear Models, Technometrics, 17, (1975) 129-132.
18. Wand, Y., and Wang, R.Y. Anchoring Data Quality Dimension in Ontological Foundations. Communications of the ACM, 39, 11, (1996) 86-95.
19. Kaya, A.: An Investigation The Analysis of Outliers in Time Series, Ph.D Thesis, Dokuz Eylül University, İzmir, Turkey (1999).
20. Fox, A. J.: Outliers in Time Series, Journal of the Royal Statistical Society , Ser. B. 43, 350-363.

Finding Maximal Similar Paths Between XML Documents Using Sequential Patterns

Jung-Won Lee and Seung-Soo Park

Dept. of Computer Science and Engineering, Ewha Womans University,
11-1 Daehyun-dong, Sudaemun-ku, Seoul, Korea
{jungwony, sspark}@ewha.ac.kr

Abstract. Techniques for storing XML documents, optimizing the query, and indexing for XML have been active subjects of research. Most of these techniques are focused on XML documents shared with the same structure (i.e., the same DTD or XML Schema). However, when XML documents from the Web or EDMS (Electronic Document Management System) are required to be merged or classified, it is very important to find the common structure among multiple documents for the process of handling documents. In this paper, we propose a new methodology for extracting common structures from XML documents and finding maximal similar paths between structures using sequential pattern mining algorithms. Correct determination of common structures between XML documents provides an important basis for a variety of applications of XML document mining and processing. Experiments with XML documents show that our adapted sequential pattern mining algorithms can find common structures and maximal similar paths between them exactly.

1   Introduction

The self-describing feature of XML, coupled with its nested structure that naturally models complex objects, makes it ideal for both representing and exchanging information over the Internet. Active subject of research related to XML is focused on moving data from Web to database system. Therefore, techniques for XML schema discovery, indexing, storing, query processing and optimization, and view materializing have been actively developed.

However, these techniques deal with a set of XML documents shared with almost similar or the same structure using single DTD or Schema. Even if they process XML documents with various structures, they try to make a fixed schema for migrating data from Web to database. For example, let's assume that our company wants to buy some products using XML-based B2B system. We first send our request form to 'A' company. The company extracts product information from its own database, generates an XML document, and gives it back to us. For exchanging these data, there may be only two DTDs such as 'OurBuyingInfo.DTD' (for the request form) and 'A-SellingInfo.DTD' (for sales information). If we want to compare with products of other companies automatically, we need to analyze formats of XML documents, which are described using another DTDs (i.e., B-SellingInfo.DTD, C-SellingInfo.DTD, and so on). They have the same data but don't conform the same

T. Yakhno (Ed.): ADVIS 2004, LNCS 3261, pp. 96–106, 2004.

structure and element names. Therefore, we have to rearrange all data from three DTDs. It is very important to figure out common structures among XML documents when we want to process XML documents with various structures.

In this paper, we propose a new methodology for finding common structures from XML documents and finding maximal similar paths between structures. We discover a unique and minimized structure from an XML document using automata theory and identify similar elements between documents. We then extract common structures and find maximal similar paths by adapting sequential pattern mining algorithms[1]. Accurate determination of common structures between XML documents can be important basis for processing XML document with various structures. This methodology can be widely used for managing and integrating XML documents for EDMS, sharing information on multiple B2B systems, building a knowledge base of a retrieval engine for XML, and mining XML documents as well.

The remainder of this paper is organized as follows. Section 2 describes background and Section 3 proposes a methodology for finding maximal similar paths between XML documents. Section 4 shows the details of algorithms. Section 5 provides experimental results and section 6 concludes the paper.

2   Background

Automatic deduction of the structures of XML documents is an essential technique for processing XML[2,3,4]. Structure discovery aims for extracting a fixed structure for migrating or storing XML data to a database. Most of researches are focused on finding an optimized structure and minimizing loss of information at the same time. However, we need to figure out a common structure between XML documents, which are written not from one DTD but with different element names and structures.

The problem of finding specific patterns on discovered structures has been researched for a long time as tree-pattern matching problem for optimization in the field of compiler[5,6]. Algorithms for tree pattern matching aim for replacing subexpression to another expressions[5]. Let's assume that we have a path like a-b-c-d. It is possible to match a-b, b-c, and c-d with some expressions partially. However, if we want to match a embedded path like a-b-d, it needs more processing and time complexity. On the other hand, to find frequent patterns like [7] examines the inside of a document. It finds frequent patterns using association rule for discovering schema from semi-structured documents. However, it is difficulty to use as it is for comparing structures between documents, which conform to different DTDs. Therefore, we need to develop a new technique for finding common structures between multiple documents.

The method for extracting common structures between XML documents is similar to the problem of detecting duplicated program codes for reuse of software. That problem has been researched for reducing the cost for software maintenance or for finding plagiarism of software. [8] uses the abstract syntax tree for finding duplicated parts of trees. However, it is dependent of parser of each programming language. Our target, XML, is a markup language, which does not have any variable names and any specific syntax or defined grammar. Furthermore, most of algorithms have time complexity, $O(N^2) \sim O(N^3)$[6]. It is not practical to process large XML documents with this complexity. Therefore, we have to develop a new methodology for extracting common structures and finding maximal similar paths between XML documents.

3   The Adaptation Process for Finding Maximal Similar Paths

In this section, we propose an adapted sequential pattern mining algorithms to find maximal similar paths between XML documents. Original sequential pattern mining algorithms[1] find maximal sequences among transaction sequences that satisfy user-defined minimum support with time complexity, $O(n)$. Transaction sequences which are random sequences of goods purchased by customers, such as 'beer', 'diaper' and 'milk'. Common structures between XML documents have semantic relationships among frequent transaction sequences. Continuously, nested XML elements on a common path also have semantic relationships with transactions on frequent sequences. Therefore, we adapt sequential pattern mining algorithms to extract common structures and find maximal paths. However, in the concept of minimum support needs to be viewed from a different perspective. In particular, minimum support for finding maximal similar paths between two documents must be 100%.

3.1   The Concept of Adaptation

There are 5 phases in original sequential pattern mining algorithms-sort, litemset, transformation, sequence, and maximal phase. Our adaptation algorithms also have 5 phases but we rename each phase correspondingly as the following Table 1. This table also summarizes the concept of adaptation.

- *Extracting Paths* : We have to preprocess for minimizing an XML structure using automata theory. From a minimized automata, we can get multiple paths from root(start state) to terminal elements(final state). Elements composed of paths are naturally expressed by the order of level.
- *Identification of Similar Elements* : We assume that XML documents have various structures and use different element names. Therefore, there are synonyms, compound words, and abbreviations between element names. In this phase we identify similar elements and define them as large 1-paths.
- *Transformation* : We rename element names of all paths with integers for keeping the level of an element and fast computing. At this time, if two elements are identified as similar, they are transformed with the same integer.
- *Finding Common Paths* : We find common paths by increasing the length of a path. We generate candidate paths by concatenating large 1-paths, prune candidates by checking that they are contained in both documents, and define remaining paths as large 2-paths. We repeat this step until we have no more candidates.
- *Extracting Maximal Similar Paths* : Maximal similar paths are found by reducing duplicated paths among the set of large paths.

Table 1. The Concept of Adaptation

	Original Algorithms		Our Adapted Algorithms
Sort	The database is sorted, with customer-id as the major key and transaction-time as the minor key.	Extracting Paths	The XML document is converted to minimized automata. Then path expressions are extracted and are sorted by level.
Litemset	An itemset with minimum support is called a large itemset(or litemset). A set of all litemsets L is found.	Identification of Similar Elements	All large 1-paths are found considering element similarity.
Transfor -mation	Each customer sequences is transformed into alternative representation.	Transfor -mation	All extracted elements of path expressions are replaced with integers. Similar elements are renamed with the same integer.
Sequence	If a sequence of length k is called k-sequence, k-sequences composed of large itemset are found.	Finding Common Paths	Large 1, 2,..n paths are found with similarity.
Maximal	Maximal sequences among the set of large sequences are found.	Extracting Maximal Similar Paths	Maximal similar paths are found among the set of large paths.

3.2   Preprocessing

Before using adapted sequential pattern mining algorithms, we have to preprocess XML documents. First, we have to discover and minimize a structure from an XML document and then build similarity measure and matrix to identify similar elements. Our prior paper[9] describes the detail of preprocessing but we explain how to preprocess briefly. We have to discover a structure directly from an XML document without using DTD or Schema because there is no standard definition for XML structure. There are a lot of methods such as DTD, XML Schema, XML-Data, DCD(Document Content Description), SOX(Schema for Object-Oriented XML), and so on for defining XML structures. If we use a specific definition for discovering XML structures, we have to develop a technique for automatic understanding and integrating of different definitions. There are several methods for formalizing the structure of semistructured data[10]. We have chosen to formalize the structure of an XML document using NFA(Non Deterministic Finite Automata). By removing repeated state transitions, we can transform NFA to DFA (Deterministic FA). We can then apply a state minimization algorithm to DFA to minimize the number of states. We extract path by connecting elements from root to terminal and can get paths, which are ordered by the levels of elements. Second, we have to define similarity measure between elements and build a similarity matrix for two sets of elements. The basis of the measure is the degree of match between two elements-complete match, partial match, synonyms, compound word and so on.

4   Algorithms

In this section, we explain the detail of algorithms of our adapted sequential pattern mining algorithms. We propose 3 algorithms for extracting paths, identifying similar elements and transformation, and finding maximal similar paths.

4.1   Extracting Paths

As a result of preprocessing, we got a minimized XML structure from an XML document. In our minimized automata, each state has a state number and transitions between states have real element names. We can get path expressions by traversing automata by depth-fist search and concatenating only labels of transitions from start to final state. The following Fig.1 shows this algorithm. For the convenience, we define a base document as B and n query document as $Q_{1..n}$.

Procedure SortStructure (B:base document, $Q_{1..n}$: query document)
    returns PE_B: set of path expressions of B,   *// path expressions are sorted by levels*
            $PE_{Q1..n}$: set of path expressions of each $Q_{1..n}$;
    begin
        convert B to NFA-XML of B;
        transform NFA-XML of B to DFA-XML of B ;
        minimize DFA-XML of B ;
        PE_B = path expressions from the minimized DFA-XML of B;
        for (k=1; k <= n; k++) **do**
        begin
            convert Q_k to NFA-XML of Q_k ;
            transform NFA-XML of Q_k to DFA-XML of Q_k ;
            minimize DFA-XML of Q_k ;
            PE_{Qk} = path expressions from the minimized DFA-XML of Q_k;
        end
    end

Fig. 1. Algorithm for Extracting Paths

< Example 1 >
In Table 3 of section 4.2, we show path expressions extracted from two minimized XML structures. Two XML documents are obtained from on-line bookseller sites and simplified by omitting a part of structures. For comparing, we define the first one as a base document(PE_B) and the second as a query document(PE_{Q1}). We show only one query document for simplicity. Transformed paths in the right column will be explained the next section.

4.2   Identification of Similar Elements and Transformation

In this section, we rename terms of paths with integers. It includes two phases-identification and transformation. The following Fig.2 shows the algorithm. In the identification phase, we have to build a mapping table with similar elements. It means that the same and similar elements are renamed with the same number in the mapping table. Here, we define elements with the same number as large 1-paths for next phase because they exist in both of two structures. Then, we replace every element with numbers by increasing order in the phase of transformation.

---

procedure Identification&Transformation (PE_B: path expressions of a base document, $PE_{Q1..n}$: path expressions of query documents, SM : similarity matrix between elements)
returns $L_1^{B \cdot Q1..n}$; // *all large 1-paths between PE_B and $PE_{Q1..n}$*
   begin
          initialize MappingTable;   // *build a mapping table*
          for (k=1; $PE_B \neq$ nil or $PE_{Q1..n} \neq$ nil; k++) **do**
          begin
                  E = read (one element from PE_B or $PE_{Q1..n}$);
                  if (E $\notin$ MappingTable)
                      then if (similar element of E in SM $\notin$ MappingTable)
                      then insert MappingTable(k , E);
                      else append MappingTable(similar element of E, E)
                              // *with the same index of similar element of E*
        end
      // *elements in path expressions are replaced by integers*
          map elements of PE_B and $PE_{Q1..n}$ to integers in MappingTable;
          generate new path expressions in which elements are represented in integers;
          for (k=1; k <= n ; k++) **do** // *find all large 1-paths $L_1^{B \cdot Q1..n}$*
                foreach element E in PE_{Qk} **do**
                    if (E $\in PE_B$) // *minimum support 100%*
                    then insert E into $L_1^{B \cdot Qk}$;   // *between PE_B and PE_{Qk}*
              end
        end
   end

Fig. 2. Algorithm for Identifying Similar Elements and Transforming

< Example 2 >
We build a mapping table, which shows renamed numbers of elements. As the mentioned above, similar elements have the same number. For example, each pair of (author, writer), (contents, TableofContents), and (rating, avg_rating) has the same number such as 16, 21, and 22 as the following Table 2. The 'bookinfo', of PE_B and PE_{Q1} surly have the same number 3.

Table 2. Mapping Table

No	Element	No	Element	No	Element	No	Element
1	book	7	date	13	list	19	reviews
2	title	8	publisher	14	our	20	customer
3	bookinfo	9	isbn	15	save	21	rating, avg_rating
4	page	10	size	16	contents, tableofcontents	22	writer, author
5	paperback	11	buyinginfo	17	section	23	name
6	edition	12	price	18	chap		

Using this table, we can transform every path expression of Table 3. as the rightmost column. Therefore, we prepare a data structure for fast computing by generating path expressions expressed with integers. Here, we can get large 1-paths as well as renamed paths. (i.e. <2>, <3>, <12>, <13>, <14>, <16>, <17>, <18>, <19>, <21>, <22>, <23>) Large 1-paths are obtained by checking whether they exist or not in both of documents.

Table 3. Transformed Paths

Doc.	Path Expressions	Transformed
PE$_B$	book.title.$\perp$	<{1} {2}>
	book.bookinfo.page.$\perp$	<{1} {3} {4}>
	book.bookinfo.paperback.$\perp$	<{1} {3} {5}>
	book.bookinfo.edition.$\perp$	<{1} {3} {6}>
	book.bookinfo.date.$\perp$	<{1} {3} {7}>
	book.bookinfo.publisher.$\perp$	<{1} {3} {8}>
	book.bookinfo.ISBN.$\perp$	<{1} {3} {9}>
	book.bookinfo.size.$\perp$	<{1} {3} {10}>
	book.buyinginfo.price.list.$\perp$	<{1} {11} {12} {13}>
	book.buyinginfo.price.our.$\perp$	<{1} {11} {12} {14}>
	book.buyinginfo.price.save.$\perp$	<{1} {11} {12} {15}>
	book.contents.section.chap.$\perp$	<{1} {16} {17} {18}>
	book.reviews.customer.rating.$\perp$	<{1} {19} {20} {21}>
	book.writer.name.$\perp$	<{1} {22} {23} >
PE$_{Q1}$	bookinfo.title.$\perp$	<{3} {2}>
	bookinfo.price.list.$\perp$	<{3} {12} {13}>
	bookinfo.price.our.$\perp$	<{3} {12} {14}>
	bookinfo.author.name.$\perp$	<{3} {22} {23}>
	bookinfo.tableofcontents.section.chap.$\perp$	<{3} {16} {17} {18}>
	bookinfo.reviews.reviews_no. $\perp$	<{3} {19} {24}>
	bookinfo.reviews.avg_rating.$\perp$	<{3} {19} {21}>

4.3   Extracting Common Structures and Finding Maximal Similar Paths

We are now ready to find common structures between two XML documents. The following algorithm involves multiple passes over the path expressions.

```
procedure Sequence&Maximal (L₁ᴮ•Q1..ⁿ : all large 1-path expressions between a base
                                        document B and each query document,
                            PE_B: path expressions of a base document,
                            PE_Q1..n : path expressions of query documents)
returns ML ᴮ•Q1..ⁿ ; // all maximal large similar paths between PE_B and PE_Q1..n
  begin
        for (i=1; i <= n; i++) do
        begin
                for (k=2; L_{k-1}^{B•Qi} ≠ ∅; k++) do
                begin      // same as apriori-generate function of sequential patterns [10]
                        C_k = New candidate-paths generated from L_{k-1}^{B•Qi};
                        foreach path expressions in PE_B and PE_Qi do // pruning
                                if (C_k ∈ PE_B and C_k ∈ PE_Qk) // exists on the both
                                then L_k^{B•Qi} = C_k ;
                        end
                        length = k; // longest length of large paths L_k^{B•Qi}
                end
                for (j = length; j >= 1; j--) do     // maximal phase
                        foreach j-large paths, L_j^{B•Qi} do
                                delete all sub-paths of L_j^{B•Qi} ;
                        end
                ML^{B•Qi} = { remained large paths in L^{B•Qi} }
        end
  end
```

Fig. 3. Algorithm for Finding Maximal Similar Paths

In the first path, we use all large 1-paths(L_1) as the seed set and generate new potential large paths, called candidate paths C_2 using a candidate-generation function. We use AprioriAll algorithm among sequential pattern mining algorithms to find $L_2, ...L_n$. In the maximal phase, we remove non-maximal paths from all large paths.

< Example >
We generate new potential large paths, called candidate paths C_2 by concatenating L_1 each by each. Then, C_2(underlined paths) remains only if they exist in both paths and are selected as L_2 in the following Table 4. Continuously, we generate C_3 by concatenating path i and j if the last element of one path(i) is matched with the first element of another path(j) among L_2. Therefore, we can get only one C_3, <16, 17, 18>, in Table 5 and this path also can be L_3 because it exists in both paths.

Table 4. Finding Large Path L_2

Large 1-Paths (L_1)	Candidate Paths (C_2)	Large 2-Paths (L_2)
<2>,<3>, <12>,<13>, <14>,<16>, <17>,<18>, <19>,<21> <22>,<23>	<2,3>, <2,12>, <2,13>, <2,14>, <2,16>, <2,17>, <2,18>, <2,19>, <2,21>, <2,22>, <2,23>, <3,12>, <3,13>, <3,14>, <3,16>, <3,17>, <3,18>,<3,19>,<3,21>, <3,22>, <3,23>, **<12,13>**, **<12,14>**, <12,16>, <12,17>, <12,18>, <12,19>, <12,21>, <12,22>, <12,23>, <13,14>, <13,16>, <13,17>, <13,18>, <13,19>, <13,21>, <13,22>, <13,23>, <14,16>, <14,17>, <14,18>, <14,19>, <14,21>, <14,22>, <14,23>, **<16,17>**, <16,18>, <16,19>, <16,21>, <16,22>, <16,23>, **<17,18>**, <17,19>, <17,21>, <17,22>, <17,23>, <18,19>, <18,21>, <18,22>, <18,23>, **<19,21>**, <19,22>, <19,23>, <21,22>, <21,23>, **<22,23>**	<12, 13> <12, 14> <16, 17> <16, 18> <17, 18> <19, 21> <22, 23>

Table 5. Finding Large Path L_3

Large 2-Paths (L_2)	Candidate Paths (C_3)	Large 3-Paths (L_3)
<12, 13>, <12, 14>, <16, 17>, <16, 18>, <17, 18>, <19, 21>, <22, 23>	<16, 17, 18 >	<16, 17, 18 >

By reducing duplicated paths among L_1, L_2, and L_3, we can get 7 maximal similar paths as Table 6. Here, we convert numbers to element names. Based on maximal similar paths, we know that two documents share structures quite a lot.

Table 6. Maximal Similar Paths

Large 1-paths	Large 2-paths	Large 3-paths
title bookinfo	price.list, price.our reviews.rating (=reviews.avg_rating) writer.name (=author.name)	contents.section.chap (=tableofcontents.section.chap)

5   Experiment

Due to difficulty in obtaining large XML documents with various structures, we chose to translate HTML documents to equivalent XML documents. In this experiment,

XML documents translated from Amazon site have the same purpose for selling some products. There are four categories such as books, electronics, music, and video. They have very similar structures but some parts of structures are different because selling items are different. The following Fig. 4 shows four minimized structures.

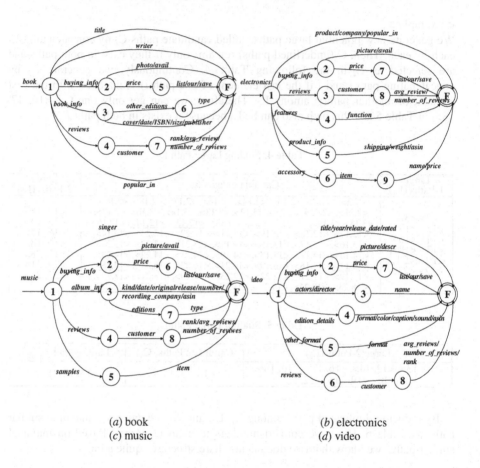

(a) book
(c) music

(b) electronics
(d) video

Fig. 4. Representative Structures of Each Category

The following table shows maximal similar paths between these structures using our adapted sequential pattern mining algorithms.

As a result, we knew that our proposed algorithms could find maximal similar paths exactly. However, element 'item' of electronics and 'item' of music have different meanings. The first one means accessory item that we have to buy together with some electronics. The last is one of music samples for CD promotion. We can differentiate this semantics by determining whether to include large 1-paths in maximal similar paths or not. These maximal similar paths can be used partially or fully according to what the application is.

Table 7. Maximal Similar Paths

books : electronics	books : music	books : video
buying_info.photo	date , buying_info.photo	title
buying_info.avail	buying_info.avail	bying_info.photo
buying_info.price.list	buying_info.price.list	buying_info.price.list
buying_info.our	buying_info.our	buying_info.our
buying_info.save	buying_info.save	buying_info.save
reviews.customer.avg_review	other_editions.type	reviews.customer.rank
reviews.customer.number_of_reviews	reviews.customer.rank	reviews.customer.avg_review
	reviews.customer.avg_review	reviews.customer.number_of_reviews
	reviews.customer.number_of_reviews	

electronics : music	electronics : video	music : video
date, item	asin, name	asin, buying_info.picture
buying_info.picture	buying_info.picture	buying_info.avail
buying_info.avail	buying_info.price.list	buying_info.price.list
buying_info.price.list	buying_info.our	buying_info.our
buying_info.our	buying_info.save	buying_info.save
buying_info.save	reviews.customer.avg_review	reviews.customer.rank
reviews.customer.avg_review	reviews.customer.number_of_reviews	reviews.customer.avg_review
reviews.customer.number_of_reviews		reviews.customer.number_of_reviews

6   Conclusion

In this paper, we proposed a new methodology for extracting common structures from XML documents and finding maximal similar paths between structures. We can extract efficiently and exactly maximal similar paths by using advantage of sequential pattern mining algorithms, which can find maximal sequences among transaction sequences with O(n). Correct determination of common structures between XML documents provides an important basis for a variety of applications of XML document mining and processing. We need further research to apply this methodology to document mining and bioinformatics.

References

1. R. Srikant and R. Agrawal.: Mining Sequential Patterns:Generalizations and Performance Improvements. In Proc. of the Int'l Conf. on Data Engineering(ICDE). March 1995.
2. Nestorov, Abiteboul, Motwani.: Extracting Schema from Semistructured Data. In Proc. of SIGMOD, pages 295-306. 1998.
3. Y. Papakonsstantinou.: XML and the Automation of Web Information Processing. Tutorial given at the International Conference on Data Engineering. 1999.
4. Deutsch, Fernandez and Suciu.: "Storing Semistructured Data with STORED. In Proc. of SIGMOD, pages 431-442. 1999.
5. C. M. Hoffmann and M. J. O'Donnell.: Pattern Matching in Trees. Journal of ACM 29(1), pages 68–95. Jan. 1982.
6. P. Kilpelainen and H. Mannila.: The Tree Inclusion Problem. In Proc. the International Joint Conference on the Theory and Practice of Software Development (TAPSOFT'91), Vol. 1: Colloqium on Trees in Algebra and Programming (CAAP '91), pages 202-214. 1991.

7. K. Wang and H. Liu.: Discovering Typical Structures of Documents: a Road Map Approach. In Proc. of SIGIR, pages 146-154. 1998.
8. I. D. Baxter, A. Yahin, L. Moura, M. Sant'Anna, and L. Bier.: Clone Detection using Abstract Syntax Tree. In Proc. of the ICSM'98. Nov. 1998.
9. J. W. Lee, K. Lee, and W. Kim.: Preparations for Semantics-based XML Mining. In Proc. of IEEE International Conference on Data Mining (ICDM '01), pages 345~352. Nov./Dec. 2001.
10. Abiteboul, Buneman, and Suciu.: Data on the web : from relations to semistructured data and XML. Morgan-Kaufmann. 2000.

Using Ontologies for Collaborative Information Management: Some Challenges and Ideas

Victor Guevara-Masis, Ozgul Unal, Ersin C. Kaletas, Hamideh Afsarmanesh, and Louis O. Hertzberger

University of Amsterdam, Informatics Institute,
Kruislaan 403, 1098 SJ Amsterdam, The Netherlands
{vguevara, ozgul, kaletas, hamideh, bob}@science.uva.nl

Abstract. Emerging collaborative networks (CNs) bring together the need for an effective collaborative information management (CIM) infrastructure. Achieving a common understanding of the concepts and entities in CNs, especially with the presence of different types of heterogeneity involved in such environments, represents a big challenge for the developers of the CIM infrastructure. This paper proposes some ontology-based solutions to this challenge in three different research domains. Among the described solutions, the first one addresses the challenges of data representation and implementation regarding the translation of semantic model into appropriate data structures, the second one suggests an ontology-based semi-automatic approach for the resolution of schematic and semantic heterogeneity, and the third one aims to assist scientists from different e-science domains when customizing their experimentation environments with user-defined experiments and data types.

1   Introduction

Currently, distributed and cooperative environments using network facilities are emerging, which offer an increasing number of applications and services. The services and the base infrastructure supporting the environment can be together referred to as *Collaborative Networks* (CNs) [1]. Several forms of collaborative networks are evolving in parallel, among which the promising types can be named as Virtual Organizations, Virtual Communities, and Virtual Laboratories. Briefly, a *Virtual Organization* (VO) is a gathering of autonomous organizations that pursue accomplishment of specific common goals [2]. *Virtual Communities* (VCs) replace the face-to-face communication with "online communication" among the members of the community [3]. A *Virtual Laboratory* (VL) provides the necessary hardware and software infrastructure to help scientists to systematically define and carry out their experiments, without regard to physical location [4].

Although each one of these virtual environments has a specific set of requirements, they all need an information management infrastructure. In this paper, the term *collaborative information management (CIM)* is used to refer to the set of (sub-)components and mechanisms that altogether constitute a *generic*

T. Yakhno (Ed.): ADVIS 2004, LNCS 3261, pp. 107–116, 2004.

framework to support the interoperation and data sharing among the members of the CN.

There are several different types of heterogeneity that play an important role for the management of information in such collaborative environments, e.g. differences in the performed activities, and in the background/expertise and the roles of involved people. Other types of heterogeneity include the system heterogeneity (e.g. hardware/software platform), the syntactic heterogeneity (e.g. data definition/manipulation/query languages), and the semantic heterogeneity (e.g. schema definitions).

Such different types of heterogeneity make it a common challenge for the developers of the CIM to achieve *a common understanding* of the concepts and entities within the domain of the collaboration.

In this paper, we propose some *ontology-based solutions* to this challenge, which are specifically targeting the problems that we encounter in our application cases, and at the same time related to the management of information in collaborative environments from different domains. The remaining of this paper first introduces the addressed problem areas in Section 2. Section 3 provides some general ideas on using ontologies in collaborative information management. Section 4 then describes the application cases, and how we use ontologies in each of them to overcome the specific problems of that domain/application. An overview of the related work is given in Section 5. Finally, Section 6 concludes the paper.

2   Problems Areas – Motivation

In this section, we introduce three research domains as motivation, which constitute the problem areas that we consider in this paper. The first one is related to tele-assistance, the second one is the biodiversity domain, and the third one is related to the e-science experimentations. For each of these domains, we solely address the problems related to the *"common understanding of concepts"* for information management.

In VOs committed to support *tele-assistance* applications, developers from multi-disciplines and different domains (e.g. health care, elderly care, ubiquitous computing, etc.) gradually build and develop an extensive set of applications and value-added services on top of a base infrastructure. Each of these applications and services has its own data model, data structures, and information sources that need to be supported by the information management component of the networked environment. Similar to the information management requirement of vertical services, developers of the base infrastructure also need to model and store their data in the database. Thus, information management for tele-assistance is, on one hand, required to support the flexibility, openness, and extensibility needed for the incremental addition of conceptual models. On the other hand, it must also provide facilities for assisting the developers of the base infrastructure to manage their information.

In the *biodiversity* domain, different organizations structure biodiversity data in different formats depending on their specific needs and preferences. Level of detail for the managed data varies, and standard data models are typically not used. These matters have resulted in a large number of independent and heterogeneous databases, scattered all over the world. Hence, demands for effective mechanisms to integrate/inter-link and homogeneously access the heterogeneous and distributed databases, and to provide a single, integrated interface for users are increasing.

In *e-science domains*, large amounts of data are generated, many steps in experiments are automated, and Information and Communication Technologies (ICT) are extensively used throughout the entire experiment life-cycle. Life sciences, physics, simulation and modeling, medical sciences, and astronomy can be named among the most active e-science domains. Following are among the most common characteristics of experiments from different e-science domains: *Diversity* (increasingly diverse experiments even in a single domain), *complexity* (longer and more complex experimental procedures), and *large data sizes* (generated by high-throughput experimental technologies). Furthermore, by nature, experiments themselves as well as the data/information they generate are *heterogeneous*. This heterogeneity further increases with *ad-hoc experimentations* driven by 'what if' questions especially during the result analysis phase of experiments, as well as with *new types of information* generated by new types of experiments.

3 Using Ontologies in Collaborative Information Management

In this section, we provide some general ideas on using ontologies in collaborative information management. Note that these do not comprise the complete set of possible usages of ontologies; rather, they represent the solutions that we applied or plan to apply in our application cases. Some other examples of how ontologies can be used in this field are provided in Section 5 as part of the related work.

An ontology refers to the set of logical definitions that express the meaning of terms for a particular domain. These conceptual definitions make use of explicit assumptions and may include semantics as well [5]. Ontologies are based on the understanding of the members of a particular domain, and help to reduce ambiguity in human-computer, human-human, and computer-computer interactions. For purposes of clarity, this paper assumes an ontology as *"descriptions of entities involved in a specific domain with a well-defined boundary, and the relationships between the entities"*.

Ontologies can be used in different ways to support the information management requirements in collaborative networks. One use of ontologies can be to resolve schematic and semantic heterogeneity when integrating/inter-linking heterogeneous data/information or when defining the integrated database schemas in a federated database system. For example, existing ontologies or semantic dictionaries can be used to create mappings between two different database schemas by determining the matching components. These mappings are then used when generating the integrated schemas or when integrating data from these databases.

In e-science domains, on the other hand, ontologies can be used to assist scientists when customizing their experimentation environments with user-defined experiments and data types. Considering the diversity of emerging e-science experiments, the former will especially help to provide a formalized description for customized experimental procedures. On the other hand, the latter type of usage will allow scientists to save the results of data analysis (i.e. interpretation/metadata), which are generally of ad-hoc and intuitive nature, where the type of output is not known in advance. Ontology entries can also be used to annotate the results. Ontology can be built up from scratch in a lab, by inserting the definitions of new terms, techniques, etc. In time, this ontology may serve as the knowledgebase for the lab.

An ontology can also be used within the context of a single project, e.g. a software development project for tele-assistance, where the entities and operations must be standardized during the software development phase. Here, the ontology will be built and used only during the life-time of the project.

4   Application Cases

This section provides an overview of the research projects that we consider as the application cases for using ontologies in collaborative information management. The three application cases described here are the TeleCARE from the tele-assistance application domain, ENBI from the biodiversity domain, and VLAM-G from the e-science domains.

4.1   TeleCARE

The IST 5FP TeleCARE project [6] designs and develops a collaborative framework solution for tele-supervision and tele-assistance, to support the elderly people. TeleCARE integrates a number of technologies and paradigms, in order to provide an open architecture supporting seamless future expansion. The base infrastructure developed for TeleCARE contains a *horizontal* platform, which provides the *multi-agent system* (MAS) and the CIM functionality, while a variety of tele-assistance applications constitute the *vertical services* built on top of the horizontal platform.

Federated Information Management plays a fundamental role within the horizontal platform. It considers the sharing and exchange of distributed information in a highly heterogeneous environment [7]. The federated approach to information management in networks of independent cooperative nodes is well suited to management of all local and distributed information handled in TeleCARE, while at the same time preserving the node autonomy and information privacy. The establishment of federated schemas and data structures is a critical task, since the information sharing is generally performed based on those schemas and data structures. In TeleCARE, to avoid both schematic and semantic heterogeneity, the CIM component uses explicit data structures specified from ontological definitions [8].

The ontological definitions in TeleCARE constitute a base collection of concepts, entities, and their inter-relationships. The concepts are established by developers of modules for the horizontal infrastructure, as well as the developers of vertical services into the *Ontology Management System*. TeleCARE uses the Protégé-2000 [9] for this purpose, which is an open source software developed at the Stanford Medical Informatics Laboratory to support the software developers and experts for development of their knowledgebase systems.

The *Dynamic Ontology-based data Structure Generator – DOSG* is a key component of the CIM module that assists developers during the process of data structure generation from the concepts in the ontology. The data structures represent the shareable information from both the base horizontal platform and the vertical services. The main task of DOSG is to transform and translate a Protégé ontology-based definition into the underlying data model of the CIM layer within the TeleCARE platform [8]. Particularly, it provides a collection of output schemas with their appropriate class definitions and interclass relationships that are used to initially specify relational database structures. As shown in Fig. 1, the DOSG tool automatically produces five different output formats, namely *(1) RDBMS Schema* with the data definition language for relational databases, *(2) Java classes* providing the source code of the data structures, *(3) XML Schema* with the specification for proper handling of XML documents, *(4) Object-relational mapping* containing the mappings that govern the conversion between Java classes and the relational database system, and *(5) XML mapping* that defines the translation between the Java classes and XML.

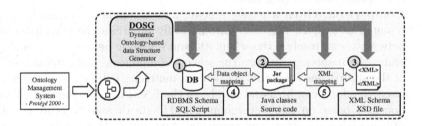

Fig. 1. Data structures generated by DOSG

4.2   ENBI

Taking into account the requirements of biodiversity domain mentioned in Section 2, our work in the European Network for Biodiversity Information (ENBI) [10] project focuses on making the European-level biodiversity data, which are scattered over distributed and heterogeneous databases, available through a common access infrastructure. Therefore, data from each provider have to comply with the common schema of the system when providing them to outside world. In other related biodiversity projects, it is usually the responsibility of the provider to manually define the mappings between his local schema and the common schema. Since the manual work is error-prone and time consuming, in ENBI we aim to provide some mechanisms to handle this process as automatically as possible by utilizing a combination of automatic schema matching techniques based on a domain ontology and the WordNet lexical database [18].

Federated Schema Management Component. The common access infrastructure of ENBI consists of two main components: the Federated Schema Management Component (FSMC) and the data/query interoperation component. The FSCM is based on using available biodiversity data standards (e.g. ABCD Schema, Darwin Core) as the "common schema" and finding the matches between this schema and the schema of legacy databases semi-automatically. These matching results are then used by the data/query interoperation component, for both translating the queries based on the common schema elements to queries on top of the legacy systems and for translating results of the queries from legacy data format to the common format.

The FSMC achieves the semi-automatic matching of schemas in three steps: 1) preparation, 2) comparison, and 3) result generation/validation. Fig. 2 shows a general overview of these steps, details of which will follow below.

1. **Preparation.** One of the distinctive features of our approach for semi-automatic resolution of schematic and semantic heterogeneity is that it is generic enough to be used with different schema types, such as the relational and the object-oriented schemas. Considering the difficulties of directly comparing two schemas represented in different schema languages, our approach first translates them into an internal graph format and then tries to find the correspondences between them.

2. **Comparison.** Given a legacy schema and a common schema, both represented as graphs, this step automatically identifies the correspondences between them, resolves the schematic and semantic heterogeneity, and generates the mappings between the schema components. An extensive survey of the approaches for automatic schema matching followed by some related research efforts can be found in [11]. In the ENBI project, the 'Match' component is based on using a combination of linguistic and structure matching utilizing label, datatype, and graph structure information, while at the same time benefiting from a domain ontology and the WordNet. We create an

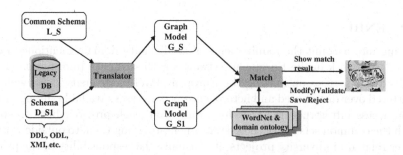

Fig. 2. Semi-automatic matching of schemas

ontology for the ENBI domain, which contains the basic concepts of this domain and their relationships. The WordNet helps to identify synonymy, antonymy, hypernymy, hyponymy, and holonymy relationships between different words.

3. **Result Generation/Validation.** After the mappings between schema elements have been automatically identified, the result of the matching process is displayed to the user. Through a user-friendly GUI, the user can modify/validate/accept/reject the suggested mappings.

4.3 VLAM-G Collaborative Experimentation Environment

The Grid-based Virtual Laboratory Amsterdam (VLAM-G) [12] is a multi-disciplinary virtual laboratory (VL) environment for experimental science domains. VLAM-G allows its users to perform experiments in a uniform and integrated environment, complement their in-vitro experiments with in-silico experiments, define customized experimental procedures and analysis flows, reuse (generic) software components, and share ICT resources as well as knowledge and experience.

The VLAM-G Experiment Model. The *experiment model* outlines the overall approach that a VL follows for supporting scientific experiments, and allows a methodological definition of complex experiments in a problem domain. The VLAM-G experiment model consists of three main components, namely *experiment procedure*, *experiment context*, and *computational processing* [13].

An *experiment procedure* defines the approach taken to solve a particular scientific problem, by defining the experiment components that are typically involved in experiments of the same type. Thus, an experiment procedure standardizes the experimental approach for such experiments. An *experiment context*, on the other hand, describes the solution. It is an instantiation of an experiment procedure, and describes the accomplishment of a particular experiment by providing descriptions of each component involved in the experiment. Processing and analysis of large data sets constitute an important part of scientific experiments, and hence require special attention. In an experiment, during its processing and analysis, data flows from one computational process to another. In VLAM-G, this data flow is represented by a directed graph. Nodes in the graph are computational processes, while the connecting arcs are the data flowing through the processes. This data flow graph is called as *computational processing*.

Customizing the VLAM-G Experimentation Environment. Currently, experiment procedures can only be defined by experts in the domain. Although this approach is useful to assist inexperienced users, it may have a restrictive effect on the experienced users in the long term. For instance, extending the application database schemas with *customized user-defined data types* is needed to save the results of user-specific experimental steps, especially during ad-hoc experimentations. Similarly, *user-defined experiment procedures* are needed to

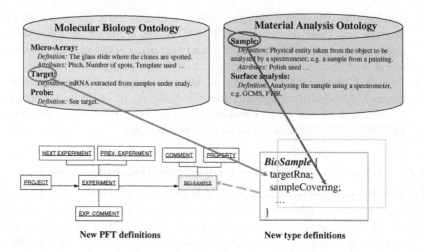

Fig. 3. Customizing the experimentation environment

represent more specialized experiments to be used by a certain group of more experienced users, or to change the procedure when the experiment is still ongoing. *Ontology management systems* can be used to assist such tasks, by providing a dictionary for formal definitions of concepts and entities (e.g. data elements, processes, and their attributes) in a specific scientific domain, and serving as the base for achieving a common understanding of these concepts and entities for *inter-disciplinary research*. Customizing the experimentation environment for a multi-disciplinary experiment is illustrated in Fig. 3. In this figure, a customized data type (namely BioSample) is defined using the definitions in two different ontologies (namely Target from the Molecular Biology Ontology and Sample from the Material Analysis Ontology), and this data type is in turn used when defining a new, customized experiment procedure. Ontologies can also be used to annotate experiment results; for instance, in order to describe a just discovered phenomenon or to explain the behavior of a subject, scientists may include pointers to the ontology terms in their interpretations/conclusions.

5   Related Work

Research in semantic interoperability of databases has now begun to make use of ontologies. These efforts have benefited from ontologies for query formulation, query processing, and query processing steps, as well as in the schema integration process so as to cope with the schematic and semantic heterogeneity.

Resolution of schematic and semantic heterogeneity is a challenge for enabling interoperability among databases. This challenge is addressed by several projects, a number of which makes use of ontologies for that purpose, such as [14, 15].

All the projects above are big steps in database interoperability research. However, they either provide limited functionalities or require the manual work of domain experts to define mappings between ontologies and data sources. Manual work is time consuming and might cause wrong results. In order to reduce the user involvement, several research projects have addressed the need for (semi-) automatic matching [16, 17].

At the same time, ontologies are being more widely used in e-science domains. Here, gene ontologies will be used as example, as they are becoming increasingly important in the analysis of results of microarray experiments. Gene ontologies are defined as (functional) annotations to genes. The Gene Ontology system, maintained by the Gene Ontology Consortium (http://www.geneontology.org), is the most widely used. The three organizing principles of Gene Ontology are molecular function, biological process and cellular component. Setting up associations between the ontologies and the genes and gene products in the collaborating databases is done by means of a set of (curated) mapping files.

Genes only make up a small portion of total DNA content of the genome. Recently it was recognized that a vocabulary of annotation of the entire sequence is needed, and the Sequence Ontology Project was set up (http://song.sourceforge.net/so.shtml). The Sequence Ontology is a set of terms used to describe features on a nucleotide or protein sequence.

Ontologies are also considered in medical domains such as clinical medicine and the biomedical sector, where complex concepts need to be modeled and integrated. A number of applications and ontologies, particularly in the domain of medical care, are used in problem-solving and decision-making, such as Health Level Seven (HL7) Reference Information Model (RIM) classes (http://www.hl7.org/) and GuideLine Interchange Format (GLIF) Ontology (http://www.glif.org/).

Other ontologies, e.g. biochemical, developmental lifetime, anatomy ontologies are being developed orthogonal to each other.

6   Conclusions

Ontologies help to reduce ambiguity in human and computer interactions. By providing a common understanding for the concepts and the relationships between them in a particular domain, ontologies represent a powerful means to support the information management requirements in collaborative networks.

In this paper, we presented some ideas of using ontologies in collaborative information management addressing the challenges we encounter in three different research projects, namely TeleCARE, ENBI, and VLAM-G. Ontologies are used in these projects to achieve a common understanding of the concepts and entities respectively in the domains of tele-assistance, biodiversity, and e-science experimentations. More specifically, they are used in automatic generation of data structures, semi-automatic resolution of schematic and semantic heterogeneity among data schemas, and assisting scientists from different e-science domains when customizing their experimentation environments with user-defined experiments and data types.

References

1. L.M. Camarinha-Matos: New Collaborative Organizations and Their Research Needs. In Proceedings of the IFIP TC5/WG5.5 Fourth Working Conference on Virtual Enterprises (PRO-VE'03) 2003 3–14
2. L.M. Camarinha-Matos et.al: Advances in Networked Enterprises - Virtual Organisations. Balanced Automation, and Systems Integration, IFIP International Federation For Information Processing: Kluwer Academic Publishers, 2000.
3. H. Afsarmanesh et.al: Virtual Community Support in TeleCARE. In Proceedings of the 4th IFIP working conference on Virtual Enterprises (PROVE'03) 2003 211–220
4. J.P. Vary: Report of the Expert Meeting on Virtual Laboratories. United Nations Educational, Scientific and Cultural Organization. Tech. Report CII-00/WS/01 2000
5. N. Michael et.al: Ontologies for Agents. IEEE Internet Computing 1996 81–83
6. TeleCARE – A Multi-Agent Tele-Supervision System for Elderly Care. http://www.uninova.pt/~telecare 2004.
7. S. Busse et.al: Federated Information Systems: Concepts, Terminology and Architectures. Berlin: Computergestutzte InformationssystemeCIS, Technische Universitat Berlin 1999
8. V. Guevara-Masis V et.al: Automatic Data Structures Generation from Ontological Definitions. Submitted to PRO-VE'04 - 5th IFIP Working Conference on Virtual Enterprises 2004
9. Stanford Medical Informatics. The Protege Project. Stanford University School of Medicine, http://protege.stanford.edu/ 2003
10. ENBI – European Network for Biodiversity Information (IST 2001-00618). http://www.enbi.info
11. E. Rahm, P.A. Bernstein: A Survey of Approaches to Automatic Schema Matching. VLDB Journal **10** 2001 334–350
12. H. Afsarmanesh et.al: VLAM-G: A Grid-based Virtual Laboratory. Scientific Programming. **10** 2002 173–181
13. E. C. Kaletas et.al: Modelling Multi-Disciplinary Scientific Experiments and Information. In Proceedings of the Eighteenth International Symposium on Computer and Information Sciences (ISCIS'03) 2003 75–82
14. R.J. Bayardo et.al: InfoSleuth: Agent-Based Semantic Integration of Information in Open and Dynamic Environments. In Proceedings of the ACM SIGMOD International Conference on Management of Data 1997
15. E. Mena et.al: OBSERVER: An Approach for Query Processing in Global Information Systems based on Interoperation across Pre-existing Ontologies. Distributed and Parallel Databases Journal **8(2)** 2000 223–271
16. H.H. Do, E. Rahm: COMA - A System for Flexible Combination of Schema Matching Approaches. VLDB 2002 610–621
17. J. Madhavan et.al: Generic Schema Matching with Cupid. VLDB 2001 49–58
18. WordNet. A Lexical Database for the English Language. http://www.cogsci.princeton.edu/~wn/

The Construction of Domain Ontology and Its Application to Document Retrieval

Soo-Yeon Lim, Mu-Hee Song, and Sang-Jo Lee

Department of Computer Engineering, Kyungpook National University,
Daegu, 702-701, Korea
nadalsy@hotmail.com, {mhsong,sjlee}@knu.ac.kr

Abstract. Ontology means terms used in a specific domain, the definition of relationships among the terms, and the expression of the relationships in a hierarchical structure. This study suggests a method of constructing domain ontology using terminology processing and applies the method to document retrieval. In order to construct ontology, it proposes an algorithm that classifies the patterns of nouns and suffices which compose terminology, in domain texts, extracts terminology, and build a hierarchical structure. The experiment used documents related to pharmacy, and the algorithm showed accuracy of 92.57% for singleton terms and 66.64% for multi-word terms on the average. Constructed ontology, which forms natural groups of senses centering on specific nouns or suffices composing the terminology with semantic information, can be utilized in approaching the knowledge of special areas such as document retrieval. According to the result of document retrieval based on the constructed ontology, the system improved accuracy by 14.28% compared to keyword-based document retrieval.

1 Introduction

With the emergence of the semantic Web, there have been active researches on ontology as the core of knowledge dealt with in the area of artificial intelligence. Ontology is composed of a set of relevant concepts representing the characteristics of a given application domain, their definitions, and relationships among the concepts. When retrieving documents or Web pages, the use of ontology improves speed and accuracy in retrieving important information.

The success of the semantic Web depends on the scalability of ontology. Ontology learning is important to reduce time and cost in constructing and updating ontology. Another critical thing is text mining technology that extracts concepts of the concerned domain and semantic relationship among the concepts [8]. Ontology learning constructs ontology semi-automatically using unstructured, semi-structured or fully structured data. Even if an automatized method is used, however, the core part of ontology, which is conceptual system, is made manually in order to construct high quality semantic knowledge base. As (semi-)automatic methods of constructing ontology, there are largely those using existing resources such as thesauruses and dictionaries [4] and those constructing base ontology and expanding it using the

T. Yakhno (Ed.): ADVIS 2004, LNCS 3261, pp. 117–127, 2004.
© Springer-Verlag Berlin Heidelberg 2004

distribution of words obtained from analyzing texts without using existing resources [5]. While the former can build knowledge base that can be utilized immediately without additional dictionary process as they use dictionaries containing a large volume of concepts, while the latter can expand concepts easily. Both methods are quite important for extracting high quality patterns of semantic relationships. In order to extract a larger number of patterns of semantic relationships, it is necessary to process terminology obtained from analyzing the form of terms appearing in texts within a corpus.

The present study classifies the patterns of terminology appearing in Korean documents in the form of compound nouns analyze their structures. In addition, it proposes an algorithm that extracts sense groups and hierarchical structure from the results of the analysis and defines semantic relationships in ontology. Terms are classified according to suffix, which is attached for forming compound nouns, or the form of noun, are naturally clustered within the corresponding domain and form sense groups. If groups of attached nouns or suffices for a concerned domain are utilized effectively and sense groups are identified properly, it is possible to approach special knowledge. This study chose the field of pharmacy and carried out experiment using drug descriptions.

2   Methods of Constructing Domain Ontology

Ontology means information used in a specific domain and relationships defined in relation to the information. Concepts and their relational structure are defined through conference with specialists in the corresponding domain, and based on them is constructed ontology.

This study purposes to suggest a method of constructing ontology semi-automatically by delimiting documents for learning to those in the domain of pharmacy and using them in training. Figure 1 in next page shows four steps of ontology construction process proposed. The first step is to structurize web documents in the relevant domain and to form a corpus. The second step is to extract concepts after simple natural language processing. The third step is to extract terminology and analyze its structure to obtain a hierarchical structure and to add extracted relationships to ontology. Each step is explained in detail later.

2.1   The Structure and Expression of Ontology

In order to set the structure of ontology to be constructed, the author chose BITDruginfo (http://www.druginfo.co. kr) as a reliable pharmacy-related database on the Web. The results of analyzing data in documents of the database were used in defining concepts and their relationships in drug ontology to be constructed. Figure 2 is a conceptual graph of ontology structure composed of defined concepts and their relationships. Concepts including drug name are obtained from analyzing the database, and drug name is sub-divided into manufacturing company, insurance code, element code, efficacy code, etc. To return drug names in response to a query with a disease name or a symptom, the system mostly relies on information <Effect> among concepts related to drug name. Thus, this study will focus analyze and process on information in <Effect> tag.

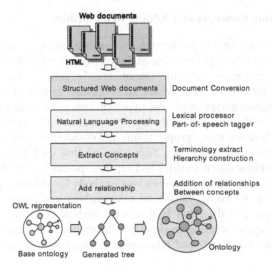

Fig. 1. Ontology construction process

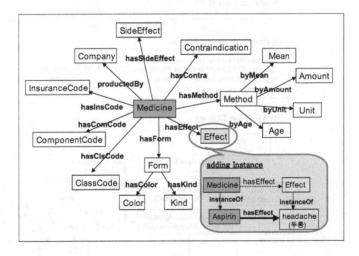

Fig. 2. Base ontology structure composed of defined concepts and relationship

In order to create a corpus for learning using semi-structured drug-related documents collected, this experiment converts the documents into the structure as Figure 2 and performs text analysis using a natural language processing technology. In case the analyzed documents include syntactic patterns containing specific contents, texts are classified and tagged by the patterns. In case of drug descriptions, documents are composed of texts tagged by pattern, and tags indicate the concept of the corresponding drugs. Concepts in ontology to be constructed and their relationships are expressed using OWL [7].

2.2   Extracting Concepts and Adding Relationships

Tagged texts in documents go through text analysis using a simple natural language parser. In the process, stop words are excluded from the texts first, and after stemming all nouns are extracted from the documents. In general, horizontal relationships between relevant objects and agents are obtained from text analysis but vertical relationships between hypernyms and hyponyms are not easy to extract from a corpus.

According to the result of analyzing nouns extracted from <Effect> texts in drug descriptions, there are many proper nouns and compound nouns representing disease names, symptoms, elements, etc. This suggests that each domain has item names indicating its unique characteristics and separate processing methods are required for the terminology. This study proposes two methods for defining relationships among concepts. One is to extract horizontal relationships using tags and verbs extracted from documents, and the other is to extract vertical relationships among concepts using terminology processing as described in section 2.3. Figure 3 shows a part of ontology to which concepts and relationships extracted from sample texts have been added.

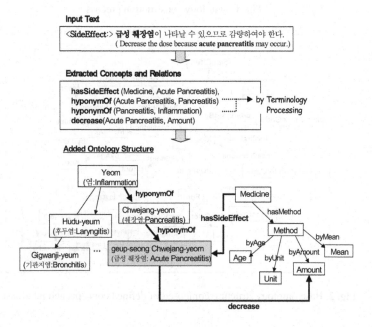

Fig. 3. Ontology (part) to which extracted concepts and relationships are added

As a result of parsing the sentence given in the figure above, concept 'acute pancreatitis and relationships 'hasSideEffect' and 'decrease' are extracted for the corresponding medicine. In particular, concept 'acute pancreatitis' is a term that does not exist in the base ontology. It goes through terminology processing and extracts hypernyms 'pancreatitis' and 'inflammation.' If he extracted hypernyms exist in the corresponding ontology, what should be done is to link using relation 'hyponymOf', but if not the hypernyms are added and link to them using the corresponding relationship. In this way, ontology is expanded. Furthermore, relationship 'hasSideEffect' is extracted from attached tag <SideEffect>, and relationship 'decrease' is extracted from extracted verb 'decrease'. Extracted relationships represent semantic relations connecting nouns appearing around. For this, verbs appearing frequently in the concerned domain are classified, semantic relations are defined based on the classification as shown in Table 1, and relation extraction rules are created.

Table 1. Sematic relations defined

Semantic Relations based on Extracting verbs	
relations	Corresponding Verbs
appear	일어나다(occur), 나타나다(appear), 발현하다(express)
beWorse	증상이 악화되다(The symptom gets worse)
inject	주사하다(inject), 근육주사하다(give an intramuscular injection)
reduce	감량하다 (decrease), 감소하다 (reduce)
rise	상승하다(rise), 증가하다 (increase)

2.3   Extracting Terminology

According to the result of analyzing texts with tag <Efficacy/Effect> in test documents, extracted terms are composed of terminology related to disease names or symptoms. It may be because the documents are from the pharmacy domain containing special knowledge. Terminology means a set of words that have meanings in a given domain. Because of their low ambiguity and high specificity, these words are useful in conceptualizing knowledge domains or creating domain ontology and facilitate the construction of ontology with rich lexical information.

This study analyzed the pattern of occurrence of terms for automatic extraction of terminology. Most terms appearing in the domain of interest occur in the form of compound noun, and are largely classified into two groups according to the form of combination. One is singleton terms and the other is multi-word terms, which contain space(s) within them and are composed of two ore more words that are semantically related with one another.

2.3.1   Singleton Terms
Many of compound nouns forming terminology in the drug domain are derived from Chinese words, and they are divided into two forms. One is the combination of nouns, and the other is the combination of a noun and a suffix. This study classified nouns and suffices, which are combined to form compound nouns, into 20 groups. They are, yeom(염)[1], jeung(증), tong(통), gyun(균), seong(성), jilhwan(질환), sok(속), yeomjeung(염증), jin(진), gam(감), jong(종), byeong(병), yeol(열), gweyang(궤양), seon(선), baekseon(백선), jeunghugun(증후군), hyeong(형), hwan(환) and gun(균). These words link semantically relevant terms. Table 2 shows a part of terminology, in which nouns are combined with suffices. In the drug domain, terms occurring in the

---

[1] 'yeom' is Korean phonetic spelling of '염'.

form of singleton are mostly hyponyms of specific nouns like 'banggwangyeom (방광염)' and 'gigwanjiyeom(기관지염)' ('yeom' indicates inflammation). Therefore, they are linked with relationship 'hyponymOf' as shown in Figure 4.

Table 2. Singleton terminology (part)

Combined Pattern		Compound Nouns
+ Noun	**-yeom**(염:inflammation)	banggwangyeom(방광염),geupseong gigwanjiyeom(급성기관지염), manseong gigwanjiyeom (만성기관지염), pyeondoyeom (편도염), jungiyeom (중이염)
	-tong(통:ache)	dutong (두통), yotong (요통), geunyuktong (근육통), gwanjeoltong (관절통), singyeongtong (신경통)
	-gyun(균:bacteria)	inpeulluenjagyun (인플루엔자균), pyeryeomgugyun (폐렴구균), podogugyun (포도구균)
	-jin(진:eczema)	seupjin(습진), dammajin(담마진), dansunpojin(단순포진)
+ Suffix	**-jeung**(증:symptom)	paehyeoljeung(패혈증), gigwanjihwakjangjeung(기관지확장증), hyeopsimjeung(협심증)
	-seong(성:nature)	ganhyeolseong(간혈성), hwakjangseong(확장성), geupseong(급성), noeseong(뇌성)
	-gam(감:feeling)	bulkwaegam(불쾌감), paengmangam(팽만감), dokgam(독감)

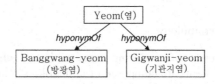

Fig. 4. Relationships in singleton terminology

Figure 5 shows an algorithm for the automatic extraction of hyponym relationships from singleton terminology as explained so far. Extracted terminology forms sense groups according to the type of nouns or suffices combined. However, there may be problems when the proposed terminology cognition method is applied to general domains. For example, 'cheoniljeyeom(천일제염:solar evaporation process)' and 'huduyeom(후두염: laryngitis)' belong to the same group. Because the two words are nothing to do with each other, they should not be linked to the same group. Therefore, it is necessary to apply restrictions in assigning relationships. For example, terms related to the human body such as "gigwanji(기관지: bronchus)' and 'hudu(후두: larynx) are in a hyponym relationship with noun 'yeom' as disease names. In this way, relationships in the constructed ontology may have rich lexical relationships.

2.3.2   Multi-word Terms
Most terms occurring in the test texts were in the form of multiple words containing a modifier and a modified like 'manseong wiyeom(만성 위염).' In many cases, multi-word terms in the test domain are composed of singleton terms. This experiment uses the relationships between the singleton terms in processing multi-word terminology, and defines and adds semantic relations in ontology. For example, in case of two-word terminology (N1 + N2), modified N2 is in a specific relationship with modifier N1 depending on the type of combination with the suffix or the particle of N1. Figure 6 shows identified patterns and plans to define relationships based on the patterns.

```
Input   : Singleton terminology with a suffix (word[1..n])
Output : Hierarchical tree of terminology

String Suffix[]={염,증,통,균,성,질환,속,염증,진,감,종,병,열,궤양,
                  선,백선,증후군,형,환,균}
boolean matrix[][];      // Hierarchical relationship matrix
// investigate if word is included in other word in all words
MakeSubTree {
    for (int i; i<n; i++)
        for (int j; j<n; j++)
            if (i!=j && (word[j].endsWith(word[i]))
                matrix[i][j]=true;
            if (word[i].length()==1) // exclude one syllable words
                matrix[i][j]=false;
}
// add sub-trees to ontology nodes
AppendSubWords {
    for (int i; i<n; i++)
        if (processed[i]=false)  // investigate if a word is a substring of another word
            boolean isSuper = true;  // add hyponyms only to the supernym
            for (int j; j<n; j++)
                if (matrix[j][i]=1)
                    isSuper=false;
                    // find the rightmost hyponym of the ith word
                    // add under I node
                    if (isSuper=true && appendSubWords(i)=null)
                        root.appendChild;
                    processed[i]=true;
}
```

Fig. 5. Algorithm to abstract hierarchical relationship from singleton terminology

Pattern	Pattern type	Example
	Plan to define relationship	
Pattern 1	N1 + { ~seong(성) , ~hyeong(형) } + N2	Geupseong gigwanjiyeom(급성 기관지염), manseong piro(만성 피로)
	Regard N1N2 as terminology expanded from N2 and Add it as a sub-concept of N2	
Pattern 2	N1 + { ~e euihan(~에 의한), ~(eui)ro inhan (~(으)로 인한), ~(eui)ro inhae yubaldoin (~(으)로 인해 유발된) } + N2 N1 + ~e ddareun (~에 따른) + N2 N1 + { ~si(eui) (~시(의)), ~sangtaeeseo (~상태에서), ~hu(eui)(~후(의)) } +N2	Nongnue uihan chulhyeol(농루에 의한 출혈), susulsi guksomachwi (수술시 국소마취)
	N2 is connected to N1 by relationship **causeTo** N2 is connected to N1 by relationship **accompanyWith** N2 is connected to N1 by relationship **stateOf**	
Pattern 3	N1+ "eui (의)" + N2, N1 + N2	Geuniwanui yuji -> geuniwanyuji (근이완의 유지 -> 근이완유지)
	Extract N1N2 as terminology	
Pattern 4	N1+ "mit (및)" + N2, N1+","+N2, N1+"ddoneun(또는)"+N2	Sohwahyosogyeolpip mit damjeupbunbichokjin -> sohwahyosogyeolpip, damjeupbunbichokjin (소화효소결핍 및 담즙분비촉진 -> 소화효소결핍, 담즙분비촉진)
	Extract N1 and N2 separately as terminology	
Pattern 5	N1(suffix_1)+ ",mit(및)"+N2(suffix_2)+N3 (if suffix_1=suffix_2)	Jiyeonhyeong·hwaldongseong manseongganyeom -> Jiyeonhyeong manseongganyeom, hwaldongseong manseongganyeom (지연형·활동성 만성간염 -> 지연형 만성간염, 활동성 만성간염)
	Extract N1N3 and N2N3 as terminology	

Fig. 6. Patterns of multi-word terminology and plan to define relationships

3   Application to Document Retrieval

The constructed ontology can be utilized in various areas. This study applies it as a means to improve the accuracy of document retrieval in order to process users' queries effectively. When ontology is used in document retrieval, the user enters key words. Then the system investigates concepts related to the input key words throughout ontology. Retrieval may be retried after the keywords are modified or new ones are added. Using ontology, the user can confirm if input keywords reflect the target concept or not and improve the efficiency of retrieval by modifying or adding keywords. Furthermore, the user may be able to use new words, which he has not thought out but are related to the target of retrieval.

This study used relative-frequency($Rf_{i,j}$) and sub-frequency($Sf_{i,j}$) in order to give a weight to keywords and set the priority of documents, and defined as follows.

Let n be the total number or document d_j, $freq_{i,j}$ be the frequency of term k_i in the document d_j , and m be the number of hyponym words of term k_i in ontology. And $w_{i,j}$ is a weight associated to the term-document pair[k_i, d_j].

$$w_{i,j} = Rf_{i,j} \times Hf_{i,j}$$

$$Rf_{i,j} = \frac{freq_{i,j}}{\sum_{i=1}^{n} freq_{i,j}} \quad , \quad Hf_{i,j} = \frac{\sum_{h=1}^{m} freq_{h,j}}{freq_{i,j}}$$

4   Experiment and Evaluation

The terminology processing method proposed for constructing drug domain ontology was applied to 21,113 documents, and extracted a total of 78,902 nouns. Among them, 55.870 nouns (70.8%) were included into the ontology. Table 3 shows the distribution of singleton terms according to the pattern of combination and accuracy for the terms.

As a result of applying the proposed algorithm, 2,864 sub-concepts were added. Evaluation of extracted terminology was made manually by two specialists. According to the result of evaluation, accuracy is measured by the percentage of terminology connected with correct relationships among the whole extracted terminology as below.

Table 4 shows the distribution of the pattern of multi-word terms and accuracy. The number of patterns in the table means the number of concepts added.

$$Accuracy = \frac{The\ number\ of\ terms\ connected\ with\ correct\ relationships}{The\ number\ of\ terms\ extracted}$$

In order to verify the efficiency of constructed ontology in document retrieval, this study compared the accuracy of keyword-based retrieval with that of ontology-based one. Figure 7 shows the result of the comparison. For 1500 documents, this experiment set the most accurate 300(30 per a query) correct documents in reply to 10 queries by the help of eight specialists. When evaluated based on the documents, the average accuracy of the keyword-based retrieval was 43.47% while that of

Table 3. Distribution of singleton terminology and accuracy

Noun/Suffix	frequency of occurrence	percentage	the number of subconcepts	accuracy
yeom(염)	5,827	23.41%	506	98.50%
jeung(증)(excluding yeomjeung)	4,306	17.30%	721	97.50%
tong(통)	3,220	12.93%	140	98.57%
gyun(균)	2,238	8.99%	217	98.15%
seong(성)	2,156	8.66%	267	94.00%
jilhwan(질환)	989	3.97%	175	93.14%
sok(속)	976	3.92%	115	92.17%
yeomjeung(염증)	748	3.00%	60	99.99%
jin(진)	705	2.83%	96	71.87%
gam(감)	648	2.60%	77	96.10%
jong(종)	596	2.39%	123	97.56%
byeong(병)	574	2.31%	107	93.46%
yeol(열)	562	2.26%	46	93.47%
gweyang(궤양)	454	1.82%	38	99.99%
seon(선) (excluding baekseon)	341	1.37%	50	78.00%
baekseon(백선)	191	0.77%	22	99.99%
jeunghugun(증후군)	163	0.65%	40	99.99%
hyeong(형)	114	0.46%	34	79.41%
hwan(환) (excluding jilhwan)	47	0.19%	18	77.78%
gun(군) (excluding jeunghugun)	41	0.16%	12	91.67%
Total	24,896	100.00%	2,864	
average accuracy				92.57%

Table 4. Distribution of multi-word terminology and accuracy

Pattern Type	Pattern Number	Frequency of Occurrence	Percentage	Accuracy
pattern 1	1,853	3,888	12.55%	90.69%
pattern 2	975	1,327	4.28%	83.91%
pattern 3	2,456	4,258	13.75%	81.79%
pattern 4	1,361	2,379	7.68%	66.76%
pattern 5	287	1,110	3.58%	76.67%
etc	–	18,012	58.15%	–
Total		30,974	100.00%	
Average Accuracy				66.64%

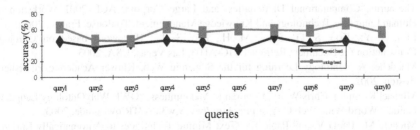

queries

Fig. 7. Comparison of accuracy between keyword-based retrieval and ontology-based one

ontology-based one was 57.75%. Accordingly, accuracy was improved in document retrieval that assigned weights considering hyponym relationships among terms occurring within the corresponding domain.

5   Conclusions

This study proposed a method of constructing ontology semi-automatically by collecting documents related to a specific domain, creating a corpus and analyzing texts in the corpus. For experiment, it used medicine-related documents collected from the Web and suggested plans for terminology processing using specific nouns or suffices in order to extract concepts and relationships necessary for constructing ontology. The constructed ontology was domain-dependent, and sense groups were clustered in it according to the form of suffices. As singleton terms combined with specific nouns or suffices were identified, 2,864 sub-concepts were added and accuracy of 92.57% was achieved on the average. In case of multi-word terms, the average accuracy was 66.64%. When the constructed ontology was applied to document retrieval, accuracy was improved by 14.28% compared to keyword-based retrieval.

As stated above, ontology constructed by analyzing texts in a specific domain adds concepts and relationships automatically. As a result, it maintains richer information, can answer various queries, and enhance the accuracy of retrieval. This suggests that concepts and rules defined in ontology may be used as the base of inference to improve the performance of retrieval. Subsequent research will be focused on how to apply the proposed method of ontology construction to general domains.

References

1. Baeza-Yates, R. and Robeiro-Neto, B.: Modern Information Retrieval. ACM Press, New York, NY, USA, 1999.
2. Bettina, B., Andreas, H., Gerd, S. : Towards Semantic Web Mining. International Semantic Web Conference, 2002.
3. Guarino, N.: Formal Ontology and Information Systems. In Proceeding of the 1st International Conference, Trento, Italy, IOS Press, 1998.
4. Kang, S. J. and Lee, J. H.: Semi-Automatic Practical Ontology Construction by Using a Thesaurus, Computational Dictionaries, and Large Corpora. ACL 2001 Workshop on Human Language Technology and Knowledge Management, Toulouse, France, 2001.
5. Lim, S. Y., Koo, S. O., Song, M. H., Lee, S, J., "Hub_word based on Ontology Construction for Document Retrieval", IC-AI'03, Las Vegas, USA, 2003.
6. Maedche, A.: Ontology Learning for the Semantic Web. Kluwer Academic Publishers, Boston, 2002.
7. Michael K. Smith, Chris Welty, Deborah L. McGuinness, "OWL Web Ontology Language Guide", World Wide Web Consortium, http://www.w3.org/TR/owl-guide, 2003.
8. Michele M., Paola V. and Paolo F., "Text Mining Techniques to Automatically Enrich a Domain Ontology", Applied Intelligence 18, 322-340, 2003.

9. Jong-Hoon Oh, Kyung-Soon Lee and Key-sun Choi, "Automatic Term Recognition using Domain Similarity and statistical Methods", Korean Journal of Cognitive Science, Vol. 29, No. 4, pp. 258-269, 2002.
10. Hyun-Min Lee, Hyuk-Ro Park, "A Reverse Segmentation Algorithm of Compound Nouns", Korea Information Processing Society Journal(B), vol. 8-B, No 4, pp.357-364, 2003.

WetDL: A Web Information Extraction Language

Benjamin Habegger[1] and Mohamed Quafafou[2]

[1] Laboratoire d'Informatique de Nantes Atlantique, Nantes, France
[2] Institut des Applications Avances de l'Internet, Marseille, France

Abstract. Many online information sources are available on the Web. Giving machine access to such sources leads to many interesting applications, such as using web data in mediators or software agents. Up to now most work in the field of information extraction from the web has concentrated on building wrappers, i.e. programs allowing to reformat presentational data in HTML into a more machine comprehensible format. While being an important part of a web information extraction application such wrappers are not sufficient to fully access a source. Indeed, it is necessary to setup an infrastructure allowing to build queries, fetch pages, extract specific links, etc. In this paper we propose a language called WetDL allowing to describe an information extraction task as a network of operators whose execution performs the desired extraction task.

1 Introduction

With the development of the web, many online sources are now available. However these sources were destinated to be viewed by human users using a web browser. Giving machine access to such information sources can yield many applications such as the integration of the extracted data into a mediator, building intelligent agents making use of such information, etc. One of the major problems of giving such a machine access is extracting the informational content from web pages, mainly in the HTML format, and restructuring this content into a machine readable and understandable format. A program translating the HTML data from a given source into a machine readable format is called a wrapper. Much research has been interested in the automatic or semi-automatic construction of wrappers [1, 2, 3, 4, 5]. However, we argue that having a wrapper is not sufficient to build web information extraction applications allowing to fully automatically access a source. Indeed, this often requires filling in forms, following specific links, etc. Writing a program allowing to access a source requires deep technical knowledge such as the HTTP protocol. This makes writing such applications a tedious task.

The contributions of this paper are threefold. Firstly, we propose to model web information extraction tasks as a network of operators. We define of a set of generic web information extraction operators (such as query building, fetching,

T. Yakhno (Ed.): ADVIS 2004, LNCS 3261, pp. 128–138, 2004.

extracting, etc.) into which an information extraction task can be decomposed. Secondly we propose, a language called WetDL (Web Extraction Task Description Language), allowing to describe a specific web information extraction task by instantiating the generic operators. Thirdly, we propose an algorithm allowing to directly execute the task described in WetDL. In this framework, the description of an extraction task is reduced to the minimum allowing the user to concentrate only on specific parts of a web information extraction task such as describing which links to extract from a given page.

The ideas we develop in this paper have been implemented in a system call WebSource. Multiple information extraction tasks, such as extracting information from the CIA World Fact Book, extracting conference listings from DBLP, etc. have been described using WetDL and correctly executed using Web-Source. However, due to space limitations, we only present the WetDL language in this paper. More detailed examples cans be found in [6]. The implementation of our framework allows to take advantage of existing XML technology such as XPath[1],XSLT[2]and DOM[3].For example, in our implementation the extraction operators use an XPath expression to specify the set of elements to extract. We also make use of XSLT to specify format transformations.

This paper is organized as follows. Section 2 presents a set of generic internet operators into which an information extraction task can be decomposed. Next, section 3 shows how to describe an instance set of these operators and their coordination for a given task in the language we propose. Then, in section 4 we propose different algorithms allowing the execution of a web extraction task network. Section 5 presents related work. Finally we conclude in section 6.

2   Decomposing a Web Extraction Task

A typical information extraction task involves querying a source, retrieving the result pages and extracting the results from them by applying a program transforming the result pages into a machine readable format. For example, figure 1 describes how the address directory superpages.com is accessed manually.

In a first step the user fills in a query form with the name of the person he/she wants the address of (1). When the form is submitted a first page of results is given. The user then writes down the addresses he is interested in (2) and continues on to the next page by following the next link (3). On the next page the same extraction and link following procedure is started over again until the user hits the last page which contains no next link. It should be noted that, in general, the user never follows all the links to the last page, and therefore may miss answers which may be of interest to him. This gives another motivation

---

[1] XML Path Language (http://www.w3.org/TR/xpath)
[2] XML Stylesheet Language Tranformations (http://www.w3.org/TR/xslt)
[3] Document Object Model (http://www.w3.org/DOM/)

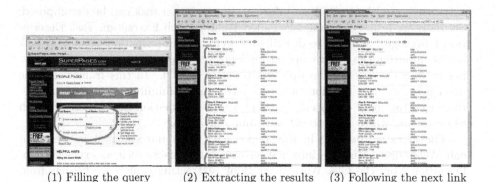

(1) Filling the query   (2) Extracting the results   (3) Following the next link

Fig. 1. Manually accessing superpages.com

to creating web information extraction tasks, since they will allow the user to integrate all the data from all the pages into an application helping him refine the search to more thoroughly answer his informational needs.

Accessing a web source requires to mimic the described steps. For each action, such as filling the form, we can define a corresponding operator. We have determined a basic set of operators, which by their coordination allows to describe web information extraction tasks. All the operators take as input some type of object (a query, an HTTP Request, a URL, a Document, etc.) and return zero, one or more results. For genericity, we define a global domain noted O and require all operators to return a list of objects of O. In the case of information extraction from the Web O can be decomposed into four sets : the set of user queries Q, the set of HTTP requests H which includes URLs, the set of XML documents[4] D, the set of parts of any XML document P (i.e. these correspond to DOM Nodes in our implementation) and the set of results (expressions of a user defined format) R. Therefore any operator σ can be defined as a function $\sigma : O \rightarrow O*$, where $O*$ denotes the set of all lists we can build from elements of O. However, these operators may only be valid for a subset of O. It should be noted that any XML document is also a document part (i.e. $D \subset P$).

Building Queries. A common operation when accessing a source is filling in a query form. A query building operator allow to mimic such an operation. This involves transforming the query in the applications logic into an HTTP request. This corresponds to the user filling in a form and the browser interpreting this form into an HTTP request. A query operator takes as its input a query and returns an HTTP request. This requires knowning the base URL of the source, the HTTP method to use (GET, POST, HEAD) and the set of parameters. We can define a generic query operator which takes three parameters : a URL, a

---

[4] HTML documents can easily be transformed into XHTML documents (many tools exist). This allows us to consider HTML documents as XML and use technologies such as XPath, XSL and DOM

method, and a mapping from the keys of application domain queries and the names of HTML form fields. Formally, such an operator can be defined as a function $\sigma_Q : Q \rightarrow H*$.

Fetching Documents. Once a an HTTP request has been built or a URL has been extracted it is necessary to fetch the document referred to. This can be done by a fetch operator. Such an operator takes an HTTP request (a URL can easily be transformed into an HTTP request) and returns a document. It can be defined as a function $\sigma_F : H \rightarrow D*$.

Extracting Data. One of the most important sub-tasks of a web extraction application is the extraction of relevant data and/or data useful for the extraction process itself. For example, in the case of extracting results form **superpages** two extraction actions were taken : the first to extract the results and the second to extract the next page link. When considering XML or parts of XML documents a useful way to specify interesting sub parts is to use a path expression language such as XPath. By considering that we have such a language to extract the parts of the document we are interested in, we can define a generic extraction operator which takes such an expression as a parameter. An extraction operator returns all the parts which match the expression. This can be defined as a function $\sigma_E : P \rightarrow P*$.

Transforming Data. The data extracted from Web pages may not be in the required format for further treatment, therefore transformations may be necessary. When considering XML data, such a transformation can be naturally described using a XSL stylesheet. Having such a language we can define a generic transformation operator which has a stylesheet as its parameter. Given input data, the operator applies the stylesheet to the data and returns the transformed results. This can also be defined as a function $\sigma_T : P \rightarrow R*$.

Filtering Data. In some cases it may be interesting to filter data which is not meaningful in further treatment or as final results. This can be especially true once the data has be reformatted and the semantics of the data clarified. For example, when extracting book results from Amazon, one might want to filter out books above a given price. This can be easily done by setting up a filter which only keeps books under the given price. Given a filter description language we can define a filter operator which takes as parameter a filter description and when applied to incoming data either returns the data or filters it out. A filter an operator can be defined as a function $\sigma_K : O \rightarrow O*$.

Coordinating the Operators. In our framework the operators are coordinated by defining a transition function over the operator set. Le Σ denote the set of operators and $\mathcal{P}(\Sigma)$ denote the set of partitions of Σ. The transition function is a function $\mu : \Sigma \rightarrow \mathcal{P}(\Sigma)$. The function μ tells us where a given operator $\sigma \in \Sigma$ should send the results it produces. Given this function it is possible to associate two sets to each operator σ_i the set of its producers $prod_\mu(\sigma_i) = \{\sigma_j \in \Sigma | \sigma_i \in \mu(\sigma_j)\}$ and the set of its consumers $cons_\mu(\sigma_i) = \{\sigma_j \in \Sigma | \sigma_j \in \mu(\sigma_i)\}$.

3   Describing a Web Extraction Task

We propose to build web information extraction tasks based on a descriptive approach. In this goal we propose and XML-based language called WetDL for Web Extraction Task Description Language. The WetDL language allows to describe instances of the generic operators described in section 2 and coordinate them building a network of operators. We will then see in section 4 how such a network can be executed to perform the desired web information extraction task.

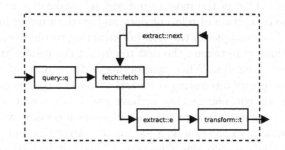

Fig. 2. WetDL network for superpages.com

In order to illustrate how to describe an information extraction task using WetDL, we will show how the superpages extraction task can be described. This task requires five operators as shown in figure 2. In this figure each rectangle corresponds to an operator. In each rectangle a string of the for Type::Name is given where Type corresponds to the type of operator and Name corresponds to a name given to the specific operator.

In WetDL, each operator is described by an XML element named according to its type. For example the query tag name declares a query building operator. Each type of operator (query, fetch, etc.) has its own set of parameters. These are described between the start and end operator tags with specific XML tags and attributes. The operator descriptions have some common properties which are describe by a common set of XML attributes in the operator tags.

name *and* forward-to *Attributes.* Each of the operator tags must have a name attribute with a unique value. This will allow to refer to the operator when describing the network. The operator tags may also have a forward-to attribute whose value must contain a blank separated list of operator names. The forward-to attributes allows to define the transition function between the operators and therefore the set of producers and consumers of each operator. For example, in the case of the superpages extraction task represented in figure 2 the operator fetch::f will be described by a fetch element which will have a name attribute with a value of "f" and a forward-to attribute with a value of "e next" (the space character being a reference list separator in XML).

query *Element.* To describe a query operator it is necessary to know where the resource to query is located by giving its URL, the HTTP method type to use and the mapping between the incoming data and the resource's parameters. In WetDL a query operator is described by a **query** element. The method is specified by defining a **method** attribute. The resource's URI is specified by a base element whose content is the URI. The mapping between the incoming data is described by a set of **param** elements under a **parameters** element. Each **param** element has three attributes : a **name** attribute which contains the name of the parameter as understood by the resource, an optional **default** value for the parameter, and a **value-of** attribute allowing to specify which part of the input data should be set as the value of the parameter.

Below is shown the form a query building operator takes as part of a WetDL description.

```
<wet:query name="_name_" forward-to="_consumers_" method="_method_">
  <base>_base_uri_</base>
  <parameters>
  <param name="_param_1_" default="_def_val_" value-of="_expr_" />
  ...
  </parameters>
</wet:query>
```

The address directory superpages can be accessed using the GET HTTP method bye sending a request to http://directory.superpages.com/wp/results.jsp. The form leading to this page allows to set different parameters such as WL for the last name, WF for the first name, T for the city, etc. In the example of figure 2, the operator q is a query operator. In the description the **method** attribute value will be set to GET and the text under the **base** element will be the URL http://directory.superpages.com/wp/results.jsp. In our description of the task the query is expressed as a set of key-value pairs with keys the in the set {"*lastname*","*firstname*","*city*","*state*"}. The q operator will have to translate a query given in this language in the set of key-value pairs understood by superpages. For example, the "*lastname*" parameter will be used to fill the WL parameter of superpages. This will be expressed by a **param** element under the **parameters** element.

fetch *Element.* A fetch operator is not as generic as the other operators. However having multiple instances of a fetch operator may be required to describe a task. Indeed what is to be done after the fetch operation may depend on the type of document (a result page, an index page, etc) it receives as input. In such cases it is necessary to have multiple instances of the same operation. A fetch operator is described as follows.

```
<wet:fetch name="_name_" forward-to="_consumers_" />
```

The f operator in figure 2 corresponds to such an operator.

extract *Element* An extraction operator applies to its input an expression allowing to extract specific parts of it. Therefore defining an extraction operator consists in specifying the expression. In WetDL an extraction operator is specified by a **extract** element. The expression (in our implementation we use XPath) is the content of a **path** element. The format of an extract operator is given below.

```
<wet:extract name="_name_" forward-to="_consumers_">
 <path>_xpath_</path>
</wet:query>
```

For **superpages**, the operators e and **next** are extraction operators. The first should allow to extract one result item from a page of results. The XPath expression `//table[3]//table[3]//tr/td[2 and font/b]` matches a set of nodes each fully containing one result. By setting this expression as the text under the **path** element of the operator declaration allows to specify an operator which will proceed to the extraction of the nodes containing the results. The **next** operator is needed to extract the URL of the next page of results. For **superpages** the XPath expression `//a[contains(.,"Next Page")/@href` can be used to extract the URL of the next page.

transform *Element.* A transformation operator allows to transform data from one format (an HTML document Node) to another (a structured result). When considering XML (HTML cans be considered as XML data by converting it to XHTML) data this can be done by using an XSL stylesheet. Therefore in WetDL the only parameter of a transformation operator is a stylesheet. The transformation operator is described by a **transform** element. The elements contained under this element is a XSLT stylesheet. Below, the format of an transformation operator is given.

```
<wet:transform name="_name_" forward-to="_consumers_">
 _xsl_stylesheet_
</wet:transform>
```

For example, a result extracted by the e operator of the **superpages** extraction task returns a node containing one result. However, this result is still described in HTML. To put it into a more structured format, for example as a tuple of the relation $address(name, street, city, state, zip)$ a transformation is necessary. This can be done by applying an XSLT stylesheet onto the input HTML node. This is what is done by the t operator of the **superpages** description.

filter *Element.* There are many ways to describe a filter. We chose to define such an operator as a sequence of tests. A test is composed of three parts : a selection expression which allows to choose which part of the input is to be used in the test, a matching expression which is a regular expression the selected data should match for the test to succeed and finally an action which can either be keep or reject determining what happens if the test succeeds. Each of the tests are applied in sequence until the input data matches one of them. Then the data is either kept and forwarded to the consumers of the current operator or kept back depending on the action associated to the test. If no test matches the data is also kept back. The filter operation is described by a `filter` element. Each of the tests are represented by a `test` element having three possible attributes `select`, `match` and `action` which respectively allow to specify the selection expression, the matching expression and the test's action. The format of a filter declaration is given below.

```
<wet:filter name="_name_" forward-to="_consumers_">
  <test select="_xpath_" match="_reg_exp_" action="_action_"/>
  ...
</wet:filter>
```

4   Executing an Information Extraction Task

Once we have described our extraction task in WetDL we should be able to execute it. In this section we show this can be done. Let $\sigma_1, \ldots, \sigma_n$ be a set of operators obtained by interpreting a WetDL description. Let μ be the transition function described by the `forward-to` attributes of the description. Executing such a network consists in associating to each operator a queue of results. When an operator receives data, it applies it's operation to the data generating a set of results which are added to the operators queue. Let $s_1, \ldots, s_n$ be the set of queues associated to each operator. For example, if we take an extraction operator, by feeding it result documents it will build on its queue a set of extracted items. At sometime these results will be forwarded to the consumers of the operator. When this is to be done depends on the strategy applied.

The strategy we use is to produce results on demand. In this case operators can be asked to produce a result. Given an operator σ_i and its queue s_i, s_i can either contain results or can be empty. Asking σ_i to produce a result when s_i is not empty consists in taking the head result out of s_i and sending it to σ_i's consumers and returning it. If no results are available on s_i then the producers of σ_i are asked to produce. Two cases can occur : either (1) at least a producer σ_j of σ_i has produced a result or (2) no producers have produced any results. In the latter case, the network will not be able to produce without more incoming data and therefore the produce call on σ_i returns no results. In the first, case the result of σ_j will have been sent to and handled by σ_i, generating a list of results. This list will be appended to s_i. We then find ourselves in the original situation where there may be results on the queue and we can return one, or none are available (the incoming results did not lead to new production). In this

---

Input :   — An operator index i
            — A list of indexes l

Output :   — A list of zero or one results R

Procedure produce_one

  $done \leftarrow i \in l$
  while $s_n = [] \land \neg done$ **do**
    $L \leftarrow []$; $done \leftarrow 1$
    for all σ_j where $\sigma_i \in \mu(\sigma_j)$ **do**
      $T \leftarrow produce\_one(j, concat([i], l))$
      if $T \neq []$ **then**
        $s_n \leftarrow concat(s_n, \sigma_i(head(T)))$
        $don \leftarrow 0$
      end if
    end for
  end while
  if $s_n = []$ **then**
    return $[]$
  else
    return $[head(s_n)]$
  end if

Algorithm 1: Executing an information extraction task

case, we need to ask the producers again for more results to handle. Algorithm 1 describes this lazy strategy.

5   Related Work

One of the main problems in extracting information from the Web is to put the Web data into a machine understandable format whether it is for storing the data into a structured database or for further treatment. A program which allows to translate Web data into a structured format is called a wrapper. Different approaches to wrapper construction have been proposed such as labeled-page based learning [1, 4, 5], structure discovery [2, 3], and knowledge-based wrappers [7]. We proposed [8] an approach based on example instances rather than labeled pages allowing go give fewer total example instances.

Another problem in extracting information form the Web is to be able to query the web-based applications by simulating form filling. Some work has been done in using machine learning to build programs allowing to transform an initial query into the form-based languages of web-based sources (see for example [9]). Some other work has tackled the problem of automatically filling Web forms in order to crawl the hidden web (i.e. the set of pages generated in response to a query)[10]. In the case of crawling, the objective is not to build an automatic access to a web source, but rather to find a set of pages relevant to a topic. Finding relevant pages, however is not sufficient to respond to an extraction need such as finding instances a relation such as *address*(*name, street, cirty, state, zip*).

Other recent work has proposed a unified framework for integrating information from the web [11]. This framework uses F-logic, a rule-based language combining object-orientation and first order logic, to build wrappers, integrate data, etc. The same language is used to represent application level data and source level data. However, mixing levels of abstraction, while powerful can get confusing. Furthermore, querying web sources has not been integrated in the web model they use. Also, the description of the application data being highly linked to the source-level data this framework is mainly useful for mediation : it is not clear how to extract once and for all data using this framework.

6   Conclusion

In this paper we have proposed WetDL a language allowing to describe web information extraction tasks. The model on which it is based, consists in a network of operators. Each operator is obtained by specifying the parameters of a generic operator such as an extraction operator, a fetch operators, etc. This allows the creator of the extraction task to concentrate on the specific parts of the task he/she is building. Furthermore, our framework makes use of existing XML technologies such as DOM, XPath and XSLT to describe extraction and transformation operators. We also give an algorithm allowing to execute any task described using WetDL. Also, this framework has been implemented and tested in a system called WebSource.

References

1. Kushmerick, N.: Wrapper induction: Efficiency and expressiveness. Artificial Intelligence (2000)
2. Chang, C.H., Hsu, C.N., Lui, S.C.: Automatic Information Extraction from Semi-Structured Web Pages by Pattern Discovery. Decision Support Systems Journal **35** (2003)
3. Crescenzi, V., Mecca, G., Merialdo, P.: RoadRunner: Towards Automatic Data Extraction from Large Web Sites. In: The VLDB Journal. (2001) 109–118
4. Hsu, C.N., Dung, M.T.: Generating Finite-State Transducers for Semi-Structured Data Extraction from the Web. Information Systems **23** (1998)
5. Muslea, I., Minton, S., Knoblock, C.A.: Hierarchical Wrapper Induction for Semistructured Information Sources. Autonomous Agents and Multi-Agent System **4** (2001)
6. Habegger, B., Quafafou, M.: Building web information extraction tasks. In: WI'2004. Proceedings of the ACM/IEEE Web Intelligence Conference, Beijing, China (2004) to appear.
7. Seo, H., Yang, J., Choi, J.: Knowledge-based Wrapper Generation by Using XML. In: IJCAI-2001 Workshop on Adaptive Text Extraction and Mining, Seattle, Washington (2001)
8. Habegger, B., Quafafou, M.: Multi-pattern wrappers for relation extraction. In van Harmelan, F., ed.: ECAI 2002. Proceedings of the 15th European Conference on Artificial Intelligence, Amsterdam, IOS Press (2002)

9. Kushmerick, N.: Learning to Invoke Web Forms. In Meersman, R., Tari, Z., Schmidt, D.C., eds.: CoopIS/DOA/ODBASE. Lecture Notes in Computer Science, Catania, Sicily, Italy, Springer Verlag (2003) 997–1013
10. Raghavan, S., Garcia-Molina, H.: Crawling the Hidden Web. In Apers, P.M.G., Atzeni, P., Ceri, S., Paraboschi, S., Ramamohanarao, K., Snodgrass, R.T., eds.: VLDB 2001, Proceedings of 27th International Conference on Very Large Data Bases, Roma, Italy, Morgan Kaufmann (2001) 129–138
11. May, W., Lausen, G.: A uniform framework for integration of information from the web. Information Systems **29** (2004)

Towards Building Knowledge Centres
on the World Wide Web

Zsolt T. Kardkovács[1], Gábor M. Surányi[2], and Sándor Gajdos[3]

[1] Budapest University of Technology and Economics,
Department of Telecommunications and Media Informatics,
Database Education Laboratory,
H-1117, Budapest, Magyar tudósok körútja 2., Hungary
kardkovacs@db.bme.hu
[2] FZI Research Center for Information Technologies,
Database Systems Research Group,
Haid-und-Neu-Strasse 10–14, D-76131 Karlsruhe, Germany
Gabor.Suranyi@fzi.de
[3] Hewlett-Packard Hungary,
H-1117, Budapest, Neumann János u. 1., Hungary,
sandor.gajdos@hp.com

Abstract. The amount of structured information published on the
World Wide Web is huge and steadily increases. The demand for uniform
management of these heterogeneous and autonomous sources is also increasing. In this paper we present a method which is capable of virtually
integrating data sources with logical rules into a catalogue and more importantly, discovering similar entities across the information sources. We
prove that the technique is algorithmically decidable. The resulting system
is primarily suitable for applications which require an integrated view of all
the distributed database components for querying only, such as web shops.

1 Introduction

The World Wide Web is no longer just a common platform for user-friendly
exchange of less structured information (simple documents) but rather the sole
interface of huge, distributed storages of *fully-structured* data. This phenomenon
is usually referred to as the Web is deep [1]. It is a natural demand that information spread among the information sources be made accessible and manageable
together. That is knowledge centres in which experience and results are accumulated should be set up.

The Semantic Web approach is an orthogonal effort as it aims at enriching
pure data (simple documents as well as portal pages) available on the Web so that
the information represented is processable by computers, too. In this context a
knowledge centre is an information store encompassing all pieces of information
contained in a certain collection of machine-processed web resources.

The goal of our research-work is to ease the integration of independent
databases, i.e. we use the term knowledge centre in the first sense. In this at-

T. Yakhno (Ed.): ADVIS 2004, LNCS 3261, pp. 139–149, 2004.
© Springer-Verlag Berlin Heidelberg 2004

tempt, however, we take into consideration that the main application area will be the presentation on the Web. It makes our approach feasible although it would not be reasonable to apply in a classical integration problem.

Previously, as published in [2] and [3], we described how so-called glossaries and generalised catalogues can be applied to reconcile differences among database schemata and set up a virtual union of *explicit data*. The union of data elements is actually well-organised and enables multi-purpose access to the items. For example, catalogues support similarity queries, i.e. elements which are the most similar to an arbitrary entity can be returned.

In general, knowledge includes not only explicit facts but *logical rules* as well. Rules enable reasoning over the facts and thus provide an efficient way to express additional information, i.e. not all pieces of the domain knowledge need to be explicitly specified. A good example is the use of derived attributes in data models. On the Semantic Web logical rules are widely employed, too (see e.g. [4]).

The type of logic and the language used by the logical rules varies strongly. The history of logic databases starts with several forms of Datalog[5]. F-logic[6] can be considered as the next bold step because it also incorporates the object-oriented features into a single solid, sound and complete framework. Nowadays, most of the attention is paid to Description Logics[7] since their expressiveness and complexity properties mean a reasonable trade-off.

In this paper we propose an extension of our catalogue organisation technique for logic databases with Datalog^{neg} formulae. However, the results can easily be adapted to F-Logic as well. This way our knowledge integration method can be applied to any of the widely-used database models including any relational or object-oriented database.[1]

The paper is organised as follows. In the next section, pre-order relations suitable for rules are introduced. They form the mathematical basis for the catalogues. In Section 3 decidability issues are addressed. Section 4 presents the catalogue structure and its key management routines. In Section 5, we demonstrate the capabilities of our extended integration method by a simple example. In the end conclusions are drawn and future work is outlined.

2   Pre-order Relations Over Predicates

Catalogues organise data elements which are in this case stored in the form of Datalog^{neg} formulae. Since we would like to discover similarities among these elements, we prefer the representation in which properties correspond to predicates

---

[1] Obviously, the database has to possess an equivalent logical form. Although any relational database based on Codd's model[8] can automatically be converted into an equivalent logic database, non-logic object-oriented databases have to be processed by hand for this purpose. In fact, only schemata are to be transformed manually in these cases, after that the transformation of data elements is straightforward and automatable.

and the owning data items are referenced in the first argument of the predicates. A further notation is that $\supset$ stands for logical implication throughout this paper.

Definition 1 (Substitutability of Ground Terms). *Let C and D be ground terms (i.e. they do not contain any variables) and denote logical identifiers of data elements. Moreover, m is a predicate symbol with arity $n\geq2$. C is substitutable by D concerning m, denoted by $C \preceq_m D$, if and only if*

$$\forall X_2 \ldots \forall X_n \; m(C, X_2, \ldots, X_n) \; \supset \; m(D, X_2, \ldots, X_n).$$

The definition expresses that properties of the substitutable entity always have to hold for the substituting entity also. Note that because of the properties of implication this substitutability relation is reflexive and transitive as required (see e.g. [2]). That means substitutability is a pre-order on ground terms.

Definition 2 (Ground Term Covering). *There is a natural extension of substitutability to a finite set M of predicate symbols with arity of at least 2. Let $M = \{m_1, \ldots, m_k\}$ where m_is are the predicate symbols. D covers C concerning M, denoted by $C \sqsubseteq_M D$, if and only if*

$$\forall m \; m \in M \supset C \preceq_m D.$$

3   Computability of the Covering Relation

Certainly, concepts are practically useless if they are theoretically uncomputable. That is why we must investigate whether ground term covering is algorithmically decidable or not. It is obvious that it is decidable if and only if so is substitutability of ground terms, because substitutability is a special case of ground term covering and ground term covering requires substitutability at a finite number of times.

In the case of substitutability of ground terms the problem can be seen as follows. Based on the previous definitions, in order to decide if $C \preceq_m D$ holds for arbitrary C and D ground terms and m predicate symbol, the question to answer is whether the formulae defining the predicate m logically imply the implication formulae of substitutability or not.

To logically imply means that the union of database formulae with head $m(\ldots)$ and the negation of the implication in the definition of substitutability has no model. This question is well-known in first-order predicate logic, it is called the decidability problem and is generally unsolvable [9].

However, here all participating formulae are universally quantified and there are no function symbols, only predicate symbols are used. This is actually the Bernays-Schönfinkel-Ramsey class, which is proven to be decidable [9]. Consequently, decidability of ground terms and ground term covering are decidable in logic databases with Datalog[neg] formulae.

Another practical computability issue is complexity. Obviously, all complexity results of (automated) theorem proving for first-order logic, specifically for this class of formulae apply (see e.g. [10]). Moreover, since our problem is decidable, we can be sure that the proof process always terminates and delivers a result within the time limits.

4   Catalogue Structure

Based on the previously introduced relations over ground terms, a common index for any number of data sets (Datalog^{neg} formulae) can be set up. Since the data sets may even reside in different databases, at first the common schema has to be established by adding the appropriate logical rules to the union of all data. Then predicate symbols for ground term covering, i.e. elements of the common schema have to be selected. As the last step of the integration process, catalogues, which provide a read-only (more precisely lookup-only) access to the participating databases, can be built the following way.

Definition 3 (Full Catalogue). *Let us call a finite set of predicate symbols the catalogue definition and denote it by K. Let the full catalogue, $G = \langle V, E \rangle$ be a directed graph. Its vertices, V are the elements of the database and $v_i \in V$ is connected to $v_j \in V$, i.e. $\langle v_i, v_j \rangle \in E$ if and only if $v_i \neq v_j$ and $v_i \sqsubseteq_K v_j$.*

As it can be seen, a full catalogue is a representation of the ground term covering relation, but reflexive edges are deleted. However, it still contains many edges as pointed out by the following proposition.

Proposition 1. *The strongly connected components of G are cliques.*

Proof. Let v_i and v_j be arbitrary but distinct elements of the same component. Since ground term covering is transitive, there exist paths of length 1 between v_i and v_j in both directions. This way all nodes are accessible in one step from all others, the component is a clique.   □

For indexing purposes, we use a reduced version of the full catalogue.

Definition 4 (Catalogue). *Let us derive the simplified catalogue (or the catalogue for short), $G' = \langle V', E' \rangle$ from G the following way: each clique of G will be a vertex and two vertices, $v'_i \in V'$ and $v'_j \in V'$ corresponding to the cliques $C_i \subseteq V$ and $C_j \subseteq V$ are connected, i.e. $\langle v'_i, v'_j \rangle \in E'$ if and only if*

$$v'_i \neq v'_j \wedge \exists v_i \exists v_j \ v_i \in C_i \wedge v_j \in C_j \wedge \langle v_i, v_j \rangle \in E$$

and

$$\neg \exists v_i \exists v_j \exists v_k \ v_i \in C_i \wedge v_j \in C_j \wedge v_k \in C_k \wedge$$
$$\wedge \quad C_i \neq C_j \wedge C_j \neq C_k \quad \wedge$$
$$\wedge \ \langle v_i, v_k \rangle \in E \wedge \langle v_k, v_j \rangle \in E$$

where $C_k \subseteq V$ is a clique of G. The latter formula disallows short cuts in the catalogue.

Catalogues are not necessarily connected graphs, i.e. they may consist of several components. Management routines (see the next section) are, however, much simpler if catalogues are one-component graphs. To this end, let a special node (the root) along with edges to all other nodes be always added to the full catalogue. Obviously, the root appears in the same role in the catalogue also.

Catalogues have another important property.

Proposition 2. G' *is a directed acyclic graph (DAG).*

Proof (Indirect). Let us assume there is a directed cycle in G'. By definition the graph does not contain any loop, i.e. the cycle has two distinct vertices, v_i' and v_j' (corresponding to distinct cliques C_i and C_j of G respectively).

Since there is a path from v_i' to v_j', there is a sequence of nodes in G' whose cliques contain data elements each covering the preceding one. The transitivity property of ground term covering ensures that elements of C_i are also covered by elements of C_j.

The same way we can infer that all elements of C_i cover all elements of C_j. The last two statements imply that one component contains all the elements of C_i and C_j. Because of Proposition 1 the component is also a clique. This contradicts the fact that the items were selected from two distinct cliques C_i and C_j. $\square$

Since $|V'| < \infty$ the acyclic property of catalogues ensures that catalogue management routines do not have to employ any checks to avoid infinite loops when they follow any number of adjacent edges.

Computers may represent catalogues in many different ways. The most efficient data structures consider V' as a partially ordered set with the partial order given by the reflexive and transitive closure of E'. Then the space allocation can be as small as $\mathcal{O}(c|V'|)$, where c stands for the number of chains in V' and is usually much smaller than $|V'|$ [11].

5   Catalogue Management

As mentioned before, the principal access method to knowledge centres is retrieval. Since catalogues can form the core of knowledge centres, they need to provide retrieval facilities, i.e. methods for searching for data elements. We thus discuss the most important search operations in this section. From now on, let the search condition (desired properties) be denoted by k. k is a function which maps predicate symbols to terms. It is to match K, i.e. has to be defined for all members occurring in K.

Algorithm (Simple Search)

1. Select an item m from k in which the current vertex differs from at least one of the successive vertices.
2. Go down until the graph ends or the values of m in k match the values of m in the vertex.

3. Select, if exists, another differentiating item from k, m, and go to step 2. Otherwise, the algorithm ends.

The search never takes infinite time since all paths are finite as proven in Section 4.

N.B. The algorithm does not specify any particular order in which elements of the search condition are to be selected. It does not specify either which edge to follow if there are two or more proper directions in Step 2. It does not matter due to the following theorem.

Theorem 1. *If there are vertices v_i' and v_j' in G' so that $v_i' \sqsubseteq_K v_j'$ but $v_i' \neq v_j'$, then there is a path from v_i' to v_j' in G'.*

Proof. Let us use induction: at every iteration split the proposition into two smaller but equivalent pieces so that they can be connected.

$v_i' \sqsubseteq_K v_j'$ does not contradict the definition of edge in G'. If there is no edge from v_i' to v_j', then

$$\exists v_i \exists v_j \exists v_l \ v_i \in C_i \wedge v_j \in C_j \wedge v_l \in C_l \wedge$$
$$\wedge \ C_i \neq C_j \wedge C_j \neq C_l \ \wedge$$
$$\wedge \ \langle v_i, v_l \rangle \in E \wedge \langle v_l, v_j \rangle \in E$$

where C_i, C_j and C_l are cliques of G and v_i' and v_j' corresponds to C_i and C_j respectively. That is, $v_i \sqsubseteq_K v_l$ and $v_l \sqsubseteq_K v_j$ according to the definition of E. Then the same applies to v_i', v_j' and v_l': $v_i' \sqsubseteq_K v_l'$ and $v_l' \sqsubseteq_K v_j'$ due to the definition of G'.

Since G' is finite, sooner or later all mentioned vertices are connected, in other words there is a path from v_i' to v_j'.   □

Because every path to the requested element is equally proper, an advanced search may examine them in parallel. It can be quicker since the search stops when the element is found on one path. If only a single processing unit is available, the maximum number of required steps is $|V'|$ [12]. Note that G' may contain $\mathcal{O}(|V'|^2)$ edges and thus a naive search would be slower. However, one may think that examining each node of G' irrespective of the edges has also $\mathcal{O}(|V'|)$ complexity. But our algorithm has the advantage that it stops as soon as it is certain that the element is not contained in the catalogue, while the algorithm which simply iterates over the vertices has to process all vertices in that case.

As mentioned before we also define a similarity notion for logic databases.

Definition 5 (Similarity of Terms). *Let C be a ground term, the logical identifier of a data element and $v \in V'$ correspond to C in V'. Let $min(v)$ be defined as*

$$\{v_i | v_i \in V' \wedge v_i \sqsubseteq_K v \wedge \forall v_j \ v_j \in V' \wedge v_i \sqsubseteq_K v_j \supset v_j \not\sqsubseteq_K v\}$$

and let $max(v)$ be defined as

$$\{v_i | v_i \in V' \wedge v \sqsubseteq_K v_i \wedge \forall v_j \ v_j \in V' \wedge v_j \sqsubseteq_K v_i \supset v \not\sqsubseteq_K v_j\}.$$

The most similar elements to C are contained in the nodes

$$max(v) \cup min(v).$$

That means these elements are covered by v but are maximal with respect to it or they cover v but are minimal with respect to that.

If $max(v)$ and $min(v)$ are the same, there are elements identical to v concerning K in the catalogue.

The complexity of computing the most similar elements is also $\mathcal{O}(|V'|)$ irrespective of the number of edges, i.e. irrespective of the complexity of the covering relation on which the catalogue is based [12].

It follows from the previous definition that every vertex divides the catalogue graph into two parts. The first part contains only elements it covers, the elements of the second part cover the divider element. That means that the graph also supports upper and lower bound queries which realise enquiries about elements fulfilling a maximum or minimum requirement, respectively.

Clearly, a catalogue has to be modified if the underlying data change. Having seen the search functions, the methods, which perform the modifications are straightforward. However, as proven in [12] they may have to modify all edges of the catalogue and are therefore very time-consuming. This is the reason why catalogues are primarily suitable to integrate knowledge sources for query purposes. Web shops for merchandise of different producers are a good example. The shops have to provide a single structure of merchandise for the customers and they do not normally modify the product details, only place orders etc. whose data reside in separate parts of the databases and need not be integrated with similar data of other producers.

6   Example

We have referred to web shops as an example of our integration method throughout this paper. In this section we consider another example, the following recruitment scenario in details: A global IT company with presence in America, Asia and Europe would like to open its first local office in Australia and is currently seeking trustworthy people for the new positions. To minimise risks, the company would welcome if its current employees filled the new roles. For this purpose the HR managers have to select candidates from their separate employee information databases located all over the world. The most obvious way to achieve this goal is to integrate the databases and perform the selection on the unified database.

Figures 1 and 2 depict excerpts of two Datalog^{neg} databases containing information on departments of local offices and their employees. Apart from many similarities, there are substantial differences between the two schemata. For instance, an employee is considered senior in the first system if they have worked

```
has_attribute(department, name, string).      has_attribute(employee, name, string).
has_attribute(department, location, string).  has_attribute(employee, location, string).
has_attribute(department, head, boss).        has_attribute(employee, department, department).
                                              has_attribute(employee, startwork, integer).
has_attribute(boss, benefits, string).        has_attribute(employee, skills, string).
                                              has_method(employee, senior, [integer]).


employee(I):- boss(I).

benefits(I, X):- boss(I), (X = car; X = cellphone).

senior(E, X):- employee(E), integer(X), startwork(E, S), S-X > 5.

location(F, L):- employee(F), department(F, D), location(D, L).

department(comp).                             employee(kate).
boss(mary).                                   employee(drew).

name(comp, 'Computing').                      name(kate, 'Kate').
location(comp, 'Berlin').                     department(kate, comp).
head(comp, mary).                             startwork(kate, 2000).
                                              skills(kate, database).

name(mary, 'Mary').                           name(drew, 'Drew').
head(mary, comp).                             department(drew, comp).
department(mary, comp).                       startwork(drew, 1997).
startwork(mary, 1996).                        skills(drew, sales).
skills(mary, logic).                          skills(drew, marketing).
skills(mary, database).
skills(mary, leadership).
```

Fig. 1. Database 1 with a department, employees and a boss

```
has_attribute(department, name, string).      has_attribute(employee, name, string).
has_attribute(department, location, string).  has_attribute(employee, location, string).
has_attribute(department, head, employee).    has_attribute(employee, department, department).
                                              has_attribute(employee, startwork, integer).
                                              has_attribute(employee, skills, string).
                                              has_method(employee, senior, [integer]).

senior(E, X):- employee(E), integer(X), startwork(E, S), S-X > 8.

location(F, L):- employee(F), department(F, D), location(D, L).

department(hard).                             department(soft).
employee(joe).          employee(sam).        employee(bob).

name(hard, 'Hardware').                       name(soft, 'Software').
location(hard, 'New York').                   location(soft, 'San Francisco').
head(hard, sam).                              head(soft, joe).

name(joe, 'Joe').                             name(bob, 'Bob').
department(joe, hard).                         department(bob, hard).
startwork(joe, 1996).                          department(bob, soft).
skills(joe, logic).                            startwork(bob, 1993).
skills(joe, database).                         skills(bob, sales).
skills(joe, leadership).                       skills(bob, database).

name(sam, 'Sam').
department(sam, soft).
startwork(sam, 1997).
skills(sam, marketing).
skills(sam, leadership).
```

Fig. 2. Database 2 with departments and employees

for more than 5 years, but more than 8 years' work is needed in the second case. Furthermore, the concept **boss** is totally unknown in Database 2.

Suppose that the managers' selection criteria are based on location, seniority and skills. Then catalogues defined by those predicates are excellent tools for making decisions. As the schemata are identical concerning the predicates used for catalogue construction, the step of establishing a common schema can be skipped.

The actual catalogues are depicted in Fig. 3. It is noteworthy that in the catalogues not only employees and bosses but departments are indexed as well. Furthermore, in accordance with our goal, the catalogues also deal with derived attributes such as location (in the case of employees) and seniority.

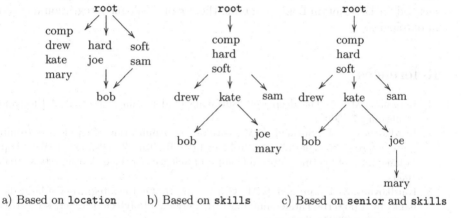

a) Based on **location**   b) Based on **skills**   c) Based on **senior** and **skills**

Fig. 3. Sample catalogues for the recruitment scenario

Regarding queries, if managers look for employees with **sales** and **database** skills, **bob** is returned by the catalogue built on **skills**. If managers try to find **senior** employees who have only **database** skills, the search in the corresponding catalogue, i.e. in the one based on **senior** and **skills** is unsuccessful. However, **kate**, **bob** and **mary** are almost adequate and answered to a similarity query. If the conditions are not so strict, i.e. **senior** employees with **database** skills are searched, a lower bound query is executed and **kate** is omitted.

7   Conclusions and Future Work

We proposed a simple decidable reorganising method for data entities with logical rules. It supports the integration of elements from different, heterogeneous information sources into knowledge centres. The method sets up a directed graph, a so-called catalogue. The structure provides a uniform, efficient query access to the participating data stores as required by most web-based and traditional services offered to customers. Similarity and lower/upper bound queries are also supported besides the basic exact search.

Like in relational databases the join, in our method the substitutability of ground terms is the key operation. The efficiency of indexing depends upon the time complexity of computing the substitutability relation, which can be performed by automated theorem provers for $Datalog^{neg}$ formulae. The search in the catalogue graph is efficient since it is suitable for parallel processing.

The work presented herein is an intermediate step of our work. It is clear that by adapting the results to F-logic, object-oriented databases can also benefit from these results. However, in our future endeavour we will propose a similar method for Description Logics enabling the use of catalogue integration methods in ontologies.

References

1. Bergman, M.K.: The deep web: Surfacing hidden value. Journal of Electronic Publishing **7** (2001)
2. Kardkovács, Zs.T., Surányi, G.M., Gajdos, S.: Application of catalogues to integrate heterogeneous data banks. In Meersman, R., Tari, Z., eds.: OTM Workshops. Volume 2889 of Lecture Notes in Computer Science., Springer-Verlag (2003) 1045–1056
3. Kardkovács, Zs.T., Surányi, G.M., Gajdos, dr., S.: On the integration of large data banks by a powerful cataloguing method. Periodica Polytechnica, Series Electrical Engineering (2004) To appear.
4. Gutirrez, C., Hurtado, C., Mendelzon, A.O.: Foundations of semantic web databases. In: Proceedings of the 23rd ACM SIGMOD-SIGACT-SIGART symposium on Principles of Database Systems (PODS), ACM Press (2004) 95–106
5. Abiteboul, S., Hull, R., Vianu, V.: Foundations of Databases. Addison-Wesley (1995)
6. Kifer, M., Lausen, G., Wu, J.: Logical foundations of object-oriented and frame-based languages. Journal of the ACM **42** (1995) 741–843
7. Baader, F., Calvanese, D., McGuinness, D.L., Nardi, D., Patel-Schneider, P.F., eds.: The Description Logic Handbook: Theory, implementation, and applications. Cambridge University Press (2003)
8. Codd, E.F.: A relational model of data for large shared data banks. Communications of the ACM **13** (1970) 377–387
9. Börger, E., Grädel, E., Gurevich, Y.: The Classical Decision Problem. 1st edn. Springer-Verlag Telos (1997)
10. Plaisted, D.A., Zhu, Y.: The Efficiency of Theorem Proving Strategies: A Comparative and Asymptotic Analysis. Second edn. Friedrich Vieweg & Sohn (2000)

11. Kardkovács, Zs.T., Surányi, G.M., Gajdos, S.: Towards more expressive query languages in web services. (Submitted for publication)
12. Surányi, G.M., Kardkovács, Zs.T., Gajdos, S.: Catalogues from a new perspective: a data structure for physical organisation. In: Advances in Databases and Informations Systems – 8th East-European Conference. Lecture Notes in Computer Science, Springer-Verlag (2004)

Navigation Modelling from a User Services Oriented Approach

Paloma Cáceres, Valeria de Castro, and Esperanza Marcos

Kybele Research Group,
Rey Juan Carlos University,
Madrid (Spain)
{pcaceres,vcastro,emarcos}@escet.urjc.es

Abstract. Traditional methodologies for Web Information Systems (WIS) development usually propose to get the navigation model from the conceptual data model. Unlike these methodologies, that follow a *structural* approach to build the navigation model, we propose to address the problem of navigation model construction from a *user services oriented* perspective. The method is based on identifying *conceptual user services*, that is specific services required by the user, and all the models are user services oriented. In this way, the navigation model is focused on the services required by the user. It also identifies just one specific *route* for each conceptual user service that guides the navigation of the user through the WIS. In this paper we explain the method and we show, by a case study, how the navigation model conceived from a user services oriented approach is more intuitive and user friendly.

1 Introduction

The construction of the navigation model is a problem addressed by most of the methodologies for Web Information System (WIS) development [1, 3, 4, 5, 7, 8, 9, 10]. Despite the differences found between them, most of them follow a similar approach to obtain the navigation model: they start from the conceptual data model [8, 9]. At best, they make reference to the need to consider use cases model [8, 10] but only as a recommendation, without indicating how to do it. Unlike the mentioned methodologies, that follow a *structural* approach to build the navigation model, we propose to address the problem of the systematic construction of the navigation model from a *user services oriented* perspective. That is, we will mainly take into account the services required by the user, called from now on *conceptual user services*. Therefore, in this paper we propose a method to obtain the navigation model starting from the *user services model*, a use cases model in which we identify conceptual user services as stereotyped use case. We also take into account the conceptual data model, but we do not start from it.

But, what are the benefits provided by a user services oriented approach with regard to a structural one? Structural approaches consider the conceptual data model

This research is carried out in the framework of the projects: EDAD (07T/0056/2003 1) financed by Regional government of Madrid and DAWIS financed by the Ministry of Science and Technology of Spain (TIC 2002-04050-C02-01).

T. Yakhno (Ed.): ADVIS 2004, LNCS 3261, pp. 150–160, 2004.

to give us information about the data to be shown on the Web. Data is grouped in meaningful pieces of information called *slices*. The slices model represents the slices and the links to navigate between them. In the navigation model the *navigational structures* (menus, indexes, guided tours, etc.) are added. This process has two main drawbacks: on one hand it is not possible to choose the navigational links based just on the information provided by the conceptual data model; on the other hand, the slice and the navigation models only represent pieces of information and navigational structures, lacking the conceptual representation of other kinds of pages, such as pages that represent the behavior provided by the WIS. Our method solves these two drawbacks proposing to obtain the *functional* and *structural* slices as well as the navigational links from an *extended use cases model* which will be explain in next section.

Besides, we want to remark that we propose a method to get the navigation model of *Web* IS. In WIS development the client is who defines the requirements of the WIS, because he knows the IS and what he wants to show or to sell to the users. Unlike the traditional IS, in WIS, the client and the users are not the same people. In the Web scope, when the user access to the WIS he does not know how to use it. The user only knows what he wants to do, but not how to do it. Therefore, the WIS and its navigation model have to be clear and intuitive to guide to the user. So for example, in the Amazon WIS a conceptual user service is "Buy a book" and this user service must be identified in the first menu of the WIS; then, to select a book, to register as client, etc., are steps required by the WIS to carry out this user service. The navigation model obtained with our approach will present a main menu with the services required by the user. Moreover, for each service, the navigation model will specify the sequence of steps to properly execute the service. This sequence of steps will be called *route*, and allows guiding the user when navigate through the WIS.

The main benefit of our method is that the navigation model is obtained from a user services oriented perspective, identifying the services required by the user and guiding him in the sequence of steps that he will have to follow. Therefore, the WIS will be more intuitive and user friendly.

In previous works [11] we have presented a first approach to a systematic method (from now on hypertext modeling method) to obtain a navigation model. Now we present the hypertext modeling method including the improvements explained before. The hypertext modeling method is part of MIDAS, a methodological framework for agile development of WIS, which proposes a Model Driven Architecture [2] based on the proposal of MDA by the Object Management. MIDAS proposes to model the WIS according to three basic aspects: *hypertext*, *content* and *behavior* (see Figure 1).

In this paper we focus on the PIM models related to the modeling of the hypertext aspect of a WIS that introduces four new models, shadowed in Figure 1: the *user services model*, the *extended use cases model*, the *extended slices model* and the *extended navigation model*. These new models will be explained in next section.

The rest of the paper is structured as follows: section 2 defines the new concepts and models proposed in our method; section 3 presents the hypertext modeling method of MIDAS by a case study, showing the main benefits of a user services oriented approach; finally, in section 4, we conclude underlying the main contribution and the future work.

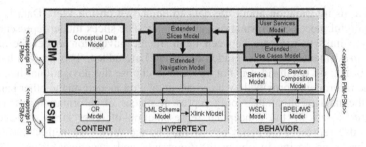

Fig. 1. Model-driven architecture of MIDAS

2   User Services Oriented Approach: Concepts and Models

The navigation modeling from a user services oriented approach introduces some new concepts and models. The *user services model* and *extended use cases model* are extensions to the use cases model in which different types of use cases are identified. The types of use case identified in our method are depicted in Figure 2.

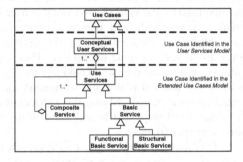

Fig. 2. Use Cases Taxonomy

2.1   Conceptual User Services: User Services Model

As you can see in Figure 2, a ***conceptual user service*** is an special type of use case that represents a service required by the user. Let's see an example based on the *ConfMaster WIS* that is the case study we will present in section 4. *ConfMaster* supports the organization of conferences allowing paper submission, assignment of papers to reviews, etc. To submit a paper the author has to login, to register the paper data, and afterwards he can send the paper. From our perspective, "Submit a Paper" is a service required by the user, whereas the "Login" is only a step required by the system to submit a paper, but it is not a service required by the user. Therefore, "Submit a Paper" is a user conceptual service.

We think that is important first, to capture the necessities of the user and then to analyze the requirements of the WIS, defined by the client, to carry out these necessities. To model these two steps, our method proposes two use cases models whit different types of use cases in each one. The first one is the *user services model* in which the conceptual user services are identified as use cases stereotyped whit <<*CUS*>>. The second one is the *extended use cases model*.

2.2   Use Services: Extended Use Cases Model

Each conceptual user service must be detailed taken into account the requirements of the WIS to carry out it. So for example, in the *ConfMaster WIS* when the user chooses "Submit a Paper", he will have to carry out three tasks in the following sequence: to login, to register data paper, and to send the paper. Each one of these actions, that are functionalities required by the system, is called *use service*. Therefore, a user conceptual service is an aggregation of use services (see figure 2) and a *use service* is also a type of use case identified in the *extended use case model*.

A use service could be implemented by means of Web services or other kind of technology. Based on the Web service classification provided in [12], a use service can be either a basic or a composite service. A *basic use service* is an atomic functionality of the WIS, for example, viewing a book catalogue. A *composite use service* is an aggregation of either basic or composite use services. From a presentational point of view, a basic use service can be functional or structural. A basic use service is *structural* when its functionality is only to provide a data view (i.e. viewing a catalogue, viewing the author's data, etc.). A basic use service is *functional*, if it implies some interaction with the user, generally requiring some input data (i.e. searching a book, adding a product to the shopping cart, paying, etc.).

The basic (structural and functional) and composite use services are identified in an *extended use cases model*. A use service is represented as a use case. For each use service (basic or composite) we define the following stereotypes: <<*CS*>> to represent a *composite use service*, <<*FBS*>> to represent a *functional basic use service* and <<*SBS*>> to represent a *structural basic use service*. We propose to model this composition of use services with a UML activity diagram.

2.3   Structural and Functional Slices: Extended Slice and Navigation Models

The *slices model* is defined in [9] as the decomposition of the system into meaningful units, called slices, and the hyperlinks between them. Our approach proposes to obtain: the slices from the extended use cases model and the information about each slice from the conceptual data model. As the extended use cases model represents two kinds of basic use services, (structural and functional) we also have to introduce two types of slices. A *structural slice* is a slice as defined above. A *functional slice* also represents a Web page, but an interactive one. Therefore, a functional slice allows the interaction with the user to be represented. An *extended slices model* is defined as a slices model in which the functional and structural slices are represented.

A *navigation model* is usually defined as a slices model plus the navigational structures. Then, an *extended navigation model* is an extended slices model and their navigational structures, that is, a navigation model which includes functional slices and structural slices. To identify the different slices, we introduce the <<*SS*>> and <<*FS*>> stereotypes that represent structural and functional slices, respectively.

2.4   Route: Signposting the Navigation Model

Travelling by car we can mark, in a road map, the route that we must follow to reach our destination, as a guide to travel. In the same way, in a navigational map of a WIS, it could be useful to mark the *route* that we must follow to carry out a task. Thus, in the hypertext modeling method of MIDAS, we defined a *route* for each conceptual user service, to guide the user in the navigation through the WIS. A *route* is the sequence of steps that the user follows to execute a conceptual user service. So for example, in the *ConfMaster WIS*, to submit a paper the author has to login, to register the paper data and afterwards he can send the paper. This sequence of steps represents the route to carry out the Submit Paper conceptual user service.

In the *extended slices model*, each route is composed by a set of slices linked between them. Each link between two slices is represented by an arrow stereotyped with *<<route>>*. Besides, a route has a tagged value to identify the conceptual user service that is carried out; thus in the above example, the route to Submit Paper is stereotyped with *<<route>> {SP}*. Moreover, a route can be forked giving rise to alternative ways at the same conceptual user service. These alternative ways are sub-routes of a route. In this case, if the route *X* has the sub-route *Y*, then the sub-route is stereotyped with *<<route>> {X.Y}*. These concepts are explained in depth in section 4 with the case study.

As we have said before, in the *extended navigation model*, the navigational structures are added. Usually, the main menu will show the conceptual user services identified in the user services model. The extended navigation model contains the routes to navigate through the WIS. This information has to be taking into account in the implementation phase, defining in the WIS the sequence of steps that the user must follow to execute a conceptual user service. This sequence of steps is transparent to the user, because he doesn't know the steps, required by the WIS, to carry out the service. So, in our example, if the user chooses "Submit Paper" in the main menu, the WIS will force him to login and to register the paper data before to allow him send the paper. In this way, the user is guided through WIS, giving rise to a more intuitive and user friendly WIS.

3   The Hypertext Modelling Method of MIDAS: A Case Study

The hypertext modeling method of MIDAS is the method to model the hypertext aspect of a WIS; it includes the new extended models explained in the previous section, the mappings between them and the process. Figure 3 shows the process of hypertext modeling method.

As you can see in Figure 3, the inputs of the method are the *user requirements* and the *conceptual data model*; and the output is the *extended navigation model*. We define three intermediate models to obtain the *extended navigation conceptual model*: the *user services model*, the *extended use cases model* and the *extended slices model*. Besides, we propose to use an *Activity Diagram* to model the composition of use services and to obtain the route. Figure 3 shows the process of the method, in which the new proposed models are shadowed.

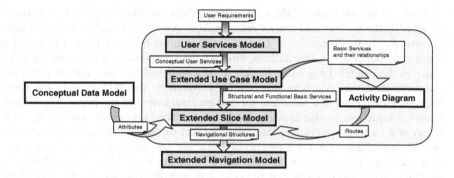

Fig. 3. The Process for the Hypertext Modeling Method

The process, models and mappings of MIDAS hypertext modeling method are illustrated in depth, through a case study. The case study we are going to present is the *ConfMaster WIS* [6], a WIS to support the organization of a conference. It allows the nomination of the Program Committee members, paper submission, assignment of papers to reviewers, etc. In this work we focus on the functionality in which the author is involved. An author must register as a new author and then it obtain a login. Then the author can submit a paper, can edit his data and can view his submitted papers.

3.1   Generating the User Services Model

As we have mentioned before, we propose the construction of the navigation model from a *user services oriented* approach. Then, we generate the user services model taking into account this approach. In our example, the real aim of an author is to submit a paper, to view their papers or to edit the author data. They are the specific services required by the author. Then, in a user services model (see Figure 4) we have identified *Submit Paper, View Papers* and *Edit Author Data* as conceptual user services and they will be stereotyped whit *<<CUS>>*.

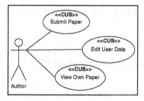

Fig. 4. (a) User Services Model

3.2   Generating the Extended Use Cases Model

The extended use cases model is obtained from de user services model. We begin *identifying the basic and composite use services* taking into account the functionality required by the WIS to carry out the conceptual user services previously identified.

Next, we *specify in detail the composite services* identified previously and finally we *identify the include and extend relationships*. As we have said, to submit a paper (*Submit Paper* in Figure 4): at first, the author must be logged in, next it has to register the paper data (other authors, abstract, etc.) and finally, it can send the paper. Then, in the extended use cases model, we decomposed *Submit Paper* in four basic use services: *Login* is a basic use service required by the WIS to send the paper, *Register Paper Data* is a basic use service necessary to send the paper, *Show Paper Data* is a basic use service showing the data introduced previously, and finally, *Send Paper* is a basic use service representing the fact of sending the paper. *Send Paper* and *Register Paper Data* are functional basic use services because they are stand-alone services that represent an interaction with the user. *Show Paper Data* is a structural basic use services that is associated with the use service *Register Paper Data* by an include relationship. *Login* is a functional basic service and is associated with the service *Send Paper*. *Login* has also associated two functional basic services by an extend relationships, *Register as New Author* and the other to *Forgot Password*.

Figure 5(a) shows the extended use cases model in which the use service implied in the *Submit Paper* conceptual user service are shadowed, in Figure 5(b) you can see the activity diagram associated to it. The same process applied to *Submit Paper* would be also applied to the conceptual user services *View Own Papers* and *Edit User Data*.

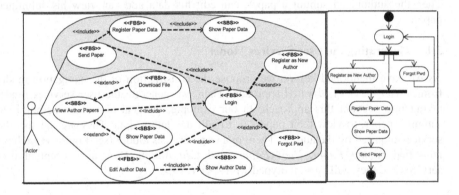

Fig. 5. (a) Extended Use Cases Model - (b) Activity Diagram for the Submit Paper Composite Service

3.3   Generating the Extended Slices Model

The extended slices model is obtained from the extended use cases model and taking into account the conceptual data model and the activity diagrams associated with each conceptual user service.

First, each *structural and functional basic service* of the extended use cases model will give rise to a structural and functional slice respectively. The relationships between basic use services will give rise to the hyperlinks. The attributes of the slices generally come from the attributes of the conceptual data model. For the sake of space limitation, the conceptual data model has been omitted. This model presents two classes: *Author* and *Paper*. So for example, attributes of the *Show Author Data* come from the class *Author*; however, some attributes of this class as Login and Password, are not represented in this slice because they will not be shown in a Web page. In fact, Login and Password will be attributes of the *Login* functional slice because they will be shown in this Web page.

Next, ***the specific route*** associated to each conceptual user service has to be identified. This route will guide to the users through the WIS, indicating the sequence of steps that must be followed. This sequence is obtained from the UML activity diagram. The route associated with *Submit Paper* (see Figure 5(a)) is identified with the tag value *{SP}* in the extended slices model (Figure 6). *Forgot Password* is a sub-route of the *<<route>> {SP}* then this sub-route is identified with *<<route>> {SP.FP}* as is shown in Figure 6. Figure 6 shows the extended slices model of *ConfMaster*.

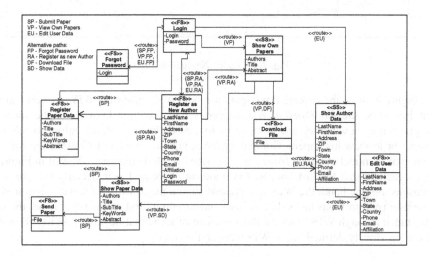

Fig. 6. Extended Slices Model

3.4   Generating the Extended Navigation Model

The extended navigation model is the result of introducing the navigational structures (index, menu, etc.) into an extended slices model.

We propose to introduce a main menu whit the services required by the user that represents the beginning of each route. As you can see in Figure 7, we represent a main menu with three entries for each conceptual user service: *Submit Paper*, *View Own Paper* and *Edit User Data*. Besides, the route of *View Own Paper*, stereotyped as *route {VP}*, also has two alternative paths for representing the *Download File* and the *Show Paper Data* slices. Then, we also represent a menu with two entries one of each slice). The navigational structures should be introduced according to the guidelines proposed in [8].

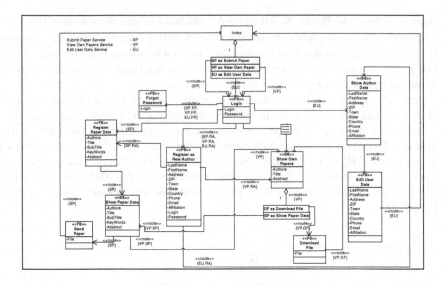

Fig. 7. Extended Navigation Model

Figure 8 show the extended navigation model of *ConfMaster WIS*. As you can see in Figure 8, the *ConfMaster WIS* supposes that the user knows that he must be registered as new author and he must be logged on in the systems before to submit a paper or to view his papers. Comparing the navigation model of *ConfMaster* with the navigation model obtained from a user service oriented approach, showed in Figure 7, we conclude that the last one, will be more intuitive and user friendly for two main reasons: on one hand, the WIS will present a main menu with the services required by the user (not previous tasks that the user must to do it) and on the other hand, the user is guided through WIS, because the sequence of steps that he will have to follow has been previously defined in the WIS through the route.

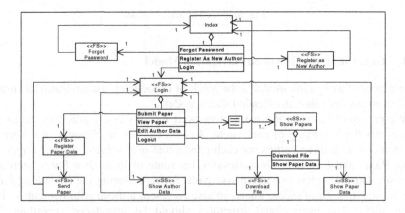

Fig. 8. Extended Navigation Model of *ConfMaster WIS*

4   Conclusions and Future Work

In this paper we have presented a method for the systematic construction of the navigation model in the framework of MIDAS, a model-driven methodology for WIS development. Unlike traditional methodologies for WIS development, that follow a *structural* approach to build the navigation model, we propose to address the problem from a *user services oriented* perspective. That is, we will mainly take into account the services required by the user, that we have called *conceptual user services*.

Usually in the Web scope when the user access to the WIS he does not know how to use it. The user only knows what he wants to do, but not how to do it. Therefore, the WIS and its navigation model have to be clear and intuitive to guide the user. For this reason we propose to model the navigation of the WIS starting form a user services model in which only the services required by the user are represented. Next, in the extended use cases model, the WIS requirements to carry out these services are represented. Thus, the navigation model obtained with our approach will present a main menu with the services required by the user. Moreover, for each service, the navigation model will specify the sequence of steps to properly execute the service. This sequence of steps will be called *route*, and allows guiding the user in the navigation through the WIS.

In this paper we have summarize the concepts of use service, structural slices and functional slices and we have also summed up the method, including the extended models with the required UML extensions to represent the new concepts. The main contributions of this work are: on one hand the introduction of a new concept, *route*, that allows to guide the user in the navigation trough the Web; on the other hand we have showed by a case study, how a use services oriented approach plus the route concept allows building a WIS more intuitive and user friendly.

At the present time, we are working on the integration of this method into MIDAS methodology. In future work we are going to implement the proposed models and mappings in a CASE tool that supports MIDAS to generate the WIS (semi-) automatically.

References

1. Atzeni, P., Merialdo, P., Mecca, G.: Data-Intensive Web Sites: Design and Maintenance. World Wide Web 4(1-2), pp. 21-47, 2001.
2. Cáceres, P., Marcos, E., Vela, B.: A MDA-Based Approach for Web Information System Development. Workshop in Software Model Engineering (WiSME) in UML'2003. Retrieved from: http://www.metamodel.com/wisme-2003/.
3. Castano, S., Palopoli, L., Torlone, R.: A General Methodological Framework for the Development of Web-Based Information Systems. Conceptual Modeling for E_Business and the Web. Liddle, S. W., Mayr, H. C., Thalheim, B. (eds.) ER 2000. Berlin (Germany), October, 2000. LNCS-1921. Springer Verlag. October, 2000.
4. Ceri, S., Fraternali, P., Matera, M.: Conceptual Modeling of data-intensive Web Applications. IEEE Internet Computing, Vol. 6 (5), pp. 20-30, 2002.
5. Conallen, J.: Building Web Applications with UML. Addison Wesley, 2000.
6. ConfMaster. Available in http://confmaster.net/phpwebsite_en/index.php, 2003.
7. Gómez, J., Cachero, C., Pastor, O.: Conceptual Modeling of Device-Independent Web Applications. IEEE Multimedia, 8 (2), pp. 26-39, 2001.

8. Hennicker, R., Koch, N.: A UML-based Methodology for Hypermedia Design. UML' 2000, LNCS 1939, pp.410-424, 2000.
9. Isakowitz, T., Kamis, A., Koufaris, M.: The Extended RMM Methodology for Web Publishing. Working Paper IS-98-18, Center for Research on Information System. Retrieved from: http://rmm-java.stern.nyu.edu/rmm/, 1998.
10. Koch, N., Kraus, A., Cachero, C., Meliá, S.: Modeling Web Business Processes with OO-H and UWE. In Third International Workshop on Web-oriented Software Technology (IWWOST03). Schwabe, D., Pastor, O., Rossi, G., Olsina, L. (eds.), 27-50, July 2003.
11. Marcos, E., Cáceres, P., De Castro, V.: An approach for Navigation Model Construction from the Use Cases Model. The 16th Conference On Advanced Information Systems Engineering. CAISE'04 FORUM, pp. 83-92.
12. Papazoglou, M.P., Georgakopoulos, D.: Serviced-Oriented Computing. Communications of ACM, Volume: 46, 10, October 2003, pp. 25-28.

Kreios: Towards Semantic Interoperable Systems[*]

Ismael Navas-Delgado, María del Mar Roldán-García,
and José Francisco Aldana-Montes

Computer Languages and Computing Science Department,
Higher Technical School of Computer Science Engineering,
University of Malaga, 29071 Málaga, Spain
`{ismael,mmar,jfam}@lcc.uma.es`

Abstract. Mediators used to be developed as monolithic systems that envelop the data source's information, such as its semantics and location. Furthermore, its architecture based on wrappers involves a high degree of coupling among the mediator's components. This coupling does not allow sharing services with other organizations or the dynamic integration of new data sources. We have proposed an architecture for conceptual mediation, which allow users to make more expressive queries and infer information from the ontology-explicit knowledge, enabling them to solve queries that a traditional mediator could not evaluate. This architecture also provides a way to achieve not only dynamic integration, but also interoperability between users/applications in the Semantic Web context by means of Semantic Fields. The latter is the focus of this paper.

Keywords: Semantic Integration, Semantic Queries, Semantic Interoperability.

1   Introduction

The amount of information in the web and the complexity of processing it in a reasonable manner has given rise to a lot of research on heterogeneous data integration. Mediator-Wrapper is the most common approach to achieve this goal. Its main objective is to allow users to make complex queries over heterogeneous data sources, as if they were a single one, using an integration schema. Mediators offer users interfaces for querying the system, based on the integration schema. These interfaces transform user queries into a set of sub-queries that are sent to the wrappers in order to be translated to the data source schema. Therefore, data sources can solve each sub-query. Usually, sub-query results are (specially those comming from Web resources) unstructured documents that are translated into structured documents following a standard format (XML, for example). XML technology makes it possible to both structure the information and to state explicitly the schema by means of an XMLSchema document. However, this information is insufficient for agents searching the Web, due to the fact that they cannot interpret these XML documents because they do not know their semantics.

---

[*] This work has been supported by the MCyT grant TIC2002-04586-C04-04.

T. Yakhno (Ed.): ADVIS 2004, LNCS 3261, pp. 161–171, 2004.

Mediation systems have evolved by means of different improvements made to traditional mediation architecture (of systems such as Manifold [1] and TSIMMIS [2]). Nonetheless, there are still several open problems in semantic heterogeneous data integration:

1. Design problems: (1) mediators and wrappers are strongly coupled; (2) they are manually designed for each new mediator by software developers; in other words, there is no reusability; (3) there is no dynamic integration; (4) it is not possible to use loose integration; and (5) software agents can not find wrappers, as they are "hidden" behind mediators.
2. Semantic problems: (1) wrapper query capabilities and semantics are not published; and (2) traditional mediators do not allow expressive queries based on semantics.

The need for systems that provide dynamic integration of data sources has led us to define a novel semantic mediation architecture [3] (Section 2). This architecture includes directories in which an ontology and several resources with semantics relevant to the domain information are published. We also improve the wrapper generation process by publishing them as web services and making their semantics accessible by means of several Web Methods. We have applied this architecture in two contexts: bioinformatics [3] and digital libraries [4].

The advantages of flexibility and openness provided by the Internet in connecting computer systems are lacking when connecting software applications. The primary techniques aimed at application interoperability are adapters (typically in Enterprise Application Integration) and exchange formats, such as Electronic Data Interchange (EDI) or Knowledge Interchange Format (KIF). Due to the limited success of existing solutions, we propose an approach that would start from the techniques mentioned above but be centrally based on a reference ontology. Using both this ontology and user needs we build semantic fields, which are a set of ontologies from (probably) several semantic directories, which are connected by means of mappings between domain ontologies.

In this paper we briefly describe our architecture (Section 2). In Section 3 we describe two use cases that help us to understand the rest of the paper. In Section 4 we present several examples about how to use this architecture for solving queries (both for biological and bibliographic data sources). Section 5 presents an extension of our proposal in order to obtain interoperability between bioinformatics and digital library directories. Finally, Section 6 presents some conclusions and future work.

2   DCRONO: A Semantic Mediation Architecture

DCRONO (Dynamic Conceptual integRation of heterOgeNeous data sOurces) is a framework architecture that seeks to make wrappers independent entities and to eliminate their ties to the mediator, thus increasing their reusability in different applications. We emulate P2P hybrid systems, which implement a directory with location information of available resources. In these systems the applications access the resources directly by means of point to point connections that the directory has provided them with. Therefore, the flow of information is greatly reduced w.r.t. the one generated in traditional client-server architectures.

Our proposal for semantic mediation stems from the need for both dynamic integration and application interoperability. This architecture introduces two main considerations concerning the basic architecture of mediation: (1) the isolation of wrappers, which are encapsulated as web services (Data Services for us); and (2) the added directory (Semantic Directory) with information about these Data Services (See Figure 1). This architecture allows wrappers to contribute data, information schemas and query capabilities in a decentralized and easily extensible way.

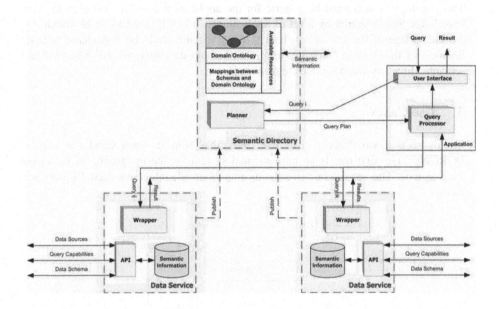

Fig. 1. Architecture for Semantic Integration

A data service needs to be registered in one or more semantic directories in order to be used by a mediator or other software agent. In other words, data services, like P2P hybrid systems, must know the location of semantic directories that are in the same application domain. Finally, public interfaces of data services and semantic directories will allow applications that share their communication protocol to take advantage of knowledge about available directory resources. Next we present the components of the proposed architecture as well as their functionality.

Semantic directories offer essential services for query processing, and data services provide the minimal elements for solving query plans. The aim of this type of component is to allow applications to access wrapper functionalities. In this way, we have designed an extensible and adaptive architecture in which we can define a data service as "a service that offers wrapper query capabilities using web protocols".

The publication of these online web services using UDDI (Universal Description Discovery Integration) [5] could allow other applications to dynamically discover wrappers by means of an easy interface. However, our data services have been devised for publication in a specialized type of directory: the semantic directory, so it is possible to find semantic information and a planner is available.

Semantic directories are at the core of this architecture because they provide essential services for solving user queries. We can define a semantic directory as "a server that offers information about available web resources (data services), a domain ontology, mappings between resource schemas and this ontology, and provides a query planner".

A semantic directory stores an ontology described with OWL [6]. The planner can use reasoning mechanisms over this ontology in order to obtain better query plans. This ontology, which must be generic for the application domain, describes the core knowledge that is shared by a set of applications. It can be seen as an abstraction of the knowledge of the resource schemas. Each schema could be considered as a refinement of the domain ontology. Information about data services will be added to a semantic directory when services register in it.

3   Use Cases

In this section we describe two use cases that help us understand the uses of DCRONO. The first one is an implemented system for the integration of biological data sources. The second one (just being implemented) integrates digital library services.

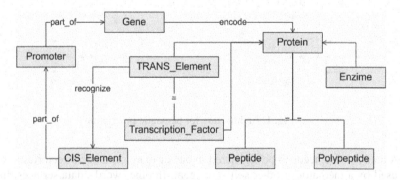

Fig. 2. Biological Ontology

3.1   Biological Data Source Integration

Let us consider a system accorded to the biological ontology (O_B) shown in Figure 2. This ontology represents a functional view of biological data. Queries will be defined over the concepts and relationships of this ontology. Examples of such kind of queries are (Note that "ans" element contains the concept instances that we want to retrieve):

Q1: "Find the nucleotide sequence of proteins encoded by some gene that contains the promoter whose id is EP17030".

ans(S) :- Protein(P), Gene(G), encode(G,P), sequence(P,S), Promoter(Po),
        part_of(Po,G), id(Po, EP17030)

Q2: "Find Transcription Factors, which are proteins that recognize CIS elements of gene promoters that encode the enzyme aldehyde dehydrogenase"

ans(T) :- Enzime(E), Gene(G), Protein(P), Transcription_Factor(T),
        CIS_element(CE),
        enzyme_name(E, "aldehyde dehydrogenase"), encode(G,P),
        part_of(P,E), is_composed(P,CE), recognize(T,CE)

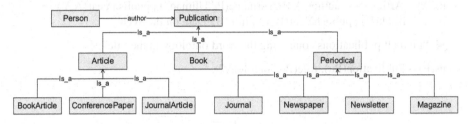

Fig. 3. Digital Library Ontology

For this case these resources envelop the access to biological sources, such as EMBL [7], SWISS-PROT [8], PDB [9], MICADO [10], DIP [11], EPD [12] and TRANSFAC [13].

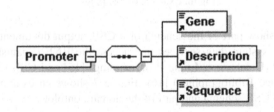

Fig. 4. EPD output schema

In Figure 4 we show part of the schema of an EPD output document. Mappings between resource schemata and the domain ontology are now obtained manually and inserted in the semantic directory when connected to a data service. An example of mappings (as logical formulas in which left side makes reference to ontology terms and right side to schemata terms) can be seen in Figure 5.

sequence(P) :- ($EPD//Sequence) (P)
part_of(P,G) :- gene_Name(G,Gn),
                ($EPD//Gene) (Gn)

Fig. 5. Example of mappings

3.2   Digital Library Services Integration

The reference ontology of the second system in our example is in Figure 3, which shows our Digital Libraries ontology (O_{DL}), that represents the domain knowledge of a group of digital library users. This ontology is based on terms described by the Dublin Core Metadata Initiative (http://dublincore.org/). Queries will be defined over the concepts and relationships of this ontology. Examples of these kinds of queries are:

Q3: "Find articles whose author is Ullman and were published the same year as the book titled 'Data on the Web'"

ans(A) :- Article(A) , author(A,P), surname(P,"Ullman") , publishYear(A,Y) ,
       Book(B) , publishYear(B,Y) , title(B,"Data on the Web")

Q4: "Find all publications containing the word ontology in the title"

ans(P) :- Publication(Pu), title(Pu,"ontology").

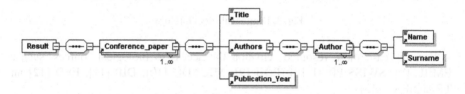

Fig. 6. Example of mappings

In Figure 6 we show part of the schema of a CSB output document. For this case we can add to our system data services that access the BNE (Spanish National Library) [14], DBLP (Database & Logic Programming) [15] and CSB (The Collection of Computer Science Bibliographies) [16]. Figure 7 shows an example of mapping between part of the CSB schema and part of the domain ontology.

Person(P) :- ($CSB//Name) (P)
title(CP,T), ConferencePaper(CP) :- ($CSB//Title) (T)

Fig. 7. Mapping example

4   Semantic Fields: The Use of DCRONO on the Semantic Web

The basic configuration of our proposal has been described with only one directory. But we will usually have distributed configurations and/or more complex architectures with several semantic directories. We are now going to present an analysis of the integration problem between semantic directories in order to obtain interoperability capabilities among several applications. We propose a two level integration solution. At a first level we use "loose" integration between close domains. For this task we take advantage of a reference ontology and use automatic matching algorithms based on semantic distance measurements. At the second level we propose "tight" integration among non closer ontologies (see Figure 8).

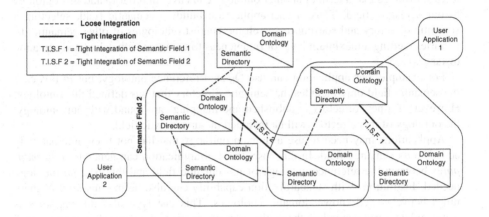

Fig. 8. Mediation on the Semantic Web

4.1   Semantic Field

Semantic directories integrate data sources taking advantage of domain ontologies, as shown in Section 2. These ontologies represent core knowledge that is shared by a set of resources and users. However, these domains will not be sufficient for several end-users, who may need to obtain information from different, but related, domains.

However, we need to define a method for allowing directories to share information/knowledge with other directories or applications. For this task we take advantage of P2P technology. That is, when a new semantic directory appears it is published in a P2P network; each semantic directory and application of this network receives information about the new directory, and the semantic distance from the ontologies in the semantic directory to the ontologies in other semantic directories of the network are calculated. Although this is an expensive process, semantic distances are static and only change when an ontology changes or a new ontology appears. Thus, each node of the P2P network will store semantic distances to a set of public ontologies, and could use then to improve its query capabilities.

Let us suppose that we have published the first directory (with the domain ontology O_B) in the P2P network, and then another developer publishes the second directory (with the domain ontology O_{DL}). Thus, the first directory receives information about this second directory and automatically calculates the similarity between terms of both ontologies. For this task we make use of the COMA framework [17]. However, this framework does not find mappings between both ontologies.

We define a semantic field as a set of ontologies related to our reference ontology through several mappings. There are two types of mappings: *loose* and *tight*. We define *loose mappings* as "mappings that can be automatically obtained without human interaction". In our case, these mappings are obtained making use of semantic distances previously calculated in a P2P network. The user/application can decide the longest distance that a term of another ontology can have in order to add this ontology to our semantic field. Thus, a user/application builds a semantic field, selecting a semantic directory and starting to search the nearest ontologies of other semantic directories (setting a maximum level of remoteness to compare with calculated semantic distances).

For example, our application can use O_B as a reference ontology, but in this case the semantic field only includes the semantic directory that has defined this ontology. However, if a new directory is published and mappings are found with our ontology, the ontology of this directory will be included in our semantic field.

Applications may need to use a domain ontology that has not been automatically added to its semantic field. In this case, the user/application can generate *tight mappings* between the reference ontology of its semantic field and the external ontology needed. Institutions with standardization capability can also define this kind of mappings between well-known domain ontologies. This last type of tight mappings is static and does not depend on the application perspective. We define "tight mappings" as "those mappings that cannot be obtained automatically and are established with human interaction". Thus, ontologies related by means of loose or tight mappings set up a semantic field, which is dynamically built up and updated for a given user-application perspective.

In this way, we can add O_{DL} to our semantic field, establishing a tight mapping between terms *gene* and *title*. Thus, our semantic field is now composed of two ontologies: O_B and O_{DL}.

Our proposal is not to obtain isolated semantic fields; instead, we hope that our solution will offer capabilities to achieve interoperable applications. In consequence, we propose using both loose and tight mappings to obtain semantic fields, and to take advantage of them to solve queries. Once the application establishes the set of semantic directories it can use, it will have defined a semantic field centered on a reference ontology (the one corresponding to the initial semantics). Next, end-user queries are decomposed to be planned for the semantic directories of the semantic field. Then these plans are combined and evaluated to return a complete result to the user/application.

Now the application may take advantage of the new semantic directory to solve its user queries, as for example: "Find Transcription Factors that recognize CIS elements of gene promoters that encode the enzyme aldehyde dehydrogenase, and publications where information about these Transcription Factors can be found". Thus, the biological part of the query is solved in the directory that has the O_B ontology, and the bibliographic information is retrieved from resources of the other directory. So it is necessary to send each part to the relevant semantic directory. Below this query is shown in logical terms:

ans(T,Pu) :- Enzime(E), Gene(G), Protein(P), Transcription_Factor(T),
      CIS_element(CE),
      enzyme_name(E, "aldehyde dehydrogenase"), encode(G,P),
      part_of(P,E), is_composed(P,CE), recognize(T,CE)
      factor_name(T,Name), Publication(Pu), title(Pu,Name).

Note that the part of the query "publications where information about these Transcription Factors can be found" has been transformed in a searching of transcription factor names in titles of publications. The query is divided in two parts.

ans(T,Name) :-   Enzime(E), Gene(G), Protein(P), Transcription_Factor(T),
                 CIS_element(CE),
                 enzyme_name(E, "aldehyde dehydrogenase"), encode(G,P),
                 part_of(P,E), is_composed(P,CE), recognize(T,CE)
                 factor_name(T,Name).
ans(Pu) :-   Publication(Pu), title(Pu,Name).

Finally, each sub-query can be evaluated in the corresponding semantic directory. In this way we have obtained semantic interoperability between systems and applications by means of semantic directories, whose domain ontologies are not very close, improving query capabilities offered by user applications.

5   Conclusions and Future Work

In this paper we have presented an architectural approach (DCRONO) in which we explicitly describe mediator and wrapper semantics. Thus, the design and use of existent technology (web services, P2P, etc.) is studied to obtain better integration systems. Our main goal is to break the mediation architecture and recompose it later, taking into account the advantages of previous experience and works.

We apply DCRONO to integrate biological and bibliographical data sources as use examples. This architecture is based on an extension of traditional mediation, called semantic mediation. A mediator typically uses an integration schema as a global view of the local schemas of the data sources that are integrated. Thus, queries are limited to the information that the integration schema provides. In our approach, the semantics introduced in the Semantic Directories allows users to make more expressive queries, viz. semantic queries. Furthermore, information inferred from the ontology-explicit knowledge is used to make queries that a traditional mediator could not evaluate.

Therefore, in several domains in which there are no technical users, such as librarians or biologists, dynamic integration is a very important issue. In this context, it is necessary to give users a simple environment for integrating data information without modifying the mediator code or schema. Directories supply an easy way to integrate data sources, opening up new directions for dynamic integration.

We also provide elements to achieve interoperability between semantic integration systems that cooperate in the same application domain or have certain relations (Kreios). We introduce a solution to integrate semantic fields and obtain better query capabilities. This will allow us to make complex queries, relating domains like Digital

Libraries and Molecular Biology. These kinds of queries will really exploit the advantages of the proposed architecture. For example, we could query a Digital Library using both the results of a biological experiment stored in a Biological data source and the related specific domain knowledge.

As future work, we intend to study the possibility of giving data services more semantics, taking into account service quality and relations with other domain ontologies. We plan to continue studying automatic mapping between schemas and ontologies, taking into account previous experience [18]. This experience can be applied to establish correspondences between a retrieved document's schemas and directory ontologies in those new systems developed using our architecture. We are also interested in establishing a semantic model to define the data service's query capabilities, which improves query planning by adding inferences about query capabilities to reasoning between schemas and the domain ontology. Finally we would obtain sound implementations in cited fields and perform practical evaluations with real users.

References

1. Levy, A., Rajaraman, A., Ordille, J.: Querying Heterogeneous Information Sources Using Source Descriptions. In Proc. VLDB, pages 251-262, Mumbai (Bombay), India, September 1996.
2. Papakonstantinou, Y., Garcia-Molina, H., Widom, J.: Object Exchange Across Heterogeneous Information Sources. In Proc. ICDE, pages 251-260, Taipei, Taiwan, March 1995.
3. Navas, I., Aldana, J.F.: Towards Conceptual Mediation. ICEIS 2004, vol. 1, pag. 169-176, Porto, Portugal.
4. Aldana-Montes, J.F., Navas-Delgado, I., Roldán-García, M.M.: Semantic Integration of Digital Libraries. ICEIS 2004, vol. 5, pag. 313-318, Porto, Portugal.
5. UDDI Spec Technical Committee Specification. http://uddi.org/pubs/uddi-v3.0.1-20031014.pdf.
6. OWL Web Ontology Language 1.0 Reference. W3C Candidate Recommendation 18 August 2003 http://www.w3.org/TR/owl-ref/
7. Wang, L., Riethoven, J.J., Robinson, A.: XEMBL – distributing EMBL data in XML format. Bioinformatics 18(8): pp. 1147-1148. 2002.
8. Bairoch, A., Apweiler, R.: The SWISS-PROT Protein Sequence Database and Its Supplement TrEMBL. Nucleic Acids Res. 28(1), pp. 45-48. 2000.
9. Bourne, P.E., Weissig, E.: Details the history, function, development, and future goals of the PDB resource. The PDB Team: Structural Bioinformatics. Wiley pp. 181-198. 2003.
10. Biaudet, V., Samson, F., Bessieres, P.: Micado a Network Oriented Database for Microbial Genomes. Com App. In BioSciences. 1997.
11. Xenarios, I., Salwínski, Ł., Joyce Duan, X., Higney, P., Kim, S., Eisenberg, D.: DIP: The Database of Interacting Proteins. A research tool for studying cellular networks of protein interactions. NAR 30:303-5. 2002.
12. Praz, V., Perier, R., Bonnard, C., Bucher, P.: The Eukaryotic Promoter Database, EPD: new entry types and links to gene expression data. Nucleic Acids Research, 2002, Vol. 30, No. 1 322-324.

13. Wingender, E., Chen, X., Fricke, E., Geffers, R., Hehl, R., Liebich, I., Krull, M., Matys, V., Michael, H., Ohnhauser, R., Pruss, M., Schacherer, F., Thiele, S., Urbach, S.: The TRANSFAC system on gene expression regulation. Nucleic Acids Res. 29, 281-283 (2001).

14. BNE (Spanish National Library).
    http://www.bne.es/cgi-bin/wsirtex?FOR=WBNCONS4#PRECISA

15. DBLP (Data base & Logic Programming). http://www.informatik.uni-trier.de/~ley/db/

16. CSB (The Collection of Computer zScience Bibliographies).

17. http://liinwww.ira.uka.de/bibliography/waisbib.html#search

18. Do, H.-H., Rahm, E.: COMA - A System for Flexible Combination of Schema Matching Approaches. In VLDB, 2002.

19. Madhavan, J., Bernstein, P.A., Domingos, P., Halevy, A.Y.: Representing and Reasoning about Mappings Between Domain Models. Proceedings of the AAAI Eighteenth National Conference on Artificial Intelligence, 2002.

Adaptive Architecture
for Web Server Survivability

Eungki Park[1], Dae-Sik Choi[1], Eul Gyu Im[1],
Jung-Tack Seo[1], and Dongkyu Kim[2]

[1] National Security Research Institute,
62-1 Hwa-am-dong, Yu-seong-gu,
Daejeon, 305-718, Republic of Korea
{ekpark,dschoi,imeg,seojt}@etri.re.kr
[2] School of Information & Computer Engineering,
Ajou University, Suwon,
Republic of Korea
dkkim@madang.ajou.ac.kr

Abstract. Internet becomes more and more popular, and most companies and institutes use web services as a fundamental tools to promote
their business. As results, Internet and web services become core infrastructure for a business and become more and more important, but
attacks against web services increase as the popularity of web services
grows. Therefore, there are increasing needs of undisturbed web services
despite of attacks. In this paper, we proposed adaptation policies for
a web-server intrusion tolerant system. Our proposed adaptation policies allow the system to provide continuous web services using various
techniques, such as intrusion tolerant types, replication degree, server
allocation mechanism, adaptive access control method and so on.

Keywords: intrusion tolerance, survivability, web services.

1 Introduction

Advances of Internet make more people to use Internet services, and among these
Internet services, web services are most popular and become important business
tools. Web services disruptions can cause many problems, such as reduced number of accesses, restoration costs, degradation of company credibility, and the
like. According to the reports of CSI/FBI in 2001, 38 percent of web sites were
affected by hacking, and among these sites 21 percent of them were not aware
of hacking in their sites [1]. The Symantec/Riptech report published in January
2002 says that 100 percent of web users experienced hacking incidents and 43
percent of users experienced serious hacking incidents in 2001 [2].

Defense directions against hacking incidents can be divided into two categories: the first one is intrusion blocking mechanisms, such as firewalls, user
authentication, and virus scanning, and the second one includes intrusion detection mechanisms.

T. Yakhno (Ed.): ADVIS 2004, LNCS 3261, pp. 172–180, 2004.

The theme of intrusion detection systems (IDS) is detection because prevention mechanism alone is no guarantee to keep intruders out. The research focus of IDS is therefore on how to detect as many attacks as possible, as soon as we can, and at the same time to reduce the false alarm rate. However, a growing recognition is that a variety of mission critical applications need to continue to operate or provide a minimal level of services even when they are under attack or have been partially compromised; hence the need for *intrusion tolerance*. [10]

Since systems and networks become more and more complicated with the advance of technologies, there are many limitations to eliminate all the vulnerabilities of computer systems and networks [3]. Because of widespread uses of integration of COTS components and various distributed resources, defense mechanisms against attacks become incomplete and more vulnerable [4].

According to CSI/FBI reports, even though 95 percent of organizations have firewalls, 61 percent of them have IDS, 90 percent of them use access control, and 42 percent of them use digital signatures, attacks still occurred. These data indicate that both intrusion detection mechanisms and intrusion blocking mechanisms apparently have limitations, so there should be new directions toward research areas, such as intrusion tolerant systems.

Intrusion tolerant systems(ITS's) are defined as systems that provide continuous services using filtering, recovery, and adaptation techniques even though attacks are occurred on the server [5, 6, 7, 8]. ITS's can be composed with the following components: a resistance module, a recognition module, a recovery module, and an adaptation module. A resistance module is used to tolerate attacks, a recognition module is used to detect intrusions, a recovery module is used to recover damages caused by attacks, and an adaptation module is used to reconfigure components for continuous services after attacks.

In this paper, we proposed adaptation policies for a web-server intrusion tolerant system. Our proposed adaptation policies allow the system to provide continuous web services using various techniques, such as intrusion tolerant types, replication degree, server allocation mechanism, adaptive access control method and so on.

The rest of this paper is organized as follows: after reviewing previous approaches in Section 2, Section 3 shows an overall structure of our Advanced Web-server Intrusion Tolerant System, each module is explained in detail in Section 4 and Section 5 shows adaptation policies, followed by conclusions and future directions in Section 6.

2 Related Work

Feiyi Wang et al. [9, 10, 11] proposed an intrusion tolerant system called SITAR. In their approach, requests are forwarded to several web servers through acceptance monitors, and responses are monitored in acceptance monitors and ballot monitors. adaptive reconfiguration module takes care of reconfiguration and adaptation when attacks are detected. There are several problems with their approach. 1) Their modules lack detailed design and implementation descriptions, and many issues are not addressed in their paper. It is not clear how the reconfiguration module works. 2) Since a request is forwarded to several web servers simultaneously, there is performance problem for handling requests.

Partha P. Pal et. al at BBN Technologies explained intrusion tolerant systems [4]. But their paper shows system strategies and requirements without any detailed system design, so it is just a preliminary report about intrusion tolerant systems.

Daesik choi et. al [12] suggests Web server Intrusion tolerant system called WITS. In their approach, WITS consists of four modules (resistance, recognition, reconstruction and adaptation) for continuous services. Detailed adaption methods are not fully discussed in their paper.

Even though there are some previous researches on intrusion tolerant systems, more research and experiments are in need, especially on adaptive policies. Therefore, after reviewing previous approaches, we designed an intrusion tolerant system and currently work on implementing a prototype.

3   Our System Overview

Figure 1 shows a logical view of our proposed system which is called AWITS, i.e. advanced web server intrusion tolerant system. An intrusion tolerant server lies in front of more than one web server which includes wrapper-based web servers, and these web servers share a database. Each server can have more than one identical web service for redundancy and diversity, and more than one web server runs simultaneously. An intrusion tolerant server acts as a proxy server, and it relays requests and responses between clients and servers.

Data flow in AWITS is as follows: for requests from each client in the Internet, a new FRM (filtering and request handling module) process and a new VOM (voting module) process are created. An FRM process forwards requests to MRM (masking and recognition module) according to policies of ARM (adaptive reconstruction module). FRM executes request validation procedures (These will be explained later), and if the request passed validation tests, the request is forwarded to a web server through MRM. Then, the MRM gets results from the web server and performs result validation procedures. If the results are ok, then they are forwarded to VOM. Otherwise, the validation test results are sent to ARM and the ARM performs filtering and reconstruction. In VOM, a selected result through voting is transmitted to the client that sent the request. AMs(admin modules) reside in web servers, and collect information about web servers.

Based on results of request and response validations, 'black' lists are maintained. These 'black' lists are created using statistical information of relations between clients and URLs or between clients and web servers, and these lists allow system administrators to establish policies of filtering requests, restricting services, or selecting a web server for a request. The policies established here are used by FRM when requests are forwarded to MRM. Unknown attacks are detected through the response validation process.

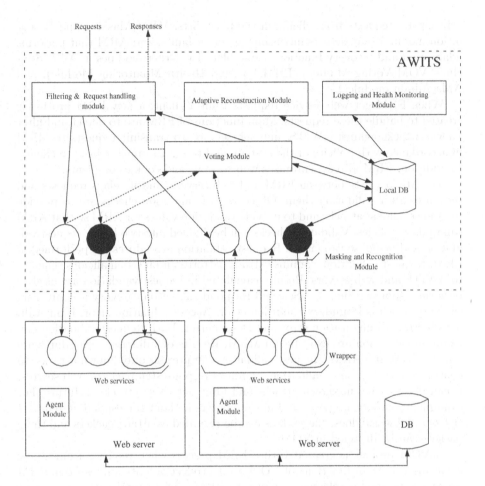

Fig. 1. Structure of Our Intrusion Tolerant System

LHM(logging and health monitoring module) is responsible for collecting logs from modules in the system as well as checking web server status or contents of web servers. To check integrity of contents, LHM keep MD5 hash values of contents that must be protected, and AM's periodically recalculate hash values and send them to LHM , monitor Web server health and modify wrapper based web server policy.

4   Advanced Web Server Intrusion Tolerant System (AWITS) Components

Our proposed intrusion tolerant system is mainly designed for web servers. In this section, we will address each module in AWITS in detail. Main modules of AWITS are FRM(Filtering and Request Handling Module) that filters known attacks and requests from clients in the black lists, MRM(Masking and Recognition module) that detects intrusions or server faults, and ARM that performs adaptation and recovery functions using blacklist. Other modules in AWITS include VOM(Voting Module), LHM(Log and Health Monitoring Module), and AMs(Admin modules).

When FRM get web service requests from a client, a new FRM process is created to handle these requests. Main functions of FRM are to detect and filter known attacks against AWITS and web servers, to transmit requests to MRM in accordance with policies of the system, and to send responses back to clients. In addition, FRM also synchronizes web sessions and cookies of clients.

The MRM exists between FRM and web servers, and it relays requests and responses after validating them. Objectives of validation checks are to provide resistance against attacks and to provide validation values for ARM so that ARM can update policies. Validation checks can be divided into two kinds: request validation and response validation. Request validation procedures are performed in FRM. Request validation examines attack patterns and filters malicious requests to AWITS and web servers. Results calculated in request validation are used to perform response validation. Selected Respond validation category is defined six category which is Boundary condition error, Access validation error, Input validation error, Configuration error and Design error. Both Request validation and response validation are executed in MRM. Results of validation procedures are sent to VOM and ARM. Request validation can prevent only known attacks. In contrast, since response validation examines responses(empact) of web servers, it can detect some unknown attacks and filter out these attacks in future. For example, if packets are generated in web servers without corresponding requests as CodeRed worm does, the packets can be regarded as attack packets and these packets can be dropped in VOM.

A VOM process is created with a FRM process when requests from a new client arrival. Main functions of VOM are to collect validity values from MRM processes, to send a selected response to FRM, and to send voting results to ARM. Voting enables AWITS to provide continuous web services even though there are attacks against some of web servers. As an example, when one web service is affected by attacks, if a request is forwarded to more than one web services, VOM can be able to select responses from unaffected web services using validity tests. Since a same attack will have different effects on different web servers, more robust web services can be provided by running diverse replicated web servers with same contents. In addition, replication of web contents gives redundancy to the system, and correct contents can be selected by validation testing despite one of contents is modified by an attacker. Moreover Wrapper based web server enhanced more continuous service using adaptive access control mechanism. The contents checking procedure compares modified time and MD5 hash values of response contents with pre-saved values. This procedure applies only to static web contents, and dynamically changing web pages cannot be examined. Statistical data generated in VOM are sent to ARM so that ARM updates policies of request filtering.

ARM gets inputs from LHM, VOM, MRM, and Admin Module, and it updates filtering policies and executes reconstructions of web servers and data flows when necessary.

AM is communicated with other modules such as Admin module, MRM, and ARM. AM exists in a web server as a process, and its main functions are the following:

- MD5 checksums are calculated for web pages, and the checksums are sent to LHM.
- AM recovers web pages when the pages are affected by attacks.
- AM examine notifies performance decrease,
- AM executes reconstructions of the web server when reconstruction requests are received from ARM.

Main functions of LHM which is executed as a process in AWITS are to monitor health of web servers and other modules as well as to save logs of AWITS. The period of health monitoring is dynamically changed based on conditions of AWITS. Other functions of LHM are as follows:

- LHM checks hash values of web pages periodically. If LHM finds errors in any web pages, it notifies AM so that AM can restore the pages.
- If LHM finds errors or performance degradation from any modules, LHM notifies ARM for reconstructions or adaptation.

5 Adaptation Policies

The most important and critical function of AWITS is how to adapt to new attacks. In this section, we proposed several adaptation policies.

Policy 1: Decision of an Intrusion Tolerant Type. In AWITS, intrusion tolerance types are divided into two types: *Prevent(active defense)* type and *Recover(Passive defence)* type. The prevent-type defense uses actively known attack model, predicts intensity of threats about attacks, and filters requests in advance. The recovery-type defense provides continuous services through impact masking, reconstruction, voting, and health monitoring. The type is determined according to several essential factors, especially threat levels.
Let the size of blacklist be B, threshold value be T, active defense be A, and passive defense be P, then
$if B \geq T \Rightarrow A \rightarrow P$
How can we decide the threshold value? This value is influenced by external alert condition, administrator's judgement, etc. This policy is adaptively selected considering security strength and performance.

Policy 2: Web Server Assignment. There are two kinds of web server assigning policies: *all active* and *primary/backup*. Initially, web servers are set to the *all active* mode. As the number of attacks increases, the assigning method is changed to the *primary/backup* mode.

Heterogeneous Web Server. Web server that is composed to AWITS is consisted of heterogeneous two kind of web server. Usually, web server more than 3 exists to single system. One of these is text-viewing server prepared to show web page of existing multiple component base to text base for continuous of service when performance decrease happens. Another one is wrapper based server that requires more robust security in condition of blacklist statistic. Wrapper based web server has access control function about request that and controls request privilege about execution, write and read.

Black List. Blacklist means statistical data to manage AWITS's whole Adaptation. This statistical data(Blacklist) is used by judgment value of whole adaptation element. Statistical data generated in VOM are sent to ARM so that ARM updates policies of request filtering. To collect statistical data, the following validity scores are collected:

- Web server : Validity scores of each server are collected, and the average scores are calculated. The higher validity score of a web server, the more requests are assigned to the server.
- URL : Validity scores per URL are collected.
- Client : Validity scores per client are collected and they are used for ARM to build the 'black' lists.
- URL vs web server : If one URL is replicated into several servers and requests to the URL are forwarded to more than one server, URL validity scores per web server are collected.
- Client vs web server : Client validity scores per web server are also collected.

Based on collected validity scores, scores per web server, URL, and client are calculated. These calculated scores are used to update policies for filtering requests, assigning MRM processes for requests, and the like. If more than one web server is running and the average validity score of a web server within a certain time frame is less than a threshold, the number of requests that the web server receives is decreased, and vice versa.

Policy 3: Reconstruction Policy. Basically, reconstruction is executed based on collected statistical data, such as web server validity, URL validity, Client validity, URL vs web server validity and client vs Web server validity. These data are used for impact masking and determination of degrees of web server redundancy.

Impact Masking. Let each request be I, A be request validation percentage, B be response validation percentage, V be Valid percentage, and threshold be T, $T_1 > T_2 > T_3$.

- if $\frac{A+B}{V} \geq T_1$ then put I to blacklist, and execute response masking.
- if $\frac{A+B}{V} \geq T_2$ then put I to blacklist, and execute request masking.
- if $\frac{A+B}{V} \geq T_3$ then put I to blacklist, and store I for future calculation.

Using this policy, AWITS can dynamically prevent exploit codes from doing malicious action.

Degree of Web Server Redundancy. To determine degrees of web server redundancy, AWITS considers information, such as web server access statistics, performance, and admin commands. Let heterogeneous web server be $W_1, W_2, ..., W_n$, voting winner for web server be VW, the validity score of url vs web server be VU, the validity score of client vs web server be VC, the voting result be V.

> if $VW \geq T_{W_n}$ then invoke $T_{W_{n+1}}$, and redirect the request flow considering VU, VC. Because heterogeneous web servers are running concurrently, AWITS reduces $W_1, W_2, ..., W_n \rightarrow W_1$ for performance efficiency.

Let the average of all voting scores be $Q_{average}$, Wrapper-based web server be WW.

> if $VW \geq Q_{average}$ then invoke WW, and redirect the request flow considering response validation which is used as a criterion for privileged read/write. If VW becomes less than $Q_{average}$, ARM invokes W, redirects the request flow, and deactivates WW.

Let request/response utilization be U, utilization threshold be T, text-based web server be TW.

> if $U \geq T$ then invoke TW, and redirect the request flow for continuous of service. If the utilization becomes normal and situation is stable, then this flow is deactivated.

6   Conclusions and Future Directions

Advances of Internet make more people use Internet services, and among these Internet services, web services are most popular and become important business tools as well as an infrastructure. Therefore, web service disruptions can cause many problems, such as reduced number of client accesses, restoration costs, degradation of company credibility, and the like.

In this paper, we proposed adaptation policies for an intrusion tolerant system, called AWITS (Advanced Web Server Intrusion Tolerant System). AWITS executes active and passive protections against attacks, and it is designed to provide continuous web services and higher availability of data. Especially, AW-ITS makes use of various adaptation element such as Wrapper based web server, text-based web server. these diversity helps more adaptively reconstruction for survivability. The main advantages of AWITS are 1) it can provide more continuous service than other IA systems, 2) it can block some unknown attacks, and 3) it can adapt against attacks.

As future directions, we need more tests and experiments on our proposed adaptation policies, and need to improve the adaptation mechanisms.

References

1. Computer Security Institute/Federal Bureau of Investigation: Computer crime and security survey (2001)
2. Symantec Corp.: Symantec internet security threat report, volume i (2002)
3. Ellison, B., Fisher, D.A., Linger, R.C., Lipson, H.F., Longstaff, T., Mead, N.R.: Survivable network systems: An emerging discipline. Technical Report CMU/SEI-97-TR-013, Carnegie-Mellon University Software Engineering Institute (1997)
4. Pal, P., Webber, F., Schantz, R.E., Loyall, J.P.: Intrusion tolerant systems. In: Proceedings of the IEEE Information Survivability Workshop, Boston, Massachusetts, U.S.A. (2000)
5. Lee, W., Fan, W.: Mining system audit data: opportunities and challenges. ACM SIGMOD Record **30** (2001) 35–44
6. Pal, P., Webber, F., Schantz, R.: Survival by defense-enabling. In: Proceedings of the 2001 workshop on New security paradigms, ACM Press (2001) 71–78
7. Rathi, M., Anjum, F., Zbib, R., Ghosh, A., Umar, A.: Investigation of intrusion tolerance for COTS middleware. In: Proceedings of the IEEE International Conference on Communications 2002. (2002) 1169–1173
8. Stavridou, V., Dutertre, B., Riemenschneider, R.A., Saidi, H.: Intrusion tolerant software architectures. In: Proceedings of the DARPA Information Survivability Conference & Exposition (DISCEX) 2001. (2001) 230–241
9. Wang, F., Upppalli, R.: SITAR: a scalable instrusion-tolerant architecture for distributed services - a technology summary. In: Proceedings of the DARPA Information Survivability Conference & Exposition (DISCEX) 2003. (2003) 153–155
10. Wang, R., Wang, F., Byrd, G.T.: Design and implementation of acceptance monitor for building scalable intrusion tolerant system. In: Proceedings of the Tenth International Conference on Computer Communications and Networks, Scottsdale, AZ, USA (2001) 200–205
11. Wang, F., Gong, F., Sargor, C., Goseva-Popstojanova, K., Trivedi, K., Jou, F.: SITAR: A scalable intrusion-tolerant architecture for distributed services. In: Proceedings of the 2001 IEEE Workshop on Information Assurance and Security, United States Military Academy, West Point, NY (2001) 38–45
12. Choi, D.S., Im, E.G., Lee, C.W.: Intrusion-tolerant system design for web server survivability. In Chae, K., Yung, M., eds.: Proceedings of the 4th International Workshop on Information Security Applications, Jeju Island, Korea, also published in *Lecture Notes in Computer Science 2908*, Springer-Verlag, Berlin (2003) 124–134

Integration and Maintenance of Heterogeneous Applications and Data Structures

Elaine Isnard[1], Enrique Perez[2], Radu Bercaru[3],
Alexandra Galatescu[3], Vladimir Florian[3],
Dan Conescu[3], Laura Costea[3], and Alexandru Stanciu[3]

[1] Prologue Software, 12, avenue des Tropiques, 91943 LES ULIS, Paris, France
eisnard@prologue-software.fr
[2] Virtual Desk, Avenida de Brasil, 17 5-a/b 28020 Madrid, Spain
eperez@virtualdesk.es
[3] National Institute for R&D in Informatics,
8-10 Averescu Avenue, Bucharest, Romania
{radu,agal,vladimir,dconescu,laura,alex}@.ici.ro

Abstract. The paper introduces an XML-based solution for the conceptual representation, integration, adaptation and maintenance of heterogeneous applications and data structures. It first presents the architecture of the XML repository and the content of the XML (meta)models that represent applications and data structures. Then, the architecture of the repository manager is given, along with its interface (the browser) and its functions for the management and maintenance of the XML models which describe applications/ data structures.

1 Introduction

Information systems (ISs) unify legacy and new applications, developed with heterogeneous software. They usually manage heterogeneous data structures [14]. The integration and maintenance of heterogeneous applications, possibly distributed, imply a great programming effort, without spectacular results. There are software engineering tools that can be used to create, integrate and maintain applications and data structures within a uniform and consistent environment, but none completely handles non-uniform solutions. Lately, the IDEs and relational DBMSs integrate version managers for tracking the versions of the objects they are able to create and update. The DBMSs can even manage heterogeneous types of versioned objects (tables, forms, reports, souce code etc). However, their versioning and maintenance abilities apply only to one producer's objects (e.g. the software configuration manager integrated with ORACLE DBMS can version and maintain only ORACLE objects).

The integration and maintenance of heterogeneous applications and data structures become much more difficult when the software companies, IT departments, application service providers (ASPs) try to meet the users need for customized solutions, which are not available in the standard software and existing applications. Application and data structure customization (adaptation) and maintenance is going to be a major business in the coming years. This extends from the customization of screens to the

T. Yakhno (Ed.): ADVIS 2004, LNCS 3261, pp. 181–191, 2004.
© Springer-Verlag Berlin Heidelberg 2004

writing of additional modules, via the redefinition of the data structures or the connection of generic and application software with different origins.

Issued from an IST project named MECASP (Maintenance and improvement of component-based applications diffused in ASP mode) (completed in December 2003), the XML-based solution described here aims to (1) integration, adaptation and maintenance of heterogeneous applications and data structures, (2) application deployment and exploitation on heterogeneous and distributed platforms. MECASP is compliant with ASP's technical requirements, but it is not limited to the ASP market.

MECASP overcomes the following *limits of the existing tools* for integration and maintenance of applications, e.g. version managers like CVS [2]: versioning of text files only; relying exclusively on a literal diff-like comparison of source file versions; using a primitive mechanism for tracking and merging the changes. A database, for instance, is treated as a binary file, without dealing with its schema and with the changes on it, from one database version to another.

Three features differentiate MECASP from such tools: (1) configuration and maintenance of heterogeneous software, based on XML models, (2) (semi)automatic and semantic comparison and merging of versions for heterogeneous objects (text and non-text- like objects), (3) rule-based decisions to solve conflicts and inconsistencies.

The *use of XML in MECASP* is, in brief, as follows:

- the definitions/ schemas of heterogeneous pieces of software are first converted and integrated into *XML meta-models* (e.g. definitions for Java source code, database schemas, graphical forms, etc).
- then, new applications are built by incorporating, in an *XML model,* definitions from existing XML meta-models.
- the user can further maintain or adapt his application by changing the definitions of the physical objects in the application (e.g. the schema of a table in a database). These changes are automatically reflected into the XML model of the respective object. They can produce a new (historical or parallel) version of the application. The XML model for the new version includes the descriptions in XML of all change actions (*deltas*) applied to the original version.
- the user can merge versions of an application. In MECASP, merging applies to the XML models, not to the physical objects (as in existing version managers).

The benefits from XML modeling in software integration and maintenance are: (1) software descriptions are independent of platform and development tool; (2) merging heterogeneous resources is possible.

The MECASP platform is divided into three layers: (1) *the browsing layer* with an advanced graphical interface, (2) *the tool layer*, composed of editors for source files, database schema, graphical forms; security manager, merger, installer, meta-model generator, import tool, wizards, etc. (3) *the repository layer*, composed of the repository and its manager. The paper focuses on the last layer.

Structure of the Paper. The basic intentions, problems and partial results of MECASP development using XML technology have been previously described in [7], [11], [12], etc. In this paper, the final results are given, along with the conclusions from the research and development activity. Section 2 gives the architecture of the XML repository and the implemented solution for the uniform representation of the software in XML. Section 3 gives the architecture of the XML repository manager, along with its interface (the browser) and the functions for the management and maintenance of XML models. Section 4 enumerates some related research results and their limits. It also compares them with the results obtained in MECASP.

2   XML-Based Integration of Applications and Data Structures

The repository layer represents the core of MECASP. It allows the uniform representation and integration of heterogeneous applications and data definitions/ schemas. It has a three level architecture:

- *XML schema* - the general architecture for all types of applications and data structures integrated and maintained with MECASP,
- *XML meta-models* - predefined or imported definitions from existing applications and data structures. They comply with the XML schema and represent templates in XML for the types of objects allowed in MECASP: Java code, databases, graphical objects, etc, or any combination of them.
- *XML models* – descriptions of customized applications and data structures maintained with MECASP. Each model results from the customization of the definitions in one or several meta-models.

The XML schema and the XML meta-models are predefined while the XML models are user-defined and application-specific. The XML (meta-)models integrate data, control and presentation levels in the application architecture.

From the *data* point of view, the (meta-)models are *object-oriented*, hierarchically organized in XML. Their common schema was conceived as general as possible, in order to comply with any type of application and data structure. It contains the following types of elements: Project, Object, Property, Attribute. The project is composed of objects, the objects are qualified by properties or attributes and can embed other (atomic or container-like) objects, and object properties are described by attributes. Relationships between objects are 'composition' and 'property inheritance'.

From the *control* point of view, the XML meta-models describe *actions*. MECASP manages predefined *change actions* upon objects. These actions can be: (1) standard actions like "create", "delete", "update", "move" objects or properties or (2) nonstandard actions like "compile" or "search and replace". In the meta-models, the actions are represented as particular types of properties of the objects upon which they are allowed to act. The actions can be executed by scripts or external tools, represented in the meta-models as particular types of objects.

From the *presentation* view point, the objects are described in meta-models by default values of their properties and attributes.

The definitions in the meta-models are copied and further customized in application- specific models. When an application is changed, the corresponding XML model is changed as well and a new version is created and managed in the repository. On the developer's request, a new version can also be created by merging two existing versions of the application. Each new version of the model contains customized definitions of the change actions applied to the original version.

XML repository architecture in MECASP differs from the existing XML-based software representations (e.g. [5], [6], [9], [13], [15]) by the meta-model level, which ensures the *reusability of the object definitions*, i.e. the definition of an object type can be used in several models and a model can contain object definitions from several meta-models. In the existing solutions, the models directly instantiate the XML Schema/ DTD. An object type must be redefined in each model it is involved in.

On the other hand, the software representation in MECASP includes explicit descriptions of the change actions and of the external tools for object changing. E.g., the action 'Search and replace' is defined in the XML meta-model as follows:

```
<Property name="__actionSandR" mandatory="true" inherit="true">
  <Attr name="type" value="__ACTION" />
  <Attr name="label" value="Search and Replace" />
  <Attr name="value" value="SearchAndReplace" />
  <Attr name="parameters" value="" />
  <Attr name="default" value="true" />
  <Attr name="launcher" value="Explorer" />
  <Attr name="Help_Message" value="" />    ... other attributes
</Property>
```

3 Management and Maintenance of XML Models in MECASP

In MECASP, all tools communicate by means of the *repository manager* (RM). RM manages the XML (meta-)models and co-ordinates the actions of the other tools in MECASP. It allows for building or extracting XML models, object versioning and deltas calculation (*deltas* contain the changes on the current version of an object).

This section describes the repository manager and its graphical interface (browser). RM implementation has raised many problems and has required new solutions, with a high degree of complexity and difficulty. The already implemented solutions have been previously mentioned, as intended solutions, in [7], [11], [12].

Open Source-Based Architecture of RM (Figure 1). For the implementation of RM, the following open source software products have been used:

- *Castor*, an open source data binding framework for Java;
- *XML:DB API* for Java development, as vendor neutral API for any XML:DB compliant database, used as storage support.
- *Slide*, a Jakarta framework which provides a consistent interface to a variety of repositories or data stores: JDBC databases, source code or document repositories, file systems etc. Its methods for content and structure management have been wrapped with MECASP RM functionality.
- *support* for (meta-)models and version graphs (Slide's content store). It can be (alternatively): (1) an XML database server, e.g. Xindice, eXist, etc or (2) a file system, or (3) a JDBC compliant relational DBMS (e.g MySQL), etc.
- *Xalan-Java*, an XSLT processor, used in MECASP for implementing the recovery from crashes.

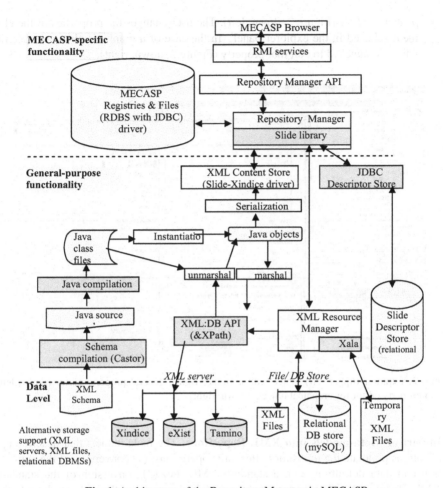

Fig. 1. Architecture of the Repository Manager in MECASP

Browser. The browser provides the interface for editing heterogeneous types of objects (e.g. Java code, database schema, graphical objects etc). It instantiates *four graphical clients*, which are views on the information inside the XML repository:

- *meta-model and model explorer.* The user navigates the list of existing meta-models and models, the hierarchy of objects in the application definition (see the left side in Figure 2).
- *object editor.* The user visualizes or edits the object selected in the explorer panel. This editor displays, using a unitary graphical representation, objects of different types (source code, DBs, forms) (see the right side in Figure 2).
- *contextual menu.* The user selects an action from a pop-up menu containing the actions allowed on the element selected in the explorer panel.

- *property editor* (Figure 2, down, left). The user changes the properties of the element selected in the explorer panel. In the case of a graphical object, a specific editor is launched to edit that property (Figure 2, down, right).

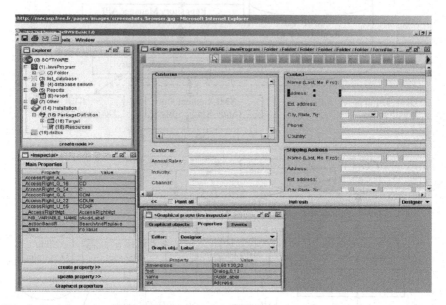

Fig. 2. Explorer (upper left), object editor (upper right), general property editor (down, left) and property editor for graphical objects (down, right)

Import of Meta-models into XML Repository. The meta-models that describe applications populate the repository after three operations: (1) conversion of the application and data definitions into a standard XML file; (2) conversion of the standard XML file into a MECASP-specific meta-model; (3) import of the meta-model into the XML repository (e.g. the import of a database schema as in Figure 3, left).

Export of Changes and Generation of the Changed Application. The changes on an XML model are transferred to the physical application described by the model. MECASP ensures the generation of the application from the model or only from a part of it. The generation process converts the nodes in the model into the corresponding files that compose the application. For instance, for the database schema imported as in Figure 3, MECASP provides a tool to generate DDL files representing the full database schema or only updates of it. The updates on the schema can be done from inside MECASP, as shown in Figure 3 (right).

Meta-model and Model Management. RM implements functions for: (1) *meta-model management*: create, delete meta-model, navigate the tree of models that instantiate a meta-model, navigate and retrieve the content of the meta-model, select definitions from the meta-model, identify the actions allowed for each object, etc; (2) *model management*: create model and create objects/ properties/ attributes according to the definitions in a meta-model, change objects/ properties/ attributes, navigate and retrieve objects/ properties/ attributes according to the selection criteria, etc.

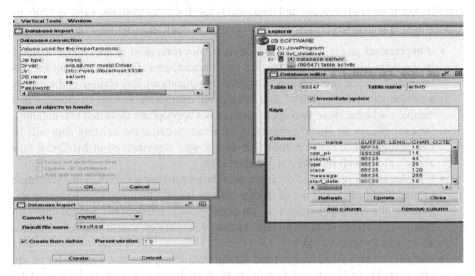

Fig. 3. Import and change of a database structure. On the left, a tool to import the database schema. On the right, a graphical interface to edit the database schema from inside MECASP

Management of Changes. When the user changes the definition of a physical object (e.g. the schema of a table in a database), the changes are reflected into the XML model for that object. Version merging applies to the versions of the model, not to the physical objects (as done by other tools).

Slide helps for version management, but not for delta management. RM provides its own mechanism for *delta management*. The deltas are bi-directional and allow merging and version restoration in both directions (forward and backward), in comparison with the existing tools, which allow only backward restoration. The bidirectional definition of the delta can be noticed in the deltas below, where old and new values are kept, in the definition of the actions 'move' and 'set attribute' for an object.

```
<Obj id="16" refObjMM="109" parentId="7">        <Obj id="14" refObjMM="114" parentId="7">
  <Attr name="type" value="delta" />              <Attr name="type" value="delta" />
  <Attr name="action"  value="moveObject" />      <Attr name="action" value="setObjectAttribute" />
  <Attr name="propagate" value="" />              <Attr name="propagate" value="" />
  <Attr name="objectId" value="726" />    ...      <Attr name="objectId" value="726" />   ...
  <Attr name="oldParentId" value="725" />         <Attr name="oldValue"value=" PositionnerDebut"/>
  <Attr name="newParentId" value="690" />         <Attr name="newValue"  value="BoiteMessage "/>
</Obj>                                            </Obj>
```

RM has its own mechanism for *delta interpretation*. For example, when a field is deleted in a table, a trigger is fired to delete the references to the field in all windows, although, in the repository, the delete action is stored only once. So, during the version restoration or version merging, the change is adapted to the current context.

The most important tool in MECASP is the merger, used for merging the changes on heterogeneous applications and data structures. It differs from the existing tools by the following features:

- it implements an algorithm for the *semantic interpretation of the change actions*. In the delta-like files of the existing version managers (files that contain the differences between two versions of the same application), any change is tracked by a combination of the 'delete' and/ or 'append' operations. In case of changes in a database schema, these two operations are not appropriate to switch two columns, for example, in an already populated database, because the existing data will be lost during 'delete'. So, a 'move' operation was implemented in MECASP (see above), along with its semantic interpretation.
- it implements a *rule-based decision mechanism for conflict resolution*. According to predefined rules, the list of change actions is simplified and the change operations in the merged versions are chronologically interleaved. Special types of change operations (e.g. compile, search and replace etc), also tracked in deltas, are treated by specific rules.
- it creates change files, further used for the installation of a new version for an application. These files depend on the type of application. For example, for a database application, they are SQL scripts and for a Java project, they compose the new executable file.

Utility Functions of the Repository Manager. Because *multi-user* is the basic MECASP working method, the product implements *locking and transaction mechanisms*. The hierarchical representation of the XML models requires specific mechanisms for locking and transaction management on XML hierarchical objects. These mechanisms are not yet implemented in the existing open source XML database servers [10]. For MECASP, they have been implemented from scratch.

MECASP also implements a synchronous *refresh mechanism*. Each user registered to certain objects in a model can refresh its screen with the definitions of those objects, as modified by the other members of the team. Repository and RM crashes are prevented by a specific mechanism for *recovery from crashes*.

4   Related Research Results. Comparison with MECASP

Many of research results are related to separate aspects of MECASP implementation: representation of software and data structures, generation of XML meta-models from existing applications, version management and merging algorithms, management of the changes in XML documents, transaction management and locking etc. MECASP is meant to solve pending issues in all these fields (see also [7], [11], [12]).

Issues regarding software integration and maintenance and software deployment using XML descriptions of the software have already been approached by the research communities. Representation languages of the software architectures (e.g. [17], [8], [20]) have been adapted to XML (e.g. [5], [6], [9]).

Research results have also been obtained for the automatic generation of XML documents from MOF meta-models [1], UML [22], relational schemas [13], for the semantic enhancement of XML schemas [15], for the XML representation of parallel adaptive components [4], etc. The basic *limits* of these XML representations of software, in comparison with the representation in MECASP, are:

- software definitions cannot be reused in several XML models, because these models directly instantiate XML Schema/ DTD. In MECASP, the reusability is solved by the intermediate XML meta-model.
- object changing behaviour is not explicitly represented. In MECASP, the change actions on objects and the external tools they might call are explicitly defined in XML meta-models.
- they either are not concerned with the representation of the changes or do not treat the changes in XML documents from the semantic point of view, but only from the literal or structural viewpoint. In MECASP, the change actions are treated from semantic viewpoint. Versioning and detecting changes in XML documents are still subject to debates (e.g. [3], [16], [18], [19]).

Transaction management and locking on XML databases (e.g. [10]) are still in an incipient research stage and do not have practical results. In MECASP, these mechanisms have been implemented from scratch.

The queries on XML documents and the existing tools for their execution usually confine to the literal or structural retrieval of the information [19], [21]. The same limit is with respect to the merging of XML documents, which confines to the textual merging and conflict resolution. Instead, in MECASP, queries and merging are semantically treated.

5   Conclusions

This paper briefly described the representation of the software and of the changes on it in MECASP-specific XML (meta-)models. It also presented the architecture and functions of the repository manager, the main components of the browser and the main functions and features of the MECASP merger.

The major advantage of MECASP based on the external XML-based description of the applications/ data structures is the possibility to maintain heterogeneous types of applications/ data structures (in comparison with the existing version managers which can maintain only text files). Another benefit is the conceptual integration of applications/ data structures in a virtual context (including in ASP mode), independently of the implementation platform. Although not relying on a standard proposal for obtaining platform independence (e.g. [20]), the simplicity and generality of the proposed representation and the portability of the tools that manage it, make it flexible and adaptable to any type of application and virtual context.

Starting in 2004, MECASP will be distributed in open source from the site http://mecasp.free.fr and from the SourceForge site.

References

1. Blanc X., Rano A., LeDelliou.: Generation automatique de structures de documents XML a partir de meta-models MOF, Notere, 2000
2. Cederqvist P. et al.: Version Management with CVS, http://www.cvshome.org/
3. Chien S-Y., Tsotras V.J., Zaniolo C.: Version Management of XML Documents. 3rd International Workshop on the Web and Databases (WebDB'2000), Texas, 2000.
4. Courtrai L., Guidec F., Maheo Y.: Gestion de ressources pour composants paralleles adaptables. Journees Composants adaptables, Oct. 2002, Grenoble
5. Dashofy E.M., Hoek A., Taylor R.: A Highly-Extensible, XML-based Architecture Description Language. Working IEE/ IFIP Conference on Software Architecture, 2001
6. Dashofy E.M.: Issues in generating Data Bindings for an XML Schema-based Language. Conf. on XML Technology and Software Engineering, 2001
7. Galatescu A., Florian V., Costea L.., Conescu D.: Issues in Implementing an Open Source-based XML Repository Manager for Application Maintenance and Adaptation. 3rd Workshop on Open Source Software Engineering, Oregon, USA, May 2003
8. Garlan D., Monroe R., Wile D.: Acme: Architectural Description of Component-Based Systems. Foundations of Component-based Systems, Cambridge Univ Press, 2000
9. Hall R.S., Heimbigner D., Wolf A.L.: Specifying the Deployable Software Description Format in XML, CU-SERL-207-99, University of Colorado
10. Helmer S., Kanne C., Moerkotte G.: Isolation in XML Bases. Technical Report of University of Mannheim, 2001.
11. Isnard E., Bercaru R., Galatescu A., Florian V., Costea L., Conescu D, Perez. E: An XML Repository Manager for Software Maintenance and Adaptation, XML Database Symp., Berlin, 2003
12. Isnard E., Mathey J., Nesnidal P., Galatescu A., Florian V., Costea L., Conescu D., Bercaru R., Perez E.: XML-based Tools for Managing the Evolution of Heterogeneous Software. Ws on Principles of Software Evolution (IWPSE 2003), Helsinki, Finland, 2003
13. Lee D., Mani M., Chu W.: Efective Schema Conversions between XML and Relational Models. Workshop on Knowledge Transformation (at ECAI), France, 2002.
14. Linthicum D.: Enterprise Application Integration. Addison-Wesley, 2000
15. Mani M., Lee D., Muntz R.: Semantic Data Modeling using XML Schemas, 20th Int'l Conf. on Conceptual Modeling (ER), Yokohama, Japan, 2001.
16. Marian A., Abiteboul S., Cobena G., Mignet L.: Change-Centric Management of Versions in an XML Warehouse, 27th Intl Conf. on Very Large DataBases, Italy, 2001
17. Open Group: Architecture Description Markup Language (ADML). 2002, http://www.opengroup.org/
18. Wang Y., DeWitt D. J., Cai J.: X-Diff: An Effective Change Detection Algorithm for XML Documents. 19th Intl. Conference on Data Engineering (ICDE 2003), India 2003,

19. Wang F., Zaniolo C.: Temporal Queries in XML Document Archives and Web Warehouses. Proc. of 10th Intl. Symp. on Temporal Representation and Reasoning and 4th International Conference on Temporal Logic, Queensland, Australia, July 2003.
20. OMG: Model Driven Architecture, http://www.omg.org/mda/
21. Papakonstantinou Y: Quering Distributed Data using XML. Talk UC Berkeley, Oct 2002.
22. Suzuki J.: UML eXchange Format, http://www.yy.ics.keio.ac.jp/~suzuki/project/uxf/

A Component Language for Hybrid Solver Cooperations*

Eric Monfroy[1] and Carlos Castro[2]

[1] LINA, Université de Nantes, France
[2] Universidad Técnica Federico Santa María, Valparaíso, Chile
Eric.Monfroy@lina.univ-nantes.fr, Carlos.Castro@inf.utfsm.cl

Abstract. In this paper, we use a simple component language to design solver cooperations for solving constrained optimisation problems. The cooperations we consider are hybrid: they use both complete and incomplete methods in order to take advantage of their respective assets. Our language enables us to carry out some more exotic cooperations than the usual "algorithmic" ones. We present some experimental results that show the benefits of such hybrid cooperations in terms of efficiency.

1 Introduction

Constraint Satisfaction Optimisation Problems (CSOP) provide a general framework for modeling many practical applications such as planning, scheduling, timetabling, and so on. Solving a CSOP consists in assigning values to variables in such a way that the constraints are satisfied and the objective function is optimised [12, 1]. We may distinguish two main classes of techniques (*solvers*) to solve this kind of problems. On one hand, *complete methods* aim at exploring the whole search space in order to find all solutions satisfying the set of constraints or to detect that the problem is unsatisfiable. Constraint Programming (based on constraint propagation and enumeration) is a complete technique that solves optimisation problems by adding constraints to impose better bounds on the objective function until an unsatisfiable problem is reached. On the other hand, *incomplete methods* mainly rely on the use of heuristics to provide a more efficient exploration of interesting areas of the search space. For example, *local search* techniques (such as Hill-Climbing) explore the search space by moving from a point to one of its neighborhood. A fitness function evaluates the benefit of such moves to guide the search towards a local optimum. Complete solvers can compute global optimum but they generally become very slow for hard problems, whereas incomplete methods can obtain some local solutions very quickly. A common idea is to build more efficient and robust solvers by making cooperate complete and incomplete methods. The benefit of the local search+constraint programming hybridization does not have to be proven (see [4, 5, 9, 10]).

---

* The authors have been partially supported by the Franco-Chilean INRIA-CONICYT project Cocars.

T. Yakhno (Ed.): ADVIS 2004, LNCS 3261, pp. 192–202, 2004.

Nowadays, very efficient constraint solvers are available. The challenge is to make them cooperate in order to: 1) solve hybrid problems that cannot be handled by a single solver, 2) improve quality of solutions (e.g., for optimisation problems), 3) improve solving efficiency (e.g., using specific solvers for parts of problems), and 4) reuse solvers to reduce implementation costs. In [6], a component language has been proposed for designing and implementing solver cooperations. These components enable one to manage computation, control, interaction, and coordination of solvers. In this paper, we are concerned with the design of hybrid cooperations (local search and constraint programming) using the component language of [6]: our goal is to design some usual "algorithmic" cooperations (such as master-slave combinations, or fixed point of solvers) and to propose some more exotic cooperations (such as parallel hybrid cooperation and concurrent hybrid cooperations). The main contribution of this paper is to show how simply exotic hybrid cooperations can be designed using our component language. We also show the benefit of such cooperations in terms of efficiency.

To this end, in Section 2 we improve the language of [6]. This language can be seen as a simple coordination language [8] for solver cooperation. It is composed of a set of interaction components that control some external agents (such as solvers) by managing the data flow. These components can be grouped into patterns to simplify the programming process and to enable code reuse. In Section 3, we consider two solvers, one based on constraint programming (Forward Checking), and the other one on local search (Hill-Climbing). We then design and specify some hybrid solver cooperations using our component language. These cooperations have been implemented and some experimental results are reported in Section 4. We conclude and give some ideas for further work in Section 5.

2   A Component Language

Our language is composed of a set of interaction components that control the execution of external agents by managing the data flow. A set of components can be seen as a simple coordination language (see e.g., [2]). External agents are computational agents that can be seen as some kinds of functions with a local memory. The data flow is composed of two types of messages: data messages, such as constraints, and control messages, such as Boolean values. In order to specify more complex behaviors, we introduce the notion of pattern as a set of connected components and patterns. Patterns also simplify the design of a solver cooperation by allowing code re-use. A formal definition of these concepts and their specification in terms of concurrent rules are given in [3].

2.1   Notion of Components

Interaction components (components in short) are entities that are connected to each other to exchange data and control messages. A component can internally use some agents: these agents can be seen as call-back functions with their own memory. Locally, a component has input and output ports, i.e., some opening to the outside world. Since ports are used as identifiers to exchange data among components, their name must be unique. Messages are stored on input ports using a buffer that is managed in a First In First Output (FIFO) way until they are read/consumed, one by one, by components. A component is represented by a term as follows:

$$\text{component\_name}([p_1, \ldots, p_n], [a_1, \ldots, a_m])$$

where $[p_1, \ldots, p_n]$ is the list of ports of the component, and $[a_1, \ldots, a_m]$ is the list of agents that can be used by the component (when the list of agents is empty it can be omitted).

A component is in a sleeping state. When the messages it is waiting for are received, it becomes active: it reads/consumes the awaited messages, then it executes some agents (if needed), and finally it sends some messages before going back in a sleeping state. Components execute concurrently and cannot be interrupted. Note that a component is not blocking and it stays in a sleeping state when only some of the messages it is waiting for have been received.

In the following, upper-case letter will represent variables (either ports of agent) whereas lower case letters will represent instances (either ports of agent).

2.2   The Language: The Set of Components

The component language that we propose in this paper is an improvement of the one introduced by ourselves in [6]. The main differences concern:

- an init component has been added to initialise data flow,
- the $y - junction$ component clarifies channel connections,
- a channel is now a component, and
- the first component has been omitted since we do not need it in this paper.

The syntax of each component is given in Table 1 and their graphical representation is given in Figure 1. We use solid lines to represent connectors carrying

Table 1. Syntax of components

connect($[In, Out]$)		
y($[In_1, In_2, Out]$)	init($[Out], [F]$)	trans($[In, Out], [F]$)
sync($[In_1, In_2, Out], [F]$)	sieve($[In_d, In_c, Out], [F]$)	dup($[In, Out_1, Out_2]$)

data messages, dashed lines for connectors carrying control messages, and dotted lines and components to represent possible (but not mandatory) components. We now explain informally the operational semantics of each of the components of our language:

Connectors. A connect component represents a directional channel linking 2 ports: a message stored on the FIFO buffer of the output port Out is forwarded

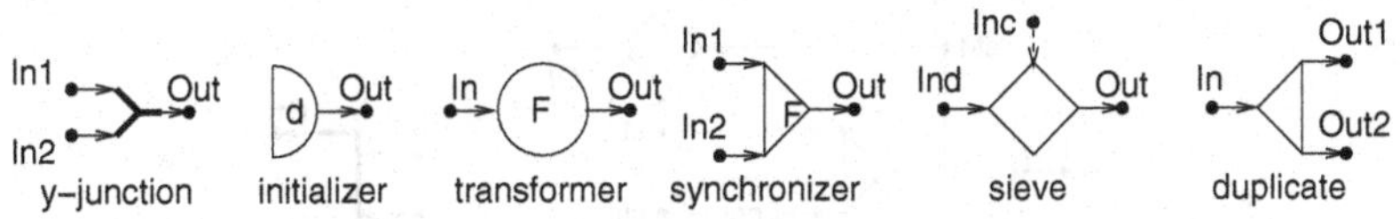

Fig. 1. Graphical description of components

to the input port In. Thus, messages transfered through a connector are read in the same order they are produced. For sake of simplicity, in order to limit the number of ports and components, we will generally omit connect components by giving the same name to an output and an input port (meaning these two ports are linked by a connector); on graphical representations, connectors will be represented by lines connecting components.

Y-Junctions. A Y-junction component links two input ports, In_1 and In_2, to the output port Out: each time there is a message on either port In_1 or port In_2 it is forwarded to the port Out.

Initializers. An init component puts data d, given by an agent producing a constant value, on an output port Out. This type of components is meant for initializing data flow, i.e., at the beginning, all channels are empty and thus no component can react.

Transformers. A component of this type has an input port In, an output port Out, and an agent parameter F: when the component receives a message X on port In, it consumes it, then it executes the agent parameter F on message X, and finally it sends the result on port Out.

Synchronizers. These components synchronize two components by the mediating of their messages: they wait for two messages, one on the input port In_1 and one on the input port In_2, then they execute an agent F using the two messages, and finally they put the result on the output port Out.

Sieve. A sieve component waits for a data message X on the input port In_d and for a control message on In_c. If a *true* value is received on In_c, then the data message X is put on Out; otherwise, X is consumed but no action is performed. Such a component blocks a message until a control message arrives, and deletes it if the control message is *false*.

Duplicate. A *duplicate* component duplicates a dataflow: when it gets a message X on the input port In, it returns a copy of X on both Out_1 and Out_2.

2.3   Patterns

A program written with this component language is restricted to a set of components. In order to simplify programming and to enable re-use of code, we

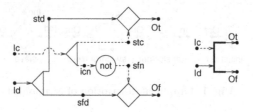

Fig. 2. Switch pattern

introduce the notion of pattern. A pattern is a parameterized piece of program defined by induction: a set of components is a pattern, and a set of patterns is a pattern. Variables appearing in the definition of a pattern are the parameters of this pattern. Port names can be seen as local variables of a pattern: several occurences of a pattern, possibly different, such as different instantiations, can appear in a program, and different patterns can use internally the same port name without referencing to the same port. Thus, we consider a naming process that uniquely renames ports used in more than one pattern.

We now present two patterns of interactions that are widely used in solver cooperation: switch and fixed point patterns. A pattern is represented by a new graphical pattern when specified, or by a square box labelled with its name.

Switch. A *switch* pattern can be graphically described as shown in Figure 2: its implementation (left) and its representation to be re-used in other patterns (right). A *switch* pattern transfers a data message to one of its two output ports depending on the value of a control message. More precisely, a switch pattern synchronizes a data message d received on Id with a control message c received on Ic: if c is *true*, d is sent to the output port Ot, otherwise d is sent to Of. This switch pattern can be defined, and thus implemented, by:

$$\text{switch}([Id, Ic, Ot, Of]) =$$
$$\left\{ \begin{array}{ll} \text{dup}([Id, icn, stc]), & \text{trans}([icn, sfn], [not]), \\ \text{dup}([Id, std, sfd]), & \text{sieve}([std, stc, Ot]), \quad \text{sieve}([sfd, sfn, Of]) \end{array} \right\}$$

Fixed Point. A fixed point pattern (see Figure 3) applies iteratively a given solver cooperation (a pattern) until the output of the cooperation does not change any more. More precisely, a data message m is received on the input

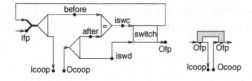

Fig. 3. Fixed point pattern: implementation (left) and representation (right)

port Ifp. This message is duplicated and forwarded to a pattern representing a cooperation by sending m to $Icoop$ (an input port of a pattern). The copy of m (on port $before$) and the result of the cooperation pattern applied on m (on port $after$) are compared in a synchronizer to test equality (using an $equal$ agent) of the two data messages. This synchronizer generates a control message $true$ or $false$ which is used in a switch to either send the result to the output of the fixed point (Ofp) or to the input port of the fixed point to treated again by the cooperation. The fixed point pattern is implemented by:

$$\mathsf{fp}([Ifp, Ofp, Icoop, Ocoop]) =$$
$$\left\{ \begin{array}{ll} \mathsf{dup}([Ifp, before, Icoop]), & \mathsf{sync}([before, after, iswc], [equal]), \\ \mathsf{dup}([Ocoop, after, iswd]), & \mathsf{switch}([iswd, iswc, Ofp, Ifp]) \end{array} \right\}$$

3 Prototyping Hybrid Cooperations

We now design some solver cooperations for optimisation problems. An optimisation problem consists in a set of constraints and an objective function to be minimised or maximised. The goal is to compute a point that optimises the objective function and satisfies the set of constraints. This is done by incrementally computing some *best bounds* for the optimisation function until the optimum is reached or the solvers cannot improve anymore the current best bound.

3.1 The Solvers

We consider $fc(t)$ and bn, two elementary solver agents. Given an optimisation problem and a current best bound for the objective function, $fc(t)$ and bn try to improve the current best bound. These agents have a local memory in which they store the optimisation problem. None of these solver agents are idempotent: if they are requested, they can try to improve again the current best bound that they computed. Thus, the solver agents have to receive only once the optimisation problem with the current best bound in order to improve the best bound. Then, each time they receive a new bound, they will produce a better bound using the problem they have in memory. When they cannot improve the bound they return the best bound they received. Sending only once the problem significantly reduces the data flow. When there is no current best bound the current best bound can be initialised to $+\infty$ or $-\infty$ for minimisation problems or maximisation problems, respectively.

$fc(t)$ and bn are encapsulated into transformer components that are used inside a solver pattern (Figure 4) in order to receive the first time they are used a problem and a best bound, and the next times only a best bound. This pattern has two input ports (Pb and Op to receive a problem and bounds respectively) and one output port (Out) to send improved best bounds. The first time the pattern is used is determined by an initializer component that sends the control message $true$ to a sieve component. The current best bound (received on Op) is forwarded to a synchronizer, in which it is combined (using the c_first agent) with the problem (received on Pb). This combination (problem and best bound)

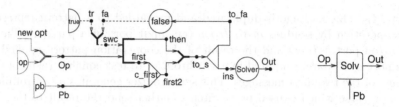

Fig. 4. Solver pattern: in terms of components (left), its representation (right)

is then sent to the solver agent that produces a new best bound (sent on *Out*). The combination is also sent to a transformer that transforms any data message into the *false* control message (*false* agent). This *false* message determines that the solver has already run (thus, it has a problem in memory and it just requires a new best bound). Using the *false* message, the sieve will forward the next current best bound (received on *Op*) to the solver and to the *false* agent (to specify again that the solver already run). The pattern is defined by:

solver($[Op, Pb, Out], [Solver]$) =

$$\left\{ \begin{array}{l} \text{init}([tr], [true]), \quad \text{y}([fa, tr, swc]), \quad \text{switch}([Op, swc, first, then]), \\ \text{sync}([first, Pb, first2], [c\_first]), \quad \text{y}([first2, then, to\_s]), \\ \text{dup}([to\_s, ins, to\_fa]), \quad \text{trans}([to\_fa, fa], [false]), \quad \text{trans}([ins, Out], [Solver]) \end{array} \right\}$$

Note that on Figure 4 components in dotted line are not part of the solver pattern: they are used to initialize and to update data of the solvers. However, this initializations and updates could come from other patterns. Similarly, on the next figures, dotted components represent possible initializations of cooperations.

We now give a brief description of the algorithms used in $fc(t)$ and bn.

fc(t) is a solver based on Forward Checking, a technique specially designed to solve CSP. Forward Checking is based on a backtracking procedure but it includes filtering to eliminate values that the variables cannot take in any solution to the set of constraints. This interleaving process between variable enumeration and local consistency verification is carried out until an assignment of values to variables satisfying all constraints is found or an empty domain is obtained for some variable due to the consistency verification. Some heuristics have been proposed in the literature to improve the search of Forward Checking. For example, in our tests we include the minimum domain criteria to select variables. $fc(t)$ is based on standard Forward Checking algorithms, but it works at most t units of time: when it finds a solution in less than t time units, it returns it; otherwise, it returns the best bound it got as an input.

bn, the best feasible neighbor, works as follow: given a feasible solution, it generates a set of neighbor solutions using the 2-opt heuristics proposed by Kernighan. In general, the notion of neighbors means the generation of a new solution by modifying an old solution. The 2-opt heuristics was proposed for problems such as the Traveling Salesperson Problem: given a tour visiting all cities a new one can obtained interchanging the position of two cities. After

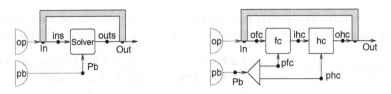

Fig. 5. Full-search pattern (right) and Fixed point of a sequential cooperation (right)

the generation of all neighbors, each solution is verified in order to select the feasible ones. The feasible solution giving the best value for the objective function is returned (this acceptance criteria is generally known as best improvement). The repeated application of *bn* until no more better neighbor can be found corresponds to a Hill-Climbing algorithm.

3.2 Full Search

fc and *bn* are not idempotent: they can be applied several times to improve their results until a fixed point is reached. This can be performed using the full-search pattern (Figure 5) based on a fp pattern:

$$\text{full-search}([In, Out, Pb], [Solver]) =$$
$$\{ \text{solver}([ins, Pb, outs], [Solver]), \quad \text{fp}([In, Out, ins, outs]) \}$$

Global Optimum. In order to compute a global optimum, one need to completely explore the search space. This can be achieved using the *fc* solver inside a full-search pattern: each time *fc* finds a new best bound (local optimum), this bound is used again by *fc* (i.e., a *cut* that constrains more the problem and states that the next bound must be better than the current one). When *fc* cannot improve the current bound, the global optimum has been found. Finding a global optimum can be done by instantiating the full-search pattern with *fc*:

$$\text{global-optimum}([In, Out, Pb]) = \{ \text{full-search}([In, Out, Pb], [fc]) \}$$

Hill-Climbing. Hill-Climbing consists in applying iteratively our *bn* solver until *bn* cannot improve anymore the current best bound. The *hc* pattern is an instantiation of the full-search pattern with *bn*:

$$\text{hc}([In, Out, Pb]) = \{ \text{full-search}([In, Out, Pb], [bn]) \}$$

3.3 Fixed Point of a Sequential Cooperation

In this cooperation, we first apply $fc(t)$ looking for a first solution; then we apply *hc* (i.e., fixed point of *bn*); and we loop on this sequence until a fixed point is reached. The idea is to give a good starting bound to *bn*. Then *bn* is exploited as much as possible since this is a fast solver. Applying again $fc(t)$ can be seen as a diversification: the bound is improved and is certainly in another part of the search space; this plays the role of a restart for hc. This cooperation pattern is:

$$\mathsf{fp\text{-}seq}([In, Out, Pb], [FC]) = \left\{ \begin{array}{l} \mathsf{solver}([ofc, pfc, ihc], [FC]), \ \mathsf{hc}([ihc, phc, ohc]), \\ \mathsf{fp}([In, Out, ofc, ohc]), \ \mathsf{dup}([Pb, pfc, phc]) \end{array} \right\}$$

where FC is an agent parameter that will be instantiated by the solver agent $fc(t)$. Note that on Figure 5, hc is a hc pattern (a fixed point of the bn agent) while fc is the solver pattern instantiated with the fc agent.

3.4 Parallel Cooperation

We now propose a parallel cooperation pattern:

$\mathsf{par}([In, Pb, Out], [FC, BN]) =$

$$\left\{ \begin{array}{l} \mathsf{fp}([In, Out, in\_coop, out\_coop]), \ \ \mathsf{dup}([in\_coop, in\_opt\_fc, in\_opt\_bn]), \\ \mathsf{solver}([in\_opt\_fc, pb\_fc, out\_fc], [FC]), \ \ \mathsf{dup}([Pb, pb\_fc, pb\_bn]), \\ \mathsf{sync}([out\_fc, out\_bn, out\_coop], [best]), \mathsf{solver}([in\_opt\_bn, pb\_bn, out\_bn], [BN]) \end{array} \right\}$$

where $best$ is an agent that takes the best of two bounds, FC and BN are parameters that will be instantiated by the solver agents $fc(t)$ an bn, respectively. In this cooperation, $fc(t)$ and bn run in parallel. When the both of them return a new bound, the best of these two bounds is sent again to $fc(t)$ and bn. And so on, until neither $fc(t)$ nor bn can improve the best bound (detected by the fixed point pattern).

The drawback of this cooperation is that $fc(t)$ and bn are synchronized. Since bn is generally faster than $fc(t)$, it will have to wait. A solution consists in setting t to a small value. But in this case, $fc(t)$ can become inefficient and useless (not enough time to compute a new bound). Note also that the global optimum is computed only when instantiating FC by $fc(\infty)$.

3.5 Concurrent Cooperative Cooperation

bn is generally faster than $fc(t)$. Hence, we do not want it to be delayed by $fc(t)$ (i.e., waiting for a solution of $fc(t)$). The cc cooperation works as follows: as soon as bn finds a new bound, it looks for a bound from $fc(t)$: if there is one,

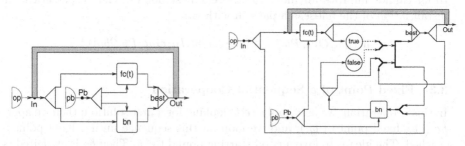

Fig. 6. Parallel cooperation (left) and Concurrent cooperative cooperation (right)

the best of both bounds is computed (using the *best* agent) and sent to bn and $fc(t)$; note that in this case, the bound is sent to bn via the sieve to "consume" the *false* control message generated by bn. Otherwise, the best bound of bn is sent again to bn so it can run without waiting for $fc(t)$.

The cooperation terminates when the fixed point of $fc(t)$ is reached. Hence, the global optimum is computed when instantiating the cc pattern with $fc(\infty)$. Note that it can happen that bn runs several times without being able to improve the best bound: this means that it reached its own fixed point, but that $fc(t)$ is still improving it; when $fc(t)$ will send a new best bound, bn will become effective again:

$$cc([In, Pb], [FC, BN]) =$$

$$\left\{ \begin{array}{l} \mathsf{dup}([Pb, pb1, pb2]), \ \mathsf{dup}([In, opt1, opt2]), \ \mathsf{fp}([opt1, Out, in\_coop, out\_coop]), \\ \mathsf{solver}([in\_coop, pb1, out\_fc], [FC]), \ \mathsf{solver}([in\_bn, pb2, out\_bn], [BN]), \\ \mathsf{y}([sfa, opt2, in\_bn]), \ \mathsf{dup}([out\_fc, to\_fa, bst2]), \ \mathsf{trans}([to\_fa, fa], [false]), \\ \mathsf{switch}([ds, cs, str, sfa]), \ \mathsf{sync}([to\_best, str, out\_best], [best]), \ \mathsf{y}([tr, fa, cs]), \\ \mathsf{dup}([out\_best, out\_coop, bst1]), \ \mathsf{trans}([to\_tr, tr], [true]), \ \mathsf{y}([bst1, bst2, ds]) \end{array} \right\}$$

4 Experimental Results

We have implemented ans tested some schemes of cooperation presented in this paper. To carry out the tests, we use the classical Capacity Vehicle Routing Problem (CVRP). Our objective is to minimise the total distance travelled by a fixed number of vehicles to satisfy all customers. Since we are just interested in evaluating cooperations, we simplified the $RC101$ problem [11] by adding capacity constraints. Table 2 presents results obtained when applying Forward Checking (FC) and Hill-Climbing (HC) alone (as defined in Section 3.2) and their cooperation schemes defined in Section 3.3. For example, we can see that the best value obtained by FC is $z = 357, 78$ after 5 instantiations in 111180 seconds. In general, applying a cooperation scheme, the results are better in terms of z than applying either FC or HC isolated. The first scheme of cooperation takes less time than the second one: the total time is mainly due to FC.

These encouraging results show the benefit of making cooperate complete and incomplete methods. The language we present in this paper gives a uniform

Table 2. Experimental results

#	FC		HC		FC + HC			FC (2 sec) + HC		
	t	z	t	z	solver	t	z	solver	t	z
1	29803	383,32	10	1108,42	FC	29803	383,32	FC	29803	383,32
2	31545	367,00	370	816,46	HC	30023	341,42	FC	31545	367,00
3	35200	364,61	661	583,33	HC	30214	294,99	FC	33200	364,61
4	109537	359,83	991	486,11				HC	35491	294,99
5	111180	357,78	1311	429,23						
6			1592	405,08						
7			1882	395,09						
8			2173	387,94						
9			2453	380,49						
10			2734	373,85						
11			3014	368,03						
12			3445	366,19						
13			3725	360,05						
14			4005	356,31						
15			4276	355,86						

and flexible way to express both complete and incomplete methods, and their cooperations as well. We are currently working on the implementation of parallel and concurrent patterns defined in Sections 3.4 and 3.5.

5 Conclusions

We improved and used the component language proposed in [6] to design some hybrid (local search and constraint programming) solver cooperations. We showed that our language is well suited to design usual sequential cooperation, but also concurrent and parallel cooperations in which more interaction between agents must be settled. The experimentations show the efficiency of cooperations designed with our language and the efficiency of hybrid constraint solving. In the future, we plan to develop a generic and complete implementation of our language in order to ease cooperation design. We also plan to design and develop some finer strategies using the model presented in [7]: in this model, basic functions of local search (neighborhood computation) and constraint programming (split and reductions) are "homogeneized" and considered at the same level, and thus, are handled by the same application mechanism.

References

1. K.R. Apt. *Principles of Constraint Programming*. Cambridge Univ. Press, 2003.
2. F. Arbab. *Manifold 2.0 Reference Manual*. CWI, The Netherlands, May 1997.
3. C. Castro, E. Monfroy, and C. Ringeissen. A Rule Language for Interaction. In *Recent Advances in Constraints 2003*, volume 3010 of *LNAI*. Springer, 2004.
4. D. Habet, C. M. Li, L. Devendeville, and M. Vasquez. A hybrid approach for sat. In *Proc. of CP'2000*, number 1894 in LNCS. Springer, 2000.
5. N. Jussien and O. Lhomme. Local search with constraint propagation and conflict-based heuristics. *Artificial Intelligence*, 2002.
6. E. Monfroy and C. Castro. Basic Components for Constraint Solver Cooperations. In *Proc. of ACM SAC'2003*. ACM Press, 2003.
7. E. Monfroy, F. Saubion, and T. Lambert. On hybridization of local search and constraint propagation. In *Proc. of ICLP'04*, number xxxx in LNCS. Springer, 2004. To appear.
8. G.A. Papadopoulos and F. Arbab. Coordination models and languages. In *Advances in Computers – The Engineering of Large Systems*, volume 46, pages 329–400. Academic Press, 1998.
9. G. Pesant and M. Gendreau. A view of local search in constraint programming. In *Proc. of CP'96*, number 1118 in LNCS. Springer, 1996.
10. P. Shaw. Using constraint programming and local search methods to solve vehicle routing problems. In *Proc. of CP'98*, number 1250 in LNCS. Springer, 1998.
11. M. Solomon. Algorithms for the vehicle routing and scheduling problem with time window constraints. *Operations Research*, pages 254–365, 1987.
12. Edward Tsang. *Foundations of Constraint Satisfaction*. Academic Press, 1993.

Non-interleaved Quadtree Node Codification*

Mariano Pérez, Marcos Fernández, and Ricardo Olanda

Institute of Robotics, University of Valencia,
Polígono de la Coma, s/n.
Aptdo. 22085, 46071-PATERNA, Spain
{Mariano.Perez, Marcos.Fernandez, Ricardo.Olanda}@uv.es

Abstract. The usual quadtree node non-pointer codification is based on inter-leaved binary representations of node coordinates, in such a way that every operation that concerns to the spatial position or to the specific orientation of the region represented by the node needs to undo this interleaving process. So, the computation time of such operations is linear with the node depth. In this paper an alternative codification is presented called "non-interleaved codification". The new codification has a simpler management and a higher intuitiveness than current codifications that use the interleaving approach. The proposed codification is more efficient than previous ones for the following set of operations: generating the node codes from the spatial coordinates, recovering original coordinates from the node codes, and performing topological operations where explicit or implicit reference is made to node location, for instance, checking if two nodes are adjacent, evaluating distances between nodes, evaluating relative orientation, etc. The proposed codification performs all these operations in $O(1)$ time, independently from the node depth.

1 Introduction

In recent years, spatially referenced information has reached a strong popularity in several fields of research and Information Technology applications. Thanks to the broad extension of these applications, a wide set of data structures has been developed to manage spatial data.

Probably, one of the most extended data structure for spatial information representation is the quadtree [9], and amongst the different kinds of quadtrees, the region quadtree [4, 7] is the most used. The region quadtrees are hierarchical data structures which present a recursive decomposition of the space in regular regions. The resulting subspaces from the partition of the original space are usually square blocks that are called quadrants. The fact that quadrants are regular makes it easy searching operations and reduces the amount of information associated with each node.

Region quadtrees can be represented in memory as a dynamic tree (using pointers), they can be stored using a set of linear codes (without using pointers) or using Depth First (DF) expressions (also without using pointers) [8]. From the linear codes and DF-expressions, it is possible to reproduce the hierarchical quadtree structure.

---

* Supported by the Spanish MCYT under Grant TIC-2003-08154-C06-04.

T. Yakhno (Ed.): ADVIS 2004, LNCS 3261, pp. 203–212, 2004.
© Springer-Verlag Berlin Heidelberg 2004

Pointer-based approach is ill-suited for implementing disk-based structures. DF-expressions are very compact but they are ill-suited to perform individual elements access operations, and there is also a lack of performance when spatial references are made. So, from now, our discussion is focused on the linear codes approach. Memory requirements in the case of linear codes is lower than using pointers, but it is possible to regenerate the whole structure from only a few leaf nodes, as it happens for linear quadtrees [2].

An important issue to take into account is the needed time to build the linear codes. This aspect becomes critical in applications like dynamic data bases, where update and access operations are performed in a mixed way. A high construction time for the linear codes may result in a serious lost of performance for data access operations [3].

2   Previous Linear Codifications

There are several ways of implementing linear codes that are able to identify the quadtree nodes, i.e. their location and their size. Usually the codification employs numbers in a base four or five digits, called locational codes. The digits of these numbers are directional codes which locates the node within the quadtree from the root node. Depending on the implementation, apart from the location code, the node level (depth of the leaf node within the quadtree) is also stored. The most popular linear implementations are the FL (Fixed Length), the FD (Fixed Depth) and the VL (Variable Length) [8]. FD codification is usually the one used in linear region quadtrees [11, 1].

All the indicated codifications hide the spatial location of the node because of the interleaving of the bits that represent x and y quadrant coordinates. In order to obtain these spatial coordinates, a process to undo the interleaving is needed. Its corresponding computation time is $O(n)$ (linear with the node level n). The same problem arises in the inverse process of de-codification.

It is possible to achieve an improvement in the computation time of the process by using bi-dimensional tables (lookup tables), which contain an entry for every possible x - y pair of values [8]. However, the amount of memory required for such a table is $2^N \times 2^N$ entries (where N is the maximum level of the quadtree nodes), but this memory size is not affordable in most of the cases. It is possible to reduce the amount of memory required for the lookup tables by decomposing the codification in group of m bits, and use a table with $2^m \times 2^m$ entries. Nevertheless, this solution is not optimal because it needs to build the table and needs to store it in memory, with the associated temporal and storage costs. Apart from this, the computation time of the codification / de-codification algorithm still is $O(n)$.

2.1   FL Locational Code

The FL locational code uses a fixed size code. This codification does not need an additional field to codify the node level. This information is implicit in the directional code. This is possible because the FL location code uses a base 5 digits, the extra digit can be set to an extra value, which is a "don't care". This value indicates the node is a leaf. Each digit can have the value 0,1,2,3,4 which indicates NW,NE, SW,SE and "don't care" directions respectively. The node level can be evaluated based on the number of digits different from the "don't care" which are present in the node codification.

2.2   VL Locational Code

The VL locational code is quite similar to FL locational code. It is also based on a base five sequence of digits. In this case, the value 0 indicates the "don't care" directional code, while the values 1,2,3, and 4 represent the directions NW, NE, SW and SE, respectively. The main difference between VL and FL is that VL has a variable length in the node codification. In this codification only the first "don't care" directional code is stored.

2.3   FD Codification

Among the three indicated codifications, the FD codification is the most popular in scientific literature. This is because is a base four code which allows the use of binary and logical operations to carry out the codification and de-codification processes. This is much more optimal than the use of the usual division operations.

FD codification is implemented as a structure with two fixed size fields. The first field, which stores the directional code, is a base 4-digit code-word call quadcode [6, 5]. The quadcode indicates the position and orientation of the node within the quadtree. The digit values are 0,1,2,3 and indicate the direction NW, NE, SW and SE, respectively. The second field indicates the node level.

The quadcode is a base 4 code. So, if N is the code length (which is the maximum number of tree levels), the code consists of a sequence of values:

$$q = q_1 q_2 ... q_N$$

where $q_i = 0, 1, 2, 3$ being $i = 1, 2, .., N$.

For each square block in which a quadrant is divided, a different number from 0 to 3 is assigned (see figure 1). Each new quadtree partition inherits the previous sequence of digits from its parent node and in the partition process a new value is added $q_i = 0, 1, 2, 3$ in order to have a unique characterization of each one of the new nodes (see figure 2).

Fig. 1. Quadrant and Quadcodes

In order to generate a quadcode q for a particular node from its spatial location, such as from its i and j relative coordinates from the left-top domain corner, it is possible to use the following equation [6]:

$$q \leftarrow \sum_{k=1}^{N} (2i_k + j_k) \cdot 4^{N-k} \tag{1}$$

Being i_k and j_k the k-binary digit of i and j.

To perform the opposite operation (recover the relative coordinates of the node from the quadcode) the following equation can be used [6]:

$$i \leftarrow \sum_{k=1}^{N} (q_k DIV 2) \cdot 2^{N-k}$$
$$j \leftarrow \sum_{k=1}^{N} (q_k MOD 2) \cdot 2^{N-k} \tag{2}$$

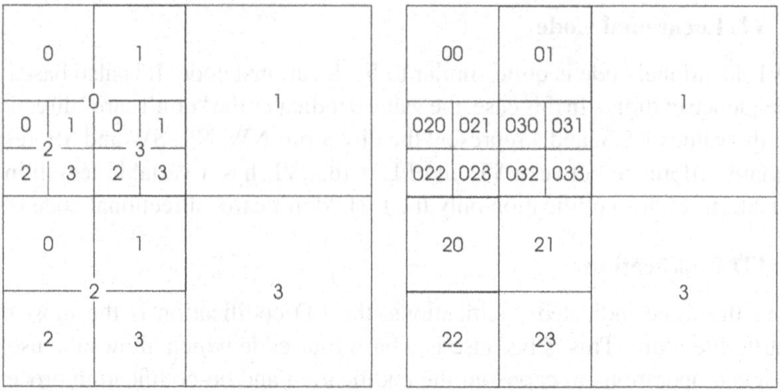

Fig. 2. Left: Quadrant Partition. Right: Quadcode partition representation

In the normal quadtree representations it is quite usual to have the need for evaluating the cartesian coordinates associated with a quadrant represented by a node in the quadtree. Also it is important to be able to evaluate neighboring relationships among nodes, for instance, when two nodes share some of its edges, which is its relative orientation; when they are not neighbors, which is the distance between them, compute etc. From the quadcode it is possible to calculate the previous values using the following procedures [6]:

- In order to evaluate the spatial location in cartesian coordinates of the left-bottom corner of a quadrant represented by a quadcode:

$$
\begin{aligned}
Pos_x(q) &= o_x + \tfrac{T}{2^N} \sum_{k=1}^{N}(q_k MOD\ 2) \cdot 2^{N-k} \\
Pos_y(q) &= o_y + \tfrac{T}{2^N} \sum_{k=1}^{N}(q_k DIV\ 2) \cdot 2^{N-k}
\end{aligned}
\tag{3}
$$

where n is the node level, T is the size of the grid, and (o_x, o_y) the cartesian position of the left-bottom square of the grid.

- To figure out the distance between two nodes p and q it is possible to use the equation:

$$
\begin{aligned}
D_x(p,q) &= |Pos_x(p) - Pos_x(q)| - L_x \\
D_y(p,q) &= |Pos_y(p) - Pos_y(q)| - L_y
\end{aligned}
\tag{4}
$$

where L_x is the length of x edge of the left node and L_y is the length of y edge of the bottom node.

- It is possible to prove that two nodes p and q are adjacent by evaluating if they simultaneously fulfill the following conditions:

$$
\begin{aligned}
D_x(p,q) \cdot D_y(p,q) &= 0 \\
D_x(p,q) + D_y(p,q) &\leq 0
\end{aligned}
\tag{5}
$$

3   Non-interleaved (NI) Codification

All the previously introduced codifications interleave the coordinates information to build the locational code in the bits sequence. As a consequence of the mixture of information, each action, where an implicit or explicit reference to spatial coordinates of the node should be made, requires a process of recovering this information (undoing the interleaving) before performing the action. This increases the computation time of the operation up to $O(n)$ (linear order with the node level).

In this section, an alternative codification is presented, where the spatial coordinates are not interleaved. Instead each coordinate is separated within the digits sequence of the code. This non-interleaved codification has variable memory size, but it is always inferior to the space required by FD, and similar or inferior to the one required by FL and VL. The new codification also integrates the node level information in the code (this property was not present in FD codification). Apart from that, the most important aspect about the new codification is its performance in the codification and de-codification processes, and also the improvement in performance to carry out operations such as evaluating the spatial position of a node, evaluating the distance between two nodes, testing if two nodes are adjacent, etc. The computation time of these operations is reduced to $O(1)$, instead of $O(n)$ offered by the previous codifications.

The new codification is based on the idea that the quadtree elements can be seen as the subset of elements of a pyramidal structure [10]. Pyramids are data structures more constrained than region quadtrees. They are usually defined as a $2^n \times 2^n$ matrices list, where n is the pyramid level $0 \leq n \leq N$. Pyramids are used as a representation of multi-resolution elements, which have an internal node of the pyramid containing an abstract of the information included in the nodes located below.

Each element in the pyramid is characterized by three integer values: (n, i, j), where n is the node level, which means the matrix index within the matrices list, and i and j are the indices within the matrix structure. The value of n is within the range of 0 to N, and the values of i and j inside of 0 to 2^n. The set of values (0,0,0) represents the root node.

The proposed codification uses the set of three values to codify the quadtree nodes, the values are sequentially packed in only one number in order to save memory storage space.

To carry out the packing process, the bits that define the code are divided into three parts. The first part (corresponding to low bits) has a fixed size and is used to store the node level. The other two parts have variable length (the same for both of them), and store the binary representation of the coordinates i and j without interleaving.

If the maximum node level in the quadtree is N (the numbering of levels start form zero for the root node), and the non-interleaved codification is used to represent a black and white image with a resolution of $2^N \times 2^N$ pixels, the number of bits used to codify the first par of the triple-value set is $\lceil \log_2(N+1) \rceil$, while the second and third parts need n bits. The length for the first part of the code is independent from the node level so it is only computed one time and this value is stored in memory, such as in a variable called S_N. The number of bits for the other two parts is variable and equal to the node level (see figure 3).

Let us see the process need for the non-interleaved codification to generate a node code from the set of values (n, i, j), and the inverse process that allows the extraction of these three values from node code. The processes required to perform other common operations on quadtrees are also revised.

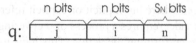

Fig. 3. Bits distribution in non-interleaved codification

The algorithm that allows the code generation from the three values representing the node is based on the following equation:

$$q \leftarrow ((j \ll (n + S_N)) + (i \ll S_N) + (n)) \tag{6}$$

where $\ll$ is the left bitwise binary operator, and S_N is the number of bits in the first part of the code. This number is the same for every node in the quadtree and its value is $\lceil \log_2(N + 1) \rceil$, where N is the maximum node level in the quadtree.

The inverse operation which recovers the values (n, i, j) from its codified format q, is based on the following equations:

$$\begin{cases} n \leftarrow (q \& M_S) \\ i \leftarrow ((q \ll n) \gg (n + S_N)) \\ j \leftarrow (q \gg (n + S_N)) \end{cases} \tag{7}$$

where $\&$ is the AND binary operator, and $\gg$ is the right bitwise operator; M_S represents a binary mask computed one time using the equation: $M_S = 2^{S_N} - 1$ and then stored in memory.

The presented codification allows to perform usual quadtree location operation in an easy way. For instance:

- To evaluate the coordinate nodes of child nodes. If we have a node (n, i, j), its child node located in the left-top quadrant has the coordinates $(n+1, 2i, 2j)$; the right-top $(n + 1, 2i + 1, 2j)$; the left-bottom $(n + 1, 2i, 2j + 1)$; and finally the right-bottom $(n + 1, 2i + 1, 2j + 1)$.
- To compute codes of neighbor nodes in the same quadtree level. If we have a node (n, i, j), another node at the same level of the quadtree, placed a distance (d_x, d_y) from the first one, has the coordinates $(n, i + d_x, j + d_y)$.
- To evaluate for a certain node with the coordinates (n, i, j), which are the coordinates (n_p, i_p, j_p) of its father node:

$$(n_p, i_p, j_p) = (n - 1, \left\lfloor \frac{i}{2} \right\rfloor, \left\lfloor \frac{j}{2} \right\rfloor)$$

where $n > 0$ is the level of the node. The division can be replaced for right bitwise operators:

$$(n_p, i_p, j_p) = (n - 1, i \gg 1, j \gg 1).$$

- To evaluate for a certain node (n, i, j), which are the coordinates (n_a, i_a, j_a) of a superior node located m levels above this node:

$$(n_a, i_a, j_a) = (n - m, i \gg m, j \gg m).$$

- Let T_x and T_y be the side values of the original domain covered by the quadrant, to evaluate the size of the grid cell associated to the node:

$$L_x = T_x/2^n$$
$$L_y = T_y/2^n$$

- To evaluate the spatial coordinates of the left-top corner of each node (n, i, j), it can be done using the following equations:

$$Pos_x(n, i, j) = o_x + (T/2^n) \cdot i$$
$$Pos_y(n, i, j) = o_y + (T/2^n) \cdot j \tag{8}$$

where (o_x, o_y) represent the spatial coordinates of the left-top coordinates of the general spatial domain represented in the quadtree.
- To evaluate the Euclidean distance between two nodes, it can be done through the equation 4.
- To check if two nodes (n_1, i_1, j_1) and (n_2, i_2, j_2) are adjacent, it can be done using the equation 5.

4   Results

4.1   Spatial Analysis

As indicated for FD and FL codifications, each code has a fixed size in memory, while VL codification and the proposed non-interleaved codification uses a variable size code depending on the level of the coded node.

The number of bits used in these codifications are based on node level n and based on the maximum achieved level N within the quadtree:

- In FD codification each quadcode has a minimum size consisting of the following number of bits [8]:
$$E(n) = \lceil \log_2(N+1) \rceil + 2N$$
- For the FL codification the number of bits required is:
$$E(n) = \lceil N \cdot \log_2 5 \rceil$$
- For VL Codification:
$$E(n) = \lceil (n+1) \cdot \log_2 5 \rceil$$
if $n < N$, or:
$$E(n) = \lceil (n) \cdot \log_2 5 \rceil$$
if $n = N$.
- And the number of bits needed for the proposed non-interleaved codification is:
$$E(n) = \lceil \log_2(N+1) \rceil + 2n \tag{9}$$

In order to compare the memory space required for each kind of codification, the average number of bits needed to codify the nodes included in fully occupied quadtrees will be considered (quatrees are selected based on its maximum level N). Results are presented in table (1).

Table 1. Average node bits for each codification based on the maximum quadtree node level N

N	1	3	5	7	10	13	16	20	25
NI	3.00	7.28	12.33	16.33	23.33	29.33	36.33	44.33	54.33
FD	3.00	8.00	13.00	17.00	24.00	30.00	37.00	45.00	55.00
FL	3.00	7.00	12.00	17.00	24.00	31.00	38.00	47.00	59.00
VL	2.50	6.78	11.81	16.77	23.77	30.77	37.77	46.82	58.77

4.2   Temporal Analysis

In this section we compare the computation time required to carry out the most common operations, needed when a quadtree representation is used. The FL and VL codifications have not been considered because they have a clear drawback compared to FD and non-interleaved codifications: they can not substitute divisions by binary bits displacement operations (they use division by 5). To evaluate the computation time associated to operations that involved the use of the quadcode, only the n digits of the quadcode have to be considered (where n is the node level) because the rest of $N - n$ are always set to zero (where N is the maximum level in the quadtree).

Codification/De-codification Operations. Both operations are described using the equations (1) and (2) for the case of quadcode. For the non-interleaved codification the equations to be used are (6) and (7)

In order to have a better idea of best-case computation time, the division, multiplication and module operations present in the equations of quadcode have been changed for their corresponding binary operations, which offer a better temporal performance.

Let s be the computation time associated to each addition operation and let b be the computation time associated to each binary operation (OR, AND or bitwise), using the previous equation it is possible to conclude that the computation time of the quadcode codification is:

$$T(n) = n \cdot (2s + 2b) \in O(n)$$

while the de-codification of the quadcode has a computation time:

$$T(n) = 2n \cdot (2s + 3b) \in O(n)$$

In the case of the non-interleaved codification, the computation time of the codification operation is:

$$T(n) = 2s + 2b \in O(1)$$

while for the de-codification process, the computation time is:

$$T(n) = 2s + 4b \in O(1) \tag{10}$$

Based on the previous results it is possible to establish that the non-interleaved codification offers a $O(1)$ time for both codification and de-codification operations, throughput all the nodes in the quadtree, while for the quadcode is $O(n)$.

Spatial Location. In equations 3 it is the described, for the case of quadcode, the process to evaluate spatial coordinates of a quadrant based on the node code. These equations are similar for the non-interleaved codification.

The computation time associated to the evaluation of spatial location using quadcode is $T(n) \in O(n)$.

While the computation time associated in the case of using non-interleaved code is $T(n) \in O(1)$.

To evaluate the computation time of these operations, the extraction time of values (n, i, j) from q (equation 10) has been considered.

Analyzing in detail this equation, it can be concluded that the computation time for the non-interleaved codification is always lower than the one for quadcode if $n > 1$, besides it is independent from the node level n.

Distance Between Nodes and Adjacency. These operations are almost equivalent to the spatial location operation, so the previous results are extensible to these cases.

The computation time of both operations using quadcode is $T(n) \in O(n)$, while the one associated in the case of using non-interleaved code is $T(n) \in O(1)$.

5 Conclusions

In this paper a new approach to codify nodes in quadtree representation has been presented. The approach is based on the use of a non-interleaved code which allows a compact representation of the node coordinates without needing the mixture of bits. This fact allows to perform some of the most usual quadtree operations in a more efficient way than previous codifications.

The computation time needed for these operations is $O(1)$ for the proposed codification, while in the previous codifications is $O(n)$. This point is specially critical in large quadtrees.

Concerning storage cost, it has also been demonstrated that the proposed codification performs better than previous codifications (table 1). Space used for non-interleaved codification is always lower than the memory used for FD codification. Compared to FL and VL codifications, this is similar for low level quadtrees and lower for high level quadtrees.

References

1. A. Corral, M. Vassilakopous, and Y. Manolopoulos. Algorithms for joining r-trees and linear region quadtrees. In *Proc. 6th International Symposium on Advances in Spatial Databases (SSD'99)*, pages 251–269, 1999.
2. Irene Gargantini. An effective way to represent quadtrees. *Communications of the ACM*, 25(12):905–910, 1982.
3. Gisli R. Hjaltason and Hanan Samet. Speeding up construction of pmr quadtree-based spatial indexes. *The VLDB Journal - The International Journal on Very Large Data Bases*, 11(2):109–137, 2002.
4. A. Klinger. *Patterns and search statistics. In Optimatizacion Methods in Statistics.* Academic Press, New York, 1971.

5. Shu-Xiang Li and Murray H. Loew. Adjacency detection using quadcodes. *Communications of the ACM*, 30(7):627–631, 1987.
6. Shu-Xiang Li and Murray H. Loew. The quadcode and its arithmetic. *Communications of the ACM*, 30(7):621–626, 1987.
7. Hanan Samet. The quadtree and related hierarchical data structures. *ACM Computing Surveys*, 16(2):187–260, 1984.
8. Hanan Samet. *Applications of spatial data structures: Computer graphics, image processing, and GIS*. Addison-Wesley Longman Publishing Co., Inc., Boston, 1990.
9. Hanan Samet. *The design and analysis of spatial data structures*. Addison-Wesley Longman Publishing Co., Inc., Boston, MA, 1990.
10. S. Tanimoto and T. Pavlidis. A hierarchical data structure for picture processing. *Computer Graphics and Image Processing*, 4(2):104–119, 1975.
11. T. Tzouramanis, M. Vassilakopoulos, and Y. Manolopoulos. Overlapping linear quadtrees: a spatio-temporal access method. In *Proc. 6th ACM Symposium on Advances in Geographic Information Systems (ACM-GIS'98)*, pages 1–7, 1998.

Parameterized Formatting of an
XML Document
by XSL Rules

Madani Kenab[1], Tayeb Ould Braham[2], and Pierre Bazex[1]

[1] IRIT, 118, Route de Narbonne 31062 Toulouse
kenab@info.unilim.fr, bazex@irit.fr
[2] MSI, 83, Rue d'Isle 87000 Limoges
ould@unilim.fr

Abstract. The possibilities of formatting offered by database management systems (DBMS) are insufficient and do not allow emphasizing the various data results. It is the same for the usual browsing of an XML document without any particular rules of formatting. The contents of the document is presented according to a basic format, which can be insufficient with regard to the needs of the user. We propose to generate automatically some XSL rules of formatting in order to improve the presentation of the contents of a document. We propose to distinguish the formatting of the various levels of elements as well as the formatting of the attributes, which are associated to them. We also emphasize the attributes and the elements corresponding to keys and reference links. These various parameters of formatting are requested from the user and eventually stored in a file. After the creation of a DOM tree of an XML document, these parameters are taken into account to create automatically XSL rules of formatting which are inserted in an XSL stylesheet. These possibilities of formatting will be applied on the document results produced by XQuery requests on XML documents or on XML views of data managed by database management systems.

Keywords: XML document, DOM tree, Parameters of formatting, XSL rules, XSLT, XHTML document.

1   Introduction

Database management systems (DBMS) offer a standard presentation of the request results. In the relational database management systems (RDBMS), these results are presented in the form of tuples containing atomic information with a simple format of display. In order to improve the quality of this display, some systems have been developed such as the system Delaunay [1]. This system is based on the visual database query language DOODLE (*Draw an Object-Oriented Database LanguagE*). According to a study made recently [6], the new DBMSs offer an access to XML, in particular those that are used for the publication of data by the Web. Some research has been carried out to give a better presentation of XML data by using a visual

T. Yakhno (Ed.): ADVIS 2004, LNCS 3261, pp. 213–222, 2004.

language [2] or by using an SMIL (*Synchronized Multimedia Integration Language*) representation [12].

XML languages allow a separation between the contents, the structure and the presentation of the documents. Some works have been carried out to only query XML views on DBMS by using XSL rules [4,7]. XSL language has been also used to compare two XML documents and generate an XSL stylesheet expressing a possible difference between them [3]. An XSLT processor can use some XSL rules to transform an XML document into another XML document [11]. It can also use some XSL rules to format an XML document to an XHTML document [9], which could be displayed thanks to a browser.

In our work, the XSL stylesheets are used to improve the presentation of an XML document or an XML result of an XQuery request. We automatically generate an XSL stylesheet from a DOM tree of an XML document and some parameters of formatting. This DOM tree is generated by a DOM parser from an XML document containing data and its XML schema, which defines the structure of these data [5] especially keys and reference links. This XSL stylesheet is used to obtain an XHTML document corresponding to an XML document thanks to the XSLT processor. This work will be applied to improve the presentation of the query results on XML views of data managed by database management systems.

This paper is organized as it follows. In a first section, we present the DOM tree, which is a memory representation of an XML document having its schema. In a second section, we illustrate the various parameters of formatting used to improve the display of a document and the emphasizing of keys and reference links. The XSL rules automatic generation method that take into account the parameters is presented in a third section. In a fourth section, we present how the display of an XHTML document is made by using an usual browser.

2 The DOM Tree of an XML Document

An XML document is represented in the memory by a DOM tree [8], which consists of nodes. A DOM parser generates this tree from an XML document and an XML schema (Figure1) when the document is validated with regard to the XML schema. A node can be an element, an attribute, a comment, a text, a document etc. Each element can have sub-elements and/or attributes.

The DOM model treats a document thanks to a hierarchy of object interfaces among which the interfaces: Node, Document, Element, Attr, Text etc. Thanks to this model, we can treat all DOM components either by their generic type Node, or by their specific type (Element, Attribute etc). Many methods of navigation are available, and thus allow navigation in the tree structure without having to worry about the specific type of the component.

The major disadvantage of the DOM tree is the important place that it takes in the memory when it is used to represent large documents. We use DOM tree to automatically generate a stylesheet in order to display XQuery request results, which generally are not represented by a large XML document.

An XML document is represented by a DOM tree of which the root is a node with a Document type, which has a son with an Element type. An element can have a value followed by sub-elements. In this case, the value of this element is the first son of this element, which is a node with a Text type. On the other hand, the value of an attribute is available in the node itself. In order to generate XSL rules, we use the in-depth prefixed order traversal algorithm of the DOM tree. We thus carry out a top to bottom then a left to right traversal.

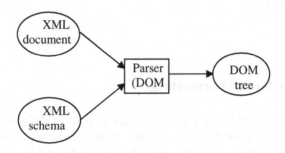

Fig. 1. The phase of analysis

Recursive algorithm of the in-depth prefixed order traversal
Traversal(n:Node)
Begin
If n is an element Then
            If n has attributes Then
                        For each attribute a of the node n Do
                                    Generate XSL rule for a;
                        EndFor;
            EndIf;
            Generate XSL rule for n;
            If n has sub-elements Then
                        For each son s of the node n Do
                                    Traversal(s); /* Recursive call*/
                        EndFor;
            EndIf;
EndIf;
End;

In an XML document, a key can be an element or an attribute with an ID type. It is possible to declare a key using the clause *key*. In the same way, a reference link can be an element or an attribute with an IDREF(S) type. It is possible to define a reference link using the clause *keyref*. However, a DOM tree does not contain any information concerning the declarations made by these clauses. In order to take into account these declarations for the formatting stage, we need to recover information related on keys and reference links from the XML schema. This latter is checked in the analysis phase by the DOM parser (Figure 1).

Algorithm of extraction of key and reference link information from the XML schema
While Not(End_of_File(XML_Schema)) Do
   Read(Tag);
   If (Tag = '<key>') or (Tag = '<keyref>') Then
      Read(Tag);
      While (Tag ≠ '</key>') and (Tag ≠ '</keyref>') Do
            Extract information concerning this declaration;
            Read(Tag);
      EndWhile;
   EndIf;
EndWhile;

3   Parameters of Formatting

In order to distinguish the display of the various parts of the document therefore the various types of node of the corresponding DOM tree, we use different parameters of formatting. The elements and the attributes are displayed with different colors. The name of a node is differentiated from its value by a boldfacing. For a better presentation of the document, we use an indentation in which a node (element or attribute) is shifted relatively to the margin according to its level of nesting. The various levels of nesting of the document are also distinguished by decreasing the size of the characters. We reserve also a particular treatment for the key values that are underlined and for the reference link values that are located with stars (*).

These parameters of formatting are stored in a file and are read by the program of formatting. They can be modified by a user request. The construction of the parameter file can be made by asking the user about his formatting needs. For example, each file record is composed of six fields (Style, Font type, Color, Size, Underlining, Boldfacing). The record number is equal to the double of the depth (level number) of the XML document. Certain parameter values can be fixed according to the level and the type of the node (element or attribute). Once the size of the character of the element of the highest level is fixed, for each under level, we decrement the size by 2 (for example). The construction of the XSL rules will be done by traversing the DOM tree and relying on the file of the parameters of formatting to decide which formats to apply.

4   Construction of XSL Rules

The XSL rules are generated during the in-depth prefixed order traversal of the DOM tree by taking into account the file of the formatting parameters. For each node of the DOM tree, if certain conditions are checked, an XSL rule is inserted in the stylesheet file intended to receive these rules. After the traversal of the DOM tree, this stylesheet file containing XSL rules will be applied to the XML document thanks to an XSLT processor to generate an XHTML corresponding document (Figure 2).

4.1   Rules of Formatting

In order to define an applicable format to a whole part of a document or to a precise tag, we place an attribute style in a tag < DIV> or < SPAN >. These tags define a zone of text corresponding to a style of formatting, which will constitute an XSL rule. The difference between < DIV > and < SPAN > is that the first involves a jump of line while the second does not. <SPAN> may modify the style of any part of text located inside a paragraph. We chose to use < SPAN > to hold the freedom of the management of the line jumps.

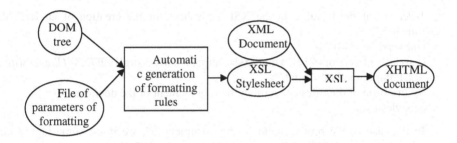

Fig. 2. Automatic generation of a stylesheet from a DOM tree

We propose the following simple formatting which can be adapted to the user's needs. The property font-style is initialized, by default, with the value: `normal'. It takes the value ' italic' for the display of the attributes. The property font-family takes its value from the font-type parameter, it will be applied to the whole document. The property color can take one of the two possible values according to the type of node of the document: attribute or element. The property font-size takes a maximum initial value from the size parameter. This value will decrease when we get down from an element to its sub-element. The property text-decoration initially takes the value 'none'. This value is replaced by 'underline' to underline the key value. The property font-weight is used to display the name of the node in bold, the value 'bold' is given to this property.

Example of formatting rule
```
<SPAN   STYLE="font-size:   '18pt';   color:'Green';   font-family='Verdana';   font-
style:'italic'">
    <SPAN STYLE="font-weight='bold'">  {NP} = </SPAN>
    <SPAN STYLE="text-decoration='underline'">123</SPAN>
</SPAN>
```

This rule of formatting produces this display: *{NP} = 123*

In this example, we used a <SPAN > element with <SPAN> sub-elements. The <SPAN> element of the first level specifies the common format to apply to a part of the document. The <SPAN> sub-elements specify the particular formats to apply to sub-parts of this part of the document.

Note: The distinct colors are visible on the screen.

4.2   Rules of Selection

In order to select one or more nodes of a DOM tree we use the Xpath language [10]. The XPath language enables to address nodes and it offers some functions that increase its capacity of expression and research. The Xpath language enables to identify a node in a tree corresponding to an XML document by using Xpath expressions.

At the beginning of the creation of the XSL stylesheet file, we insert a heading in the XSL file by specifying "html" for the attribute *method* of the XSL element *output*, because we want to generate an XHTML document, as it follows:

```
/* Insertion of the heading in the XSL stylesheet for the creation of an XHTML
document */
<?xml version ="1.0"?>
<xsl:stylesheet version="1.0" xmlns:xsl="http://www.w3.org/1999/XSL/Transform">
    <xsl:output method="html"/>
    /* Insertion of the rules concerning the root element of the document */
</xsl:stylesheet>
```

In the case of the root element of the document "/", we insert some tags which enable to create an HTML document (<HTML> and </HTML>). We insert also some tags which define the heading and the title of the document (<HEAD> and </HEAD>, <TITLE> and </TITLE>), some tags which delimit the body of the document (<BODY> and </BODY>) and some tags which specify the style of the used characters (element SPAN with an attribute STYLE in which we give a value to font-family, Verdana, for example), as it follows:

```
/* Insertion of the rules concerning the root element of the document */
<xsl:template match="/">
    <HTML>
        <HEAD>
            <TITLE>Representation of an XML document in a formatted XHTML
            document </TITLE>
        </HEAD>
        <BODY>
            <SPAN STYLE="font-family='Font_Type'">
            /* Insertion of XSL rules concerning all the descendants of the element
            (root) having sub-elements */
            </SPAN>
        </BODY>
    </HTML>
</xsl:template>
```

For each element, which has sub-elements, we insert the following XSL rule, by defining the position of the occurrence of this element in the DOM tree relatively to the other occurrences of the element, because an element could have several occurrences. This Xpath expression will distinguish two different nodes having the same name.

/* Insertion of XSL rules concerning the descendants of the element having sub-elements */
```
<xsl:for-each select="Element_Xpath">
    <xsl:if test="position()=Element_Position">
                [Element_Name]
                /* Insert XSL rules concerning the sub-elements of this element */
    </xsl:if>
</xsl:for-each>
```

The research of the position of the occurrence of an element (Element_Position) in the DOM tree and the building of its Xpath expression (Element_Xpath) are done according to the following algorithm.

XPATH : Array of paths of nodes (distinct); /* Initialized with null strings : "" */
Position : Array of integer;   /* Initialized to 1 */
Path : String;
n : Node;
index : integer;
/* Building of the path expression (XPATH) of the current node */
n ← current_node;
Path ← "/" + Name(n);
While (Name(Parent(n)) ≠"DOCUMENT") Do
        n ← Parent(n);
        Path ← "/" + Name(n) + Path;
EndWhile;
/* Checking if the current node is already visited */
index ← 0;
While ((XPATH[index] ≠ "") and (XPATH[index] ≠ Path)) Do
        index ← index + 1;
EndWhile;
/* Incrementing of the position of the current node if it is already visited */
If (XPATH[index] = Path) Then
        Position[index] ← Position[index]+1;
Else
    If (XPATH[index] = "") Then
        XPATH[index] ← Path;
        EndIf;
EndIf;

For all the elements having attributes, we insert for each attribute pertaining to this element the following XSL rule.

/* Insertion of XSL rule concerning the attribute of an element */
{Attribute_Name} = <xsl:value-of select="@Attribute_Name"/>

In the case of an elementary element (which do not have sub-elements), we add the following XSL rule:

/* Insertion of XSL rule concerning the element which do not have sub-element */
[Element_Name] = <xsl:value-of select="Element_Name"/>

The rules of formatting will contain the rules of selection according to the level of nesting of the node, its type (element or attribute) and its constraints of uniqueness and reference (key, reference link). The following algorithm summarizes the previous insertions of XSL rules of selection for the current element.

Algorithm of XSL rules generation
If the current node is an element Then
    If the current node has sub-elements Then
        Insert('<xsl:for-each select="Element_Xpath">');
      Insert('<xsl:if test="position()=Element_Position">[Element_Name]');
    Else
        Insert('[Element_Name] = <xsl:value-of select="Element_Name"/>');
    EndIf;
    If the current node has attributes Then
        Insert('{Attribute_Name} = <xsl:value-of select="@Attribute_Name"/>');
    EndIf;
/*At the end of the traversal of all the descendants of an element having sub-elements */
 Insert('</xsl:if></xsl:for-each>');
EndIf;

5   Display of an XHTML Document

In Figure 3, we present the display of an XHTML document produced by XSLT processor from an XML document and an XSL stylesheet generated according to algorithms described in the previous section. This XHTML document is the representation of the database PURCHASE_DB in which the various relations (PRODUCT, CUSTOMER, and PURCHASE) are elements and the fields of each relation are attributes. This document can be displayed by using an Internet browser (Internet Explorer for example).

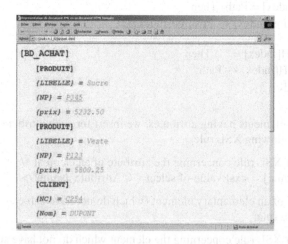

Fig. 3. XHTML document generated from the XML document db2.xml

On the other hand, the Figure 4 illustrates the representation of the same database PURCHASE_DB in which the relations (PRODUCT, CUSTOMER, and PURCHASE) are elements and the fields of each relation are sub-elements.

Note: The distinct colors are visible with the screen. The different formatting using attributes or sub-elements are shown in Figure 3 and Figure 4.

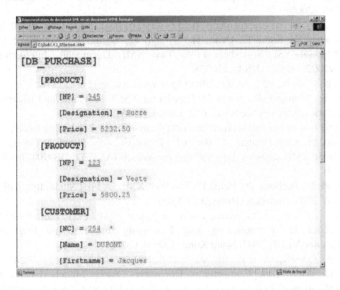

Fig. 4. XHTML document generated from the XML document purchase_db.xml

6   Conclusion

We showed the feasibility of an automatic generation of XSL rules in order to format the contents of a document by taking into account formatting parameters provided by the user. We suppose that any document is described by a schema. Before to display a document, we check that its contents is in conformity with its schema by creating its DOM tree.

In our example of displaying (figure3 and figure4) we have used a whole document but this formatting could be applied to a part of the document having its temporary schema. Our work is intended to format and display the request results put in the form of XML documents.

In our example of formatting we used only some properties of formatting among the broad range offered by the XSL language. Among others properties, there are those related to the pagination, to the scrolling and edging. They could be taken into account by adding them as formatting parameters.

We have worked on an XML document containing only structured data, but we will be able to generalize these possibilities of formatting on non-structured data. This work will constitute a layer of presentation on a system offering documentary views on different types of databases.

References

1. Averbuch, M., Cruz, I. F., Lucas, W. T., Radzyminski, M., Zhang K.: Delaunay: a Database Visualization System. ACM SIGMOD, Arizona (USA), (1997) http://www.cs.brown.edu/people/ifc/IEEE/sigmodrev.ps
2. Erwig, M.: A Visual Language for XML. IEEE Symp. on Visual Languages, Washington (USA), (2000) http://cs.oregonstate.edu/~erwig/papers/Xing_VL00.pdf
3. Ishikawa, N., Kato, T., Ueno, H., Sumino H., Suzuki H.: Automatic Generation of a Differential XSL Stylesheet From Two XML Documents. International conference www2002, Hawaii (USA), (2002) http://www2002.org/CDROM/poster/36.pdf
4. Jain, S., Mahajan, R., Suciu D.:Translating XSLT Programs to Efficient SQL Queries. International conference www2002, Hawaii (USA), (2002) http://www.cs.washington.edu/homes/ratul/papers/www2002-xslt.ps
5. Kenab, M., Ould Braham, T., Bazex P.: Evaluation of a document database description by different XML schemas. International conference IASTED: DBA'04, Innsbruck (Austria), (2004)
6. Mignet, L., Barbosa, D., Veltri P.: The Web XML: A First Study. International conference WWW 2003, Budapest (Hungary), (2003)
7. http://www.cs.toronto.edu/~mignet/Publications/www2003.pdf
8. Moerkotte G.: Incorporating XSL Processing Into Database Engines. International conference VLDB 2002, Hong Kong (China), (2002) http://www.cs.ust.hk/vldb2002/VLDB2002-papers/S04P03.pdf
9. World Wide Web Consortium: Document Object Model (DOM) Level 2 Core Specification. (2000) http://www.w3.org/TR/DOM-Level-2-Core/
10. World Wide Web Consortium: XHTML 1.0 : The Extensible HyperText Markup Language. W3C Recommendation, (2002) http://www.w3.org/TR/xhtml1/
11. World Wide Web Consortium: XML Path Language (XPath) 2.0. (2003) http://www.w3.org/TR/xpath20/
12. World Wide Web Consortium: XSL Transformations (XSLT). (2003) http://www.w3.org/TR/xslt20/
13. Zhang, K., Zhang, D.Q., Deng, Y.: A Visual Approach to XML Document Design and Transformation. International conference HCC'2001, Stresa (Italy), (2001)
14. http://www.utdallas.edu/~kzhang/Publications/HCC01.ps.gz

A Middleware Approach to Storing and Querying XML Documents in Relational Databases

Zülal Şevkli, Mine Mercan, and Atakan Kurt

Dept. of Computer Eng.,
Fatih University,
Istanbul, Turkey
{zsevkli, minemercan, akurt}@fatih.edu.tr

Abstract. In this paper we present a middleware for storing and retrieving XML documents in relational databases. To store XML documents in RDBMS, several mapping approaches can be used. We chose structure independent approach. This approach stores XML documents in fixed-schema tables and does not require a direct extension of SQL. So the middleware can be used with any RDBMS with minor changes in the interface. The middleware offers two alternative methods -namely XRel and Edge- for storing XML in the database. The Edge method is a straightforward method, while XRel utilizes path summary information for faster query processing. We present a comparative experimental study on the performance of insertion and retrieval of two types of XML documents along with a set of XPath queries executed though the XPath query processor which is a part of the middleware.

1 Introduction

XML is eXtensible Markup Language [3] emerged as a major standard for representing data on the World Wide Web. Despite the excitement XML has produced, there are important problems to tackle with regarding the management of large amounts of XML documents efficiently in a database. Recently native-XML databases such as Tamino have emerged in the market; however native-XML databases usually have limited support for relational data.

Taking up emerging requirements, database vendors such as IBM, Oracle and Microsoft are enabling their products for XML. XML-Enabled databases have mature and proven techniques for relational data processing but XML-extensions have not been mature enough yet. Since there are many relational databases systems on the market, a middleware approach [1] can be used until most relational systems have XML-support. The key to middleware approach is to store XML documents in a relational database through a user interface and with an XPath query processor.

There are various approaches for effective, automatic conversion and storage of XML documents into relational databases [7], [9], [11], [17], [15], [20], [22]. Generally, we can classify all studies on XML storage in two categories as in [10]. The first one is *integral storage*, which normally keeps the unparsed document intact

T. Yakhno (Ed.): ADVIS 2004, LNCS 3261, pp. 223–233, 2004.
© Springer-Verlag Berlin Heidelberg 2004

and stores it as a BLOB in a database or a file in the file system. With this approach, access to individual elements is realized by parsing, and therefore it is inefficient. This approach is appropriate for retrieving documents, but requires specific index structures for query processing. The second one is *dispersed storage*; in which the documents are shredded and shredded items are stored in tables. When XML documents are stored via dispersed storage, a problem occurs about schema design. The problem of a storage model design becomes a database schema design problem. In [11], the authors categorize such database schemas into two categories: *structure dependent mapping approach* and *structure-independent-mapping approach*. In the former, the design of database schema is based on the understanding of DTD (Document Type Descriptor). In the latter, a fixed database schema is used to store all XML documents regardless of DTDs.

Vendors such as IBM, Oracle, and Microsoft either use structure dependent mapping approach or store unparsed documents in a CLOB field. For details about XML support in DB2, Oracle and SQL Server, please refer to [4], [7], and [15].

In this study, we present a middleware that takes advantage of the structure independent mapping approach. We adapted PhpMyAdmin 2.4.0 web base interface for storing and retrieving XML documents in MySQL open source database. With this implementation, users can store XML documents regardless of structure of documents. The application gives users two alternatives (XRel and Edge) for database schema design. We compared with storage and retrieval time of a set of XML documents. We also present an experiment with a set of XPath queries. The results seem to be satisfactory in most cases, very good in some cases, and acceptable in other cases.

The remainder of this paper is organized as follows. Section 2 presents structure independent mapping approaches. We describe the middleware in Section 3. Experimental results are discussed in Section 4. The conclusions are drawn in Section 5.

2   Structure Independent Mapping Approach

In this section, the structure independent mapping approach is explained with a sample XML document shown in Figure 1. In this paper, we employ the data model of XPath [5] to represent XML documents. In the XPath data model, XML documents are modeled as an ordered and directed labeled tree. There are seven types of nodes. In this paper, we consider only the following four types of nodes for the sake of simplicity: root, element, text and attribute. The root node is a virtual node pointing to the root element of an XML document. Elements in an XML document are represented as an element node. Element nodes can have other elements or text as its children. Text nodes are string-valued leaf-nodes. An element node can have a set of attribute nodes. An attribute node has an attribute-name and an attribute-value.

Figure 2 shows an XML tree such that a left-to-right and depth-first traversal describes the order of the XML content within our document in Figure 1.

2.1 The Edge Method

The Edge method stores all edges of an XML tree in a single table named Edge [9]. The table schema is given below

Edge (Source, Ordinal, Target, Name, Flag, Value)

An edge is specified by two node identifiers, namely Source and Target. The Name attribute stores the element or attribute name. The Ordinal attribute records the ordinal of the node among its siblings. A flag value indicates whether the target node is an inter-object reference (ref) or points to a value (val). Table 1 shows the Edge table for the XML document in Figure 2. The tuple, (5, 2, 8, given, val, "Paul"), means the element with name "given" and value "Paul". The parent node of this element is 5 and its ordinal is 2. This approach is quite simple. It stores parent-child relationship. A large number of joins may be required during retrieval of the original document from the records stored in the table if the tree is not shallow. The same can be said for processing long XPath queries on data stored with this method.

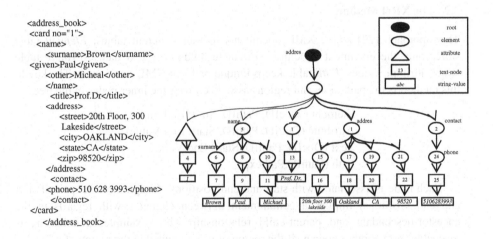

Fig. 1. Sample XML   **Fig. 2.** The XML Tree the sample XML

As a variation of the Edge approach, the XML tree can be stored in multiple tables in [16]. That method partitions the Edge table according to all possible label-paths. For each unique path, the method creates a table. This method is also a structure independent approach, but the number of tables is not fixed. So it is difficult to support database schema for dynamic XML documents.

Table 1. Edge Table

Source	Ordinal	Target	Name	Flag	Value
0	1	1	address_book	ref	-
1	1	2	card	ref	-
2	1	3	@no	val	"1"
2	2	5	name	ref	-
5	1	6	surname	val	"Brown"
5	2	8	given	val	"Paul"
5	3	10	other	val	"Michael"
2	3	12	title	val	"Prof.Dr."
2	4	14	address	ref	-
14	1	15	street	val	"20th floor 300 Lakeside"
14	2	17	city	val	"oakland"
14	3	19	state	val	"CA"
14	4	21	zip	val	"98520"
2	5	23	contact	ref	-
23	1	24	phone	val	"510 628 39 93"

2.2 The XRel Method

This approach [22] stores XML documents in four different tables; *Element* table stores only the document structure. *Text* table holds only text data. *Attribute* table stores attribute values. *Path* table keeps unique paths in XML documents. The key to this method is the path table and regions associated with the inner nodes in the tree.

> Element (DocID, PathID, Start, End, Index)
> Attribute (DocID, PathID, Start, End, Value)
> Text (DocID, PathID, Start, End, Value)
> Path (PathID, Pathexp)

Each node is associated with start and end positions. A region (or the pair of start and end positions) implies a containment between elements with regards to the ancestor-descendant and parent-child relationships. For example, a node, n_i, is reachable from another node n_j, if the region of n_i is included in the region of n_j.

In our study, we modified some attributes of tables in XRel approach: we added a ParentID column to Element, Attribute, and Text tables to find parent nodes easily. We put NodeID and last descendant node id (EndDescID) attributes instead of start and end columns in Element table. The XRel tables can be seen in Table 2 for the XML document given in Figure 1:

Table 2. Tables of XREL

PathID	PathExp
1	/address_book
2	/address_book/card
3	/address_book/card/@no
4	/address_book/card/name
5	/address_book/card/name/surname
6	/address_book/card/name/given
7	/address_book/card/name/other
8	/address_book/card/title
9	/address_book/card/address
10	/address_book/card/address/street
11	/address_book/card/address/city
12	/address_book/card/address/state
13	/address_book/card/address/zip
14	/address_book/card/contact
15	/address_book/card/contact/phone

(a) Path Table

NodeId	EndDescID	PathID	ParentID	Ordinal
1	51	1	0	1
2	25	2	1	1
5	11	4	2	1
6	7	5	5	1
8	9	6	5	1
10	11	7	5	1
12	13	8	2	1
14	22	9	2	1
15	16	10	14	1
17	18	11	14	1
19	20	12	14	1
21	22	13	14	1
23	25	14	2	1
24	25	15	23	1

(b) Element Table

NodeId	PathID	ParentID	Value
7	5	6	Brown
9	6	8	Paul
11	7	10	Michael
13	8	12	Prof.Dr.
16	9	15	20th floor 300 Lakeside
18	10	17	Oakland
20	11	19	CA
22	12	21	98520
25	15	24	5106283993

(c) Text Table

NodeId	PathID	ParentID	Value
3	3	2	1

(d) Attribute Table

3 Implementation: Middleware for XML Support on MySql

We used MySQL as the DBMS for storing and retrieving XML documents using structure independent mapping approaches. To realize this, we develop a middleware and embed it into PhpMyAdmin program which is a web based interface between MySQL and users.

In Section 2, we discussed three different methods that we can use in structure independent mapping approach. There are variations of these methods as well. We chose the Edge and XRel methods, because Edge is a simple method to implement, and XRel is more complex with the path summary for faster XPath query processing. So our initial expectation was that XRel should be several times faster than Edge. However the results are somewhat unexpected. In some cases Edge seems to do better, in some other cases it displays performance comparable to XRel.

Figure 3 outlines the architecture of the middleware which adds XML support to the MySQL database system. The three main classes (Collection, Document, XPath) can be used to adapt the same interface to other databases systems.

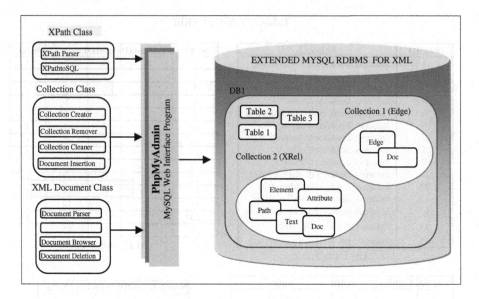

Fig. 3. The middleware architecture

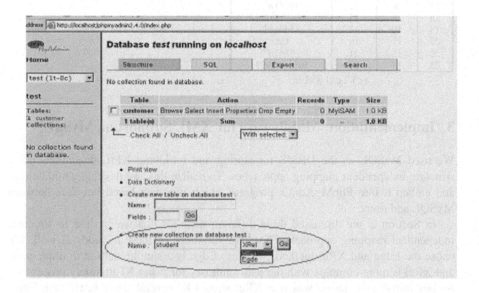

Fig. 4. Creating collection in PhpMyAdmin

Our implementation adds *collection* support to XML into the MySQL database. A collection is a set of similar XML documents stored in fixed schema of tables, sometimes referred to as *XML repository*. In reality, MySQL database model does not change, but from the user point of view, a database can contain *tables* and *collections*. Fig. 4 shows a screenshot during collection creation. Users can not modify or access the tables behind collections directly. Users can manipulate XML data through collections only. A collection can store document using either Edge or XRel method. Users can create, drop or browse collections, insert, delete, or browse XML documents in a collection.

4 Experimental Result

This section discusses the experimental results of storage and retrieval time of XML documents and a set of XPath queries using XRel and Edge methods. All the experiments were conducted on a Pentium IV 350 MHz PC with 1 GB RAM 30GB hard disk. We used Windows XP, MYSQL 4.0.13, Php 4, Apache 1.3.29, and PhpMyAdmin 2.4.0 for the experiments.

Generally, we can classify XML documents in two categories as in [21]: *data-centric* and *text-centric*. Text-centric documents have more irregular structure. They can contain long and variable-length text and the order of siblings is always important. Data-centric documents are usually used for XML-encoding relational data. We used Catalog.xml [21] as a sample of *data-centric documents* and Shakespeare's plays [2] documents as sample *of text-centric documents*. Although Shakespeare's plays are well-structured, they contain variable-length strings like dictionary file in [21]. So they can be considered text-centric documents. Tables were indexed on their key fields and the fields used in join. Insertion and retrieval results are given below, for details please refer to [19].

4.1 XML Insertion

The insertion time of both types of document using EDGE and XREL methods are given in Figure 5. As seen in the figure, the Edge method is at least twice as fast as the XRel method. The reason could be that the data is stored in one table only in the Edge method, while the XRel method has to store path summary and end_descendant_id which requires more complex processing.

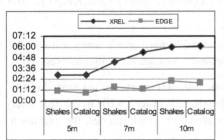

Fig. 5. Insertion time (mm:ss) of docs

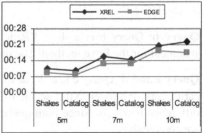

Fig. 6. Reconstruction time (mm:ss) of docs

4.2 XML Reconstruction

The retrieval times are given in Figure 6. The results are close. Edge seems to be a little faster than XRel. The retrieval time is roughly proportional to file size. We think that the results are affected by the number of inner node as well. The XRel method needs to join 3 different tables, while Edge table joins with itself.

4.3 Query Results

A set of 13 queries executed on Catalog and Shakespeare documents. Below we only present 6 queries on Shakespeare documents and skip queries on catalog documents because of space limitations. Please refer to [14] for a full presentation. The results are shown in Figure 7 for both methods. The XPath queries were automatically converted to SQL by the query processor. The execution times do not include sorting nodes according to document order, and conversion to text with XML tags. Time is given in milliseconds.

Query a is a long XPath query. Query b represents a short XPath query. Query c is a (//) descendant-or-self query. Query d has a wild card (*) which represents any single element. Query e and f contains equality and range predicates on text-values.

Query a: Query a requires one join in each step (5 steps total) in the XPath query using the Edge method, however the XRel uses the path information in the Path table, as a result XRel is faster in the long XPath query as expected. The SQL statements for Edge and XRel methods respectively generated by the query processor are given below:

SELECT e5.* FROM edgecol_edge as e1,edgecol_edge as e2,edgecol_edge as e3,edgecol_edge as e4,edgecol_edge as e5 WHERE e1.name='plays' AND e1.parentID=0 AND e1.docID=3 AND e1.flg!='att' AND e2.name='play' AND e2.parentID=e1.nodeID AND e2.flg!='att'AND e2.docID=3 AND e3.name='act' AND e3.parentID=e2.nodeID AND e3.flg!='att'AND e3.docID=3 AND e4.name='scene' AND e4.parentID=e3.nodeID AND e4.flg!='att'AND e4.docID=3 AND e5.name='title' AND e5.parentID=e4.nodeID AND e5.flg!='att'AND e5.docID=3

SELECT e1.* FROM xrelcol_Path p1,xrelcol_Element e1 WHERE p1.pathexp LIKE '#/plays#/play#/act#/scene#/title' AND e1.DocID=1 AND e1.pathID=p1.pathID AND p1.DocID=1

Query b: Query b is a short XPath query. So there aren't many joins in the SQL statement for the Edge method. The response times are very close as expected.

Query c and d: Query c is a '//' descendant-or-self query, while Query d is a '*' wild card query. Although XRel seems to be slightly faster (%10) in the first query, this difference is trivial. Since both queries are short XPath queries, the execution times are comparable.

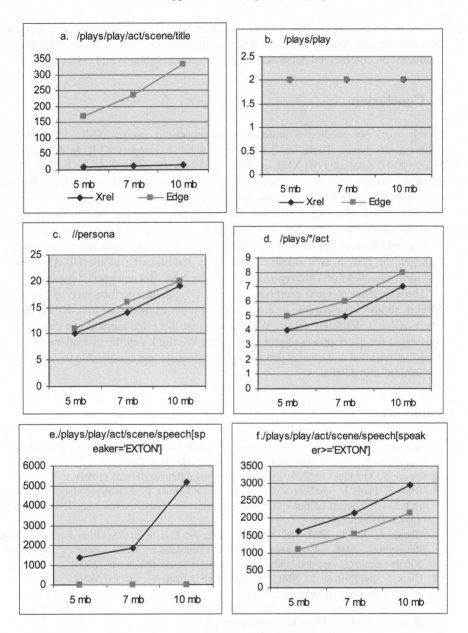

Fig. 7. Retrieval time (milliseconds) of XML documents

Query e and f: Both queries contain predicates on text values. The objective is to see how fast the query processing is with text not with structure as with previous queries. Edge seems to do better than XRel on these queries.

We think that the executions times for insertion, retrieval and queries processing are adequate and comparable to commercial applications and databases. Experiments conducted on commercial databases support this observation [12], [13].

5 Conclusion

In this work we studied a middleware approach to storing XML documents in relational databases. There are 2 main approaches to support XML in databases (i) Native XML databases (ii) XML-enabled databases. Since there are several relational databases on the market, a middleware approach can be used as an affordable and quick solution until XML data processing matures. The key to middleware approach is storing XML documents in a relational database, providing a user interface for XML manipulation, and adding an XPath query processor for XML querying.

The middleware implemented in this study can be used with any other database management system as it doesn't require any modification to the DBMS itself. It provides *collections* or *XML repositories* to store XML documents in a database.

The experiments yield promising results. Overall the performance of Edge and XRel methods is comparable in most cases with the exception of long XPath queries where XRel is definitely faster. We can say that the Edge method can certainly be considered for query processing in most cases. We think that the executions times for insertion, retrieval and queries processing are adequate and comparable to commercial applications and databases.

References

1. Bourret, R. P.: Middleware for Transfering Data Between XML Documents and Relational Databases. http://www.rpbourret.com/xmldbms/index.htm (2001)
2. Bosak, J.: The Plays of Shakespeare. http://www.ibiblio.org/bosak/ (1999)
3. Bray, T., Paoli, J., Sperberg-McQueen, C. M., and Maler, E.: Extensible Markup Language (XML) 1.0 (Second Edition), W3C Recommendation. http://www.w3.orglTR2OOOlREC-xml-200010061. (2000)
4. Cheng, J., Xu, J.: IBM DB2 XML Extender-An End to End Solution for Storing and Retrieving XML Documents, IBM Corporation white paper, http://www-306.ibm.com/software/data/db2/extenders/xmlext/xmllextbroch.pdf (2000)
5. Clark, J., and DeRose, S., XML Path Language (XPath) Version 1.0, W3C Recommendation 16 November 1999,
   http://www.w3.org/TR1999/REC-xpatb-19991116
6. Dayen, I.: Storing XML in Relational Databases.
   http://www.xml.com/pub/a/2001/06/20/databases.html. (2001)
7. Deutsch, A., Fernandez, M. and Suciu, D.: Storing Semistructured Data with STORED. In Proc. of ACM SIGMOD, Philadelphia, PN, (1999)
8. Drake, M.: Oracle XML DB White Paper,
   http://otn.oracle.com/tech/xml/xmldb/Current/TWP.pdf (2004)
9. Florescu, D., and Kossmann, D.: Storing and quering xml data using an RDBMS. IEEE Data Engineering Bulletin 22, 3, (1999) 27-34
10. Goldfarb, C., F., Prescod, P.: XML Handbook, Prentice Hall 4th Edition (2001)

11. Jiang, H., and Lu, H.: Path Materialization Revisited: An Efficient Storage Model for XML Data, 2nd Australian Institute of Computer Ethics Conference, Canberra (2001)
12. Kentel, E.: A Performance Study on XPath Queries in Commercial Databases, Senior Project, Dept. of Computer Eng. Fatih University, Istanbul Turkey (2003)
13. Kurt, A., Atay, M.: An Experimental Study on Query Processing Efficiency of Native-XML and XML-Enabled Database Systems, in Databases in Networked Information Systems, LNCS Volume 2544, Editors: S. Bhalla, Springer-Verlag Heidelberg, (2002) pp 268-284
14. Mercan, M.: An Implementation of an XPath Query Processor for XRel and Edge Methods, MS Thesis, Fatih University, Istanbul Turkey (2004)
15. OPENXML: Retrieving and Writing XML Data.
    http://msdn.microsoft.com/library/default.asp?url=/library/
    en-us/xmlsql/ac_openxml_759d.asp (2004)
16. Schmit, A., Kersten, M. L., Windhouwer, M., and Wass, F.: Efficient Relational Storage and Retrieval of XML documents. In WebDB (Informal Proceedings), (2000) pp 47-52
17. Shanmugasundaram, J., Tatarinov, I., Shekita, E., Kiernan, J., Viglas, E. and Naughton, J.: A General Technique for Querying XML Documents using a Relational Database System, SIGMOD (2001)
18. Shanmugasundaram, J., Zhang, C., Tufte, K., He, G., DeWitt and D., Naughton, J.: Relational Databases for Querying XML Documents: Limitations and Opportunities. Proceeding of the 25th VLDB Conference, Edinburgh, Scotland (1999)
19. Su, A. Z.: An Implementation of Storage and Retrieval Methods for XML Documents in Relational RDBMSs, MS Thesis, Fatih University, Istanbul Turkey (2003)
20. Tatarinov, I., and Iglas, S., D., V.: Storing and Quering Ordered XML Using a Relational Database System, ACM SIGMOD, Wisconsin, USA (2002)
21. Yao, B. B., Özsu, M. T., and Keenleyside J.: XBench -- A Family of Benchmarks for XML DBMSs, In Proceedings of EEXTT 2002 and DiWeb 2002, Lecture Notes in Computer Science Volume 2590, S. Bressan, A. B. Chaudhri, M. L. Lee, J. Yu, Z. Lacroix (eds), Springer-Verlag, (2002) pp 162-164.
22. YoshiKawa, M. and Amagasa, T.: XRel: A Path -based approach to storage and retrieval of XML documents using relational databases, ACM Trans. on Internet Technology (2001)

On Families of New Adaptive Compression Algorithms Suitable for Time-Varying Source Data

Luis Rueda[1,*] and B. John Oommen[2,**]

[1] School of Computer Science, University of Windsor,
401 Sunset Avenue, Windsor, ON, N9B 3P4, Canada
lrueda@uwindsor.ca
[2] School of Computer Science, Carleton University,
1125 Colonel By Dr., Ottawa, ON, K1S 5B6, Canada
oommen@scs.carleton.ca

Abstract. In this paper, we introduce a new approach to adaptive coding which utilizes *Stochastic Learning-based Weak Estimation (SLWE)* techniques to adaptively update the probabilities of the source symbols. We present the corresponding encoding and decoding algorithms, as well as the details of the probability updating mechanisms. Once these probabilities are estimated, they can be used in a variety of data encoding schemes, and we have demonstrated this, in particular, for the adaptive *Fano* scheme *and* and an adaptive *entropy-based* scheme that resembles the well-known arithmetic coding. We include empirical results using the latter adaptive schemes on real-life files that possess a fair degree of *non-stationarity*. As opposed to higher-order statistical models, our schemes require *linear space complexity*, and compress with nearly 10% better efficiency than the traditional adaptive coding methods.

1 Introduction

The problem that we address in this paper is the following. We are given an input sequence, $\mathcal{X} = x(1) \ldots x(M)$, where each input symbol, $x(i)$, is drawn from a source alphabet, $\mathcal{S} = \{s_i, \ldots, s_m\}$, whose probabilities are $\mathcal{P} = [p_1, \ldots, p_m]^T$. The encoding process is rendered by transforming $\mathcal{X}$ into an output sequence, $\mathcal{Y} = y(1) \ldots y(R)$, where each output symbol, $y(i)$, is drawn from a code alphabet, $\mathcal{A} = \{a_1, \ldots, a_r\}$. The intent of the exercise is to determine an encoding scheme that minimizes the size of $\mathcal{Y}$, in such a way that $\mathcal{X}$ is completely recovered by the decompression process. The encoding process is rendered adaptive, and thus, the data is encoded by performing a single pass. This is carried out by assuming that $\mathcal{P} = [p_1, \ldots, p_m]^T$ is unknown, as opposed to the static coding algorithms which require two passes – the first to learn the probabilities, and the second to accomplish the encoding. Adaptive coding is the best

---

* Member of the IEEE. Partially supported by NSERC, the Natural Science and Engineering Research Council of Canada.
** *Fellow of the IEEE.* Partially supported by NSERC, the Natural Science and Engineering Research Council of Canada.

T. Yakhno (Ed.): ADVIS 2004, LNCS 3261, pp. 234–244, 2004.
© Springer-Verlag Berlin Heidelberg 2004

choice in many applications that require on-line compression such as in communication networks, LANs, internet applications, e-mail, ftp, e-commerce, and digital television.

A crucial problem that has received little attention in the literature is that of compressing data, which "simultaneously" comes from different sources, or perhaps, possesses different stochastic characteristics. Examples of data that exhibit this kind of behavior can be found in real-life data files, including text files containing tables, figures, and Object Linking and Embedding (OLE), postscript files containing text, equations, and figures, Windows executable files, dynamic link libraries, and font format files. A few efforts have been made to develop techniques that utilize higher-order statistical models for stationary distributions. The most well-known adaptive coding technique is Huffman's algorithm and its enhancements [4, 8]. Other important adaptive encoding methods include *arithmetic coding* [5], *interval coding* and *recency rank encoding* [5, 9]. In [12], greedy adaptive Fano coding algorithms for binary code (and r-ary) alphabets have been introduced. Adaptive coding approaches that use higher-order statistical models, and other structural models, include *dictionary techniques* (LZ and its enhancements) [14], *prediction with partial matching* (PPM) and its enhancements [6]. Other static coding methods which are worth mentioning include *block sorting compression* [3], and *grammar based compression* (GBC) [7].

On the other hand, little work has been done to enhance the probability updating phase, so that the updates obtained yield better estimates of the true probabilities of the data coming from potentially *time-varying* sources and probability distributions. One of the reported approaches consists of periodically multiplying each counter by a positive real number less than unity [4]. Another approach, suggests that the probabilities of occurrence should be real numbers to represent the frequency counters [2]. These authors proposed an exponential incrementing of the counters by choosing a multiplication factor $\alpha > 1$, suggesting a value of α slightly greater than unity, e.g. $\alpha = 1.01$. A third method utilizes a window as a circular buffer, in which the last t symbols encoded are stored [1]. All these approaches lack from a sound theoretical basis, and hence are limited to produce *only marginal* improvements in compressing time-varying source data.

A recent work that (in our opinion) has made a significant contribution to the above-mentioned problem is the new family of "weak" estimators introduced recently [11], referred to as Stochastic Learning Weak Estimators (SLWE), and which are developed by using the principles of stochastic learning. While the former paper is theoretical and only solves the general problem of SLWE for non-stationary environments, this paper provides the first potential application of the scheme. We introduce a novel adaptive encoding scheme that utilizes the principles of the SLWE to update the probabilities of the input symbols. The new approach is capable of dealing with data coming from different and time-varying sources, and thus, it is appropriate for a wide variety of files, which are currently being transmitted or stored in state-of-the-art computer systems. Thus, our contribution can be summed up in the following sentences: *We present a compression paradigm in which the SLWE estimates can be used in conjunction with any established encoding scheme to enhance its performance, whenever the data which is characterized by a non-stationary distribution. We have demonstrated this fact by utilizing it in the context of the adaptive Fano scheme, and also in the context of an entropy-based scheme, adaptive arithmetic coding.*

2   The Stochastic Learning-Based Weak Estimator

We consider a source alphabet $\mathcal{S} = \{s_1, \ldots, s_m\}$, where $m \geq 2$, with probabilities of occurrence $\mathcal{P} = [p_1, \ldots, p_m]^T$, the *binary* code alphabet $\mathcal{A} = \{0, 1\}$, and the input sequence $\mathcal{X} = x(1) \ldots x(M)$. First of all, we assume that we start with arbitrary probabilities for the source symbols. The set $\mathcal{S}$ is considered as a list sorted in a non-increasing order of the occurrence probabilities. Since the *actual* probabilities for the symbols are unknown, we will rather use estimates, namely $\hat{\mathcal{P}}(n) = [\hat{p}_1(n), \ldots, \hat{p}_m(n)]^T$, which are obtained in a well-specified manner. Additionally, to establish a convention between the encoder and the decoder, the initial estimated probabilities are initialized to $\frac{1}{m}$.

When dealing with an alphabet of m source symbols, whose probabilities have to be estimated "on the fly", i.e. during the encoding phase, the best model is to assume that the input symbol is drawn from a multinomial random variable. The problem of estimating the parameters of a multinomial distribution has been efficiently solved by the recently introduced SLWE [11]. The multinomial distribution is characterized by two parameters, namely, the *number* of trials, and a probability vector which determines the probability of a specific event (from a pre-specified set of events) occurring. In this regard, we assume that the number of observations is the number of trials. Therefore, the problem is to estimate the latter probability *vector* associated with the set of possible outcomes or trials.

Let X be a multinomially distributed random variable, which takes on the values from the set $\{s_1, s_2, \ldots, s_m\}$. We assume that X is governed by the probability distribution $\mathcal{P} = [p_1, p_2, \ldots, p_m]^T$ as follows:
$X = s_i$ with probability p_i, where $\sum_{i=1}^{m} p_i = 1$.

Also, let $x(n)$ be a concrete realization of X at time 'n'. The intent of the exercise is to estimate $\mathcal{P}$, i.e., p_i for $i = 1, \ldots, m$. We achieve this by maintaining a running estimate $\hat{\mathcal{P}}(n) = [\hat{p}_1(n), \ldots, \hat{p}_m(n)]^T$ of $\mathcal{P}$, where $\hat{p}_i(n)$ is the estimate of p_i at time 'n', for $i = 1, \ldots, m$. Then, the value of $\hat{p}_1(n)$ is updated as per the following simple rule (the rules for other values of $\hat{p}_j(n)$ are similar):

$$\hat{p}_1(n+1) \leftarrow \hat{p}_1 + (1 - \lambda) \sum_{j \neq 1} \hat{p}_j \quad \text{when } x(n) = s_1 \qquad (1)$$

$$\leftarrow \lambda \hat{p}_1 \qquad \text{when } x(n) \neq s_1 \qquad (2)$$

where λ is the parameter of the scheme, with $0 \leq \lambda \leq 1$.

In the rest of the paper, the vector $\hat{\mathcal{P}}(n) = [\hat{p}_1(n), \hat{p}_2(n), \ldots, \hat{p}_m(n)]^T$ refers to the estimate of $\mathcal{P} = [p_1, p_2, \ldots, p_r]^T$ at time 'n', and we will omit the reference to time 'n' in $\hat{\mathcal{P}}(n)$ whenever there is no confusion. The first result that has been shown is that the distribution of $\mathrm{E}\left[\hat{\mathcal{P}}(n+1)\right]$ follows $\mathrm{E}\left[\hat{\mathcal{P}}(n)\right]$ in a Markovian manner. This leads to two results, namely that of the limiting distribution of the chain, and that which concerns the rate of convergence of the chain. In [11], it has been shown that the former is *independent* of the learning parameter, λ, and the latter is *only* determined by it (and not a function of it). The formal results concerning the SLWE are stated below. The proofs of the results are found in [11], and omitted here to avoid repetition.

Theorem 1. *Let* X *be a multinomially distributed random variable governed by the distribution* $\mathcal{P}$, *and* $\hat{\mathcal{P}}(n)$ *be the estimate of* $\mathcal{P}$ *at time 'n' obtained by (1) and (2). Then,*
$$E\left[\hat{\mathcal{P}}(\infty)\right] = \mathcal{P}.$$
$\square$

It has also been shown that the convergence of $\hat{\mathcal{P}}$ to $\mathcal{P}$ occurs in a Markovian manner, and so we now derive the explicit form of the underlying Markovian matrix, say, M. The result is formalized as follows.

Theorem 2. *Let* X *be a multinomially distributed random variable governed by the distribution* $\mathcal{P}$, *and* $\hat{\mathcal{P}}(n)$ *be the estimate of* $\mathcal{P}$ *at time 'n' obtained by (1) and (2). Then, the expected estimated probability vector follows a Markovian behavior in which every off-diagonal term of the underlying Markov matrix has the* same *multiplicative factor,* $(1 - \lambda)$. *Furthermore, the final expected solution is independent of* λ. $\square$

Finally, the convergence and eigenvalue properties of M follow.

Theorem 3. *Let* X *be a multinomially distributed random variable governed by the distribution* $\mathcal{P}$, *and* $\hat{\mathcal{P}}(n)$ *be the estimate of* $\mathcal{P}$ *at time 'n' obtained by (1) and (2). Then, all the non-unity eigenvalues of* M *are exactly* λ, *and thus the rate of converge of* $\mathcal{P}$ *is fully* determined by λ. $\square$

A small value of λ leads to fast convergence and a large variance. On the contrary, a large value of λ leads to slow convergence and a small variance. Although the results we have derived are asymptotic, and thus, are valid only as $n \rightarrow \infty$, realistically, and for all practical purposes, the convergence takes place after a relatively small value of n. If λ is even as "small" as 0.9, after 50 iterations, the variation from the asymptotic value will be of the order of 10^{-50}, because λ also determines the rate of convergence, which again, occurs in a geometric manner [10]. In other words, even if the environment switches its multinomial probability vector after 50 steps, the SLWE will be able to track this change.

3   Adaptive Coding Utilizing the SLWE Schemes

3.1   A *Generic* Estimate-Based Adaptive Fano Coding Scheme

We shall first show how we can implement the adaptive Fano method using an "arbitrary" *generic* estimation process. Let us consider first, the implementation of the encoding procedure for the greedy adaptive version for Fano coding, which is given in [13]. At each time step, the encoding (or decoding) algorithm invokes a procedure to update the symbol probabilities, which utilizes a generic estimation process. To instantiate this generic process to a specific method, we use two variants of the SLWE, namely the model based on the linear reward-inaction (L_{RI}) and nonlinear[1] reward-inaction (N_{RI}) learning automata schemes respectively [10]. Assuming that the nth symbol from the input is unknown, our method encodes the symbol using the estimates for the probabilities at time $n - 1$, $\hat{\mathcal{P}}(n - 1)$, and updates the probabilities using the SLWE.

The scheme that utilizes a linear scheme implements the estimation procedure discussed in Section 2. That is, the probabilities of the symbols for the next encoding step are updated as per Equations (1) and (2). The procedure for updating the probabilities at time 'n', which is invoked by the encoding and decoding algorithms, is implemented in Algorithm **Probability_Updating** shown below. The probabilities of the symbols at time 'n' are maintained in a vector, $\hat{\mathcal{P}}(n)$, which is updated in the algorithm. After the probability update takes place, the list of symbols, $\mathcal{S}(n)$, is sorted in a non-increasing order of the estimates of the occurrence probabilities. Note that this order is not mandatory when using Fano coding or arithmetic coding. The reason for invoking this sorting here is only to achieve a stylistic pattern.

Algorithm 1 Probability_Updating

Input: The source alphabet, probabilities and input symbol at time 'n', $\mathcal{S}(n)$, $\hat{\mathcal{P}}(n)$ and $x(n)$.
Output: The updated probabilities, $\hat{\mathcal{P}}(n + 1)$.
Method:
    procedure UpdateProbabilities(**var** $\mathcal{S}(n)$,$\hat{\mathcal{P}}(n)$: list, $x(n)$: symbol)
        $i \leftarrow$ index of $x(n)$ in $\mathcal{S}(n)$
        for $j \leftarrow 1$ **to** m **do**
          if $i = j$ **then**
            $\hat{p}_i(n + 1) \leftarrow \hat{p}_i - (1 - \lambda) \sum_{k \neq 1} \hat{p}_k$
          else
            $\hat{p}_i(n + 1) \leftarrow \lambda \hat{p}_i$
          endif
        endfor
        Swap s_i and the top-most symbol in $\mathcal{S}(n)$ whose probability is less than $\hat{p}_i(n + 1)$
          (Do the same updating for $\hat{\mathcal{P}}(n + 1)$)
    endprocedure
  end Algorithm Probability_Updating

The implementation of the nonlinear scheme for estimating the probabilities is based on an N_{RI} learning automaton. As in the linear case, we let X be a multinomially distributed random variable, which takes on the values from the set $\{s_1, s_2, \ldots, s_m\}$. We assume that X is governed by the probability distribution $\mathcal{P} = [p_1, p_2, \ldots, p_m]^T$ as follows:

$$X = s_i \text{ with probability } p_i, \text{ where } \sum_{i=1}^{m} p_i = 1.$$

---

[1] Although the properties of the nonlinear SLWE family have not been proven, we believe that they are analogous to those proven for the linear scheme. In any case, the experimental results seem to demonstrate this conjecture.

Let $x(n)$ be a concrete realization of x at time 'n'. The aim is to estimate $\mathcal{P}$, i.e., p_i for $i = 1, \ldots, m$, by maintaining a running estimate $\hat{\mathcal{P}}(n) = [\hat{p}_1(n), \ldots, \hat{p}_m(n)]^T$ of $\mathcal{P}$. Thus, the value of $\hat{p}_1(n+1)$ is updated as per the following nonlinear rule (the rules for other values of $\hat{p}_j(n+1)$ are similar):

$$\hat{p}_1(n+1) \leftarrow \hat{p}_1 + \sum_{j \neq 1} \hat{p}_j - \theta_j\left(\hat{\mathcal{P}}\right) \quad \text{when } x(n) = s_1 \qquad (3)$$

$$\leftarrow \theta_j\left(\hat{\mathcal{P}}\right) \qquad\qquad \text{when } x(n) \neq s_1 \qquad (4)$$

where $\theta_j\left(\hat{\mathcal{P}}\right)$ is a *nonlinear* function of $\hat{p}_1, \ldots, \hat{p}_m$. In our implementation, we use the function $\theta_j\left(\hat{\mathcal{P}}\right) = (\hat{p}_j)^\kappa$, where κ is a positive real number. In practice, κ is typically chosen to be near 2.0.

The algorithm for updating the probabilities by using a nonlinear SLWE scheme is similar to the linear case, except that the updating rule is changed to be that of (3) and (4) in Algorithm **Probability_Updating**. This substitution is trivial and is omitted to avoid repetition.

The analysis of convergence of the SLWE that utilizes a nonlinear updating function, such as the one in (3) and (4) constitutes an open problem that we are currently investigating. Our empirical results in the next section show that the nonlinear scheme works slightly better than the linear one.

3.2   An SLWE-Based Adaptive Entropy Coding Scheme

The results discussed above explain how the SLWE can be incorporated to yield schemes which are (soon shown to be) more efficient than those that estimate using a traditional (for example, maximum likelihood counter-based) estimation method. They, albeit, "sit on top of" a sub-optimal compression method, in this case the Fano coding method. However, with little imagination, we can see how we can easily generalize this strategy for any compression method, where the estimation is achieved using the SLWE and not a traditional estimator. Indeed, we now demonstrate that even better results can be obtained, if the Fano coding method is substituted by an *entropy-based* method, such as *arithmetic coding*. To make the model simpler, we assume that the symbol at time 'n', say s_i, is encoded using a number of bits determined by its information amount, $-\log_2 \hat{p}_i(n)$, which in essence assumes that all symbols in $\mathcal{X}$ occur independently of each other. Under this assumption, the entire input sequence, $\mathcal{X}$, can be encoded using $\left\lceil -\log_2 \prod_{n=1}^{M} \hat{p}(x(n)) \right\rceil = \left\lceil -\sum_{n=1}^{M} \log_2 \hat{p}(x(n)) \right\rceil$ bits.

The formal algorithm to achieve this is straightforward – it merely involves substituting the estimation phase of the entropy-based compression with the SLWE. It is thus omitted here. The corresponding encoding schemes using those entropy based methods for the traditional adaptive encoding, and the encoding that use linear and nonlinear estimation schemes are referred to as[2] *Traditional Estimator Adaptive Entropy-based*

---

[2] We have used the letter 'H' to refer to the term "entropy", as it is widely used in the literature.

(TEAH), Linear-SLWE Estimator Adaptive Entropy-based (LEAH) and *Nonlinear-SLWE Estimator Adaptive Entropy-based (NEAH)* respectively[3].

4   Empirical Results

To demonstrate the power of our encoding schemes, we have conducted some experiments on various real-life files taken from different sources. The set of files that we have chosen include Microsoft word documents containing tables, figures, and OLE objects, postscript files containing text, equations, and figures, Windows executable files, dynamic link libraries, and font format files. The list of the files and their descriptions are given in [13][4]. Note that we have not used standard benchmarks, such as the Canterbury corpus, because of the non-stationary nature of the data we want to examine.

In our simulations, we have implemented the traditional adaptive Fano coding algorithm as proposed in [12], namely TEAF. We have also implemented the adaptive Fano coding approaches introduced in this paper using the linear and nonlinear schemes, which we have called *Linear-SLWE Estimator Adaptive Fano (LEAF)* and *Nonlinear-SLWE Estimator Adaptive Fano (NEAF)* respectively. For the LEAF we have set the value[5] of λ to be 0.999, and for the NEAF the value of κ was set to be 2.0. The empirical results obtained from the simulations on the files described above are shown in Table 1. The first and second columns contain the names of the files and their original size. The subsequent columns contain the results for the three coding methods tested, grouped in two columns each; the first column contains the size (in bytes) of the compressed file, and the second column contains the compression ratio, calculated as $\rho = \left(1 - \frac{\ell_y}{l_x}\right) 100$, where l_x is the length of the input file, and ℓ_y is the length of the compressed file. The last row shows the *total* for each column representing the file sizes, and the *weighted average* for the columns containing the compression ratios.

The results from the table show that the LEAF and the NEAF compress approximately 8% and 9% (respectively) more than the traditional adaptive Fano coding, TEAF. The best results for the LEAF have been obtained in compressing postscript and word document files. We also observe that the NEAF achieves much better compression ratios than the TEAF in word document files, and in file ariali.ttf.

---

[3] This is in contrast to the *Linear-SLWE Estimator Adaptive Fano (LEAF)* and *Nonlinear-SLWE Estimator Adaptive Fano (NEAF)* methods defined for the Fano scheme.

[4] The complete list of the files and their descriptions can be found in this reference, which is the unabridged version of the paper. This paper is also electronically available at:

    http://davinci.newcs.uwindsor.ca/~lrueda/papers/FanoSLWEJnl.pdf.

To assist readers in benchmarking, the following files can be made available upon request: authinst.doc, expaper.doc, fanocode.ps, grantapp.doc, lncsinst.doc, and oplclass.ps. The rest of the benchmark files cannot be made publicly available due to the fact that they are copyrighted. They have to be obtained from the corresponding software packages as tabulated in [13].

[5] A value of λ close to unity is typically used in the field of stochastic learning automata. While setting this value is problem dependent, we have empirically found that 0.999 works well in adaptive data compression.

Table 1. Compression ratio and compressed file sizes for the traditional adaptive Fano coding scheme, the LEAF and NEAF coding schemes on real-life data files

File name	Orig. size (bytes)	TEAF ℓ_y	$\rho\,(\%)$	LEAF ℓ_y	$\rho\,(\%)$	NEAF ℓ_y	$\rho\,(\%)$
agentsvr.exe	242,448	191,922	20.84	179,533	25.95	182,418	24.76
ariali.ttf	200,684	173,210	13.69	157,356	21.59	153,102	23.71
authinst.doc	630,784	203,365	67.76	158,642	74.85	149,370	76.32
expaper.doc	62,976	43,712	30.59	37,949	39.74	36,463	42.10
fanocode.ps	165,149	108,206	34.48	94,085	43.03	98,363	40.44
faxocm.dll	77,584	49,793	35.82	42,958	44.63	43,183	44.34
grantapp.doc	126,976	81,849	35.54	66,980	47.25	68,770	45.84
lncsinst.doc	104,448	86,713	16.98	74,994	28.20	76,320	26.93
oplclass.ps	167,772	110,998	33.84	93,097	44.51	96,251	42.63
timesbi.ttf	233,892	203,463	13.01	186,318	20.34	181,968	22.20
twain.dll	94,784	80,102	15.49	71,998	24.04	72,690	23.31
vcmd.exe	362,256	298,426	17.62	263,722	27.20	271,547	25.04
Avg. — Total	2,469,753	1,631,758	33.93	1,445,534	41.47	1,430,445	42.08

The empirical results for the entropy-based adaptive coding methods are shown in Table 2. The results show that if enhanced by using the linear and nonlinear SLWE schemes, a gain of nearly 9% and 10% (respectively) is obtained with respect to the traditional entropy-based encoding scheme. As can be expected, we observe that the entropy-based encoding methods achieve more efficient compression than the Fano coding. We also notice that the LEAH and the NEAH achieve the best results for word documents, dynamic link libraries, and postscript files. As opposed to this, it can be seen that the NEAH works slightly less efficiently in executable files. This behavior indeed demonstrates that encoding methods which are enhanced with SLWE schemes work much better for data which show a substantially *high degree of non-stationarity*. This is the case of the word documents used in the testing, which contain fragments of text, followed by a table or a figure, followed by text again, and so on. A similar scenario occurs in the postscript files used in the testing, which contain text, figures, tables and mathematical equations. These two types of files are the ones in which the learning schemes achieve superior compression ratio.

Although a zeroth-order statistical model has been implemented, it is easy to see that the adaptive encoding schemes introduced in this paper can also be implemented using higher-order models, such as the LZ algorithms, PPM, and Markov models. It is also important to point out that our schemes achieve much better compression ratio than the traditional encoding, and still use *linear* space complexity, as opposed to k^{th}-order statistical models, which require $O(m^k)$ space complexity.

5 Discussions

From our perspective, we would like to emphasize that the compression schemes introduced in this paper constitute a possibly emerging paradigm, which are in an extreme

Table 2. Empirical results obtained after testing the entropy-based coding utilizing the traditional probability updating method, the LEAH and NEAH learning schemes on real-life data files

File name	Orig. size	TEAH		LEAH		NEAH	
	(bytes)	ℓ_y	$\rho\,(\%)$	ℓ_y	$\rho\,(\%)$	ℓ_y	$\rho\,(\%)$
agentsvr.exe	242,448	190,249	21.43	178,054	26.56	180,260	25.65
ariali.ttf	200,684	171,966	14.31	156,373	22.08	151,516	24.50
authinst.doc	630,784	201,094	68.12	132,149	79.05	113,289	82.04
expaper.doc	62,976	43,082	31.59	36,778	41.60	34,989	44.44
fanocode.ps	165,149	107,264	35.05	93,177	43.58	97,520	40.95
faxocm.dll	77,584	48,195	37.88	40,716	47.52	40,569	47.71
grantapp.doc	126,976	78,268	38.36	64,669	49.07	65,761	48.21
lncsinst.doc	104,448	85,261	18.37	73,375	29.75	74,283	28.88
oplclass.ps	167,772	109,874	34.51	92,023	45.15	94,724	43.54
timesbi.ttf	233,892	202,013	13.63	185,102	20.86	180,167	22.97
twain.dll	94,784	79,401	16.23	71,249	24.83	71,638	24.42
vcmd.exe	362,256	296,507	18.15	261,404	27.84	268,287	25.94
Avg. — Total	2,469,753	1,613,173	34.68	1,385,069	43.92	1,373,004	44.41

preliminary stage. We thus believe that the use of the techniques introduced here and the files used in the testing are quite promising, which could lead to a vast amount of potential research in the near future. To highlight these advantages, we itemize below a few possible research directions for this novel paradigm:

- Within the SLWE schemes, there are numerous different learning automata schemes that could be used, including linear, nonlinear, continuous, discretized, pursuit learning, and estimator algorithms. The use of these variants of learning models in conjunction with adaptive coding techniques is worth investigating.
- The analysis of the convergence of the nonlinear reward-inaction SLWE schemes for stationary and nonstationary sources is a problem that we are currently investigating.
- In our encoding schemes, we have considered a zeroth-order statistical model. This can be easily extended by incorporating SLWE schemes to enhance encoding techniques that utilize higher-order statistical models, including Markov models, LZ algorithms, and PPM.
- Although our schemes have shown (in our opinion) amazing results for the set of files used for the testing, there is still a fair amount of work to be done in the analysis of *stationarity*. In other words, the question of how we can theoretically evaluate our schemes on non-stationary sources, and how we can measure the degree of stationarity (or non-stationarity) in data remains open. The characterization of such a model, and its analysis are far from trivial.
- Another potential model for the encoding models introduced in this paper is the extension of the encoding algorithms to multi-symbol code alphabets. This will be an extension to the work found in [12].

- Finally, we believe that the set of files utilized in our simulations, which show some degree of "non-stationarity", constitute the starting point for a benchmark that contains relevant files to be used in testing new encoding schemes.

6 Conclusions

In this paper, we have introduced two novel adaptive encoding models, which were obtained by introducing SLWE techniques to update probabilities in the traditional adaptive encoding algorithms. We have proposed the corresponding encoding and decoding algorithms that implement the adaptive Fano coding method, and adaptively update the probabilities of the source symbols using versions of the linear and nonlinear SLWE schemes. For the two learning schemes utilized in our model, we have introduced the corresponding updating functions and adjusted the relevant parameters that make our model work efficiently in real-life data files.

Our empirical results show that the introduction of SLWE schemes to the adaptive Fano coding leads to gains of 8% and 9% in compression ratio. When entropy-based methods are enhanced using linear and nonlinear SLWE schemes, the gain in compression with respect to the traditional adaptive coding is 9% and 10% respectively on the set of files used for the testing. We have also observed that the maximal gain in compression efficiency is exhibited in files that contain data from different sources and probability distributions, such as word documents and postscript files, which include figures, tables, and equations. In particular, we emphasize that we have used a zeroth order statistical model to yield quite good results, although it requires only *linear* space complexity, as opposed to higher-order models, such as Markov models, which require *exponential* space complexity.

References

1. T. Bell, J. Cleary, and I. Witten. *Text Compression*. Prentice-Hall, 1990.
2. G. Cormack and R. Horspool. Algorithms for Adaptive Huffman Codes. *Information Processing Letters*, pages 169–165, 1984.
3. M. Effros, K. Visweswariah, S. Kulkarni, and Sergio Verdú. Universal Lossless Source Coding With the Burrows Wheeler Transform. *IEEE Transactions on Information Theory*, 48(5):1061–1081, 2002.
4. R. Gallager. Variations on a Theme by Huffman. *IEEE Transactions on Information Theory*, 24(6):668–674, 1978.
5. D. Hankerson, G. Harris, and P. Johnson Jr. *Introduction to Information Theory and Data Compression*. CRC Press, 1998.
6. P. Jacquet, W. Szpankowski, and I. Apostol. A Universal Predictor Based on Pattern Matching. *IEEE Transactions on Information Theory*, 48(6):1462–1472, 2002.
7. J. C. Kieffer and E. Yang. Grammar-Bassed Codes: A new Class of Universal Lossless Source Codes. *IEEE Transactions on Information Theory*, 46(3):737–754, 2000.
8. D. Knuth. Dynamic Huffman Coding. *Journal of Algorithms*, 6:163–180, 1985.
9. J. Muramatsu. On the Performance of Recency Rank and Block Sorting Universal Lossless Data Compression Algorithms. *IEEE Transactions on Information Theory*, 48(9):2621–2625, 2002.

10. K. Narendra and M. Thathachar. *Learning Automata. An Introduction*. Prentice Hall, 1989.
11. B.J. Oommen and L. Rueda. Stochastic Learning-based Weak Estimation of Multinomial Random Variables and Its Applications to Non-stationary Environments. (Submitted for Publication).
12. L. Rueda and B. J. Oommen. Greedy Adaptive Fano Coding. In *Proceedings of the 2002 IEEE Aerospace Conference*, BigSky, MT, USA. Track 10.0407, March 2002.
13. L. Rueda and B.J. Oommen. Weak Estimator-based Novel Adaptive Compression Techniques Applicable for Files with Non-Stationary Distributions. (Submitted for Publication).
14. M. J. Weinberger and E. Ordentlich. On Delayed Prediction of Individual Sequences. *IEEE Transactions on Information Theory*, 48(7):1959–1976, 2002.

Text Summarization and Singular Value Decomposition

Josef Steinberger and Karel Ježek

University of West Bohemia in Pilsen,
Department of Computer Science and Engineering,
30614, Univerzitni 22, Plzeň, Czech Republic
{jstein, jezek_ka}@kiv.zcu.cz

Abstract. In this paper we present the usage of singular value decomposition (SVD) in text summarization. Firstly, we mention the taxonomy of generic text summarization methods. Then we describe principles of the SVD and its possibilities to identify semantically important parts of a text. We propose a modification of the SVD-based summarization, which improves the quality of generated extracts. In the second part we propose two new evaluation methods based on SVD, which measure content similarity between an original document and its summary. In evaluation part, our summarization approach is compared with 5 other available summarizers. For evaluation of a summary quality we used, apart from a classical content-based evaluator, both newly developed SVD-based evaluators. Finally, we study the influence of the summary length on its quality from the angle of the three evaluation methods mentioned.

1 Introduction

The actual huge amount of electronic information has to be reduced to enable the users to handle this information more effectively. Short summaries can be presented to users, for example, in place of full-length documents found by search engine in response to a user's query. In section 2 we mention prior approaches to text summarization and section 3 covers our previous research focus. In section 4 we describe the method based on SVD which has been recently published. We have further modified and improved this method. One of the most controversial fields in the summary research is its evaluation process. Next part of the article deals with possibilities of summary evaluation. We propose there two new evaluation methods based on SVD, which measure a content similarity between an original document and its summary. At the end of the paper we present evaluation results and further research directions.

2 Approaches in Automatic Text Summarization

We can begin with classical approaches that include the use of surface level indicators of informative relevance and corpus statistics that can be applied to unrestricted text. Luhn [7] developed the first sentence extraction algorithm which uses term frequencies to measure sentence relevance. Kupiec et al. [5] implemented a trainable

T. Yakhno (Ed.): ADVIS 2004, LNCS 3261, pp. 245–254, 2004.
© Springer-Verlag Berlin Heidelberg 2004

Bayesian classifier that computes the probability that a sentence in a source document should be included in a summary. The next group consists of methods which take the text cohesion into account. An example is the lexical chains method which searches for chains of context words in the text [6]. Ono et al. [11] and Marcu [8] made use of Rhetorical Structure Theory, which is a descriptive theory about text organization, as the bases for text summarization. The approach consists in the construction of a rhetorical tree for a given text. Knowledge intensive approaches are based on the extensive encoding of world knowledge about specific situations. These methods base the selection of information not on the surface level properties of the text, but on expected information about a well known situation. The next approach is mapping natural language into predefined, structured representations, that, when instantiated, represent the key information from the original source (e. g. Concept-based abstracting [9]). While sentence extraction is a currently wide-spread and useful technique, more research in summarization is now moving towards summarization by generation. Jing and McKeown [10] proposed a *cut-and-paste* strategy as a computational process of automatic abstracting and a sentence reduction strategy in order to produce concise sentences. A quite new approach in text summarization uses the singular value decomposition.

3   Our Previous Summarization Research

Our recent research has been focused namely on the use of inductive machine learning methods for automatic document summarization. We analyzed various approaches to document summarization, using some existing algorithms and combining these with a novel use of itemsets. The resulted summarizer was evaluated by comparing classification of original documents and that of summary generated automatically [3]. Now we decided to investigate possibilities of using singular value decomposition in both creating a summary and its evaluation.

4   SVD-Based Summarization

Yihong Gong and Xin Liu have published the idea of using SVD in text summarization in 2002 [1]. The process starts with creation of a term by sentences matrix $A = [A_1, A_2, ..., A_n]$ with each column vector A_i, representing the weighted term-frequency vector of sentence i in the document under consideration. If there are a total of m terms and n sentences in the document, then we will have an $m \times n$ matrix A for the document. Since every word does not normally appear in each sentence, the matrix A is sparse.

Given an $m \times n$ matrix A, where without loss of generality $m \geq n$, the SVD of A is defined as:

$$A = U \Sigma V^T, \tag{1}$$

where $U = [u_{ij}]$ is an $m \times n$ column-orthonormal matrix whose columns are called left singular vectors; $\Sigma = \text{diag}(\sigma_1, \sigma_2, ..., \sigma_n)$ is an $n \times n$ diagonal matrix, whose diagonal elements are non-negative singular values sorted in descending order, and $\mathbf{V} = [v_{ij}]$ is an $n \times n$ orthonormal matrix, whose columns are called right singular vectors (see figure 1). If rank($\mathbf{A}$) = r, then (see [4]) Σ satisfies:

$$\sigma_1 \geq \sigma_2 ... \geq \sigma_r > \sigma_{r+1} = ... = \sigma_n = 0 \cdot \qquad (2)$$

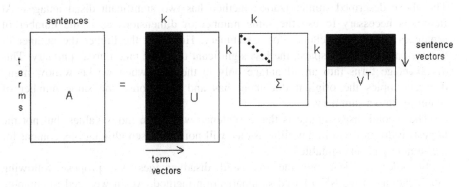

Fig. 1. Singular value decomposition

The interpretation of applying the SVD to the terms by sentences matrix $\mathbf{A}$ can be made from two different viewpoints. From transformation point of view, the SVD derives a mapping between the m-dimensional space spawned by the weighted term-frequency vectors and the r-dimensional singular vector space. From semantic point of view, the SVD derives the latent semantic structure from the document represented by matrix $\mathbf{A}$. This operation reflects a breakdown of the original document into r linearly-independent base vectors or concepts. Each term and sentence from the document is jointly indexed by these base vectors/concepts. A unique SVD feature is that it is capable of capturing and modelling interrelationships among terms so that it can semantically cluster terms and sentences. Furthermore, as demonstrated in [4], if a word combination pattern is salient and recurring in document, this pattern will be captured and represented by one of the singular vectors. The magnitude of the corresponding singular value indicates the importance degree of this pattern within the document. Any sentences containing this word combination pattern will be projected along this singular vector, and the sentence that best represents this pattern will have the largest index value with this vector.

As each particular word combination pattern describes a certain topic/concept in the document, the facts described above naturally lead to the hypothesis that each singular vector represents a salient topic/concept of the document, and the magnitude of its corresponding singular value represents the degree of importance of the salient topic/concept.

Based on the above discussion, authors [1] proposed a summarization method which uses the matrix $\mathbf{V}^{\mathrm{T}}$. This matrix describes an importance degree of each topic in each sentence. The summarization process chooses the most informative sentence for each topic. It means that the k'th sentence we choose has the largest index value in k'th right singular vector in matrix $\mathbf{V}^\mathrm{T}$.

5 Modified SVD-Based Summarization

The above described summarization method has two significant disadvantages. At first it is necessary to use the same number of dimensions as is the number of sentences we want to choose for a summary. However, the higher the number of dimensions of reduced space, the less significant topic we take into a summary. This disadvantage turns into an advantage only in the case when we know how many different topics the original document has and we choose the same number of sentences into a summary.

The second disadvantage is that a sentence with large index values, but not the largest (it doesn't win in any dimension), will not be chosen although its content for the summary is very suitable.

In order to clear out the discussed disadvantages, we propose following modifications in the SVD-based summarization method. Again we need to compute SVD of a term by sentences matrix. We get the three matrices as shown in figure 1.

For each sentence vector in matrix $\mathbf{V}$ (its components are multiplied by corresponding singular values) we compute its length. The reason of the multiplication is to favour the index values in the matrix $\mathbf{V}$ that correspond to the highest singular values (the most significant topics).

Formally:

$$s_k = \sqrt{\sum_{i=1}^{n} v_{k,i}^2 \cdot \sigma_i^2} \, , \tag{3}$$

where s_k is the length of the vector of k'th sentence in the modified latent vector space. It is its significance score for summarization too. n is a number of dimensions of the new space. This value is independent of the number of summary sentences (it is a parameter of the method). In our experiments we chose the dimensions whose singular values didn't fall under the half of the highest singular value (but it is possible to set a different strategy). Finally, we put into the summary the sentences with the highest values in vector s.

6 Summary Evaluation Approaches

Evaluation of automatic summarization in a standard and inexpensive way is a difficult task. It is an equally important area as the own summarization process and that's why many evaluation approaches were developed [2].

Co-selection measures include precision and recall of co-selected sentences. These methods require having at one's disposal the "right extract" (to which we could compute precision and recall). We can obtain this extract in several ways. The most common way is to obtain some human (manual) extracts and to declare the average of these extracts as the "ideal (right) extract". However, obtaining human extracts is usually problematic. Another problem is that two manual summaries of the same input do not share in general many identical sentences.

We can clear out the above discussed weakness of co-selection measures by content-based similarity measures. These methods compute the similarity between two documents at a more fine-grained level than just sentences. The basic method evaluates the similarity between the full text document and its summary with the cosine similarity measure, computed by the following formula:

$$\cos(X,Y) = \frac{\sum x_i * y_i}{\sqrt{\sum (x_i)^2} * \sqrt{\sum (y_i)^2}} , \qquad (4)$$

where X and Y are representations based on the vector space model.

Relevance correlation is a measure for accessing the relative decrease in retrieval performance when indexing summaries instead of full documents [2].

Task-based evaluations measure human performance using the summaries for a certain task (*after* the summaries are created). We can for example measure the suitability of using summaries instead of full texts for text categorization [3]. This evaluation requires a classified corpus of texts.

7   Using SVD in Summary Evaluation

We classify this new evaluation method to a content-based category because, like the classical cosine content-based approach (see 6.), it evaluates a summary quality via content similarity between a full text and its summary.

Our method uses SVD of the terms by sentences matrix (see 4.), exactly the matrix **U**. This matrix represents the degree of importance of terms in salient topics/concepts. In evaluation we measure the similarity between the matrix **U** derived from the SVD performed on the original document and the matrix **U** derived from the SVD performed on the summary. For appraising this similarity we have proposed two measures.

7.1   First Left Singular Vector Similarity

This method compares first left singular vectors of the full text SVD (i. e. SVD performed on the original document) and the summary SVD (i. e. SVD performed on the summary). These vectors correspond to the most salient word pattern in the full text and its summary (we can call it the main topic).

Then we measure the angle between the first left singular vectors. They are normalized, so we can use the following formula:

$$\cos \varphi = \sum_{i=1}^{n} ue_i \cdot uf_i , \qquad (5)$$

where uf is the first left singular vector of the full text SVD, ue is the first left singular vector of the summary SVD (values, which correspond to particular terms, are sorted up the full text terms and instead of missing terms are zeroes), n is a number of unique terms in the full text.

7.2 U.Σ -Based Similarity

This evaluation method compares a summary with the original document from an angle of n most salient topics. We propose the following process:

- Perform the SVD on a document matrix (see 4).
- For each term vector in matrix **U** (its components are multiplied by corresponding singular values) compute its length. The reason of the multiplication is to favour the index values in the matrix **U** that correspond to the highest singular values (the most significant topics). Formally:

$$s_k = \sqrt{\sum_{i=1}^{n} u_{k,i}^2 \cdot \sigma_i^2} , \tag{6}$$

where s_k is the length of the k'st term vector in the modified latent vector space, n is a number of dimensions of the new space. In our experiments we chose the dimensions whose singular values didn't fall under the half of the highest singular value (by analogy to the summary method described above).

- From the lengths of the term vectors (s_k) make a resulting term vector, whose index values hold an information about the term significance in the modified latent space (see figure 2).
- Normalize the resulting vector.

This process is performed on the original document and on its summary (for the same number of dimensions according to the summary) (see figure 2). In the result, we get one vector corresponding to the term vector lengths of the full text and one of its summary. As a similarity measure we use again the angle between resulting vectors (see 7.1).

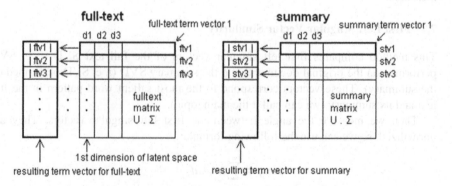

Fig. 2. Creation of a resulting term vectors of a full text and a summary

This evaluation method has the following advantage above the previous one. Suppose, an original document contains two topics with the virtually the same significance (corresponding singular values are almost the same). When the second significant topic outweighs the first one in a summary, the main topic of the summary will not be consistent with the main topic of the original. Taking more singular vectors (than just one) into account removes this weakness.

8 Experiments

8.1 Testing Collection

We tested our document summarizer using the Reuters Corpus Volume 1 (RCV1) collection (the first "official" collection Reuters corpus released to the community of researches, containing over 800 thousand documents). We prepared a collection by selecting RCV1 documents with the length of at least 20 sentences. The selected documents had to be suitable for the summarization task. Table 1 contains details about our collection.

Table 1. Testing collection – details

Number of documents	115
Minimum number of sentences in document	20
Maximum number of sentences in document	61
Average number of sentences per document	29
Average number of words per document	775
Average number of significant words per document	301
Average number of distinct significant words per document	187

8.2 Results and Discussion

We evaluated the following summarizers:

- Gong + Liu SVD summarizer (SVD–G+L)
- SVD summarizer based on our approach (SVD–OUR)
- RANDOM – evaluation based on the average of 10 random extracts
- LEAD – first n sentences
- 1-ITEMSET – based on itemsets method [3]
- TF.IDF – based on frequency method [3]

These summarizers were evaluated by the following three evaluation methods:

- Cosine similarity – classical content-based method
- SVD similarity – First left singular vector similarity
- SVD similarity – U.Σ-Based similarity

The summarization ratio was set to 20 %. Results are presented in the following table. Values are averages of cosines of angles between a full text and its summary.

Table 2. Summary quality evaluation

Evaluator	Summarizer					
	SVD-L+G	SVD-OUR	RANDOM	LEAD	1-ITEMSET	TF.IDF
Cosine similarity	0.761	**0.765**	0.642	0.689	0.759	0.750
First left sing. vector simil.	0.799	**0.824**	0.516	0.656	0.796	0.774
U.Σ-Based similarity	0.846	**0.848**	0.545	0.613	0.810	0.809

The classical cosine evaluator shows only small differences between summarizers (the best summarizer – 0.765 and the worst (random) – 0.642). It is caused by a shallow level of this evaluation method which takes into account only term counts in compared documents. The evaluation based on SVD is a more fine-grained approach. It is possible to say that it evaluates a summary via term co-occurrences in sentences.

Figures 3-5 show the dependencies of a summary quality on the summarization ratio and the evaluation methods for our SVD-based and random summarizer.

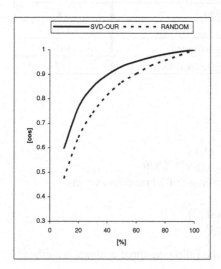

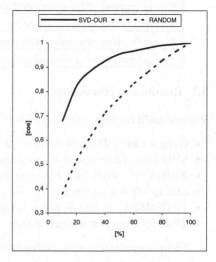

Fig. 3. Cosine similarity evaluation

Fig. 4. First singular vector similarity evaluation

In the evaluation by the first left singular vector we noticed the disadvantage discussed in 6.2 (proved in 10% of documents). The U.Σ -Based evaluation removes this weakness.

In the following graphs we can see a big difference between random and our summarizer by SVD evaluation approaches.

Next, we observed from the evaluation, the SVD summarizer has been shown as the expressively best with the evaluator (3). This property was expected.

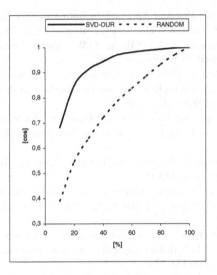

Fig. 5. U.Σ -Based similarity evaluation

9 Conclusion

This paper introduced a new approach to automatic text summarization and summary evaluation. The practical tests proved that our summarizing method outperforms the other examined methods. Our other experiments showed that SVD is very sensitive on a stoplist and a lemmatization process. Therefore we are working on improved versions of lemmatizers for English and Czech languages. In future research we plan to try other weighing schemes and a normalization of a sentence vector on the SVD input. Of course, other evaluations are needed, especially on longer texts than the Reuters documents are. Our final goal is to integrate our summarizer into a natural language processing system capable of searching and presenting web documents in a concise and coherent form.

This work has been partly supported by grants No. MSM 235200005 and ME494.

References

1. Gong, Y., Liu, X.: Generic Text Summarization Using Relevance Measure and Latent Semantic Analysis. Proceedings of the 24th ACM SIGIR conference on Research and development in information retrieval, New Orleans, Louisiana, United States (2001) 19-25
2. Radev, R., Teufel, S., Saggion, H., Lam, W., Blitzer, J., Qi, H., Celebi, A., Liu, D., Drabek, E.: Evaluation Challenges in Large-scale Document Summarization. Proceeding of the 41st meeting of the Association for Computational Linguistics, Sapporo, Japan (2003) 375-382
3. Hynek, J., Ježek, K.: Practical Approach to Automatic Text Summarization. Proceedings of the ELPUB '03 conference, Guimaraes, Portugal (2003) 378-388
4. Berry, M.W., Dumais, S.T., O'Brien, G.W.: Using Linear Algebra for Intelligent Information Retrieval. SIAM Review (1995)
5. Kupiec, J., Pedersen, J., Chen, F.: A trainable Document Summarizer. Proceedings of the ACM SIGIR Conference on Research and Development in Information Retrieval, Seattle, Washington, United States (1995) 68-73
6. Barzilay, R., Elhadad, M.: Using Lexical Chains for Text Summarization. Proceedings of the Intelligent Scalable Text Summarization Workshop (ISTS'97), ACL Madrid, Spain (1997)
7. Luhn, H. P.: Automatic Creation of Literature Abstracts. IBM Journal and Research Development 2(2) (1958) 159-165
8. Marcu D.: From Discourse Structures to Text Summaries. Proceedings of the ACL'97/EACL'97 Workshop on Intelligent Scalable Text Summarization, Madrid, Spain (1997) 82-88
9. Jones, P.A., Paice, C.D.: A 'select and generate' Approach to Automatic Abstracting. Proceeding of the 14th British Computer Society Information Retrieval Colloquium, Springer Verlag (1992) 151-154
10. Jing, H., McKeown, K.: Cut and Paste Text Summarization. Proceedings of the 1st meeting of the North Americat Chapter of the Association for Computational Linguistics, Seattle, Washington, USA (2000) 178-185
11. Ono, K., Sumita, K., Miike, S.: Abstract Generation Based on Rhetorical Structure Extraction. Proceedings of the 15th International Conference on Computational Linguistics, Kyoto, Japan (1994) 344-348

Sentence Boundary Detection in Turkish

B. Taner Dinçer and Bahar Karaoğlan

Ege Üniversitesi, Uluslararası Bilgisayar Enstitüsü , 35100 Bornova, İzmir, Türkiye
{dtaner, bahar}@ube.ege.edu.tr

Abstract. In this paper, we describe a solution method for sentence boundary detection in Turkish. The method exploits simple heuristic knowledge of Turkish syllabication and its phonetic rules for disambiguation of dots. The test accuracy of the algorithm is measured as 96.02%. The main contribution of this study is considered as presenting a new lexicon free method for differentiating EOS (end of sentence) dots from the ones that are used for other purposes.

1 Introduction

The sentence boundary detection is a dilemma of text normalization task that is the main issue of many text processing (i.e., syntactic parsing, information extraction, machine translation, text alignment, document summarization etc.) and information retrieval applications. Sentences should always end with punctuation: exclamation sign, question mark, or a period. The sentence boundary detection (or sentence boundary disambiguation, period disambiguation for tokenization, sentence segmentation, or sentence splitting) is a trivial task when the sentence ends with an exclamation point or a question mark. However, a dot may not always signal the end of a sentence. In some cases, it is not trivial to decide whether a dot is a full stop, a part of an abbreviation or both. In this respect, the sentence boundary detection is simply a problem of identifying the dots, which are full stops.

In this paper, we present a heuristic scheme for period disambiguation in written Turkish texts. The Turkish syllabication and the phonetic rules are used collectively to resolve ambiguous cases. The accuracy of our approach is 96.02%.

This paper is organized as follows: In section 2, after giving a brief overview on sentence boundary detection related work, we introduce our approach. In section 3, we present our test results, and section 4 is the conclusion.

2 Sentence Boundary Detection

2.1 Previous Works

In computational linguistic literature, the problem of sentence boundary detection is attacked in two major approached: 1-) Rule-based approaches and 2-) Machine Learning approaches. The rule based approach exploits manually constructed rules

T. Yakhno (Ed.): ADVIS 2004, LNCS 3261, pp. 255–262, 2004.

that are usually encoded in terms of regular expression grammars and supplementary lists of abbreviations, common words, proper names, and appropriate feature sets of syntactic information. For instance, Aberdeen et al. [2] uses a sentence-splitting module, which contains about 100 regular-expression rules, in the Alembic workbench study. In the Rule-based systems, there are two shortcomings: the first one is developing a good rule base is an ambiguous task itself, and the second one is that the systems are closely tailored to a particular training corpus and are not easily portable to other domains. There are several approaches to the problem of sentence boundary detection using Machine Learning techniques. The examples include the Maximum Entropy approach of Reynar and Ratnaparki [3], the Decision Tree Classifier approach of Riley [4], and Neural Network approach of Palmer and Hearst [5]. In addition, there are hybrid systems such as the Mikheev's work [6], which integrates part-of-speech tagging task based on Hidden Markov model of the language and the Maximum Entropy into sentence boundary detection.

In the field of sentence boundary detection for written Turkish texts, the first noticeable published work is seen as a module in Tür's study [1]. This system is a combination of two language models: word based and morphology based. Word based model produces the probability of being a sentence boundary for each word from the surface form of that word. It uses a supplementary lexicon of Turkish word forms. In addition, morphological analysis of each word is produced with a morphological parser based on a two-level language model of Turkish. In the same time, all possible morphological parse (all possible part-of-speech combinations) of each word is assigned a probability of being a sentence boundary. After all, these two probabilities are interpolated under a Hidden Markov Model. However, the word model has a lexicon, which has a high space complexity for Turkish as stated in Hankamer's work [12]. On the top, two-level language model, theoretically, is a NP-hard problem as stated in the Barton's work [11]. Although this model is very accurate, it is, unfortunately, very complex. Others include Oflazer et al. [7] and the LC-STAR project [8].

2.2 Evaluation Metric

Evaluation metric of our test is based on error rates of the period disambiguation process. The formula for error rate is:

$$ER = \frac{(\#\ of\ false\ alarms)\ +\ (\#\ of\ misses)}{(total\ \#\ of\ dots)} \tag{1}$$

In equation 1, the number of false alarms is the count of the dots that our algorithms detects as full stops but actually are not. Conversely, the number of misses is the count of full stop dots that our algorithm fails to detect. The total number of dots is the count of all dots in the corpus.

2.3 Syllabication in Turkish

Turkish is an agglutinative and a free constituent order language, with high productive morphology, which has a rich set of derivational and inflectional suffixes. In Turkish, syllabication is a well-defined system composed of few simple rules. An ordinary

Turkish word may be composed of a sequence of one or more six predefined syllable patterns: V, VC, VCC, CV, CVC, and CVCC (C: consonant; V: vowel). The first three patterns may only appear in the beginning of a word. The remaining last three patterns may appear anywhere in an ordinary Turkish word. Hence, a word has a Turkish syllabication if one can find a sequence of these patterns in combination in the given word. Dalkılıç and Dalkılıç [10] study is a good reference for an extended statistical analysis of Turkish n-gram letter patterns. There are 8 vowels (*a, e, i, ı, u* and *ü*) and 21 consonants (*b, c, ç, d, f, g, ğ, h, j, k, l, m, n, p, r, s, ş, t, v, y* and *z*) in Turkish alphabet. Some examples of Turkish syllabication are given in Table 1.

Table 1. Examples of Turkish syllabication

Word	Pattern	Syllables
Türkçe	CVCC-CV	Türk-çe
zonklamak	CVCC-CV-CVC	zonk-la-mak
alkış	VC-CVC	al-kış
ürkmek	VCC-CVC	ürk-mek

2.4 Our Approach

We represented all possible combinations around a dot with a triplet. For example, *[w * W]* denotes the situation where a letter sequence *w* which starts with a lower-case character, is followed by a dot (represented by asterisk "*") which is then followed by a letter sequence *W* which starts with an uppercase character. The symbols and their meanings in our notation are listed in Table 2.

Table 2. Notation

Symbol	Meaning
w	All letter sequences starting with a lowercase character.
W	All letter sequences start with an uppercase character
#	All number sequences. (Real, integer cardinal or ordinal, date, time, telephones, etc.)
T	Apostrophe (')
TT	Quote character (")
K	Dash (-)
V	Comma (,)
(	Open parentheses
)	Close parentheses
:	Colon
;	Semi colon
P	All punctuation including not listed ones such as %, &, $, etc.
EOS	End of Sentence
~EOS	Not End of Sentence
∞	All kind of tokens (w, W, #, T, TT, K, V, "(", ")", P)

In Table 3, the triplets that occur in our test corpus are listed with their frequencies. In this listing, punctuation combinations *[P * ∞]* which appear with a frequency of 495 as EOS is excluded for simplicity. Zero frequency cases in either *EOS* or *~EOS* column mean that there is no instance of this particular combination in our test corpus. Nevertheless, it does not mean that these combinations can never be seen and should be excluded from the consideration. These cases are ignored due to their little effect on the decision process on sentence boundary detection.

Table 3. The frequency table of the triplets in test corpus with respect to being EOS

Case	EOS	~EOS	Case	EOS	~EOS	Case	EOS	~EOS
[w * w]	8	10	[W * w]	0	10	[# * w]	0	267
[w * W]	9395	1	[W * W]	739	183	[# * W]	36	106
[w * #]	320	2	[W * #]	44	1	[# * #]	1	27
[w * T]	41	1	[W * T]	3	5	[# * T]	0	1
[w * TT]	601	0	[W * TT]	41	1	[# * TT]	0	16
[w * ( ]	57	0	[W * ( ]	9	0	[# * ( ]	0	1
[w *)]	19	0	[W *)]	3	0	[# *)]	1	3
[w * K]	174	0	[W * K]	38	0	[# * K]	0	8
[w * /]	1	0	[W * V]	0	3	[# * V]	0	28
Total	**10616**	**14**		**877**	**203**		**38**	**457**

We concentrate our discussion on none zero frequency cases, especially on the cases having high degree of ambiguity such as *[W * W]*. All the ambiguous cases that we countered are:

1. *[w * w]*: The dot is preceded by a letter sequence which starts with a lower-case character and followed by a letter sequence which again starts with a lower-case character. This case may be marked as ~EOS, because the 10 detected EOS triplets have the same kind of pattern:"... *yapıldı. c-) Başkanlıklar ....*". These are item characters and they can be identified and eliminated by regular expressions at tokenization phase.
2. *[W * W]*: The dot is preceded by a letter sequence that starts with an upper-case character and followed by a letter sequence that starts with an upper-case character. This is the most ambiguous and high frequent situation in our corpus. The instances mostly consist of abbreviations such as titles "*Prof. Dr. Mustafa ...*", and abbreviation of personal first middle and last names" ... *küçük A. H. yalnız ...*", etc.
3. *[# * W]*: The dot is preceded by a numeric token and followed by a letter sequence that starts with an upper-case character. This is again a heavy weighted ambiguous case, but the ~EOS case is more dominant, like in the ordinals such as "... *2. Tümen ...*". However, counter examples to ~EOS cases, i.e. EOS cases, are common as well: "... *ölenlerin sayısı en az 28. Fransa'da 10 ...*", etc.
4. *[# * P]*: The dot is preceded by a numeric token and followed by any punctuation. The dominant instances are of ~EOS cases such as "... *2.'lik için mücadele ...*", etc. However, some counter examples, EOS cases, do exist such as "... *(...kitabı sf. 27.). ...*", etc. Since this treatment causes just a 0.017% (1 EOS out of 57 ~EOS) expected error rate for itself and a negligible error rate of 1/12700 for the test corpus, it may be efficient, with respect to computational complexity, to treat all the cases as ~EOS without loosing a large amount of accuracy according to our corpus statistics.

5. *[W * TT]* and *[w * TT]*: An uppercase or lowercase first letter word, a dot and quote character are a special construct for Turkish. In particular, newspapers use quote character, ", and, ", to quote some one's utterances. It is also used in place of apostrophe (i.e. proper noun suffix separator, or to stress on meaning of an utterance). Although, we have encountered only one instance of the *[W * TT]* triplet in our corpus "... *yerine "Gelme"nin* ...", intuitively, this situation is not rare in Turkish written texts (news). Therefore, special attention must be paid to this case in the tokenization phase.

Above cases contribute with the value of 303 out of 310 to the total ambiguity of our test corpus. The heuristic driven from these cases to resolve ambiguity is as follows:

• Mark the dot as a full stop (EOS), if the token preceded and followed by a dot belongs to one of these triplets: *[w * W], [w * #], [w * P], [W * #], [W * TT, (,), K], [P * ∞]*

• Mark the dot as a non full stop (~EOS), if the token preceded and followed by a dot belongs to the one of these triplets: *[W * w], [W * V], [# * w], [# * W], [# * #]*

• Otherwise, further process the case for disambiguation.

In the following sections, we give our proposed disambiguation process and test of efficiency considerations against ambiguities enumerated in this part.

3   Results and Discussion

3.1   Properties of the Test Corpus

Our test corpus is a collection of Turkish news texts having 168,375 tokens, including punctuations, and 12,026 sentences, which are morphologically analyzed and disambiguated by Hakkani-Tür et al. [9]. Properties of the corpus are given in Table 4. Since exclamation sign (!) and question mark (?) are absolute sentence boundary representatives, they are treated as a full stop and marked as period in the original annotated form in the corpus. We have also made a second check on all sentences manually to ensure that our test collection is free from any sentence boundary errors. In this process, we have left out other errors that appear in any written texts such as spelling, untouched.

Table 4. Properties of the Turkish text corpus used

# of Tokens	Non Full-Stop periods	Full-Stop periods	Total
168,375	674	12,026	12,700

The column labeled as *Non Full-Stop periods* shows the total number of periods that are not a full stop as 674. The *Full-Stop periods* column shows the number of periods that are coherent sentence ends. Both values sum up to 12,700, which is the total number of dots appearing in the corpus.

3.2 Results

Without any further processing in addition to our proposed heuristic and marking "otherwise" cases as EOS, we have achieved 94.69% of accuracy. We, now, present solutions to the ambiguities listed in the section 2.4 in the decreasing order of magnitude of ambiguity.

- *[W * W]*: The dot is preceded by a letter sequence, which starts with an upper-case character, and followed by a letter sequence that starts with an upper-case character. If the 739 instances of [W * W] are accepted as the evidence to mark this case as EOS, there are 183 ~EOS instances on the counter part. Totally, this case has, itself, an error rate of 19.84% (183 false alarms over 922) and has a contribution of 1.44% (183 false alarms over 12700) to the whole corpus error rate of 5.31%. Since the instances of this type mostly consist of abbreviations, we propose syllabication for further disambiguation. We state that if a dot immediately follows an abbreviation, the sequence is expected not to be a valid Turkish word hence it does not have a valid syllabication. The syllabication disambiguation results are shown in the Table 5. At first glance, the error rate of 6.8% (i.e., 27+36/922) means a 65.5% reduction from the original error rate of 19.84% and a proportional reduction from the corpus error rate of 1.44% to about 0.5%. In addition, when we analyze more intensively our false alarms, we may identify further regularities. The 18 out of 27 false alarms appear personal first middle and last names, which have a syllabication of the form *V* (a single vowel). This evidence enhances syllabication results to an error rate of 4.8% in the case and about 0.35% in the corpus. Our final success ratio is, now, 95.78% (94.69 + 1.09). The source of misses is mainly due to foreign words, and the source of false alarms is abbreviations that have valid Turkish syllabications such as "Gen." for General, "Av." for lawyer, etc.

Table 5. Disambiguation result of the [W * W] triplet with Syllabication

	Syllabicate	Not Syllabicate	Total
EOS	703	36 (miss)	**739**
~EOS	27 (false alarm)	156	**183**

- *[# * W]:* The dot is preceded by a numeric token and followed by a letter sequence that starts with an upper-case character. The instances of this triplet are mostly seen as ~EOS with a count of 106. EOS instances of this type case have a frequency of 36. Assuming the dots of this triplet as a ~EOS, results in an error rate of 25% in itself and of 0.28% in the corpus. According to our findings, 5 of these 36 misses have suffixes after proper apostrophe separator like "... 3.'lük Aydın, ...", etc which are a tokenization phase issue, because selecting "3.'lük" as a number token is solely a choice of tokenizer. Hence, when this stream is processed, it results a *[# * W]* triplet, for the reason that the first token of stream is number, next token has an uppercase letter and stream has a dot. Note that, this case is also a recursion from the *[# * P]* case, with respect to the first token. In this sense, identifying as a feature whether the dot is an in-place token, may resolve this ambiguity in the to-kenization phase before they appear recursively in the phase of sentence boundary detection. The five of the misses have internal semi colon to indicate time, like "... *suare 18:30. Harbiye ...*". The left out 26 have instances such as "... *Zafer yılı : 1996. Fenerbahçe ...*", "... *kazanan ilk üç numara 7 4 6. ...*", and telephone numbers " *Tel: 0312 555 55 55. ...*". The help of the given observations one may identify the first 10 misses. In addition, the remaining 26 instances are examined in detail, there seems enough evidence that one can infer the situation as a generality that if the sentence including the current *[# * W]* case has any of the words *sayı, numara, rakam, yıl, sene, tarih (number, year, date etc.)*, these instances should mark as EOS. This assumption, at least for our corpus, disambiguates 13 out of 26 of the cases. Further, detecting telephone numbers disambiguates 4 instances and summing up to 17 out of 26 misses. As a result, a reduction of 17 miss cases, increases our total sentence boundary detection to a 96.02% (95.78 + 0.24 "0.28 – 0.04")).

4 Conclusion

Our results show that exploiting syllabication information and phonetic rules makes possible a simple but efficient rule based period disambiguation task for Turkish. Our method has a linear computational complexity, which is crucial for IR tasks that are dealing with an unlimited amount of written texts. The accuracy of 96.02% is above the accuracy of 95.66% as in Tür's work [1] which has not a linear computational complexity. Thus far, more research is required to improve our simple heuristic. The first contribution of our approach is to keep the task of sentence boundary detection free from any lexicon, probability table, and abbreviation list, and the second one is to describe a method, which has a linear computational complexity.

References

1. Gökhan Tür, *A Statistical Information Extraction System.* PhD Thesis, Bilkent University, Ankara, Turkey, 2000.
2. Aberdeen, J., J Burger, D. Day, L. Hirschman, P. Robinson, and M. Vilain. Mitre: *Description of the alembic system used for muc-6.* In The Proceedings of the Sixth Message Under-standing Conference (MUC-6), Columbia, Maryland. Morgan Kaufmann, 1995.
3. Reynar, J. C. and A. Ratnaparkhi. *A maximum entropy approach to identifying sentence boundaries.* In Proceedings of the Fifth A CL Conference on Applied Natural Language Processing (ANLP'97), Washington, D.C., 1997.
4. Riley, M.D. *Some applications of tree-based modeling to speech and language indexing.* In Proceedings of the DARPA Speech and Natural Language Workshop, pages 339-352. Morgan Kaufman, 1989.
5. Palmer, D. D. and M. A. Hearst. *Adaptive multilingual sentence boundary disambiguation.* Computational Linguistics, 1997.

6. Mikheev, A. *Tagging Sentence Boundaries*. Language Technology Group, University of Edinburgh , 1997.
7. Kemal Oflazer, Bilge Say, Dilek Hakkani-Tür, Gokhan Tur, *Building a Turkish Treebank*, Chapter in Building and Using Parsed Corpora, Anne Abeillé (Ed.), Kluwer Academic Publishers, 2003.
8. Ziegenhain, U. Arranz, V. Bisani, M, Bonafonte, A. Castell, C. Conejero, D. Hartikainen, E. Maltese, G. Oflazer, K. Rabie, A. Razumikin, D. Shammass, S. Zong C. The *LC-STAR: Lexica and Corpora for Speech-to-Speech Translation Technologies*. Technical Report, IST-2001-32216, Siemens AG, CT IC 5, München, Germany, 2003. http://www.lc-star.com
9. Hakkani-Tür, D.Z., Oflazer, K. and Tür, G. *Statistical Morphological Disambiguation for Agglutinative Languages*. Computers and the Humanities, 2002.
10. Dalkılıç, M.E. and Dalkılıç, G. Basılı Türkçe'nin önemli bazı istatistiksel özellikleri. *İstatistik Araştırma Dergisi* 1(1): 113-130, 2002.
11. Barton, G. Edward.: Computational Complexity in Two-Level morphology. In: ACL Proceedings, 24th Annual Meeting, 1986.
12. Hankamer, J.: Turkish generative morphology and morphological parsing. In: Second International Conference on Turkish Linguistics. Istanbul, Turkey, 1984.

Multiple Sets of Rules for Text Categorization

Yaxin Bi[1,2], Terry Anderson[3], and Sally McClean[3]

[1]School of Computer Science,
Queen's University of Belfast, Belfast, BT7 1NN, UK
[2]School of Biomedical Science,
University of Ulster, Coleraine, Londonderry, BT52 1SA, UK
[3]Faculty of Engineering,
University of Ulster, Newtownabbey, Co. Antrim, BT37 0QB, UK
`y.bi@qub.ac.uk`, {`tj.anderson`, `si.mcclean`}`@ulster.ac.uk`

Abstract. This paper concerns how multiple sets of rules can be generated using a rough sets-based inductive learning method and how they can be combined for text categorization by using Dempster's rule of combination. We first propose a boosting-like technique for generating multiple sets of rules based on rough set theory, and then model outcomes inferred from rules as pieces of evidence. The various experiments have been carried out on 10 out of the 20-newsgroups – a benchmark data collection – individually and in combination. Our experimental results support the claim that "k experts may be better than any one if their individual judgements are appropriately combined".

1 Introduction

Appropriately combining evidence sources to form a more effective output than any of the individual sources has been investigated in many fields. The challenges of integrating evidence have gone under pattern recognition [1], sensor fusion [2], and a variety of ensemble methods [3]. Ensemble methods first solve a classification or regression problem by creating multiple classifiers that each attempts to solve the task independently, then use the procedure specified by the particular ensemble method for selecting or combining the individual classifiers. The two most popular ensemble methods include bagging and boosting [4]. In this research, we investigate an approach for combining multiple decisions derived from multiple sets of rules based on Demspter's rule of combination. Each set of rules is generated by a single rough sets-based inductive learning method, and is referred to as a classifier as in the boosting method. The advantage of our approach is its ability to combine multiple sets of rules into a highly accurate classification rule by modelling the accumulation of evidence.

We apply these methods to 10 out of the 20-newsgroups – a benchmark data collection – individually and in combination. Our experimental results show that the performance of the best combination of the multiple sets of rules on the 10 groups of the benchmark data can achieve 80.47% classification accuracy, which is 3.24% better than that of the best single set of rules.

T. Yakhno (Ed.): ADVIS 2004, LNCS 3261, pp. 263–272, 2004.
© Springer-Verlag Berlin Heidelberg 2004

2 Rough Sets for Generating Text Classifier

Inductive learning can be loosely defined as *learning general rules* from specific instances [5]. In other words, inductive learning can be seen as a process of synthesizing mappings from a sample space consisting of individual instances. The result often is to reduce the space containing individual instances, leading to a new smaller space containing a set of representative instances, which serves the same role as the original one. By contrast, a rough sets-based inductive learning is aimed at learning a covering set of attributes in terms of a reduct, which is a minimal sufficient subset of a set of condition attributes. It preserves the dependency degree with respect to a set of decision attributes that has the same ability to discriminate concepts as a full set of attributes.

A rough set-based approach to inductive learning consists of a two-step process. The first step is to find multiple single covering solutions for all training instances held in a decision table. Specifically, given a set of condition attributes A and a subset $B \subseteq A$, a covering attribute set is found directly by computing its dependency degree with the decision attribute. The direct solution involves adding an attribute at a time, removing the attribute covered by the attribute set, and then the process is repeated until the dependency of B is equal to that of A. At the end of the induction of conjunctive attributes, more than one covering set – reduct – will be found.

The second step is to transform rules from multiple sets of reducts and weight each rule based on counting the identical attribute values. As a result, a number of rule sets will be produced, denoted by $\Re = \{R_1, R_2, \ldots, R_{|\Re|}\}$, where $R_i = \{ r_{i1}, r_{i2,\ldots,} r_{|Ri|} \}$, $1 \leq i \leq |\Re|$. Each set of rules is called a *intrinsic* rule set, referred to as a classifier. It plays an independent role in classifying unseen instances. The relation between two sets of intrinsic rules is in disjunctive normal form (DNF) as are the rules within R_i. To examine the effectiveness of using multiple classifiers to classify unseen cases, our approach does not involve any rule optimzation between multiple sets of rules. More details about these algorithms can be found in [6].

A general DNF model does not require mutual exclusivity of rules within a set of intrinsic rules and/or between different sets of intrinsic rules. The DNF used in this context differs from the conventional way in which only one of the rules is satisfied with a new instance. Instead, all the rules will be evaluated on a new instance. Rules for either the same classes or different classes can potentially be satisfied simultaneously. In the case of different classes, conflicting conclusions occur. One solution for this is to rank rules for each class according to a class priority as established in some way, such as *information gain*, where the latest class is taken as the final class [7, 8]. The other solution is based on the majority voting principle, in which the conflicting conclusions are resolved by identifying the most satisfied rules [9]. In contrast, our approach makes use of as much rule-based evidence as possible to cope with conflicting conclusions through Dempster's rule of combination.

3 Demspter Shafer Theory of Evidence

The Demsper-Shafer (D-S) theory of evidence allows us to combine pieces of evidence from subsets of the frame of discernment that consists of a number of exhaustive and mutually exclusive propositions h_i, i = 1, .., n. These propositions form a universal set Θ. For any subset $H_i = \{h_{i1}, ..., h_{ik}\} \subseteq \Theta$, h_{ir} (0< r ≤ k) represents a proposition, called a *focal element*. When H_i is a one element subset, i.e. $H_i = \{h_i\}$, it is called a *singleton*. All the subsets of Θ constitute powerset 2^Θ, i.e. $H \subseteq \Theta$, if and only if $H \in 2^\Theta$. The D-S theory uses a numeric value in the range [0, 1] to represent the strength of some evidence supporting a subset $H \subseteq \Theta$ based on a given piece of evidence, denoted by $m(H)$, called the *mass function*, and uses a sum of the strengths for all subsets of H to indicate the strength of belief about proposition H on the basis of the same evidence, denoted by $bel(H)$, often called the *belief function*. Notice that $bel(H)$ is equal to $m(H)$ if the subset H is a singleton [10].

4.1 Derive Mass Functions

In the previous section, we have given a general form of a text classifier, R. As stated in Section 2, given multiple reducts obtained from a collection of documents, the multiple corresponding sets of intrinsic rules will be generated, denoted by $\mathfrak{R} = \{R_1, R_2,..., R_{|\mathfrak{R}|}\}$, where $R_i = \{r_{i1}, r_{i2,...}, r_{|Ri|}\}$ and $1 \le i \le |\mathfrak{R}|$. We now examine how to connect each classifier to a piece of evidence in order to formulate a mass function.

Let $\Theta = \{c_1, c_2, ..., c_{|\Theta|}\}$ be a frame of discernment, and let $R_i = \{r_{i1}, r_{i2,...}, r_{i|Ri|}\}$ be a set of intrinsic rules as above. Given a test document d, if k rules are activated, i.e. $r_{ij+1}, r_{ij+2}, ..., r_{ij+q}$ where $1 \le j, q \le |R_i|$, then q decisions are inferred from R_i. Formally, this inference process can be expressed by $r_{ij+1}(d) \rightarrow h_1 | stg_{j+1}$, $r_{ij+2}(d) \rightarrow h_2 | stg_{j+2}$, ..., $r_{ij+q}(e) \rightarrow h_q | stg_{j+q}$, where $h_s \in 2^\Theta$, $s \le q$, and stg_{j+s} are rule strengths expressing the extent to which documents belong to the respective categories in terms of degrees of confidence. At the end of the inference process, a set of decisions will be obtained, and denoted by $H' = \{h_1, ..., h_q\}$, where $H' \subseteq 2^\Theta$.

With respect of the number of the rules fired, there are two situations, i.e. either $q = |R_i|$ or $q < |R_i|$. When $q = |R_i|$, his means all the rules in R_i are completely satisfied with a given document. We exclude this case since it may not play any role in classifying any documents. When $q < |R_i|$, $stg_{j+1} + stg_{j+2} + ...+ stg_{j+q} < 1$, so H' does not constitute a frame of discernment. Therefore Demspter's rule of combination can be not applied. To use Demspter's rule of combination appropriately to pool all the conclusions to draw a final decision, we need a way to normalize the outcomes obtained. For convenience later, we define a function ϖ such that $\varpi(h_j) = stg_{i+j}$.

The normalization process starts by finding the duplicate conclusions within H', and then the corresponding rule strengths are added up, resulting in a new set of the decisions. Formally, for any two h_j, $h_{i+s} \in H'$, if $h_j = h_s$, j ≠ s, then $\varpi(h_j) \leftarrow \varpi(h_j) + \varpi(h_s)$ and h_s is eliminated. After this processing, a set of decisions is reconstructed, denoted by $H = \{h_1, h_2, ..., h_{|H|}\}$, where $H \subseteq 2^\Theta$. The definition of a mass function for H is as follows:

Definition 5. A mass function is defined as $m: H \rightarrow [0,1]$. There are four different situations based on the inclusive relations between Θ and H.

1) if $\Theta \in H$, then we define a mass function as follows:

$$m(\{h_i\}) = \frac{\varpi(h_i)}{\sum\limits_{j=1}^{|H|} \varpi(h_j)} \quad (1 \le i \le |H|) \tag{1}$$

2) if $\Theta \notin H$, and $|H| < 2$, then $H \leftarrow H \cup \Theta$ and we define a mass function as follows:

$$m(\{h_i\}) = \varpi(h_i) \, (1 \le i \le |H|-1) \tag{2}$$

$$m(\Theta) = 1 - \sum_{i=1}^{|H|-1} \varpi(h_i) \tag{3}$$

3) if $H = \Theta$, and $\varpi(h_i) \ne 0$ for any element $h_i \in H$ ($1 \le i \le |H|$) then we define:

$$m(\{h_i\}) = \varpi(h_i) \, (1 \le i \le |H|) \tag{4}$$

4) if $H = \Theta$, and $\varpi(h_i) = 0$ for any element $h_i \in H$ ($1 \le i \le |H|$) then we define: $m(H) = 1$.

We have elsewhere provided a proof that the rule strength satisfies the condition of a mass function [6]. However, as in the first case above, some conclusions cannot be inferred from a specific piece of evidence, so these conclusions remains unspecified. Thus it is necessary to redistribute mass among known conclusions. We believe such a redistribution for the unknown state of hypotheses could be valuable in the coherent modeling and basic assignment of probabilities to potential hypotheses and for making decisions over an incomplete frame of discernment.

The second case means that the added Θ represents our ignorance about the unknown state of hypotheses in inference processes. It absorbs the unassigned portion of the belief after the commitment to H. The addition of ignorance about the likelihood of future hypotheses provides us with all the information we need for the inference process. This also means that the system does not require complete knowledge about all potential hypotheses since we represent an implicit set of unmodeled future hypotheses by including an additional Θ.

For the third case, the conclusions obtained are exactly the same as these integral hypotheses within Θ, through we directly replace strengths with a mass function.

The fourth case means that the conclusion obtained does not have knowledge about any individual hypotheses within the frame of discernment Θ, and its complement is an empty element. In this situation, we reassign its degree of total belief as 1.0.

4.2 Decision Fusion

Having defined the mass function, now we examine the problem of combining multiple classifiers. Suppose we are given multiple classifiers $\Re = \{R_1, R_2, ..., R_{|\Re|}\}$ and a set of categories $\Theta = \{c_1, c_2, ..., c_{|\Theta|}\}$, for a new document d, the category predictions of multiple classifiers R_1, R_2, ..., $R_{|\Re|}$ will be applied to the document, resulting in $R_i(d) = H_i$. If only one of the classifiers is activated, such as $R_1(d) = H_1$, then H_1 will be ranked in decreasing order. If the top choice of H_1 is a singleton, it will be assigned to the new document, otherwise lower ranked decisions will be considered for further selection. When K classifiers are activated, the multiple sets of classification decisions H_1, H_2, ..., H_K are obtained, where $H_i = \{h_{i1}, h_{i2}, ..., h_{i|H_i|}\}$, $H_i \subseteq 2^C$, and the corresponding rule strengths are $\varpi(H_i) = \{\varpi_i(h_{i1}), \varpi_i(h_{i2}), ..., \varpi_i(h_{i|H_i|})\}$. After normalizing $\varpi(H_i)$ by using the method introduced in Section 4.1, we can obtain K mass functions, denoted m_1, m_2, ..., m_K. With all of these outcomes along with the mass functions, we can gradually combine them to decide the final decisions using Equation (4) as follows:

$$[...[m_1 \oplus m_2] \oplus ... \oplus m_K] \tag{5}$$

The combined results will be ranked and the final decision will be made by Equation (6). Notice that we are interested in the case where h_{ij} is a singleton, i.e. a single category, given H_i, so we have $m(h_{ij}) = bel(h_{ij})$ as stated in Section 3.

$$D(x) = H \quad \text{if } bel(H) = max_{H \in C} \, bel(H) \tag{6}$$

5 Experiment and Evaluation

There are a number of methods for evaluating the performance of learning algorithms. Among these methods, one widely used in information retrieval and text categorization is a pair of measures called precision and recall, and denoted by p and r respectively. Precision is the ratio of the true category documents to the total predicted category documents. Recall is the ratio of the predicated category documents to the true category documents. To compute overall performance on all the categories, we use the other measure the micro-averaged F_1 which is defined on the basis of the concepts of precision and recall as follows:

$$\text{micro-averged } F_1 = \frac{\sum_{i=1}^{m} F_1(c_i)}{m} \tag{7}$$

where

$$F_1(c_i) = \frac{2pr}{p+r} \tag{8}$$

The F_1 measure, initially introduced in [11], it combines Precision and Recall as a harmonic mean of the two measures. This measure will be used as an evaluation criterion in this experiment.

5.1 Newsgroup Data

For our experiments, we have chosen a benchmark dataset, often referred to as 20-newsgroup. It consists of 20 categories, and each category has 1,000 documents (Usenet articles), so the dataset contains 20,000 documents in total. Except for a small fraction of the articles (4%), each article belongs to exactly one category [12].

In this work, we have used 10 categories of documents, 10,000 documents in total, to reduce the computational requirements. The documents within each category are further randomly split into two groups, one consisting of 800 documents for training, and the other including 200 documents, but only 100 of the 200 documents are selected for testing.

5.2 The Experiment Results

For our experiments, we use information gain to select about 270 keywords after removing stopwords and applying stemming. By using the algorithms described in Section 2, ten reducts have been generated, and ten corresponding sets of intrinsic rules in turn have been constructed, denoted by R_0, R_1, ..., R_9. In the following, we will not distinguish between the concepts of rules and reducts if no confusion occurs.

Prior to the experiments for evaluating the effectiveness of different combinations of reducts, we first carried out the experiments on individual reducts. Figure 1 presents the performance of each set of intrinsic rules. It can be seen that the best performing reduct is R_4.

To examine of the effectiveness of combined reducts in classification, we rank these reducts in decreasing order based on their classification accuracy, and then divide the 10 reducts into two groups to see the effect of the combinations of the reducts with high and low predictive accuracy, respectively. The first group consists of R_1, R_2, R_3, R_4, R_6 and R_7, and the second group includes R_0, R_5, R_8 and R_9. For the first group of reducts, we first take R_4 with the best performance, and then combine it with R_1, R_2, R_3, R_6, R_7. The combined results are denoted by R_{41}, R_{42}, R_{43}, R_{46}, R_{47} and they will be ranked. The best performing combination R_{46} is chosen, and in turn is combined with R_1, R_2, R_3, R_7, resulting in ranked combinations of R_{461}, R_{462}, R_{463}, R_{467}. As illustrated in Figure 2, in comparison with R_{46}, their classification accuracy performance has dropped. To examine the change in performance with the addition of more reducts, R_{461} and R_{463} are taken for further combinations, it is surprising that the performance increases. However, the performance degrades again with more reducts being combined. Therefore, it can be concluded that the combination of the best individual reduct with a reduct having a fairly modest performance is the best combination in achieving the highest predictive performance, and the performance of the best combination is 3.24% better than the best individual in the first group.

For the second group of reducts, we use the same method as the first group to examine behaviour of the combined reducts. We first take R_9 to combine with R_0, R_5, R_8. The performance of the combined reducts is shown in Figure 3. Following the same principle as above, we combine R_{59} with R_0, R_8, and combine R_{58} with R_0. As

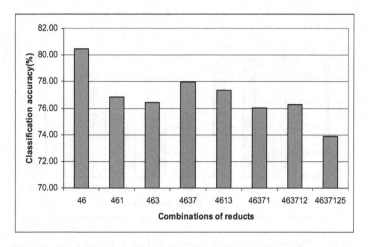

Fig. 1. The performance of different sets of intrinsic rules

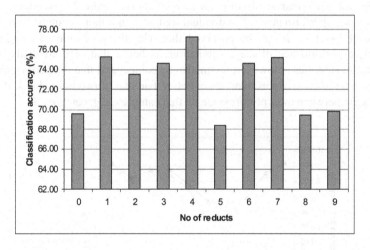

Fig. 2. The performance of the combined reducts from the first group

can be seen, the performance of these combinations drops by about 2% on average relative to R_{59} and R_{58}. However, when four reducts are combined, the performance increases again. A similar pattern to the first group of reducts is observed for this group. To analyze the effect of adding more reducts, we take the best performing R_4 and worst performing R_2 from the first group to combine with R_{5890}. The performance of this combination is not better than the previous one, this is a similar outcome to the first group of reducts.

To investigate how the performance improvement has been achieved when multiple reductes are combined, we base the outcome of the first group of reducts to

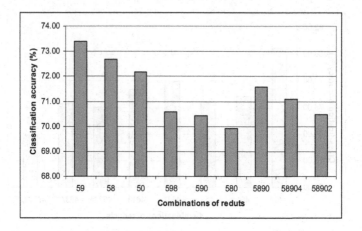

Fig. 3. The performance of the combined reducts from the second group

examine the performance variation on each category. Figure 4 presents a comparison between the performance of individual reducts and their combinations on each document category. It can be observed that with the exception of category 3, the predictive performance of the combinations is better that of individuals on all the document categories. However, it can also be conjectured that the performance of the combination of two reducts may be not better than that of two individuals, if there is a big margin between their performance on that category, e.g. category 3.

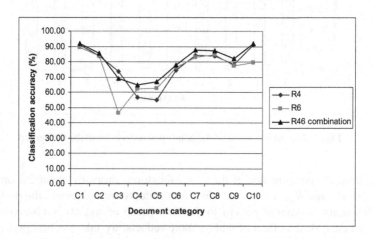

Fig. 4. The performance of reducts R4 and R6 vz the combined reducts 46

In Figure 5, we put the four combined reducts R_{46}, R_{463}, R_{4637} and R_{46371} on one graph to see the effect of the different combinations. The performance of the best com bination is mainly determined by the performance on categories C2, C3, C5, and C6.

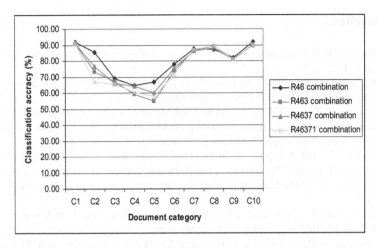

Fig. 5. The performance of the different combinations of reducts

Although R_{4637} performs better than R_{463} and R_{14637}, still worse than R_{46}, and its trend seems not provide an indication that it could be competitive to R_{46} on each category.

6 Conclusion

In this work, we have presented a boosting-like method for generating multiple sets of rules which is built on Rough Set theory, and a novel combination function for combining classification decisions derived from multiple sets of rule classifiers based on Dempster's combination rule. Preliminary experiments have been carried out on 10 of 20-newsgroups benchmark data, individually and in combination. We found that the combination which can achieve the highest predictive performance is a combination of two reduts of which one is the best, and the other should have reasonable predictive performance. The finding of which combining more 'weak learners' outperforms any individuals is consistent with the results obtained by Quinlan, and Freund and Schapire [13, 14].

To our knowledge, this work is the first attempt to use Dempster's rule of combination as a combining function for integrating multiple sets of decision rules in boosting-like methods and for text categorization. The experimental results have shown the promise of our approach. To consolidate this work, more comprehensive comparisons with the other combining functions of weighted linear and majority voting methods, and with previous results published in the literature will be carried.

Acknowledgements. This work was partly funded by the Centre for Software Process Technologies at the University of Ulster which is supported by the EU Programme for Peace and Reconciliation in Northern Ireland and The Border Region of Ireland (PEACE II).

References

1. Duda R, Hart P and Stork D (2001) Pattern classification. New York, NY: John Wiley & Sons, Inc.
2. Klein LA (1999) Sensor and data fusion concepts and applications. Society of Photo-optical Instrumentation Engineers. 2nd edition.
3. Dietterich, T. G. (2000a). Ensemble Methods in Machine Learning. In J. Kittler and F. Roli (Ed.) First International Workshop on Multiple Classifier Systems, Lecture Notes in Computer Science, pp1-15, © Springer-Verlag.
4. Freund, Y and Schapire, R.(1996). Experiments with a new boosting algorithm. In Machine Learning: Proceedings of the Thirteenth International Conference, pp148-156.
5. Mitchell, T. (1999). Machine learning and data mining. Communications of ACM. Vol. 42 (11).
6. Bi, Y. (2004). Combining Multiple Piece of Evidence for Text Categorization using Dempster's rule of combination. Internal report.
7. Quinlan, J. R. (1993). C4.5: Programs for Machine Learning. San Matero: Morgan Kaufmann.
8. Apte, C., Damerau, F., Weiss, S. (1994). Automated Learning of Decision Text Categorization. ACM Transactions on Information Systems, Vol. 12 (3), pp 233-251.
9. Weiss, S. M. and Indurkhya, N. (2000). Lightweight Rule Induction. Proceedings of the International Conference on Machine Learning (ICML).
10. Shafer, G.(1976). A Mathematical Theory of Evidence, Princeton University Press, Princeton, New Jersey.
11. van Rijsbergen, C. J. (1979). Information Retrieval (second edition). Butterworths.
12. Joachims, T. (1998). Text categorization With Support Vector Machines: Learning With Many Relevant Features. In Proceedings 10th European Conference on Machine Learning (ECML), Springer Verlag, 1998.
13. Quinlan, J, R. (1996). Bagging, boosting, and C4.5. In Proceedings of the Thirteenth National Conference on Artificial Intelligence, pages725–730, 1996.
14. Freund, Y. and Schapire, R. E. (1997). A decision-theoretic generalization of on-line learning and an application to boosting. Journal of Computer and System Sciences, 55(1), pp119–139.

Zipf's Law and Mandelbrot's Constants for Turkish Language Using Turkish Corpus (TurCo)

Gökhan Dalkılıç and Yalçın Çebi

Computer Engineering Dept., Dokuz Eylul University, 35100 Bornova, Izmir, Turkey
{dalkilic, yalcin}@cs.deu.edu.tr
http://www.cs.deu.edu.tr

Abstract. Zipf's Law is a common law applied for different kinds of observations. Many investigations were carried out to find the correspondences between Zipf's Law and different languages. This study deals with the correspondence of Turkish with Zipf's Law and finding Mandelbrot constants (c and B) by using a large scale Turkish corpus (TurCo). In order to determine these constants, coefficient of determination was used, and different c and B values were examined. As both languages show agglutinative characteristics, the most suitable B value was found smaller than 1 for Turkish like Korean, and c value was found as 0.27.

1 Introduction

Investigation of statistical properties of a language is useful for cryptanalysis, compression processes, optical character and speech recognition, etc. For this purpose, a corpus, which is large enough to represent a language, should be created. Turkish Corpus (TurCo), which is ~360 MB capacity and has more than 50M words, was created, and n-gram analysis have been carried out by applying different algorithms on this corpus [1–3].

Besides n-gram analysis, the correspondence between a given language and the commonly accepted rules, such as Zipf's Law, which is one of the most common laws for different kinds of observations, should also have been investigated. Most of these investigations were carried out for English language [4, 5] and there is no previous work found for Zipf's Law investigation on Turkish. In Section 2, the results for this investigation for Turkish by using TurCo were given.

The common deficiency of Zipf's Law is its generality, which is not suitable for word frequency analysis of a language. In order to overcome this problem, Mandelbrot added some constants to Zipf's Law's formula. Section 3 deals with the Mandelbrot's constants for TurCo and its comparison with Korean as they are both agglutinative languages.

2 Zipf's Law

George Zipf, a psycholinguist, stated in *"Human behaviour and the principle of least effort"* book in 1949 that word frequencies and lots of other observations, follow

T. Yakhno (Ed.): ADVIS 2004, LNCS 3261, pp. 273–282, 2004.
© Springer-Verlag Berlin Heidelberg 2004

hypergeometric laws ([6] as cited in [4] and [7]). After analyzing the word frequencies for the novel *Ulysses* manually, Zipf claimed his best known "Zipf's Law" [8].

According to Zipf, when the probability list of the words is sorted in descending order and numbered from 1, 2, to n, which are called the *rank* (*r*), then the product of *rank* and the *probability* (*P(r)*) of the corresponding word will be *constant* (μ) for each word [7]. This is called Zipf's Law and given in Formula 1.

$$P(r) = \frac{\mu}{r} \text{ , r = 1, 2, ..., n .}$$ (1)

Using Formula 1 and the definition of *P(r)*, Formula 2 can be generated.

$$P(r) = \frac{F(r)}{Number\ of\ Words} = \frac{\mu}{r} \Rightarrow F(r) = \frac{\mu * Number\ of\ Words}{r} \text{ , r = 1, 2, ..., n .}$$ (2)

where *F(r)* is the frequency of the word which has rank r. As μ, μ *Number of Words (NOW)* will also give a constant.

Word frequency and rank distribution graph for Brown corpus, the most known corpus for English language, is given in Figure 1 [5]. The straight line shows Zipf's Law. The other dotted points are the actual values.

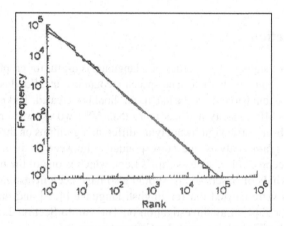

Fig. 1. Word Frequency Data from the Brown Corpus and Zipf Distribution [5]

2.1 Sampling f*r for English and Turkish

According to Zipf's Law, *f*r* is constant [7]. In order to check if a language obeys Zipf's Law, word rank-frequency values of that language can be sampled. Some samples of word monogram values of English language are given in Table 1.

The data in Table 1 nearly matches Zipf's Law. The first three values and the values in the middle (r=90,100,200) tend to bulge. Except those values f*r is approximately constant as the Zipf's Law states [9].

When the same analysis was done for Turkish on TurCo, it was seen that, f*r increases until the rank 300, and Zipf's Law holds between 300 and 4000. After 4000, it decreases linearly as seen in Table 2.

Table 1. f*r values on Tom Sawyer [9]

Word	Freq.(f)	Rank (r)	f*r	Word	Freq.(f)	Rank (r)	f*r
the	3332	1	3332	turned	51	200	10200
and	2972	2	5944	you'll	30	300	9000
a	1775	3	5325	name	21	400	8400
he	877	10	8770	comes	16	500	8000
but	410	20	8200	group	13	600	7800
be	294	30	8820	lead	11	700	7700
there	222	40	8880	friends	10	800	8000
one	172	50	8600	begin	9	900	8100
about	158	60	9480	family	8	1000	8000
more	138	70	9660	brushed	4	2000	8000
never	124	80	9920	sins	2	3000	6000
oh	116	90	10440	could	2	4000	8000
two	104	100	10400	applausive	1	8000	8000

Table 2. f*r values on word monograms of TurCo

Word	Freq.(f)	Rank (r)	f*r	Word	Freq.(f)	Rank (r)	f*r
ve	1137582	1	1137582	sağlamak	6354	1000	6354000
bir	803553	2	1607106	başarı	3205	2000	6410000
bu	646620	3	1939860	önergeler	2100	3000	6300000
n	169675	10	1696750	koşulları	1587	4000	6348000
büyük	116978	20	2339560	incelediğini	712	8000	5696000
dünya	96287	30	2888610	böyledir	552	10000	5520000
göre	81062	40	3242480	yapılabileceği	228	20000	4560000
ki	74659	50	3732950	gittiğimiz	131	30000	3930000
durumu	69049	60	4142940	giyimli	87	40000	3480000
ilk	59241	70	4146870	önlenmiştir	62	50000	3100000
olduğu	56229	80	4498320	istihdamdaki	46	60000	2760000
bugün	52326	90	4709340	kaydetme	36	70000	2520000
diye	46981	100	4698100	dönebilen	29	80000	2320000
milyar	28999	200	5799800	durmamış	24	90000	2160000
sohbet	20733	300	6219900	egem	20	100000	2000000
eb	15967	400	6386800	sekseni	10	150000	1500000
mu	12778	500	6389000	görmemişsiniz	5	200000	1000000
saygıyla	10967	600	6580200	güçleştireceği	2	300000	600000
halde	9295	700	6506500	gönülaydın	1	393709	393709
savaş	8166	800	6532800	götürebiliyorum	1	400000	400000
geniş	7200	900	6480000				

2.2   Actual f, r Values for English and Turkish

In order to get accurate results, all word monograms, bigrams, and trigrams should be used. To show this graphically, rank-frequency graphs can be drawn. The rank-frequency graph of monograms (types), bigrams and trigrams for English from Brown Corpus is given in Figure 2 [4]. As the values on the graph cannot show linearity, English can not be said to have a *"perfect match"* with Zipf's Law.

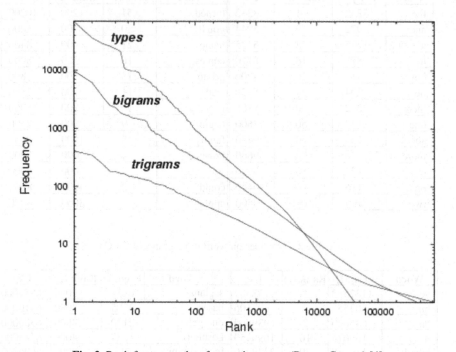

Fig. 2. Rank frequency data for word n-grams (Brown Corpus) [4]

For Turkish, word analysis processes were carried out for different types of corpora [1–3]. The graphs for two different corpora of Turkish are given in Figure 3 and Figure 4. The rank-frequency graph of Novels and Stories, a collection of 118 novels and stories of 110 different authors and having 4,668,306 words, is given as Figure 3.

The monogram, bigram and trigram graphs are said to be similar to their correspondings for English, and they obey Zipf's Law, but not perfectly. As the corpus size is not big enough to obtain more accurate results, the tetragram and pentagram graphs do not show obeyence to Zipf's Law.

The rank-frequency graph of TurCo, which is the main corpus with a word count of 50,111,828, is given as Figure 4. The monogram, bigram, trigram and tetragram graphs are said to be obeying Zipf's Law with some bulges, but not perfectly.

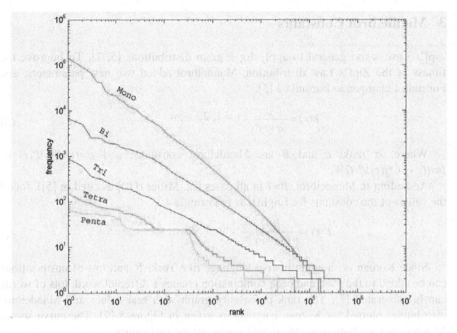

Fig. 3. Rank frequency graph for Novels & Stories

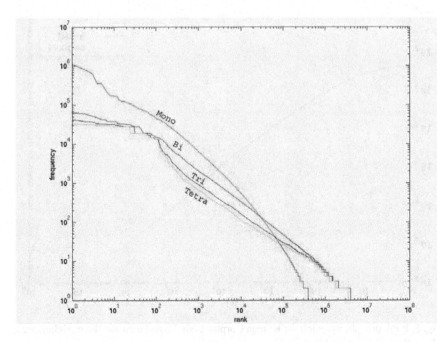

Fig. 4. Rank frequency graph for TurCo

3 Mandelbrot Constants

Zipf's Law is too general to apply for n-gram distributions [5, 7]. To improve the fitness of the Zipf's Law distribution, Mandelbrot added two new parameters, and Formula 1 changed to Formula 3 [5].

$$P(r) = \frac{\mu}{(c+r)^B} \, , r = 1, 2, ..., n \,. \tag{3}$$

Where, r: rank; c and B are Mandelbrot constants; and $\mu=(c+r)^B*P(r)$ or $\mu=((c+r)^B*f(r))/NOW$.

According to Mandelbrot, $B>1$ in all cases [7]. Miller ([10] as cited in [5]), found the values of the constants for English as in Formula 4.

$$P(r) = \frac{0.11}{(0.54+r)^{1.06}} \, , r = 1, 2, ..., n \,. \tag{4}$$

Since Korean is an agglutinative language like Turkish, and lots of postpositions can be added to the root, and each combination creates a different word, lots of words can be generated [7]. The rank-probability graph with real values and Mandelbrot distribution plotted for Korean language is given in Figure 5 [7]. The curve shows Mandelbrot distribution and the dotted points are the real values.

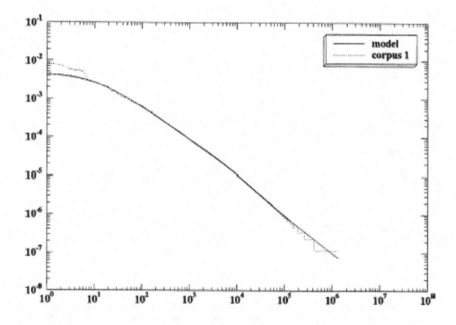

Fig. 5. Rank probability graph for Korean Corpus, both the real data and the modeling used Mandelbrot distribution [7]

As seen in Figure 5, the model graph, generated by using Formula 4, nearly matches the actual values, except for the starting and ending values where it has much more fluctuations.

In order to determine the c and B values for Turkish, the similarity between the graphs of actual and by Formula 3 created values, should be investigated. This similarity can be better determined by using statistical methods.

In statistics, after plotting the points, in order to find the formula of the distribution, which can help to predict the unknown values, regression analysis can be used. R^2 value, which is called "*coefficient of determination*" and shows the closeness of the estimated values with the actual data, can be calculated.

R^2 is the proportion of the variance in dependent variable y attributable to the variance in independent variable x as shown in Formula 5. As R^2 gets larger, by introducing the independent variable x, the more total variation in the dependent variable y reduced. If there is a perfect match between two variables, then $R^2=1$. If $R^2=0$, then none of the variation in y is being explained by x. So, the closeness to 1, the greater the linear association between x and y. For any regression data set, R^2 shows how close the raw regression data points are to the theoretical data [11].

$$R^2 = \frac{\left(\sum(x-\bar{x})(y-\bar{y})\right)^2}{\sum(x-\bar{x})^2\sum(y-\bar{y})^2}.$$ (5)

By using average f*r and NOW, μ was calculated as 0.063, with an average $f*r$ of 292,440 (Formula 6).

$$\mu = \frac{Average\ of\ f*r}{NOW} = \frac{292,440}{4,668,306} = 0.063.$$ (6)

For Turkish, different c and B values were tried to find the most appropriate R^2 values, and the best R^2 and the corresponding c and B values are given in Table 3. For Novels and Stories, c is found between 0.26 and 0.35 with an average of 0.30, and B is found as 0.90, both of which have the best R^2 value with 0.9958.

Table 3. Mandelbrot Constants

Novels and Stories				TurCo		
c	B	R^2		c	B	R^2
0.35	0.90	0.9958		0.28	0.78	0.9883
0.33	0.90	0.9958		0.27	0.78	0.9883
0.30	0.90	0.9958		0.29	0.78	0.9882
0.29	0.90	0.9958		0.28	0.79	0.9882
0.27	0.90	0.9958		0.29	0.79	0.9881
0.26	0.90	0.9958		0.28	0.77	0.9881
0.38	0.90	0.9957		0.30	0.77	0.9880
0.37	0.90	0.9957		0.30	0.80	0.9878
0.25	0.90	0.9957		0.27	0.80	0.9878
0.25	0.90	0.9957		0.25	0.80	0.9878

By substituting the c and *B* values in Formula 3 with the values given in Table 3, and using the calculated μ value, the probability formula can be rewritten for Turkish Novels and Stories as:

$$P(r) = \frac{0.063}{(0.30 + r)^{0.90}} \quad , r = 1, 2, ..., n \;. \tag{7}$$

The graph, obtained for Novels and Stories after adding Mandelbrot constants to Zipf's Law, is given in Figure 6.

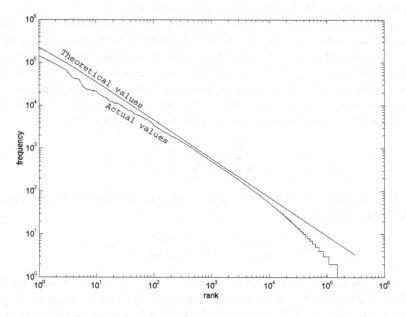

Fig. 6. Graph of actual and theoretical values with c=0.30, B=0.90 for Turkish Novels and Stories

For TurCo, c is found as 0.27, and *B* is found as 0.78 with an R^2 value of 0.9883, as given in Table 3. By substituting the values found for TurCo with the values in formulae 6 and 7, the formulae 8 and 9 were obtained.

$$\mu = \frac{Average \; of \; f * r}{NOW} = \frac{1,176,000}{50,111,828} = 0.024 \; \cdot \tag{8}$$

$$P(r) = \frac{0.024}{(0.27 + r)^{0.78}} \quad , r = 1, 2, ..., n \;. \tag{9}$$

The graph, obtained for TurCo after adding Mandelbrot constants to Zipf's Law, is given in Figure 7.

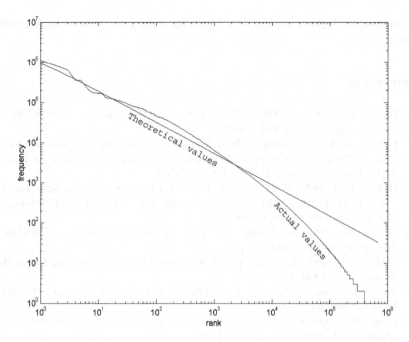

Fig. 7. Graph of actual and theoretical values with c=0.27, B=0.78 for TurCo

When Figure 6 and 7, and their corresponding R^2 values compared, a better match was found for Novels and Stories. The corpus for Figure 6 (Novels and Stories) includes fewer duplicated words than the corpus TurCo. At the same time, Turco includes different types of text, which causes strong stair effect at the beginning ($10^{0.5}$ thru 10^1) and end (>10^5) of the rank, and a bow more then Figure 6 between 10^1-10^4. When both corpora are compared to the rank 10^4, it can be said that Figure 6 matches Zipf's Law with Mandelbrot correction more than Figure 7.

4 Conclusion

Although, there is a similarity between Zipf's Law's rank-frequency graph and the actual rank-frequency graph of Turkish word n-grams, it can be said that, since Zipf's Law is a general law for various kinds of observations, there is not any perfect match. Mandelbrot added some constants (c and B) to Zipf's Law to apply for word distributions, and these constants vary from language to language and corpus to corpus.

Although Mandelbrot states that "*B>1 in all the usual cases*" ([10] as cited in [7]), B value in Mandelbrot's Law for Turkish was found as 0.78, and c value was found as 0.27. The agglutinative behaviours of Turkish and Korean cause the B values to be smaller than 1, unlike English [5, 7]. In Turkish, by adding different suffixes to a predicate (verb or adjective), different words, each having different meanings, can be generated. This results a more bowed actual value curve as shown in Figure 7 [7].

In general, Turkish obeys Zipf's Law with some modifications by Mandelbrot's constants.

References

1. Dalkılıç, G., Çebi Y.: A 300MB Turkish Corpus and Word Analysis. ADVIS 2002. LNCS 2457, Springer Verlag. (2002) 205-212
2. Çebi Y., Dalkılıç, G.: Turkish Word N-gram Analyzing Algorithms for a Large Scale Turkish Corpus – TurCo. ITCC 2004, IEEE International Conference on Information Technology. (2004) accepted and will be published
3. Dalkılıç, G., Çebi Y.: Word Statistics of Turkish Language on a Large Scale Text Corpus – TurCo. ITCC 2004, IEEE International Conference on Information Technology, accepted and will be published (2004)
4. Teahan, W.J.: Modeling English Text. Ph.D. Dissertation. The Univ. of Waikato. New Zealand (1998) 50-52, 64-69
5. Witten, I. H., Bell, T.C.: Source models for natural language text. Int J Man-Machine Studies. 32:5. (1990) 545-579
6. Zipf, G.K: Human behavior and the principle of least effort. Reading, MA. Addison-Wesley Publishing, USA. (1949)
7. Choi, S.W.: Some Statistical Properties and Zipf's Law in Korean Text Corpus. Journal of Quantitative Linguistics, 7:1. (2000) 19-30
8. Le Quan Ha, Sicilia-Garcia E. I., Ji Ming; Smith F. J.: Extension of Zipf's Law to Words and Phrases. The 17th International Conference on Computational Linguistics. (2002)
9. Manning, C. D., Schütze H.: Foundations of Statistical Natural Language Processing. The MIT press. (2000) 119
10. Miller G.A., Newman E.B., Fiedman, E.A.: Some effects of intermittent silence. American Journal of Psychology. (1957) 70, 311-313
11. Robbins J.L., Daneman J.C: The Best Known Statistic – Coefficient of Determination (r2): What it does and does not do in Regression Analysis. National Estimator Fall 2002. (2002) 18-27

Letter Based Text Scoring Method
for Language Identification

Hidayet Takcı and İbrahim Soğukpınar

Gebze Institute of Technology, 41400 Gebze /Kocaeli
{htakci, ispinar}@bilmuh.gyte.edu.tr

Abstract. In recent years, an unexpected amount of growth has been observed in the volume of text documents on the internet, intranet, digital libraries and news groups. It is an important issue to obtain useful information and meaningful patterns from these documents. Identification of Languages of these text documents is an important problem which is studied by many researchers. In these researches generally words (terms) have been used for language identification. Researchers have studied on different approaches like linguistic and statistical based. In this work, Letter Based Text Scoring Method has been proposed for language identification. This method is based on letter distributions of texts. Text scoring has been performed to identify the language of each text document. Text scores are calculated by using letter distributions of new text document. Besides its acceptable accuracy proposed method is easier and faster than short terms and n-gram methods.

1 Introduction

Language identification is the first step of understanding text documents which is written in. It is one of the text mining applications [8]. It can be seen as a specific instance of the more general problem of an item classification through its attributes. Text documents are classified by language identification method based on language categories. Therefore we can solve language identification problem by using of text classification algorithms. There are many algorithms for text classification [1]. Recently, due to its linear time complexity centroid-based (CB) text classification algorithm has been used for text classification [6].

In language identification, generally, short words or common words [9], n-grams [3, 11], unique letter combinations [10] etc. have been used. In addition to these methods, letter distributions of texts can be used for language identification of text documents. It has already been mentioned that, letters could be used for characterization of text documents [4]. Letter distributions can be used as an additional solution and this solution can be used to reduce the size of feature set [12].

In this study, letter based text scoring method has been proposed for language identification of text documents. In our method, text scores have been calculated by using letter distributions of texts. Text scoring has increased the speed of language identification. In the experiments successful results has been obtained by using this method.

T. Yakhno (Ed.): ADVIS 2004, LNCS 3261, pp. 283–290, 2004.
© Springer-Verlag Berlin Heidelberg 2004

In the proposed method, firstly letter distributions of new text document (observed values) are calculated. Then these letter distributions are multiplied by average letter distributions of languages (estimated values). Average letter distributions have been obtained from training documents. Letter distributions for all languages are used from the ref. [7]. There is an average letter distribution for each of languages. These values are named as centroid values for CB algorithm. k numbers (k is equal to the number of different languages) of text scores are calculated for each new text document. The unit score of each letter is different from the others. Where, unit score is frequency of each letter in centroid values. If one of text scores is maximum then text is mapped into related class, else if there are two or more maximum text scores then text cannot be mapped into anyone class. Maximum text score is used to identify the language of new text document.

The rest of the paper is organized as follows: in the second section of this paper, using letters in language identification has been described. In the third chapter, text scoring system has been explained. In the fourth section, experimental results and analysis have given. The last section contains conclusions.

2 Using Letters in Language Identification

Short terms, n-grams, or unique letter combinations are used generally in the language identification. However, the sizes of feature set of these methods are large and preprocessing costs are very much. Therefore, reducing of their dimension and preprocessing costs is necessary.

Dimension and preprocessing problems can be indeed solved by using letters in the language identification. For example, the feature set sizes of n-grams are estimated as 2550-3560 and common words are 980-2750 [2]. The size of our method is only 30 – 40. Our method uses alphabet and the other methods use dictionary. Document-term frequencies are used by other methods whereas document-letter frequencies are used by proposed method in this work. In letter based language identification, documents are represented by letter distributions.

Letter distributions can be used to distinguish of documents. Figure 1 shows the differences of letter distributions among different languages. The reason of closeness of distributions of some letters is from the neighbor of languages. This situation is from the historical basis of languages. Figure 1 obviously depicts that letters provide distinguishing information for text documents. Letter distributions in documents depend not only on language but also on subject and writer as well.

3 Letter Based Text Scoring Method

Proposed method for language identification is a statistical based method. In our method, text scores are calculated for text classification. Text scores are obtained from letter distributions (D_{LF}) of new text document and average letter distributions (L_l) of languages. After calculating language scores of new text document they are compared with each other. Then max language score gives the class of new text document.

Architecture of the proposed system explained following paragraphs is shown in Figure 2.

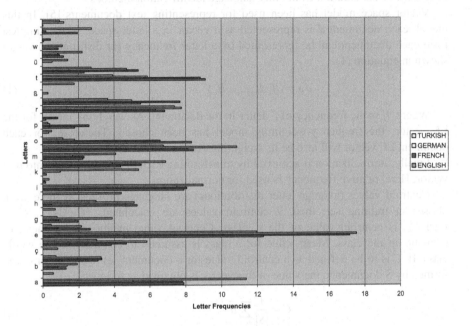

Fig. 1. Letter frequencies of each language

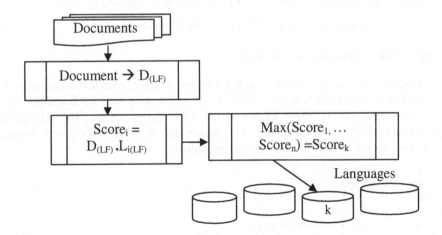

Fig. 2. Proposed language identification system

Firstly, raw text documents are transformed to letter distributions ($D_{(LF)}$). These distributions are called as document profiles. Document profiles are multiplied with centroid values of languages ($L_{i(LF)}$). If k^{th} text score is max score, new text document is assigned into k^{th} class. Using letter based text scoring is the most important difference of our solution from other language identification methods.

Vector space model has been used for representing text documents [5]. In this model, each document d is represented as a vector in a letter space. In the simplest form each document can be represented by a letter frequency (or distribution) vector shown in equation (1),

$$\vec{d}_{lf} = (lf_1, lf_2, \ldots, lf_n) \tag{1}$$

Where, lf_i is the frequency of ith letter in the document. As weighting model for the LF vector, the frequency-weighting model has been chosen. Therefore, for each document LF vector will also be its weighting vector.

Finally, normalization is achieved by transforming each document vector into unit vector. Here, relative frequency is used for normalization.

Centroid values (average letter distributions) are language profiles. If there are k classes in training set, then, k centroid values are calculated. $\{\vec{C}_1, \vec{C}_2, \ldots, \vec{C}_k\}$, Each $\vec{C}_i$, is centroid value of the ith class. Centroid value mentioned the mean of elements in the class. Mean value for a class is assumed to characterize the whole class. If $\vec{C}$ is to be defined as a centroid value for a document set (category or class) formed by S documents, the value of this vector is obtained as follows:

$$\vec{C} = \frac{1}{|S|} \sum_{d \in S} \vec{d} \tag{2}$$

This centroid value has been used to calculate text score value. This score value computed with equation (3) is used for identification of language of texts.

$$\text{Score}_i = D_{(LF)} . L_{i(LF)} \text{ (dot product multiplication)} \tag{3}$$

3.1 Using Letters and Text Scoring

Text scoring is a score computing task. Language scores of each text are computed as letter based. Average frequencies of letters are unit letter scores for languages. Texts are classified into language classes based on language scores. The text scoring algorithm which is shown in Fig. 2 is represented in the following pseudo-codes. Firstly some terms used in algorithm are presented

D	: *Document*
ch	: *Letter*
lf_i	: *letter frequency of ith letter*
letter_i	: *ith letter*
n	: *the size of letter features*
k	: *the size of language categories*
weight_ij	: *the weight of ith letter according to jth language*
Score_j	: *language scores of document*
Max	: *Maximum language score*

```
Open a text document // D
...
Read ch;
    Case ch of
   Letterᵢ : lfᵢ:= lfᵢ+1;
    ...
           end;
for j:=1 to k do
 for i:=1 to n do
   scoreⱼ:=scoreⱼ+ lfᵢ * weightᵢⱼ;
Max:=0;
For j:=1 to k do Begin
   If dj>Max then Begin Max:=scoreⱼ; Class_No=j; End;
   End;
If Max>0 Then Write('Document is assigned to class
number ',Class_No)
```

4 Experimental Results and Analysis

In order to obtain successful results from language identification, training set must contain as much text documents as possible. Today it is obvious that the biggest data and documents storage is the Internet. Therefore, it is the most practical solution to get training documents from the Internet. To accomplish language identification 36285 letters have been selected from documents, distributions of letters are in Table 1.

Table 1. The sample sizes of letters according to languages

Language	Sample Letter Count
English	8502
French	9415
German	9831
Turkish	8537

In the test, English, French, German, and Turkish were used as document languages. Firstly, language scores are computed for each of texts. To compute the language scores of texts we have a score table. In this table there is a unit score of each letter according to languages. These unit scores are shown in Table 2. In fact these values are centroid values.

Table 2. The unit scores of letters

Centroid	A	Ä	B	C	Ç	D	E	F	G	Ğ	H	...	W	X	Y	Z
English	8	0	1	3	0	4	12	3	2	0	5	...	1	0	2	0
French	8	0	1	3	0	5	17	1	1	0	0	...	0	0	0	0
German	5	1	1	3	0	6	18	2	4	0	5	...	1	0	0	1
Turkish	11	0	2	1	1	3	12	0	1	1	3	...	0	0	3	1

Language scores of text are computed from the values of score table and letter distributions. Letter distributions for a text document are shown in Table 3.

Table 3. Letter frequencies of text documents

Letter Frequencies	A	Ä	B	C	Ç	D	E	F	G	Ğ	H	...	W	X	Y	Z
Dlf$_1$	8	0	1	3	0	4	12	3	2	0	5	...	1	0	2	0
Dlf$_2$...Dlf$_{n-1}$	...	...	...	...	...	...	...	...	...	...	...	...	...	...	...	...
Dlf$_n$	11	0	2	1	1	3	12	0	1	1	3	...	0	0	3	1

Maximum language score are used for language identification. If all of the language scores are equal to zero or some of language scores are equal to each other then classification cannot be performed.

After representing documents in the form of LF as in Table 3, centroid values are found for each class. Centroid values are vectors formed by mean values belonging to classes. Centroid values for classes are shown in Table 2. In this system centroid values are unit scores.

This study is the modified method of "Centroid-Based Language Identification Using Letter Feature Set" [12]. At the paper letter distributions have been used for language identification. [12] In this study, we joined text scoring method into letter based language identification system. Classification accuracy of language identification has been increased by this new method. Some of the experimental results have been presented in Table 4. As it will be seen from the table 4 detection rates for letter based language identification are acceptable.

In addition to, we have also tested two methods for Turkish documents. In comparison of the results of proposed new method with results of the Letter based method in ref [12] the more accurate result has been obtained. Its classification accuracy is presented in Table 5.

Main advantage of our method is in detection speeds. We may take the size of the features of these methods for speeds of the methods. Thus, it can be claimed that when centroid based document classification is supported with letter feature set, its existing better performance is further increased and operation time is further lowered. The operation costs of three methods are presented in Table 6.

Table 4. The comparison of letter based language identification and the other techniques

	Number of words in sentence						
	1-2	3-5	6-10	11-15	16-20	21-30	31 >
English							
3gram	78.9	97.2	99.5	99.9	99.9	100.0	99.9
Short	52.6	87.7	97.3	99.8	99.9	100.0	99.9
Letter Based	54.0	78.2	96.0	99.0	99.0	99.0	100.0
Text Scoring	60.0	80	93.0	96.0	98.0	99.0	100.0
French							
3gram	69.2	93.0	94.5	93.6	99.8	100.0	99.9
Short	30.8	81.8	96.0	97.2	99.8	100.0	100.0
Letter Based	66.0	92.0	96.0	95.0	97.0	100.0	100.0
Text Scoring	85.0	98.0	100.0	100.0	100.0	100.0	100.0
German							
3gram	90.3	97.2	99.3	99.8	99.9	100.0	100.0
Short	30.8	81.8	96.0	97.2	99.8	100.0	100.0
Letter Based	65.0	90.0	92.0	95.0	96.0	100.0	100.0
Text Scoring	75.0	83.0	99.0	98.0	100.0	100.0	100.0

Table 5. The comparison of letter based language identification and text scoring

	Number of words in sentence						
	1-2	3-5	6-10	11-15	16-20	21-30	31 >
Turkish							
Letter Based	76.0	93.0	96.0	100.0	100.0	100.0	100.0
Text Scoring	93.0	97.0	99.0	100.0	100.0	100.0	100.0

Table 6. Operation costs of Language identification systems

Operation cost	
3gram	2550 ops.
Short	980 ops.
Text Scoring	37 ops.

It is assumed that operation costs depend on the size of feature sets of language identification systems.

5 Conclusions

Data mining is a partially new technique of finding meaningful information and useful patterns from large amount of data. It has been applied generally to structural data stored at database. Therefore, data mining is considered as one of knowledge discovery steps from databases. After realizing that concepts of data mining can be applied also to data, which are not structural, text mining is born as a new field. Text categorization is being at an important position at text mining. Therefore, text documents can be automatically assigned to previously defined classes by this technique. In text categorization operation, documents are represented according to frequency information of words that are concerned in these documents and in that way documents enter into the classification process.

In this study, we have proposed that documents could be represented by letter frequencies instead of word frequencies. Text scoring method has been used for language identification. Experiments have been conducted for four languages. Pleased results are achieved in the end of this experiment. Thus, it has been revealed that letter feature set can be used for language based recognition types. As a result, it is shown that the usage of letter feature sets can be used for language identification of text documents. For future study, experiments can be extended for more different languages.

References

1. Dumas, S., Plat, J., Heckerman, D., and Sahami, M.: Inductive learning algorithms and representation for text categorization. In Proceedings of CIKM-98, 7th ACM International Conference on Information and Knowledge Management, pages 148-155, 1998.
2. Grefenstette, G.,: Comparing two language identification schemes, in Proceedings of the 3rd International Conference on the Statistical Analysis of Textual Data (JADT?95), Rome, Italy, December 1995.
3. Cavnar, W *and* Trenkle, J. : "N-gram-based text categorization," in Proceedings of SDAIR-94, 3rd Annual Symposium on Document Analysis and Information Retrieval, pp.161--175, 1994.
4. Benedetto, D., Caglioti, E. and Loreto, V.: Language trees and zipping. Physical Review Letters, 88:4(2002).
5. Salton, G.: Automatic Text Processing: The Transformation, Analysis, and Retrieval of Information by Computer. Addison-Wesley, 1989
6. Han, E.-H. and Karypis, G.: Centroid-based document classification: Analysis and experimental results. In Principles of Data Mining and Knowledge Discovery, pages 424--431, 2000.
7. Pawlowski, B.,: Letter Frequency Statistics, URL : //www.ultrasw.com/pawlowski/brendan/Frequencies.html
8. Visa,A.: Technology of Text Mining, (MLDM 2001), Perner, P. (Ed.), LNAI 2123, pp. 1–11, 2001.
9. Johnson, S.,: Solving the problem of language recognition Technical report, School of Computer Studies, University of Leeds, 1993
10. Churcher, G.,: Distinctive character sequences, Personal communication, 1994
11. Hayes, J.,: Language Recognition using two and three letter clusters. Technical report, School of Computer Studies, University of Leeds, 1993
12. Takçı, H., Soğukpınar, İ.,: Centroid-Based Language Identification Using Letter Feature Set, Lecture Notes in Computer Science, (CICLING 2004) Springer-Verlag, Vol. 2945/2004, pages 635-645, February 2004

Parallel Implementation of a VQ-Based Text-Independent Speaker Identification

Ruhsar Soğancı[1], Fikret Gürgen[1], and Haluk Topcuoğlu[2]

[1]Department of Computer Engineering, Boğaziçi University Bebek, Istanbul, Turkey
{ruhsar.soganci,gurgen}@boun.edu.tr
[2]Department of Computer Engineering, Marmara University, Göztepe,
İstanbul, Turkey
haluk@eng.marmara.edu.tr

Abstract. This study presents parallel implementation of a vector quantization (VQ) based text-independent speaker identification system that uses Mel-frequency cepstrum coefficients (MFCC) for feature extraction, Linde-Buzo-Gray (LBG) VQ algorithm for pattern matching and Euclidean distance for match score calculation. Comparing meaningful characteristics of voice samples and matching them with similar ones requires large amount of transformations and comparisons, which result in large memory usage and disk access. When the cost of computations is considered, it states the main motivation for a parallel speaker identification implementation, where the parallelism is achieved using domain decomposition. In this paper, we present a set of experiments using the YOHO speaker corpus and observe the effects of several parameters as VQ size, number of MFCC filter banks and threshold value. First we focus on the serial algorithm and improve the algorithm to give the best success rates and provide a strong base for parallel implementation, where a clear performance improvement on speedup is obtained.

1 Introduction

Biometrics can be used to authenticate a person's claim to a certain identity or establish a person's identity from a large database. Biometrics based authentication is emerging as a reliable method that can overcome some of the limitations of traditional automatic personal identification technologies. Automated biometrics deal with physiological and/or behavioral characteristics.

Voice is an advantageous physiological characteristic as voice samples can be collected by a simple microphone attached to the PC or by a phone. Voice recognition can be divided into two according to its purpose as speaker identification and verification. In speaker identification, the goal is to recognize an unknown speaker from a set of N known speakers. The system decides who the person is, or it finds that person is unknown. On the other hand, for speaker verification, there is a claim of speaker. So verification system compares input speech with only claimed reference model. If similarity is above a threshold value, the system authenticates user; otherwise, it rejects user [1–3].

T. Yakhno (Ed.): ADVIS 2004, LNCS 3261, pp. 291–300, 2004.
© Springer-Verlag Berlin Heidelberg 2004

A speaker identification system contains transformation of the input voice samples from time domain to frequency domain. It also requires large amount of comparisons between the input and the data set. The cost of computation and time required to do the comparisons are important concerns of implementation. The system should be able to response (accept the user or reject the user) in a reasonable time. Growing data set sizes forces disk based algorithms due to main memory size limitations; but the disk based algorithms increases the recognition time.

Using a set of computers to do the computations in parallel provides main memories of all processing elements instead a disk based algorithm and it may give better results compared with serial applications.

In this study, the performance of a parallel implementation of a VQ-based text independent speaker identification system is evaluated to see the effects of parallel processing on the response time, and inclination of identification tasks to parallelism. Experiments show that sharing tasks between processor reduces running time as expected. For 100 speakers and 16 processors running time reduces by a factor of 13.83.

The rest of the paper is organized as follows: Section 2 defines the speaker recognition systems and their usage. Our speaker identification algorithm and its serial and parallel implementations are discussed in Section 3. In Section 4, the experiments to demonstrate the effects of several parameters on the algorithm are presented; and Section 5 concludes the paper.

2   Speaker Recognition Systems

Speech processing is a field with many applications that are based on analysis and synthesis [2]. Some applications are speech modification, speech coding, speech enhancement, speech recognition, language recognition, speech synthesis from text, and speaker recognition. Speaker recognition (SR) is use of a machine to verify a persons claimed identity from his voice. Some speaker recognition based applications are voice dialing, banking by telephone, telephone shopping, database access services, information services, security control, voice mail and remote access to computers.

Speech is a complicated signal which contains speaker specific characteristics resulting from physical differences and learned habits, but there are also some error sources such as misspoken phases, extreme emotional states, time varying microphone placement, poor room acoustics, mismatch handsets, sickness and aging. The input utterance either belongs to a customer or an impostor and system has to decide to accept or reject the user so there are four conditional probabilities: probability of correct acceptance (CA), probability of false acceptance (FA), probability of false rejection (FR) and probability of correct rejection (CR).

Speaker recognition can be categorized as text-independent, text-dependent and text-prompted according to what the speaker says as an input. Recognition is based on speaking one or more specific phrases in text-dependent systems, while in text-independent systems the input utterance may be any random phrases. In text-prompted systems, each user is prompted a new key utterance every time system is used.

2.1 Feature Extraction

First step of speech processing is modeling the signal to obtain feature set that exhibits low intra-speaker variability and high inter-speaker variability. This is called as feature selection or feature extraction. One method for this is LP analysis, which represents the signal as a linear combination of its past values and a scaled input. Another method is the Mel-Frequency Cepstrum Coefficients (MFCC). In MFCC modeling, signal is divided into frames and spectrum of the signal is obtained by taking Fast Fourier Transform (FFT); then mel-scale logarithmic transformation is used before taking inverse FFT that produces MFCC coefficients. The MFCC coefficients represent the local spectral properties of the signal. In our speaker identification system, MFCC is preferred for feature extraction.

2.2 Speaker Identification

After model construction to authenticate incoming speech, speech signal is compared with model of claimed user and a match score is calculated. In stochastic models such as Gaussian mixture model (GMM) and hidden Markov model (HMM), matching score is the probability of observation being generated by claimed speaker. In template models such as Vector quantization (VQ), pattern matching is deterministic and it is a measure of similarity between two patterns: an input vector and a model.

In our implementation, Euclidean distance is used for match score calculation. The purpose of VQ is mapping the vectors from a large vector space to finite number of regions in that space. Each region is called a cluster and can be represented by its center called a codeword. The collection of all codewords is called a codebook. The VQ method used in our project is Linde-Buzo-Gray (LBG) VQ, which is also named as Generalized Lloyd Algorithm. The algorithm starts with an initial codebook and it improves iteratively until a local minimum is reached. First, each feature vector (MFCC coefficients in our case) is mapped to the nearest code vector in current codebook. Secondly, code vectors are recalculated as the centroids of new partitions.

After the computation of match scores, the system has to choose one of the two hypotheses: user is the claimed speaker or user is an impostor. To decide on hypotheses a threshold value is set, and the following cases are used for a decision.

```
If (macthscore> thresholdValue )
        {Report as False Rejection}
else if (Train speaker i matches with test speaker i)
        {Report SUCCESS}
else    {Report False Acceptance};
```

The determination of the threshold value is important. If flexibility of system is increased to accept valid users who are in flue, crying or under stress, false rejection will decrease, but this will be an advantage to wolves who try attacks on system and will increase false acceptance. Similarly if system is too strict and tries to find almost exact match then imposters will be avoided but valid users may also be rejected.

2.3   Related Work

There is a considerable speaker recognition activity in industry, national laboratories, and universities. Some recent studies made on YOHO corpora are: CAVE speaker recognition project for telephone banking implemented by D.James, HP.Hutter, and F.Bimbo at 1997 using MFCC, HMM and GMM and achieve a 0.061% EER [4]. In 1998 B.Pellom and J.Hansen worked on a novel algorithm to reduce the computational complexity of GMM and reduce the search time by a factor of six [5]. In 2002 A.Park and T.Hazen compared the performances of several methods such as GMM, phone classing, speaker adaptive and multiple classifiers and obtain EER ranging from 0.25%-0.83% according to the method used [6]. General trend shows accuracy improvements over time with larger data sets and increasing the duration of speech segment reduces IE and VE [7].

3   Proposed Framework

Our framework is a text independent speaker identification system in which speech signals are modeled with MFCC. LBG VQ method is considered to compare input speech signal with data set by calculating match score with Euclidean distance. We start with a serial MATLAB code, since MATLAB provides enhanced methods for handling voice. There are several alternatives to extend a MATLAB code with multiprocessing capabilities: using MPI toolbox for MATLAB [8], using MultiMATLAB [9] and converting MATLAB code to C code by using MATLAB compiler provided with MATLAB 6.5. In our work, we consider the last approach. The generated C code of this alternative is a C-Mex code that uses some libraries provided by MATLAB.

In our framework, both serial and parallel implementations contain two phases: training and testing. There are two non-identical speech files for each speaker. The first file is in training set, and the second one is in testing set. When, our system matches two files of same speaker, it recognizes the speaker.

Our experimentation is based on the YOHO database, which consists of 106 male speakers and 32 female speakers. Speech signals of the database were collected with a STU-III electro-microphone telephone handset over a three-month period in a real world office environment. There were four enrollment sessions per subject with 24 phrases per session and ten verification sessions per subject at approximately 3-day intervals with four phrases per session. The corpus contains 1380 validated test sessions sampled with 8 kHz and 3.8 kHz analog bandwidth [1].

3.1   Serial Implementation

In the training phase of our framework, each speech file in the train set is sampled, and 320 data points per file are obtained. The MFCC values are computed by using the data points; MFCC values are then passed to VQ function to form regions and centroids of the data. In the testing phase, speech files are read one by one, and their MFCC's are calculated similarly. Then Euclidean distance between MFCC of files and the LBG VQ data are calculated. Finally, test and train files with the minimum distances are matched. Figure 1 gives the operational flow of our proposed speaker identification system.

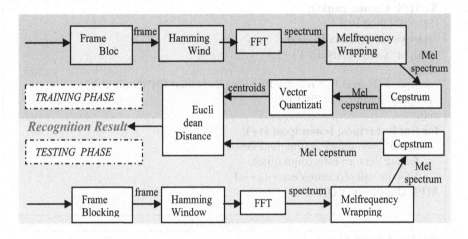

Fig. 1. Operational flow of speaker verification system

Changing several parameters such as the VQ size, threshold and number of MFCC filter banks changes both the recognition accuracy rate and the runtime. A detailed set of experiments on these parameters is presented at Section 4.

3.2   Parallel Implementation

The parallel speaker recognition algorithm presented in this work uses domain decomposition based on file sharing, where the data is divided among the processes by considering approximately the same size on each processor.

Source code written in Matlab is transferred to C-Mex code using Matlab compiler, and parallelism is achieved by message passing interface (MPI) calls. MPI is a library of functions that has more than one freely available quality implementation and has full asynchronous communication. MPI computation consists of a cluster of processor with local memory. Figure 2 shows the steps of our parallel implementation.

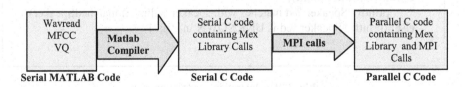

Fig. 2. Parallel implementation of the framework

Figure 3 gives a pseudo code of parallel implementation with a data set of N speakers, and tries to match M speakers.

Training Part

P=MPI_Comm_size();
X=MPI_Comm_rank();
if (x < (N mod P)){
  startpos=X*((N Div P) +1)+1;
  endpos=startpos+(N div P) +1;}
else{
  startpos= (N mod P) * ((N div P))+1)+ (X-(N mod P))*(N div P)+1;
  endpos= startpos+(N div P);}
r=0;
for (int i=startpos; i<=endpos; i++){
    digitalfile=sampleFile(trainingFiles(i));
    featureVector= mfcc(digitalfile);
    VQ[r]= vqlbg(featureVector); r++;}
MPI_allgatherv(VQ);

Testing Part

P=MPI_Comm_size();
X=MPI_Comm_rank();
if (x < (M mod P)){   startpos=X*((M Div P) +1)+1; endpos=startpos+(M div P)
+1;}
else{
  startpos= (M mod P) * ((M div P))+1)+ (X-(M mod P))*(M div P)+1;
  endpos= startpos+(M div P);
}
threshold=somePredefinedValue;
for (int i=startpos; i<=endpos; i++){
    digitalfile=sampleFile(testingFiles(i));   featureVector= mfcc(digitalFile);
    minDist= infinity; matchedSpeaker=0;
    for (int j=1; j<=N; j++){
    distance=euclidean(featureVector , VQ[i]);
      if (distance< minDist){
        minDist=distance;
        matchedSpeaker=j; }
    }
    if (minDist<threshold){
        printf("Speaker %d matches with speaker %d\n", i; matchedSpeaker);}
    else{ printf("Speaker %d is UNKNOWN \n", i); }
}

Fig. 3. Parallel training and testing part

Parallel implementation shows equal accuracy rate with sequential implementation because it uses the same algorithm and functions. The main difference is sharing the files and computations between processors. Load sharing results in good speed-up in our implementation.

4   Experimental Study

In this section, we first present measure the effects of various parameters in our speaker identification framework, which is followed by measuring the performance of parallel implementations. In the first part, we observe the effects of the VQ size, number of filter banks and threshold value on the performance of our framework. The experimental study is based on YOHO corpus using the ASMA cluster system in Bogazici University, which contains 42 nodes that are connected with fast Ethernet. We used a set of 16 identical processors (p2-400 nodes with 128 MB RAM and 6 GB Hard disk) in our studies.

Figure 4 shows effects of VQ size for 50 speakers. Increasing number of filterbanks increases computational complexity and results with increase in success rate and running time. In order to limit the running time, VQ size is set to 16 in our implementation.

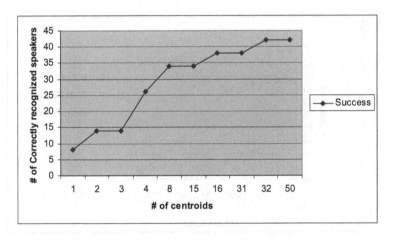

Fig. 4. VQ size effect for N=50, M=50

Another parameter is the number of filter banks used in MFCC calculation. In our system 20 filter banks are used, but different number of filter banks is also tested to see its effect on runtime and recognition accuracy. For 50 speakers, increasing the number of filter banks up to 30, results in better success rate and less error rate; but there is an increase in running time for more than 20 filter banks. Since, there is a decrease in success rate for more than 30 filter banks; we consider 20 filter banks for the case of 50 speakers, in our experiments. Figure 5 gives the normalized results that are obtained by taking 5 filterbanks as a reference for the value 1.

In our identification system there is no threshold value, i.e., threshold is infinite; therefore, the system finds the most similar speaker for the given input. When we set threshold value, we observe false rejection.

Figure 6 gives the number of successes, number of false acceptance and number of false rejections, for the case of 50 speakers by considering different threshold values.

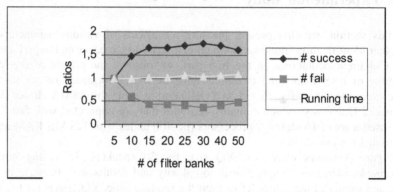

Fig. 5. MFCC size effect for 50 speakers

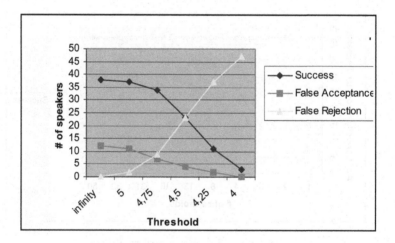

Fig. 6. Effect of threshold value for 50 speakers

Setting threshold value reduces both false acceptance and success rate, but increases false rejection. The decrease in false acceptance is higher then the decrease in success for threshold 4.75 so it seems a suitable threshold value. Using a threshold that produces equal false acceptance and false rejection errors is called equal error rate. Results also show that threshold value 4.75 produces equal error rate.

Finally several experiments are performed on the cluster system to see effect of domain decomposition on running time. For parallel implementation, using one processor causes a slight increase in runtime compared with serial implementation, because of additional calculations for sharing data among processors. The experiments on changing population and cluster sizes result in significant decrease for running time.

Figure 7 shows running time cluster size relations in terms of 1000 clocks, while Figure 8 shows the speed up of the tests.

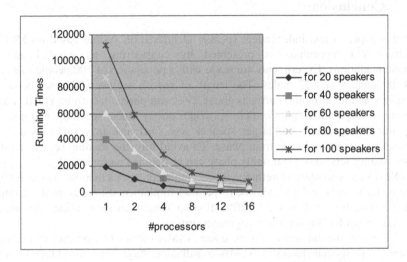

Fig. 7. Runtime results for parallel implementation

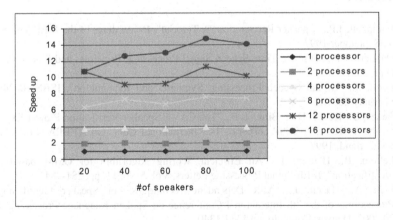

Fig. 8. Speedup results for parallel implementation

Load balancing is based on distribution of speaker files, and the number of speakers per processors in our system and it affects the running time severely. If there are equal number of files for each processor then idle time is minimized and speed up increases, for example in 8 processors system, test with 40 and 80 speakers show better speed up than tests with 20,60 and 100 speakers as seen in Figure 8. Also reducing the maximum number of speakers per processor increases speed up, For 20 speakers using 16 processors does not improve performance compared with using 12 processors, because in both cases maximum number of speakers per processor is two.

5   Conclusion

In this paper, a text independent speaker identification system based on MFCC and (LBG) VQ algorithms is presented by considering its parallel and serial implementations. Experiments are made with a population of 100 people that consists of 28 females and 72 males. The length of speech segments changes between 1-5 seconds and identification error is about 25% with phone data from YOHO database. In our tests, parallel implementation provides nearly linear speed-up, and good scale-up for 100 speakers. For larger speaker sets, network may suffer as a result of broadcast operation in the train phase. To avoid this, the training set can be divided into smaller sets, and the training phase can be handled incrementally.

Next step is to search alternative serial implementations that may result with better recognition rates and provide their parallel implementations, as well. Combining face recognition with voice identification so strengthen recognition rates may be a starting point for human-like recognition systems.

The experimental study is done using ASMA cluster of Bogazici University. We express our special thanks to ASMA coordinator, Assc. Prof. Can Ozturan, and lab members, A.Burak Gürdağ and A.Haydar Özer.

References

1. Campbell, J.P., "Speaker Recognition: A Tutorial", Proceedings of the IEEE,Vol. 85, No. 9 , September 1997.
2. Quatieri, T.F., "Discrete-Time Speech Signal Processing: Principles and Practice", Prentice Hall, 2001.
3. Furui, S., "Digital Speech Processing, Synthesis and Recognition", ISBN: 0824704525, February 2001.
4. James, D., Hutter, H.P., Bimbot, F., "The CAVE Speaker Verification Project-Experiments on the YOHO and SESP corpora", 1st Inernational Conf. On AVBPA, Crans-Montana, Switzerland, 1997.
5. Pellom, B., Hansen, J., "An Efficient Scoring Algorithm for GMM based Speaker Identification", IEEE Signal Processing Letters, Vol. 5 No. 11, pp. 281-284.
6. Park, A., Hazen, J., "ASR Dependent Techniques For Speaker Identification", In Proceedings of the 7th Internatonal Conference on Spoken Kanguage Processing, Sep.16-20,2002, Denver, Colorado, pp.1337-1340.
7. Zilca, R.D., "Text-independent speaker verification using covariance modeling", IEEE Signal Processing Letters, Vol. 8, No. 4, April 2001.
8. MPITB, http://atc.ugr.es/javier-bin/mpitb_eng, 2004.
9. MultiMatlab, http://www.cs.cornell.edu/Info/People/lnt/multimatlab.html, 2004.

A Distributed Model of Neuronal Regulators Based on Message-Driven Software Component Architecture

Francisco Maciá Pérez, Antonio Soriano Payá, Jerónimo Mora Pascual,
and Juan Manuel García Chamizo

Department of Computing and Information Technology, University of Alicante,
P.O. 99, Alicante, Spain
{pmacia, soriano, jeronimo, juanma}@dtic.ua.es
http://www.ua.es/i2rc

Abstract. The neuronal regulators of biological systems are very difficult to deal with since they present non-structured problems. The software component approach can attend to this type of systems in a simple way. In this paper, a software component-based architecture of neuronal regulators is presented. The main approach will be the modelling of each neuronal centre involved with a message-driven component. As an example, we will discuss a model of the neuronal regulator of the lower urinary tract. A monitor has been developed to validate the proposed models. Several experiments have been carried out using the proposed model, and the results have been validated by comparing them with real data, exhibiting an equivalent behaviour to that of the modelled biological system.

1 Introduction

The main theories developed so far to control complex systems incorporating non-linear aspects and that presenting unknown parameters are the optimal control, the adaptive control and the robust control [1]. Their feature in common is its sound mathematical foundation. The neuronal regulators of the biological systems, however, cannot be merely described by means of mathematical models as the data available are incomplete and vague and, furthermore most of the information is qualitative. The situation gets still more complex if distributed systems and emergent behaviour intervene as is the case with the neuronal regulators.

With the aim of concentrating on the use of the proposed model, we will analyze the particular instance of the neuronal regulator of the lower urinary tract. Several models of this tract have been published [2–5], where the problem is examined from a centralized approach. This present study considers problem from a distributed viewpoint, with emergent characteristics.

It is in this context where the software component architecture offers a greater level of abstraction reducing the complexity of the problem. Software component architecture provides a framework capable of supplying reasonable expressive capacity to tackle the development of such distributed systems, accounting for a wide range

T. Yakhno (Ed.): ADVIS 2004, LNCS 3261, pp. 301–311, 2004.

of contingencies, emerging behaviour, and the possibility of structure modification as new advances are being made in neurological research.

In the following sections, a design pattern [6] which will enable us to define the model of the neuronal regulator of the biological system is proposed; in section 3, this pattern is applied, as an example, to the specific case of the neuronal regulator of the lower urinary tract; the results are shown in section 4; and, in last section, we extract our conclusions, and offer an outline of the different research areas we are currently involved.

2 System Architecture

At a general level, let's assume that a biological system is made up of a mechanical system (MS), a neuronal regulator system (NRS) that controls the mechanical system and an interface ($^{MS}I_{NRS}$) communicating both systems. Formally,

$$\text{Biological\_System} = \langle \text{MS, NRS, } ^{MS}I_{NRS} \rangle \tag{1}$$

The model is based on software components. The software components, which makes up the distributed system, correspond to the NRS neuronal centres. These components collect information from the MS and process/transmit it back towards the mechanical system. Each component makes a contribution, called an influence, to the system in such a way that contributions of the different influences will determine the overall state of the system by activation or non-activation signals involved. The next step will identify each one of the elements that forms the biological system.

Neuronal regulators consist of sets of neuronal centres. Each neuronal centre receives electrical signals, and depending on the signals and on its internal state, the centre activates or inhibits its outputs.

$$\text{NRS} = \langle nc_1, nc_2, \ldots, nc_n \rangle \tag{2}$$

A software component $nc \in NRS$ can be formally described using the structure:

$$nc = \langle \Phi_{nc}, S_{nc}, \text{Percept}_{nc}, \text{Mem}_{nc}, \text{Decision}_{nc}, \text{Exec}_{nc} \rangle \tag{3}$$

where Φ_{nc} corresponds to the set of perceptions; S_{nc} to the set of internal status; Percept_{nc} provides the centre with information about the state of the system; Mem_{nc} allows the centre to show awareness of the state, Decision_{nc} selects the next influence; and Exec_{nc} represents the intention of centres of acting on the system. These functions present a general structure that rests on each component specified sets and functions [7].

The proposed approach models every neuronal centre with a message-driven software component (MDC). A MDC is an asynchronous message consumer looking at its behaviour; however, a MDC is similar to the stateless session component in that a MDC has no conversational state. Unlike session components an entity components however, MDCs do not have a home or remote interface [8]. We can appreciate the internal structure of a software component in fig. 1.

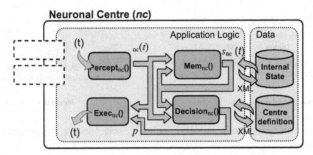

Fig. 1. Internal structure of a neuronal centre software component

This type of component is extremely useful to represent the way the different neuronal centres communicate among themselves and with their environment —by small electric discharges in a very loosely coupled way.

The interface regards the biological system as a system of actions and reactions, using the following structure:

$$^{MS}I_{NRS} = \langle \Sigma, \Gamma, A \rangle \tag{4}$$

where Σ represents the set of possible states of the system. Γ identifies the set made up of the possible intentions of actions on the system. The entities do not have overall control of the system but they are subjected to combining their objectives with other entities objectives so that the result of each action will be represented as an intention of action on the system. Finally, A is the set of all the possible activities that the components can perform on the system.

The most general communication model would be defined by a message-driven component of the publish/suscribe type where the component output is sent to a topic, a kind of collective mailbox which acts as if it were an asynchronous broadcasting element. The neuronal centres waiting for emitted (published) signals by another centre will just connect (subscribe) to its related topic and then communication will take place by way of messages.

A slightly simplified communication model uses MDCs Point-to-Point; that is, components that develop an asynchronous message queue to which another neuronal system is subscribe (only one centre per queue). This queue acts as an asynchronous mailbox for the subscribe centre (fig. 2).

The communicated messages among the centres follow a name-value layout and it will be codified by XML structures.

Each centre is constantly perceiving, deliberating and executing with the aim of accomplishing a specific assigned job —its portion of application logic, also defined in XML — and it is the exchange of these messages which manages, indirectly, the overall behaviour of the system.

At any rate, an external co-ordinator is also provided to perform secondary tasks, like starting/stopping the regulation process or providing information about the state of the system. This co-ordinator will manage access to users to perform system managing and monitoring tasks.

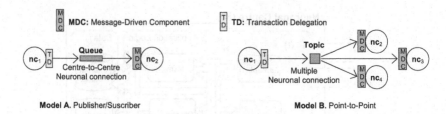

Model A. Publisher/Suscriber   **Model B.** Point-to-Point

Fig. 2. Two communications models among message-driven components which represent neuronal centres

This paper focuses on the neuronal regulator of a biological system. However, since the mechanical system (MS) and the neuronal regulator system are so closely connected, let's introduce the function of the mechanical system in this context: it generates afferent signal from a given set of efferent signals. This function complies with the dynamics of the mechanical system and is carried out through accomplishment of actions with the aim of transforming one state into another. The resulting changes are regarded as reaction of the system under different influences.

Function MS provides the information about the current state of the system subjected to the influences from different entities:

$$MS : \Sigma \times \Gamma \to \Sigma \tag{5}$$

Taking into account the above definition for a neuronal centre, and the perception of the environment at a certain point, the new state of the system results as the assessment of influences from the different software components when they are concurrently performing their tasks:

$$\sigma(t+1) = MS(\sigma(t), \prod_i^n Exec_i (Decision_i(\phi_i(t), s_i(t)), \phi_i(t))) \tag{6}$$

$$s_1(t+1) = Mem_1(\phi_1(t), s_1(t));$$

$$\dots$$

$$s_n(t+1) = Mem_n(\phi_n(t), s_n(t))$$

2.2 Regulation Model

Having been the elements that make up a system defined, it is time to see the way they are organized to define a control model. The neuronal regulator can conceptually be divided into three parts:

- The behaviour of each component, capable of handling its portion of application logic. For example, one activity notifies the bladder of the sacral storage status while a different activity regulates the pontine storage and the preoptic area components.

- The inputs of each component. They define the queues or topics to which every subscriber must subscribe so as to have access to nervous signals to be able to perceive their environment.
- The outputs of each component. They define the queues or topics which each component must set up to broadcast their nervous signals. Transition delegates handle the detail of transitioning to the next activity. They prepare messages and send them to destinations.

Taking into account this conceptual definition, the regulation model is completely distributed. In a conventional model, a workflow process coordinates the activities in the regulator process. However, the proposed approach lacks a process manager to handle the entire workflow process; then, the behaviour is said to be emergent.

This approach simplifies the definition of the system using declarative (not imperative) languages.

In our case, every component exhibits the general structure and behaviour defined in previous sections. Thus the particular behaviour and the relations among them are defined by an XML structure which the component itself stores.

3 The Biological System

The lower urinary tract (LUT) carries out two main functions; namely, the storage of urine in the bladder and the expulsion of urine through the urethra (micturition process). Micturition depends mainly on coordination between the detrusor muscle and the external sphincter [7]. This coordination is carried out by neuronal control which involves a complex system of interconnections and neuronal centres. The LUT can be divided into two parts: the mechanical system (MSLUT) and the neuronal regulator (RLUT). The first system describes the biomechanics of the LUT and has to do with the anatomy and physiology of the muscles and tissues that make it up. The second one is referred to the anatomy and physiology of the neuronal control pathways, retransmission centres and exciting and inhibitory areas associated with micturition [9].

The input and output signals of the model, as well as the interconnections between centres, change with time. In the storage phase, as urine enters into the bladder (Qi), vesical pressure (Pves) increases and the pressure on the bladder wall rises. In order to retain urine in this phase, as detrusor pressure increases so do the disabling micturition neuronal signals. When the micturition process begins, clear coordination between the retaining elements (internal sphincter (IS) and external sphincter (ES)) and the emptying elements (detrusor) can be seen. This happens in such a way that the internal and external sphincter neuronal signals are reduced almost to nil while the detrusor neuronal signal increases considerably. The changes in pressure lead to the expulsion of urine (Qo) from the bladder to the urethra and form there to the outside. This process is achieved by the afferent (detrusor afferent (Ad) and urethral afferent (Au)) and efferent (stimulation internal sphincter (SIS), inhibition internal sphincter (IIS) and stimulation external sphincter (SEE)) neuronal signals.

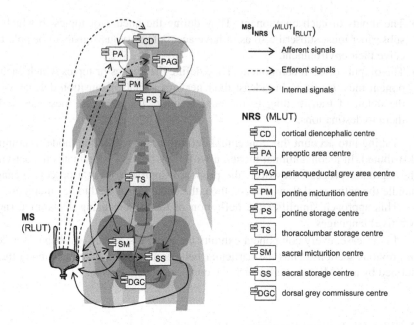

Fig. 3. Structure of the biological neuronal regulator (RLUT) and its relation with the mechanical system (MLUT)

Fig. 4 shows the evolution of the main signals in the filling and emptying phases. These phases allow us to determine five different states in the system, which are sequential and periodical.

State s'_0 represents a state of transition randomly produced by a disruption, such as a cough, sneeze, blow in the abdomen, etc.

States s_4 and s_5 are related, voluntary (and therefore, optional) and can be produced more than once. These states represent a model refinement; for this reason, it is out of scope of the present paper.

On the ground of the formal framework as proposed in section 2, we formally define the lower urinary tract (LUT) using the tupla:

$$LUT = \langle MLUT, RLUT, {}^{MLUT}I_{RLUT} \rangle \tag{7}$$

where the MLUT models the mechanical system of the lower urinary tract, the RLUT, the neuronal regulator of the lower urinary tract, and finally, the ${}^{MLUT}I_{RLUT}$ correlates them.

The neuronal regulator of the lower urinary tract consists of the set of neuronal centres that are constantly perceiving, deliberating and executing.

The states of system (σ_i) are a list of pairs consisting of the afferent and efferent neuronal signals with their corresponding values. The influences of a neuronal centre (γ_i) are stated by a list of pairs of its efferent neuronal signals together with the new values that the neuronal centre wants to obtain. The activities performed by a component at a certain moment are associated with the influence the component wants to exert on the system.

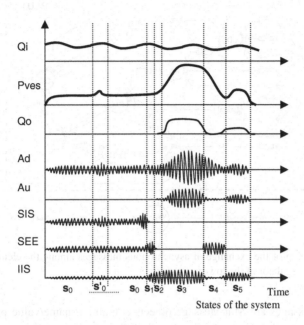

Fig. 4. Signals main and states of the model. s_0 — Storage. Detrusor relaxation and sphincter contraction; s'_0 — Storage. More sphincter contraction. Transition state: cough, sneeze, etc.; s_1 — Storage. Detrusor relaxation and external sphincter voluntary contraction; s_2 — Star micturition. Sphincter relaxation and detrusor contraction. s_3 — Micturition. Urine outflow; s_4 — Micturition. Voluntary stoppage of micturition to improve bladder emptying.; s_5 — Micturition. End of micturition and beginning of storage

Following the design pattern defined in the second section, and the LUT model proposed in the third one, fig. 5 shows the message-driven components involved, together with the relationships among themselves.

4 Experiments

To validate the model of the LUT, a detailed system has been developed using Java and J2EE platform as middleware. The monitoring system and the user interface follow the model 2 — so called, the MVC (Model-View-Controller) design pattern — in which the controller users servlets 2.3, JSP 1.2 for viewings and EJB 2.0 components for the model. The software components to model each neuronal centre are message-driven beans (MDB), a new type of component available with EJB 2.0. Java Message Service (JMS 1.0.2) serves as transaction delegate. XML datasheets specifies each MDB component behaviour and their interconnection network, as discussed in section 2. Fig. 6 shows the system general architecture.

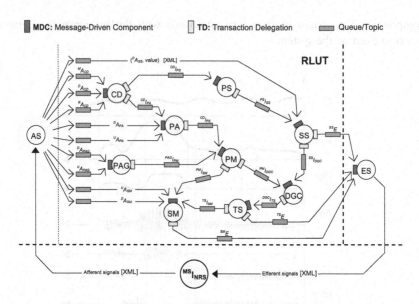

Fig. 5. Diagram of the exchange of asynchronous messages among the elements that make up the neuronal regulator of the lower urinary tract

The messages are MapMessage objects containing name/value pairs, where each name corresponds to a string object — the name of a neuronal connection among the centres already defined by the interface $^{MS}I_{NRS}$.

The mechanical system that requires regulation has been simulated by using the Simulink 3.0 package for Matlab 6.1. This system has been considered, in the general architecture, as a legacy system. To achieve the best level of integration with regard to the J2EE platform elements, the MS component package has been conceived as a set of legacy components using EJB with bean-managed persistence (BMP entity beans), following the application adapter design pattern for the access and integration of legacy systems.

Users can remotely access the system by a standard browser and assign or modify its operating parameters. Furthermore, they can graphically observe the regulator behaviour with urodynamic graphs (figs. 7 and 8).

Taking the simulation and monitoring systems as a starting point, we have carried out different LUT simulations with data regarding both healthy individuals and those with dysfunctions due to neurological causes.

The result of the tests in average working conditions, without dysfunctions, can be observed in fig. 7. In the storage phase, the centre remains inhibited, allowing the bladder to be filled. During the emptying phase, the person activates the micturition centres to contract the detrusor to expel the urine.

In the first step of the storage phase, we can observe that an increase in urine generates exponential increases in pressure because of the initial stretching of the muscle. When the micturition begins, a contraction of the detrusor takes place generating a great increase in vesical pressure, reaching values of 40 cm of H_2O. At the end of the process, the bladder will have practically emptied, maintaining a basal pressure. The urine flows out when the external sphincter is opened. The output flow of urine is observed to increase to 23 ml/seg. The graphs in fig. 7 show urodynamic curves fall within the permitted ranges for the International Continence Society [12].

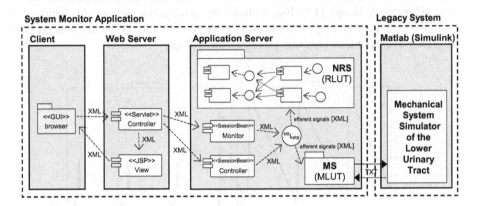

Fig. 6. Monitoring system tier map with internal structure and relationship with the legacy simulator system

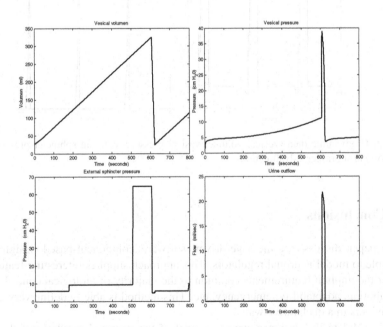

Fig. 7. Urodynamic data (vesical volume, vesical pressure, external sphincter pressure, urine outflow) in a situation without dysfunctions

When there is a lesion that affects interaction among the sacral centres and the rest of the neuronal centres (thoracolumbar centre, pontine centre and suprapontine centres), interaction ceases. The LUT no longer controls voluntary and involuntary areas, but the vesicosomatic guarding reflex and the vesicosimpatic and urethralparasympathetic reflexes of micturition remain. A lesion of this type usually generates a detrusor- sphincter disinergy [13]. Fig. 4 shows the urodynamic curves of a suprasacral lesion, where a detrusor-sphincter disinergy can be observed. When detrusor pressure is greater than sphincter pressure, urine loss takes place.

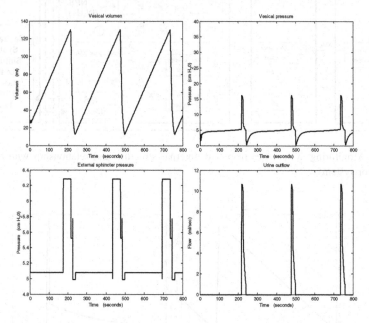

Fig. 8. Urodynamic data (vesical volume, vesical pressure, external sphincter pressure, urine outflow) in suprasacral dysfunctions

5   Conclusions

This paper discusses a message-driven software component-based design pattern suitable to model neuronal regulators. This approach supplies interesting features that cover the implicit requirements common to the majority of biological control models: distribution, adaptability, emergency, etc. This method is able to define very complex behaviours in a declarative way.

To validate the design pattern, a model of the neuronal regulator of the human LUT has been proposed and a web application has been developed by means of which we have obtained urodynamic graphs and compared them with real data from healthy individuals.

We are presently developing a specification and deployment platform for neuronal regulators enabling a straight forward definition, from their XML datasheets.

Acknowledgements. This study has been supported as part of the research project CTIDIA/2002/112 by the Office of Science and Technology of the Autonomous Government of Valencia (Spain).

References

1. Aström, K.J. (ed.): Control of Complex Systems. Spinger-Verlag (2000)
2. Bastiaanssen, E.H.C., van Leeuwen, J.L., Vanderschoot, J., Redert, P.A.: A Myocybernetic Model of the Lower Urinary Tract. J. Theor Biol. Vol. 178 (1996) 113-133
3. van Duin, F., Rosier, P.F., Bemelmans, B.L., Wijkstra, H., Debruyne, F.M., van Oosterom, A.: Comparison of Different Computer Models of the Neuronal Control System of the Lower Urinary Tract. Neurourol Urodyn. Vol 19 (2000) 203-222
4. Soriano, A., García, J.M., Ibarra, F., Maciá, F.: Urodynamic Model of the Lower Urinary Tract. Proceedings of Computational Intelligence for Modelling, Control & Automation (1999) 123-128
5. Valentini, F.A., Besson, G.R., Nelson, P.P., Zimmern, P.E.: A mathematical micturition model to restore simple flow recordings in healthy and symptomatic individuals and enhance uroflow interpretation. Neurourol Urodyn. Vol. 19 (2000) 153-176
6. Marinescu, F.: EJB Design Patterns. Advanced Patterns, Processes and Idioms. Wiley Computer Publishing (2002).
7. Soriano, A.: Modelado y Simulación del Regulador Neuronal del Tracto Urinario Inferior. Thesis of University of Alicante (2001)
8. Kurniawan, B.: Java for the Web with Servlets, JSP, and EJB. New Riders (2002).
9. Kinder, M.V., Bastiaanssen, E.H.C., Janknegt, R.A., Marani, E.: The Neuronal Control of the Lower Urinary Tract: A Model of Architecture and Control Mechanisms. Archives of Physiology. 107 (1999) 203-222
10. Micheli, F., Nogués, M.A., Asconapé, J.J., Pardal, M.M.F., Biller, J.: Tratado de Neurología Clínica. Ed. Panamericana (2002)
11. García, J.M., Soriano, A., Maciá, F., Ruiz, D.: Modelling of the Sacral Micturition Centre Using a Deliberative Intelligent Agent. Proceedings of the IV International Workshop on Biosignal Interpretation (2002) 451-454
12. Castro, D.: Urodinámica. Generalidades y terminología de la función del tracto urinario inferior. In Salinas, J., Romero, J. (eds): Urodinámica Clínica. Merck Sharp & Dohme (1995) 61-78
13. Sotolongo, J.R.: Causes and treatment of neurogenic bladder dysfunction. In Krane, R.J. et al (eds): Clinical Urology. J.B. Lippincott Company (1994) 558-568

Winsim: A Tool for Performance Evaluation of Parallel and Distributed Systems

Alexander Kostin[1] and Ljudmila Ilushechkina[2]

[1] Department of Computer Engineering, Eastern Mediterranean University,
Magusa, KKTC, via Mersin 10, Turkey
Alexander.Kostin@emu.edu.tr
[2] Department of Software Engineering, Moscow Institute of Electronic Technology,
Moscow, Russia
ljuda_il@fromru.com

Abstract. A simulation system Winsim for modeling of parallel and distributed systems is presented. Winsim is based on a class of extended Petri nets, has a simple graphical user interface, high level programming language possibilities for complex data processing, enables simulation of systems consisting of a large number of processes, and provides fast simulation. The paper considers the basic features of the system, outlines its architecture, and gives an example of a simulation model of a distributed mutual exclusion algorithm developed and implemented in Winsim.

1 Introduction

For the analysis and performance evaluation of parallel and distributed systems, Petri nets are becoming increasingly popular. To use Petri nets as a mathematical tool for the investigation of structural and behavioral properties of systems, a number of corresponding software packages have been developed. A comprehensive source of information on them is available at the web site [1].

The existing Petri-net-based tools belong to one of two basic classes. The first class includes the tools intended for investigation of structural properties of Petri nets and for reachability analysis. The tools of the second class are designed mainly for discrete event simulation of dynamic systems. The proposed tool Winsim is intended for performance evaluation of parallel and distributed systems by simulation modeling. Such orientation of the tool gave the possibility to make it simple for use and fast which is essential for large models.

The extended Petri nets used in Winsim are high-level timed coloured Petri nets with two types of places - simple places (S-places) and queue places (Q-places), attributed tokens and fixed set of so called elementary nets which serve as primitive building blocks to create nets of arbitrary size and complexity. In these nets, time is associated with transitions. The basic types of elementary nets are carefully chosen to support all constructs of structured, parallel, and distributed programming [2]. One of the types of elementary nets is the interruptible net, which is essential for modeling and simulation of distributed systems, especially of communication protocols with

T. Yakhno (Ed.): ADVIS 2004, LNCS 3261, pp. 312–321, 2004.
© Springer-Verlag Berlin Heidelberg 2004

time-outs. All these features provide the increased efficiency of extended Petri nets for simulation purposes and make them a convenient and easy-to-use modeling tool which combines the advantages of the original Petri nets with those of high level programming languages. The formal aspects of extended Petri nets, used in Winsim, are presented in [3].

Winsim runs in the environment of MS Windows 95/98/NT/2000/XP operating systems. The basic features of the system are:

1. Possibilities of high level programming languages are available for data processing during simulation.
2. Direct execution of the compiled model's code provides high simulation speed.
3. Parameters and data in the compiled model can be set and changed without re-compiling and re-linking the ready model.
4. Models can be built of practically unlimited size.
5. Several models can be run concurrently.
6. A simulation can be saved in any state and continued later.

Winsim was included in the list of Petri nets tools at the web site [1].

The rest of the paper is structured in the following way. Section 2 summarizes the basic features of extended Petri nets. Section 3 describes two languages used in the system, model description language and modeling control language. Section 4 outlines the architecture and implementation of the proposed system. Finally, Section 5 presents as an example a simulation model of a distributed mutual exclusion protocol developed and investigated with the use of Winsim.

2 Features of Extended Petri Nets

The minimal structural elements in extended Petri nets are places, transitions and directed arcs which connect places and transitions in accordance with the rules of a bipartite directed graph. From the structural point of view, this type of Petri nets may be considered as marked graphs [4], with the relaxed condition that each place may have one input transition or one output transition or both. The number of arcs which may be incident to a transition is theoretically unlimited.

In a graphical representation, simple places and queue places are depicted by circles and ovals, respectively. A simple place can hold at most one token at a time. A queue place has theoretically unlimited capacity and hence it can hold any number of tokens at any moment of time. A minimal, functionally complete, structural component of the used Petri nets is an elementary net, which is a graph consisting of a transition and associated input and output places pertaining to the given transition. Formally, we define an elementary net $E(t)$ of a transition t as

$$E(t) = \; < C, P_1, P_2, r_1, r_2, d, m >,$$

where C is a necessary (but generally not sufficient) condition to fire transition t; P_1 and P_2 are finite sets of input and output places for t, with $P_1 \cap P_2 = \varnothing$ and $P_1 \cup P_2 \neq \varnothing$; r_1 and r_2 are functions of input selection and output selection respectively; d is a delay function; and m is a data transformation function.

These features allow to express in terms of E-nets the four fundamental processes in information systems - information transfer, time (delays), data transformation and control - and make them very powerful and effective apparatus for the formalized description and simulation of information systems.

There are many possible structures of elementary nets. It was proved in [5] that, to model any data processing system in terms of extended Petri nets, it is sufficient to have the basic set of types of elementary nets given in Fig. 1. For the area of data processing systems, the proposed basic set is functionally complete, even though it is not minimal. Connecting elementary nets from the proposed basic set with each other, we can build nets of any size and complexity.

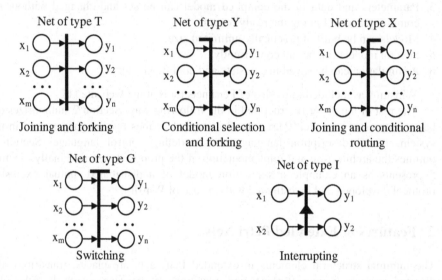

Fig. 1. The basic set of types of elementary nets

Tokens exist only in places, and the values of token attributes are stored in the place which is occupied by the corresponding token. For this purpose, each place may be assigned a number of memory slots. All transitions are timed, even though the activity interval may be zero for some firing transitions. The duration of the activity interval of a firing is allowed to be deterministic or random, with a desired probability distribution. For this purpose the implemented simulation system has a collection of random number generators. There are defaults for all functions in the definition of an elementary net. The defaults are used if the corresponding functions are not given explicitly for the elementary net. This possibility simplifies the creation of models.

3 Model Description Language and Modeling Control Language

Model Description Language (MDL) and Modeling Control Language (MCL) are the main tools for creation of models and interaction of a user with the simulation system during the execution of models. MDL gives the possibility to describe a simulation model and its components as a sequence of statements in terms of extended Petri nets. The minimal model unit, that can be expressed in MDL and then compiled, is called a segment. The concept of a segment in MDL is similar to the concept of a module in an ordinary programming language. MCL is intended for setting and changing of parameters and data in the compiled model that is ready for execution. It is important to note that the changes done by MCL statements in the ready model do not require re-compiling and re-linking of the model. This capability essentially decreases the time for carrying out simulation experiments with the compiled model.

Therefore, MDL is used on the stage of creation of models, while MCL is necessary on the stage of running of compiled models. The detailed description of MDL and MCL, with numerous examples of models, is given in [3].

Generally, a complete Petri net model consists of one, two or more interlinked segments. Each segment is a unit of work for the MDL compiler. The information links between segments in a Petri-net-based model are provided only by attributed tokens flowing from one segment into another via external places chosen for linking of the corresponding segments to build the complete model.

Segments are structurally linked together on the stage of preparation of the executable model. Any global variables and common memory locations for different segments in a Petri net model are not provided by MDL. This is consistent with the contemporary view on the organization of open systems and, in particular, with the ideas of the object-oriented design according to which the communication between different modules, or objects, should be carried out only by means of messages.

The possibility of using multiple copies of the same segment in models considerably simplifies the development of the model having many identical components. For example, the protocol of distributed mutual exclusion deals with many identical processes running in a distributed system. In this case, the modeler needs to develop only one segment representing one generic process and then to specify the necessary number of its copies and links between the copies in the model. The creation of the desired number of segment copies corresponding to identical processes is done by the executive subsystem automatically.

MDL is implemented as an extension of a high level programming language and hence has all its power to process data which is important for simulation purposes. Elements of the extension are declarations of token attributes and of so called net variables, the descriptions of elementary nets (with all explicitly defined functions in the definition of the corresponding elementary nets), statements for attaching and linking of segments.

Before running a ready Petri net model, it is quite usual to put tokens in some places and assign values to attributes of these tokens. This is done by means of the MCL. MCL is used immediately before starting a ready model or during the run. Its purpose is to manage different kinds of user's interaction with the ready model, such as setting an initial state of the model, watching and controlling of the simulation run.

Each MCL statement generally requires some set of parameters. All MCL statements can be input in an interactive command line mode or in a batch mode. In the last case, a user has to prepare the desired sequence of MCL statements in a text file with JZP extension and to supply the name of this file before starting the simulation run. The possibility to make parametric changes in a ready Petri net model considerably simplifies the work of users. Quite often, when a model is ready, many subsequent changes in that model require only those operations that are supported by MCL. With MCL, one does not need to recompile modified segments and carry out other activities to prepare the complete Petri net model. This saves a lot of time and efforts for a modeler during the simulation.

4   Architectural Features and Implementation of Winsim

Winsim supports all stages in the development of Petri-net-based models, their compilation and execution, with the gathering of detailed statistical information about the model. Fig. 2 presents the structure of the system and the sequence of steps in the model's development.

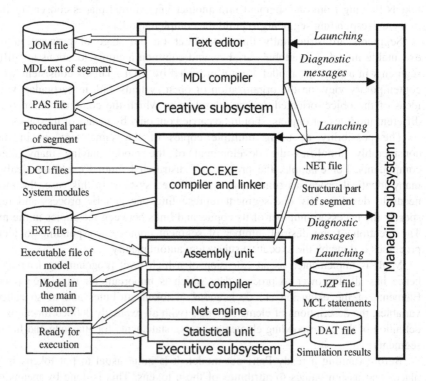

Fig. 2. Structure of the Winsim simulation system

Winsim consists of three main subsystems: a managing subsystem (manager), a creative subsystem, and an executive subsystem. The managing subsystem plays the role of a system's control program. It provides a graphical user interface and is responsible for the launch of the other two subsystems. The creative subsystem is intended for the development and compilation of segments of models. It includes a text editor and the MDL compiler. For each segment of a model, the MDL compiler produces two files. One file contains the procedural component of the compiled segment and the other file (NET-file) includes net variables declared in the segment and data structures representing elementary nets of the segment and their interlinks.

As a result of compilation and linking, an executable file of the model is created. It also contains some service units. These units implement the MCL compiler, the net engine, and different random variates (uniform, exponential, normal, binomial, Poisson, tabular, Markovian and some others) for the use by the model during simulation runs. The random number generator, implemented in Winsim, provides 100 streams of high quality random numbers.

```
SEGMENT A, ...;          SEGMENT        B,    SEGMENT           C,
ATTRIBUTES               ...;                 ...;
  A1: REAL;              ATTRIBUTES           ATTRIBUTES
  A2: INTEGER;             A11: REAL;           A21: REAL;
  A3: REAL;               A12:                  A22:
  . . .                  INTEGER;             INTEGER;
  ATTACH B/B1,B2/, C;      A13: REAL;           . . .
  LINK A,A.B1: S1,S3;      . . .               SEGEND.
  LINK A,A.B2: S2,S3;     ATTACH  D;
  LINK                    SEGEND.
A.B1,A.C:S4,S5;
  LINK
A.B2,A.C:S4,S6;
  SEGEND.
```

(a)

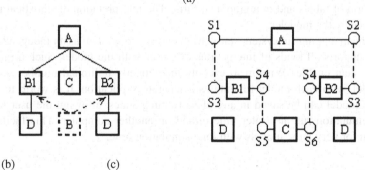

(b)   (c)

Fig. 3. A multi-segment model: *a)* the fragments of the description of three segments in MDL; *b)* the hierarchical structure of the model; *c)* the links between the segments

The model is created in Winsim as a hierarchical structure of segments. If the same segment is present in a few nodes of the overall model structure, then the executive subsystem prepares multiple copies of the file with data structures of this segment, but only one copy of the file with procedural component will be used by identical copies of the segment. An example of a model structure is shown in Fig. 3.

The model consists of three explicitly defined segments — A, B, and C, with segment A as the root. Segments A and B contain the MDL statements ATTACH for including additional segments or their copies. In particular, segment A includes two copies of segment B (with names B1 and B2) and segment C. Segment B (and each of its copies) includes segment D. The statements LINK in segment A (Fig. 3, *a*) specify the links between the segments via indicated places. Each segment in a statement LINK is referenced by its full path name in the hierarchical structure of the model. Note that segment D is included twice with the same name but the two instances of this segment have different full path names A.B1.D and A.B2.D and therefore can be easily localized by the user with MCL statements. In different segments of the same model the number of token attributes may be different but, for any pair of linked segments, their attributes must be declared with the same ordering of data types. This is illustrated in Fig. 3, *a*, in which segments A and B have the same number and types of attributes, but only two attributes are declared in segment C.

After executable file of a model is created, a user can start the simulation. This is done in the executive subsystem which prepares model for simulation by loading NET-files of every segment, applies MCL statements, performs the simulation run of the model, collects and outputs statistics. The executive subsystem provides two modes of simulation — fast simulation and step-by-step simulation, or tracing. The latter is especially useful at the debugging stage and for tracing time diagrams of complex communication protocols.

During the simulation run, different statistics are gathered and evaluated in Winsim. This statistics include measures on transitions (number of firings, mean firing times, intervals between firings, utilization) and places (number of passed tokens, mean token waiting times, mean and maximum numbers of tokens in Q-places) in the form of tables with fixed formats. Winsim also produces histograms in the form of tables and in a graphical form. The interpretation of statistical results will be done by the modeler.

The managing subsystem starts the executive subsystem as an independent process that supports all kinds of interactions of a user with the model. Such arrangement of the system enables Winsim to execute theoretically unlimited number of models in parallel, with each model running as a separate application. It is worth to note that a ready model can be saved in any of its running states, allowing the user to complete the simulation run at a later time or/and on another computer. This facility may be useful for very large models with long simulation time.

5   The Example of a Simulation Model

A large number of simulation models have been developed in Winsim. These incl ude different communication protocols, local area networks, components of flexible manufacturing systems, logistics functions, different schemes of distributed mutual exclusion, data flow processors, components of operating systems, distributed data processing algorithms, distributed queuing systems etc [6], [7].

Due to space limitation, only a brief description of a simulation model of the distributed mutual exclusion (ME) algorithm proposed by Ricart and Agrawala [8] is given in this section. Distributed ME is concerned with the granting of access to a shared resource (SR) in a distributed system consisting of many nodes. Since there is no shared memory or global clock in a distributed system [9], the synchronization of serial access of the nodes in the distributed system to the SR is carried out by message passing. As performance metrics, the number of messages per use of SR and the average response time for a process were used [10]. With n processes, the Ricart and Agrawala algorithm requires $2*(n - 1)$ message exchanges for each ME invocation or exactly n messages if there is a support for multicast. The model (Fig. 4) consists of one network segment, and n identical segments of processes.

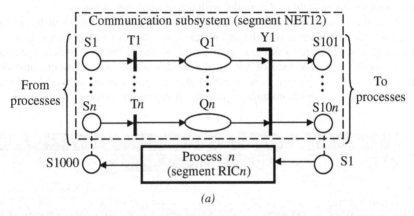

(a)

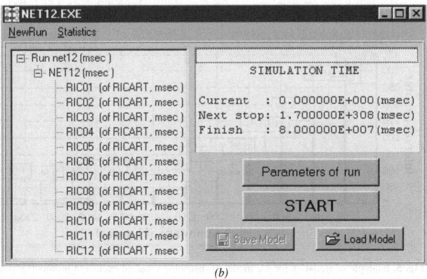

(b)

Fig. 4. The structure of the model of the distributed ME protocol: *a*) the network segment with segments of twelve processes; *b*) the view of the run window before the start of simulation

The model of the network, shown in Fig. 4, *a*, simulates by transition Y1 multicasting mode of communication. When transition Y1 fires, tokens will appear, after some random delay, in all its output places, so that each process receives a multicast message. The scheme of the process' model and the full description of the model are given in [3].

The window shown in Fig. 4, *b* corresponds to 12 processes, but it can be easily extended for an arbitrary number of processes. In this case, it should be necessary to change only the network segment, representing the communication subsystem, adding the corresponding number of queues and attaching the desirable number of new copies of the process's segment. These copies will be created automatically by executive subsystem before simulation. With MCL, it is possible to do a number of changes in the model without its re-compiling. For this example, before starting a simulation run, the user can change, in particular, the load of the SR. The user can also specify initial state of the model with initial marking of places.

With this model, the performance study has been carried out for different loads of the SR (low, medium, and high) and different numbers of processes (3, 6, 9, ..., 21). Fig. 5 shows a histogram of the response time of one of the processes in the model for 12 processes and low load of SR. In the model, a process' segment consists of 11 transitions and 15 places; a segment of the communication subsystem (Fig. 4, *a*) consists of $n + 1$ transitions and $3n$ places, where n is the number of processes.

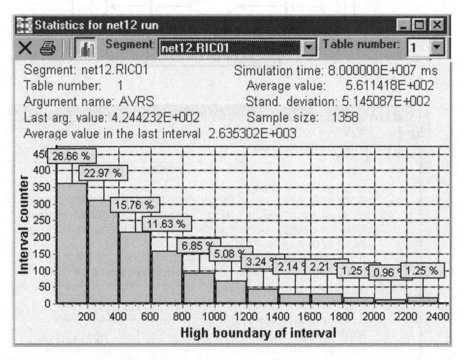

Fig. 5. Example of statistics for the model of distributed mutual exclusion protocol: histogram of response time

The simulation run for 12 processes took about 17 sec on the Pentium IV 1.4 GHz computer for $8 \cdot 10^7$ ms of simulation time. During this period each of 12 processes had about 1300 - 1400 accesses to SR. The entire number of events in the model was about 860000. Therefore, the processing of one event required about 19.8 microseconds of computer time on average. The execution of a model in Winsim is quite fast, and according to our benchmark experiments, is about four times faster than in GPSS Word simulation system for similar models.

6 Conclusion

The developed simulation system Winsim implements a class of extended Petri nets with attributed tokens and associated functions of time, data transformation and control in transitions. Winsim was successfully applied for simulation of many different information systems and their components. It is especially useful for modeling and simulation of parallel and distributed systems and the related algorithms. For such systems, characterized by extensive concurrency of events and processes and complex patterns of interprocess interactions, the developed tool is a natural choice.

References

1. Data base on Petri nets tools. http://www.daimi.au.dk/PetriNets/tools/complete_db.html (2002)
2. Andrews, G.R.: Foundations of Multithreaded, Parallel, and Distributed Programming. Addison-Wesley (2000)
3. Simulation System Winsim Based on Extended Petri Nets: User Manual.
4. http://www.daimi.au.dk/PetriNets/tools/complete_db.html (2002)
5. Murata, T.: Petri Nets: Properties, Analysis and Applications. Proc. IEEE, vol. 77, no. 4 (1989) 541 – 580
6. Kostin, A.E.: Models and Algorithms for Organization of Distributed Data Processing in Information Systems. Diss. DSc , Moscow Institute of Electronic Technology (1989) (in Russian)
7. Kostin, A.E., Aybay, I., and Oz, G.: A Randomized Contention-Based Load Balancing Protocol for a Distributed Multiserver Queuing System. IEEE Trans. on Parallel and Distributed Systems, vol. 11, no. 12 (2000) 1252 - 1273
8. Kostin, A.E., Aybay, I., and Oz, G.: A Paradigm of Alternating Sequential/Parallel Computation in a Distributed-Memory System over a Shared Transmission Media. Proc. of the 13th International Symposium on Computer and Information Sciences ISCIS'98, 26 - 28 October 1998, Belek-Antalya, Turkey. IOS Press, Amsterdam (1998) 342 - 351
9. Ricart, G., and Agrawala, A.K.: An Optimal Algorithm for Mutual Exclusion in Computer Networks. Communications of the ACM, vol. 24, no. 1, (1981) 9 - 17
10. Coulouris, G., Dollimore, J., and Kindberg, T.: Distributed Systems: Concepts and Design. 3rd ed. Addison-Wesley (2001)
11. Singhal, M.: A Taxonomy of distributed mutual exclusion. Journal of Parallel and Distributed Computing, vol. 18, (1993) 94 - 101

Integrating Distributed Composite Objects
into Java Environment

Guray Yilmaz[1] and Nadia Erdogan[2]

[1] Turkish Air Force Academy, Computer Eng. Dept., Yeşilyurt,
34149 İstanbul, Turkey
g.yilmaz@hho.edu.tr
[2] Istanbul Technical University, Electrical-Electronics Faculty,
Computer Engineering Dept., Ayazaga,
80626 İstanbul, Turkey
erdogan@cs.itu.edu.tr

Abstract. This paper introduces a new programming model for distributed systems, distributed composite objects (DCO), to meet efficient implementation, transparency, and performance demands of distributed applications with cooperating users connected through the internet. It allows the representation of an object as a collection of sub-objects and enhances the object distribution concept by implementing replication at the sub-object level and only when demanded. DCOBE, a DCO-based programming environment, conceals implementation details of the DCO model behind its interface and provides basic mechanisms. An important feature of the programming framework is transparency.

1 Introduction

This paper introduces a new programming model for distributed systems, *distributed composite objects (DCO),* to meet efficient implementation, transparency, fault tolerance and performance demands of cooperative applications with users connected through the internet. DCO model incorporates two basic concepts. The first concept is **composition,** by which an object is partitioned into *sub-objects (SO)* that together constitute a single *composite object (CO).* The second basic concept is **replication**. Replication extends the object concept to the distributed environment. Sub-objects of a composite object are replicated on different address spaces to ensure availability and quick local access. Decomposition of an object into sub-objects reduces the granularity of replication. To a client, a DCO appears to be a local object. However, the distributed clients of a DCO are, in fact, each associated with local copies of one or more sub-objects and the set of replicated sub-objects distributed over multiple address spaces form a single distributed composite object.

A software layer, *Distributed Composite Object Based Environment (DCOBE)* provides a programming framework that is based on the DCO model [5]. DCOBE is a middleware built on Java Virtual Machine and presents functionalities that facilitate

T. Yakhno (Ed.): ADVIS 2004, LNCS 3261, pp. 322–331, 2004.

the development of internet wide distributed applications, through a well-defined interface.

An important feature of the programming framework is transparency. Users of DCOs acquire the benefits of a centralized environment as DCOBE takes care of issues such as distribution and replication of object state, management of consistency, and concurrency control. They are automatically programmed separately from the application code, thus enabling developers to concentrate on the semantics of the application they are working on.

The paper is organized into six sections. Section 2 presents the distributed composite object model. The structure of a DCO is explained in Section 3. Section 4 presents developing steps of a DCO. Related work is explained in Section 5. Finally, Section 6 presents our conclusion.

2 Distributed Composite Object Model

The DCO model allows applications to describe and to access shared data in terms of objects whose implementation details are embedded in several sub-objects. Each sub-object is an elementary object, with a centralized representation, or may itself be a composite object. Several sub-objects are grouped together in a container object to form a composite object.

The developer of the composite object distributes the object's state between multiple sub-objects and uses them to implement the features of the composite object. SOs of a composite object are replicated on different address spaces to ensure availability and quick local access. A CO is first created on a single address space with its constituent SOs. When a client application on another address space invokes an operation on a CO which triggers a method of a particular SO, the state of that SO only, rather than that of the whole CO, is copied to the client environment. With this replication scheme, SOs are replicated dynamically on remote address spaces upon method invocation requests. The set of SOs replicated on a certain address space represents the CO on that site. Thus, the state of a CO is physically distributed over several address spaces. Active copies of parts, or whole, of a composite object can reside on multiple address spaces simultaneously. We call this conceptual representation over multiple address spaces a *distributed composite object*.

Fig.1 depicts a DCO that spreads over four address spaces. It is initially created on *Site2* with all of its sub-objects (SO1, SO2, and SO3), and is later replicated on three other sites, with SO1 on *Site1*, SO2 and SO3 on *Site3*, and SO1 and SO3 on *Site4*. The three sites contribute to the representation of the DCO. The set of address spaces on which a DCO resides evolves dynamically as client applications start interactions on the target CO.

Clients see the interface, which the developer has defined for the composite object, rather than the interfaces from the collection of embedded sub-objects. Therefore, from the client's point of view, a composite object is a single shared object that has only one access point, a single interface. He is not aware of its internal composition and, hence, has no explicit access to the sub-objects that make up its state. This restriction is an important aspect of our model and allows the object developer to dynamically adapt composite objects to changing conditions. The developer may add new sub-objects to a composite object to extend its design, remove existing ones or modify the implementation of some, without affecting the interface of the composite object. Thus, dynamic adaptation of the object over time becomes possible, without affecting the applications that use it.

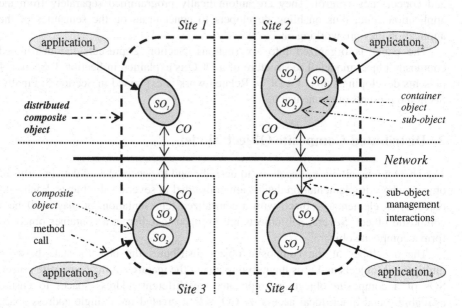

Fig. 1. A distributed composite object that spreads over three sites

Clients of a DCO are aware neither of its composition, nor of its distribution. As the objects in our model are passive objects, a client accesses a DCO by invoking methods in the interface provided by the object. Invocations are ordinary local object invocations as the client has a local implementation of the object in its address space. Multiple clients may access the same object simultaneously. When the state of an object is modified, all replicas are kept consistent through consistency management protocols that involve remote interactions.

3 The Structure of a DCO

We have defined an enhanced object structure to deal with implementation issues and thus provide the object developer and its clients with complete transparency of distribution, replication and consistency management. This structure includes two intermediate objects, namely, *a connective object* and *a control object*, which are inserted between the container object and each target sub-object.

Connective and control objects cooperate to enable client invocations on DCOs. A connective object is responsible for dynamic client to object binding which results in the placement of a valid replica of a sub-object in the caller's address space. A control object is a wrapper that controls accesses to its associated replica. It implements coherence protocols to ensure consistency of sub-object state. A client object invocation follows a path through these intermediate objects to reach the target sub-object after certain control actions.

An Automatic Class Generator (ACG) that has been developed in the context of this work is used to generate classes for connective and control objects from interface descriptions of sub-objects. Hence, the developer has to focus only on the design of the sub-objects that make up a composite object. The others are generated automatically, according to the coherence protocol specified by the developer.

3.1 Connective Object

The connective object is the target of all local client invocation requests. Structurally, it is an object with the same abstract type and implements the same interface as the sub-object it is associated with. For a client invocation to be possible, it is necessary that the client bind to that object. Each connective object contains a reference that points to the control object of the referenced sub-object. If the reference is bound, it means the control object is already present. The connective object forwards the invocation request to the control object. It is the control object's task to make a valid replica of the sub-object available locally. In case the reference is null, a copy of the control object is fetched and the reference is updated.

3.2 Control Object

The control object is located between the connective object and the local implementation of the sub-object and exports the same interface as the sub-object. It receives both local and remote invocation requests and directs them to the local sub-object. Consistency problems arise as sub-object replicas on different address spaces are modified. The control object is responsible for the management of consistency of object state and concurrency control to ensure mutually exclusive access. It implements certain coherence and access synchronization protocols before actually allowing a method invocation request to execute on the sub-object it is associated with. The system uses *entry consistency* [4] for memory coherency.

There are two approaches in the synchronization of write accesses to objects so that no client reads old data once a write access has been completed on some replica: *write-update* and *write-invalidate* [2]. Write-update broadcasts the effects of all write accesses to all address spaces that hold replicas of the target object. In the write-invalidate scheme, on the other hand, an invalidation message is sent to all address spaces that hold a replica before doing an update. Upon receipt of an invalidation message, objects are simply marked invalid, but not immediately retrieved. Clients ask for updates as they need them. DCO model implements both coherence protocols. The developer chooses the one which suits the requirements of his application the best and the control object's class is generated accordingly by the ACG.

The interface of a control object is divided into two parts. The first part is identical to that of the sub-object and its methods are called by the connective object to access the sub-object replica. The second part is an upcall interface that is used to implement the coherence and access synchronization protocols. Control objects on different sites communicate through this interface to keep the object state consistent.

The control object implements a method invocation request in three main steps. They are briefly explained below, omitting specific details.

Step 1. Get access permission: This step involves a set of actions, possibly including communication with remote control objects, to obtain access permission to the sub-object. It is blocking in nature, and once activity is allowed, it proceeds to step 2. The control object recognizes the type of the operation the method invocation involves, either a write *(W)* operation that modifies the state of the object or a read *(R)* operation that does not, and proceeds with this information. The object developer specifies the access type of each method with an appropriate keyword *(R/W)* that follows the method signature in the interface declaration of a sub-object. For a *R-type* of invocation request, the actions are similar for both types of coherence protocols. They result in the placement of a valid sub-object copy in the local address space if one is not already present and return a permission to proceed, if currently there is no active writer to the object and the list of pending requests is empty. The client is added to the valid list of the target sub-object. If those conditions do not hold, the client is suspended temporarily and the request is queued in a waiting list.

A *W-type* of invocation request is queued for both coherence protocols, if a writer is already active or the pending list of requests is not empty. Otherwise, for the write-invalidate protocol, all reader clients in the valid list are sent an invalidation message and the valid list is purged. The operation returns a valid copy of the target sub-object on the caller's address space, if not already present, along with its ownership granting write access permission to the invoker.

Step 2. Invoke method: This is the step when the method invocation on the local sub-object takes place. After receiving permission to access the target sub-object, the control object issues a call which received from the connective object.

Step 3. Complete invocation: This step completes the method invocation after issuing update requests for remote replicas on the valid list to meet the requirements of write-update protocol. After the call returns, the control object activates invocation requests that have blocked on the object. The classical multiple-reader/single-writer scheme is implemented, with waiting readers given priority over waiting writers after a write access completes and a waiting writer given priority over waiting readers after the last read access completes.

4 Developing a New DCO

In this section, we will demonstrate with an example how a DCO is created and how it is accessed from a remote Java application. No language extensions or system support classes are required during coding. The developer generates code as he does for a conventional centralized application. As an example, we assume a DCO named Employee, whose state and implementation is distributed between three sub-objects: Person, Account, and Job. Fig.2 shows the class definition a developer would prepare for the container object Employee.

```
public class Employee {
    //Definitions of the sub-objects and other variables
    Connective_Account bankAccount;
    Connective_Person  person;
    Connective_Job     job;
    float              amount;
    . . . . .          . . . . . . .
    public Employee() {
            bankAccount = new Connective_Account();
            person      = new Connective_Person();
            job         = new Connective_Job();
            amount      = 0;
            . . . . . . . . . . . . . . . . . .
    }
    public void deposit_BankAccount(float amount) {
            bankAccount.deposit(amount);
    }
    public void withdraw_BankAccount(float amount) {
            bankAccount.withdraw(amount);
    }
    public float balance_BankAccount() {
            amount = bankAccount.balance();
            return amount;
    }
    . . . . . . . . . . . . . . . . . . . . . . . .
}
```

Fig. 2. Container class definition for DCO Employee

```
public class Sub_Account {
    float total = 0;
    public void deposite(float amount) {
            total = total + amount;
    }
    public void witdraw(float amount) {
            total = total - amount;
    }
    public float balance() {
            return total;
    }
}
```

Fig. 3. Code for sub-object class Sub_Account

In this example, for clarity, we have only included methods that utilize the sub-object class Account and their contents are extremely simplified as to include only a single method invocation on the target sub-object. Actually, there is no restriction on the semantics of the methods of a DCO. Next, the class definitions and interface descriptions for each sub-object are prepared. Class definitions are typical Java definitions, except for the prefix 'Sub_' that precedes the name of the class. Fig.3 shows the code for sub-object Sub_Account .

Interface descriptions list the methods the sub-object implements for internal use. At this point, the developer is required to identify, for each method, the type of operation its invocation involves using an appropriate symbol: W (short for Write) for one that modifies the state of the object and R (short for Read) for one that does not. This is the only difference between an RMI and DCO interface description. Fig.4 shows the interface description for sub-object Sub_Account.

```
public interface Sub_Account {
      public void deposit_W(float amount);
      public void withdraw_W(float amount);
      public float balance_R();
}
```

Fig. 4. Interface description for class Sub_Account

The next step involves the generation of class definitions for connective and control objects of each sub-object. The Automatic Class Generator creates them automatically using the information extracted from interface descriptions of the sub-objects. Fig.5 and Fig.6 show the class definitions for the connective object and the control object generated respectively from interface Account.

```
public class Connective_Account {
      int obj_id;
      Control_Account control_object;

      public Connective_Account() {
            control_object = new Control_Account ();
            obj_id = control_object.get_id();
      }

      public void deposite(float amount) { ....... }

      public void witdraw(float amount)   { ....... }

      public float balance() {
            if (control_object == null) (1)
                control_object = (Control_Account)
                dcobe_server.get_control_object(obj_id);(2)
            return control_object.balance();(3)
      }
}
```

Fig. 5. Class definition for the connective object; Connective_Account

The connective object of Sub_Account is named as Account and implements the same interface as Sub_Account because a method invocation on a sub-object is actually directed to its connective object first. It contains a pointer to the control object. Whenever one of its methods is activated, it first checks the binding of the reference to the control object ((1) in Fig. 5). If the reference has not yet been bound, a call is issued, which returns copies of both the control object and the sub-object (2). The method invocation is then forwarded to the control object (3).

```
public class Control_Account {
    Sub_Account   subObject;
    int    obj_id, server_id;

    public Control_Account() {
        subObject = new Sub_Account();
        server_id = dcobe_server.get_serverId();
        obj_id = dcobe_server.
                      register_object(this, subObject);(1)
    }

    public void deposite(float amount) { ....... }

    public void witdraw(float amount)  { ....... }

    public float balance() {
        access_right(R);   (2)
        float account = subObject.balance();(3)
        access_end(server_id, R);
        return account;
    }
}
```

Fig. 6. Class definition for the control object; `Control_Account`

The control object registers the sub-object and, in return, receives a unique identifier, obj_id ((1) in Fig.6), which is used by the connective and control objects on successive accesses to the sub-object. Control object implements coherence protocols to ensure consistency of the sub-object's state. After getting access permission through a lock (2), the method is invoked on the sub-object (3). The control object also includes internal methods (upcalls not presented in Fig.6) that may be invoked by DCOBE_Server in order to check the status of the lock on the sub-object and block a lock request from a remote node until the lock is explicitly released.

After completing the class definitions for a composite object class, these class files are made available to other nodes by an HTTP-server so that they may be dynamically loaded from remote addresses. The following piece of code first instantiates a composite object in an application program. Immediately afterwards, connective objects, control objects and the sub-objects are automatically created on that node (1). Second, the newly created composite object is registered with a name (2), and third, in order to make class definitions dynamically loadable, class base information is also registered (3).

```
(1) employee = new Employee();
(2) dcobe_server.register(employee, "John");
(3) dcobe_server.register_class("Employee",
                               "http://Class_Base/");
```

For a DCO to be accessible from a remote node, a user has to bind to the object through a lookup operation, that is, a registered composite object needs to installed in its address space. With this process, connective objects are also installed on the requesting node automatically. However, a local method invocation on the object becomes possible only after the control object and a replica of a sub-object is loaded.

The following piece of code loads the class Employee dynamically (4), and binds to one of its instances, John, (5). Now, the remote user is ready to invoke a method on the distributed composite object (6). Only a replica of the sub-object bankAccount will be loaded to the user's address space. In addition, according to the coherence protocol, all other replicas of bankAccount will either be invalidated or updated after this method completes.

```
(4) Employee = dcobe_server.load_class("Employee");
(5) employee = dcobe_server.lookup("John");
(6) employee.deposit_BankAccount(1000);
```

5   Related Work

Our work has been influenced closely by the SOS [1] and Globe [6] projects, which support state distribution through physically distributed shared objects. The SOS system is based on the Fragmented Object (FO) model [3]. The FO model is a structure for distributed objects that naturally extends the proxy principle. FO is a set of *fragment objects* local to an address space, connected together by a *connective object*. Fragments export the FO interface, while connective objects implement the interactions between fragments. A connective object embodies the consistency and coherence properties of the distributed object and provides an internal communication substrate for the FO. Even though the work hides the cooperation between fragments of a FO from the clients, the programmer is responsible to control the details of the cooperation. He has to decide if a fragment locally implements the service or is just a stub to a remote server fragment. FO hides data replication and consistency management from the user, but those details are exposed to the implementer.

One of the key concepts of the Globe system is its model of *Distributed Shared Objects* (DSOs) [6]. A DSO is physically distributed, meaning that its state might be partitioned and replicated across multiple machines at the same time. However, all implementation aspects are part of the object and hidden behind its interface. For an object invocation to be possible, a local object is bound in the client's address space. A local object may implement an interface by forwarding all invocations, as in RPC client stubs, or through operations on a replica of the object state. Local objects are partitioned into sub-objects, which implement distribution issues such as replication and communication, so developers concentrate on the semantics of the object.

The major difference between our work and above projects is that, they both do not support the composite object model and caching is restricted to the state of the entire object. However, the DCO model allows the representation of an object as a collection of sub-objects and enhances the object distribution concept by implementing replication at the sub-object level, providing a finer granularity. To the best of our knowledge, there is no programming framework that supports replication at the sub-object level. Also, in both projects, deciding where and when to create a replica is left to the application. Even though Globe provides a general mechanism for associating replication strategies with objects, at present, a developer has to write his own implementation of a replication sub-object. DCO, in contrast, replicates sub-objects at all sites they are used and management of consistency of state and concurrency control is transparent to both object developers and users. Dynamic loading of sub-objects is also a feature that is not supported by either of the projects. Another important difference is that, DCO developer may add new sub-objects to a composite object to extend its design, remove existing ones or modify the implementation of some sub-objects without affecting its users.

6 Conclusion

In this study, we proposed a new object model, distributed composite object, for internet-wide collaborative computing. This distributed composite object model allows users to describe applications in terms of a single composite object whose implementation details are embedded and encapsulated in different types of sub-objects. In this model, a distributed object is not an entity running on a single machine, possibly with full copies on other machines, it is partitioned on several sub-objects and these sub-objects are replicated across multiple sites at the same time.

Applications are developed using Java language as centralized manner and made available on the internet. Applications are dynamically deployed on client nodes and the distributed objects are transparently shared among applications. This allows users to deal with the diverse environments that exist in a wide area network and to separate applications from the implementation of the objects. Application programmers may really concentrate on the application specific logic. This approach makes distribution and replication almost transparent to the application programmers.

References

1. Shapiro, M., Gourhant, Y., Herbert, S., Mosseri, L., Ruffin, M. and Valot, C.: SOS: An Object-Oriented Operating System-Assessment and Perspectives. Computing Systems, Dec. 2(4) (1989) 287-338.
2. Mosberger, D.: Memory consistency models. Operating Systems Review, Jan. (1993) 18-26.
3. Makpangou, M., Gourhant, Y., LeNarzul J.P. and Shaphiro, M.: Fragmented Objects for Distributed Abstractions. in: T.L. Casavant and M. Singhal (eds.), Readings in Distributed Computing Systems, IEEE Computer Society Press (1994) 170-186.
4. J. B. Carter, J. K. Bennett, and W. Zwaenepoel. Techniques for reducing consistency-related communication in distributed shared-memory systems. ACM Transactions on Computer Systems, Aug. 13(3) (1995) 205–243.
5. Yılmaz G., Distributed Composite Object Model for Distributed Object-Based Systems. PhD Thesis, Istanbul Technical University Institute of Science and Technology, Istanbul, Turkey (2002).
6. Bakker, A., Kuz, I., Steen, M.V., Tanenbaum, A.S. and Verkaik. P.: Design and Implementation of the Globe Middleware. Technical Report IR-CS-003, June (2003).

Content-Based Distribution for Load Sharing in Locally Clustered Web Servers

Ji Yung Chung[1] and Sungsoo Kim[2]

[1] Department of Computer Science and Information, Myongji College, 356-1,
Honguen-Dong, Seodaemun-Gu, Seoul, 120-776, Korea
abback@mail.mjc.ac.kr
[2] Graduate School of Information and Communication, Ajou University,
Wonchun-Dong, Paldal-Gu, Suwon, Kyunggi-Do, 442-749, Korea
sskim@madang.ajou.ac.kr

Abstract. A cluster consists of a collection of interconnected stand-alone computers working together and provides a high-availability solution in application areas such as web services or information systems. With the growing popularity of the Internet, services using the World Wide Web are increasing, and it is certain that web server clusters will be the basic architecture. The Layer-4 distribution algorithms of web server clusters have widely studied, but they are content information blind. They select the target server when the client establishes the TCP/IP connection. On the contrary, content-based load distribution uses the detailed data found in the application layer to intelligently route user requests among web servers. In this paper, we propose an effective content-based load distribution algorithm that considers cache hit and load information of the web servers under the web server clusters. In addition, we expand this algorithm in order to manage user requests for dynamic file. Specially, our algorithm does not keep track of any frequency of access information or try to model the contents of the caches of the web servers.

1 Introduction

Recent applications request more computing power than a sequential computer can process. One method that solves this limit is to improve the speed of processors, memory and other components. However, it is constrained by the speed of light. A practical and cost-effective alternative solution is to improve computing power by coordinating multiple computers together [1].

With the growing popularity of the Internet, services using the web are increasing. However, the overall increase in traffic on the web causes a disproportionate increase in client requests to popular web sites. Performance and high availability are important at web sites that receive large numbers of requests.

Although the web is becoming a widely accepted medium, it provides relatively poor performance and low availability. In order to provide the required levels of reliability and availability, many service providers have traditionally built their servers on top of fault tolerant computers [2, 3]. Typically, these systems use self-

T. Yakhno (Ed.): ADVIS 2004, LNCS 3261, pp. 332–341, 2004.
© Springer-Verlag Berlin Heidelberg 2004

checking replicated hardware, which is very expensive. On the contrary, cluster systems provide not only a low cost but also a flexible alternative to fault tolerant computers for applications that require high throughput and high availability [4, 5].

Another advantage of clustered systems is scalability. Interconnections in traditional supercomputers have a fixed network topology. However cluster systems are more dynamic. With the increasing demand for computing, more and more nodes can be added in cluster systems.

A common approach adopted by popular web sites to handle millions of accesses per day has one virtual URL interface and uses a distributed server architecture that is hidden from the user [6]. These systems provide scalability and transparency, but require some internal mechanism that assigns client requests to the web server that can offer the best service.

Load balancing over a network uses a special node to distribute workload or network traffic load across the cluster systems. The decision to distribute the load to a particular node can be static or dynamic depending upon the current network status.

Layer-7 dispatching algorithms can establish a complete TCP connection with the client and examine the HTTP request prior to choosing the target server. They accomplish content-based routing by letting the load balancer inspect the HTTP request and then route it to the target server. In particular, the potential advantages of content-based dispatching algorithms involve the possibility to achieve higher cache hit rate and to partition the web content among heterogeneous servers. Also, layer-7 dispatching policies can have special-purpose back-end nodes for certain types of requests. For these reasons, it seems clear that in the future, layer-7 dispatching solutions will continue to dominate products in terms of performance and cost.

In this paper, we propose an effective content-based dispatching algorithm that takes into account load information of the web servers and cache hit under the web server clusters. Also, this algorithm is expanded to manage user requests for dynamic files.

The remainder of the paper is organized as follows. In section 2, we present work related to content-based load balancing algorithm. Section 3 describes our load balancing algorithm in comparison to the other algorithms. In section 4, we describe the model used to simulate performance and present the results of the simulation. Finally, section 5 summarizes with concluding remarks.

2 Related Work

Over the past few years, a lot of researches have proposed methods for distributing the user requests in web server clusters [7, 8]. TCP connection routing is the most widely used method as the content-blind dispatching policy. It decides the target server before client sends out the HTTP request. In this method, the client establishes a TCP connection to the server if the IP address is resolved. The load balancer sends the user requests on different server to appear as a virtual service on a single IP address.

HTTP redirection is achieved by returning the IP address of the selected server instead of returning the requested data. It can be used for content-based routing, but it is not proper because it exposes IP addresses of the target server and adds client round-trip latency [9].

While layer-4 clustering may be considered a solved problem, a lot of research is currently ongoing in the area of layer-7 clustering [10]. Typically, these methods use information involved in OSI layer-7. This is also known as content-based routing because it behaves based on the contents of the client request.

LARD(Locality Aware Request Distribution) has much influenced related work as an early attempt for content-based routing in web server clusters [11]. In particular, it focuses on the high cache hit rate and locality is increased by dynamically subdividing the server's working set. The load balancer maintains a one-to-one mapping of targets to each node in the web server clusters. If the first request arrives for a given target, it is assigned a server by selecting a lightly loaded server. After that, subsequent requests are directed to a target's assigned server, if that node is not overloaded. That is to say, the existing methods assign user requests to the least loaded node but LARD reassigns targets only when there is a significant load imbalance. LARD appears to focus entirely on the static file case.

HACC(Harvard Array of Clustered Computers) proposed for locality enhancement supports for dynamic files [12]. Client requests that arrive in the web server cluster are distributed among the servers in order to enhance the locality of reference. By improving locality, it can reduce working set size and achieve high performance.

When the web site provides heterogeneous services that make an intensive use of different web server resources, most load sharing problems occur. To improve load sharing in web server clusters that provide multiple services, the CAP(Client Aware Policy) looks only at client requests instead of server states [13]. It classifies the client requests on the basis of their expected impact on server resources, that is, CPU, disk, network interface. By doing so, most of the page latency time can be half of that of commonly used dynamic load balancing, such as Weighted Round Robin and LARD. Because the service classes are determined in advance CAP does not require a hard tuning of parameters that is typical of most dynamic policies.

The basic idea of this paper is to effectively merge load information and cache hit rate in order to improve the performance of web server clusters. Also, we expand this algorithm to manage user requests for dynamically generated content.

3   Load Distribution Algorithm

In order to handle millions of accesses, a general approach adopted by popular web sites is to preserve one virtual URL (Uniform Resource Locator) interface and use a distributed server architecture that is hidden from the user.

Thus, we consider the architecture of a cluster system that consists of the load balancer and a set of document servers. Each of the document servers is a HTTP (Hyper Text Transfer Protocol) server.

Figure 1 presents the web server cluster architecture. In this architecture, the load balancer has a single, virtual IP (Internet Protocol) address and request routing among servers is transparent. Every request from the clients is delivered into the load balancer over the Internet. The load balancer redirects the request to a target server that is selected by load distribution algorithm.

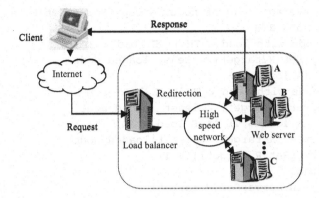

Fig. 1. Clustered web server architecture

In content-based routing, the load balancer directs all requests for file A in the first node and all requests for file B in the second node. By doing so, content-based routing can improve locality in the main memory caches of servers.

When the first request arrives for a given target, the load balancer assigns a node by selecting a lightly loaded node and adds it to the set of the service node. The load balancer maintains a mapping from the target to a set of nodes that serve the target. Subsequent requests are directed to a target's assigned node, if that node is not overloaded. If the requested file's service set exists, requests for a target are assigned to the least loaded node in the target's service set. Also, if the average load of nodes in service set exceeds threshold value, the load balancer picks a new lightly loaded node except service set and adds that node to the service set for the target.

If this service set strategy is not used, a node can go into an overloaded state. That is, when one extremely popular target exists, only one node serves the target and a new service node is assigned as often as the overloaded situation occurs. This decreases the system performance. On the contrary, if service set strategy is used, multiple servers can serve a given target.

On the other hand, if a request target has several nodes and its access rate is decreased enough, the load balancer removes one node from the target's service set. This ensures that the degree of replication for a target does not remain unnecessarily high if it is requested less often. The pseudo code for this strategy is inserted in line 18 to 24.

```
Load Distribution Algorithm : CUL
1 while (true)
2fetch next request R
3if (ServerSet[R.target] = NULL)
4L, ServerSet[R.target] ← least loaded node
5else
6L ← least loaded node in ServerSet[R.target]
7M ← most loaded node in ServerSet[R.target]
8A.load ← average load of nodes in ServerSet[R.target]
```

```
9E.load ← average load of nodes except ServerSet[R.target]
10if (A.load > 2TH)
11if (∀ node with load < TH || E.load < 2TH)
12L, ServerSet[R.target] ← least loaded node
13else if (A.load > TH)
14if (∀ node with load < TL || E.load < TH)
15L,ServerSet[R.target] ← least loaded node
16else if (A.load > TL && E.load < TL)
17L, ServerSet[R.target] ← least loaded node
18if (|ServerSet[R.target]| > 1)
19if (A.load <= TL)
20remove M in ServerSet[R.target]
21else if (A.load <= TH && ∀ node with load > 2TH)
22remove M in ServerSet[R.target]
23else if (A.load <= 2TH && E.load > 2TH)
24remove M in ServerSet[R.target]
25send R to L
```

LARD diverges from this strategy and reassigns target servers only when there is a significant load imbalance. However, this method has a problem that a node can reach serious load even though another node is idle. A 'significant load imbalance' means that a node has a load larger than TH when every other node has a load less than TL. Where, TH is the load above which a node is likely to cause substantial delay in serving requests and TL is the load below which a node is likely to have idle resources. That is, LARD focuses more on locality enhancement rather than load balancing.

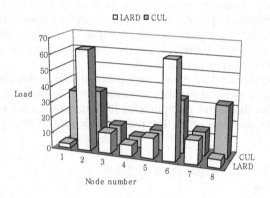

Fig. 2. Example: LARD Vs. CUL

However, we can see that this condition is inefficient in the example of Figure 2. When the load of node 2 and 6 is larger than TH (65 connections) and the load of every other node is less than TL (25 connections), LARD does not reassign the requests for node 2. In the same case, the proposed algorithm CUL (Content-based

Useful Load distribution) distributes the load by adding node 1 to the service set that serves the target. The following algorithm proposed in this paper does not have bias toward any side of load balancing and locality as the hybrid of the existing methods.

Our proposed algorithm does not keep track of any frequency of access information or try to model the contents of the caches of the web servers. In particular, this method is dependent on the local replacement policy used by the nodes.

Much of recent research effort has been directed at support for static files. Even though research for dynamic file tries, but additional research is needed. Therefore, we develop a DCUL algorithm that expands a CUL algorithm in order to manage user requests for dynamic files efficiently. This algorithm classifies the user requests on the basis of their expected impact on server resources. That is to say, we distinguish web requests as static file service that is cacheable to memory, disk bound service such as web transaction, CPU bound service and CPU and disk bound service such as web commerce.

```
Load Distribution Algorithm : DCUL
1 while (true)
2fetch next request R
3if (R.class = Static)
4execute CUL algorithm line 3 to 24
5if (R.class = CPU)
6L ← node that has the smallest C_count
7L.C_count = L.C_count + 1
8if (R.class = Disk)
9L ← node that has the smallest D_count
10L.D_count = L.D_count + 1
11if (R.class = Disk & CPU)
12for each node
13if (C_count > D_count)
14DC_count = C_count
15else
16DC_count = D_count
17L ← node that has the smallest DC_count
18L.C_count = L.C_count + 1
19L.D_count = L.D_count + 1
20send R to L
```

In this algorithm, a single component of a server such as the CPU or disk is not exceedingly overloaded. The service components are determined in advance, and the scheduling choice is decided statically. To begin with, user request R is classified as each class. Then, if the class of R is static it executes line 3 to 24 of a CUL algorithm. If R is a request related to a CPU or disk the node that has the smallest number in the corresponding class is selected. By using DCUL assignment, each server has a similar number of requests for each class of service.

Also, if the class of R is a CPU and disk it selects a high number of C_count and D_count in each node. Then, the node that has a small number of selected values is selected.

4   Performance Evaluation

As indicated by the title, this section is devoted to a description of the simulation results which we obtained using our proposed algorithm for web server clusters. Table 1 presents the simulation parameters. In our simulation model, web server clusters consist of the load balancer and several nodes. Each node in the cluster is modeled as a separate component with its CPU, memory and disk. We use real parameters to setup the system. For example, the disk is parameterized with the values of a real disk having a transfer rate equal to 10 MBps, seek time to 9msec, rotational latency to 8msec. For simplicity of simulation, caching is executed on a whole-file basis. The main memory transfer rate is set to 100MBps. In addition, the assumed threshold value TH and TL are 65 and 25, relatively.

Table 1. Simulation parameters

Parameter	Value
Number of nodes	1-10
Memory per node	64MB
Memory transfer rate	100MB
Disk transfer rate	10MB
Seek time	9ms
Rotational latency	8ms
File size	64KB
Connection establishment and teardown	1.5ms
Zipfian Distribution	skew=1.5

The assumption is that the load balancer and networks are fast enough not to limit the cluster's performance. Web requests a user will submit to the web site are modeled according to the exponential distribution. In general, the access frequencies of web documents closely resemble a Zifpian distribution. In this distribution, the shape of the curve is decided by the skew parameter. When skew is 0 the access frequencies of web documents are uniform, and when the skew parameter is 2 the access frequencies of web documents are skewed.

The every user requests arrive at the queue of the load balancer and are assigned a node by a load distribution algorithm. If the requested file exists in the memory, it is serviced immediately. If the file is absent in the memory, it is served from the disk. Multiple requests for the same file from disk are processed with only one disk read. The processing steps for a given request are performed in sequence. However, the CPU and disk times can be overlapped. As the main measure for analyzing the performance of the web server clusters we use the requests per second.

Figure 3 presents the throughput as a function of the number of nodes. In WLC(Weighted Least Connection), the load balancer keeps track of all currently active connections assigned to each node in the cluster and assigns the next new incoming connection request to the node that currently has the least connections. WLC achieves the lowest throughput because it ignores locality. Since LARD focuses on the cache hit rate, the throughput achieved with that exceeds the value of WLC. CUL accomplishes the highest throughput by considering load balancing and locality simultaneously.

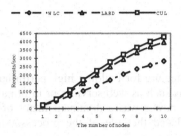

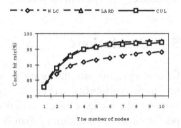

Fig. 3. Throughput : static workload

Fig. 4. Cache hit rate

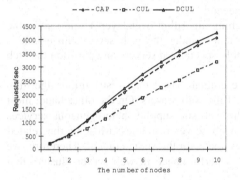

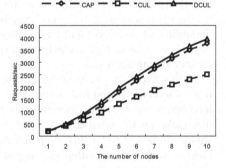

Fig. 5. Throughput : light dynamic

Fig. 6. Throughput : intensive dynamic

Figure 4 shows the cache hit rate as a function of the number of nodes. The cache hit rate is the number of requests that hit in a node's memory divided by the number of requests. Because LARD reassigns target only when there is a significant load imbalance focuses on the high cache hit rate higher than that of CUL that has the highest throughput. That is to say, CUL distributes the load by using idle nodes properly rather than tries for the high cache hit rate. This means that the high cache hit rate or good load balancing does not improve performance.

In order to observe the performance of DCUL that expands CUL algorithm, we performed additional experiments for dynamically generated content. In figure 5 and 6, 85% and 70% of requests are used for the static object. That is, 15% and 30% are used for dynamic services, respectively. The dynamic requests are classified as CPU(5%, 10%), disk(5%, 10%) and CPU & disk(5%, 10%).

In figure 5, we compare the performance of CAP, CUL and DCUL under light dynamic workload. Figure 6 is compared under intensive dynamic workload. The CAP that looks at only client requests instead of server states outperforms CUL that does not consider dynamic files. However, the DCUL that merges client and server states effectively has the best performance. That is, when comparing DCUL with CAP the load balancing achieved by DCUL has the better performance.

In addition, as user requests for dynamic files are increased, the performance of CUL is decreased. Meanwhile, we can see that CAP and DCUL are almost not influenced on dynamic contents.

5   Conclusions

Cluster systems are emerging as a viable architecture for building high performance and high availability servers in application areas such as web services or information systems. In initial cluster systems, processing power was a dominant factor of the performance, but memory bandwidth has replaced the role of the processor as a performance bottleneck.

The web is becoming the standard interface for accessing remote services, and there is no doubt that web server clusters will be the basic architecture. The load balancing algorithm of web server clusters should be considered carefully since it influences the system performance. Also, because it is not a commonly used standard or established protocol, more studies are needed.

The main advantage of layer-7 dispatching algorithm over layer-4 solutions is the possibility of using content-based information under the web server clusters. It is possible to achieve high cache hit rate, apply specialized servers and partition the web content among the nodes.

In this paper, we propose an effective content-based load distribution algorithm that uses cache hit and load information of the web servers. On the other hand, most load balancing problems happen when the web site supplies heterogeneous services that make an intensive use of different web server resources. Most of the related studies do not consider this issue and they focus on the static content. Therefore, we propose a DCUL algorithm that improves performance in web server clusters that provide multiple services.

The area of content-based dispatching algorithm that effectively combines server and client information needs further research. Also, combining load balancing and caching of dynamic content is worthy of further research.

Acknowledgement. This research is supported by the Ubiquitous Autonomic Computing and Network Project, the Ministry of Science and Technology (MOST) 21st Century Frontier R&D Program in Korea.

References

1. Buyya, R.: High Performance Cluster Computing: Architectures and Systems. Prentice-Hall, Upper Saddle River, New Jersey (1999)
2. Friedman, R. and Mosse, D.: Load Balancing Schemes for High-Throughput Distributed Fault-Tolerant Servers. Journal of Parallel and Distributed Computing (1999) 475-488

3. Wong, A. and Dillon, T.: Load Balancing to Improve Dependability and Performance for Program Objects in Distributed Real-time Co-operation over the Internet. The 3rd IEEE International Symposium on Object-Oriented Real-time Distributed Computing (2000)
4. Iyengar, A. et al.: High-Performance Web Site Design Techniques. IEEE Internet Computing (2000) 17-26
5. Zhu, H. et al.: Adaptive Load Sharing for Clustered Digital Library Servers. Proceedings of the Seventh IEEE International Symposium on High Performance Distributed Computing (1998) 28-31
6. Cardellini, V. et al.: Redirection Algorithms for Load Sharing in Distributed Web-server Systems. Proceedings of the 19th IEEE International Conference on Distributed Computing Systems (1999) 528-535
7. Hunt, G.D.H. et al.: Network Dispatcher: A connection Router for Scalable Internet Services. Proceedings of the 7th International World Wide Web Conference (1998)
8. Chung, J.Y. and Kim, S.: Efficient Memory Page Replacement on Web Server Clusters. Lecture Notes in Computer Science, Vol. 2331. Springer-Verlag (2002) 1042-1050
9. Yang, C.-S. and Luo, M.-Y.: Efficient Support for Content-based Routing in Web Server Clusters. Proceedings of the 2nd USENIX Symposium on Internet Technologies and Systems (1999)
10. Carzaniga, A. and Wolf, A.L.: Content-based Networking: A New Communication Infrastructure. Lecture Notes in Computer Science Vol. 2538. (2002) 59-68
11. Pai, V.S. et al.: Locality-aware Request Distribution in Cluster-based Network Servers. Proceedings of the 8th ACM Conference on Architecture Support for Programming Languages (1998)
12. Zhang, X. et al.: HACC: An Architecture for Cluster-based Web Servers. Proceedings of the 3rd USENIX Windows NT Symposium (1999)
13. Casalicchio, E. and Colajanni, M.: A Client-aware Dispatching Algorithm for Web Clusters Providing Multiple Services. Proceedings of the 10th International World Wide Web Conference (2001)

A Study on Grid Partition for Declustering High-Dimensional Data

Tae-Wan Kim[1], Hak-Cheol Kim[2], and Ki-Joune Li[2]

[1] Research Institute of Computer Information and Communication,
Pusan National University, Korea
twkim@quantos.cs.pusan.ac.kr
[2] Department of Computer Science, Pusan National University, Korea
{hkckim, lik}@pusan.ac.kr

Abstract. Most of the previous work on declustering have been focused on proposing good mapping functions under the assumption that the data space is partitioned equally for all dimensions. In this paper, we relax equal partition restriction on all dimensions by choosing smaller number of dimensions as split axes and study the effects of grid-like partitioning methods on the performance of a mapping function which is widely used for declustering algorithms. For this, we propose a cost model to expect the number of grid cells intersecting a range query and apply the best mapping scheme so far to the partitioned grid cells. Experiments show that our cost model gives remarkable accuracy for all ranges of selectivities and dimensions. By applying different partitioning schemes on the Kronecker sequence mapping function[5], which is known to be the best mapping function for high-dimensional data so far, we can achieve up to 23 times performance gain. Thus we can conclude that the performance of a mapping function is highly dependent on partitioning schemes applied. And our cost model gives clear criteria on how to select the number of split dimensions out of d dimensions to achieve better performance of a mapping function on declustering.

1 Introduction

Modern scientific database management systems such as CAD, information retrieval systems, geographic information systems, remote sensing databases, etc., store and handle massive amount of high dimensional data. While storing tera bytes of data is now achievable, time-efficient retrieval methods remain a crucial challenge. A lot of work have been done to improve I/O performance of these systems by distributing data across multiple parallel disks. This problem is termed as *declustering* in the fields of database. Most of declustering algorithms consist of two steps. First, one must organize data onto a physical disk block (data block) by the number of a blocking factor at most. To do this, they assume that the data space is partitioned into disjoint regular tiles or grid cells. And each of grid cells corresponds to a physical data block. Second, each data block must be assigned a disk number. To do this, they use

T. Yakhno (Ed.): ADVIS 2004, LNCS 3261, pp. 342–352, 2004.

mapping functions that map a grid cell to a disk number. Approaches that follow mentioned above are Disk-Modulo [6], Field-wise Xor [13], Error Correcting Code [8], Hilbert Curve Allocation Method [7], Cyclic Allocation Method [16], Coloring method [1], Generalized Disk Modulo [10], Golden-Ratio Sequence [3], Discrepancy based Numbering [4], Kronecker Sequence Mapping [5]. Among them, the Kronecker Sequence based mapping function [5] has been reported to outperforms others for high dimensional data. Beside above works, little efforts have been done to decluster non-uniform high dimensional data based on graph theory [9, 14, 15]. They treat data objects or data blocks as nodes of a graph and represent the weight of an edge as similarity between data blocks. Another approach is also proposed in [11, 12]. Authors suggested to partition data into a set of clusters where each cluster is generated based on Euclidean distance.

For high-dimensional data, all of them do not mention about how to construct d-dimensional grid cells, where d is large enough to generate more grid cells than the number of data blocks required. We focus on this problem and suggest how to select the number of dimensions and disjoint intervals at each dimension to construct uniform grid cells that optimize the range query performance of a mapping function. It seems sufficient to do binary partition for high dimensional data. However, it has potential drawbacks. Since as the dimensionality of data grows, the side length of a range query Q becomes extremely large even for a small selectivity due to 'Curse of Dimensionality'. As a result, all of the grid cells are accessed by Q. And thus a simple scheme that allocates in round-robin fashion could be the best since it allocates disk numbers evenly. Our approach is to *partition more than two times along the smaller number of dimensions*. For this, we have several alternatives and it is crucial to select an appropriate number of dimensions and splits, together with a good mapping function, for the performance of declustering.

In this paper, we propose a cost model that estimates the number of grid cells intersecting a range query. Our model is based on the Minkowski-sum cost model, which is a generalization of a geometric probability by taking into account a boundary effect[2]. Based on our model, we can apply an appropriate grid partitioning scheme among the possible alternatives. Experimental results show that our cost model gives an accuracy less than 0.5% error ratio. Furthermore, we improve the performance of well-known declustering algorithm[5] up to 23 times by applying a good partitioning scheme which is chosen by the cost model.

This paper is organized as follows: in the next section, we give preliminaries of the declustering problem and present our motivations. In section 3, we propose a cost model that expects the number of grid cells intersecting a range query. In section 4, we validate our cost model and show the effects of grid partitioning method on the declustering algorithm by several experiments. Finally, we conclude this paper in section 5.

2   Preliminaries and Motivations

In this section, we give preliminaries of a declustering problem and our motivations.

2.1   Preliminaries

To decluster data across multiple disks, one must group them by several buckets. Formally, we define bucketing of data set π for a given disk blocking factor $|B|$ as follows:

Definition 1. *Bucketing of Data*
A bucketing of data π is a collection of groups $G_1, G_2, \cdots, G_P$ where $\mid G_i \mid \leq |B|$,
$\bigcup_{i=1}^{P} G_i = \pi$ *and* $G_i \cap G_j = \varnothing$ *for* $i \neq j$ □

Based on this definition, we view a declustering algorithm as the following two steps for given M disks.

- **step 1. Bucketing:** $\{v \mid v \in \pi\} \rightarrow \{ G_1, G_2, \cdots, G_P \}$
- **step 2. Allocation:** $\{ G_1, G_2, \cdots, G_P \} \rightarrow \{0, 1, 2, \cdots, M\text{-}1\}$

When we distribute data across multiple disks, response time of a query $\mathcal{Q}$ is defined as the maximum number of disk blocks retrieved from any one of the disks. We formally define response time of a declustering scheme as follows:

Definition 2. *Response time of a declustering algorithm*
For a given query $\mathcal{Q}$, the number of disk accesses $DA(\mathcal{Q})$, i.e, response time of a declustering algorithm, is determined as follows.

$$DA(\mathcal{Q}) = \max\{DA_i(\mathcal{Q})\} \forall i, 1 \leq i \leq M$$

where $DA_i(\mathcal{Q})$ is the i-th disk accesses to process a query $\mathcal{Q}$ □

Definition 2 means that a good declustering algorithm should access the same number of data blocks on any disk to process a query. Based on this notion, we define a strictly optimal declustering algorithm as follows:

Definition 3. *Strictly optimal declustering algorithm*
A declustering algorithm is strictly optimal if

$$\forall \mathcal{Q}, DA(\mathcal{Q}) = \lceil \tfrac{B_{\mathcal{Q}}}{M} \rceil$$

where $B_{\mathcal{Q}}$ is the number of data blocks touched by a query $\mathcal{Q}$ □

It has been known to be NP-complete to achieve response time in definition 3 for all queries without restrictions. Hence, any declustering algorithm has an additive error $\epsilon (> 0)$ and its actual response time is given as follows:

$$DA(\mathcal{Q}) = \lceil \frac{B_{\mathcal{Q}}}{M} \rceil + \epsilon \qquad (1)$$

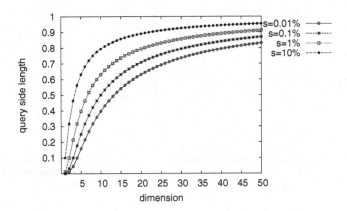

Fig. 1. Query side length *vs* Dimension: *s* means selectivity

2.2 Motivations

There are three factors that affect the performance of the declustering algorithm in equation (1), which are B_Q, M, and ϵ. B_Q is the number data blocks touched by a query Q, M is the number of parallel disks and ϵ is an additive error which is determined by an allocation scheme. Since M is a constant factor, B_Q and ϵ mostly influence the performance of declustering.

Most of the previous work focused on proposing efficient methods for the allocation step and rather ignored the effects of the bucketing step. They assume that data is bucketized into grid cells which are constructed by assuming each dimension is split into equal number of disjoint intervals. Under this assumption and suppose the number of grid cells $\mathcal{P}$ is 2^d, it seems sufficient to partition the data space binary for all dimensions to bucketize high dimensional data. However, it has potential drawbacks to process range queries on binary partitioned high dimensional data space due to so called 'Curse of Dimension'. Since as the dimensionality of data grows, the side length of a range query Q becomes extremely large even for a small selectivity s, which is shown in Fig 1. As a result, all of the grid cells may be intersected by Q. In this case all allocation methods show equal performance if they distribute disk numbers fairly or evenly. If we partition more than two times along the smaller number of dimensions than needed for binary partition, the number of intersecting grid cells could be reduced since larger grid cells have more probability to include small range queries. This fact is shown in Fig 2. In this figure, we assume that 14 dimensions are needed for binary partition. As we can see, it is quite clear that we can achieve better performance by selecting appropriate number of splits which is less that 14. Thus the problem we have to solve is *how to choose the number of dimensions to split that minimizes the result size of an arbitrary range query*. In the next section, we propose a cost model that estimates the number of grid cells intersecting a range query for the given selectivity. Based on this we can construct *better* grid cells to allocate disk numbers.

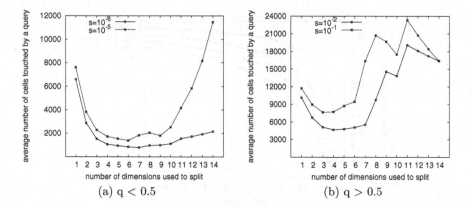

Fig. 2. Average number of grid cells intersected by range queries according to the number of dimensions used to split where $d = 16$ and $\mathcal{P} = 2^{14}$

3   A Cost Model of Grid Partition

We assume that a grid method partitions a data space $[0, 1]^d$ into equal-sized cells and thus equal number of intervals at each dimension. We call it GRID, for short. In table 1 we define symbols and meaning of parameters to be used. In our cost model, we calculate the expected value of each cell based on the Minkowski-sum cost model[2]. By observations on this model, we can infer that the expected values of the cells are different by which type of hypercubes the cells are intersecting or contained in. In the two-dimensional case, there are three different types of partitioned areas when $q \geq 0.5$: those of which the side lengths are all $1 - q$, all $2q - 1$, and one $1 - q$ and one $2q - 1$ (when $q < 0.5$ we substitute $2q - 1$ to $1 - 2q$). Figure 3 shows two-dimensional case. Each of H_1, H_2, and H_3 matches $(1 - q)^2$, $(1 - q)(2q - 1)$, and $(2q - 1)^2$, respectively. We can rewrite the volume of a d-dimensional unit hypercube in terms of q, $Vol(cube, q)$, as follows:

$$Vol(cube, q) = [(2q - 1) + 2(1 - q)]^d = \sum_{i=0}^{d} C(d, i) \cdot (2q - 1)^i \cdot (2(1 - q))^{d-i}$$

$$= \sum_{i=0}^{d} C(d, i) 2^{d-i} (1 - q)^{d-i} (2q - 1)^i \qquad (2)$$

Table 1. Symbols and their meaning

Symbol	Meaning
d	Dimensionality of the data
$\mathcal{P}$	Number of blocks(cells) to be generated
q	Side length of a range query $\mathcal{Q}$ (assume $0 < q < 1$)
Y	Number of blocks (cells) of partition intersected by $\mathcal{Q}$

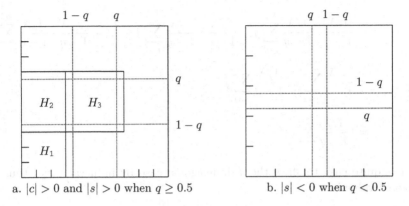

a. $|c| > 0$ and $|s| > 0$ when $q \geq 0.5$ b. $|s| < 0$ when $q < 0.5$

Fig. 3. Different types of a hypercube partitioned by q in two-dimensional case

Equation (2) implies that there are $d + 1$ different types of hypercubes and there are $C(d, i)2^{d-i}$ numbers of a hypercube whose volume is $(1-q)^{d-i}(2q-1)^i$. For simplicity, we rewrite the number of the same type of hypercubes as:

$$Coef(d, i) = C(d, i) \cdot 2^{d-i} \ where \ 0 \leq i \leq d \tag{3}$$

Suppose that the number of partition at each dimension is $\lambda (\geq 2)$ and there is an integer n satisfying $\prod_{i=1}^{n} \lambda = \mathcal{P}$ where $n \leq d$. When $q \geq 0.5$, let $|c|$ be $\lfloor \frac{1-q}{1/\lambda} \rfloor$ and $|s|$ be $\lambda - 2|c|$. To show the expected number of cells intersecting a range query $\mathcal{Q}$, we calculate the expected value of cells contained in or intersecting $d + 1$ different types of hypercubes.

Lemma 1 *Among $d + 1$ types of hypercubes induced by $q \geq 0.5$, the expected value of cells intersecting or contained in a hypercube H which has $i(0 \leq i \leq d)$ numbers of $2q - 1$ interval lengths and $d - i$ numbers of interval lengths $1 - q$ is:*

$$E(H, \mathcal{Q}) = |s|^i \cdot \left(\frac{1/\lambda}{1-q} \cdot \sum_{j=1}^{|c|} j \right)^{d-i} \tag{4}$$

Proof. We first show the expected value for the two-dimensional case and generalize it for the d-dimensional case. For simplicity, we assume $|c| > 0$ and $|s| > 0$. When $i = 0$, H is $(1 - q)^2$ which is the case of H_1 in Figure 3.a. The expected value of the cells contained in this hypercube is:

$$E(H, \mathcal{Q}) = \frac{1/\lambda}{1-q} \cdot \frac{1/\lambda}{1-q} + \frac{1/\lambda}{1-q} \cdot \frac{2/\lambda}{1-q} + \ldots + \frac{1/\lambda}{1-q} \cdot \frac{|c|/\lambda}{1-q} +$$
$$\frac{2/\lambda}{1-q} \cdot \frac{1/\lambda}{1-q} + \frac{2/\lambda}{1-q} \cdot \frac{2/\lambda}{1-q} + \ldots + \frac{2/\lambda}{1-q} \cdot \frac{|c|/\lambda}{1-q} +$$
$$\ldots$$
$$\frac{|c|/\lambda}{1-q} \cdot \frac{1/\lambda}{1-q} + \frac{|c|/\lambda}{1-q} \cdot \frac{2/\lambda}{1-q} + \ldots + \frac{|c|/\lambda}{1-q} \cdot \frac{|c|/\lambda}{1-q}$$

$$= \frac{1/\lambda}{1-q} \cdot \frac{1/\lambda}{1-q} \sum_{j=1}^{|c|} j + \frac{2/\lambda}{1-q} \cdot \frac{1/\lambda}{1-q} \sum_{j=1}^{|c|} j + \ldots + \frac{|c|/\lambda}{1-q} \cdot \frac{1/\lambda}{1-q} \sum_{j=1}^{|c|} j$$

$$= \frac{1/\lambda}{1-q} \sum_{j=1}^{|c|} j \cdot \frac{1/\lambda}{1-q} \sum_{j=1}^{|c|} j$$

$$= (\frac{1/\lambda}{1-q} \sum_{j=1}^{|c|} j)^2. \tag{5}$$

It is quite easy to show the d-dimensional case by induction, and thus the expected value is:

$$E(H, Q) = (\frac{1/\lambda}{1-q} \sum_{j=1}^{|c|} j)^d. \tag{6}$$

When $i = 1$, H is $(2q-1)(1-q)$ which is the case of H_2 in Figure 3.a. The expected value of cells intersecting $(2q-1)$ and contained in $(1-q)$ is:

$$E(H, Q) = \frac{1/\lambda}{1-q} \cdot |s| + \frac{2/\lambda}{1-q} \cdot |s| + \ldots + \frac{|c|/\lambda}{1-q} \cdot |s|$$

$$= \frac{1/\lambda}{1-q} \sum_{j=1}^{|c|} j \cdot |s| \tag{7}$$

When $i = 2$, H is $(2q-1)^2$ which is the case of H_3 in Figure 3.a. The expected value of cells intersecting $(2q-1)$ is:

$$E(H, Q) = 1 \cdot |s| + 1 \cdot |s| + \ldots + 1 \cdot |s| = |s|^2 \tag{8}$$

For d-dimensional case, the intervals contained in $(1-q)$ contribute $((1/\lambda)/(1-q) \sum_{j=1}^{|c|} j)$ and the intervals intersecting $(2q-1)$ contribute $|s|$ to the expected value independently. Thus the expected value of cells contained in or intersecting one of $d+1$ types of hypercubes is:

$$E(H, Q) = |s|^i (\frac{1/\lambda}{1-q} \sum_{j=1}^{|c|} j)^{d-i} \tag{9}$$

$\square$

Lemma 2 *Given $\prod_{i=1}^{d} \lambda = P$ grid cells, the number of cells intersecting a range query Q when $q \geq 0.5$ is:*

$$E[Y] = \sum_{i=0}^{d} Coef(d, i) |s|^i (\frac{1/\lambda}{1-q} \sum_{j=1}^{|c|} j)^{d-i} \tag{10}$$

Proof. Since $Coef(d, i)$ denotes the number of $(1-q)^i(2q-1)^{d-i}$ type of hypercubes and we know the expected value of a $(1-q)^i(2q-1)^{d-i}$ hypercube, it holds. $\square$

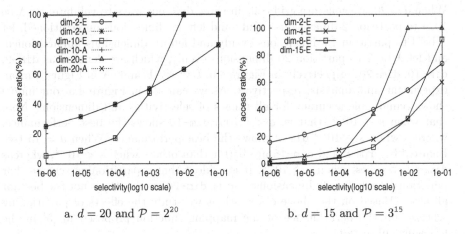

a. $d = 20$ and $\mathcal{P} = 2^{20}$ b. $d = 15$ and $\mathcal{P} = 3^{15}$

Fig. 4. Validation of analysis and different selection of λ when $d = 20$ and $d = 15$

So far we have shown the expected value when $q \geq 0.5$. Now we show it when $q < 0.5$. In this case, let $|c|$ be $\lceil \frac{q}{1/\lambda} \rceil$ and $|s|$ be $\lambda - 2|c|$.

Lemma 3 *Given $\prod_{i=1}^{d} \lambda = \mathcal{P}$ grid cells, the number of cells intersecting a range query $\mathcal{Q}$ when $q < 0.5$ is:*

$$E[Y] = \begin{cases} \sum_{i=0}^{d} Coef(d,i)(\frac{1/\lambda}{1-q} \sum_{j=1}^{|c|-1} j)^{d-i} & \text{if } |s| < 0, \\ \sum_{i=0}^{d} Coef(d,i)(\frac{1/\lambda+q}{1-q} |s|)^{i} (\frac{1/\lambda}{1-q} \sum_{j=1}^{|c|} j)^{d-i} & \text{if } |s| \geq 0 \end{cases} \tag{11}$$

Proof. The proof is similar to those of lemma 1 and lemma 2. □

A special case when $|s| < 0$ is shown in Figure 3.b for understanding.

4 Experiments

In this section, we show experimental results. For a query set, we decide a side length q of $\mathcal{Q}$ as a function of the selectivity s since a fixed query side length has different meaning at different dimensions. That, $q = 0.2$ means 4% selectivity at two-dimensional space but 10^{-5}% selectivity at ten-dimensional space. Thus in our experiments, we define q as $s^{1/d}$ and vary selectivities from 10^{-6} to 10^{-1} for dimensions varying from 2 to 20. Now, we show experimental results validating our cost model.

4.1 Validation of Cost Model

To validate our analysis of GRID, we perform range queries on $\mathcal{P}$ cells which tile $[0,1]^d$ data space. We set the value of $\mathcal{P}$ be 2^{20} for $d = 20$ and $\mathcal{P}$ be 3^{15} for $d = 15$.

When $d = 20$, we generate grid cells in three different ways to validate: let λ be 1024 to partition 2 dimensions evenly and left 18 dimensions unpartitioned, let λ be 4 to partition 10 dimensions evenly and left 10 dimensions unpartitioned, and let λ be 2 to partition 20 dimensions evenly, which are denoted as dim-2, dim-10, dim-20, respectively in Figure 4.a. Letters -E and -A in Figure 4 mean experiment and analysis, respectively. As we can see in Figure 4.a, our model shows remarkable accuracy for all ranges of selectivities and dimensions. Note that when $s < 10^{-3}$ (that is, $q < 0.709$) dim-10 shows the best performance, whereas when $s \geq 10^{-3}$ dim-2 shows the best performance. When $d = 15$ (see Figure 4.b), dim-8 and dim-15 are better than others when $s < 10^{-4}$, whereas dim-4 is the best when $s \geq 10^{-2}$. It is evident that a partitioning scheme that partitions evenly for all dimensions(that is, dim-20 or dim-15) is not the best for all cases. Based on the above observations we study the effects of partitioning schemes on the performance of the mapping function proposed in [5] in the following subsection.

4.2   The Effects of Partitioning Scheme on Declustering Performance

In this subsection, we show the effects of a partitioning scheme on the mapping function based declustering algorithm called Kronecker sequence [5], which has been known the best allocation scheme for high dimensional data. We assume that we have 16 dimensional 10^6 data and $|B|$ is 64. Thus, we need at least 15,625 data blocks($= \lceil 10^6/64 \rceil$) to store these data and 14 dimensions($= \lceil log_2 15625 \rceil$) are sufficient for binary partition. However, we can reduce the number of grid cells touched by a range query by choosing less dimensions than needed for binary partitioning and split more than 2 times along those dimensions. As we see in Fig 2, the number of data blocks to be retrieved highly depends on the number of dimensions used to split data space.

One may apply a good GRID partitioning scheme for the given query size. In this case, we have 14 different partitioning choices and we can count the number of grid cells intersected by a range query using the proposed cost model. As we can see in Fig 5.a through Fig 5.c, the mapping function can achieve better performance by selecting less number of split dimensions (denoted d_p). In Fig 5.d, we show overall performance gain over binary partition by applying varying number of diks and query sizes. We can improve the performance of Kronecker sequence based declustering algorithm up to 23 times by applying an appropriate partitioning method. Experimental results also show that we can achieve no performance gain by increasing the number of disks when the data space is binary partitioned.

5   Conclusions

A lot of work have been done to improve I/O performance by distributing data across multiple parallel disks and access them in parallel. Most of them focused

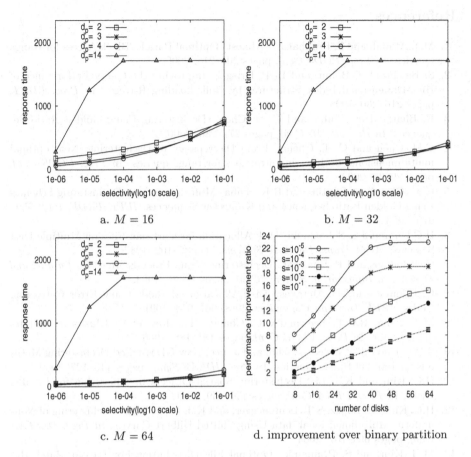

a. $M = 16$

b. $M = 32$

c. $M = 64$

d. improvement over binary partition

Fig. 5. Response time of Kronecker sequence by varying d_p and M when $d = 16$ and $\mathcal{P} = 2^{14}$

on proposing efficient methods at the allocation step and rather ignored the effects at the bucketing step. To study the effects of bucketing step, we proposed a cost model that estimates the number of grid cells intersecting range queries, which give less than 0.5% error ratio. Thus we know by our cost model how to construct grid cells to improve the performance of declustering method. In our work we choose Kronecker sequence based declustering algorithm [5], since it has been known the best mapping function for high dimensional data. By experiments, we achieve up to 23 times performance gain compared to binary partition by selecting proper number of split dimensions. Thus, we can conclude that our approach suggested give clear criteria how to select the number of split dimensions for declustering. Currently, our proposed cost model can be applied only when each dimension is split into equal numbers. Thus, our future study will suggest a cost model that allow arbitrary number of splits at each dimension.

References

1. M.J. Atallah and S. Prabhakar. (Almost) Optimal Parallel Block Access for Range Queries. In *Proc. PODS Conf*, pages 205–215, 2000.
2. S. Berchtold, C.Böhm, and H-.P. Kriegel. Improving the Query Performance of High-Dimensional Index Structures by Bulk Loading R-trees. In *Proc. EDBT*, pages 216–230, 1998.
3. R. Bhatia, R.K. Sinha, and C.-M. Chen. Declustering Using Golden Ratio Sequences. In *Proc. ICDE Conf*, pages 271–280, 2000.
4. C.M. Chen and C. T. Cheng. From Discrepancy to Declustering: Near optimal multidimensional declustering strategies for range queries. In *Proc. PODS Conf*, pages 29–38, 2002.
5. C-M. Chend, R. Bhatia, and R.K. Sinha. Multidimensional Declustering Schemes Using Golden Ratio Sequence and Kronecker Sequences. *IEEE TKDE*, 15(3):659–670, 2003.
6. H.C Du and J.S. Sobolewski. Disk Allocation for Cartisian Files on Multiple-Disk Systems. *ACM Trans. Database Systems*, 7(1):82–102, 1982.
7. C. Faloutsos and P. Bhagwat. Declustering Using Fractals. In *Proc. Parallel and Distributed Information Systems Conf*, pages 18–25, 1993.
8. C. Faloutsos and D. Metaxas. Disk Allocation Methods Using Error Correcting Codes. *IEEE Trans on Computers*, 40(8):907–914, 1991.
9. M.T. Fang, R.C.T. Lee, and C.C. Chang. The Idea of De-Clustering and Its applications. In *Proc. VLDB Conf*, pages 181–188, 1986.
10. S-Wk. Kao, M. Winslee, Y. Cho, and J. Lee. New GDM-based Declustering Methods for Parallel Range Queries. In *Proc. IDEAS Symp*, pages 119–127, 1999.
11. H.C. Kim and K.J. Li. Declustering Spatial Objects by Clustering for Parallel Disks. In *Proc. DEXA Conf*, pages 450–459, 2001.
12. H.C. Kim, M. Lopez, S.T. Leutenegger, and K.J. Li. Efficient Declustering of Non-uniform Multidimensional data Using Shifted Hilbert Curves. In *Proc. DASFAA Conf*, pages 694–707, 2004.
13. M.H. Kim and S. Pramanik. Optimal File Distribution For Partial Match Retrieval. In *Proc. SIGMOD Conf*, pages 173–182, 1988.
14. D.R. Liu and S. Shekhar. Partitioning Similarity Graphs: A Framework for Declustering Problems. *International Journal Information System*, 21(6):475–496, 1996.
15. D.R. Liu and M.Y. Wu. A Hypergraph Based Approach to Declustering Problems. *Distributed and Parallel Databases*, 10(3):269–288, 2001.
16. S. Prabhakar, K. Abdel-Ghaffar, and A. El Abbadi. Cyclic Allocation of Two-Dimensional Data. In *Proc. ICDE Conf*, pages 94–101, 1998.

Design and Implementation of a Real-Time Static Locking Protocol for Main-Memory Database Systems

Jin-Ho Kim[1], Young-Chul Kim[2], Han-Yang You[2], June Kim[2], and Soo-Ho Ok[3]

[1] Kangwon National University, Hyoja-Dong, Chunchon, Republic of Korea
jhkim@kangwon.ac.kr
[2] Electronic and Telecommunications Research Institute, Daeduk-Gu, Daejeon,
Republic of Korea
{yckim,hyyou,jkim}@etri.re.kr
[3] Kosin University, Yeongdo-Gu, Busan, Republic of Korea
shok@kosin.ac.kr

Abstract. Main-memory database systems reside whole databases into main memory thus they process transactions in very short time. These high-speed main-memory database transactions incur low probability of lock conflict. If the traditional two-phase locking (2PL) as concurrency control protocol is used to handle the main-memory database transactions, its lock operations become relatively big overhead in total transaction processing time. In this paper, we designed a real-time static locking (RT-SL) protocol which minimizes the lock operation overhead and handles the priority of transactions. We also implemented the proposed protocol on a main-memory database system, Mr.RT (Main-memory Resident Real-Time) DBMS and then we evaluated its performance with the existing real-time locking protocols based on 2PL such as 2PL-PI (Priority Inheritance) and 2PL-HP (High Priority). Through experiments, we show that the proposed RT-SL outperforms the existing ones in most cases.

1 Introduction

Main-memory database systems maintain all data into main memory and they process their transactions in very short time. Thus main-memory database technology has been widely used in recent database applications such as mobile computing, embedded systems, and real-time processing. The main-memory databases remove the overheads and the uncertainty occurred by disk I/O thus they can provide the high performance required in those applications [2, 4, 6]. The transactions issued by the applications should be scheduled (i.e., their execution sequence be rearranged) in order to finish every transactions within their timing constraints (i.e., deadlines) or to process more urgent transactions earlier. The transactions can be scheduled by using real-time scheduling policies such as EDF (Earliest Deadline First), LSF (Least Slack First), and RM (Rate Monotonic) [3]. However database systems employ concurrency control mechanisms to

T. Yakhno (Ed.): ADVIS 2004, LNCS 3261, pp. 353–362, 2004.

guarantee the consistency of databases accessed by multiple transactions concurrently, which can block higher-priority transactions accessing some data locked by lower-priority transactions. This situation incurs priority inversion problem and transactions cannot be executed in their scheduling sequence.

In order to resolve the priority inversion problem and to ensure the scheduling sequence, several real-time concurrency control algorithms such as 2PL-PI (priority inheritance), 2PL-CPI (conditional priority inheritance), 2PL-HP (high priority), and 2PL-CR (conditional start) have been developed [1, 2, 3, 5, 6]. These previous real-time concurrency control algorithms are based on the two-phase locking protocol which has been designed for disk-resident database systems. This protocol sets a lock on each data object, whenever a transaction accesses the data object, and it releases all the locks at once, when the transaction is finished. Therefore it incurs a quite big burden for frequent locking operations (such as checking lock conflict, setting locks, etc.) and the maintenance of lock tables. In disk-resident database systems, locking operations take less time than disk I/O thus the locking overhead is not a big portion of the total transaction processing time. In main-memory database systems, however, transactions are executed very quickly without employing any disk accesses. Therefore, main-memory database transactions hold their locks for shorter periods and have the lower probability of lock conflicts. Locking operations will be a big burden in main-memory databases and the cost of locking operations could be sometimes bigger than that of actual transaction processing.

On the other hand, static locking protocol requires that each transaction gets all locks at the beginning of the transaction. Because a transaction can start its execution after getting all locks on data objects to be accessed by the transaction, it can complete the whole execution without waiting any locks after it starts. If a transaction cannot acquire all of the required locks, it waits without holding any of the locks. Thus the locking management of this protocol becomes very simple, because transactions process all of the locking operations at once before they start to execute. Because of this advantage, the static locking protocol has been studied as a real-time concurrency control method in [1]. But this study has only simulated the performance of the real-time static locking algorithm on distributed real-time databases, and they didn't implement nor evaluated it on a real main-memory database management system. In this paper, we developed a real-time static locking (RT-SL) protocol which reduces the cost of locking operations in main-memory databases and handles the priority of real-time transactions. We also implemented the proposed RT-SL protocol on a main-memory database management system, Mr.RT (Main-memory Resident Real-Time) DBMS and then we evaluated its performance with the existing real-time locking algorithms based on 2PL such as 2PL-PI (Priority Inheritance) and 2PL-HP (High Priority) under the Mr.RT DBMS environment. From the experiments, we observed that the proposed RT-SL protocol outperforms the existing ones in most cases.

The rest of the paper is organized as follows. Section 2 describes the lock request algorithm and the lock release algorithm of the proposed RT-SL protocol in main-memory real-time databases. In section 3, we describe the implementation details of the RT-SL in the Mr.RT DBMS. Section 4 presents the results of the performance evaluation. Finally, section 5 summarizes our conclusions and further research issues.

2   Design of Real-Time Static Locking Strategy

2.1   Locking Granularity

In disk-resident database systems, locking operations take much less time than disk I/Os accessing data objects. Thus these disk-resident database systems use records as locking granularity in order to decrease locking conflict and increase concurrency of transactions. This small locking granularity increases the overhead of concurrency control by invoking locking operations frequently. In main-memory databases, transactions will be executed very quickly thus the cost of frequent locking operations will be relatively high over the total transaction execution time. Therefore bigger granularity such as table (i.e., relation) or database will be recommendable in main-memory database systems [6]. Therefore we determine tables as locking granularity and we also permit two types of locking modes such as shared lock (S-lock) and exclusive lock (X-lock).

2.2   Locking Data

We use tables as the locking granularity. We can find which tables each transaction accesses from SQL statements included in the transaction. Thus the RT-SL algorithm we propose in this paper gets the table names to be accessed by a transaction, before the transaction begin to execute.

The locking information for each table is maintained into the system catalogue, which consists of the following information:

- *locking modes* granted to a table (i.e., S-lock, X-lock, or No-Lock)
- *the number of transactions* holding the lock, and
- *the pointer* to the list of transactions waiting the lock.

Whenever a transaction cannot get a lock because of lock conflict, it is inserted into the list of waiting transactions and each entry of the list includes the following information:

- *transaction identifier*,
- *transaction priority*, and
- *the number of the locks* that were requested by the transaction but not granted.

All transactions running in the system maintains the information related to locking such as the number of tables accessed by the transactions, the pointers to the entries of the system catalog for the tables, and the locking modes the transactions request.

2.3   Lock Request Protocol

In the proposed RT-SL protocol, lock conflicts are determined by considering the current lock mode of a table, the priority of the transaction requesting a lock for the table, T_{req}, and the priority of the transactions waiting a lock for the table, T_{wait}. Even though a table has No-Lock or S-Lock mode, a S-Lock is not granted to a transaction whose priority is lower than that of any transaction in T_{wait}. If this lock request is granted to the transaction, the transactions in T_{wait} with higher priority will be delayed by the transaction with lower priority. Thus this policy of the RT-SL protocol can reduce the delay time of higher priority transaction. In the static locking, there are some waiting transactions (i.e., T_{wait}) in a table which has No-Lock mode, because a transaction can get none of its locks and has to wait when it cannot get all of the locks.Table 1 shows the lock compatibility matrix of the RT-SL protocol.

Table 1. Lock compatibility matrix

Lock granted \ Lock requested		S-lock	X-lock
No-lock	T_{wait} doesn't exist	O	O
	$Prio(T_{req}) < Prio(T_{wait})$	X	X
	$Prio(T_{req}) > Prio(T_{wait})$	O	O
S-lock	T_{wait} doesn't exist	O	X
	$Prio(T_{req}) < Prio(T_{wait})$	X	X
	$Prio(T_{req}) > Prio(T_{wait})$	O	X
X-lock		X	X

In the Table 1, $Prio(T_{req})$ represents the priority of the transaction requesting a lock on the given table and $Prio(T_{wait})$ the highest priority among the transactions waiting a lock on the table. O and X denote *Compatible* and *Conflict*, respectively. From the Table 1, we can see that lock conflict is determined by the lock mode granted on a table, the lock mode requested by a transaction, and the priorities of requesting and waiting transactions.

Example 1: We assume that transactions, T1, T2, T3, and T4 request X-lock on tables (R2, R5), (R1, R2), (R2, R4), and (R1, R3) respectively, and their priority order is T1 < T2 < T3 < T4. Fig. 1 (a) shows the execution sequence of these transactions when locks are granted to them without considering the priority of waiting transactions. Under the RT-SL, on the other hand, the execution sequence of these transactions is determined as shown in Fig. 1 (b) by considering the priority of waiting transactions.

In Fig. 1 (a), T4 acquires the locks for R1 and R3 at t0 and continues its execution. When T2 requests the locks for R1 and R2 at t1, R2 is not in conflict but R1 is already held by T4 as X-lock. Thus T2 turns to waiting status. T1 requests the locks for R2 and R5 at t2 and acquires them. T3 requests the locks for R2 and R4 at t3 but it turns to waiting status because R2 is already held by T1. At t4, T1 completes and releases the lock for R1. But T2 still has to

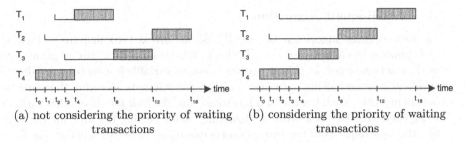

(a) not considering the priority of waiting transactions   (b) considering the priority of waiting transactions

Fig. 1. Execution sequence of transactions in Example 1

remain at the waiting status because R2 is being used by T1. Because the locks were granted to T1 without considering the priority of T2 which is waiting, the transactions T2 and T3 with higher priority are delayed by T1 with lower priority.

In the case of Fig. 1 (b) considering the priority of waiting transactions, T1 requests the locks for R2 and R2 at t2. There is no lock conflict but the lock for R2 is not granted to T1 because T2 with higher priority is waiting the locks for both R2 and R4. Thus T1 also turns to waiting status. T3 will acquire the locks for R2 and R4 at t3. After T3 finishes at t8, T2 gets its locks and finishes at t12. T2 and T3 can complete their execution without being delayed by T1.

2.4   Lock Release Protocol

Each transaction releases the locks for all tables accessed by itself after its completion or abortion. Then the released locks should be granted to the transactions waiting the locks. We have designed the lock release protocol of the RT-SL to determine next transactions acquiring the released locks according to the priorities of the waiting transactions. When a S-Lock is released, it is granted to the waiting transactions whose have higher priority than any transaction waiting a X-Lock. Thus the RT-SL grants released locks to higher priority transactions in order not to be delayed by lower transactions.

3   Implementation of Real-Time Static Locking Strategy

The proposed RT-SL protocol is implemented on a main-memory real-time database, Mr.RT developed by the ETRI (Electronic and Telecommunication Research Institute of Korea). The Mr.RT stores entire databases into main-memory, and provides several features such as storage management, transaction management, concurrency control, and recovery, which is implemented in C++ language. The Mr.RT server has a multi-thread structure to process transactions requested by multiple users concurrently. Transactions running on the Mr.RT server are assigned to one of three kind of priorities (HIGH, MID, LOW) and they are scheduled by transaction scheduler based on their priorities.

3.1   Lock Request Algorithm

The lock request algorithm of the RT-SL is invoked to acquire a lock at the beginning of each transaction. It checks whether the lock can be granted to the transaction or not. In this algorithm, a *mutex* variable is used to maintain the consistency of the locking data over multiple transactions accessing the same table concurrently. Each transaction has to acquire the lock for this *mutex* variable before executing the lock request algorithm. After getting the lock for the variable, the lock requests of the transaction is examined to decide whether the locks are granted or conflicted. If finishing the lock request algorithm, the transaction releases the lock of the *mutex* so that another transaction may invoke the lock request algorithm. The Fig. 2 shows the detailed description of the lock request algorithm, where T_{req} denotes as a transaction requesting a lock, and T_{wait} denotes as a transaction which has the highest priority among waiting transactions.

3.2   Lock Release Algorithm

When transaction is completed or aborted, all locks acquired by the transaction are released. The RT-SL protocol includes the lock release algorithm which releases the locks held by a transaction and awakes another one of waiting trans-

```
MODULE Lock_Request(T_req)
BEGIN
    lock mutex;
    conflict := FALSE;
    FOR each relation to be accessed by T_req
        IF T_wait exists
            IF (lock granted = N-lock) and (Prio(T_req) > Prio(T_wait))
                increment waiting count of T_wait;
            ELSE IF (lock granted = X-lock) or
                    (lock requested by T_req = X-lock) or
                    ((lock requested by T_req = S-lock) and (Prio(T_req) <= Prio(T_wait)))
                    conflict := TRUE;
                    increment waiting count of T_req;
            ENDIF
        ELSE IF (lock granted = X-lock) or
                ((lock granted = S-lock) and (lock requested by T_req = X-lock))
                conflict := TRUE;
                increment waiting count of T_req;
        ENDIF
    ENDFOR

    IF conflict = TRUE
        create lock requester for T_req;
        FOR each relation to be accessed by T_req
            create node of lock requester for T_req;
            insert node of lock requester for T_req into waiting list;
        ENDFOR
        unlock mutex;
        wait lock released;
    ELSE
        FOR each relation to be accessed by T_req
            set lock granted to lock requested by T_req;
            increment holder count;
        ENDFOR
        unlock mutex;
    ENDIF
END
```

Fig. 2. Lock request algorithm

```
MODULE Unlock(T_hold)
BEGIN
    FOR each relation to be released by T_hold
        lock mutex;
        decrement holder count;
        IF holder count = 0
            set lock granted to N-lock;
            IF T_wait exists
                decrement waiting count of T_wait;
                IF waiting count of Twait = 0
                    IF lock requested by T_wait = X-lock
                        FOR each relation to be accessed by T_wait
                            delete node of lock requester for T_wait from waiting list;
                            set lock granted to lock requested by T_wait;
                            increment holder count;
                        ENDFOR
                        wake up T_wait;
                    ELSE
                        WHILE lock requested by next T_wait in waiting list = S-lock
                            decrement waiting count of next T_wait;
                            IF waiting count of next T_wait = 0
                                FOR each relation to be accessed by next T_wait
                                    delete node of lock requester for next T_wait from waiting list;
                                    set lock granted to lock requested by next T_wait;
                                    increment holder count;
                                ENDFOR
                                wake up next T_wait;
                            ENDIF
                        ENDWHILE
                    ENDIF
                ENDIF
            ENDIF
        ENDIF
        unlock mutex;
    ENDFOR
END
```

Fig. 3. Lock release algorithm

actions. This lock release algorithm uses the same *mutex* variable used in the lock request algorithm in order that the lock release algorithm is accessed mutually by multiple transaction thus the locking data is consistent.

Fig. 3 shows the implementation of the lock release algorithm, where T_{hold} denotes the transaction releasing a lock and T_{wait} denotes the transaction which has the highest priority among waiting transactions. The lock release algorithm decreases the *holder count*, representing the number of transactions holding the lock for a table, by 1. If the count becomes zero, it means that no transaction holds any lock for the table thus the lock mode of the table is set to No-Lock. If there are any transactions waiting the lock, then we select one of them (i.e., T_{wait}) and decrease the *waiting count*, representing the number of tables T_{wait} waits for their locks, by 1. If the *waiting count* is zero, it means that T_{wait} got all locks for the tables. Thus T_{wait} is waken up and starts its execution.

4 Performance Evaluation

4.1 Parameters

In this section, we present the results of the performance evaluation of the RT-SL protocol. Its performance is compared with two real-time concurrency control algorithms based on the traditional two-phase locking protocol: 2PL-PI and 2PL-HP.

The transactions used in the experiments include read and/or write operations on databases. We assume that the transactions arrive at the system by exponential distribution over the given average arriving rate. Each transaction has a priority, tables to access, and the average number of records to read or write as parameters. The basic parameters for this evaluation are shown in Table 2.

4.2   Results of Performance Evaluation

In the experiments, we measured the deadline miss rate of transactions over average transaction arrival time for uniform distribution of transaction priorities. We also analyze the deadline miss rate of transactions by varying the ratio of read-only transactions and the slack rate of transactions.

Fig. 4 shows the deadline miss rate of transactions over their average arrival time in the case that the priorities of transactions have a uniform distribution. This result shows that the RT-SL has lower deadline miss rate than 2PL-PI and 2PL-HP. Because the RT-SL has lower cost of lock operations and doesn't involve any overheads caused by deadlock. On the other hand, 2PL-HP has

Table 2. Performance evaluating parameters

parameters	values
size of database	30 relations
average of tables accessed by transaction	3 relation
average expected time of transaction execution	6 ms
average arrival rate of transaction	$2 \sim 16$ trans./sec
rate of read-only transaction	$0 \sim 80$ %
slack rate	$1 \sim 8$
numbers of action processing threads	50

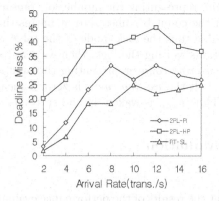

Fig. 4. Deadline miss over transaction arrival rate

the highest miss rate, because some of transactions with lower priority may be aborted repeatedly by other transactions with higher priority thus they can miss their deadlines.

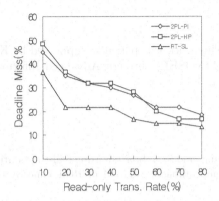

Fig. 5. Deadline miss over read-only ratio

If the ratio of read-only transactions is higher, the possibility of lock conflict becomes lower thus the deadline miss rate can be also decreased. The deadline miss rate over the ratio of read-only transactions is shown in Fig. 5. From this graph, we can also observe that the RT-SL has lower rate of deadline miss than other algorithms in all range of read-only transaction ratio. When the read-only transaction ratio is increased, however, the gap of the deadline miss rate between the RT-SL and the others is decreased, because the possibility of lock conflict is reduced and the effect of concurrency control is also reduced.

5   Conclusion

In order to reduce the overhead of locking operations in main-memory databases which process transactions in very short time without invoking any disk I/Os, we designed and implemented a real-time static locking algorithm, called the RT-SL, adequate to main-memory database systems. The RT-SL algorithm is based on static locking protocol that each transaction gets every locks of all data objects. In the protocol, transactions don't involve any delay caused by lock conflict and the management of locks will be simpler. In this paper, we implemented the proposed RT-SL algorithm on a main-memory real-time database management system, called Mr.RT.

In order to evaluate the proposed algorithm, we measured and compared its performance with 2PL-PI and 2PL-HP which are traditional real-time concurrency control algorithms based on the dynamic 2PL. From our experiments, we observed that the proposed RT-SL has lower deadline miss rate than 2PL-PI and 2PL-HP.

For future researches, we are going to evaluate the performance under the workload of real applications in main-memory real-time databases. We are also going to compare its performance with the real-time optimistic concurrency control algorithms.

Acknowledgement. This work was partially supported by Korea Science and Engineering Foundation (KOSEF) through Advanced Information Technology Research Center (AITrc).

References

1. Kam-Yiu Lam, S. L. Hung, and S. H. Son. On using real-time static locking protocols for distributed real-time databases. Journal of Real-Time Systems, Vol 13 No 2 (1997) 141–166, Sep.
2. Özgür Ulusoy and A. Buchmann. A real-time concurrency control protocol for main-memory database systems. Information Systems, Vol 23, No 2, (1998) 109–125
3. Anindya Datta and S. H. Son. A Study of Concurrency Control in Real-Time, Active Database Systems. IEEE Trans. on Knowledge and Data Engineering, Vol 14, No 3, (2002)
4. Hector Garcia-Molina and K. Salem. Main Memory Database Systems: An Overview. IEEE Trans. on Knowledge and Data Engineering, 4 (6), (1992)
5. Jiandong Huang, J. Stankovic, K. Ramamritham, and D. Towsley. On Using Priority Inheritance in Real-Time Databases. Proc. IEEE Real-Time Systems Symp., 1991.
6. Özgür Ulusoy and A. Buchmann. Exploiting Main Memory DBMS Features to Improve Real-Time concurrency Control Protocols. ACM SIGMOD Record, Vol 25, No 1, (1996)

Integrated Querying of Images by Color, Shape, and Texture Content of Salient Objects*

Ediz Şaykol, Uğur Güdükbay, and Özgür Ulusoy

Department of Computer Engineering, Bilkent University,
06800 Bilkent, Ankara, Turkey
{ediz, gudukbay, oulusoy}@cs.bilkent.edu.tr

Abstract. The growing prevalence of multimedia systems is bringing the need for efficient techniques for storing and retrieving images into and from a database. In order to satisfy the information need of the users, it is of vital importance to effectively and efficiently adapt the retrieval process to each user. Considering this fact, an application for querying the images via their color, shape, and texture features in order to retrieve the similar salient objects is proposed. The features employed in content-based retrieval are most often simple low-level representations, while a human observer judges similarity between images based on high-level semantic properties. Using color, shape, and texture as an example, we show that a more accurate description of the underlying distribution of low-level features improves the retrieval quality. The performance experiments show that our application is effective in retrieval quality and has low processing cost.

1 Introduction

Over the last few years, retrieving images from large collections using image content has been a very important topic. The need to find a desired image from a collection is shared by many professional groups, including medicine, graphic design, criminology, publishing, etc. A considerable amount of information exists in images. Thus, the quick visual access to the stored images would be very advantageous for efficient navigation through image collections. That's why the problems of image retrieval have become widely recognized, and the search for solutions has become an important research area.

Content-based image retrieval systems provide a facility to retrieve the suitable images from the image database for a given query (e.g., [1]). A very common way for query specification is query-by-example. Returning a relevance-ordered list of database images for the query is generally accepted by the researchers. The basic need is to embed a dissimilarity metric among the objects, hence to

* This work is supported in part by Turkish State Planning Organization (DPT) under grant number 2004K120720, and European Commission 6th Framework Program MUSCLE Network of Excellence Project with grant number FP6-507752.

T. Yakhno (Ed.): ADVIS 2004, LNCS 3261, pp. 363–371, 2004.

differentiate them, and rank them. Various dissimilarity metrics have been used in the literature (e.g., histogram intersection [2]). These metrics generally rely on feature vectors extracted from the visual content of the images. The feature vectors generally store information based on the color, shape, and texture contents.

In this paper, we present an application that provides an integrated mechanism to query images by color, shape, and texture content of the salient objects. Querying salient objects rather than whole images is more interesting, since users may want to focus on some specific parts of the images for querying purposes. By this type of querying, multiple object regions can be queried on a single image. Video frames can also be processed by our application after the salient objects in frames are extracted by an object extraction tool [3]. The object extraction mechanism is an improved version of the one presented in [4]. The object regions can be determined by simple mouse clicks, polygon specifications, or bounding rectangle drawings. The extracted features (color, shape, and texture vectors) are stored in an object-feature database. In our application, the color vector is based on color histograms but the pixels are probabilistically distance-weighted during computations. Shape vector is a combination of two vectors: the first one is the angular distribution of the pixels around the centroid of the salient object. The second vector is the accumulation of the pixels in the concentric circles centered at the centroid of the object. This type of shape description is very close to the human visual system [5]. Our texture vector is based on Gabor filter banks, which are widely employed in face recognition, vehicle recognition, defect detection, automatic speech recognition, fingerprint matching, etc.

The paper is organized as follows: Section 2 presents the literature summary on low-level object features. We explain our design principles for integrated querying application in Section 3. The performance experiments are discussed in Section 4, and Section 5 concludes the paper.

2   Low-Level Features of Salient Objects

Color, shape, and texture are known as the low-level features in content-based querying terminology. The low-level feature content of the images, or salient objects residing in images, are generally encoded in feature vectors. The feature vectors that we have employed are invariant under scale, rotation, and translation.

2.1   Color

Image data represent physical quantities such as *chromaticity* and *luminance*. Chromaticity is the color quality of light defined by its wavelength. Luminance is the amount of light. To the viewer (i.e., human), these physical quantities are perceived by such attributes as color and brightness [5]. It is the HSI (Hue-Saturation-Intensity) model that represents the colors in a very close way to the human color perception. It is an intuitive representation since it corresponds to how a painter mixes colors on a palette. Image processing applications – such as histogram operations, intensity transformations, and convolutions – operate only on an image's intensity. These operations are performed much easier on an image in the HSI color space.

Traditional color histograms [1] generally suffer from low retrieval effectiveness. The retrieval effectiveness can be improved by taking the spatial distribution of the colors into consideration. Color correlograms [6] store the spatial correlation of color regions as well as the global distribution of local spatial correlation of colors in a tabular structure. Although its retrieval effectiveness is better than the traditional color histograms, it is computationally very expensive. In [7], the contributions of the pixels to the color histogram are weighted according to the *Laplacian, probabilistic,* and *fuzzy* measures. The weighting is related to a local measure of color non-uniformity (or color activity) determined by some neighborhood of pixels. This weighting approach, without changing the sizes of the histograms, is found to be more effective and its computational complexity is not excessive.

2.2 Shape

The human vision system identifies objects with the edges they contain, both on the boundary and in the interior based on the intensity differences among pixels [5]. These intensity differences are captured as the shape content of salient objects with respect to their centeroids in images.

The shape descriptors are classified in two groups: *contour-based* (e.g., Turning Angle representation [8] and Fourier descriptors [9]) and *region-based* (e.g., moment descriptors [10], generic Fourier descriptors [11], and grid descriptors [12]). The former type of descriptors only deals with the object's boundary and has some major limitations. The latter type of descriptors deals with both the interior and the boundary of the objects, thus can be employed in more general shape retrieval applications. In [11], generic Fourier descriptors are shown to be a more effective shape descriptor than the other contour-based and region-based descriptors.

2.3 Texture

Texture is an important feature since the images can be considered as the composition of different texture regions. There are various techniques for texture feature extraction. The statistical approaches make use of the intensity values of each pixel in an image, and apply various statistical formulae to the pixels in order to calculate feature descriptors [13]. Some systems employ three Tamura [14] texture measures, *coarseness, contrast,* and *orientation* (e.g., QBIC system [1]). Photobook [15] exploits texture content based on Wold decomposition; the texture components are *periodicity, directionality,* and *randomness.*

Manjunath and Ma [16] have shown that Gabor filter banks are very effective for texture retrieval. They are widely-used in various areas, such as face recognition, vehicle recognition, fingerprint matching, etc. Their use is mainly as follows: texture features are found by calculating the mean and variation of the Gabor filtered image, processed within a bandpass filter. After applying normalization by a circular shift of the feature elements, the images are re-oriented according to the dominant direction. Then, these feature elements are used to encode the texture content of the image. A comparison of Gabor-filter based texture features can be found in [17].

3   Integrated Querying of Salient Objects

In this paper, we present an application that provides an integrated mechanism to query images by color, shape, and texture content of the salient objects. Querying salient objects rather than whole images is more interesting, since users may want to focus on some specific parts of the images. Moreover, in some application domains, the classification of the salient objects is crucial (e.g., surveillance). Hence, the visual content of the salient objects can be employed for classification.

In our application, we have employed a semi-automatic object extraction scheme to extract object regions. The object extraction scheme is an improved version of the one presented in [4]. The object regions can be determined by simple mouse clicks, polygon specifications, or bounding rectangle drawings. The extracted features (color, shape, and texture vectors) for salient objects are stored in an object-feature database. Video frames can also be processed by our application once the salient objects are extracted by our object extraction tool [3].

In our application, the color vector is based on color histograms but the pixels are probabilistically distance-weighted during computations. Shape vector is a combination of two vectors: the first one is the angular distribution of the pixels around the centroid of the salient object. The second vector is the accumulation of the pixels in the concentric circles centered at the centroid of the object. Our texture vector is based on Gabor filters.

3.1   Color Vector

We have used HSI color space in the computation of the color vector. The main reasons are its perceptual uniformity and its similarity to the human vision system principles. A circular quantization of 20° steps sufficiently separates the hues such that the six primary colors are represented with three sub-divisions. Saturation and intensity are quantized to 3 levels leading to a proper perceptual tolerance along these dimensions. Hence, 18 hues, 3 saturations, 3 intensities, and 4 gray levels are encoded yielding 166 unique colors, i.e., a color feature vector of 166 dimensions (see [18] for details). This color quantization also reduces the effects of noise on the images.

Traditional color histogram technique accumulates pixel intensities into an array of uniquely available intensity values. Since this technique is shown to be not efficient enough in retrieval of similar objects, various techniques have been developed to increase the retrieval effectiveness. We employ a probabilistic distance weighting-scheme similar to [7] for the extracted color vector of salient objects. The effects of the closer pixels are increased in pixel weight calculation among the neighborhood. In this approach, the contribution of uniform regions is decreased and that of singular points is increased according to the following formula: $w_p = \frac{1}{N_p(c)}$, where w_p is the weight of pixel p, and $N_p(c)$ is the number of pixels having color c as p within the neighborhood of p.

3.2 Shape Vector

The human vision system identifies objects with the edges they contain, both on the boundary and in the interior based on the intensity differences among pixels [5]. These intensity differences, i.e., the shape content, can be captured with respect to the center of mass of these pixels. For this purpose, two specialized feature vectors can be used to encode the shape content of the objects: *distance vector* and *angle vector*.

Distance Vector stores the Euclidean distance between the centeroid (c_m) and all of the pixels within the salient object. The distance between a pixel p_i and c_m is re-scaled with respect to the maximum distance among the pixels (i.e., the distance of the farthest pair of pixels). This type of scaled-distance storage in distance vector satisfies scale invariance directly.

Angle Vector stores the counter-clockwise angle between pixel vectors and the unit vector on the x-axis (e_x). The pixel vector v_{p_i} for a pixel p_i is a vector directed from c_m to p_i. The unit vector e_x is translated to c_m. α_{p_i} is the polar angle for p_i. This type of information storage provides an easy and intuitive way to capture angular distribution of the pixels around a fixed object point (c_m).

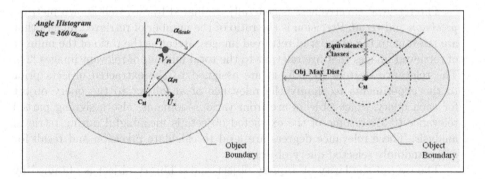

Fig. 1. Visualization of angle and distance vector computations

These two shape vectors are illustrated in Figure 1. The dimension of the angle vector is $\frac{360}{\alpha_{scale}}$. In the experiments, α_{scale} is set to 5. The dimension of the distance vector is fixed at 10, and the radial increments are determined by dynamically-computed `ObjMaxDist` parameter.

3.3 Texture Vector

We have employed a Gabor-filter based texture vector for the texture content of the salient objects. It is shown in [16] that Gabor filter banks are very effective in texture retrieval, and outperform most of the other methods in the literature. Gabor filters are composed of wavelets. Wavelets are a class of functions used to localize a given function in both space and scaling. Wavelets are especially useful for compressing image data. Each wavelet in a Gabor filter holds the energy at a specific frequency and a specific direction. Gabor filters estimate the strength of certain frequency bands and orientations at each location in the image. This gives a result in the spatial domain. The spatial distribution of edges is useful for image querying when the underlying texture is not homogeneous. Processing through a bank of these Gabor filters is approximately equivalent to extracting line edges and bars in the images, at different scales and orientations. Then, the mean and standard deviation of the filtered outputs can be used as features. The details of the Gabor texture feature extraction can be found in [16].

We have selected 5 levels of scales and 6 levels of orientations for the texture feature vector. For each scale and orientation pair, the mean and the standard deviation are calculated. Hence, the dimension of our texture feature vector is 60.

4 Performance Experiments

We have conducted performance experiments on an image library of 100 Brodatz textures [19], 48 carpet patterns gathered from various urls, and 1490 Corel images [20]. The image library contains rotated and scaled versions of the images to validate the invariants of the feature vectors. The experiments were conducted on a 1800 MHz PC with 512 MB RAM.

The retrieval effectiveness is generally evaluated by two well-known metrics, *precision* and *recall*. Precision is the ratio of the number of retrieved images that are relevant to the number of retrieved images. Recall is the ratio of the number of retrieved images that are relevant to the total number of relevant images [21]. The relevance degrees (0, 0.5, 1) are assigned to the extracted objects prior to the experiments to signify the relevance of an object to the query object for each query. Since objects are from various domains, also assigning partial relevance (0.5) to some of the extracted objects is meaningful during retrieval analysis. These relevance degrees are used to calculate precision and recall for each randomly selected query object.

The overall similarity of a query object and a library object is obtained by linearly combining the partial feature vector similarities. Feature vector similarities are computed by histogram intersection method [2]. The weights assigned during the linear combination are set by the user through the interface. In the experiments, we have assigned the following weights: color vector (0.3), angle vector (0.18), distance vector (0.12), and texture vector (0.4). Figure 2 and 3 show two sample query executions corresponding to a scaled Corel image and a carpet pattern, respectively.

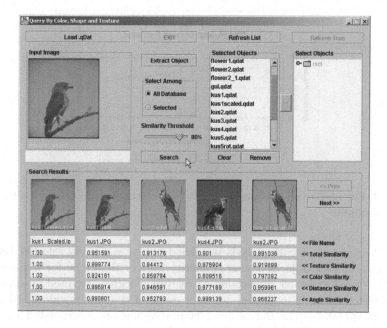

Fig. 2. Sample query 1, a Corel image. The retrieved objects are shown five-by-five

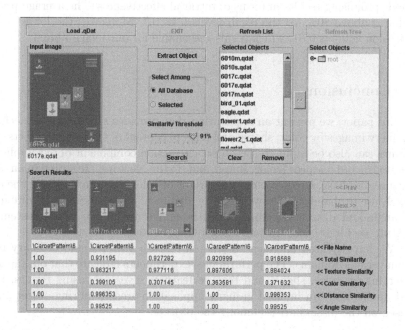

Fig. 3. Sample query 2, a carpet pattern. The retrieved objects are shown five-by-five

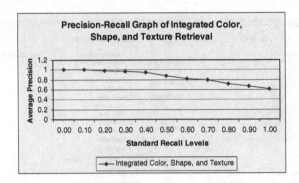

Fig. 4. Precision-recall analysis for integrated querying by color, shape, and texture of salient objects

The precision-recall analysis is carried out by randomly selected 100 query objects. Library objects having similarity greater than 0.80 for a query object are retrieved and their corresponding relevance degrees are used in calculations. The effectiveness is evaluated as the average of the results calculated for each query separately. The individual precision values are interpolated to a set of 11 standard recall levels (0, 0.1, 0.2, ..., 1) to ease the computation of average precision and recall values [21]. Figure 4 presents the precision-recall analysis of our integrated querying application. The results show that our querying methods yields promising results in terms of retrieval effectiveness. The average precision value is above 80% for the recall levels 0 to 0.7. Moreover, the lowest average precision value is 0.61, which seems reasonable for our image library.

5   Conclusion

In this paper, we present an application that provides an integrated mechanism to query images by color, shape, and texture content of the salient objects. Video frames can also be input to the object extraction component of our application. The extracted features (color, shape, and texture vectors) are stored in an object-feature database. Color vector is a variant of color histograms where the object pixels are probabilistically weighted by distance. Shape vector is a combination of angle and distance vectors, which is similar to human visual system. Our texture vector is based on well-known Gabor filters.

We have created an Image library of texture patterns and ordinary images from various domains. The performance experiments indicate that our integrated querying by color, shape, and texture features gives promising results. Hence, our application can be used in many application areas requiring object analysis based on the dissimilarities among the objects.

Acknowledgement. We are grateful to K. Oral Cansızlar, S. Gönül Kızılelma, and Ö. Nurcan Subakan, who worked in the implementation of the system.

References

1. Flickner, M.: Query by image content: the QBIC system. In: IEEE Computer Magazine. Volume 28. (1995) 23–32
2. Swain, M., Ballard, D.: Color indexing. Int. J. of Computer Vision **7** (1991) 11–32
3. Dönderler, M., Şaykol, E., Ulusoy, Ö., Güdükbay, U.: BilVideo: A video database management system. IEEE Multimedia **10** (2003) 66–70
4. Şaykol, E., Güdükbay, U., Ulusoy, Ö.: A semi-automatic object extraction tool for querying in multimedia databases. In Adali, S., Tripathi, S., eds.: 7th Workshop on Multimedia Information Systems MIS'01. (2001) 11–20
5. Buser, P., Imbert, M.: Vision. MIT Press, Cambridge, Massachusetts (1992)
6. Huang, J., Kumar, S., Mitra, M., Zhu, W., Zabih, R.: Image indexing using color correlograms. In: Proc. of IEEE Conf. on Com. Vis. and Pat. Rec. (1997) 762–768
7. Boujemaa, N., Vertan, C.: Integrated color texture signature for image retrieval. In: Proc. of Int. Conf. on Image and Signal Processing. (2001) 404–411
8. Arkin, E., Chew, P., Huttenlocher, D., Kedem, K., Mitchel, J.: An efficiently computable metric for comparing polygonal shapes. IEEE Trans. on Pattern Analysis and Machine Intelligence **13** (1991) 209–215
9. Zahn, C., Roskies, R.: Fourier descriptors for plane closed curves. IEEE Trans. on Computer **C-21** (1972) 269–281
10. Kim, H., Kim, J.: Region-based shape descriptor invariant to rotation, scale and translation. Signal Processing: Image Communication **16** (2000) 87–93
11. Zhang, D., Lu, G.: Shape based image retrieval using generic fourier descriptors. Signal Processing: Image Communication **17** (2002) 825–848
12. Lu, G., Sajjanhar, A.: Region-based shape representation and similarity measure suitable for content-based image retrieval. Multimedia Systems **7** (1999) 165–174
13. Haralick, R., Shanmugam, K., Dinstein, I.: Textural features for image classification. IEEE Trans. on Systems, Man and Cybernetics **3** (1973) 610–621
14. Tamura, H., Mori, S.: Textural features corresponding to visual perception. IEEE Trans. on Systems, Man, and Cybernetics **8** (1978)
15. Pentland, A., Picard, R., Scarloff, S.: Photobook: Tools for content-based manipulation of image databases. In: Proc. of Storage and Retrieval for Image and Video Databases II, SPIE. Volume 2. (1994) 34–47
16. Manjunath, B., Ma, W.: Texture features for browsing and retrieval of image data. IEEE Trans. on Pattern Analysis and Machine Intelligence **18** (1996) 837–842
17. Grigorescu, S., Petkov, N., Kruizinga, P.: Comparison of texture features based on gabor filters. IEEE Trans. on Image Processing **11** (2002)
18. Smith, J., Chang, S.: Tools and techniques for color image retrieval. In: Proc. of Sto. and Retr. for Im. and Vid. Databases IV. Volume 2670. (1996) 426–437
19. Brodatz, P.: Textures–A Photographic Album for Artists and Designers. Dover Publications, New York (1966)
20. Corel: Image Library, University of California, Berkeley.
http://elib.cs.berkeley.edu/photos/corel/ (accessed in 2003)
21. K.S.Jones: Information Retrieval Experiment. Butterworth and Co. (1981)

Trajectory-Based Video Retrieval for Multimedia Information Systems

Choon-Bo Shim[1], Jae-Woo Chang[2], and Young-Chang Kim[2]

[1]School of Computer Information Engineering, Catholic University of Pusan,
Pusan, 609-757, South Korea
cbsim@cup.ac.kr
[2]Dept. of Computer Engineering, Research Center for Advanced LBS Applications,
Chonbuk National University, Chonju, Chonbuk 561-756, South Korea
{jwchang,yckim}@dblab.chonbuk.ac.kr

Abstract. In this paper, we develop a trajectory-based video retrieval system. To achieve it, we first design a spatio-temporal representation scheme for modeling the trajectories of moving objects in video databases. In addition, we present an efficient trajectory-based retrieval scheme using a k-warping distance algorithm. Finally, we propose a new signature-based access method which can provide good retrieval performance on a trajectory-based query. To show the usefulness of applying our above schemes to a real video database application, we implement a trajectory-based soccer video retrieval system because soccer video data generally contain a lot of motions according to a salient object called soccer ball. Our soccer video retrieval system provides graphic user interfaces for both indexing and retrieval. We also provide the performance analysis of our trajectory-based video retrieval scheme.

1 Introduction

Recently, a lot of interests in content-based (or similarity-based) retrieval have been increased in multimedia information systems. Unlike image data, one of the most important features of video data is the trajectory of moving objects. The trajectory of a moving object can be represented as a spatio-temporal relationship which combines spatial properties between moving objects in each frame with temporal properties among a set of frames. A user query for trajectory-based retrieval using moving objects in video databases is as follows: *"Find all video shots whose trajectory is similar to the trajectory sketched in a graphic user interface."* Thus, it is necessary to support trajectory-based retrieval using a sequence of locations of moving objects. The initial research issues on the trajectory-based video retrieval have highly concentrated on a data representation scheme which can model trajectory content extracted from video data [1].

In this paper, we develop a trajectory-based video retrieval system. To achieve it, we first present a spatio-temporal representation scheme for modeling the trajectories of moving objects in video databases. Our scheme takes distance property into

T. Yakhno (Ed.): ADVIS 2004, LNCS 3261, pp. 372–382, 2004.

account additionally while the traditional schemes consider direction property, time interval property and spatial relation property. In addition, we present an efficient trajectory-based retrieval scheme using a k-warping distance algorithm. This algorithm is used to measure a similarity between two trajectories of moving objects, which is newly made by applying the concept of time warping distance in time-series databases to the trajectory data of moving objects. Finally, we design a new signature-based access method which can provide good retrieval performance on a trajectory-based query. To show the usefulness of applying our above schemes to a real video database application, we implement a trajectory-based soccer video retrieval system because soccer video data generally contain a lot of motions according to a salient object called soccer ball. Our soccer video retrieval system provides graphic user interfaces for both indexing and retrieval.

This paper is organized as follows. In Section 2, we introduce the related work on video retrieval using moving objects' trajectories. In Section 3, we design a trajectory-based video retrieval system using moving objects. In Section 4, we implement our trajectory-based soccer videos retrieval system as an application. In Section 5, we provide the performance analysis of our trajectory-based video retrieval scheme. Finally, we draw our conclusion in Section 6.

2 Related Work

There have been two main researches on trajectory-based retrieval by measuring a similarity between a given query trajectory and data trajectories, i.e., Li's scheme and Shan's scheme. First, Li et al. [2,3] represented the trajectory of a moving object as eight directions, such as North(NT), Northwest(NW), Northeast(NE), West(WT), Southwest(SW), East(ET), Southeast(SE), and Southwest(SW). They represented as (S_i, d_i, I_i) the trajectory of a moving object A over a given time interval I_i where S_i is the displacement of A and d_i is a direction. For a set of time interval $<I_1, I_2, \cdots, I_n>$, the trajectories of A can be represented as a list of motions, like $<(S_1, d_1, I_1), (S_2, d_2, I_2), \ldots, (S_n, d_n, I_n)>$. Based on the representation for moving objects' trajectories, they present a similarity measures to computes the similarity of spatio-temporal relationships between two moving object. In addition, Shan and Lee [4] represented the trajectory of a moving object as a sequence of segments, each being expressed as the slope with real angle ranging from 0 to 360 degree for content-based retrieval. They also proposed two similarity measure algorithms, OCM (Optimal Consecutive Mapping) and OCMR (Optimal Consecutive Mapping with Replication), which can measure similarity between query trajectory $Q=(q_1, q_2, \ldots, q_M)$ and data trajectory $V=(v_1, v_2, \ldots, v_N)$. The OCM algorithm that supports exact matching measures the similarity for one-to-one segment mapping between query trajectory and data trajectory. The OCMR algorithm supports approximate matching. In order to measure the similarity, each motion of query trajectory can be permitted to map with more than one motions of data trajectory.

Meanwhile, similar sub-sequence retrieval [5,6] is an operation that finds data sequences whose changing patterns are similar to that of a given query sequence. The sequence database is a set of data sequence, each of which is an ordered list of elements. In a sequence $S(=<s[1], s[2], ..., s[|S|])$, $|S|$ is the length of S and $s[i]$ is its i-th element. $s[i:j]$ and $s[i:-]$ is a sub-sequence of S that includes the elements from i-th element to j-th element and from i-th element to the end, respectively. () denotes an empty sequence or null sequence. For efficient similar sub-sequence retrieval, time warping transformation was proposed. The time warping is a generalization of classical algorithms for comparing discrete sequences with sequences of continuous values and enables each element of a sequence to match one or more neighboring elements of the other sequence. It supports the approximate matching which guarantees a result to be retrieved based on the modification of a user query within some threshold for an inaccurate query. The time warping distance is defined as the smallest distance between two sequences transformed by time warping. Given two sequence S and Q, the time warping distance D_{tw} is defined recursively as follows. Here, D_{base} can be any Lp function that returns a distance between two elements.

$$D_{tw}((), ()) = 0, D_{tw}(S, ()) = D_{tw}((), Q) = \infty$$
$$D_{tw}(S, Q) = D_{base}(S[1], Q[1]) + min(D_{tw}((S, Q[2:-]), D_{tw}(S[2:-], Q), D_{tw}(S[2:-], Q[2:-]))$$
$$D_{base}(a, b) = |a-b|$$

3 Trajectory-Based Video Retrieval

3.1 Modeling for Moving Objects' Trajectories

Moving objects are salient objects which are continuously changing its locations over time interval. To effectively deal with moving objects, it is necessary to consider both spatial and temporal relationships. Existing schemes, like Li's scheme and Shan's scheme, consider only directional and topological information for modeling the trajectory of moving objects. But, our representation scheme takes distance information into account additionally. The trajectory is defined as a set of motions of moving objects over time interval. We will define a spatio-temporal representation scheme for the trajectory of moving objects.

Definition 1. For a given ordered list of time interval I_0, I_1, $\cdots$, I_{n-1}, the single trajectory information of a moving object A, ST(A), is defined as follows:

$$ST(A) = MPS(A) + SPS(A)$$

Here, $MPS(A) = \{M_0(A), M_1(A), \cdots, M_{n-1}(A)\}$ is a motion property information for a moving object A over all the time intervals where $M_i(A) = (R_i(A), D_i(A), I_i)$ for a time interval $I_i=[t_i,t_{i+1}]$. $R_i(A)$ is a moving direction over I_i, being represented as a real angle with a range of 0 to 360 degree. $D_i(A)$ is a moving distance over I_i, being represented as an absolute Euclidean distance. In addition, $SPS(A) = \{S_0(A), S_1(A), \cdots, S_n(A)\}$ is a stationary property information for a moving object A over all the time instances where $S_i(A) = ([L_i(A)], [O_i(A)])$ at time t_i, $L_i(A)$ is a location information of the moving object A, being describes as a real XY-coordinate. $O_i(A)$ is an object information related with the moving object A, e.g., palyer having a ball. Here, [] means an optional operator. Figure 1 represents the modeling of a single trajectory.

We define multiple trajectories as the trajectories of two or more moving objects. For this, we first define a relationship trajectory between two objects.

Definition 2. Let at least one of object A and object B be a moving object. For a given ordered list of time interval I_0, I_1, $\cdots$, I_{n-1}, the relationship trajectory information between A and B, RT(A, B), is defined as follows:

$$RT(A, B) = MPM(A, B) + SPM(A, B)$$

Here, MPM(A, B) = $\{M_0(A, B), M_1(A, B), \cdots, M_{n-1}(A, B)\}$ is a motion property information for A and B over all the time interval where $M_i(A, B) = (D_i(A, B), I_i)$ for a time interval I_i ($[t_i, t_{i+1}]$), $D_i(A, B)$ is a relative moving distance of A over B for I_i, being ranged from 0 to 100. That is, $D_i(A, B)$ is ranged from 50 to 100 if the moving distance of A is equal to or greater than that of B while ranging from 0 to 49 if the moving distance of A is less than that of B. In addition, SPM(A, B) = $\{S_0(A, B), S_1(A, B), \cdots, S_n(A, B)\}$ is a stationary property information for A and B over all the time instances where $S_i(A, B) = ([L_i(A)], [O_i(A)], ([L_i(B)], [O_i(B)], T_i(A, B), R_i(A, B))$ at time t_i. $L_i(A)$ and $L_i(B)$ are the location information of moving object A and B, respectively while $O_i(A)$ and $O_i(B)$ are the actors having moving objects A and B. $T_i(A, B)$ is a spatial (topological) relations on XY-coordinate from A to B, being represented as one of seven topological relations operator: FA(FarAway), DJ(DisJoint), ME(MEet), OL(OverLap), CL(is-inCLuded-by), IN(INclude), and SA(SAme). Finally, $R_i(A, B)$ means a directional relations from A to B, being ranged from 0 to 360 degree.

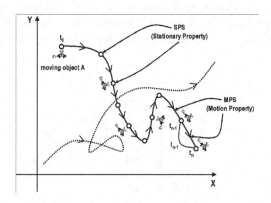

Fig. 1. Representation for the single trajectory of a moving object A

Based on Definition 1 and 2, the multiple trajectory information of multiple moving objects, MT(A_1, A_2, $\cdots$, A_n), can be represented as a combination of the relationship trajectory information (RT) and the single trajectory information (ST).

Definition 3. Among objects A_1, A_2, $\cdots$, A_n, let i be the number of moving objects and j be the number of stationary objects, i.e., n=i+j. The multiple trajectory information of A_1, A_2, $\cdots$, A_n, MT(A_1, A_2, $\cdots$, A_n), is defined as follows:

$$MT(A_1, A_2, ..., A_n) = \{ST(A_p)|p = 1, ..., i\} + \{RT(A_q, A_{q+1})|q = 1, ..., k\}, k = {}_nC_2 - {}_jC_2$$

Here, $ST(A_i)$ is the single trajectory information of an object A_i. $RT(A_k, A_{k+1})$ is the relationship trajectory information between object A_k and A_{k+1} where k is the number of relationship trajectories between two moving objects.

3.2 Trajectory-Based Retrieval Scheme

To measure a similarity between two trajectories of moving objects in video databases, we need an efficient trajectory-based retrieval scheme. For this, we present a k-warping distance algorithm which is newly made by applying the concept of time warping distance in time-series databases to the trajectory data of moving objects.

Definition 4. Given two trajectory of moving objects S and Q, the k-warping distance D_{kw} is defined recursively as follows:

$$D_{kw}(0, 0) = 0, D_{kw}(S, 0) = D_{kw}(0, Q) = \infty$$
$$D_{kw}(S, Q) = D_{base}(S[1], Q[1]) + \min(\{D_{kw}((S[2+i:-], Q), 0 \le i \le k), D_{kw}(S[2:-], Q[2:-])\})$$
$$D_{base}(a, b) = d_{df}(a, b)$$

Figure 2 depicts an example of our k-warping distance algorithm which can calculate a similarity between trajectory S and Q when k is 2. We can permit up to 2(=k) times replications for an arbitrary motion of only query trajectory Q. In the above example, we can obtain the minimum distance value, that is, the maximum similarity value, between S and Q when q[1] of trajectory Q is mapped to each s[1], s[2], and s[3] of trajectory S, instead of the exact matching, namely, one-to-one mapping between trajectory S and Q. Therefore, it is shown that the approximate matching is superior to the exact mating for calculating the similarity between trajectories.

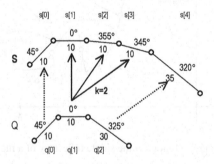

Fig. 2. Mapping of motions between S and Q when k=2

Based on our k-warping distance algorithm, we define a distance function between two motions, $d_{df}(q[i], s[j])$, when we measure a similarity between i-th motion in query trajectory Q and j-th motion in data trajectory S.

Definition 5. A distance function, $d_{df}(q[i], s[j])$, to measure a similarity between an arbitrary motion $s[i]$ of a data trajectory S and a given motion $q[j]$ of a query trajectory Q is defined as follows.

$$d_{dis}(s[i,2], q[j,2]) = |\ s[i, 2] - q[j, 2]\ |$$
$$\text{if}\ |\ s[i, 1] - q[j, 1]\ | > 180\ \text{then}\ d_{ang}(s[i, 1], q[j, 1]) = (360 - |\ s[i, 1] - q[j, 1]\ |)$$
$$\text{else}\ d_{ang}(s[i, 1], q[j, 1]) = |\ s[i, 1] - q[j, 1]\ |$$
$$d_{df}(s[i], q[j]) = (\ ((d_{ang} / 180) * \alpha) + ((d_{dis}/100) * \beta)\ )$$

Here, d_{ang} is a distance function for a direction (angle) property for all the motions of a trajectory and d_{dis} is a distance function for a distance property. $s[i, 1]$ and $s[i, 2]$ are the direction and the distance value of the i-th motion in a trajectory S, respectively. α and β mean a direction and distance weight, respectively, when $\alpha+\beta=1.0$.

3.3 Access Method for Moving Objects' Trajectories

To design an access method for moving objects' trajectories, we propose a new signature-based access method for moving objects' trajectories, called SAMOT. SAMOT can deal with a large amount of database and can support efficient retrieval on a trajectory-based query. Before doing a sequential search on the information of moving objects' trajectories, we access a signature file in our SAMOT and then do filtering with its signatures, thus the number of disk accesses for the data file being minimized to a large extent. As a result, we can support fast retrieval with little storage overhead according to the characteristics of signature files [7]. Our SAMOT can be divided into two parts: data file and signature file. The data file is to store the information of moving objects' trajectories extracted from video shot. The signature file for moving objects' trajectories is composed of two parts. A trajectory signature file (Trajectory Signature File) stores the signatures of all the trajectories of moving objects in a database while an object signature file (relObj Signature File) stores signatures corresponding to the objects of moving objects. Finally, a link file connects the above signature files with a trajectory data file. The overall architecture of our SAMOT is shown in Figure 3.

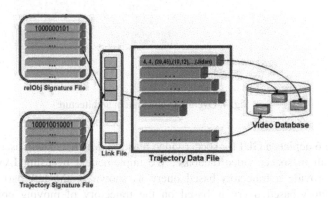

Fig. 3. The overall architecture of SAMOT access method

4   Trajectory-Based Soccer Video Retrieval System

Since soccer video data have a lot of motions according to a soccer ball, we develop a trajectory-based soccer video retrieval system, called TSVR. Figure 4 shows the overall TSVR system architecture being composed of seven managers: *repository, preprocessing, spatio-temporal representation, index(SAMOT), query analysis* and *retrieval manager.* We implement TSVR system under Windows 2000 O.S with Pentium III-800 and 512 MB memory by using Microsoft Visual C++ 6.0 compiler. Figure 5 shows a graphic user interface (GUI) for soccer video indexing which can help users to semi-automatically extract the trajectory information of soccer ball from soccer video data, e.g. moving direction, moving distance, # of frame, player name, and so on. Our GUI for soccer video indexing is composed of two windows: main window and soccer ground window. The former is to browse raw soccer video data formatted as mpeg as well as to extract the trajectory of a soccer ball. The latter is to transform the location of soccer ball in raw video data into an absolute location on the coordinate of soccer ground field. For this, we make use of so-called affined transformation algorithm which is mainly used in computer vision or image processing fields [8].

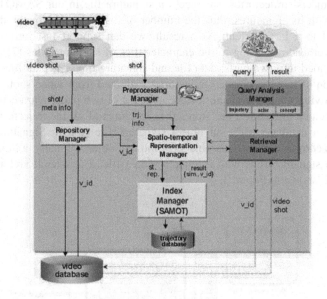

Fig. 4. Overall TSVR system architecture

Figure 6 depicts a GUI for soccer video retrieval which can help users to retrieve a query result in soccer video database. We implement it by using JAVA language. We can provide a trajectory-based query as shown in the left part of Figure 6. The trajectory-based query is based on the trajectory of moving objects, namely soccer ball, as the following: *"Finds all video shots whose trajectory is similar to the*

Fig. 5. GUI for soccer video indexing in TSVR system

trajectory sketched by a user on soccer video retrieval interface". The retrieved result for answering a user query is provided in the form of trajectory images with a similar trajectory as shown in the right part of Figure 6. We can browse them in the order of the degree of relevance to a user query. The real soccer video shot corresponding to the retrieved trajectory image can be shown by clicking its trajectory image with a left mouse button.

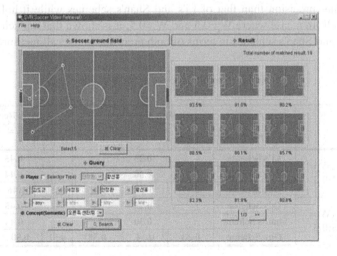

Fig. 6. GUI for soccer video retrieval in TSVR system

5 Performance Analysis

To verify the usefulness of our trajectory-based retrieval scheme using our k-warping distance algorithm, we do its performance analysis by using real soccer video data because soccer video data contain a lot of trajectories of soccer balls. We extract the trajectories of a soccer ball by manually tracing the ball in a ground field. Our experimental data used are as follows: the number of data is about 300, the average motion number of data trajectory is about 9, the number of query is 20, the average motion number of query trajectory is about 4. For our performance analysis, we do experiment under Windows 2000 O.S with Pentium III-800 and 512 MB memory and compare our scheme with the Li's and Shan's ones in terms of retrieval effectiveness, that is, average precision and recall measures [9]. The precision is defined as the proportion of retrieved data being relevant while the recall is defined as the proportion of relevant data being retrieved. In order to obtain a relevant data set to a given query, we make a test panel of 10 graduate school students which selects relevant data manually from the database. For our performance comparison, we adopt the 11-point measure [10], which is most widely used for measuring the precision and recall. For a single trajectory, we consider the weight of angle (W_a) and that of distance (W_d). We also take into account the number of replications (k) since k is a very important parameter, depending on an application area. Here we do our experiment when k=0, 1, and 2 owing to the characteristics of the trajectory of the soccer ball in soccer video data. k=0 is exact matching and k=1 and 2 is approximate matching. We show from our experiment that there is no difference on retrieval effectiveness when k is greater than 2. Table 1 shows the retrieval effectiveness of our scheme, Li's scheme, and Shan's scheme. In a case where we consider the weight of angle about two times greater than that of distance (W_a =0.7 and W_d=0.3), it is shown that our scheme achieves about 15-20% higher precision than that of Li's and Shan's schemes while it holds about the same recall. In a case where W_a=0.5 and W_d=0.5, it is shown that our scheme is better than Li's and Shan's schemes in terms of both precision and recall measures.

Table 1. Performance result for single trajectory

	# of warping	Avg. Precision			Avg. Recall		
		k = 0	k = 1	k = 2	k = 1	K = 1	k = 2
W_a:W_d= 0.7:0.3	Li's Scheme		0.25			0.45	
	Shan's Scheme		0.30			0.44	
	Our Scheme	0.39	0.44	0.45	0.50	0.46	0.47
W_a:W_d= 0.5:0.5	Li's Scheme		0.25			0.45	
	Shan's Scheme		0.30			0.44	
	Our Scheme	0.33	0.34	0.38	0.51	0.50	0.51

For multiple trajectories, we consider the weight of angle (W_a), that of distance (W_d) and that of topological relations (W_t). When k is greater than 1, it is very difficult to obtain a relevant set for the multiple trajectories of a given query. Thus, we do our experiment for multiple trajectories when k=0 and 1. Table 2 depicts the performance results for multiple trajectories in our scheme, Li's scheme, and Shan's scheme. In a case where we consider the angle and the topological relation about two times more importantly than the distance (W_a=0.4, W_d=0.2, and W_t=0.4), it is shown that our scheme achieves about 20% higher precision than that of Li's and Shan's schemes while it holds about the same recall.

Table 2. Performance result for multiple trajectories

		Avg. Precision		Avg. Recall	
	# of warping	k = 0	k = 1	k = 0	k=1
W_a:W_d:W_t = 0.4:0.2:0.4	Li's Scheme	0.25		0.49	
	Shan's Scheme	0.30		0.41	
	Our Scheme	0.45	0.53	0.51	0.54
W_a:W_d:W_t = 0.4:0.3:0.3	Li's Scheme	0.25		0.49	
	Shan's Scheme	0.30		0.41	
	Our Scheme	0.41	0.46	0.51	0.52

6 Conclusions

We designed a trajectory-based video retrieval system for multimedia information systems. For this, we first presented a spatio-temporal representation scheme for modeling the trajectories of moving objects in video databases. Secondly, we described an efficient trajectory-based retrieval scheme based on our k-warping distance algorithm in order to support both exact and approximate matching of the trajectories of moving objects. Finally, we presented a new signature-based access method which can deal with a large amount of database and can support efficient retrieval on a trajectory-based query. To show the usefulness of applying our above schemes to a real video database application, we implement a trajectory-based soccer video retrieval system, called TSVR. It is shown from our performance analysis that our trajectory-based retrieval scheme achieves about 15-20% higher precision than that of Li's and Shan's schemes while it holds about the same recall.

References

[1] Z. Aghbari, K. Kaneko, and A. Makinouchi, "Modeling and Querying Videos by Content Trajectories", In Proceedings of the International Conference and Multimedia Expo, pp. 463-466, 2000.

[2] J. Z. Li, M. T. Ozsu, and D. Szafron, "Modeling Video Temporal Relationships in an Object Database Management System," in Proceedings of Multimedia Computing and Networking(MMCN97), pp. 80-91, 1997.

[3] J. Z. Li, M. T. Ozsu, and D. Szafron, "Modeling of Video Spatial Relationships in an Objectbase Management System," in Proceedings of International Workshop on Multimedia DBMS, pp. 124-133, 1996.

[4] M. K. Shan and S. Y. Lee, "Content-based Video Retrieval via Motion Trajectories," in Proceedings of SPIE Electronic Imaging and Multimedia System II, Vol. 3561, pp. 52-61, 1998.

[5] S. H. Park, et al.,"Efficient Searches for Simialr Subsequence of Difference Lengths in Sequence Databases," In Proc. Int'l. Conf. on Data Engineering. IEEE, pp. 23-32, 2000.

[6] S. W. Kim, S. H. Park, and W. W. Chu, "An Index-Based Approach for Similarity Search Supporting Time Warping in Large Sequence Databases," In Proc. Int'l. Conf. on Data Engineering. IEEE, pp. 607-614, 2001.

[7] C. Faloutsos and S. Christodoulakis, "Signature files : An access methods for documents and its anylytical performance evaluation," ACM Transaction on Database Systems, Vol. 2, No. 4 pp. 267-288, 1984.

[8] H. S. Yoon, J. Soh, B. W. Min, and Y. K. Yang, "Soccer image sequence mosaicing using reverse affine transform," In Proc. of Int'l Technical Conference on Circuits/Systems, Computers and Communications, pp. 877-880, 2000.

[9] G. Salton and M. McGill, An introduction to Modern Information Retrieval, McGraw-Hill, 1993.

Using an Exact Radial Basis Function Artificial Neural Network for Impulsive Noise Suppression from Highly Distorted Image Databases

Pınar Çivicioğlu[1], Mustafa Alçı[2], and Erkan Beşdok[3]

[1] Erciyes University, Civil Aviation School,
Avionics Dept., Kayseri, Turkey
[2] Erciyes University, Enginering Faculty,
Electronic Engineering Dept., Kayseri, Turkey
[3] Erciyes University, Enginering Faculty, Geodesy and
Photogrammetry Engineering Dept., Kayseri, Turkey
{civici, malci, ebesdok}@erciyes.edu.tr

Abstract. In this paper, a new filter, RM, which is based on exact radial basis function artificial neural networks, is proposed for the impulsive noise suppression from highly distorted images. The RM uses Chi-Squared based *goodness-of-fit test* in order to find corrupted pixels more accurately. The proposed filter shows a high performance at the restoration of images distorted by impulsive noise. The extensive simulation results show that the proposed filter achieves a superior performance to the other filters mentioned in this paper in the cases of being effective in noise suppression and detail preservation, especially when the noise density is very high.

Noise is one of the undesired factors causing the corruption of images and therefore recovery of an image from noisy data is a fundamental step in every image analyzing process. Degradation of images by impulsive noise is usually caused by the errors originating from noisy sensors or communication channels. Generally, suppression of noise in the images must be performed before subsequent processes, like edge detection, image segmentation and object recognition because the success of many applications, such as medical imaging and robotics depends on the results of these operations. There is a large variety of literature work on this field and various types of techniques have been proposed [1, 2, 3, 4, 5, 6, 7, 8, 9, 10, 11, 12, 13]. The images corrupted by impulsive noise typically have nonstationary statistical characteristics and are formed through a nonlinear system process. Therefore, nonlinear filters have been successfully applied in smoothing images corrupted by impulsive noise and they are preferred to linear filters because these techniques achieve better image enhancement and restoration while preserving high frequency features of the original images such as edges. There exist various adaptive and nonlinear image restoration methods

T. Yakhno (Ed.): ADVIS 2004, LNCS 3261, pp. 383–391, 2004.

concerning the variations in the local statistical characteristics. Order statistics based nonlinear filters have demonstrated excellent robustness properties, and they are conceptually simple and easy to implement. The first and the well known member of the order statistics based filters is the Standard Median Filter (SMF), which has been proved to be a powerful method in removing impulsive noise [5]. In the past two decades, median-based filters have attracted much attention due to their simplicity and their capability of preserving image edges. SMF uses the rank-order information of the input data to remove impulsive noise by changing the considered pixel with the middle-position element of the reordered input data. The problem with the median filter is that it tends to alter pixels undisturbed by impulsive noise and remove fine details in the image, such as corners and thin lines, especially when the noise ratio is high. Recently, different modifications of the median filter, such as center weighted median filters [9, 10], switching median filters [6], rank ordered median filters [7] and iterative median filters [6] have been introduced in order to overcome this drawback and also detection-based median filters [1, 2, 3, 4, 5] with thresholding operations have been proposed. Furthermore, the switching scheme is introduced by some of the recently published papers [6] where the algorithms of impulse detection are employed before filtering and the detection results are used to control whether a pixel should be modified or not. Recently, artificial neural networks based or neuro-fuzzy based systems [11, 12, 13] have been proposed as attractive alternatives to classical approaches in impulsive noise suppression. Neural networks are very effective tools for solving various problems in different areas of engineering. They can be trained to perform complicated functions in a wide variety of fields including pattern recognition, identification, classification, noise reduction and control systems. The popularity of this technique among engineering community is because of its simplicity in application and reliability in the results it produces. Recently, neural network based techniques have been developed for the restoration of images contaminated by impulsive noise and suppression of noise is successfully performed by using these techniques [11, 12, 13].

In this paper, a new filter, which is based on exact radial basis function artificial neural network, is proposed for the impulsive noise suppression from highly distorted images. In order to evaluate the performance of the proposed method, it is compared with SMF [5], and the recently introduced complex structured impulsive noise removal filters: Iterative Median Filter (IMF) [6], Progressive Switching Median Filter (PSM) [6], Signal Dependent Rank Order Mean Filter (SDROM) [7], Two-state Recursive Signal Dependent Rank Order Mean Filter (SDROMR) [7], Impulse Rejecting Filter (IRF) [8], Non-Recursive Adaptive-Center Weighted Median Filter (ACWM) [9], Center Weighted Median Filter (CWM) [10] and the Russo's Neuro-Fuzzy Filter (RUSSO) [11].

The rest of the paper is organized as follows: The detail of the exact radial basis function artificial neural network and noise detection is given in Sections 2 and 3, respectively. The proposed filter is defined in Section 4 and finally, experiments and conclusions are presented in Sections 5 and 6, respectively.

1 Exact Radial Basis Function Artificial Neural Network

An alternative network architecture to the Multilayered Perceptrons [20, 21] is the Radial Basis Function Artificial Neural Network (RBFN), which can be represented with radially symmetric hidden neurons [14, 15, 16, 17, 18, 19, 20, 21]. The topology of the RBFN is similar to the three-layered MLP but the characteristics of the hidden neurons are different. RBFNs require more neurons than standard feed-forward backpropagation networks, but they can be usually designed in a less time than it takes to train standard feed-forward networks. RBFNs can be employed to approximate functions and they work best when many training arrays are used. Basically, the structure of an RBFN involves three different layers. The input layer is made up of source neurons. The second layer is a hidden layer of high dimension serving a different purpose from that of an MLP. This layer consists of an array of neurons where each neuron contains a parameter vector called a center. The neurons calculate the Euclidean distance between the center and the network input vector, and then passes the result through a nonlinear function. The output layer, which supplies the response of the network, is a set of linear combiners. The transformation from input layer to the hidden layer is nonlinear but the transformation from the hidden layer to the output layer is linear. The output of a hidden layer is a function of the distance between the input vector and the stored center, which is calculated as,

$$O_k = \|A - C_k\| = \sqrt{\sum_{j=1}^{T} \left(A_j - C_{k_j}\right)^2} \tag{1}$$

The learning phase consists of using a clustering algorithm and a nearest neighbour heuristic in order to determine the C_k cluster centers. The weights from the hidden layer to the output layer are determined by using linear regression or a gradient descent algorithm. Exact design of RBFN constitutes a radial basis network very quickly with zero error on the design vectors [14, 15, 16, 17, 18, 19, 20, 21].

2 Noise Detection

Pixels do not distribute randomly or uniformly over the image canvas in real world images. There exist more sophisticated relationships between the pixels and in general, real images have spatial uniformity (small differences from pixel to pixel). Furthermore, image acquisition sensors are generally affected by undesired factors (i.e., multipath effects, atmospheric effects, etc.) uniformly. Thus, the pixels, whose gray values are uniformly distributed, are suspected to be corrupted pixels and the Chi-square test [21] can be used to find out the uniformly distributed gray levels in distorted images. The chi-square test requires dividing the data interval into n subintervals of equal length. The data includes the total number of gray values within the unoverlapping blocks. The test uses the statistic rule of,

$$J = \sum_{p=1}^{b} \frac{(J_p - E(J_p))^2}{E(J_p)} \tag{2}$$

where J_p is the number of realizations in the pth subinterval. If B is the total number of observations then $E(J_p) = B/b$ is obtained. Under the null hypothesis of uniformity of the realizations, it can be shown that the distribution of J is approximately the chi-square distribution with b - 1 degrees of freedom. So the value of J is compared with the α -percentile of the chi-square distribution with b-1 degrees of freedom to conclude whether the null hypothesis should be rejected or not. Here, α is the significance level of the test.

3   Proposed Filter

The proposed filter, RM, is a finite-element-based filter [22, 23] and it uses the Delaunay triangles (as seen in Fig.1) [22] as finite elements. The RM involves four main steps: image padding, Delaunay triangulation, interpolation and image reconstruction.

For the implementation of RM, the image is padded with 5 pixels reflected copy of itself on the sides in order to cover the whole image with Delaunay network. Then the triangulation phase is achieved by using the spatial positions

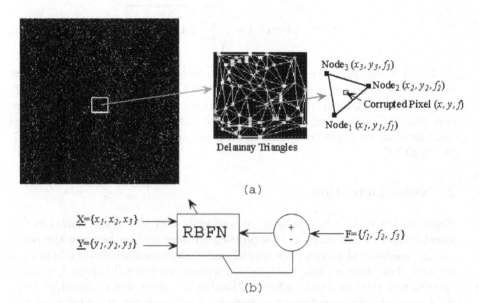

Fig. 1. Delaunay triangles and the used RBFN structure: (a) The noisy Lena image for the noise density of 80 % (*Corrupted pixels are shown as black for illustration at left*) and a Delaunay triangle at right (*The nodes of the triangle are centred at uncorrupted pixels*), (b) The RBFN with the data set (*two inputs/one output*) of the selected Delaunay triangle at (a)

of the non-uniformly distributed pixels. The convex-hull and Delaunay triangles are both obtained over the image after the Delaunay triangulation phase as expressed in [22, 23]. Then RBFN is used as an interpolant for each Delaunay triangle to get the estimated gray values of uniformly distributed pixels. The estimations of gray values are made for only uniformly distributed pixels.

The original gray values of the non-uniformly distributed pixels and the estimated gray values of the corrupted pixels are reorganized in order to obtain the restored image. In order to find out the uniformly distributed gray levels within corrupted image, the well-known Chi-Square test has been used. Then the corrupted image surface is divided into [32x32] pixel sized unoverlapping blocks and the total amount of the gray levels of allowable dynamic range within these blocks are counted. Then, the Chi-Square significance probability is computed for each gray level by using the total amount of gray levels in each block. Extensive simulations show that the Chi-Square significance probability [21] values that are greater than 0.001 ± 0.0005 correspond to uniformly distributed pixels.

All the neural structures used in this study have two inputs and one output as illustrated in Fig.1. The inputs and the output of the neural structures have been derived from the tie points of the delaunay triangles. Training phase has been realized in the Matlab [21] environment.

The computational algorithm of the RM is expressed below step-by-step:

1. Pad the image with 5 pixels reflected copy of itself on the sides in order to cover the whole image with Delaunay network.
2. Find the image coordinates, (x, y), of the non-unifomly distributed pixels.
3. Constitute the delaunay triangulation network over the noisy image by using (x, y) values.
   For each delaunay triangle repeat the following steps,
4. Find the $\underline{X} = \{x_1, x_2, x_3\}$, $\underline{Y} = \{y_1, y_2, y_3\}$ and $\underline{F} = \{f_1, f_2, f_3\}$ values of the delunay triangle where $\underline{X}$, $\underline{Y}$ denote the spatial coordinates of the tie points of the delunay triangle and $\underline{F}$ denotes the intensity value at the related tie points (see Fig.1).
5. Train the RBFN by using the $\underline{X}$, $\underline{Y}$, and $\underline{F}$ values.
6. Use the trained-RBFN in order to get the restored gray values of the corrupted pixels within the delaunay triangle (The trained-RBFN uses spatial coordinates of corrupted pixels within the delaunay triangle in order to get restored gray values of the related corrupted pixels).
7. Delete the padded pixels in order to obtain the restored image at the size of the original noisy image.

4   Experiments

A number of experiments were achieved in order to evaluate the performance of the proposed RM in comparison with the recently introduced and highly approved filters for impulsive noise suppression. The experiments were carried out on the well known Test Images; *The Lena, The Mandrill* and *The Peppers*

388   P. Çivicioğlu et al.

images, which are [256x256] pixel sized and 8 bit per pixel images. The Test
Images were corrupted by impulsive noise at various noise densities ranging
from 10% to 80%. The *noise density* term denotes the proportion of corruption
of image pixels. If noise density is equal to 10% then it means that the 10%
of the image pixels were corrupted. The restoration results of the noisy Lena
images for the noise densities of 80% are illustrated in Fig. 2. It is easily seen

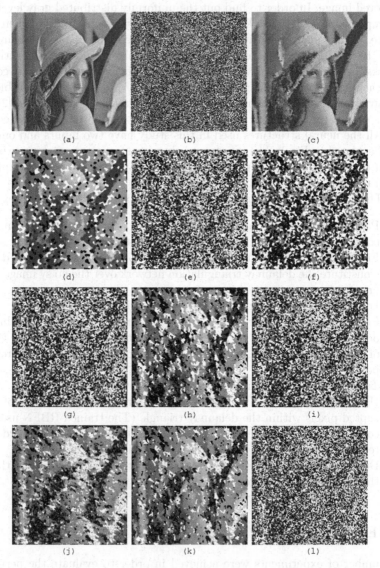

Fig. 2. The restored images of Noisy Lena for =80%: (a) The noise-free Lena, (b)
Noisy Lena for noise density=80%, (c) RM (Proposed), (d) IMF, (e) SMF, (f) PSM,
(g) SDROM, (h) SDROMR, (i) IRF, (j) RUSSO, (k) ACWMR, (l) CWM

from Fig. 2 that, noise suppression and detail preservation are satisfactorily compromised by using the proposed RM even if noise density is very high (i.e., noise density=80%). Restoration performances are quantitatively measured by the Mean-Squared-Error (MSE), which is defined as,

$$MSE = \frac{1}{MN} \sum_{x=1}^{M} \sum_{y=1}^{N} (NFI_{(x,y)} - RI_{(x,y)})^2 \tag{3}$$

where $NFI_{(x,y)}$ and $RI_{(x,y)}$ denote the original noise-free image pixels and the restored image pixels, respectively. Here $1 \leq x \leq M$, $1 \leq y \leq N$ and M, N denote the sizes at horizontal and vertical directions of the corrupted image.

The SMF, IMF, PSM, SDROM, SDROMR, IRF, RUSSO, ACWM, ACWMR, and CWM have been simulated as well for performance comparison. The major improvement achieved by the proposed filter has been demonstrated with extensive simulations of the mentioned test images corrupted at different noise densities. It is seen from Tables 1-3 that the RM provides a substantial improvement compared with the simulated filters, especially at the high noise densities. The impulsive noise removal and detail preservation are best compromised by the RM. Robustness is one of the most important requirements of modern image enhancement filters and the Tables 1-3 indicate that RM provides robustness substantially across a wide variation of noise densities.

5   Conclusions

Simulation results show that the proposed filter, RM, supplies absolutely better restoration results and a higher resolution in the restored images than all the comparison filters mentioned in this paper. The proposed filter yields satisfactory results in suppressing impulsive noise with no blurring while requiring a simple computational structure. The effectiveness of the proposed filter in processing different images can easily be evaluated by appreciating the Tables 1-3 which

Table 1. Restoration results in MSE for The Lena Image

Method	Noise Density							
	10%	20%	30%	40%	50%	60%	70%	80%
Noisy Image	1852.70	3767.60	5563.60	7451.50	9268.40	11152.00	13078.00	14769.00
RM (Proposed)	**12.02**	**22.57**	**39.45**	**58.26**	**85.83**	**119.33**	**176.09**	**277.17**
IMF	124.05	140.06	158.84	203.36	261.87	491.57	1402.70	3971.50
SMF	87.09	148.82	353.46	958.83	2046.10	3856.60	6769.10	9938.00
PSM	54.92	85.76	132.48	272.63	647.30	1938.30	5036.00	9495.10
SDROM	60.52	136.35	408.80	1105.70	2339.10	4322.30	7404.70	10619.00
SDROMR	56.79	91.21	171.88	287.33	553.76	1071.80	2452.10	5615.90
IRF	61.15	127.84	366.24	981.06	2098.80	3918.50	6821.70	9982.40
RUSSO	51.44	111.90	208.57	346.21	605.95	1114.93	2175.52	4372.28
ACWMR	46.95	85.67	170.71	299.57	536.23	1007.80	2042.30	4230.20
CWM	76.27	259.94	727.17	1729.30	3273.40	5431.60	8350.40	11291.00

Table 2. Restoration results in MSE for The Mandrill Image

Method	Noise Density							
	10%	20%	30%	40%	50%	60%	70%	80%
Noisy Image	1766.50	3585.30	5351.70	7093.50	8898.20	10623.00	12415.00	14201.00
RM (Proposed)	**28.25**	**63.49**	**98.11**	**143.92**	**187.97**	**257.82**	**344.81**	**463.38**
IMF	324.10	340.02	358.99	386.60	456.02	657.79	1653.40	4082.50
SMF	271.04	329.47	560.00	1094.30	2184.30	3836.80	6583.00	9739.10
PSM	108.39	147.80	205.12	335.73	736.27	1932.40	5146.60	9665.40
SDROM	165.39	259.65	544.67	1187.70	2443.10	4264.30	7185.30	10451.00
SDROMR	171.74	224.09	312.82	429.68	692.46	1122.90	2482.90	5432.60
IRF	171.56	252.63	497.92	1071.00	2190.20	3856.00	6614.30	9786.60
RUSSO	73.80	139.75	240.86	376.19	628.35	1114.40	2045.51	4217.16
ACWMR	115.20	176.27	263.32	381.32	620.87	975.77	1888.50	3713.40
CWM	184.00	348.50	836.76	1795.20	3319.70	5272.30	8037.50	10960.00

Table 3. Restoration results in MSE for The Peppers Image

Method	Noise Density							
	10%	20%	30%	40%	50%	60%	70%	80%
Noisy Image	1766.50	3585.30	5351.70	7093.50	8898.20	10623.00	12415.00	14201.00
RM (Proposed)	**11.94**	**25.00**	**40.94**	**63.56**	**90.53**	**135.67**	**207.26**	**380.64**
IMF	324.10	340.02	358.99	386.60	456.02	657.79	1653.40	4082.50
SMF	271.04	329.47	560.00	1094.30	2184.30	3836.80	6583.00	9739.10
PSM	108.39	147.80	205.12	335.73	736.27	1932.40	5146.60	9665.40
SDROM	165.39	259.65	544.67	1187.70	2443.10	4264.30	7185.30	10451.00
SDROMR	171.74	224.09	312.82	429.68	692.46	1122.90	2482.90	5432.60
IRF	171.56	252.63	497.92	1071.00	2190.20	3856.00	6614.30	9786.60
RUSSO	72.12	160.29	297.64	507.32	820.94	1420.30	2528.36	4767.72
ACWMR	115.20	176.27	263.32	381.32	620.87	975.77	1888.50	3713.40
CWM	184.00	348.50	836.76	1795.20	3319.70	5272.30	8037.50	10960.00

are given to present the restoration results of RM and the comparison filters for images degraded by impulsive noise, where noise density ranges from 10% to 80%. As can be clearly seen from the Tables 1–3 that the MSE values of the proposed RM is far more smaller than the MSE values of comparison filters for all of the test images. In addition, the proposed RM supplies more pleasing restoration results aspect of visual perception and also provides the best trade-off between noise suppression and image enhancement for detail preservation, as can be seen from the Fig 2.

References

1. L. Breveglieri, V. Piuri, Digital median filters, Journal of VLSI Signal Processing Systems for Signal, Image, and Video Technology, 31, (2002), 191-206.
2. T.A. Nodes, N.C. Gallagher, Median filters: some modifications and their properties, IEEE Trans. Acoust., Speech, Signal Processing, 30 (5), (1982), 739-746.

3. T. Sun, Y. Neuvo, Detail-preserving median based filters in image processing, Pattern Recognit. Lett., 15, (1994), 341-347.
4. H. Lin and A. N. Willson, Median filter with adaptive length, IEEE Trans. Circuits Syst., 35, (1988), 675-690.
5. J.W. Tukey, Nonlinear (nonsuperposable) methods for smoothing data, Cong. Rec. EASCON'74, (1974), 673.
6. Z. Wang, D. Zhang, Progressive switching median filter for the removal of impulse noise from highly corrupted images, IEEE Trans. on Circuits and Systems-II: Analog and Digital Signal Processing, 46 (1), (1999), 78-80.
7. E. Abreu, et.al., A new efficient approach for the removal of impulse noise from highly corrupted images, IEEE Trans. Image Processing, 5 (6), (1996), 1012-1025.
8. T. Chen, H.R. Wu, A new class of median based impulse rejecting filters, IEEE International Conference on Image Processing, 1, (2000), 916-919.
9. T. Chen., et.al., Adaptive impulse detection using center weighted median filters, IEEE Signal Processing Letters, 8 (1), (2001), 1-3.
10. S.J. Ko, Y. H. Lee, Center weighted median filters and their applications to image enhancement, IEEE Trans. Circuits Systems II, 43 (3), (1996), 157-192.
11. F. Russo, G. Ramponi, A Fuzzy Filter for Images Corrupted By Impulse Noise, IEEE Signal Processing Letters, 6 (3), (1996), 168-170.
12. F. Russo, Evolutionary neural fuzzy systems for data filtering, IEEE Instrumentation and Measurement Technology Conference, 2, (1998), 826-830.
13. I. Potamitis, N.D. Fakotakis, G. Kokkinakis, Impulsive noise suppression using neural networks, IEEE International Conference on Acoustics, Speech, and Signal Processing, 3, (2000), 1871-1874.
14. F.M.A. Acosta, Radial basis function and related models: An overview, Signal Processing, Elsevier Science Publishers, 45, (1995), 37-58.
15. S.A. Billings and C.F. Fung, Recurrent radial basis function networks for adaptive noise cancellation, Neural Networks, Elsevier Science Publishers, 8 (2), (1995), 273-290.
16. I. Cha and S.A. Kassam, Channel equalization using adaptive complex radial basis function networks, IEEE Journal on Selected Areas in Communications, 13 (1), (1995), 122-131.
17. I. Cha and S.A. Kassam, Interference cancellation using radial basis function networks, Signal Processing, Elsevier Science Publishers, 47, (1995), 247-268.
18. S. Chen, Nonlinear time series modelling and prediction using Gaussian RBF networks with enhanced clustering and RLS learning, Electronics Letters, 31 (2), (1995), 117-118.
19. S. Chen, B. Mulgrew, and P.M. Grant, A clustering technique for digital communications channel equalization using radial basis function networks, IEEE Transactions on Neural Networks, 4 (4), (1993), 570-579.
20. S. Haykin, Neural networks, Macmillan, New York, (1994).
21. MathWorks, MATLAB the language of technical computing, MATLAB Function Reference. New York: The MathWorks, Inc., (2002).
22. T.Y. Yang, Finite element structural analysis, Prentice Hall, Englewood Cliffs, NJ, (1986), 446-449.
23. D.F. Watson, Contouring: A guide to the analysis and display of spacial data, Pergamon, New York, (1994), 101-161.

A Histogram Smoothing Method for Digital Subtraction Radiography

Aydin Ozturk[1], Cengiz Gungor[1], Pelin Güneri[2], Zuhal Tuğsel[2], and Selin Göğüş[2]

[1]Ege University, International Computer Institute, 35100 Izmir, Turkey
[2]Ege University, School of Dentistry, 35100 Izmir, Turkey

Abstract. Digital subtraction radiography is a powerful technique for the detection of changes in serial radiographs. Among the others, contrast correction is a basic step for comparing the radiographs. Ruttimann's algorithm is widely used for contrast correction. In this study we propose a technique which is based on smoothing the empirical distribution of the reference image to improve Ruttimann's algorithm. Cardinal splines were used for smoothing the empirical distribution. Results based on clinical and simulated data showed that the proposed technique has outperformed the Ruttimann's algorithm. Relationship between the color depth and contrast differences was also investigated in terms of peak to signal ratio metric.

1 Introduction

Digital image subtraction is an efficient method for comparing and analyzing the images of the same object. Since the introduction of the *image subtraction* by Zeides des Plantes in the 1930s [1], various methods have been developed to detect the changes in serial radiographs. Among these, digital subtraction radiography for example, has been used successfully for monitoring the results of periodontal therapy [2].

A meaningful comparison can be made between two images of an object when they have the same geometric orientation, and the same color contrast. However, in most practical applications, discrepancies between the images occur due to some external conditions such as projection geometry, mismatches in X-ray tube settings, film developing and digitization procedures. Geometric transformations have been successfully used for aligning the images and thus eliminating the corresponding variation in gray levels between the images [1]. However, some additional efforts must be spent to reduce this variation by making contrast correction for the image which is to be subtracted from the reference image.

A number of parametric and non-parametric contrast correction methods have been proposed for serial radiographs. Parametric methods generally are based on polynomial regression models [3], [4], [5]. Non-linear models including logarithmic models are also used to model the relationship between the gray level pixel values of the two images. In all these models parameter estimates are obtained by using the least squares method. A major short coming involved in parametric methods is that they require that two images are aligned correctly before they are contrast corrected [6].

T. Yakhno (Ed.): ADVIS 2004, LNCS 3261, pp. 392–399, 2004.

Non-parametric methods are mainly based on transforming the empirical distribution of gray levels of pixels of the subsequent image in order to approximate it to that of the reference image. In this category, Ruttimann's algorithm for film contrast correction has been widely used in subtracting radiography [7]. Given the cumulative frequency histograms of the reference image and the image to be modified with the same number of gray levels g, the corresponding cumulative frequencies ($\tilde{p}_i$, $i=0$, 1, 2, ..., g-1) of gray levels of the image to be modified are matched to the cumulative frequencies ($\hat{p}_j$, $j=0$, 1, 2,..., g-1) of the reference image such that

$$\max_i\{\hat{p}_{j-1} < \tilde{p}_i \le \hat{p}_j\} \tag{1}$$

where $\hat{p}_0 = 0$. This equation defines the relationship between i and j and the corresponding transformation.

Ruttimann's algorithm not only provides a robust procedure for correcting film contrast differences but also introduces a simple way of gray level transformation from the frequency histograms of the corresponding radiographs. However, the discrete nature of the problem causes some loss of information when the empirical distribution of an image is forced to match as closely as possible to the reference image. For a given gray level i with cumulative frequency $\tilde{p}_i$ the corresponding probability transformation i is

$$i' = F^{-1}(\tilde{p}_i) \tag{2}$$

where $F(\cdot)$ is the empirical cumulative probability distribution function of gray levels of the test image and $F^{-1}(\cdot)$ is the inverse function of it. It is obvious that although the gray level value i is an integer, its transform i' is not necessarily an integer value. Ruttimann's algorithm assumes that $F(\cdot)$ is a discrete function defined at $i=0,1,2, ...,$ g-1 where g is the number of the gray levels in the images and matching is made in such a way that the resulting value of $i-1'$ always is an integer at the expense of loosing some accuracy of matching the distributions of the two images.

In this study we introduce a new approach based on smoothing the empirical distribution function of the test image to reduce the contrast mismatches. To investigate the contrast correction effect of smoothing, the influences of external conditions and physical noise are eliminated by simulating contrast variation in the reference radiographic image. Results are discussed in terms of PSNR which is proposed to measure the adequacy of the transformed image.

2 Transformation Based on Smoothing

Let $\hat{p}_i$ and $\tilde{p}_j$ denote the empirical cumulative probabilities at gray level i ($i=0$, 1, 2, ..., g-1) of the reference image and the image to be modified respectively. We assume that the distribution of the gray levels of the reference image is continuous and the empirical probabilities $\hat{p}_0, \hat{p}_1,...\hat{p}_{g-1}$ are the estimates of the associated probabilities evaluated at $i=0$, 1, 2, ..., g-1. It is well known in probability theory that a random variable X whose distribution function is $G(x)$ can be transformed into another variable Y whose distribution function is $F(y)$ by the following equation

$$Y = F^{-1}\{G(X)\} \tag{3}$$

For a given value of X that is $X=i$ the corresponding estimate of $G(i)$ simply is $\tilde{p}_i$. Substituting this in the equation above we obtain that $i' = F^{-1}(\tilde{p}_i)$. Thus, i' is the transformed value and must be approximated to the nearest integer by

$$j = \lfloor i' + 0.5 \rfloor \tag{4}$$

where $\lfloor \cdot \rfloor$ is the *floor* function which returns the greatest integer less than or equal to its argument. Thus the gray level i of every pixel position is replaced with the corresponding gray level j in the image and the resulting image is expected to have contrast values close to the test image (Figure 1).

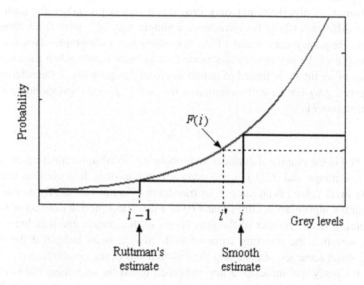

Fig. 1. Smooth histogram matching. A magnified section of the distribution function of the reference image is shown. Correspondence between the Ruttimann's transformation and the proposed transformation is illustrated

If the theoretical probability distribution of the gray levels of the test image was known then the parameters of the distribution could be estimated from the image data directly. This would enable us to make a smooth transformation for contrast correction. However, examination of the frequency histograms of the image data indicates that the underlying distribution usually consists of some mixture of distribution and identifying procedure of each distribution together with their mixture parameters is a difficult problem. We proceed to overcome this difficulty by employing spline curves which are commonly used to smooth functions or curves through a given set of points.

An illustrative empirical cumulative distribution of an image with 8 gray levels is shown in Figure 2. The points $\mathbf{p}_i = (i, \hat{p}_i)$, $(i = 0, 1, \cdots, 7)$, represent the coordinate positions of the cumulative frequencies and the corresponding gray levels. To draw a smooth curve through these points, polynomial functions are fitted to each pair of points in such a way that smooth transition from one section to the next one is provided. These techniques are known as *interpolation splines* and widely used in Computer graphics applications [8]. In this study so called *Cardinal Splines* are selected and explained below briefly [8].

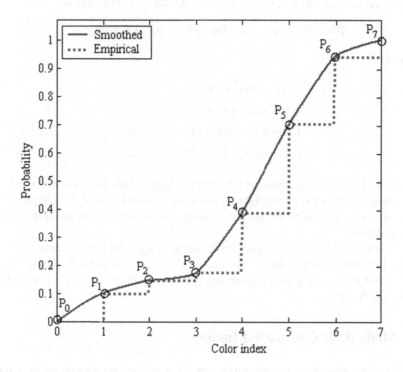

Fig. 2. A cubic cardinal spline interpolation for cumulative frequencies at 8 gray level points

Cardinal splines interpolates piecewise cubic polynomials with predetermined values of tangents at the connection points. The following parametric cubic polynomial is fitted between each pair of points

$$i(u) = a_i u^3 + b_i u^2 + c_i u + d_i$$
$$\hat{p}(u) = a_{\hat{p}} u^3 + b_{\hat{p}} u^2 + c_{\hat{p}} u + d_{\hat{p}} \qquad 0 \leq u \leq 1 \tag{5}$$

Let $\mathbf{P}(u) = \{i(u), \hat{p}(u)\}$ be the parametric cubic function between the points $\mathbf{p}_k$ and $\mathbf{p}_{k+1}$. To fit this polynomial with eight unknown parameters, at least four points must be known. A cardinal spline is specified with four consecutive points. By definition $\mathbf{P}(0) = \mathbf{p}_k$ and $\mathbf{P}(1) = \mathbf{p}_{k+1}$, ($k=0, 1, \ldots$). The endpoint tangents are defined as

$$\mathbf{P}'(0) = \frac{1}{2}(1-t)(\mathbf{p}_{k+1} - \mathbf{p}_{k-1})$$

$$\mathbf{P}'(1) = \frac{1}{2}(1-t)(\mathbf{p}_{k+2} - \mathbf{p}_k)$$

(6)

Using these boundary conditions the corresponding cubic polynomial $\mathbf{P}(u)$ can be expressed in terms of cardinal functions $C_i(u), (i=0, 1, 2, 3)$ as follows

$$\mathbf{P}(u) = C_0(u)\mathbf{p}_{k-1} + C_1(u)\mathbf{p}_k + C_2(u)\mathbf{p}_{k+1} + C_3(u)\mathbf{p}_{k+2}$$

(7)

where

$$\begin{aligned}
C_0(u) &= -su^3 + 2su^2 - su \\
C_1(u) &= (2-s)u^3 + (s-3)u^2 + 1 \\
C_2(u) &= (s-2)u^3 + (3-2s)u^2 + su \\
C_3(u) &= su^3 - 2su^2
\end{aligned}$$

(8)

with $s = (1 - t) / 2$. The choice of t dictates the shape of the fitted curve. Looser curves are obtained when $t < 0$, and tighter curves are obtained when $t > 0$. Applying cardinal splines to cumulative frequencies require special handling for the first and the last curve sections.

Given the value of $\tilde{p}_i$ at gray level i of an image which is supposed to be modified, the corresponding value i' in equation (2) can be computed by letting $\hat{p}(u) = \tilde{p}_i$ in (5) and then solving the equation for u. Then, resulting value of u is used to compute $i(u)$ that gives i'.

3   Method for Comparing Images

When comparing the reference image and the modified image one needs a standard metric to measure the overall difference between the two images. We propose a well known measure which is commonly used to assess the quality of reconstructed images compared with the original ones that is the peak signal to noise ratio (PSNR). The PSNR is defined as

$$PSNR = 20\log_{10} \frac{2^d - 1}{\left[\frac{1}{n}\sum_{k=1}^{n}(i_k - j_k)^2\right]^{\frac{1}{2}}}$$

(9)

where d is the color depth, i_k and j_k are the pixel intensities at position k of the test and the modified images respectively, and n is the total number of pixels in the image [9]. It can be seen that this measure is dimensionless and the better the modified image resembles the reference image, the bigger should be the resulting value. For a gray scale image with d bits per pixel, the typical PSNR values range between 20 and 40.

4 Material

The periapical radiographic images were taken from the left first and second molar region of a dried adult male mandible. In order to keep the geometric relationship between the X-ray source and the object constant, mandible was placed on a platform which was made up of silicone material. A 4.5 cm length groove was prepared in silicone material on the lingual side of the molar teeth to place the films in a standard position during exposures. E speed periapical films were exposed at 65 kVp, 8 mA and with a 30 cm FFD for 0.50 second using a Trophy Radiologie 77437 Croissy-Beabourg dental X-ray unit with 2 mm of aluminum filtration. In order to simulate soft tissue effects, a 1 cm thick fiberglass was placed in the route of the central X-ray beam, perpendicular to the X-ray tube. Films were processed under highly controlled conditions using hand processing solutions.

Radiographs were digitized on a flatbad scanner at 2400 dpi and 256 grey levels, and were saved as Tagged Image File Format. Then, radiographic images were cropped to 512×512 pixels and converted to Bitmap format with Adobe Photoshop 6.

5 Results

To evaluate the proposed algorithm, a reference radiograph obtained from a clinical study was used. Images with different color depth and contrasts were simulated from this reference image. Gamma correction method which is based on the transformation

$$l' = l^{1/\lambda}, \quad 0 \le l \le 1 \tag{10}$$

where l is the normalized gray level of a pixel in the reference image, is utilized to generate new images. Simulated images were used instead of the serial clinical radiographs to eliminate the influences of physical noise and some external factors. 500×500 reference image and the simulated images both with 8 color depth (256 gray levels) are displayed in Figure 3. The simulated image was generated from the reference image with $\lambda = 1.7$. The mean and the standard deviation of gray levels of the reference image were found to be 108.33 and 41.16 respectively. The simulated image has a higher mean intensity and lower contrast as expected with respective mean and standard deviation 154.30 and 39.81. The lower left of Figure 3 displays the simulated image after contrast correction. The mean and standard deviations for this image were 108.52 and 41.26 respectively. The corresponding statistics for Ruttimann's algorithm were found to be 107.52 and 41.26. These results indicate that the transformation of gray levels by smoothing provided better contrast correction for the modified image.

Gray levels $i=0,1,\ldots, 255$ of the subtraction image which is displayed in the lower right of Figure 3, were obtained by the following transformation

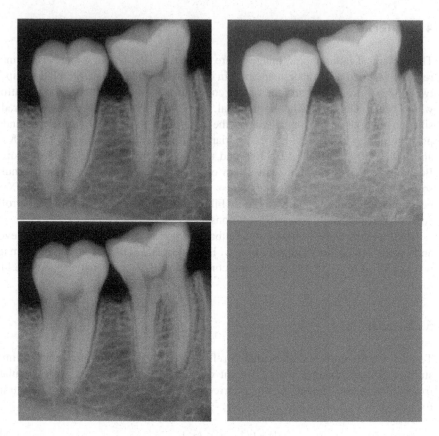

Fig. 3. Upper left: The reference image. Upper right: Simulated image. Lower left: Simulated image after contrast correction. Lower right: Subtraction image

$$d_i = (i_{reference} - i_{mod\,ified})/2 + 128 \qquad (11)$$

in order to visualize the adequate brightness changes in the image. If the two images were exactly the same then the average intensity would expected to be 128. The mean gray level of the subtracting image was 127.81 with a standard deviation of 0.39. Smaller standard deviation indicates lower contrast difference.

In order to investigate the effect of color depth on the quality of contrast correction, the test image and the simulated image were transformed to have new images with a specified color depth. 7 color depths (i=2, 3, 4, 5, 6, 7, and 8) were selected and contrast correction algorithms applied to each pair of images. The corresponding results are illustrated in Figure 4. It can be seen from the figure that the proposed algorithm has resulted higher PSNR values than that of the Ruttimann's algorithm for all color depths.

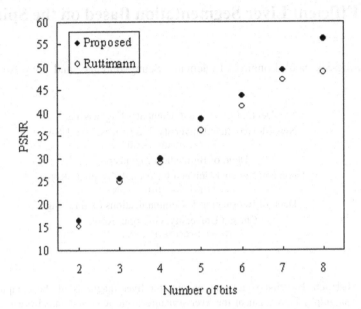

Fig. 4. Relationship between PSNR values and color depths obtained by the proposed method and the Ruttimann's algorithm

References

1. Lehmann, T. M.: Computer based registration for digital subtraction in dental radiology. Dentomaxillofacial Radiology 29 (2000) 323-346
2. Ruttimann, U. E., Webber, R. L., Schmit, E.: A robust digital method for film contrast correction in subtraction radiography. J. Periodontal Research. 21 (1986) 486-495
3. Allen, K. M., Hausmann, E.: Analytical methodology in quantitative digital subtruction radiography: Analyses of the aluminum reference wedge. J. Priodontal. 67 (1996) 1317-1321
4. Bragger, U, Pasquali L., Rylander H., Carnes, D., Kornman, K.S.: Computer-assisted densitometric image analysis in periodontal radiography. A methodological study. J. Clin Periodontal 15 (1988) 27-37
5. Ruttimann, U. E., Okano, T., Grondahl, K., Weber, R.L.: Exposure geometry and film contrast differences as bases for incomplete cancellation of irrelevant structures in dental subtraction radiography. Proc. SPIE 314 (1981) 372-377
6. Likar, B., Pernus, F.: Evaluation of three contrast correction methods for digital subtraction in dental radiology: An in vitro study. Med. Phys. 24 (1997) 299-307
7. Hidebolt, C. F., Walkup, R. K., Conover, G. L., Yokoyama-Crothers, N., Bartlett, T. Q., Vannier, M.W., Shrout, M.K., Camp, J. J.: Histogram-matching and histogram-flattening methods: a comparison. Dentomaxillofacial Radiology 25 (1996) 42-47
8. Hearn, D. Baker, P.: *Computer Graphics with OpenGL.* Pearson Educational International Inc. (2004), 420-458
9. Solomon, D.: *Data compression. The complete reference.* Springer-Verlag Inc. (2000) 240-242 `

Efficient Liver Segmentation Based on the Spine

Kyung-Sik Seo[1], Lonnie C. Ludeman[1], Seung-Jin Park[2], and Jong-An Park[3]

[1] Dept. of Electrical & Computer Engineering,
New Mexico State University, Las Cruces, NM, USA
kseo@nmsu.edu
[2] Dept. of Biomedical Engineering,
Chonnam National University Hospital, Gwangju, Korea
sjinpark@cnuh.com
[3] Dept. of Information & Communications Engineering,
Chosun University, Gwangju, Korea
japark@chosun.ac.kr

Abstract. The first significant process for liver diagnosis of the computed tomography is to segment the liver structure from other abdominal organs. In this paper, we propose an efficient liver segmentation algorithm using the spine as a reference point without the reference image and training data. A multi-modal threshold method based on piecewise linear interpolation extracts ranges of regions of interest. Spine segmentation is performed to find the reference point providing geometrical coordinates. C-class maximum a posteriori decision using the reference point selects the liver region. Then binary morphological filtering is processed to provide better segmentation and boundary smoothing. In order to evaluate automatically segmented results of the proposed algorithm, the area error rate and rotational binary region projection matching method are applied. Evaluation results suggest proposed liver segmentation has strong similarity performance as the manual method of a medical doctor.

1 Introduction

A computed tomography (CT) is currently a conventional and excellent tool for diagnosis of the liver in medical imaging technology. The CT provides the detailed image and characteristics of a tumor and cancer for resection and transplantation of the liver. Periodical monitoring of the CT after treatment and cure helps a patient obtain full recovery from the cancer. If the CT is analyzed for early detection, treatment and curing is easy and human life is prolonged. The first significant process for liver diagnosis of the CT is to segment the liver structure from other abdominal organs.

Liver segmentation using the CT has been performed often. Bae et al. [1] used priori information about liver morphology and image processing techniques such as

T. Yakhno (Ed.): ADVIS 2004, LNCS 3261, pp. 400–409, 2004.
© Springer-Verlag Berlin Heidelberg 2004

gray-level thresholding, Gaussian smoothing, mathematical morphology techniques, and B-splines. Gao et al. [2] developed automatic liver segmentation using a global histogram, morphologic operations, and the parametrically deformable contour model. Tsai [3] proposed an alternative segmentation method using an artificial neural network to classify each pixel into three categories. Also, Husain et al. [4] used neural networks for feature-based recognition of liver region. However, most of researches have depended on semi-automatic liver segmentation. Prior to the automatic segmentation process, a reference image was interactively chosen by a user [1] and data of neural networks trained [2-4].

In this paper, we propose an efficient liver segmentation algorithm using the spine as a reference point without the reference image and training data. The reference point provides fully automatic and geometric information for processing cost and time reduction. This paper is organized in the following orders. In section 2, the proposed algorithm is described for liver segmentation. In section 3, we demonstrate experimental methods. In next section, experimental results are described. In the last section, the conclusion will be given.

2   Proposed Algorithm for Liver Segmentation

A multi-modal threshold (MMT) method based on piecewise linear interpolation (PLI) is first described to find ranges of regions of interest (ROIs) in the liver region. Spine segmentation is performed to find the reference point providing geometrical coordinates. C-class maximum a posteriori (MAP) decision is utilized for selecting the liver region. Then binary morphological (BM) filtering is processed to provide better segmentation and boundary smoothing.

2.1   MMT Method

A histogram is used simply to provide statistical information like mean, median, standard deviation, and energy. The histogram is a one-dimensional statistical transformation obtained by counting total pixel numbers for each gray level. Let $I: Z^2 \rightarrow Z$ be a gray-level CT image and (m,n) be a pixel location. Then, $I(m,n) \in Z$. The histogram, $h(k): Z \rightarrow Z$, is defined as [5]

$$h(k) = \{(m,n) \mid I(m,n) = k\} \tag{1}$$

where k is a gray-level value. The transformed histogram h_s from the $h(k)$ is obtained by one-dimensional convolution and scaling [6]. Then we find a global peak in the multi-modal histogram. The left and right valleys are calculated using a PLI method [7], which is given as

$$f_k = \frac{h_s(k+\gamma) - h_s(k)}{(k+\gamma) - k} \tag{2}$$

where γ is an integer. Each valley is founded at the turning point from a negative value to a positive value because each point represents the slope. Ranges of the spine and liver from obtained valleys are created and located conventionally and experimentally in the right side of the histogram. Each $ROI : Z^2 \rightarrow Z^2$ of the spine and liver is defined as

$$ROI_{spine} = \{(m,n) \mid T_{spine\_l} \le I(m,n) \le T_{spine\_u}\} \qquad (3)$$

$$ROI_{liver} = \{(m,n) \mid T_{liver\_l} \le I(m,n) \le T_{liver\_u}\} \qquad (4)$$

Figure 1 shows the MMT method. Fig. 1(a) and 1(b) are the gray-level CT image and histogram $h(k)$ with multi-modal distribution based on gray-level values. Fig. 1(c) shows the transformed histogram h_s using convolution and scaling. Fig. 1(d) and (e) are ROIs of the spine and liver after the MMT method.

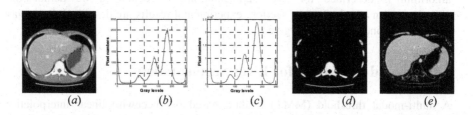

$$(a) \qquad\qquad (b) \qquad\qquad (c) \qquad\qquad (d) \qquad\qquad (e)$$

Fig. 1. Multi-modal threshold method. (*a*) Gray-level CT image. (*b*) Histogram $h(k)$. (*c*) Transformed histogram. (*d*) ROI of the spine. (e) ROI of the liver

2.2 Spine Segmentation

Spine segmentation for finding the reference point is important because a spine provides geometrical criterion for fully automatic segmentation of the liver. In past research, skin utilized as the reference point caused problems because of the complicated segmentation process and alternative location that relied upon patient breathing. In contrast, the spine has no influence from the patient's situation and is always located at the center of the horizon. Also, as coordinating pixels of the spine have little variation, it is easier to segregate than skin. To extract the spine, the ROI_{spine} is transformed to the binary image, $B : Z^2 \rightarrow Z^2$, as shown in Fig. 2 (a) and B is defined as

$$B = \begin{cases} 1 & if \quad T_{spine\_l} \le I(m,n) \le T_{spine\_u} \\ 0 & if \qquad\qquad otherwise \end{cases} \qquad (5)$$

From B, small objects such as vessels are excluded by pixel area estimation as shown in 2(b). The patient's table is removed by comparing the major axis length because the table has the longest length as shown in Fig. 2(c). In order to remove left and right ribs, a centroid [5] formulated by Eq. (6) is used because the spine is always located in the center of the horizontal axis as shown in Fig. 2(d).

$$(\overline{m}, \overline{n}) = (\frac{1}{a} \sum_{(m,n) \in B} m, \frac{1}{a} \sum_{(m,n) \in B} n) \tag{6}$$

where a is area and B is an arbitrary binary image. Finally, the centroid of the spine is defined as the reference point for extracting liver structure and it is displayed in Fig. 3 (e).

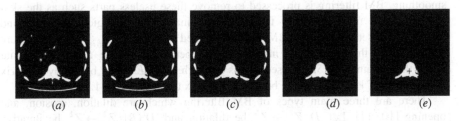

(a)   (b)   (c)   (d)   (e)

Fig. 2. Spine segmentation. (*a*) Binary image. (*b*) Small region removal. (*c*) Patient's table removal. (*d*) Rib removal. (*e*) A reference point

2.3   C-Class MAP Decision

The ROI_{liver} obtained by the MMT method is transformed into the binary image. The binary image, B, is defined as

$$B = \begin{cases} 1 & if \quad T_{liver\_l} \leq I(m,n) \leq T_{liver\_u} \\ 0 & if \qquad otherwise \end{cases} \tag{7}$$

If small objects in B are excluded, B consists of abdominal objects such as the liver, stomach, heart, and kidneys. Then B is defined as $B = \{B_1, B_2, ..., B_C\}$ with C-class where B_C is the binary image of abdominal organs.

C-class MAP decision is proposed to select the binary liver region. If geometric information of abdominal organs is used, the liver is posed at the left side of the reference point and has a bigger area than other organs. Let a reference region, $R \subset Z^2$, be the left region created from the reference point. Then the reference region includes most of liver. If R is given, then the liver has the biggest region in R. That is, if the biggest region among B_C is founded in R, B_C including this region is considered the liver, $B_{liver} \subset Z^2$.

Using this criterion, the C-class MAP decision [8] for finding the liver structure is defined as

$$B_{liver} \text{ exists if } P(B_u \mid R) > P(B_v \mid R) \text{ for all } u \neq v \tag{8}$$

where $P(B_u \mid R)$ is a posteriori probabilities and is defined as

$$P(B_u \mid R) = \frac{p(R \mid B_u)P(B_u)}{p(R)} \tag{9}$$

where $P(R)$ is the total probability.

2.4 BM Filtering

The selected B_{liver} has BM filtering to help better segmentation and boundary smoothing. BM filtering is processed to remove these useless parts such as the skin and ribs. BM filtering comes from the combination of biological structure and mathematical set theories [9]. BM filtering is used to combine B_{liver} with a structure element, SE, through various morphological operations. As the SE is the spatial mask, the 8-connected SE is used in this research. Let $SE_2 \subset Z^2$ be a 2 by 2 matrix that consists of 1 and $SE_3 \subset Z^2$ be a 3 by 3 matrix that consists of 1.

There are three main types of BM filtering which are dilation, erosion, and opening [10, 11]. Let $D : Z^2 \to Z^2$ be dilation and $D^i(B) : Z^2 \to Z^2$ be iterative dilation (ID) to extend a region. Let $E : Z^2 \to Z^2$ be erosion and $E^i(B) : Z^2 \to Z^2$ be iterative erosion (IE) to reduce a region. Let $OP : Z^2 \to Z^2$ be opening and $OP^i(B) : Z^2 \to Z^2$ be iterative opening (IO) to smooth thin protrusions. Each filtering is defined as

$$D = \{B \oplus SE\} \text{ and } D^i(B) = \{...((B \oplus SE) \oplus SE)...) \oplus SE\} \tag{10}$$

$$E = \{B \ominus SE\} \text{ and } E^i(B) = \{...((B \ominus SE) \ominus SE)...) \ominus SE\} \tag{11}$$

$$OP = \{B \circ SE\} = \{(B \ominus SE) \oplus SE\} \text{ and}$$

$$OP^i(B) = \{...((B \circ SE) \circ SE)...) \circ SE\} \tag{12}$$

where B is a binary input image and i is a iteration number. Let $D^1(B) = D$, $E^1(B) = E$, $OP^1(B) = OP$, $CL^1(B) = CL$, $D^i(B) = D^i$, $E^i(B) = E^i$, $OP^i(B) = OP^i$, and $CL^i(B) = CL^i$.

The combination of each filtering has a specific order because the combination order affects region reduction and expansion. Let $CO(B) : Z^2 \to Z^2$ be an ordered combination function of BM filtering. $CO(B)$ used in this research is $\{OP, E, D\}$. In order to smooth the boundary, OP^{10} by SE_3 is first used. Then E^2 by SE_2 is performed to reduce the region and small regions such as the skin and ribs are removed. Also, D^2 by SE_2 is processed to reconstruct the reduction region.

The binary image obtained by BM filtering is transformed to the gray-level image. Let $I_{liver} \subset Z^2$ be a gray-level image. Assuming that B and I have the same size, I_{liver} is obtained by pixel-by-pixel multiplication defined as

$$I_{liver} = \{(m,n) \mid B(m,n) \otimes I(m,n)\} \tag{13}$$

Figure 3 shows an example of liver segmentation. The binary image B is shown in Fig. 3(a) and the reference point found by spine segmentation is displayed in Fig. 3(b). The reference region created by the reference point is shown in Fig. 3(c) and the liver B_{liver} selected by the C-class MAP decision is shown in Fig. 3(d). After BM filtering and gray-level transformation, I_{liver} is created as shown in Fig. 3(e).

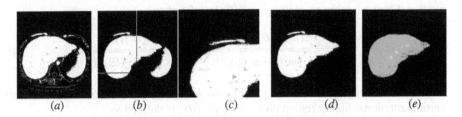

    (a)   (b)   (c)   (d)   (e)

Fig. 3. Liver segmentation. (a) Binary image, B. (b) Reference point in B. (c) Reference region, R. (d) Extracted liver B_{liver} by the C-class MAP decision. (e) Gray-level liver I_{liver}

3   Experimental Methods

In order to evaluate automatically segmented results of the proposed algorithm, area error rate (AER) and rotational binary region projection matching (RBRPM) method are applied. CT images to be used in this research were provided by Chonnam National University Hospital in Gwangju city, Korea.

3.1   Area Error Rate

AER is an evaluation method comparing degree of pixel area difference. This area difference is between an automatic segmented region (ASR) and a manual segmented region (MSR). Let $B_{auto} \subset Z^2$ be a binary region created by automatic segmentation. Let $B_{manual} \subset Z^2$ be a binary region created by manual segmentation. Let $B_{manual} \cup B_{auto}$ be the union region (UR) and $B_{manual} \cap B_{auto}$ be the intersection region (IR). AER is defined as

$$AER = \frac{a_{UR} - a_{IR}}{a_{MSR}} \times 100\% \tag{14}$$

where a_{UR} is the pixel area of UR, a_{IR} is the pixel area of IR, and a_{MSR} is the pixel area of the manual segmented region.

3.2   Rotational Binary Region Projection Matching

The RBRPM method is another method to compare mis-registration of different binary images. The RBRPM method correlates two rotating binary images by horizontal and vertical projection histograms [5, 12]. Comparative binary images do not have holes with 0 pixel values in their region. Horizontal and vertical projecttion histograms have the same basis axis even though images are rotated. The nearest neighbor interpolation as a simple interpolation method is used to rotate images. Angles for rotation are tested within $0° \leq \theta \leq 90°$.

Let $h_x(m)$ and $h_y(m)$ be the horizontal and vertical histogram of the ASR. Let $h_x'(m)$ and $h_y'(n)$ be the horizontal and vertical histogram of the MSR. Let $h_x(m,\theta)$ and $h_y(n,\theta)$ be rotated $h_x(m)$ and $h_y(m)$ by θ. Let $h_x'(m,\theta)$ and $h_y'(n,\theta)$ be rotated $h_x'(m)$ and $h_y'(n)$ by θ. Then, the correlation coefficient (CC) of the horizontal rotational binary region projection, $cc_x(\theta)$, is defined as

$$cc_x(\theta) = \frac{\sum((h_x(m,\theta)-\mu_x(\theta))(h_x'(m,\theta)-\mu_x'(\theta)))}{\sqrt{(\sum(h_x(m,\theta)-\mu_x(\theta))^2)(\sum(h_x'(m,\theta)-\mu_x'(\theta))^2)}}$$ (15)

where $\mu_x(\theta)$ and $\mu_x'(\theta)$ are mean values of $h_x(m,\theta)$ and $h_x'(m,\theta)$. The CC of the vertical rotational binary region projection, $cc_y(\theta)$, is defined as

$$cc_y(\theta) = \frac{\sum((h_y(n,\theta)-\mu_y(\theta))(h_y'(n,\theta)-\mu_y'(\theta)))}{\sqrt{(\sum(h_y(n,\theta)-\mu_y(\theta))^2)(\sum(h_y'(n,\theta)-\mu_y'(\theta))^2)}}$$ (16)

where $\mu_y(\theta)$ and $\mu_y'(\theta)$ are mean values of $h_y(n,\theta)$ and $h_y'(n,\theta)$.

4 Results

The CT scans were obtained by using a LightSpeed Qx/i, which was produced by GE Medical Systems. Scanning was performed with intravenous contrast enhancement. Also, the scanning parameters used a tube current of 230 mAs ad 120 kVp, a 30 cm field of view, 5 mm collimation, and a table speed of 15 mm/sec (pitch factor, 1:3).

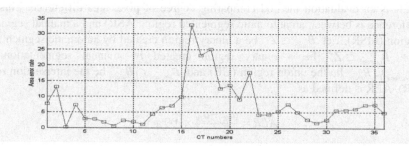

Fig. 4. Area error rate

Seven patients (193 slices) were selected for testing the new proposed algorithm to segment a liver structure. CT images of each patient were processed slice by slice. Also, one excellent radiologists in Chonnam National University Hospital took a part in this research in order to segment the liver structure by the manual method. The horizontal CC(correlation coefficient) and vertical CC were calculated by rotating

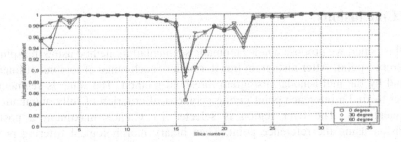

Fig. 5. Horizontal correlation coefficient

binary regions with angles of 0, 30, and 60 degrees. Figure 4 ~ 6 show the AER and CCs of one patient. Segmentation of upper and middle parts of the liver has caused problems because of neighboring abdominal organs such as the heart and pancreas. However, segmentation results of most of slices had small AER and higher CCs. Table 1 shows average AER and CCs of each patient. Total average AER is 10.8054 % and total average horizontal and vertical CC are 0.9884 and 0.9864. This evaluation results show proposed liver segmentation has strong similarity performance as the manual method of a medical doctor.

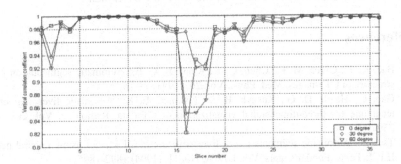

Fig. 6. Vertical correlation coefficient

Table 1. Experimental results of seven patients

	Number of slices	Average of AER (%)	Average of horizontal CC	Average of Vertical CC
Patient 01	36	11.8583	0.9847	0.9817
Patient 02	27	8.0761	0.9937	0.9921
Patient 03	23	9.8731	0.9914	0.9905
Patient 04	26	10.8479	0.9919	0.9890
Patient 05	23	12.7798	0.9854	0.9780
Patient 06	26	9.4430	0.9891	0.9909
Patient 07	32	12.7595	0.9825	0.9828
Total	193	10.8054	0.9884	0.9864

5 Conclusions

In this paper, we propose a new automatic segmentation method using the spine as a reference point. After histogram transformation, each range of regions of interest is found by the multi-modal histogram threshold method. The spine is segmented in order to find a reference point giving geometrical criterion of fully automatic liver segmentation. The liver region is selected by C-class maximum a posteriori decision using the reference point. Then binary morphological filtering provides better segmentation and boundary smoothing.

Seven patients are selected for testing the new proposed method and one excellent radiologist for manual liver segmentation takes a part in this research. As evaluation methods, area error rate (AER) and rotational binary region projection matching (RBRPM) method are applied. Total average AER is 10.8054 % and total average horizontal and vertical CCs are 0.9884 and 0.9864. This evaluation results suggest proposed liver segmentation has strong similarity performance as the manual method of a medical doctor.

Acknowledgement. This research was supported by the Program for the Training of Graduate Students in Regional Innovation which was conducted by the Ministry of Commerce, Industry and Energy of the Korean Government.

References

1. Bae, K. T., Giger, M. L., Chen, C. T., Kahn, Jr. C. E.: Automatic segmentation of liver structure in CT images. Med. Phys., Vol. 20. (1993) 71-78.
2. Gao, L., Heath, D. G., Kuszyk, B. S., Fishman, E. K.: Automatic liver segmentation technique for three-dimensional visualization of CT data. Radiology, Vol. 201. (1996) 359-364.
3. Tsai, D.: Automatic segmentation of liver structure in CT images using a neural network. IEICE Trans. Fundamentals, Vol. E77-A. No. 11. (1994) 1892-1895.
4. Husain, S. A., Shigeru, E.: Use of neural networks for feature based recognition of liver region on CT images. Neural Networks for Sig. Proc.-Proceedings of the IEEE Work., Vol 2. (2000) 831-840.
5. Shapiro, L. G., Stockman, G.. C.: Computer Vision. Prentice-Hall, Upper Saddle River NJ (2001).
6. Orfanidis, S. J.: Introduction to signal processing. Prentice Hall, Upper Saddle River NJ (1996).
7. Schilling, R. J., Harris, S. L.: Applied Numerical Methods for Engineers. Brooks/Cole Publishing Com., Pacific Grove CA (2000).
8. Ludeman, L. C.: Random Processes: Filtering, Estimation, and Detection. Wiley & Sons, Inc., Hoboken NJ (2003).
9. Gonzalez, R. C., Woods, R. E.: Digital Image Processing. 2nd. edn. Prentice-Hall Inc., Upper Saddle River. NJ. (2002).
10. Pitas, I.: Digital Image Processing Algorithms and Applications. Wiley & Sons, Inc. New York NY (2000).

11. Jahne, B.: Digital Image Processing. 5th. Edn. Springer-Verlag, Berlin Heidelberg (2002).
12. Sonka, M., Hlavac, V., Boyle, R.: Image Processing, Analysis, and Machine Vision. 2nd. edn. Brooks/Cole Publishing Com., Pacific Grove CA (1999).

Practical and Secure E-Mail System (PractiSES)

Albert Levi and Mahmut Özcan

Sabanci University,
Faculty of Engineering and Natural Sciences, Orhanli,
Tuzla, TR-34956 Istanbul, Turkey
levi@sabanciuniv.edu
mozcan@sampas.com.tr

Abstract. In this paper, a practical and secure e-mail system (called "PractiSES") that performs public key distribution and management in a unique way is proposed. PractiSES is a network of several domains. At the domain level, a designated PractiSES server, which is trusted by all users of that domain, distributes the public keys. If a user needs another user's public key at a different domain, then inter-domain communication is carried out. PractiSES clients manage their public keys and obtain public keys of other users by using unique, secure and user-transparent protocols. PractiSES clients can exchange e-mails in encrypted and/or signed fashion. Since on-demand fetching of public keys is aimed in PractiSES, use of certificates is limited for inter-domain communications only; no certificates are used within a domain. Our simulations show that a state-of-the-art PC would be sufficient to serve as PractiSES server of a medium-size organization.

1 Introduction

E-mail is one of the most commonly used communication mechanisms. Most of the recipients and senders desire secure e-mail exchange. Senders want to make sure that the recipient is really the intended recipient, and the message arrives to the recipient confidentially. On the other hand, recipients want to make sure that the sender is the entity who it claims to be, and the arrived message has not been maliciously modified and examined during transmission. These requirements can be satisfied by the e-mail applications that use public key cryptosystem (PKC) as the security base, such as S/MIME [1] and PGP [2]. The main handicap behind the deployment of applications that use PKC is the problem of public key distribution with a legitimate binding with its owner. Moreover, public key management features, such as update, delete operations must be performed in a secure way.

S/MIME is a standard mechanism that provides secure Internet message exchange between parties. S/MIME applications use digital certificates for public key distribution. Certificates [3] are digital documents that are used as bindings between users' identities and their public keys. Use of certificates may be inconvenient for several reasons. Certificates can be downloaded from certificate repositories and e-mail addresses in certificates may be collected by e-mail address collectors for mass

T. Yakhno (Ed.): ADVIS 2004, LNCS 3261, pp. 410–419, 2004.

mailing. Privacy sensitive people criticize this situation. Certificates that are issued by well-known Certification Authorities (CAs) are not free. Certificates are used in offline manner, so revocation of them is a troublesome process.

There is no common trusted third party in PGP [2]. Rather, every user can certify another user. Therefore, a message from a user, who is certified by another user not known to the receiver, may cause the receiver to hesitate. PGP has a network of public key servers, but key authenticity decisions are eventually given by the user itself. Thus, PGP key management and distribution mechanisms assume knowledgeable users.

In this paper, under the light of PGP and S/MIME experience, we propose a new secure e-mail system, *Practical and Secure E-Mail System* (*PractiSES*), that is somehow similar to a two-tiered Public Key Infrastructure (PKI) with online key servers. At the top level of PractiSES system, there is a Certificate Authority (CA), called *PractiSES CA*, to provide public key certificates for online PractiSES domain servers. Public keys of users of a specific domain are stored, distributed and managed in a centralized manner by employing a domain server and a public key storage of that domain. No certificates are used for such intra-domain public key distribution. Users belong to different domains exchange their public keys via inter-domain communication in which domain server certificates are used.

The rationale behind the design of PractiSES is explained in Section 2. Design of PractiSES and its protocols are given in Section 3. Implementation and performance details are explained in Section 4. Finally, conclusions and discussions on PractiSES are given in Section 5.

2   The Rationale Behind PractiSES

While designing PractiSES as a secure and practical e-mail system, we have considered two facts about e-mail systems.

First, we have realized that an e-mail security system is useless unless both parties use it. If a recipient does not use a secure e-mail client, sender's signature over a message is worthless. Both PGP and S/MIME suffer from this fact. A good system should be aware of the recipient's capabilities while sending a secure e-mail.

Second, we have realized that neither PGP nor S/MIME achieved a critical mass in order to be considered as default e-mail security mechanisms. Certificate requirement is the shortcoming of S/MIME. PGP's problem is at its complexity. So we need a user friendly and simple system that does not require end user certificates and eliminates the related problems.

These two observations led us to a centralized approach for e-mail security. In PractiSES, a centralized server could store the public keys and distribute them on-demand basis to the other users in an online manner. In this way, we eliminate all certificate related problems. Since this server is a trusted one, users do not bother with complex trust decision systems. Another attractiveness of such a centralized approach for closed groups is that it is plausible to assume the system knows its potential users. In this way, potential users' e-mail addresses and semi-secret information, such as mother's maiden name and SSN, can be stored in the server's database. This information is later used for authentication during the initial registration.

The above-described centralized approach solves the problem only within a domain of users. It is obvious that all potential users cannot exist within a single domain, so inter-domain end user public-key transfers are needed. We prefer to use a certificate-based mechanism, which will be detailed in the coming sections, for inter-domain secure communication. One may argue that it is contradictory to use certificates for domains while the design decision was not to use end user certificates. However, we believe that since the number of domains is not too much (especially as compared to the number of end users), the managerial problems of using certificates for domains become tractable. Moreover, the domain certificates are used transparent to the end users. When a domain certificate is revoked, which is quite unlikely, only other domain servers should handle this, not the end users. In such a case, PractiSES CA informs all the domain servers.

3   Design of Practical and Secure E-mail System (PractiSES)

From a high-level point of view, PractiSES is a network of several *PractiSES domains* and a *PractiSES Certificate Authority* (*CA*). Every PractiSES domain has a server, called *PractiSES Server*, which holds its key pair and PractiSES CA's self-signed root certificate, which may come with the server software package. Moreover, each server, consequently each domain, has a key pair and public key is available to other domains via a domain certificate pre-issued by PractiSES CA. Thus, there is a certification relationship between a PractiSES domain and CA. The trust between servers of different domains is established by using those certificates. Whenever an end user public key is to be exchanged between two domains, domain servers authenticate themselves via a protocol, key obtainment protocol, in which certificates are involved. Figure 1 shows a high-level overview of an example PractiSES system with three domains (X, Y and Z).

3.1   PractiSES Domain Architecture and Client Module

A PractiSES Domain has a centralized architecture. A designated domain server, *PractiSES Server*, acts as a key distribution center for the whole domain users. Most of those users are expected to be affiliated with the same institution, but this is not a must; any user can be served in the domain of a PractiSES Server. Public keys are eventually stored in *Public Key Storage*, but that storage initially does not contain public keys but contains values of ID, name, last name, e-mail address and semi-secret information (e.g. mother's maiden name), etc. of the potential users. It is assumed that such information exists in organization's records and can easily be conveyed to the public key storage. This potential user information will be used for authentication during the initialization protocol to upload the public keys of the users.

Moreover, each client obtains the public key of its domain server. This is necessary to authenticate the messages coming from the server and to send encrypted messages to it. This public key is stored in self-signed format and downloaded from a designated web or ftp site with a manual key digest crosscheck to make sure about the authentication of the key. Should a domain key is revoked, domain users are informed with a signed e-mail from a domain server so that they download new public key from the same site.

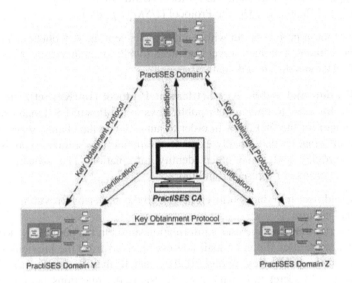

Fig. 1. Practical and Secure Email System (PractiSES)

As can be seen from the above discussion, PractiSES protocols assume pre-distribution of server public and CA public keys in an offline manner. This is a general problem for all security applications and solution generally requires sacrificing security to some extent. For example, as explained in [10], the root CA certificates for the well-known SSL (Secure Socket Layer) protocol come with browsers and installed automatically without the consent of the user. In that respect, PractiSES follows the commonsense.

The Client Module (CM) is an application, which is used as an e-mail client with additional security options. It has two functionalities with different security features. One functionality is for key management. The other functionality is secure e-mail transfer. Key management is implemented as a set of secure protocols that will be examined in Section 3.2 in detail. They are used for key pair generation, initialization and public key upload, key obtainment, key update, and key removal purposes. Secure e-mail exchange is implemented in the CM as the capabilities of sending and receiving signed and/or encrypted e-mails on top of normal e-mail client operations.

3.2 Connection Protocols

Connection protocols are designed to accomplish different key management and distribution operations in a secure way. They are listed below:

1. Initialization and Public Key Settlement Protocol (*InitKeySet*)
2. Public Key Obtainment Protocol (*KeyObt*)
3. Public Key Update Protocol (*KeyUpdate*)
4. Public Key Removal Protocol (*KeyRem*)
5. Unsigned Public Key Removal Protocol (*USKeyRem*)
6. Unsigned Public Key Update Protocol (*USKeyUpdate*)

All of these protocols run within a domain except the key obtainment protocol. In *KeyObt* protocol, a domain server may need to talk to another domain server if public key of a user at a different domain is needed.

Initialization and Public Key Settlement Protocol (InitKeySet). This protocol is designed for users to upload their public keys to the PractiSES domain server (public key storage) for the first time. In order to authenticate the clients, server uses clients' private information that already exists in the public key storage, such as ID, shared-secret, birthday and some other identity information. The sequence diagram of *InitKeySet* protocol is presented in Figure 2.

1. The end user introduces himself/herself to the server by providing his/her ID and e-mail address.
2. The server retrieves the user's information stored in the public key storage. Then it matches the user ID and e-mail address received from the previous step with the ones in the public key storage. If they match, then the server asks the user for shared semi-secret information. Server signs the questions before sending them out.
3. User verifies server's signature over the questions. If valid, then he/she encrypts the answers using a randomly generated secret key and encrypts the same secret key using server's public key. The user sends all these encrypted data to the server.
4. Server decrypts the secret key using its own private key. Then it decrypts the user's answers using the secret key. The answers are compared to the corresponding information stored in the server's database. If they match, then the server sends an e-mail that contains a server-given Message Authentication Code (MAC) [4] password encrypted with the same secret key. Otherwise protocol stops.
5. The user accesses his/her inbox and retrieves the e-mail that contains the encrypted MAC password. The, he/she decrypts the MAC password using the secret key that he/she already knows from previous steps. This password is used to provide integrity and authenticity for the message that contains user's public key.
6. Server checks the MAC within the message that contains the user's public key. If verified, then public key is deemed legitimate and stored in the public key storage. Server sends a confirmation message about successful/unsuccessful key upload.

Security of the Protocol. An attacker who eavesdrops on the communication link between the client and the server cannot upload a fake public key since such an upload requires knowing the MAC password and consequently the secret key, which is generated by the client and encrypted using server's public key. The attacker cannot obtain those secrets.

Authentication of the client to the PractiSES server is a challenging issue since we do not assume that there is pre-shared full secret (such as a PIN number) between them due to practical difficulty of distributing them. However, if such a secret is pre-distributed, then the server always asks that value in step 2 of the protocol, so that authentication can be 100% assured. In the protocol, we assume semi-secrets shared between client and the server. An attacker who knows these secrets may try to impersonate a client starting with the beginning of the protocol. However, the attacker cannot fool the server to use an e-mail address for the client other than the one stored in its records. Thus, the attacker should have a continuous access to the client's actual inbox not only to obtain the MAC password to upload the bogus public key, but also to utilize the attack after the fake upload. We believe that such an environment, in which the attacker knows the semi-secrets and has the access to the client's inbox that is separately secured with traditional username/password mechanism, is not so likely in practice.

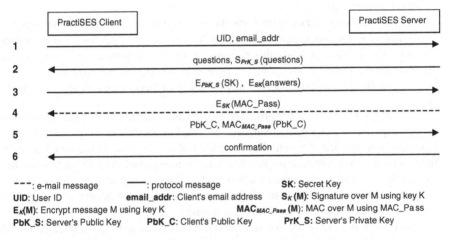

Fig. 2. Sequence diagram of InitKeySet protocol

Public Key Obtainment Protocol (KeyObt). *KeyObt* protocol is designed to obtain another user's public key from the public key storage with the server's signature on it. If the user of the public key requested belongs to the same domain with the requester, then the request is responded by the server of the home domain. If a public key owned by a user in a different domain is needed, then the home domain server needs to contact server of target user's domain. This protocol is presented in Figure 3.

1. Requesting end user sends the e-mail address of the target user (the user whose public key is being sought), the common name of the target user's domain and a randomly generated nonce value.

   Then the home server checks the domain's common name. If it is the same with home domain, then home server retrieves target's public key from its public key storage and continues with step 4. If the common name is foreign, then home server contacts with the server of foreign domain and continues with step 2.

2. Home server sends target user's e-mail address, common name of target user's domain, and newly generated nonce value of home server to the foreign server.
3. First foreign server retrieves target user's public key from its public key storage. Then, it responses to the home server with a message, which comprises from data and signature parts. Data part includes the values of the name, last name, e-mail address, and public key of the target user, the received nonce value of home server, and the certificate of foreign server issued by PractiSES CA. Here, certificate is a digitally signed document that provides a binding between foreign server's common name and its public key. The common name and public key of foreign server, validity period of the document and other fields (issuer name, serial number, etc.) constitute the certificate of foreign server. Foreign server signs the data part with its private key. In this way, home server makes sure about the legitimacy of the public key and the other information it received. Home server takes the response of foreign server, checks the correctness and validity of foreign server's certificate.
4. At this step, home server constructs the response message, which comprises from the name, last name, e-mail address, public key of the target user and the client's nonce value. Then it sends this message to the client with a signature generated using home server's private key. Client gets the signed message and verifies it using home server's public key. The public key of target user is ready for e-mail.

Security of the Protocol. In the protocol, nonce values are used to assure the freshness of the response of responders. Suppose an attacker records a server response for a key. Also assume that the same key is deleted at a later time. If the attacker replays the recorded server response for that key back to a requester after the deletion time, it can easily reintroduce the invalid key as valid. Using a nonce value in the protocol prevents such replay attacks since the requester would not accept a response that includes a nonce value it did not generate recently.

Since the public keys are not secrets, clients need not to be authenticated in order to request other users' public keys. However, the server should authenticate its response, which is implemented by the digital signature in steps 3.2 and 4. An attacker cannot forge that signature since it does not know of the private keys of the servers. Therefore, the attacker cannot present a fake public key as valid.

Other Protocols. The details of other protocols (*KeyUpdate, KeyRem, USKeyRem* and *USKeyUpdate*) are skipped for the sake of brevity. *KeyRem* and *KeyUpdate* are designed for the clients to remove and update their public keys at the PractiSES server, respectively. The security of the update/remove requests sent from client to server is provided by signing them using client's current private key. *USKeyRem* and *USKeyUpdate* are designed also for removing and updating public keys. The difference of these protocols from *KeyRem* and *KeyUpdate* is that *USKeyRem* and *USKeyUpdate* use Message Authentication Code (MAC) instead of digital signatures for integrity and authentication of the request. As in the *InitKeySet* protocol, the MAC password is sent out in an e-mail after a semi-secret-check type of authentication. In this way, the users can remove and update their keys securely even if they cannot authenticate themselves by using their private keys due to loss or compromise.

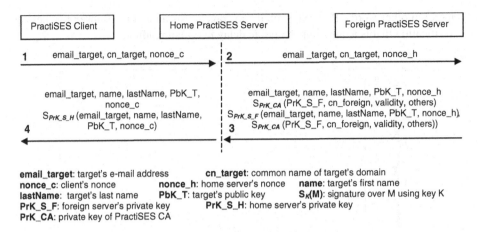

Fig. 3. Sequence diagram of KeyObt protocol

4   Performance and Implementation Issues

Connection protocols and secure e-mail client are implemented in Java. The protocols are leveraged on the TCP/IP protocol stack. PractiSES uses the Java Cryptographic Environment (JCE 1.2.2) for cryptographic primitives such as (i) 2048-bit RSA [5, 7] algorithm for public key encryption/decryption and together with SHA-1 [8] for digital signatures, (ii) Triple-DES (3-DES) [6] for conventional encryption and decryption, and (iii) Hash-Based MAC (HMAC) [9] function to provide message integrity and authentication.

In our simulations, we evaluate the performance PractiSES by analyzing the throughput of the PractiSES server and end-to-end latency. As the server, we use an ordinary PC with 2.5 GHz P4 processor, and as the client a PC with 1GHz P3 processor. Figure 4 shows that the server throughput decreases due to increased queuing delay as the number of key obtainment requests increase. For example, when the average key obtainment request is 35 requests/sec, the average server throughput is 24.35, that corresponds to 1000/24.35 ≈ 41 msec of average total server residency time (including waiting and processing times) per request. Since the server processing time is about 20 msec/request under light loads, and extra 21 msec would be considered as a good trade-off for having an average of 35 requests/sec that corresponds to about 1 million key requests per 8-hour period which is a reasonable daily load for a medium size organization.

The latency as seen by the client is another performance indicator. This latency includes key obtainment protocol run, cryptographic processing over the message and networking delays. The most important factor is, as in the previous analysis, is the load on the server. Figure 5 shows how the latency of message verification increases as the load on server gets larger. For the average load of 35 requests/second, which we used in our example for the previous analysis, the end-to-end latency is about 320 msec; in other words, PractiSES, on the average, costs an extra 320 msec for message verification that is a quite imperceptible delay in e-mail reading.

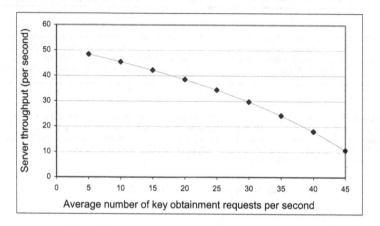

Fig. 4. The change of server throughput in terms of requests processed per second as average number of key requests changes

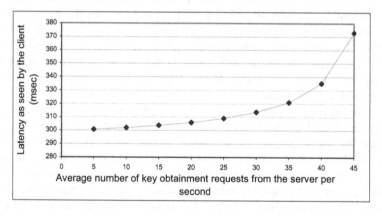

Fig. 5. The change of message verification latency as seen by the client while the average load on the server increases

5 Discussions and Conclusions

In this paper, we proposed an e-mail system, named PractiSES, for key distribution and management in secure e-mail processing. In this system, trusted centralized servers store the public keys and distribute them in an authentic way. We have implemented both server and client interfaces of PractiSES using Java programming language. Besides key management and distribution features, client part includes message encryption/decryption and signature/verification functions as well. PractiSES

Server distributes public keys on demand by sending out the requested public keys with its signature on it. It is a practical key distribution mechanism that does not require revocation control at the client side.

PractiSES takes advantage over S/MIME applications by escaping use of certificates for masses and over PGP by less complicated trust mechanism based on a trusted third party.

Every key operation, even initialization, is performed in an online manner in PractiSES. Moreover, decryption, signature verification and key obtainment services are performed transparent to the users. In other words, the client module senses the security requirements of each message and responds to those requirements automatically. This response is an intelligent one too; e.g. if the recipient cannot process a digitally signed e-mail, the sender's client module detects this by talking to the server and sends a normal message instead of a signed one.

Disclosure of e-mail addresses and other personal information in an uncontrolled fashion is not a problem of PractiSES.

Fortunately in PractiSES, it is not necessary to employ an extra mechanism for revocation control of end user public keys. Revocation of an end user public key in PractiSES is as easy as a database record update.

Our simulations show that a state-of-the-art PC can be used as the domain server for a medium-size organization with up to a traffic of one million e-mail messages per day. For larger organizations with higher e-mail traffic, it is always possible to use a more powerful server or several replicated servers that share the load. Thus the scalability problem of PractiSES due to load on server is not more than any server based application and thus tractable with a proper investment.

References

1. Ramsdell, B. (editor), S/MIME Version 3 Message Specification, RFC 2633, June 1999.
2. Network Associates, "PGP Freeware for Windows 95, Windows 98,Windows NT, Windows 2000 & Windows Millennium User's Guide Version 7.0", available from http://www.pgpi.org/doc/guide/7.0/en/win/, 2001.
3. Housley, R., W. Ford, W.Polk, and D. Solo, "Internet X.509 Public Key Infrastructure Certificate and CRL profile", RFC 2459, 1999.
4. Stallings, W., "Cryptography and Network Security, 3/E", Chapter 11, Prentice Hall, 2003.
5. J. Jonsson, B. Kaliski, "Public-Key Cryptography Standards (PKCS) #1: RSA Cryptography Specifications Version 2.1", RFC 3447, February 2003.
6. National Institute of Standards and Technology (NIST), "FIPS Publication 46-2: Data Encryption Standard", 1993.
7. Rivest, R., A. Shamir and L. Adleman, "A Method for Obtaining Digital Signatures and Public Key Cryptosystems", Comm. of the ACM, vol. 21, no. 2, pp. 120-126, Feb. 1978.
8. National Institute of Standards and Technology (NIST), "FIPS Publication 180-1: Secure Hash Standard", 1995.
9. Krawczyk, H., M. Bellare, and R. Canetti, "HMAC: Keyed-Hashing for Message Authentication", RFC2104, 1997.
10. Levi A., "How Secure is Secure Web Browsing", Comm. of the ACM, vol. 46, no. 7, pp. 152, July 2003.

A Preprocessor Adding Security to and Improving the Performances of Arithmetic and Huffman Codings

Ebru Celikel and Mehmet Emin Dalkılıç

Ege University, International Computer Institute, 35100 Bornova-Izmir, Turkey
{celikel, dalkilic}@ube.ege.edu.tr

Abstract. Arithmetic Coding and Huffman Coding are among the most common lossless compression algorithms. Their compression performances are relatively low as compared to some other tools. Still, they have widespread acceptance due to their high throughput rates. Both algorithms exploit symbol frequencies to achieve compression, which can be increased by redistributing the symbol statistics in a recoverable manner. We introduce a symbol redistributing scheme to serve as a preprocessor to improve compression. The preprocessor itself is an encryption machine providing compression and simple security. The preprocessor is succeeded by conventional compression tool to offer further compression. The overall scheme is called the Secure Compressor (*SeCom*). The system employing Arithmetic or Huffman Coding as compressor has been implemented and tested on sample texts in English and Turkish. Results show that *SeCom* considerably improves compression performances of both algorithms and introduces security to the system, as well.

1 Introduction

Compression is one of the most practical ways of optimal data storage and transfer. If the compression is lossless, then original data recovery is possible. In cases when the data of type text, compression is needed to be lossess. Because, only then the text is reobtained as it was. Arithmetic Coding [1] and Huffman Coding [2] are among the earliest lossless text compression tools. With publicly known algorithms, they provide compression to similar degrees on text.

In the following section, text compression performances of the conventional Arithmetic Coding and Huffman Coding algorithms are given. In the third section, a new scheme called SeCom, which increases the performances of both tools when used as a preprocessor, is introduced and explained in detail. Improved performance values measured with SeCom are given in the same section. The last section is the conclusion and suggests some ideas for further study on the subject.

2 Arithmetic and Huffman Codings as Conventional Lossless Compression Tools

Compression is basically an encoding in that, it represents the input data in another form, which is to require less space. To determine how to represent the input stream, the

T. Yakhno (Ed.): ADVIS 2004, LNCS 3261, pp. 420–429, 2004.
© Springer-Verlag Berlin Heidelberg 2004

encoder needs a model. The same model is then used by decoder to recover the original data. Both Arithmetic Coding and Huffman Coding algorithms use a statistics based model as seen on Figure 1 to compress data [3].

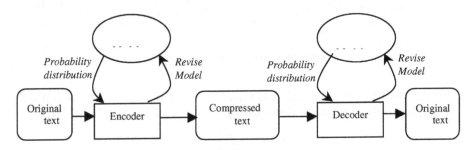

Fig. 1. A Statistical Model based lossless text compression

Arithmetic Coding replaces a stream of input symbols with a single floating point output number between 0 and 1 to obtain compression [4]. As the input text is encoded, this interval becomes narrower. On the other hand, as the interval becomes smaller, the number of bits needed to specify it grows. A high probability symbol narrows the interval less than a low probability message, so that high probability symbols contribute fewer bits to the coded message [5]. The Arithmetic Coder uses the symbol statistics provided by the model similar to the one on Figure 1.

Huffman Coding utilizes the statistical property of alphabets in the source stream and then produces respective codes for these alphabets. These codes are of variable length using integral number of bits [6]. The key to Huffman Coding is that, the codes for symbols having higher probability of occurrence are shorter than those codes for symbols with lower probability. This simple idea causes a reduction in the average code length, and thus the overall size of the compressed data is smaller than the original [7].

In Arithmetic Coding the codewords do not need to be integral number of bits, while in Huffman Coding they are integral number of bits.

2.1 Performances of Arithmetic and Huffman Codings

Using text files from standard English Calgary [8] and Canterbury [9] Corpora, and from Turkish YTU [10] and Uber [11] Corpora, we compressed them with Arithmetic Coding. We then calculated the compression performance of Arithmetic Coding on each text file. For that, we used the bits per character (*bpc*) measure. The results are shown in Figure 2.

Using pointwise compression values in Figure 2, we see that Arithmetic Coding has an average compression rate of 4.15 bpc on English and 4.38 bpc on Turkish texts. Results indicate that English texts can be compressed more than Turkish texts. One of the reasons why English is more compressible than Turkish is due to the fact

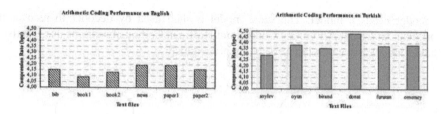

Fig. 2. Performance of Arithmetic Coding on English and Turkish texts

that English language has higher redundancy than Turkish and compression is achieved by exploiting the redundancy. Redundancy is defined by the formula in Eq. 1[12]:

$$R = 1 - \frac{H}{\log_2 P[s]} \tag{1}$$

According to Eq.1, having lower entropy causes a language to have more redundancy. Entropy (H) is a measure of the average information per letter in a meaningful string of plaintext and it is calculated by the formula:

$$H = \sum \left(-P[s] \times \log_2 P[s] \right) \tag{2}$$

Assuming that in Eq.2 the symbol probabilities, i.e. $P[s]$ of the source alphabet are equal, we get entropy values of $\log_2 27 = 4.75$ bpc and $\log_2 30 = 4.91$ bpc for English and Turkish, respectively. If we go further with symbol probabilities using digram, trigram, ..., n-gram contexts, as was done in Shannon's experiment [13], we get an entropy rate of 1.25 bpc for English. The same experiment repeated on Turkish texts has yielded 1.47 bpc for Turkish [14]. Using Eq. 1, the redundancy values calculated for English and Turkish are 73.68% and 70.06%, respectively.

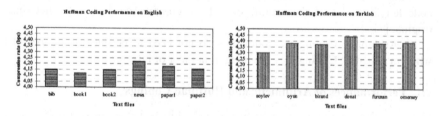

Fig. 3. Performance of Huffman Coding on English and Turkish texts

On the same sample texts, we measured the compression performance of Huffman Coding algorithm. The performance results obtained are listed in Fig. 3:

Figure 3 reveals that compression performance of Huffman Coding is very similar to that of Arithmetic Coding. The table also shows that the difference between English and Turkish text performances (Figure 2) is retained for Huffman Coding, as well. This means that both Arithmetic Coding and Huffman Coding compression performances are influenced by the source languages.

As Figures 2 and 3 indicates, we can get average compression rates of around 4 bpc with original Arithmetic Coding and Huffman Coding algorithms. To get better rates, we preceded them with a preprocessor, which is basically an encryption tool. This preprocessor encrypts, as well as compresses, the input text. It is then combined with a conventional compression algorithm to further compress the text. Whenever this compression tool is Arithmetic Coding or Huffman Coding, the system improves their compression performances. The preprocessor, in that sense, provides security to some degree while compressing. This is why it is called the secure compressor, i.e. *SeCom*. In the following section, the *SeCom* scheme is explained in detail.

3 Secure Compression (*SeCom*) Scheme

Compression is achieved by exploiting redundancy in input data. Motivated by the fact that the more redundant the input data, the higher the compression, we designed and developed a system to redistribute the symbol frequencies in the input stream. The developed system provides security to some degree, which is not considered much by the conventional compression tools. This is why it is called the secure compressor, i.e. *SeCom*.

The *SeCom* system is composed of encoder and decoder sides as seen on Figure 4. In the encoder side, preprocessing and compression phases are executed one after the other. In the former phase before encoding, the *plaintext* is first divided into n equal parts, where n is a predetermined text division index and is greater than 1. In this manner, $|P|/n$ n-grams are generated out of input text. For small n, the system provides low level of security with fast execution speed. On the other hand, larger n introduces higher levels of security while increasing the complexity and the execution time of the scheme.

Both encoder and decoder process the *plaintext* in a symbolwise manner, i.e. step by step. For encoding, the system does a simple table lookup: At each *encoding* step, the *encoder* takes the ith *n-gram* and finds the corresponding *cipher symbol (C_i)* via the *encryption matrix*. This encoding provides an initial compression given in Eq.3:

$$\left(1 - \left[\frac{(|P|-|P|/n)}{|P|}\right]\right) \times 100 = \% \left[100 \times \left(\frac{n-1}{n}\right)\right] \tag{3}$$

In order to make the *ciphertext* uniquely decodable by the decoder, a varying length special bitstream, called the *help string (H)*, is created. *Help string* encoding is performed in a symbolwise manner, as well. It means that, for each *n-gram$_i$*, *help string* bits are generated individually. At the end of $|P|/n$ *encoding* steps, C_is and H_is are combined to form the *intermediate output* θ_i, where $\theta_i = C||H$. Although using *help string* degrades the *initial compression ratio* (Eq.3), it makes *ciphertext* uniquely decodable.

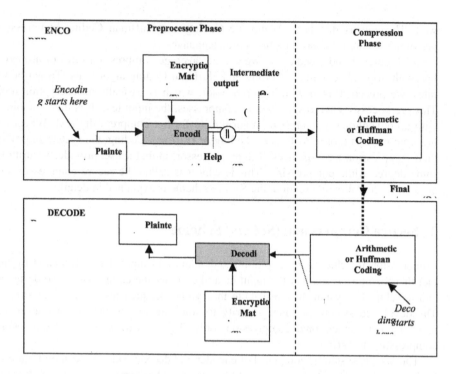

Fig. 4. Secure Compression (*SeCom*) scheme

Let's encode the sample plaintext P='spacecraft~to~mars' with *SeCom* scheme. For the given plaintext |P|=18. Assume that, the text division index $n=2$ and the encryption matrix is generated out of digram statistics of the source language, i.e. English. The encryption matrix is shown in Figure 5.

Table 1. *Encoding* of a sample English text with *SeCom*

	1	2	3	4	5	6	7	8	9
P	s	a	e	r	f	~	o	m	r
P	p	c	c	a	t	T	~	a	s
C	I	I	J	D	G	~	B	B	F
H	10100	01	0000011	00001111	0100	001	0110	01100	110

Encoding is performed as follows: We first divide P into 2 parts and obtain 18/2=9 *digrams* (Table 1). Then, we determine *cipher symbols* corresponding to each *digram* with simple table lookup through the encryption matrix shown in Figure 4. The *ciphertext* obtained is C='IIJDG~BBF'.

For *receiver* to uniquely decode the *plaintext*, a varying length special bitstream called *help string* (H) is generated for each *n-gram* encoded. *Help string encoding* is carried out in a dynamic fashion to minimize its length. In general, while *encoding n-gram_i*, the corresponding *help string* bits (H_i) are constructed based on a length-*m* *context*. Since no *context* exists for the very first *n-gram* (i.e., *n-gram_1*), *help string* for it (H_1) needs to be encoded differently: It is encoded as *n-gram_1*'s *row index* in the encryption matrix.

For the ongoing example, the very first step is to encode the *digram_1*='sp'. *Help string* H_1 for *digram_1*='sp' is encoded as '10100', since 's' occurs in the 20th row of the encryption matrix. The reason why H_1 is encoded with 5 bits is that, each *cipher symbol* occurs 27 times within the encryption matrix shown in Figure 5. So, minimum of $\lceil \log_2(27) \rceil$=5 bits are needed to uniquely identify it.

For generating other help string bits, i.e. H_i (*i*>1), a length-*m context* is used. If we choose *m*=*n*, then the *context* becomes *n-gram_{i-1}*. First, *n-gram_i* that is mapped into C_i is searched within the *n-gram_{i-1}*'s *successors-list*, which is the list of *n-grams* that follow the *context* and are mapped into the same *cipher symbol* as C_i. This list is constructed by using *q-gram* statistics of the source language, where *q*=*m*+*n*. If, for example, *m*=*n*=2 then we need to use *fourgram* statistics. To eliminate the cost of storing the full *fourgram* list with $|A|^4$ entries, where $|A|$ is the source alphabet size, we applied *SeCom* by employing the most frequent 24.688 *fourgrams*.

Following the *context n-gram_{i-1}*, the number of *n-grams* (denoted by d_i) that are mapped into the same *cipher symbol* as C_i determines H_i's length. If *n-gram_i* is found within the *context*'s *successors-list*, then its index in that list is encoded as H_i with $\lceil \log_2(d_i) \rceil$ bits.

If the ith *n-gram* is not found in the ith *context*'s *successors-list*, first an *escape sequence* (H_{esc}), which is a special bit stream consisting of all-zeros, is issued using as many number of bits as $\lceil \log_2(d_i) \rceil$. Second, the encryption matrix row index of the not found *n-gram* is emitted as H_i with $\lceil \log_2(r_i) \rceil$ bits, where r_i is the number of times C_i occurs in E. In fact, we subtract the number of C_i-encoded *n-grams* occurring in the *context*'s *successors-list* from r_i. Finally, the not found *n-gram* is appended to the end of the *context*'s *successors-list*. Thus, next time we encode the *help string* for the same *n-gram* following the same *context*, no *escape sequence* would be needed, meaning fewer bits in the *help string* (H). This is why *help string* encoding is called *dynamic*.

In the second encoding step, we utilize the *help string* encoding scheme described above, to encode the second *digram* of the sample text, i.e. *digram_2*='ac' (with C_2='I'). For that, we search 'ac' within its *context*'s ('sp') *successors-list*. There are two *digrams* ('ac' and 'ir') that are mapped into the same *cipher symbol* as C_2, i.e. 'I'. We also need to consider an extra case when the searched *n-gram* is not found within the current *context*'s *successors-list*. Therefore, we have 3 cases that follow the current *context* ('sp') in our example, leading to need for $\lceil \log_2(3) \rceil$=2 bits to encode the corresponding *help string* bits. Since 'ac' is the first *digram* in that list, then H_2='01'.

	~	a	b	c	d	e	f	g	h	i	j	k	l	m	n	o	p	q	r	s	t	u	v	w	x	y	z
~	Z	A	G	J	L	O	I	Q	D	C	U	T	M	H	N	E	K	W	P	B	~	R	V	F	Y	S	X
a	E	V	L	I	G	T	R	M	S	F	Y	N	B	H	~	X	O	Z	C	D	A	P	K	Q	W	J	U
b	H	E	L	S	N	~	W	V	P	G	J	Y	C	M	O	B	T	Z	D	I	K	A	Q	R	X	F	U
c	F	C	Y	K	P	B	R	X	A	E	T	I	H	S	W	~	N	Q	G	M	D	J	O	V	Z	L	U
d	~	D	R	P	H	A	T	K	V	B	S	W	I	L	M	C	O	Y	F	E	U	G	Q	N	Z	J	X
e	~	E	U	J	D	H	O	R	T	M	Z	X	F	I	B	S	N	V	A	C	G	W	K	Q	P	L	Y
f	~	E	W	L	N	D	F	O	V	C	U	S	H	M	Q	A	P	Y	B	K	G	I	X	T	Z	J	R
g	~	E	Q	S	L	B	U	M	A	F	X	R	I	N	J	C	P	Z	D	H	O	G	V	T	Y	K	W
h	B	A	N	U	Q	~	O	W	R	C	X	T	K	L	J	D	S	V	G	I	E	H	Y	M	Z	F	P
i	F	M	P	D	H	J	N	K	X	V	W	Q	C	G	~	E	O	U	I	B	A	T	L	Z	S	Y	R
j	D	C	T	H	M	A	X	R	P	E	V	K	I	J	Q	B	F	Y	G	O	U	~	L	N	Z	S	W
k	A	F	P	N	U	~	S	R	L	B	V	O	J	D	C	G	T	Z	M	E	Q	K	W	I	Y	H	X
l	~	D	O	Q	G	A	K	S	V	C	Y	M	B	N	U	E	P	Z	T	I	H	J	L	R	X	F	W
m	A	B	G	L	R	~	M	U	Q	C	W	S	O	I	K	D	F	Z	N	J	P	H	V	T	X	E	Y
n	~	G	X	H	A	D	O	B	S	I	V	K	L	P	M	E	T	W	U	F	C	N	Q	R	Z	J	Y
o	B	Q	R	N	I	T	D	S	V	O	W	P	H	E	~	J	M	Z	A	K	F	C	L	G	X	U	Y
p	D	C	S	N	O	~	Q	T	H	G	W	V	E	M	R	B	I	Y	A	K	J	F	U	P	Z	L	X
q	A	B	J	S	K	L	T	M	N	C	U	V	G	D	O	I	P	E	H	W	Q	~	X	F	Y	R	Z
r	~	D	T	M	G	A	S	N	U	C	X	O	P	K	I	B	R	Z	L	F	E	J	Q	V	Y	H	W
s	~	E	U	J	S	B	T	R	C	F	Y	P	K	N	Q	D	I	V	O	G	A	H	W	M	Z	L	X
t	A	E	T	M	U	C	P	W	~	D	Y	V	K	O	N	B	Q	Z	F	G	J	H	R	L	X	I	S
u	E	M	N	H	I	J	O	G	V	L	Y	P	D	K	~	R	F	Z	A	B	C	Q	W	X	T	U	S
v	D	B	V	O	M	~	U	S	R	A	Y	P	H	K	G	C	L	Z	J	E	N	I	Q	T	W	F	X
w	D	B	P	O	N	C	K	U	A	~	X	R	J	M	F	E	S	Z	G	H	I	Q	W	T	V	L	Y
x	~	F	U	C	S	D	P	W	G	E	X	Y	N	R	V	K	A	Q	J	M	B	H	O	T	I	L	Z
y	~	E	L	N	P	B	Q	S	U	D	Y	T	G	H	K	A	F	Z	J	C	I	O	V	M	X	W	R
z	B	A	L	P	V	~	Y	R	G	C	X	S	J	K	Q	D	N	Z	H	M	W	F	O	T	U	I	E

Fig. 5. Encryption matrix using digram statistics ($n=2$)

In the third encoding step, we encode $digram_3=$'ec' which maps to $C_3=$'J'. Since 'ec' does not exist within the *context* $(digram_2)=$'ac's *successors-list*, we first need to issue an *escape sequence* as '00', because $d=3$ and $\lceil \log_2(3) \rceil = 2$. Then, we encode the non-existing *digram*'s row index in the encryption matrix, excluding the already *successor-list* existing ones, as '00011'. H_3 is the combination of *escape sequence* with the *index*, i.e. '0000011'. Encoding of the following *n-grams* continues likewise. At the end of $|P|/n$ encoding steps, *ciphertext* (C) together with *help string* (H) forms the *intermediate output* (θ_1).

Upon successful completion of encoding in the preprocessor phase, we continue with the compression phase. For that, a compression tool which can be any efficient conventional lossless compression algorithm is used to compress the *intermediate output* further. By compressing the *intermediate output*, the *final output* (θ_2) is obtained. This *final output* is then sent to the *decoder*.

Within the *SeCom* scheme while generating the encryption matrix, language statistics can be reflected to obtain more compressible *ciphertexts*.

SeCom scheme adds security to some degree to the overall compression system. Because, each *n-gram* of the *plaintext* is represented with a single *cipher symbol* and if the encryption matrix is kept secret, it would be hard to recover the *plaintext*.

For practical reasons, we have implemented and tested *SeCom* on text files. Nevertheless, simply by extending the encryption matrix to include other (non-letter) symbols, *SeCom* can well be applied to any input data type.

While implementing the scheme, for the preprocessor phase we selected $n=2$ for faster execution and used digram statistics of the source language to generate the encryption matrix. For the compression phase, we employed once Arithmetic Coding and then Huffman Coding as the compression algorithm. Results indicate that *Secom* improves the compression performances of both of these algorithms. In the following subsections, these improvements are presented.

3.1 Combining *SeCom* with Arithmetic Coding

When we applied the *SeCom* with Arithmetic Coding on English and Turkish texts, compressing the *help string* by Arithmetic Coding caused it to expand. For this reason, we only compressed the *ciphertext* of the *intermediate output* and left the *help string* intact. So, the compression rates given in Table 2 (as well as in Table 3) are calculated over compressed *ciphertext* and uncompressed *help string* values:

Table 2. Performance comparison of original Arithmetic Coding and ours on English

ENGLISH	Filename	Original	SeCom/Arithmetic	improvement %
ARTH	bib	4.15	3.59	13.45%
	book1	4.09	3.45	15.66%
	book2	4.13	3.41	17.38%
	news	4.19	3.64	13.18%
	paper1	4.19	3.50	16.57%
	paper2	4.16	3.46	16.77%
Average		4.15	3.51	15.50%

As seen on Table 2, using *SeCom* followed by Arithmetic Coding improves the original compression performance by 15.50% on English texts, on the average.

We repeated the above experiment on Turkish sample text files. The results yielded are listed in Table 3:

Table 3. Performance comparison of original Arithmetic Coding and ours on Turkish

TURKISH	Filename	Original	SeCom/Arithmetic	improvement %
ARTH	soylev	4.29	3.54	17.55%
	oyun	4.38	3.58	18.33%
	birand	4.35	3.48	19.99%
	donat	4.48	4.14	7.60%
	furuzan	4.37	3.53	19.19%
	omersey	4.38	3.56	18.83%
Average		4.38	3.64	16.92%

As Table 3 indicates, a better improvement is achieved with Arithmetic Coding on Turkish texts than on English texts (with improvement percentages being 16.92% and 15.50% for Turkish and English, respectively).

3.2   Combining SeCom with Huffman Coding

We this time applied the *SeCom* scheme with Huffman Coding being the compression algorithm on English and Turkish texts. The results on English texts are listed in Table 4. The compression rates in this table are calculated over compressed *ciphertext* and compressed *help string* values.

Improvement with Huffman Coding on English texts is almost as much as the improvement with Arithmetic Coding on English texts. As Table 4 shows, the average compression performance improvement is 14.98% on English texts.

Table 4. Performance Comparison of original Huffman Coding and ours on English

ENGLISH	Filename	Original	SeCom/Huffman	improvement %
HUFF	bib	4.15	3.62	12.86%
	book1	4.12	3.54	14.12%
	book2	4.15	3.46	16.56%
	news	4.22	3.70	12.21%
	paper1	4.18	3.46	17.33%
	paper2	4.16	3.46	16.80%
Average		**4.16**	**3.54**	**14.98%**

Repeating the same experiment on Turkish sample text files, we obtained the Table 5 below:

Table 5. Performance comparison of original Huffman Coding and ours on Turkish

TURKISH	Filename	Original	SeCom/Huffman	improvement %
HUFF	soylev	4.30	3.54	17.68%
	oyun	4.38	3.59	18.08%
	birand	4.37	3.54	18.92%
	donat	4.44	4.04	9.02%
	furuzan	4.38	3.58	18.26%
	omersey	4.39	3.61	17.84%
Average		**4.38**	**3.65**	**16.63%**

As Table 5 indicates, the improvement with Huffman Coding on Turkish texts is better than the improvement with Huffman Coding on English texts (with 16.63% and 14.98%, respectively). This difference is caused by different redundancy levels of these languages.

4   Conclusion

Arithmetic Coding and Huffman Coding are among the standard lossless compression tools. Although they are not as good as some other compression tools like PPM (Prediction by Partial Matching) [15] or BWT (Burrows Wheeler Transform) [16], they are quite fast. The average compression rate achieved by Arithmetic Coding and Huffman Coding are around 4 bpc on text, while PPM and BWT provide compression rates at around 2 bpc. The reason why Arithmetic Coding and Huffman Coding are so widely used today is the high throughput rate provided by them.

In order to increase the compression performance of Arithmetic Coding and Huffman Coding, we developed a new system, called the Secure Compressor (*SeCom*). It is a preprocessor which precedes the compression tool being either Arithmetic Coding or Huffman Coding. We implemented the scheme and measured the compression rates on English and Turkish texts. The results indicate that *SeCom* does improve the compression performance of both algorithms. Further studies can be carried out with other lossless compression tools.

References

1. Nelson, M.: Arith. Coding+Stat. Modeling=Data Comp., Dr. Dobb's Journal (1991)
2. Smith, S.W.: The Scientist and Engineer's Guide to Digital Signal Processing, Ch: 27: Data Compression, USA (2000)
3. Teahan, W.J.: "Modelling English Text", D.Phil. thesis, The University of Waikato, Hamilton, New Zealand (1998)
4. Nelson, M.: The Data Compression Book, M&T Publishing, New York, USA, (1996)
5. Lelewer, D. A., Hirschberg, D. S.: Data Compression, ACM Computing Surveys, Vol. 19, No. 3, September (1987)
6. Chiang, L.: Lossless and Lossy Image Compression, Digital Data Compression, PhD Thesis, http://www.image.cityu.edu.hk/~loben/thesis.node2.htm, Febr., (1998)
7. Witten, I., Moffat, A. Bell, T.C.: Managing Gigabytes Compressing and Indexing Documents and Images, 2nd ed., Morgan Kauffman Publishers, Inc., San Francisco, California, USA, (1999)
8. Calgary Corpus URL: ftp.cpcs.ucalgary.ca/pub/projects/text.compression.corpus
9. Canterbury Corpus URL: http://corpus.canterbury.ac.nz
10. Diri B.: "A System Based on the Analysis, Complying With the Turkish Language Structure, and Dynamic Word Based Lossless Compression of Turkish Texts", PhD Thesis (in Turkish) , Yildiz Technical University, Istanbul, Turkey (1999)
11. Celikel E.: "Modelling and Compression of Turkish Texts", PhD Thesis (in Turkish), Ege University, International Computer Institute, Izmir, Turkey, (2004)
12. Stinson, D. R.: Cryptography Theory and Practice, CRC Press, USA (1995)
13. Shannon, C.: A Mathematical Theory of Communication", The Bell Sytem Technical Journal, Vol. 27, pp. 379-423, 623-656, October, (1948)
14. Dalkilic, M.E., Dalkilic, G.: 2000, "On the Entropy, Redundancy and Compression of Contemporary Printed Turkish", Proceedings of International Symposium on Computer and Information Sciences (ISCIS) XV, pp. 60-67, 11-13   October, Yildiz Technical University, Istanbul, Turkey, (2000)
15. Burrows, M., Wheeler, D. J.: A Block-Sorting Lossless Data Compression Algorithm", Digital Systems Research Center, 130 Lytton Avenue, Palo Alto, California, USA, (1994)
16. PPM ftp://ftp.cs.waikato.ac.nz/pub/compression.ppm

Performance Evaluation of Digital Audio Watermarking Techniques Designed in Time, Frequency and Cepstrum Domains

Murat Şehirli[1], Fikret Gürgen[1], and Serhat Ikizoğlu[2]

[1]Boğaziçi University, Systems Control and Computer Eng. Dept.,
Bebek 34342 Istanbul, Turkey
{sehirli, gurgen}@boun.edu.tr
[2]Istanbul Technical University, Electrical Eng. Dept.,
Maslak 34469 Istanbul, Turkey
ikizoglu@elk.itu.edu.tr

Abstract. This study investigates the performances of a variety of audio watermarking techniques designed in time, frequency and cepstrum domains. A framework of comparison is performed with respect to bit error rate (BER), objective and subjective perceptual quality, computational complexity and robustness to signal processing such as low-pass filtering, requantization and MPEG Layer 3 (MP3) compression. It is observed that the cepstrum domain technique is superior to other techniques in terms of almost all criteria. Additionally, a new watermark embedding technique is introduced that combines frequency hopping spread spectrum (FHSS) and frequency masking (FM) techniques. It is experimentally concluded that the proposed technique performs fairly well and is robust to MP3 compression.

1 Introduction

In the last years, a necessity has arisen for copyright protection of electronic media such as audio, image, video, etc. The efficiency and easiness of distribution, reproduction and manipulation of multimedia content over the Internet at very low cost has caused significant problems associated with copyright protection. Illegal and unlimited distribution of digital data without loss of fidelity is undesirable since it may cause considerable financial loss [1]. A typical example of this problem is the piracy of high-quality music across the Internet in MP3 format. Digital watermarking is proposed as a partial solution of the problem of protection of the intellectual property rights (IPR) of digital multimedia data and digital libraries serving to identify the owner or the distributor.

Digital watermarking allows media producers to embed sideband data into a host signal, such as author or copyright information. Various techniques have been proposed for watermarking audio, image and video, and comprehensive surveys of these technologies may be seen in the literature [1-11]. In the case of audio watermarking, some evaluation frameworks were recently described [12, 13]. Among these, [12] is

T. Yakhno (Ed.): ADVIS 2004, LNCS 3261, pp. 430–440, 2004.

limited to five approaches that are proposed formerly. Consequently, some recently proposed approaches [4,7-9] are not incorporated. On the other hand, [13] mainly studies the detection performance for MP3 and MPEG-2/4 AAC bitstream watermarking before and after applying selected attacks. Our study extends and generalizes the comparison results of the previous evaluation algorithms by including recent ones and additionally introducing a new one. This performance evaluation framework is used to evaluate nine audio watermarking algorithms from the literature in the vicinity of the proposed algorithm.

In Section 2, we summarize the time, frequency and cepstrum domain watermarking techniques with a common convention. In Section 3 we introduce the proposed technique developed as a combination of two formerly projected frequency domain techniques. In Section 4, we present the evaluation framework as a set of criteria. In Section 5, we provide experimental data and an analysis of the evaluated algorithms. Finally, in Section 6, we conclude our discussion.

2   Time, Frequency and Cepstrum Domain Audio Watermarking Techniques

The digital watermark (WM) is a digital code, which is robustly and imperceptibly embedded in the host data and typically has information about the origin of the data [1]. The WM, $w(n)$ is inserted into the host signal, $x(n)$ to produce the watermarked signal, $\bar{x}(n)$. Three natural formulae have been proposed by Cox *et al.* [2] for WM embedding where α represents the strength of the WM:

$$\bar{x}(n) = x(n) + \alpha.w(n) \tag{1}$$

$$\bar{x}(n) = x(n)\big(1 + \alpha.w(n)\big) \tag{2}$$

$$\bar{x}(n) = x(n)\big(e^{\alpha.w(n)}\big) \tag{3}$$

Eqn. (1) may not be appropriate when $x(n)$ values vary widely. Equations (2) and (3) give similar results when $\alpha w(n)$ is small [2]. Also for positive $x(n)$, (3) may be viewed as an application of (1) where the logarithms of the original values are used. For most cases (2) is suitable.

The WM is a sequence which consists of plus and minus ones: $w(m)\epsilon(-1,+1)$. One way of embedding the WM is to break the host signal into blocks and embed one bit of the WM sequence to each block sequentially. The watermarked signal $\bar{x}(n)$ is the combination of all independently encoded signal blocks in sequence. In the formulations m denotes the index of the blocks; n and k stand for the indexes of the samples in a block of an audio signal. The number of the blocks is $M=TS/N$ with TS representing the total number of the samples in the host signal and N the total number of the samples in a block. Thus: $1 \leq n$, $k \leq N$ and $1 \leq m \leq M$.

The WM can be embedded in time, frequency and cepstrum domains. In time domain techniques the samples of the host signal are modified according to a special rule depending on the technique. For frequency and cepstrum domain techniques, we need a transformation before modifying the samples of the host signal. Typically discrete Fourier transform (DFT), discrete cosine transform (DCT) or cepstrum transform are used for this purpose.

Audio signals are represented by much less samples per time interval compared with image and video signals. As a result, in audio watermarking the amount of the WM to be embedded robustly and inaudibly into the host signal, is considerably less. Moreover the human auditory system (HAS) is much more sensitive than the human visual system (HVS), which causes the satisfaction of the imperceptibility requirement to be far more difficult to achieve in audio watermarking in comparison to that for image and video [1].

Following audio watermarking techniques are investigated in this study: changing the least significant bit technique (LSB), phase changing technique. (PHASE), echo hiding technique (ECHO), DC-level shifting technique (DCSHIFT), direct sequence spread spectrum technique (DSSS), frequency hopping spread spectrum technique (FHSS), time hopping spread spectrum technique (THSS), cepstrum domain technique (CEPS), frequency masking (FM) and frequency hopping spread spectrum with frequency masking technique (FMFHSS). Among these, LSB, ECHO, DSSS, THSS and DCSHIFT are time domain techniques, whereas PHASE, FHSS, FM and FMFHSS are frequency domain techniques; CEPS proceeds in cepstrum domain.

The common feature of time domain techniques is to create a WM signal and to embed it into the original signal in time domain. Bender *et al.* [3] have discussed about a few techniques like low bit coding, phase coding, echo data hiding and a spread spectrum technique based on direct sequence spread spectrum. The simplest watermarking technique is the LSB [3]. Here the WM is hidden in the *LSB* plane. In this technique, there is no significant audible difference between the original and the watermarked signals. Nevertheless the main disadvantage is its poor immunity to manipulation and its weakness in channel noise and requantization.

In the ECHO [3], the WM is embedded into the host audio signal by introducing an echo with duration of about 1/1000 of a second. A delay time of δ_{+1} second and δ_{-1} second are used to embed +1 and −1 respectively. The delayed signal is multiplied by α. The DSSS and THSS techniques use a pseudo-noise (PN) sequence like the other spread spectrum techniques [3]. A key is used to encode the information in the transmitter and the same key is needed to decode it at the receiver side. The key is mostly the initial value and length of the PN sequence. The THSS is a modification of the DSSS. It also uses the PN sequence, where only a selected number of the components are modified in each block. The DCSHIFT is proposed by Uludağ *et al.* [4] which is based on shifting the DC level of each blocks of the host audio signal to positive or negative levels to indicate the WM bits +1 or −1. In this method α determines the amount of the DC-level shift while the normalized power of each block is used for inaudibility purposes.

Several techniques embed the WM into the host signal in the frequency domain. The PHASE [3] is based on changing the phase of a certain number of samples in the audio signal. This technique has no dependency on α scale. The audio signal is broken into blocks of length N and each block is divided into sub-blocks of length N_q.

The phase values of the samples in one of the sub-blocks are replaced with a new phase value, ϕ_w that is multiplied by the WM bit.

The FHSS proposed by Cox et al. [2] uses PN sequence like the DSSS and THSS techniques; however the embedding is realized in the frequency domain. A selected set of DCT coefficients is changed in each block. Also Barni et al. [5] have proposed a similar DCT domain technique.

One major advantage of the frequency domain is to employ human perceptual properties for watermarking. Swanson et al. [6] have proposed an audio watermarking technique that directly exploits temporal and frequency perceptual masking to guarantee the embedded WM to be inaudible and robust. The WM is embedded by breaking the host audio signal into blocks and by adding the product of a perceptually shaped PN sequence and the WM bit. For the FM, the masking model defined in ISO-MPEG Audio Psycho-acoustic Model 1 for Layer 1 [10] is used as suggested in [6]. Ho and Wang [7] suggest applying the quantization index modulation (QIM) algorithm to embed the WM in order to obtain high recovery rate after the attack by commonly used audio data manipulations, such as D/A conversion, low-pass filtering etc. Cvejic and Seppanen [8] present a scheme based on the frequency hopping in the spectral domain and uses attack characterization. They proclaim that compared to standard direct sequence approach, they achieve higher robustness against standard WM attacks.

Li and Yu have proposed an audio watermarking technique in the cepstrum domain [9]. They embed the WM by manipulating the mean of the cepstrum coefficients. The audio signal is broken into blocks with length N. The cepstrum coefficients of each block are calculated. The mean of the real part of the cepstrum coefficients in each block is set to zero. The cepstrum coefficients remain unchanged if the WM bit is a -1, whereas a bias is added to the cepstrum coefficients if the WM bit is a $+1$. The watermarked signal is obtained from the inverse cepstrum procedure for each block.

3 Proposed Frequency Domain Watermarking Technique

A frequency hopping spread spectrum with frequency masking technique (FMFHSS) is proposed in this study. The FMFHSS utilizes the advantages of the FHSS and the FM techniques. The WM embedding method is shown in Figure 1. The host audio signal is broken into blocks with a length of N=512 samples. The power spectrum is calculated and by using the MPEG Layer 1 model, minimum-masking threshold, MMT is found for each block. PN sequence is weighted by the MMT in the frequency domain as:

$$\overline{PN}(k) = PN(k) \cdot MMT(k) \tag{4}$$

where $PN(k) = FFT\{pn(n)\}$ and $\overline{pn}(n) = IFFT\{\overline{PN}(k)\}$.

Additionally a temporal masking is applied for inaudibility purposes in the time domain. Here, the temporal masking effects are approximated by using the envelope of the host audio signal for each block. The estimated envelope increases with the signal and decays as $e^{-\beta}$ [6]. As an additive process the DCT of each block is computed:

$$X_m(k) = DCT\{x_m(n)\} \tag{5}$$

In each block, the WM is embedded by using only a selected set of DCT coefficients. The embedding can be formulated as (6) with K representing the set of selected components in a block. Here for each block, if the related coefficient belongs to K, then the WM bit is multiplied by the shaped PN sequence coefficient, $\overline{pn}(n)$ and attenuated by α, also shaped by the temporal mask, $temp_m(n)$ in the time domain and finally added to the DCT coefficient of the host signal. In case the related coefficient does not belong to K, it is left unchanged:

$$\overline{X}_m(k) = \begin{cases} X_m(k) + s_m(k) & \text{if } k \in K \\ X_m(k) & \text{if } k \notin K \end{cases} \tag{6}$$

where

$$s_m(n) = \alpha.w(m)\,\overline{pn}(n).temp_m(n).$$

The watermarked signal is obtained by performing the inverse DCT (IDCT):

$$\overline{x}_m(n) = IDCT\{\overline{X}_m(k)\} \tag{7}$$

In the detection phase, first the watermarked signal is broken into blocks with length $N = 512$. Then the DCT of each block is computed. The WM is decoded according to the sign of the correlation, $\rho(\overline{X}_m', pn)$ between the DCT coefficients of the selected components that belong to the set K of each block and the PN sequence as:

$$\overline{w}(m) = \begin{cases} -1 & \text{if } \rho(\overline{X}_m', pn) < 0 \\ +1 & \text{if } \rho(\overline{X}_m', pn) > 0 \end{cases} \tag{8}$$

with $\overline{X}_m(k) = DCT\{\overline{x}_m(n)\}$ and $\overline{X}_m'(k) = \overline{X}_m(k)$ $\quad$ if $k \in K$.

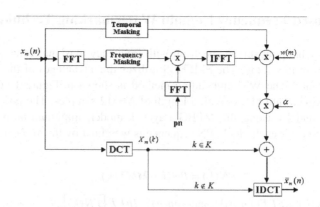

Fig. 1. Watermark embedding process in the frequency hopping spread spectrum with frequency masking technique (FMFHSS)

This method uses frequency and temporal masking, so it fits better to the conditions of listening as in the case of the FM technique [6]. It is observed that this method gives better results than those of FM since it also uses FHSS features.

4 Evaluation Criteria

4.1 Bit Error Rate (BER)

BER is the amount of WM data that may be reliably embedded within a host signal. For embedded $w(m)$ and extracted $\overline{w}(m)$ WM sequences of length M bits, the BER (in percent) is defined as:

$$BER = \frac{100}{M} \sum_{m=1}^{M} \begin{cases} 1 \; if \; \overline{w}(m) \neq w(m) \\ 0 \; if \; \overline{w}(m) = w(m) \end{cases} \tag{9}$$

4.2 Objective and Subjective Perceptual Quality

The perceptual quality is related to imperceptibility of embedded WM data within the host signal per unit time. This ensures that the quality of the host signal is not perceivably distorted or the WM is imperceptible to a listener. For this purpose, we use signal-to-noise ratio (SNR) as an objective measure and a listening test as a subjective measure. SNR is calculated as follows:

$$SNR = 10.\log_{10} \left\{ \frac{\sum_{m=1}^{M} x^2(m)}{\sum_{m=1}^{M} [\overline{x}(m) - x(m)]^2} \right\} \tag{10}$$

A subjective listening test similar to the one in [11] is performed to compare the audio watermarking techniques due to the listening quality of the watermarked audio, in other words, imperceptibility of the WM.

4.3 Computational Complexity

The embedding time is defined as the time that is needed to embed the WM into the host signal and the extracting time is the period that elapses for the extraction of the WM data from the watermarked signal.

4.4 Robustness to Signal Processing

Watermarked signals may commonly face conditioning such as low-pass filtering, re-quantization and MP3 compression. Although these operations might not affect the perceived quality of the host signal, they may cause to corruption of the WM data.

5 Experimental Data and Results

The performance analysis of ten audio watermarking techniques is carried out that a comparison is made according to BER, objective and subjective perceptual quality, robustness to some signal processing operations and computational complexity. Four different audio signals are used as host signals. These are chosen from four different classes of music: classic, jazz, pop and rock, which have different spectral properties. Each signal of duration of 10 seconds is sampled at 44100 Hz, and represented by 16 bits per sample. In the experiments, the methodology was common for all techniques: Ten different WMs are first embedded into a host signal one at each time and then extracted back from each marked signal. The original and the extracted WMs are compared and the BER is calculated according to (9) for each WM. This process is repeated for each technique and each host signal. For all of the techniques it is assumed that in the decoder parts the host and the watermarked signals are synchronized.

Each audio watermarking algorithm is implemented in MATLAB 5.3 and the experiments are carried out by using an Intel Pentium IV PC with a 1.4 GHz processor. For the techniques FHSS, THSS and FMFHSS, $N/64$ samples in a block are modified in the experiments. For all of the techniques except PHASE and LSB, which do not depend on α, α is set to a critical value so that the BER is less than 1% with the possible maximum SNR value.

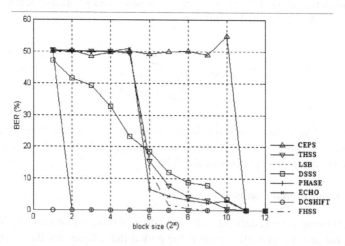

Fig. 2. Bit error rate (BER) as a function of block size

Fig. 2 illustrates the BER as a function of the block size (N) for eight of the ten techniques. It is noticeable that the BER decreases with the increase of the block size for the techniques FHSS, DSSS, ECHO and THSS. On the other hand, the block size determines the length of the embedded WM in an audio signal. In this study, during the WM embedding process one bit of the WM sequence is embedded into each block of the host signal for all of the techniques. The point should also be mentioned that the computation time decreases as the block size increases. Since FM and FMFHSS techniques use the MPEG Layer 1 model that is based on a block size of $N=512$ [6,10], this size is used in the experiments for these two techniques. BER is acceptable for a block size of $N=2048$ for the rest of the techniques as it is also suggested in [4,9,12]. LSB and DCSHIFT techniques have 0% BERs for all block sizes.

Table 1 gives the computation times of different techniques. The FM and FMFHSS techniques require the highest embedding times due to costly computation time of the MPEG Layer 1 model. As a result of not using a transform process, time domain techniques show the highest performance for the computation time in the embedding process. THSS technique gives the least embedding time, while DCSHIFT, PHASE, THSS and LSB techniques possess the least extracting times.

Signal-to-noise ratio (SNR) values of the marked signals for different techniques are also listed in Table 1. Each SNR value is computed as the mean of the SNR values of four different audio signals, each marked by ten different WMs. The LSB technique has the highest SNR value since the difference between the host and the marked signals is only in the least significant bit per sample. The CEPS and the FMFHSS techniques that are more robust than the LSB also provide high SNR values.

Table 1. Computation times and SNR values for various techniques

Technq.	Embed. time(sec)	Extract. time(sec)	SNR (dB)	Technq.	Embed. time(sec)	Extract. time(sec)	SNR (dB)
DCSHIFT	11.65	0.43	21.24	THSS	0.88	0.43	23.13
ECHO	4.66	21.74	4.82	FM	170.64	4.83	12.87
PHASE	40.53	0.38	12.20	FMFHSS	179.88	14.92	34.18
DSSS	4.17	4.82	21.68	CEPS	47.73	22.19	33.77
FHSS	9.61	4.87	28.59	LSB	1.26	0.4	67.91

Figure 3 illustrates BERs due to sample requantization for different techniques as a function of bits per sample. We notice that for bit rates higher than 10 bits per sample, all techniques give BER less than 3% with the exception of LSB technique, where the WM is hidden in last bit of each sample. It's remarkable that THSS, FM, PHASE, DSSS and FHSS techniques show very good performances.

Studies of some other effects on BER for different techniques lead to following conclusions: For BERs due to additive white Gaussian noise as a function of SNR, where SNR is defined as the ratio of the power of the watermarked signal to the noise power, we notice that above 30 dB SNR all the techniques except the LSB provide acceptable values. Here, THSS, FM and DSSS appear remarkably superior to others.

When analyzing BERs due to low-pass filtering with a cutoff frequency of 2.2 kHz we observe that the BER also increases with the increase of the filter order. Here, ECHO and CEPS techniques are observed to be superior among the others. Also inspection of BERs due to low-pass filtering with a cutoff frequency of 4.4 kHz exposes the advantage of the ECHO and CEPS techniques. Here we notice that BER decreases for most of the techniques compared with the low-pass filtering with 2.2 kHz.

For the assessment of BERs due to MP3 coding, each watermarked signal is first converted to a MPEG Layer 3 (MP3) file and then back to a WAV file. Afterwards the WM is extracted and compared with the original WM. Consequently the BER is calculated as in eqn. (9). This process is repeated for different bit rates of MP3 conversion. The software Musicmatch Jukebox 6.0 is used For MP3-WAV and WAV-MP3 conversions. The results put forward that CEPS, FMFHSS, THSS and FHSS techniques have the best performances.

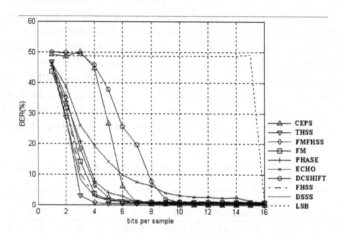

Fig. 3. Bit error rate due to sample requantization

A subjective listening test akin to that in [12] is performed to compare the audio watermarking techniques according to the listening quality of the watermarked audio, in other words, imperceptibility of the WM. The four different audio signals — classic, pop, rock and jazz music — with duration of 10 seconds each are marked with the same WM using different audio watermarking techniques with each watermarked signal having a BER of less than 1%. The listeners are asked to compare the watermarked signal with the original one in terms of the listening quality and to give a grade according to following criterion: Imperceptible-Grade 5, perceptible, but not annoying-4, slightly annoying-3, annoying-2, very annoying-1.

The test is performed in office conditions with the participation of twelve listeners. The experiments are carried out for WAV-type files and MP3 type files with a bit rate of 128 kbps.

The average values of the given grades for each technique are listed in Table 2. We observe that the CEPS, LSB and FMFHSS techniques receive good grades. For the signals, which are watermarked using the DCSHIFT, ECHO, PHASE, DSSS and THSS techniques, listeners gave lower grades for WAV type files than for MP3 type files, and vice versa for the rest of the techniques. Overall, CEPS, LSB, FHSS and FMFHSS techniques emerge as recommendable.

Table 2. The average values of the listening test with WAV and MP3 files

| Technique | WAV | MP3 (128 kbps) | Technique | WAV | MP3 (128 kbps) |
	Grade	Grade		Grade	Grade
DCSHIFT	3.35	3.39	THSS	2.96	3.21
ECHO	3.60	3.81	FM	3.02	2.93
PHASE	2.44	2.58	FMFHSS	4.40	4.21
DSSS	3.48	3.60	CEPS	4.94	4.85
FHSS	4.46	4.31	LSB	4.90	4.87

6 Conclusions

Evaluation of audio watermarking techniques includes two aspects: robustness to various intentional and non-intentional attacks and subjective listening quality.

In this study ten audio watermarking techniques of time, frequency and cepstrum domains are investigated and compared according to their imperceptibility, robustness to some signal processing operations and computational cost. It is observed that there is a trade-off between the imperceptibility and the robustness of the WM. Obviously the imperceptibility of the watermarked audio increases significantly if one is satisfied with a BER higher than 0%. Several experiments are performed in order to compare the robustness of the techniques to some signal processing operations. A new technique, the FMFHSS is introduced as a combination of the FM and FHSS techniques. This technique possesses a high SNR value and it is robust against the MP3 compression, which can be considered as a non-intentional and common attack. Also CEPS and FHSS techniques receive high grades in the listening test. Their performances are also verified with high SNR values and robustness to MP3 compression.

Audio watermarking field is very active and solutions are being deployed in many applications.

References

1. Swanson, M. D., Kobayashi, M., Tewfik, A. H.: Multimedia Data-Embedding and Watermarking Technologies. Proceedings of the IEEE, Vol. 86, No. 6 (1998) 1064-1087
2. Cox, I. J., Kilian, J., Leighton T., Shamoon, T.: Secure Spread Spectrum Watermarking for Multimedia. IEEE Transactions on Image Processing, Vol. 6, No.12 (1997) 1673-1687
3. Bender, W., Gruhl D., Morimoto, N.: Techniques for Data Hiding. IBM Systems Journal, Vol. 35, No. 3 (1996) 313
4. Uludag, U., Arslan, L.: Audio Watermarking Using DC-Level Shifting. Project Report, Bogazici Univ. (2001). http://busim.ee.boun.edu.tr/~speech/publications/audio_ watermarking/uu_la_audio_wm2001.pdf
5. Barni, M., Bartolini, F., Cappellini, V., Piva, A.: A DCT-Domain System For Robust Image Watermarking. Signal Processing, Vol. 66, No. 3 (1998) 357-372
6. Swanson, M. D., Zhu, B., Tewfik A. H., Boney, L.: Robust Audio Watermarking Using Perceptual Masking. Signal Processing, Vol. 66, No. 3 (1998) 337-355

7. Ho, Y., Wang, H.: An Audio Watermarking Algorithm Based on Significant Component Modulation. Proceedings of the IEEE International Symposium on Consumer Electronics, ISCE (2003) 212-213

8. Cvejic, N., Seppanen, T.: Spread Spectrum Audio Watermarking Using Frequency Hopping and Attack Characterization. Signal Processing, v84, n1 (2004) 207-213

9. Li, X., Yu, H. H.: Transparent and Robust Audio Data Hiding in Cepstrum Domain. IEEE International Conf. on Multimedia and Expo (ICME), Vol. 1, New York (2000) 397-400

10. ISO/IEC 11172-3. Psychoacoustic Model 1, Layer 1 (1993)

11. Arnold, M.: Audio Watermarking: Features, Applications and Algorithms. IEEE International Conference on Multimedia and Expo (ICME), New York, Vol. 2 (2000) 1013-1016

12. Gordy, J. D., Bruton, L. T.: Performance Evaluation of Digital Audio Watermarking Algorithms. Proceedings of the IEEE 43rd Midwest Symposium on Circuits and Systems (MWSCAS 2000), Michigan, USA, Vol. 1 (2000) 456-459

13. Neubauer, C., Steinebach, M., Siebenhaar, F., Pickel, J.: Robustness Evaluation of Transactional Audio Watermarking Systems. Proceedings of SPIE-The International Society for Optical Engineering, v5020 (2003) 12-20

A Hybrid Genetic Algorithm for Packing in 3D with Deepest Bottom Left with Fill Method

Korhan Karabulut and Mustafa Murat İnceoğlu

Ege University, Department of Computer Engineering,
Bornova, Izmir, Turkey
{korhan,inceoglu}@bornova.ege.edu.tr

Abstract. Three dimensional bin packing problems arise in industrial applications like container ship loading, pallet loading, plane cargo management and warehouse management, etc. In this paper, a hybrid genetic algorithm (GA) is used for regular 3D strip packing. The Genetic Algorithm is hybridized with the presented Deepest Bottom Left with Fill (DBLF) method. Several heuristic methods have also been used for comparison with the hybrid GA.

1 Introduction

The bin packing problem can be defined as finding an arrangement for n objects, each with some weight, into a minimum number of larger containing objects (or bins), such that the total weight of the item(s) in the bin does not exceed the capacity of the bin. The bin packing problems arise in forms of one, two and three dimensions. Though a lot of research has gone into 1D and 2D, 3D bin packing is relatively less researched [1]. The bin packing problem is NP-hard and is based on the partition problem [2].

In classical three dimensional bin packing problem, there is a set of n rectangular shaped boxes, each with integer values of width w_i, height h_i and depth d_i. The problem is to pack boxes into a minimum number of bin(s) with width W, height H and depth D. The main objective in 3D bin packing is to maximize the number of items placed in the bin(s), hence, minimize the unused or wasted volume. One of the versions of this problem is the knapsack loading problem where the boxes have an associated profit, and the problem is to maximize the profit of boxes packed into a single bin [3]. Another version of the bin packing problem is strip packing, where the objective is to pack all boxes into a single bin with fixed width and height but with a variable depth; the problem is to minimize this depth.

An algorithm designed for 3D bin packing must consider the constraints and automate the packing process so that the algorithm could be applied to different versions of the problem easily. The algorithm must ensure that there is no overlap between boxes. Intelligent methods can be applied to find good packing patterns. Genetic algorithms are such customizable and adaptive general-purpose intelligent methods that allow exploration of a large search space when compared to specialized placement rules.

T. Yakhno (Ed.): ADVIS 2004, LNCS 3261, pp. 441–450, 2004.
© Springer-Verlag Berlin Heidelberg 2004

Heuristics for 3D bin packing problem can be divided into construction and local search heuristics. Construction heuristics add one box at a time to an existing partial packing until all boxes are placed. The boxes are pre-sorted by one of their dimensions and added using a particular strategy, e.g., variants of first fit or best fit methods [3]. The designed hybrid genetic algorithm maintains a population of solutions and iteratively tries to find better solutions.

Our work presented in this paper is about three dimensional strip packing problem that arise in industrial applications like container ship loading, pallet loading, plane cargo management and warehouse management, etc.

Several researchers have studied on different versions of the three-dimensional bin packing problem. Corcoran and Wainwright [4] have proposed a hybrid genetic algorithm based on a 2D method called level technique that is extended to 3D for the classical bin packing problem. The bin is divided into slices along the height and levels along the length. Next fit and first fit heuristics are used to place the items. They reported a maximum of %76.9 bin utilization. Ilkka Ikonen et al. [5] present a genetic algorithm for packing of three-dimensional objects with complex shapes.

Silvano Martello, et al. [6] presents an exact branch-and-bound algorithm that is able to solve instances with up to 90 items optimally within reasonable time. Günther R. Raidl [7] presents a weight-coded genetic algorithm for the multiple container packing problem with similarities to the bin packing problem. He uses two decoding heuristics for filling multiple bins. Oluf Faroe, et al. [3] uses guided local search method.

In this paper, a 3D packing method called Deepest Bottom Left with Fill (DBLF) is presented. DBLF is used within a hybrid genetic algorithm and several heuristics are also used for comparison.

2   Genetic Algorithms

Genetic Algorithms (GAs) are adaptive methods that may be used to solve search and optimization problems [8]. The principles of the evolution of biological organisms are the main idea behind genetic algorithms. Genetic algorithms are first introduced by Holland in 1975 [9] and are studied by many researchers.

Genetic algorithms are based on the simulation of the natural evolution. The building blocks or elements in genetic algorithms are "individuals" which are candidate solutions for a problem. Each of the individuals is called either a "genotype" [9] or a "chromosome" [10]. They are usually coded as binary bit strings.

A genetic algorithm is an iterative process and is composed of several steps. Generally, a random initialization step is required. Then the iterative process begins with assigning a "fitness score" to each individual according to how good it fits as a solution to the problem. A "fitter" individual is given a higher score. Then, each individual is given a chance to "reproduce". Fitter individuals are given higher chances to reproduce but less fitting elements still have a chance. Several individuals are selected from the new population to mate through a process called "crossover".

Crossover produces new children (or offsprings) with some features from each parent. Since less fitting members have smaller chances to reproduce, they fade away from the population during iterations. After recombination, a mutation operator can be applied. Each bit in the population can be mutated (flipped) with a low probability generally smaller than 1%. It may be a fixed value or can be a function of population size.

A good GA will converge to an optimal solution after several iterations. This basic implementation is called a Simple Genetic Algorithm (SGA) [11]. Genetic algorithms are not guaranteed to find the global optimum solution to a problem but they are generally good at finding "acceptably good" solutions to problems "acceptably quickly" [8].

Typical applications of genetic algorithms are numerical function optimization, scheduling, game playing, adaptive control, transportation problems, traveling salesman problems, bin packing and time tabling, etc.

3   The DBLF Method

Genetic algorithms are robust and can deal with a wide range of problem areas that can be difficult to solve with other methods. This is yet a weakness of the genetic algorithms. Since GAs are general methods, they do not contain valuable domain information; so hybridization with domain information can dramatically increase the quality of the solution and the performance of the genetic algorithm by "smarter" exploration the search space.

In the literature, researchers generally use some form of layering technique for 3D bin packing, in which a bin is packed layer by layer. However, layering algorithms have one drawback: their performance degrades if the input forces fragmentation of the loading surface in the early stages of the algorithm [12]. Our method packs the bin box by box. This method also has the disadvantage that decisions about where to place a box can only be made by local criteria so that algorithm may end up with a poor packing. To overcome this problem, genetic algorithms have been used to maintain a population of different packings.

Bottom Left (BL) and Bottom Left with Fill (BLF) methods are used in 2D bin packing. In BL, introduced by Jakobs [16], each item is moved as far as possible to the bottom of the object and then as far as possible to the left. BL is relatively a fast algorithm with complexity $O(n^2)$. The major disadvantage of the method is; empty areas in the layout are generated. Hopper [1], to overcome this disadvantage, develops the BLF algorithm. This algorithm allocates each object to the lowest possible region of the bin thus fills the empty areas in the layout. The major disadvantage of this algorithm is its $O(n^3)$ complexity.

Deepest BLF is an extension of the BLF method to cover 3D bin packing problems. An object is moved to the deepest available position (smallest z value) in the layout, and then as far as possible to the bottom (smallest y value) and then as far as possible left (smallest x value).

Since the complexity of the BLF algorithm is high, a computer efficient implementation of this algorithm is needed. Below is the Deepest BLF algorithm used in this work.

repeat
    get next box
    repeat
        get next position *from the empty volumes list*
        check if the empty volume is large enough
        if assigned empty volume is **large enough**
            intersection test *with all boxes that could intersect at that position*
                stopped *when* **intersection is detected**
            if **intersection true**
                update *size of the empty volume at this position*
            if **intersection false**
                insert box *at this position*
                iterate box *into a deepest bottom-left position*
                update position list *by removing the inserted box's*
volume from that   *position*
                delete *unnecessary positions from list*
                sort *list of positions in deepest bottom left order*
      until **all positions are tried AND intersection is true**
    until **all boxes placed**

Alg. 1. The deepest BLF algorithm in pseudo code

In the beginning, the empty list has only one empty volume with dimensions same as the bin. As the algorithm iterates, new empty volumes are added to the list. The next box from the list is chosen to work on. Then each position in the list is checked to see if the current box fits in. If the empty volume is large enough, the position is checked for intersection with other boxes that were placed before. This check is needed because for an efficient implementation, all the volumes in list are not up to date. If there is no intersection at the chosen position, the box is inserted at this position and is iterated to the deepest bottom left position. Then the position list is updated and checked to see if there is any unnecessary position. In the final step, the new list is sorted in deepest bottom left order. Then the next box is taken from the list and the same selection procedure is repeated. Also as an additional constraint, the boxes are not allowed to rotate.

4   Generation of Test Data

Due to lack of shared test data for these kinds of studies, self generated test data are used. Three classes of test data are generated. The problems are generated with extension to algorithms used by [1] in 2D problem generation. These problem classes are generated so that an optimal solution is known for each problem. First two classes of problems are guillotineable (can be generated by straight cuts through remaining volumes). The algorithms are listed in Alg. 2 and 3.

user input (number of boxes to produce)
calculate number of rectangles to produce ($n = 1 + 7 * i$)
    *where **i** is the number of loops required*
repeat
    select randomly *one of the existing boxes*
    if start
        use object as large box
    place random point *into large box*
    construct 3 lines *that intersect the box's width,length and height*
    create *8 new boxes*
until number of rectangles reached

Alg. 2. Algorithm for the creation of a guillotineable problem instance in pseudo code (method 1)

user input (number of boxes to produce)
calculate number of rectangles to produce ($n = 1 + 3 * i$)
    where i is the number of loops required
repeat
    select randomly *one of the existing boxes*
    if start
        use object as large box
    select a random side *of large box*
    place a random point *on this side*
    select a random point along z axis
    construct 2 lines *perpendicular to the point on the side and through the z point*
    create *4 new boxes*
until number of rectangles reached

Alg. 3. Algorithm for the creation of a guillotineable problem instance in pseudo code (method 2)

The third class of problems is non-guillotineable; hence are more difficult to solve. The algorithm is listed in Alg. 4.

user input (number of boxes to produce)
calculate number of rectangles to produce ($n = 1 + 10 * i$)
    where i is the number of loops required
repeat
    select randomly *one of the existing boxes*
    if start
        use object as large box
    place two random points *into large box*
    create a small box *within these points*
    extend from these two points to three axis and create 9 new boxes
until number of rectangles reached

Alg. 4. Algorithm for the creation of a nonguillotineable problem instance in pseudo code

Generated problems in each category have the following number of elements:

Table 1. Number of problems and dimensions in different categories

	Category 1 (Generated using algorithm 1)	Category 2 (Generated using algorithm 2)	Category 3 (Generated using algorithm 3)
Problem 1	15 (20 x 20 x 20)	16 (20 x 20 x 20)	21 (20 x 20 x 20)
Problem 2	29 (50 x 50 x 50)	25 (50 x 50 x 50)	31 (50 x 50 x 50)
Problem 3	50 (100 x 100 x 100)	52 (100 x 100 x 100)	51 (100 x 100 x 100)
Problem 4	106 (200 x 200 x 200)	100 (200 x 200 x 200)	101 (200 x 200 x 200)
Problem 5	155 (300 x 300 x 300)	151 (300 x 300 x 300)	151 (300 x 300 x 300)

The first number in the columns is the number of objects in the problem and the other three numbers in parentheses are the dimensions of the large box used as the basis for the algorithms. The differences of item numbers in the same class of problems in different categories are due to algorithms used in generation.

5 Implementation

The hybrid genetic algorithm used in this study consists of two stages. First, a genetic algorithm with order based encoding (OBE) is used to explore the search space using the encoded chromosomes. Then DBLF decoding algorithm is used to evaluate the fitness or the "quality" of the proposed packing pattern and transforms the pattern into the corresponding physical layout.

Order based encoding [15] is used for encoding of chromosomes in the algorithm. In OBE, each chromosome in the algorithm represents a candidate solution and is a permutation of all items in the problem. Hence the hybrid GA uses permutation representation.

The genetic algorithm starts by placing objects into chromosomes by feeding using the heuristics used for comparison, other chromosomes are generated randomly. The population is evaluated by a fitness function. Four different fitness functions are used in this work for comparison with each other: maximum height of the bin, the amount of wasted volume, ratio of volume of packed items to wasted volume and a combination of maximum height and ratio of packed items (70% of height and 30% of the ratio of packed items). Fitness functions are based on evaluation results from the Deepest Bottom Left with Fill method.

Each candidate solution is also checked for availability of reduction. If there is a subset of placement scheme so that there is no wasted value, that subset is marked in the algorithm so that those boxes in that subset are reduced from the problem space only for that specific solution. This knowledge is also kept during crossover and mutation operations (the genetic algorithm does not manipulate the reduced part of the solution). The main problem with reduction is: when some items are removed from the solution, it may not be possible to obtain the optimal solution; so reduction is applied on chromosome basis not on all of the population.

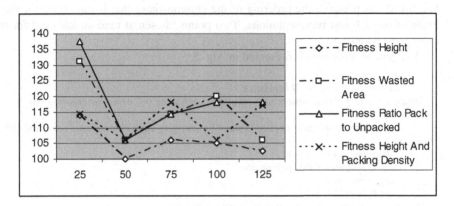

Fig. 1. Genetic algorithm solutions for the 3rd problem in the 1st category using different population sizes

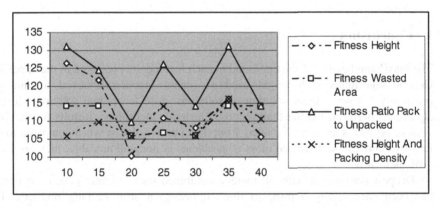

Fig. 2. Genetic algorithm solutions for the 3rd problem in the 1st category using different crossover rates

Population size used in this work is 50. A temporary population is generated using roulette wheel selection method. This method, as its name implies, simulates a roulette wheel. All chromosomes are placed on a wheel proportional to their fitness and new chromosomes are selected randomly. Elitist selection is used to preserve the best individual from the previous step. Crossover and mutation operators are applied with probabilities 20% and 0.05% respectively. The maximum number of generations is 1000. The algorithm stops if the optimal solution is found or number of generations is reached. Several experiments have been made to determine the population size and crossover rate. Solutions obtained for different population sizes and crossover rates are presented in Fig. 1 and Fig. 2.

OX operator proposed by Davis [13] is used for crossover operations. OX builds offsprings by choosing sublets of packages from one parent and preserving the relative order of other sub packages from the other parent. OX operator is chosen because it can preserve the ordering of the chromosomes that is important for these kinds of order based representations. Two points chosen at random are used for the crossover operator.

The genetic algorithm is presented in Alg. 5:

seed 4 chromosomes using 4 heuristics
initialize the rest of chromosomes by randomly exchaning two items per chromosome
repeat
        calculate each fitness of chromosome by decoding each chromosome using the DBLF
algorithm
        setup the roulette wheel
        select temporary new population
        apply crossover
        apply mutation
        use temporary new population as new population
until number of generations are reached or optimal solution is found

Alg. 5. The hybrid genetic algorithm

6   Conclusion

The maximum heights of the bin found in each method are presented in the appendix. Genetic algorithms with height used as fitness function achieved to find the previously known optimal solution or solutions close to optimal solution. Genetic algorithms performed better than proposed heuristic algorithms. Results for the third class of problems are some far away from the optimal solution when compared to the first two classes. As the third class of problems is nonguillotineable, they are more difficult to solve.

Deepest bottom left with fill method combined with a hybrid genetic algorithm has been successfully applied to three dimensional strip packing problem. The proposed method produced high utilization rates. Genetic algorithms performed better than the heuristics methods as expected. Among the genetic algorithms, maximum height fitness function performed better than the other functions.

References

1. Hopper, E: Two-dimensional Packing Utilising Evolutionary Algorithms and other Meta-Heuristic Methods., A Thesis submitted to University of Wales for the Degree of Doctor of Philosophy (2000).
2. Fowler, R.J., Paterson, M. S. and, Tatimoto, S.L.: Optimal Packing and Covering in the Plane Are NP-Complete. Information Processing Letters, Vol. 12 (1981) 133-137.

3. Oluf Faroe, David Pisinger, Martin Zachariasen: Guided Local Search for the Three-Dimensional Bin Packing Problem. INFORMS Journal on Computing (2002).
4. Corcoran III A. L. and Wainwrigth R. L.: Genetic algorithm for packing in three dimensions. Proceedings of the 1992 ACM/SIGAPP Symposium on Applied Computing SAC'92, Kansas City (1992) 1021-1030.
5. Ikonen, Ilkka and Kumar, A.: A Genetic Algorithm for Packing Three-Dimensional Non-Convex Objects Having Cavities and Holes. Proceedings of the 7th International Conference on Genetic Algorithms (1998) 591-598.
6. Martello, Silvano, Pisinger, David, Vigo, Daniele: The Three-Dimensional Bin Packing Problem. Operations Research, Vol. 48 (2000) 256-267.
7. Günther R. Raidl: A Weight-Coded Genetic Algorithm for the Multiple Container Packing Problem. SAC'99 San Antonio, Texas (1999).
8. David Beasley, David R. Bull and Ralph R. Martin: an Overview of Genetic Algorithms: Part 1, Fundamentals. University Computing, Vol. 15(2) (1993) 58-69.
9. Holland, J.H.: Adaptation in Natural and Artificial Systems. University of Michigan Press, Ann Arbor (1975).
10. Schaffer, J.D., and Selman, L.: Some Effects of Selection Procedures on Hyper plane sampling by Genetic Algorithms. Genetic Algorithms and Simulated Annealing (1987).
11. Goldberg, D: Genetic Algorithms in Search, Optimization and Machine Learning. Reading, MA, Addison-Wesley (1989).
12. Bram Verweij: Multiple Destination Bin Packing, Report, http://citeseer.ist.psu.edu/verweij96multiple.html (1996).
13. Davis L.: Applying adaptive search algorithms to epistatic domains. Proceedings of the 9th International Joint Conference on Artificial Intelligence, Los Angeles (1985) 162-164.
14. Jakobs, S: On Genetic Algorithms for the Packing of Polygons. European Journal of Operational Research Vol 88 (1996) 165-181.
15. Raidl G. R., Kodydek, G: Genetic Algorithms for the Multiple Container Packing Problem. Proceedings of the 5th Int. Conference on Parallel Problem Solving from Nature, Amsterdam, The Netherlands, (1998) 875-884.

Appendix: Test Results

Table 2. Problem class 1 test results

Method	Prob. 1 optimal: 20	Prob. 2 optimal: 50	Prob. 3 optimal: 100	Prob. 4 optimal: 200	Prob. 5 optimal: 300
GA with Fit. Fn: Height	20	50	100	204	300
GA w. Fit. Fn:Wasted Area	24	62	104	262	350
GA w. Fit. Fn: Ratio Packed – Unpacked	20	58	112	264	352
GA w. Fit. Fn: Height & Packing Dens.	24	57	112	256	342
Heuristic: Sorted by Height	24	71	124	348	435
Heuristic: Sorted by Width	32	75	136	437	448
Heuristic: Sorted by Volume	24	85	112	296	403
Heuristic: Sorted by Bottom Area	28	86	118	476	440

Table 3. Problem class 2 test results

Method	Prob. 1 optimal: 20	Prob. 2 optimal: 50	Prob. 3 optimal: 100	Prob. 4 optimal: 200	Prob. 5 optimal: 300
GA with Fit. Fn: Height	20	54	101	208	312
GA w. Fit. Fn:Wasted Area	22	62	112	251	339
GA w. Fit. Fn: Ratio Packed – Unpacked	20	62	112	251	339
GA w. Fit. Fn: Height & Packing Dens.	20	62	109	247	338
Heuristic: Sorted by Height	22	83	116	281	352
Heuristic: Sorted by Width	25	73	151	457	447
Heuristic: Sorted by Volume	23	66	126	343	437
Heuristic: Sorted by Bottom Area	24	84	133	404	405

Table 4. Problem class 3 test results

Method	Prob. 1 optimal: 20	Prob. 2 optimal: 50	Prob. 3 optimal: 100	Prob. 4 optimal: 200	Prob. 5 optimal: 300
GA with Fit. Fn: Height	20	53	108	219	330
GA w. Fit. Fn:Wasted Area	20	62	124	231	362
GA w. Fit. Fn: Ratio Packed – Unpacked	20	63	137	246	358
GA w. Fit. Fn: Height & Packing Dens.	20	63	138	248	339
Heuristic: Sorted by Height	31	77	188	388	484
Heuristic: Sorted by Width	31	75	237	388	525
Heuristic: Sorted by Volume	30	63	154	376	514
Heuristic: Sorted by Bottom Area	28	63	225	394	584

Multi-objective Genetic Algorithm Based Clustering Approach and Its Application to Gene Expression Data

Tansel Özyer, Yimin Liu, Reda Alhajj, and Ken Barker

Department of Computer Science, University of Calgary,
Calgary, Alberta, Canada
{ozyer, liuyi, alhajj, barker}@cpsc.ucalgary.ca

Abstract. Gene clustering is a common methodology for analyzing similar data based on expression trajectories. Clustering algorithms in general need the number of clusters as a priori, and this is mostly hard to estimate, even by domain experts. In this paper, we use Niched Pareto k-means Genetic Algorithm (GA) for clustering m-RNA data. After running the multi-objective GA, we get the pareto-optimal front that gives alternatives for the optimal number of clusters as a solution set. We analyze the clustering results under two cluster validity techniques commonly cited in the literature, namely DB index and SD index. This gives an idea about ranking the optimal numbers of clusters for each validity index. We tested the proposed clustering approach by conducting experiments using three data sets, namely figure2data, cancer (NCI60) and Leukaemia data. The obtained results are promising; they demonstrate the applicability and effectiveness of the proposed approach.

Keywords: multi-objective genetic algorithm, clustering, validity analysis, gene expression data analysis.

1 Introduction

The central role of the DNA microarray technology in biological and biomedical domains enabled researchers to observe transcription levels of many thousands of genes. Information gathered by analyzing the genes at different levels (stages of the process) is used for the gene function, the reconstruction of the gene network, diagnosis of disease conditions and inference of medical treatment [23].

Data mining methods and techniques have a great deal of interest and application areas including bioinformatics. They are designed for extracting previously unknown significant relationships and regularities out of huge heaps of details in large data collections [6]. The identified gene expression levels reflecting the biological processes of interest are frequently used to analyze the inference of differentially expressed genes and clustering. The main step in the analysis of gene expression data is to identify groups of genes based on some notion of similarity. Two leading data mining tasks classification and clustering exhibit the capability of grouping the genes.

Classification is one of the known mining techniques. It has two main aspects: discrimination and clustering. In discrimination analysis, also known as supervised

T. Yakhno (Ed.): ADVIS 2004, LNCS 3261, pp. 451–461, 2004.

clustering, observations are known to belong to the pre-specified classes. The task is to allocate predictors for the new coming instances in order to be able to classify them correctly. In contrast to classification, in clustering, also known as unsupervised clustering, the classes are unknown a priori and the task is to determine them from the data instances. Clustering is used to describe methods to group unlabeled data. Several clustering approaches have been proposed so far [15]. By clustering, we aim at discovering gene groups that enable us to discover for example the functional role or the existence of a regulatory novel gene among the members in a group.

As described in the literature, different assumptions and terminologies are considered for components of the clustering process and the context in which clustering is used. There exist fuzzy clustering techniques as well as hard clustering techniques. The latter assigns a label l_i to each object x_i identifying its class label. The set of all labels for the object set is $\{l_1, l_2, ..., l_n\}$, where $l_i \in \{l_1, l_2, ..., l_k\}$, and k is the number of clusters. In the former, an object may belong to more than one cluster, but with different degree of membership; an object x_i is assigned to cluster j based on the value of the corresponding function f_{ij}. The membership of an object may not be precisely defined; there is likelihood that each object may or may not be member of some clusters. The presence of noise in the data set may be quite high.

Our approach presented in this paper has been designed to handle the clustering process by using multi-objective genetic algorithm without requiring the number of clusters be known beforehand; and the developed approach has been utilized for clustering gene expression data.

Multi-objective genetic algorithms involve the simultaneous optimization of several goals, and it is not guaranteed to satisfy the optimality of all the objectives. A solution may be inferior regarding one objective while optimal regarding the other objectives. Instead of a unique solution, a set of solutions is proposed such that there are no other solutions superior to them by considering all the objectives. This solution set is called the pareto-optimal set. Solutions to a multi-objective optimization method are mathematically expressed in terms of non-dominated or superior points. In a minimization problem, a vector $x^{(1)}$ is partially less than another vector $x^{(2)}$, denoted $x^{(1)} \prec x^{(2)}$, when no value of $x^{(2)}$ is less than $x^{(1)}$ and at least one value of $x^{(2)}$ is strictly greater than $x^{(1)}$. If $x^{(1)}$ is partially less than $x^{(2)}$, we say that $x^{(1)}$ dominates $x^{(2)}$ or the solution $x^{(2)}$ is inferior to $x^{(1)}$. Any vector which is not dominated by any other vectors is said to be non-dominated or non-inferior. The optimal solutions to a multi-objective optimization problem are non-dominated solutions [25].

In the existing clustering approaches, the number of clusters is mostly given a-priori. This motivated us to consider the idea of proposing multi-objective k-means genetic algorithm (MOKGA) approach in order to present to the user several alternative solutions without taking the weight values into account. Otherwise, the user will have to consider several trials weighting with different values until a satisfactory result is obtained. We evaluate the obtained candidate optimal numbers of clusters by applying some of the well-known cluster validity techniques, namely DB index and SD index. Finally, the proposed approach has been tested using three data sets, namely figure2data, cancer (NCI60) and Leukaemia data sets available at Genomics Department of Stanford University, UCI machine learning repository, and

Genome Research at MIT. The obtained results are promising demonstrate the applicability and effectiveness of the proposed approach.

The rest of the paper is as follows. Section 2 is an overview of the related work. Section 3 describes the proposed multi-objective genetic algorithm based clustering approach and the employed cluster validity analysis. Section 4 reports the experimental results. Section 5 is the conclusions.

2   Related Work

As reported in the literature, the development of new clustering techniques has attracted several research groups. Existing clustering techniques may be classified into traditional clustering algorithms, including hierarchical clustering [11], k-means [16] and self-organizing maps [19]; and recently emerging clustering techniques such as graph-based [2] and model-based [1, 27] approaches. Some of the existing clustering techniques have been successfully employed in clustering and analyzing gene expression data.

Hierarchical clustering is a very well known method by biologists. A tree structure called dendogram is used to illustrate the hierarchical clustering. Relationships among genes are represented by the tree using a degree of similarity symbolized with the branch lengths. As stated by statisticians, hierarchical clustering suffers from different aspects, including robustness, non-uniqueness and inverse interpretation of the hierarchy [24]. Second, the tree structure is prone to error since there is multi-way for expressing the similarity; this worsens as the data size gets larger [20]. Once a gene is assigned to a cluster, there is no possibility of assigning it to another cluster to see whether there are better results.

K-means clustering algorithm is another proposed technique that has been utilized in analayzing gene expression data. The number of clusters is given a-priori. It is an iterative process where the genes are moved among sets of cluster. Initially, a number of points equal to the desired number of clusters and reciprocally farthest apart from each other is chosen as the cluster centroids. Each gene in the dataset is assigned to the closest cluster and centroids are recalculated at every insertion of genes into clusters. This process is repeated until the total error criteria converges. The shortcoming of this method is that it finds the local optimum, and hence it may miss the global optimum. This clustering process is not a stable one because of the initial phase, so that at every run it is probable to obtain different clustering results.

Self organizing maps (SOM) is a neural network approach using competitive unsupervised learning and eventually winner-takes-all approach to assign each gene to a cluster. There is one input layer and a competitive layer, so each input neuron is used for the output result of each competitive layer neuron. Two dimensional grid is used to evaluate the results. Each input neuron is connected with an arc to every neuron at the competitive layer with different weights and competitive neurons are evaluated with an activation function. It is good because input neurons feed the copmpetitive neurons with the varying weights in parallel as by product of perceptron learning. The shortcoming of SOM is the size of the two dimensional grid and the number of nodes have to be predetermined. It suits well when the prior information about the distribution of the data is not available.

Model based approach is a promising technique assuming that data is generated by a mixture of finite number of probability distributions. There is a tradeoff between the complexity of the probability model and the number of clusters. For instance, if a complex probability model is used, a small number of clusters may suffice; while a larger number of clusters may be needed for a simple model in order to appropriately fit all the data.

Graph-based methods propose a way of partitioning the data space into subgraphs with respect to some geometric properties. The study in [2] tries to make cliques for the clustering purpose. There are shortcomings with this approach. Although the number of clusters is not given, there is a pre-specified threshold used for the clustering; and after the convergence, each gene moves to the cluster with the highest average similarity. This is a very expensive cleaning step.

Our method assumes that a clustering process may have many objectives by nature and it is difficult to find the optimal solution to the satisfaction of all the objectives. Here, rather than using a fixed threshold value and/or fixed number of clusters as apriori, we are keen on giving a range of number of clusters parameter and finding a set of pareto optimal solution set in order to find the superior results in the sense that there is no other point that can be superior to our pareto-optimal solution. Our idea differs from the traditional multi-objective genetic algorithms that scalarize the objectives by assigning subjective weights to each. Hence, weights of objectives existing in the pareto-optimal are decided inherently by the system. In addition to those, using genetic algorithm with recombination and mutation, likelihood of finding global optimum solution is deemed to have succeeded with the appropriate system run parameters.

3   The Proposed Approach

The proposed Multi-Objective Genetic K-means Algorithm (MOKGA) aims at finding the optimal numbers of clusters as a solution set. In this approach, we used the pareto optimal front which involves considering the optimality of every sub goal defined in the problem. Although we tested our approach on gene expression data, it is a general purpose approach for clustering datasets in other areas [17]. Also this method can be used with different sub goals changing the proximity values as distance or non-decreasing similarity function according to the requirements of the dataset to be clustered.

Concerning our approach, after running MOKGA, we get the pareto-optimal front that gives the optimal numbers of clusters as a solution set. Then, the system analyzes the determined clustering results under two of the most commonly cited cluster validity techniques, namely SD index, DB index.

3.1   Multi-objective Genetic K-Means Algorithm

MOKGA is basically the combination of the Fast Genetic K-means Algorithm (FGKA) [18] and Niched Pareto Genetic Algorithm [12]. It uses a list of parameters to drive the evaluation procedure as in the other genetic types of algorithms: including population size (number of chromosomes), number of comparison set (t_dom) representing the assumed non-dominated set, crossover, mutation probability, termination convergence threshold and the number of iterations that the execution of the algorithm needs to obtain the result.

Sub-goals can be defined as fitness functions; and instead of scalarizing them to find the goal as the overall fitness function with the user defined weight values, we expect the system to find the set of best solutions, i.e., the pareto-optimal front. By using the specified formulas, at each generation, each chromosome in the population is evaluated and assigned a value for each fitness function.

The coding of our individual population is a chromosome of length n. Each gene is used to represent an instance. It stores a value from the set $\{1, 2, ..., K\}$. Such value indicates the cluster that the corresponding instance belongs to. In the population, each chromosome exhibits a solution for clustering. For instance, if the chromosome has k clusters, then each gene a_n (n=1 to N) takes different values from the interval $[1..K]$. Initial population is randomly generated. At every generation, the next population is generated using the current population, and generation number is incremented by 1. During this process, the current population performs the pareto domination tournament to get rid of the worst solutions from the population, crossover, mutation and k-means operator [18] to reorganize each object's assigned cluster number. Finally, we will have twice the number of individuals after the pareto domination tournament. We apply the ranking mechanism used in [11] to satisfy the elitism and diversity preservation. By using this method the number of individuals is halved. This process is depicted in the next steps.

1. Initially, assign the *current generation* to zero. Each chromosome takes number of clusters parameter within the range 1 to the maximum number of clusters specified by the user. A population with the specified number of chromosomes is created randomly by using the method in [21]: Data points are randomly assigned to each cluster at the beginning; then the rest of the points are randomly assigned to clusters. By using this method, we can avoid generating illegal strings, which means some clusters do not have any pattern in the string.

2. Generate the next population and increment the current generation by 1.

   a. The first step in the construction of the next generation is the selection using pareto domination tournaments. In this step, two candidate items picked among (*population size-t_{dom}*) individuals participate in the pareto domination tournament against the t_{dom} individuals for the survival of each in the population. In the selection part, t_{dom} individuals are randomly picked from the population. With two randomly selected chromosome candidates in (*population size-t_{dom}*) individuals, each of the candidates is compared against each individual in the comparison set, t_{dom}. If one candidate has a larger total within-cluster variation fitness value and a larger number of cluster values than all of the chromosomes in the comparison set, this means it is already dominated by the comparison set and will be deleted from the population permanently. Otherwise, it resides in the population for subsequent iterations.

b. Pareto-front at each generation is preserved to be compared in order to find the best current pareto-optimal individuals at step 2-e. The best individuals of the current generation will survive for the next generation. One-point crossover operator is applied to the population with the crossover rate p_c. After the crossover, the assigned cluster number for each gene is renumbered beginning from a_1 to a_n. For example, if the following two chromosomes, one has 3 and the other has 5 clusters need to have a crossover at the third location:

    Number of clusters=3: 1 2 3 3 3;   Number of clusters=5:   1 4 3 2 5

We will get 1 2 3 2 5 and 1 4 3 3 3, as the new chromosomes; they are renumbered to get the new number of clusters parameters:

    Number of clusters=4: 1 2 3 2 4 (for 1 2 3 2 5)

    Number of clusters=3:   1 2 3 3 3 (for 1 4 3 3 3)

The reason for choosing one-point crossover is because we realized that it produced better results compared to multi-point after some initial experiments.

c. The mutation on the current population is performed following the pareto dominant tournaments. During mutation, we replace each gene value a_n by a_n' with respect to the probability distribution, for $n=1$ to N simultaneously. a_n' is a cluster number randomly selected from the set $\{1, \ldots, K\}$ with corresponding probability distributions $\{p_1, p_2, \ldots, p_K\}$ defined by:

$$p_i = \frac{1.5 * d_{max}(X_n) - d(X_n, c_k)}{\sum_{k=1}^{K} 1.5 * d_{max}(X_n) - d(X_n, c_k)} \tag{1}$$

where $i \in [1..k]$ and $d(X_n, C_k)$ denotes Euclidean distance between pattern X_n and the centroid C_k of the k-th cluster. $d_{max}(X_n) = \max_k\{d(X_n, C_k)\}$, p_i represents the probability interval of mutating gene assigned to cluster i (e.g., Roulette Wheel).

d. Finally, k-means operator is performed. K-means operator is used to re-analyze each chromosome gene's assigned cluster value; it calculates the cluster centre for each cluster; and then it re-assigns each gene to the closest cluster to the instance in the gene. Hence, k-means operator is used to speed up the convergence process by replacing a_n by a_n' for $n=1$ to N simultaneously, where a_n' is the closest to object X_n in Euclidean distance.

e. In addition to the original population, by applying steps 2-a, 2-b, 2-c, 2-d, we get a new population of the same size or smaller because of 2-a. Our approach picks the first l individuals by considering the elitism and diversity among $2l$ individuals. Pareto fronts are ranked. Basically, we find the pareto-optimal front and remove the individuals of the pareto-optimal front from $2l$ set and place it in the population to be run in the next generation. In the remaining set, again we get the first pareto-optimal front and we put it in the population and so on. Since we try to get the first l individuals, the last pareto-optimal front may have more individuals required to complete the number of individuals to l, we handle the diversity automatically. We rank them and reduce the objective dimension into one. Then, we sum the normalized values of the objective functions of each individual. We sort them in increasing order and find each individual's total difference from its individual pairs, the one with the closest smaller summed values and the one with the closest greater summed values. After sorting the individuals in terms of total difference in decreasing order, we keep placing from the top as many individuals as we need to complete the number of population to l. The reason for doing this is to take the crowding factor into account automatically, so that individuals occurring closer to others are unlikely to be picked. Solutions far apart from the others will be considered for the necessity of diversity. Further details about this process are given in [4]. This method was also suggested as a solution for the elitism and diversity for improvement in NSGA-II.

3. Finally, exit if the maximum number of generations is reached or the pre-specified threshold is satisfied; otherwise the next generation is performed.

During our clustering process, we defined two objective functions: minimizing the number of clusters and minimizing the partitioning error. To partition the N pattern points into K clusters one goal is to minimize the Total Within-Cluster Variation:

$$TWCV = \sum_{n=1}^{N} \sum_{d=1}^{D} X_{nd}^2 - \sum_{k=1}^{K} \frac{1}{Z_k} \sum_{d=1}^{D} SF_{kd}^2 \tag{2}$$

where $X_1, X_2, \ldots, X_N$ are the N objects, X_{nd} denotes feature d of pattern X_n ($n = 1$ to N). SF_{kd} is the sum of the d-th features of all the patterns in cluster k (G_k) and Z_k denote the number of patterns in cluster k (G_k) and SF_{kd} is computed as:

$$SF_{kd} = \sum_{X_n \in G_k} X_{nd}, \quad (d = 1, 2, \ldots D). \tag{3}$$

The other objective function is to minimize the *number of clusters* parameter. By using these two objective functions, after running the proposed algorithm, we aim at obtaining the first pareto optimal front having the best partition with the least numbers of clusters as optimal solution set.

3.2 Cluster Validity Techniques

Clustering as an unsupervised task needs to be checked concerning the validity of the outcome from the process. The criteria widely accepted by the clustering algorithms are the compactness of the cluster and their well-separateness. Those criteria should be validated and optimal clusters should be found, so the correct input parameters must be given to the satisfaction of optimal clusters. Basically, with the other clustering approaches, the number of clusters is given as a priori in general. However, pareto-optimal solution set for the clustering results is obtained in our approach, MOKGA. We argue that these are considered as good clustering outcome and we use the cluster validity indexes to analyze the outcome. The target is to see the overall picture of those validity indexes value changes for each number of clusters parameter value in the solution set. In our system, we considered two cluster validity techniques widely used for the validation task, namely DB index [3] and SD index [9]. Based on the validated results, the optimal number of clusters can be determined.

DB uses the ratio of within scatter of objects to the scatter of cluster centers. It considers the average case by using the average error of each class.

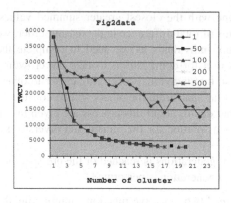

Fig. 1. Pareto-fronts for fig2data

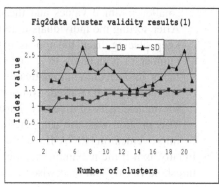

Fig. 2. Cluster validity for fig2data

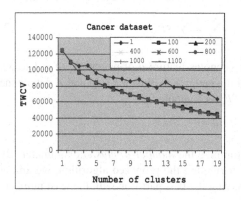

Fig. 3. Pareto-fronts for cancer data

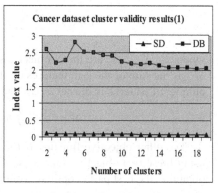

Fig. 4. Cluster validity for cancer data

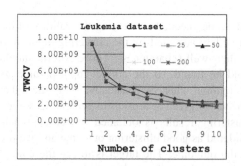

Fig. 5. Pareto-fronts for leukemia data

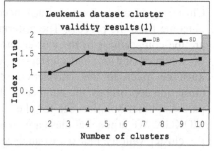

Fig. 6. Cluster validity for leukemia data

Pareto-optimal front changes during the process are given in Figure 1, Figure 2 and Figure 3 for the three analyzed data sets. The reason for getting a stabilized front for the three datasets is because of the k-means operator and the mutation which was also used in [18]. In the work described in [18], they used 517 instances with 19 attributes and their study achieved stabilization after 20 generations. However, objective functions do not converge in the first 20 generations; the partitioning error keeps reducing slightly because of both k-means and mutation. We make sure it converged with a small threshold value as in [17].

4 Experiments

We conducted our experiments on Intel® 4, 2.00 GHz CPU, with 512 MB RAM and running Windows XP. The proposed MOKGA approach and the utilized two cluster validity indexes have been implemented using Microsoft Visual Studio 6.0 C++. We used three data sets in the evaluation process. The first data set is the time course of serum stimulation of primary human fibroblasts. It contains the expression data for 517 genes of which expression changed substantially in response to serum. Each gene has 19 expression data ranging from 15 minutes to 24 hours [7, 14]. The second data set is a gene expression database for the molecular pharmacology of cancer; it contains 728 genes and 60 cell lines [22]. The third dataset is Leukemia dataset [8], it has 38 acute leukemia samples and 50 genes.

We used the following parameters for the proposed GA based approach: population size=300, number of comparison set (t_dom=10), crossover=0.6, mutation=0.005 and we used 300, 200 and 200 generations for fig2data, cancer and leukemia, respectively.

After running the algorithm for each of the three datasets, changes in the pareto-optimal front are plotted in Figures 2, 3, and 4, respectively, for different generations, demonstrating how the system converges to an optimal pareto-optimal front. Here, we tested, analyzed and compared our results with those reported in [8, 18, 22].

According to [18], the optimal number of clusters found for fig2data is 10. Although we found that value within our pareto optimal set, it is one of the promising outcomes for the SD index as can be seen in Figure 4.

For the cancer (NCI60) dataset, Figure 5 shows that we have 15 in our pareto optimal front. We got the value 15 ranking first by the DB index and second by the SD index. This is consistent with the result reported in [22].

According to the study in [8], optimal number of clusters for leukemia 2, which we consistent with the results reported in Figure 6. More interesting, we found 2 as the best number of clusters value after the validity analysis with both indices.

5 Conclusions

In this paper, we proposed a multi-objective genetic k-means algorithm MOKGA for clustering. This method is the combination of the niched pareto optimal and fast k-means genetic algorithm. We tested our system for biological data using figure2data, cancer (NCI60) and Leukaemia. Our results are promising. This way, we overcome the difficulty of determining the weight of each objective function taking part in the fitness. Otherwise, the user is expected to do several trials with different weighting of objectives as in traditional genetic algorithms. By using MOKGA, our purpose is to find the pareto-optimal front so that the user will be able to see many alternative solutions at once. Finally, cluster validity index values are evaluated for each pareto-optimal front value which is the number of clusters considered as optimal. The results reported in this paper are promising; they demonstrate the effectiveness and applicability of the proposed approach.

References

1. Y. Barash and N. Friedman. Context-specific Bayesian clustering for gene expression data. *Proc. of RECOMB*, pp.12-21, 2001.
2. Ben-Dor, R. Shamir, and Z. Yakhini, Clustering gene expression patterns, *Journal of Computatonal Biology,* 1999.
3. D.L. Davies and D.W. Bouldin, A cluster separation measure, *IEEE Transactions on Pattern Recognition and Machine Intelligence*, No.1, pp.224-227, 1979.
4. K. Deb, et al., "A Fast Elitist Non-Dominated Sorting Genetic Algorithm for Multi-Objective Optimization: NSGA-II," *Proc. of the Parallel Problem Solving from Nature. Springer LNCS No. 1917*, Paris, France, 2000.
5. J. Dunn, Well separated clusters and optimal fuzzy partitions, *Journal of Cybernetics*, Vol.4, pp.95-104, 1974.
6. J. Grabmeier, et al, Techniques of Cluster Algorithms in Data Mining, Kluwer Academic Publishers, *Data Mining and Knowledge Discovery*, Vol.6, pp.303-360, 2003.
7. Gene Expression Data of the Genomic Resources, University of Stanford (Available at: http://genome-www.stanford.edu/serum/data.html, downloaded in May 2004).
8. T.R. Golub, et al, Molecular classification of cancer: class discovery and class prediction by gene expression monitoring, *Science,* 286, pp.531-537, 1999.
9. M. Halkidi, M. Vazirgiannis and I. Batistakis, Quality scheme assessment in the clustering process, *Proceedings of PKDD*, Lyon, France, 2000.
10. M. Halkidi, M. Vazirgiannis, Clustering Validity Assessment: Finding the optimal partitioning of a data set, *Proceedings of IEEE ICDM*, California, Nov. 2001.
11. J.A. Hartigan, *Clustering Algorithms*, New York: John Wiley and Sons, 1975.
12. J. Horn, N. Nafpliotis, and D. E. Goldberg, A niched pareto genetic algorithm for multiobjective optimization, *Proceedings of IEEE CEC, IEEE World Congress on Computational Computation*, Vol.1, pp.82-87, Piscataway, NJ., 1994.
13. L. Hubert and J. Schultz, Quadratic assignment as a general data-analysis strategy. *British Journal of Mathematical and Statistical Psychologies*, Vol.29, pp.190-241, 1976.
14. V.R. Iyer, et al, The transcriptional program in the response of human fibroblasts to serum, *Science* 283(5398), pp.83-7, 1999.
15. K. Jain, et al, Data Clustering: A Review, *ACM Surveys*, Vol.31, No.3, 1999.
16. T. Kohonen, *Self-organizing Maps*, Berlin/Heidelberg: Springer-Verlag, 1997.
17. Y. Liu, T. Özyer, R. Alhajj, and K. Barker, Validity Analysis of Clustering Obtained Using Multi-Objective Genetic Algorithm, *Proc. of IEEE ISDA*, 2004 .
18. Y. Lu, et al, FGKA: A Fast Genetic K-means Clustering Algorithm, *Proc. of ACM Symposium on Applied Computing*, pp.162-163, Nicosia, Cyprus, 2004.
19. J. MacQueen, Some methods for classification and analysis of multivariate observations, *Proc. of Berkeley Symposium on Math Stat Probability (Edited by: University of California Press)*, Cam LML, Neyman J, pp.281-297, 1965.

20. B.J.T. Morgan and A.P.G Ray, Non-uniqueness and inversions in cluster analysis, *Applied Statisics*, Vol.44, pp.114-134.
21. P.J. Rousseeuw, Silhouettes: a graphical aid to the interpretation and validation of cluster analysis, *Journal of Comp App. Math*, Vol.20, pp.53-65, 1987.
22. U. Scherf, et al, A Gene Expression Database for the Molecular Pharmacology of Cancer, *Nat Genet* 24, pp.236-44, 2000.
23. R. Shamir and R. Sharan, *Algorithmic approaches to clustering gene expression data: Current Topics in Computational Biology*, MIT Press, 2001
24. P. Tamayo, et al, Interpreting patterns of gene expression with self-organizing maps: Methods and application to hematopoietic differentiation, *Proc. of. Nat'l Acad Sci USA*, 96, pp.2907-2912, 1999.
25. K. Tamura, et al, Necessary and Sufficient Conditions for Local and Global Non-Dominated Solutions in Decision Problems with Multi-objectives, *Journal of Optimization Theory and Applications*, Vol.27, pp.509-523, 1979.
26. S. Theodoridis and K. Koutroumbas, *Pattern Recognition*, Academic Press, 1998.
27. K.Y. Yeung, et al, Model-based clustering and data transformations for gene expression data. *Bioinformatics*, Vol.17, pp.977-987, 2001.

An Application of Support Vector Machine in Bioinformatics: Automated Recognition of Epileptiform Patterns in EEG Using SVM Classifier Designed by a Perturbation Method

Nurettin Acır and Cüneyt Güzeliş

Dokuz Eylül University, Electrical and Electronics Engineering Department,
35160, İzmir, Turkey
nurettin.acir@eee.deu.edu.tr, cuneyt.guzelis@eee.deu.edu.tr

Abstract. We introduce an approach based on perturbation method for input dimension reduction in Support Vector Machine (SVM) classifiers. If there exists redundant data components in training data set, they can be discarded by analyzing the total disturbance of the SVM output corresponding to the perturbed inputs. Thus, input dimension size is reduced and network becomes smaller. Algorithm for input dimension reduction is first formulated and then applied to real electroencephalography (EEG) data for recognition of epileptiform patterns.

1 Introduction

SVM is a widely used tool for data classification [1], function approximation [2] etc., due to its generalization ability. SVM maps input data into a high dimensional feature space where it may become linearly separable. Recently, SVM has been applied to a wide variety of domains such as bioinformatics and pattern recognition [3] with great success.

Different approaches for data reduction were presented for models trained in a supervised way [4]. Duplicative data pairs should be removed from the training sets with a little or no loss of accuracy. In contrast, the data carrying conflicting information decrease the performance of the system. Our aim in this paper is to exploit the redundancy in input data vector for improving the efficiency of the SVM classification algorithm.

To determine which input data components are necessary for a satisfactory neural network performance, a measure known as sensitivity was introduced in [5]. The sensitivity method was adapted to determine the irrelevant features for multilayer perceptron networks in [6].

For irrelevant features which provide little information to the classifier, the output produces a small value of sensitivity measure which indicates that the output is insensitive to those features. On the other hand, the output produces a large value of sensitivity measure for important features.

T. Yakhno (Ed.): ADVIS 2004, LNCS 3261, pp. 462–471, 2004.

This paper focuses on a perturbation method, for reduction of input dimension for SVM providing continuous mapping. Perturbation method for discarding redundant inputs of perceptron networks was introduced in [7] which highly motivated us to apply the perturbation method onto the SVM classification.

In this study, the sensitivities of SVM output with respect to inputs are calculated and used for obtaining sensitivity measure, then used to evaluate the importance of features. First, the sensitivity of the output to the inputs in SVM is derived. Then, a recursive algorithm is presented not only to remove irrelevant features but also to find the optimal solution. A real EEG data set for classification is evaluated in the experiments. Experiments' results show that perturbation method for input dimension reduction in SVM can be used successfully in pattern classification problems.

2 Support Vector Machines

Support Vector Machine (SVM) is a powerful widely used technique for solving supervised classification problems due to its generalization ability. In essence, SVM classifiers maximize the margin between the training data and the decision boundary, which can be formulated as a quadratic optimization problem in the feature space. The subsets of patterns that are closest to the decision boundary are called support vectors.

For a linearly separable binary classification problem, the construction of a hyperplane $\mathbf{w}^T\mathbf{x} + b = 0$ so that the margin between the hyperplane and the nearest point is maximized can be posed as the following quadratic optimization problem [8]:

$$\min_{\mathbf{w}} \frac{1}{2}(\mathbf{w}^T\mathbf{w}) \tag{1}$$

subject to

$$d^i((\mathbf{w}^T\mathbf{x}^i) + b) \geq 1 \text{ with } i = 1,\ldots,N \tag{2}$$

where $d^i \in \{-1,1\}$ stands for the i'th desired output, $x^i \in R^P$ stands for the i'th input sample of the training data set $\{x^i, d^i\}_{i=1}^N$. Eq. (2) forces a rescaling on $(\mathbf{w},b)$ so that the point closest to the hyperplane has a distance of $\frac{1}{\|w\|}$ [8]. Maximizing the margin corresponds to minimizing the Euclidean norm of the weight vector. Often in practice, a separating hyperplane does not exist. Hence the constraint (2) is relaxed by introducing slack variables $\xi_i \geq 0$, $i = 1,\ldots,N$. The optimization problem now becomes as follows (for a user defined positive finite constant C):

$$\min_{\mathbf{w},\xi} \frac{1}{2}(\mathbf{w}^T\mathbf{w}) + C\sum_{i=1}^N \xi_i \tag{3}$$

subject to

$$d^i((\mathbf{w}^T\mathbf{x}^i) + b) \geq 1 - \xi_i \tag{4}$$

$$\xi_i \geq 0 \text{ with } i = 1,\ldots,N \tag{5}$$

The C controls the tradeoff between the robustness of the machine and the number of non-separable points.

By introducing Lagrange multipliers α_i and using the Karush-Kuhn-Tucker theorem of optimization theory [9], the decision function, for the vector $\mathbf{x}$, then becomes [8]:

$$f(\mathbf{x}) = \text{sgn}\left(\sum_{i=1}^{N} d^i \alpha_i < \mathbf{x}, \mathbf{x}^i > + b\right) \tag{6}$$

By replacing the inner product $< \mathbf{x}, \mathbf{x}^i > = (\mathbf{x}^T)(\mathbf{x}^i)$ with kernel function $K(\mathbf{x}, \mathbf{x}^i)$, the input data are mapped to a higher dimensional space. It is then in this higher dimensional space that a separating hyperplane is constructed to maximize the margin. In the lower dimensional data space, this hyperplane becomes a non-linear separating function.

3 Perturbation Method and the Statement of the Problem

The mappings in SVM are $R^P \to R$ with continuous and differentiable output $y(\mathbf{x}) = \sum^{N} d^i \alpha_i K(\mathbf{x}, \mathbf{x}^i) + b$, where $\mathbf{x} \in R^P$. Let us consider an SVM classifier which is assumed to perform a nonlinear, differentiable mapping $\Gamma : R^P \to R$, $y = \Gamma(\mathbf{x})$, where $y \in R$, and $\mathbf{x} \in R^P$ is output and input vector, respectively. In a further discussion, we assume that some certain inputs carry none or little relationship to the output. Therefore, they can be discarded. The main aim here is to reduce the original dimension of input vector $\mathbf{x}$. Thus, a smaller SVM network can be modeled with a little or no loss of accuracy.

Let $y : R^P \to R$ be a function $y(\cdot)$. Suppose $\mathbf{x}^i \in \Omega$, where Ω is an open set needed for differentiability of y at $\mathbf{x}^i$. Since y is differentiable at $\mathbf{x}^i$, we can expand $y(\mathbf{x}^i + \Delta\mathbf{x})$ into the Taylor series for linearization as follows:

$$y(\mathbf{x}^i + \Delta\mathbf{x}) = y(\mathbf{x}^i) + \nabla^T y(\mathbf{x}^i)\Delta\mathbf{x} + h(\Delta\mathbf{x}) \tag{7}$$

where

$$\nabla y(\mathbf{x}^i) = \begin{bmatrix} \dfrac{\partial y}{\partial x_1} \\ \dfrac{\partial y}{\partial x_2} \\ \vdots \\ \dfrac{\partial y}{\partial x_P} \end{bmatrix}$$

is the gradient vector and $h(\Delta\mathbf{x})$ represents the higher order terms.

And

$$\lim_{\Delta\mathbf{x} \to 0} \frac{h(\Delta\mathbf{x})}{|\Delta\mathbf{x}|} = 0 \tag{8}$$

In Eq. (7), $y(\mathbf{x}^i)$ is a point which represents the response of the SVM for the i-th component of the training set, $\mathbf{x}^i$. On the other hand, $y(\mathbf{x}^i + \Delta\mathbf{x})$ is the perturbed response due to the disturbance $\Delta\mathbf{x}$ of the input vector.

Let assume now that the SVM network with input $\mathbf{x}$ is perturbed by a sufficiently small $\Delta\mathbf{x}$. After perturbation procedure, the first term of Eq. (7) is fixed and the third term $h(\Delta\mathbf{x})$ which corresponds higher order derivatives is vanished in accordance with Eq. (8). Consequently, the only remaining component in Eq. (7) is the linear term, $\nabla^T y(\mathbf{x}^i)\Delta\mathbf{x}$. For normalized $\Delta\mathbf{x}$ displacement, the vector $\nabla^T y(\mathbf{x}^i)$ provides the first-order directional information about the non-zero displacement $y(\mathbf{x}^i + \Delta\mathbf{x}) - y(\mathbf{x}^i)$.

Now the aim is to evaluate the displacements as a consequence of perturbation procedure over the entire training set $T = \left\{ \mathbf{x}^1, \mathbf{x}^2, \ldots, \mathbf{x}^N \right\}$.

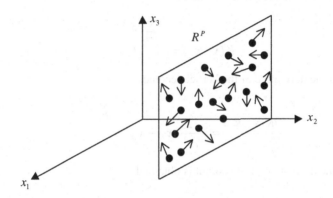

Fig. 1. A geometrical view of perturbation effects in an input space R^P with $P = 3$. Example illustrates a redundant x_2 component

The arrows in Fig. 1 shows the input space projections of the output displacements due to sufficiently small normalized input displacements $\Delta\mathbf{x}$. Then it is asked whether all P dimensions of input vectors contribute to the output changes or not. In the example illustrated by Fig. 1, the variable x_2 does not contribute to the output changes $y(\mathbf{x}^j + \Delta\mathbf{x})$. In other words, the output is constant in x_2. See [7] for a similar geometric representation for perceptron networks.

Consequently, if the output is insensitive to the j-th variable of input vector $\mathbf{x} \in R^P$, the j-th variable of the gradient vector can be discarded. The insensitivity to the j-th variable should hold for the entire training set T, thus the j-th component can be zeroed for $\nabla^T y(\mathbf{x}^i)$, $i = 1, 2, \ldots, N$. On the other hand, in real world problems, qualitative methods other than zeroing are necessary to rank the significance of each individual component of input vector over the training set. Such a method is formulated and an algorithm is presented in following sections.

4 Measurement of Sensitivity

The purpose of measuring sensitivity is to rank the significance of feature inputs over the entire training set. Notice that the elements of the gradient vector defined in Eq. (7) can be considered as sensitivity coefficients. So, the sensitivity of the output to the inputs in SVM is derived by solving the following partial derivative:

$$\frac{\partial y(\mathbf{x}_i)}{\partial x_{ik}} = \frac{\partial \left(\sum_{s=1}^{N_s} \alpha_s d^s K(\mathbf{x}_i, \mathbf{x}_s) + b \right)}{\partial x_{ik}} = \frac{\partial \left(\sum_{s=1}^{N_s} \alpha_s d^s K(\mathbf{x}_i, \mathbf{x}_s) \right)}{\partial x_{ik}} \tag{9}$$

where N_s is the number of support vectors corresponding to non-zero Lagrange multipliers and $k = 1, 2, \ldots, P$.

Let us assume the kernel is Gaussian:

$$K(\mathbf{x}_i, \mathbf{x}_s) = e^{\frac{-\sum_{l=1}^{P} (x_{il} - x_{sl})^2}{\sigma^2}} \tag{10}$$

Then the derivative of the kernel becomes:

$$\frac{\partial K(\mathbf{x}_i, \mathbf{x}_s)}{\partial x_{ik}} = -\frac{2}{\sigma^2} (x_{ik} - x_{sk}) e^{\frac{-\sum_{l=1}^{P} (x_{il} - x_{sl})^2}{\sigma^2}} \tag{11}$$

So, the derivative of the output is obtained:

$$\frac{\partial y(\mathbf{x}_i)}{\partial x_{ik}} = -\frac{2}{\sigma^2} \sum_{s=1}^{N_s} \alpha_s d^s (x_{ik} - x_{sk}) e^{\frac{-\sum_{l=1}^{P} (x_{il} - x_{sl})^2}{\sigma^2}} \tag{12}$$

The sensitivity can be calculated for any type of kernel function in accordance with Eq. (9), and its value depends upon the input feature x_{ik}, the support vectors x_s as well as the non-zero Lagrange multipliers α_s.

Then, the sensitivity measure of each feature is calculated for k-th component ($k = 1, 2, \ldots, P$) via Eq. 13.

$$S_k = \frac{\sum_{i=1}^{N} \left| \frac{\partial y(\mathbf{x}_i)}{\partial x_{ik}} \right|}{N} \tag{13}$$

See [6] for other useful measure of sensitivity used for the evaluation of input sensitivity. All these techniques can be used to obtain the relative significance of each input feature to the output.

The calculated sensitivity values are used to rank the relative significance of input features. However, sensitivity measure does not give a definite number of feature components which are to be discarded. So a recursive algorithm is needed to be proposed not only to discard redundant features but also to find optimal solution such a proposition is as follows:

Algorithm:

Step 1   Begin with setting $k = P$ in Eq. (12) and (13), where P is the dimension of the feature vector ($\mathbf{x} \in R^P$).

Step 2   Choose an n value which could be taken one for small k or more than one for large k.

Step3   If $k > n$, then
 - Train SVM using the feature set of sample vectors of k dimension and measure its generalization performance using test data.
 - Store the obtained test performance value.
 - Calculate the sensitivity measure S_i for $i = 1, 2, \ldots, k$ by using Eq. (12) and (13) for each feature candidate.
 - Rank the sensitivity values S_i in a descending order, $(S_1 > S_2 > \cdots > S_k)$
 - Delete n feature components with smallest sensitivity values, $S_{k+1-n}, \ldots, S_k$.
 - Train SVM by using the remaining features and measure the generalization performance.
 - Store the test performance value.
 - Set $k = k - n$ after reindexing the remaining feature components.

Step 4   Go to Step 2 and continue until $k \leq n$.

After the iterative implementation is concluded, the feature set that produces the best performance in SVM is obtained by evaluating stored performance values. Herein, accuracy, sensitivity and specificity which will be defined below can be considered as performance values.

5   Application

5.1   Recognition of Epileptiform Patterns in EEG

This application presents the classification of epileptiform patterns (EPs) in a one dimensional and single-channel EEG signal. SVM is used to classify the patterns into two subgroups: i) EPs and ii) non-EPs.

19 EEG records which contain 127 EPs and 184 non-EPs are used to train the SVM while a different set of 10 records with 76 EPs and 89 non-EPs are reserved for testing purposes.

The patterns are aimed to be separated from each other by a nonlinear SVM that would function as a classifier whose input is a vector of 70 consecutive sample values obtained from each peak. An EEG EP, which is different from the background activity, has a pointed peak and duration of 20 to 70 ms [10]. Although it may occur alone, an EP is usually followed by a slow wave, which lasts 150-350 ms, together forming what is known as a "spike and slow wave complex" [11].

The proposed perturbation method will be examined for two different feature extraction techniques based on:

- The discrete cosine transform (DCT) of each extracted pattern for creating Feature Set I.
- The discrete wavelet transform (DWT) of each extracted patterns for creating Feature Set II at second, third and fourth level.

Using the above procedure, two feature sets are prepared by extracting the EPs from the original signal and taking the transform of them for each extracted patterns.

The classification performance of the system is determined by measuring the sensitivity, specificity and accuracy. Sensitivity is the ratio of true positives to the total number of EPs determined by expert as "EP". Specificity is the ratio of "false positive" to the summing of false positive with correct rejections. Accuracy is the ratio of total number of true positives and false positives to the total number of true positives, false positives, true negatives and false negatives [12].

In this study, then, the performance of two feature sets from the same records is comparatively examined to justify the invariance of the proposed perturbation method with respect to the used feature extraction technique. The best features are selected by applying the adaptive feature selection method, which is proposed with the algorithm in Section 4 in detail, for each two feature sets separately. In feature selection procedure, in accordance with the recursive algorithm in Section 4, SVM is firstly trained using the whole features with 70 DCT coefficients. After testing and calculating the performance of the system, sensitivity values are calculated by using Eq. 12 and Eq. 13. Two feature components corresponding to the smallest sensitivity values are deleted, after sensitivity values are ranked in a descending order. Then, SVM is retrained with remaining features after deleting the redundant feature components (with 68 DCT coefficients). This iterative implementation is repeated until two feature components remain. At each loop in the algorithm, the classification performance of the system is tested by using test data and stored for determining the best features. So, the optimal input size is also determined as the number of the most significant feature components. If the dimension of feature vector is large, the number of deleting components corresponding to the smallest sensitivity values can be increased. Due to the nature of the algorithm, the SVM is also trained and tested while the feature selection is implemented. All these implementations are done for each two feature sets separately in the same way.

The feature extraction of the first feature set involves the DCT coefficients of data. From 70 DCT coefficient values, the best classification performance is obtained for a subset of the most significant 18 DCT coefficients. The ordering of components in each feature set is in terms of sensitivity measures:

K_1	k_2	k_3	k_4	k_5	k_6	k_7	k_8	k_9	k_{10}	k_{11}	k_{12}	k_{13}	k_{14}	k_{15}	k_{16}	k_{17}	k_{18}
d_4	d_5	d_3	d_1	d_6	d_9	d_2	d_{10}	d_{13}	d_{16}	d_{15}	d_{18}	d_{22}	d_{34}	d_{37}	d_{53}	d_{54}	d_{58}

$\mathbf{k} = [k_1, k_2, \ldots, k_{18}]^T$ is the new 18-dimensional feature vector. $\mathbf{d} = [d_1, d_2, \ldots, d_{70}]^T$ is the vector representing the DCT coefficients of each pattern.

The feature extraction of second feature set involves DWT coefficients of data. Feature vectors are formed using Daubechies-2 wavelet [13]. For each feature vector, wavelet approximation coefficients at the second, third and fourth levels (19+11+7=37 in total) are calculated. From 37 wavelet coefficients, 13 features give the highest performance of the system. Sensitivity analysis in this feature set has shown the fourth level wavelet coefficients to be more significant than others.

K_1	k_2	k_3	k_4	k_5	k_6	k_7	k_8	k_9	k_{10}	k_{11}	k_{12}	k_{13}
a_4^4	a_5^4	a_1^4	a_6^3	a_7^4	a_8^3	a_6^4	a_3^4	a_9^2	a_{11}^3	a_2^3	a_{14}^2	a_6^2

$$\mathbf{k} = [k_1, k_2, \ldots, k_{13}]^T \text{ and } \mathbf{a} = [a_1^2, a_2^2, \ldots, a_{19}^2, a_1^3, a_2^3, \ldots, a_{11}^3, a_1^4, a_2^4, \ldots, a_7^4]^T$$

where $\mathbf{k}$ represents 13-dimensional new feature vector and $\mathbf{a}$ is a vector representing the wavelet approximation coefficients at 2-th, 3-rd and 4-th levels.

Consequently, the most significant features for two different feature sets are determined by using sensitivity analysis based on SVM. Thus, not only the system is optimized for having the best performance, but also the input dimension is reduced. So, computing time is reduced and the network is become smaller and simple.

After the feature extraction, the real data feature sets are fed to SVM for classification of EPs. EPs and non-EPs are represented by +1 and −1, respectively, for both training and testing procedures. First feature set involving DCT coefficients explained above is fed to the SVM. The C is initially set to 100. The SVM is trained until finding the best result in accordance with the algorithm presented in Section 4. The best result is obtained for 18 coefficients. Thus, the input dimension is reduced to 18 by selecting the best feature components. Then, the SVM classifier is performed for different C values with determined 18 features. The best result is obtained for $C = 100$ with 22 support vectors. Testing the SVM in the system shows a sensitivity of 96.0%, specificity of 92.1% and accuracy of 93.9%.

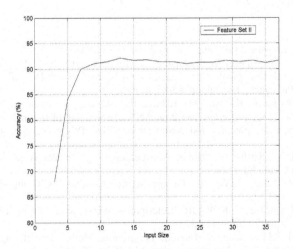

Fig. 2. The effect of the input size, determined at each iterations of adaptive feature selection algorithm, on the accuracy rate for Feature Set II

For second feature set, involving DWT approximation coefficients, the same training and feature selection implementations are repeated without any change. After, the C value initially set to 100, the algorithm is applied to the set. Then, the best result is obtained for 13 coefficients (Fig. 2). So, the input size is reduced to 13 by selecting the most significant feature components. Then, the SVM classifier is again performed for different C values with determined 13 features. The best result is obtained for C=100 which is the same as first feature set. The number of support vectors is 16 which also corresponds to the number of hidden neurons. For second feature set, the performance of the system results in a sensitivity of 94.7%, specificity of 89.9% and accuracy of 92.1%.

Consequently, proposed method is successfully performed in a classification example. In result, the best performance is obtained for DCT coefficients with a reduced input size. So, the proposed method can be generally used in pattern classification tasks.

6 Conclusion

Using perturbation based sensitivity approach for input dimension reduction in SVM is particularly useful when the training data involves a large amount of redundant data. If the redundancy in training data vectors exist, the proposed technique based on perturbation method for input size reduction allows for building more efficient SVM network models. This can be achieved at a relatively low computational cost and a simple SVM modeling as outlined in the paper. The proposed method is applied to the automated recognition of EPs in EEG. The results of application show that it performs very good for classification problems in bioinformatics.

References

1. Vapnik, V.: Statistical Learning Theory. John Wiley, NY, (1998).
2. Vapnik V.: The support vector method of function estimation. In: J.A.K. Suykens, J. Vandewalle (Eds.), Nonlinear Modelling: Advanced Black-Box Techniques. Kluwer Academic Publishers, Boston, pp. 55-85, (1998).
3. Acır, N., Öztura, İ., Kuntalp, M., Baklan, B., Güzeliş, C.: Automatic spike detection in EEG by a two stage procedure based on ANNs. Proceeding of International Conference on Artificial Neural Networks and Neural Information Processing, pp. 445-448, Istanbul, (2003).
4. Devijver, P.A., Kittler, J.: Pattern Recognition: A Statistical Approach, Prentice-Hall, Englewood Cliffs, NJ, (1982).
5. Steppe, J.M., Bauer, K.W., JR.: Feature Sensitivity Measures. Computers Math. Applic. 23-8 (1997) 109-126.
6. Belue, L.M. and Bauer, K.W.- JR.: Determining input features for multilayer perceptrons. Neurocomputing. 7 (1995) 111-121.
7. Zurada, J.M., Malinowski, A., Usui, S.: Perturbation Method for deleting redundant inputs of perceptron networks. Neurocomputing. 14 (1997) 177-193.
8. Haykin S.: Neural Networks: A comprehensive foundation. Prentice Hall, New Jersey, (1999).
9. Bertsekas, D.P.: Nonlinear Programming. Athenas Scientific, Belmont, (1995).

10. Chatrian, E., Bergamini, L., Dondey, M., Klass, D.W., Lennox-Buchthal, M., Petersen, I.:
    A glossary of terms most commonly used by clinical electroencephalographers.
    Electroencephalogr. Clin. Neurophysiol., 37 (1974) 538-548.
11. Kalaycı, T., and Özdamar, Ö.: Wavelet preprocessing for automated neural network
    detection of EEG spikes. IEEE Eng. Med. Biol., 14-2 (1995) 160-166.
12. McNeil, B.J., Keeler, E., Adelstein, J.: Primer on certain elements of medical decision
    making. Journal of medicine (The New England), 293-5 (1975) 211-215.
13. Daubechies, I.: Ten lectures on wavelets. Capital city press, Montpelier, VT, (1992).

Selection of Optimal Dimensionality Reduction Methods for Face Recognition Using Genetic Algorithms

Önsen Toygar and Adnan Acan

Computer Engineering Department, Eastern Mediterranean University,
Gazimağusa, T.R.N.C., Mersin 10, Turkey
{onsen.toygar, adnan.acan}@emu.edu.tr

Abstract. A new approach for optimal selection of dimensionality reduction methods for individual classifiers within a multiple classifier system is introduced for the face recognition problem. Principal Component Analysis (PCA), Linear Discriminant Analysis (LDA) and Independent Component Analysis (ICA) are used as the appearance-based statistical methods for dimensionality reduction. A face is partitioned into five segments and each segment is processed by a particular dimensionality reduction method. This results in a low-complexity divide-and-conquer approach, implemented as a multiple-classifier system where distance-based individual classifiers are built using appearance-based statistical methods. The decisions of individual classifiers are unified by an appropriate combination method. Genetic Algorithms (GAs) are used to select the optimal dimensionality reduction method for each individual classifier. Experiments are conducted to show that the proposed approach outperforms the holistic methods.

1 Introduction

Genetic Algorithms (GAs) are biologically inspired search procedures used for the solution of hard numerical and combinatorial optimization problems. The power and success of GAs are mainly achieved by diversity of individuals of a population which evolve following the Darwinian principle of 'survival of the fittest'. In the standard implementation of GAs, the diversity of individuals is achieved using the genetic operators mutation and crossover which facilitate the search for high quality solutions without being trapped into local optimal points [1-3].

Appearance-based statistical methods, namely Principal Component Analysis (PCA), Linear Discriminant Analysis (LDA) and Independent Component Analysis (ICA) are well-known and the most widely used dimensionality reduction methods applied for the solution of face recognition problem. PCA, also known as Eigenspace Projection, is used mainly for dimensionality reduction in compression and recognition problems [4-6]. It tries to find the eigenvectors of the covariance matrix in order to find the basis of the representation space. The eigenvectors correspond to the directions of the principal components of the original data, their statistical significance is given by their corresponding eigenvalues [4-6]. Linear Discriminant Analysis (LDA),

T. Yakhno (Ed.): ADVIS 2004, LNCS 3261, pp. 472–481, 2004.

also known as Fisher's Discriminant Analysis, searches for those vectors in the underlying space that best discriminate among classes [4-6]. The basic idea of LDA is to find a linear transformation such that feature clusters are into a number of equal width separable after the transformation which can be achieved through scatter matrix analysis [4-6]. The aim is to maximize the Between-class scatter matrix measure while minimizing the Within-class scatter matrix measure [5]. Another powerful method is Independent Component Analysis (ICA) which is a special case of redundancy reduction techniques and represents the data in terms of statistically independent variables [6-9]. ICA of a random vector consists of searching for a linear transformation that minimizes the statistical dependence between its components [8].

Face recognition is one of the well-known problems in the field of image analysis and understanding. An unknown person is recognized from his/her face image by comparing the unknown face with the known faces from a face database. The interest of researchers and engineers to develop efficient methods for the solution of the face recognition problem has grown rapidly in the recent years since there is a wide range of commercial and law enforcement applications in this field [10-12].

In this study, a face is partitioned into a number of equal-width horizontal segments and each horizontal segment is processed by a different appearance-based statistical method. A multiple classifier system in which each individual classifier is associated with a particular horizontal segment is formed and a multiple-classifier combination method is used to combine individual classifier outputs to determine the resulting face recognized. GAs are used to select the optimal dimensionality reduction method for each segment of a face image. In order to compare the performance of the proposed approach with the above mentioned holistic methods, the standard FERET (FacE REcognition Technology) database and the FERET Evaluation Methodology [13,14] are used in all experimental evaluations.

This paper is organized as follows: The proposed approach is described in the following section. Problem model and application of Genetic Algorithms are presented in Sections 3 and 4, respectively. Then, the experimental results are given in Section 5. Finally, Section 6 concludes this paper.

2   The Proposed Approach

A novel and fast divide-and-conquer approach, implemented as a multiple-classifier system using PCA, LDA, and ICA algorithms as dimensionality reduction methods, is proposed. The aim is to improve the computational efficiency and recognition performance of the holistic appearance-based statistical methods. The main difficulties of applying appearance-based statistical face recognition algorithms, such as high computation time and memory requirements, are due to their holistic approach for feature extraction. Holistic approaches aim to find a reduced dimensional representation for a facial image using features extracted from the image as a whole. However, the most important characteristic features for face recognition are those extracted from the facial image between eyebrows and chin. Hence, extraction of these features considering more localized portions of the original image may provide better representations for the improvement of recognition performance. Consequently, one can partition an input image into a number of smaller parts for the extraction of locally important features more efficiently; which may obviously result in improved recognition performance, faster computational procedures, and smaller storage space requirement. This way, face recognition using holistic face images and one classifier method is reduced to feature extraction over a number of smaller facial segments and recognition using multiple classifiers with one or more classifier methods and dedicated output combination approaches. Consequently, instead of having a single holistic classifier, a number of lower-complexity classifiers, employing locally important features for classification, are used. The final decision for face recognition requires a multiple-classifier combination method to combine individual classifier outputs into one decision for classification. It is well known that the classifier performance obtained by combining the outputs of several individual classifiers, can be better than the performance of a more powerful single classifier [15,16]. These are the main inspirations behind the proposed approach, the success of which is demonstrated by theoretical analysis and experimental evaluations using benchmark face databases.

In the implementation of the proposed approach, multiple classifiers with different number of individual classifiers and different output combination methods are considered. For this purpose, a face image is divided into a number of equal-width horizontal segments. Each horizontal segment is associated with a particular classifier for feature extraction and classification purposes. The classifier output of each classifier is computed separately followed by a multiple-classifier combination procedure, which produces the final classifier or recognition output. In this paper, multiple-classifiers with five individual classifiers is used for experimental evaluations. Also, Borda Count method [15,16] is considered as the classifier combination method due to its better performance over the other tested combination procedures. The reason why a multiple-classifier with five individuals provides the best overall performance can be explained by the fact that when a normalized facial image is subdivided into five equal-width horizontal segments, distinctive features of the face such as the forehead, eyes, nose, mouth and the chin are placed into the same horizontal segments, from which locally important features are extracted in a better way than when they are extracted by holistic counterparts.

In this study, an input face image is cropped into a normalized size with predetermined number of rows and columns. Then, the facial image is divided into equal-width horizontal segments as shown in Fig. 1. Eventually, each horizontal segment is associated with an individual classifier which uses a particular appearance-based statistical method for feature extraction and classification (i.e. recognition). In our evaluations, GAs are used to select the optimal dimensionality reduction method for each face segment to obtain the best recognition performance. Application of GAs are explained in Sections 3 and 4. The same horizontal partitioning is applied to training and test images. The proposed approach can also be very suitable for partial face recognition; even one part of a facial image is damaged, obscured, or blurred, other parts may provide quite useful features for recognition.

Considering a set of MxN holistic face images, with K images in the training set, computational and storage space efficiencies of holistic PCA, LDA and ICA approaches and the proposed multiple-classifier approach, in which individual classifiers use a particular appearance-based statistical algorithm as the classification method, are evaluated [18]. The time efficiencies of the holistic PCA, LDA and ICA approaches are found to be $O(K(MN)^3)$. The proposed approach improves the time efficiencies to $O(K((MN)^3/P^2))$. Therefore, the theoretical speedup of the proposed approach is evaluated to be P^2.

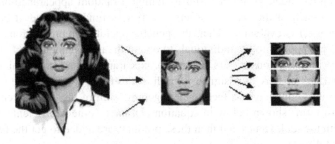

Fig. 1. The original face image, cropped image and five horizontal segments of the divided face

On the other hand, storage space complexities of the holistic PCA, LDA and ICA approaches are $O((MN)^2)$ and the proposed approach improves the storage space efficiencies to $O((MN)^2/P)$. According to these storage space efficiencies, the theoretical improvement achieved by the proposed approach becomes P [18].

3 Problem Model with Genetic Algorithms

In this study, GAs are used to select the optimal dimensionality reduction method for each horizontal segment of a partitioned face image. A population of individuals is initialized randomly where an individual is a quintuple of labels of dimensionality reduction methods associated with each horizontal segment. In this respect, the appearance-based statistical methods PCA, LDA and ICA are labeled with integers 1, 2 and 3, respectively. The algorithm assigns a random method among the three appearance-based statistical methods for each of the five classifiers. A method can be assigned to more than one classifier or none of the classifiers.

Method for Horizontal Segment 1	Method for Horizontal Segment 2	Method for Horizontal Segment 3	Method for Horizontal Segment 4	Method for Horizontal Segment 5

Fig. 2. Description of a chromosome for a partitioned facial image

To apply a Genetic Algorithm to the horizontal partitions of a face recognition problem, a population of potential solutions is randomly initialized. Each chromosome is composed of genes, each of which represents a particular appearance-based statistical method to be used for the corresponding face partition. The description of a chromosome is illustrated in Fig. 2.

4   Application of Genetic Algorithms to Select the Optimal Dimensionality Reduction Method for Each Face Segment

The Genetic Algorithm applied to the horizontal partitions of the face recognition problem, starts with a random initialization of chromosomes (individuals) each of which is a candidate solution. After assigning a random appearance-based statistical method to each of the five classifiers, the fitness function value of each individual (chromosome) is evaluated. Then the genetic operators reproduction, crossover and mutation are applied to the individuals to obtain the new generation of chromosomes.

In the initialization process, a random appearance-based statistical method, either PCA, or LDA or ICA, is assigned to each of the five classifiers. The objective function or fitness function of a face is the algebraic sum of the 20 different costs. All of these cost terms shown below in equation (1), have some coefficients that are multiplied with the rank values and then these products are added to get the fitness function value as follows:

$$f(face) = (Coefficient_1 {}^*Rank_1\_value + Coefficient_2 {}^*Rank_2\_value + Coefficient_3 {}^*Rank_3\_value +......+ Coefficient_{20} {}^*Rank_{20}\_value) \tag{1}$$

where the first coefficient (Coefficient 1) has the largest integer value and then the other coefficient values decrease by 10 units and the last coefficient (Coefficient 20) has the smallest integer value. The fitness function value must be maximized in order to obtain the best recognition performance and to find the appropriate appearance-based statistical method for each face partition.

After the calculation of fitness function value, selection, crossover, reproduction and mutation operations are applied to the individuals to obtain the new generation of chromosomes. In the selection process, two individuals are selected according to the Tournament Selection with a tournament size equal to (0.25 * Population size). That is, the individuals are selected randomly among the best 25% of the individuals. Then the selected individuals are applied Uniform Crossover with the crossover probability 0.65. For each partition, one of the parents are selected randomly and put into the new offspring. The two offspring are obtained by repeating the above process. Reproduction operation assigns the best individuals as the offspring with the probability 0.35. That is, the same individuals among the best ones survive in the next generation. Finally, mutation operation assigns a new random appearance-based statistical method for horizontal partitions according to the mutation probability which is 0.05. For each partition, a new random number is generated and the assignment is done accordingly.

5   Experimental Results

Recognition performance of the new approach is measured using the FERET database and the FERET Evaluation Methodology. FERET Large gallery test, which measures an algorithm's performance against large databases, is followed in all of the experimental evaluations. Large gallery test results are represented by a performance statistics known as 'Cumulative Matched versus Rank' or 'Cumulative match' score. In this representation, the tested algorithm reports the top Q matches for each probe in a gallery of R images, in a rank-ordered list. From this list, one can determine if the correct answer for a particular probe is in the top Q matches, and if so, how far down the list is the correct match. In our experiments, the test case for which Q=20 and R=50 is followed.

The set of facial images used in this study, consists of male and female images of different racial origins. Some of the individuals have glasses and some of the male individuals have beards. Eight-bit gray-scale images are used which are cropped so that they only include the head of the individuals. These images are scaled down, without affecting the recognition performance, to speedup the computations and reduce the memory requirements.

As the first step of experimental evaluations, all faces in the database are cropped into a standard size of 45 rows and 35 columns, from the original size of 384x256. Then, each facial image is divided into P equal-width horizontal segments. As a result of evaluations and explanations in Section 2, recognition performance of the proposed approach is tested with five horizontal segments. This selection achieves reasonably higher performance for low-rank values while demonstrating close to the best performance for high-rank cases.

Following the first step, a particular appearance-based approach is considered and a multiple classifier system with five individual classifiers, where each individual classifier uses the selected appearance-based approach as the classification method, is constructed. In this way, a MCS with five classifiers and 50 classes is established. The five different classifier outputs, one for each horizontal segment, are combined using a particular classifier combination method. Combination of classifier outputs is obtained with Borda Count method [15,16].

In the experimental studies, the probe set consists of different samples of all the individuals in the gallery. The gallery consists of 50 frontal images with two samples per person, whereas the probe set includes 50 different samples of the same individuals' images. The large gallery test results, shown as Cumulative match score, are presented in Fig. 3, Fig. 4 and Fig. 5. Results on the recognition performance are for frontal images. Table 1 presents the CPU time and memory space used by different holistic algorithms and the proposed approach using a personal computer with a 400 MHz clock speed and 128 MB memory.

Results presented in Table 1 indicate that the presented approach reduces the overall CPU time ~35 times for PCA, ~19 times for LDA, and ~16 times for ICA. On the other hand, the reduction in the required memory space is ~4 times for PCA, ~5 times for LDA, and ~4 times for ICA. These results demonstrate that the proposed method outperforms the holistic appearance-based statistical approaches in both computational and storage space efficiencies. Compared to the theoretical values in computation time improvement and storage space reduction for five individual classifiers, which are 25 and 5 respectively, the obtained experimental results are compatible with the theoretical expected values.

The recognition performance of the proposed approach, compared to the performance of holistic appearance-based statistical methods, is illustrated on Fig. 3, Fig. 4 and Fig. 5. Experiments demonstrate that the proposed approach achieves almost tsame performance with PCA, and outperforms LDA and ICA. Particularly, when compared to ICA, our approach achieves an incomparable success level. Our approach also shows much better performance than LDA, especially for ranks below 12.

Table 1. Computation time and space requirements of the holistic and proposed PCA, LDA and ICA approaches

Holistic Appearance-based Statistical Approach			The Proposed MCS Approach (with five classifiers)		
Algorithm	CPU Time (seconds)	Memory Space used (MB)	Classifier Method	CPU Time (seconds)	Memory Space used (MB)
PCA	691	99	PCA	20	26
LDA	782	586	LDA	41	121
ICA	329	27.2	ICA	21	6.65

In order to improve the performance results of the proposed approach, GAs are used to select the optimal dimensionality reduction method for each face segment. Therefore, the method to be assigned for each classifier is decided by using GAs.

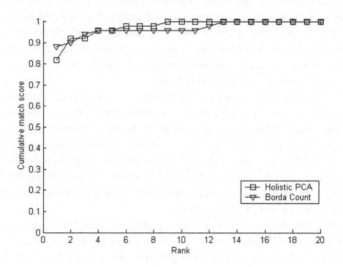

Fig. 3. PCA large gallery test: FA versus FB scores

After the application of GAs, the best performance is found using PCA method for the first four classifiers and LDA method for the last classifier. Using this arrangement of methods for each classifier, the performance results are shown below in Fig. 6. For comparison with the proposed MCS approach on PCA, LDA and ICA, all the performance results are simultaneously shown in Fig. 6. From that figure, it is seen that the optimal arrangement of methods found with GAs improves the recognition performance compared to the proposed MCS approaches.

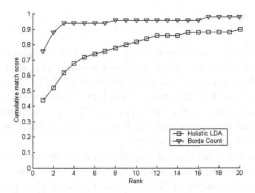

Fig. 4. LDA large gallery test: FA versus FB scores

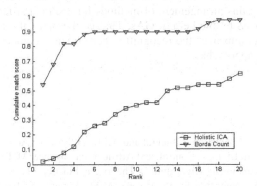

Fig. 5. ICA large gallery test: FA versus FB scores

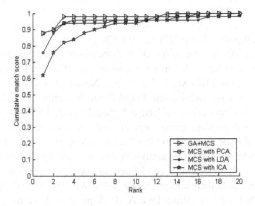

Fig. 6. Proposed MCS approach and GAs results

6 Conclusions

Recognition of faces is performed using a new, low-complexity and fast divide-and-conquer approach which is implemented as a multiple classifier system. The proposed approach uses dimensionality reduction methods PCA, LDA and ICA as the classification methods on the face recognition problem. Further, GAs are used to improve the recognition performance of the new approach. The experiments were carried out using five individual classifiers and the Borda Count method on the FERET database using FERET Evaluation Methodology.

Theoretical evaluations and the experimental results demonstrate that the new approach significantly improves computational efficiency, memory requirements and the recognition performance of these holistic methods. GAs are used to select the optimal dimensionality reduction method for each classifier to improve the recognition performance. Experimental results show that the best recognition performance is found using PCA method for the first four classifiers and LDA method for the last classifier. Using this arrangement of methods for each classifier, the performance results are improved by the help of GAs. That is, the optimal arrangement of methods found with GAs improves the recognition performance compared to the holistic and proposed MCS approaches.

References

1. Holland, J.H.: Adaptation in Natural and Artificial Systems: An introductory Analysis with Applications to Biology, Control, and Artificial Intelligence. MIT Press (1992)
2. Back, T.: Evolutionary Algorithms in Theory and Practice. Oxford University Press (1996)
3. Miettinen, K., Neitaanmaki, P., Makela, M.M., Periaux, J.: Evolutionary Algorithms in Engineering and Computer Science. John Wiley & Sons Ltd. (1999)
4. Yambor, W.S.: Analysis of PCA-Based and Fisher Discriminant-Based Image Recognition Algorithms. Technical Report CS-00-103, Computer Science Department, Colorado State University (July 2000)
5. Martinez, A. M., Kak, A.C.: PCA versus LDA. IEEE Transactions on Pattern Analysis and Machine Intelligence, Vol. 23(2). (2001) 228-233
6. Toygar, Ö., Acan, A.: An Analysis of Appearance-based Statistical Methods and Auto-associative Neural Networks on Face Recognition. The 2003 International Conference on Artificial Intelligence (IC-AI'03), Las Vegas, Nevada, USA (June 2003)
7. Hyvärinen, A.: Fast and Robust Fixed-Point Algorithms for Independent Component Analysis. IEEE Transactions on Neural Networks, Vol. 10(3). (1999) 626-634
8. Comon, P.: 'Independent component analysis: a new concept?'. Signal Processing, Elsevier, Special issue on Higher-Order Statistics, Vol. 36. (April 1994) 287-314
9. Liu, C., Wechsler, H.: Comparative Assessment of Independent Component Analysis (ICA) for Face Recognition. Second International Conference on Audio- and Video-based Biometric Person Authentication (AVBPA'99), Washington D.C., USA (March 1999)
10. Zhao, W., Chellappa, R., Rosenfeld, A., Phillips, P. J.: Face recognition: A literature survey. Technical Report CAR-TR-948, CS-TR-4167, N00014-95-1-0521 (October 2000)
11. Chellappa, R., Sirohey, S., Wilson, C.L., Barnes, C.S.: Human and Machine Recognition of Faces: A Survey, Proceedings of IEEE, Vol. 83. (May 1995) 705-740

12. Fromherz, T., Stucki, P., Bichsel, M.: A Survey of Face Recognition. MML Technical Report, No 97.01, Department of Computer Science, University of Zurich (1997)
13. Phillips, P.J., Wechsler, H., Huang, J., Rauss, P.: The FERET database and evaluation procedure for face recognition algorithms. Image and Vision Computing Journal, Vol. 16(5). (1998) 295-306
14. Phillips, P.J., Rauss, P.J., Der, S.Z.: FERET (Face Recognition Technology) Recognition-Algorithm Development and Test Results. Army Research Laboratory Technical Report, AR-TR-995 (October 1996)
15. Achermann, B., Bunke, H.: Combination of face recognition classifiers for person identification. Proceedings of 13th IAPR International Conference in Pattern Recognition (ICPR'96), Vol. 3.Vienna, Austria, (August 1996) 416-420
16. Ho, T., Hull,,J., Srihari, S.: Decision combination in multiple classifier systems, IEEE Transactions on Pattern Analysis and Machine Intelligence, Vol. 16(1). (1994) 66-75
17. Cormen, T.H., Leiserson, C.E., Rivest, R.L.: Introduction to Algorithms. The MIT Electrical Engineering and Computer Science Series (1990)
18. Toygar, Ö., Acan, A.: Multiple Classifier Implementation of a Divide-and-Conquer Approach Using Appearance-based Statistical Methods for Face Recognition. Pattern Recognition Letters, 2004 (accepted for publication)

Performance Comparison of Genetic and Differential Evolution Algorithms for Digital FIR Filter Design

Nurhan Karaboga and Bahadir Cetinkaya

Erciyes University, Department of Electronic Engineering,
38039, Melikgazi, Kayseri, Turkey
cetinkaya@erciyes.edu.tr

Abstract. Differential Evolution (DE) algorithm is a new heuristic approach mainly having three advantages; finding the true global minimum of a multi modal search space regardless of the initial parameter values, fast convergence, and using a few control parameters. DE algorithm which has been proposed particulary for numeric optimization problems is a population based algorithm like genetic algorithms using the similar operators; crossover, mutation and selection. In this work, DE algorithm has been applied to the design of digital Finite Impulse Response filters and compared its performance to that of genetic algorithm.

1 Introduction

Heuristic optimization algorithms such as genetic algorithm, tabu search and simulated annealing algorithms have been widely used in the optimal design of digital filters. When considering global optimization methods for digital filter design, the GA seems to have attracted considerable attention. Filters designed by GA have the potential of obtaining near global optimum solution [1,2]. Although standard GAs have a good performance for finding the promising regions of the search space, they are not so successful at determining local minimum in terms of convergence speed.

In order to overcome this disadvantage of GA in numeric optimization problems, Differential evolution algorithm has been introduced by Storn and Price [3]. Differential evolution algorithm is a new heuristic approach mainly having three advantages; finding the true global minimum of a multi modal search space regardless of the initial parameter values, fast convergence, and using a few control parameters. DE algorithm is a population based algorithm like genetic algorithms using the similar operators; crossover, mutation and selection. The studies on the design of optimal digital filters by using DE algorithm are not as common as GA. In literature, there are only a few studies related to the application of DE algorithm to the digital filter design. In this work, the performance comparison of the design methods based on Differential Evolution and Genetic algorithms is presented for digital FIR filters since DE algorithm is very similar to, but much simpler than GA. The paper is organized as follows. Section 2

T. Yakhno (Ed.): ADVIS 2004, LNCS 3261, pp. 482–488, 2004.

contains a review of genetic algorithm. Section 3 presents a basic differential evolution algorithm. Section 4 describes the application of algorithms to the design of digital FIR filters. Section 5 presents the simulation results and discussion.

2 Basic Genetic Algorithm

The genetic algorithm is an artificial genetic system based on the process of natural selection and genetic operators. It is also a heuristic algorithm which tries to find the optimal results by decreasing the value of objective function (error function) continuously [4]. A simplified GA cycle is shown in Fig.1.

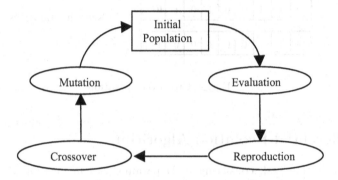

Fig. 1. A simplified GA cycle

Initial population consists of a collection of chromosomes [5]. In practice these chromosomes represent a set of solutions for the problem. The chromosome which produces the minimum error function value represents the best solution. The chromosomes which represent the better solutions are selected by the reproduction operator and then sent to the crossover operation. In this operation, two new chromosomes are produced from two chromosomes existing in the population. A common point in the selected chromosomes is randomly chosen and their corresponding digits are exchanged. Thus, new chromosomes which represent the new solutions are produced. The process in a simple crossover (single-point) operation is shown in Fig. 2.

The next operator is mutation. Generally, over a period of several generations, the genes tend to become more and more homogenous. Therefore, many chromosomes can not continue to evolve before they reach their optimal state. In the mutation process, some bits of the chromosomes mutate randomly. Namely, certain digits will be altered from either '0' to '1' or '1' to '0' in binary encoding [6].

In addition to the operators mentioned above GA also contains 'Elite' operator. By means of Elite operator, the best solution is always kept. In the evaluation process, the solutions in the population are evaluated and a fitness value associated with each solution is calculated. These fitness values are used by the selection operator. Roulette Wheel method is employed for the selection process.

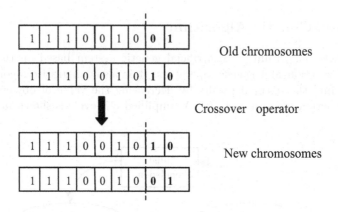

Fig. 2. Crossover operation

3   Differential Evolution Algorithm

An optimization task consisting of D parameters can be represented by a D dimensional vector. In DE, a population of NP solution vectors is randomly created at the start. This population is successfully improved by applying mutation, crossover and selection operators.

The main steps of a basic DE algorithm is given below:

> *Initialization*
> *Evolution*
> *Repeat*
>   *Mutation*
>   *Recombination*
>   *Evolution*
>   *Selection*
> *Until (termination criteria are met)*

3.1   Mutation

For each target vector $x_{i,G}$, a mutant vector is produced by

$$v_{i,G+1} = x_{i,G} + K \cdot (x_{r1,G} - x_{i,G}) + F \cdot (x_{r2,G} - x_{r3,G}) \qquad (1)$$

where $i, r_1, r_2, r_{r3} \in \{1, 2, ..., NP\}$ that randomly chosen and must be different from each other. In Eq(1), F is the scaling factor $\in [0, 2]$ affecting on difference vector $(x_{r2,G} - x_{r3,G})$, K is the combination factor.

3.2 Crossover

The parent vector is mixed with the mutated vector to produce trial vector $u_{ji,G+1}$

$$u_{ji,G+1} = \begin{cases} v_{ji,G+1} & , \text{if } (rnd_j \leq CR) \text{ or } j = rn_i \\ x_{ji,G} & , \text{if } (rnd_j > CR) \text{ and } j \neq rn_i \end{cases} \tag{2}$$

where $j = 1, 2, ..., D$; $r_j \in [0, 1]$ random number; CR stands for the crossover constant $\in [0, 1]$ and $rn_i \in (1, 2, ..., D)$ randomly chosen index.

3.3 Selection

Performance of the trial vector and its parent is compared and the better one is selected. This method is usually named greedy selection. All solutions have the same chance of being selected as parents without dependence of their fitness value. The better one of the trial solution and its parent wins the competition providing significant advantage of converging performance over genetic algorithms.

4 Application of Algorithms to the Problem

The transfer function of a FIR filter is given by Equation (3),

$$H(z) = \sum_{n=0}^{N} a_n z^{-n} \tag{3}$$

a_n represents the filter parameters to be determined in the design process and N represents the polynomial order of the function. In the design of FIR filter by using GA or DE, firstly the solutions must be represented in the string form of parameters. The representation scheme used in this work is shown in Fig.3.

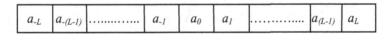

Fig. 3. Representation of solutions in string form

In order to evaluate the strings representing possible FIR filters, Least Mean Squared (LMS) error is used. The strings which have higher evaluation values represent the better filters, i.e. the filters with better frequency response. The expression of LMS function is given below:

$$LMS = \left\{ \sum_f [|H_D(f)| - |H_I(f)|]^2 \right\}^{\frac{1}{2}} \tag{4}$$

where $H_I(f)$ is the magnitude response of the ideal filter and $H_D(f)$ is the magnitude response of the designed filter. The fitness function to be maximized is defined depending on LMS function as the following,

$$Fitness_i = \frac{1}{LMS_i} \tag{5}$$

where $fitness_i$ is the fitness value of the solution i and LMS_i is the LMS error value calculated when the solution i is used for the filter.

5   Simulation Results

The simulations are realized for the filters with the order 14. In the simulations, the sampling frequency was chosen as $f_s = 1Hz$. Also, for all the simulations the sampling number was taken as 100. The control parameter values of DE and GA used in this work are given in Table 1.

Table 1. Control parameter values of DE and GA algorithms

Differential Evolution Algorithm	Genetic Algorithm
Population size = 100	Population size = 100
Crossover rate = 0.8	Crossover rate = 0.8
Scaling factor (F) = 0.8 Combination factor (K) = 0.8	Mutation rate = 0.01
Generation number = 500	Generation number = 500

The magnitude responses of the designed digital FIR filters by using DE and GA algorithms for the filter of 14th order are demonstrated in Fig.4.

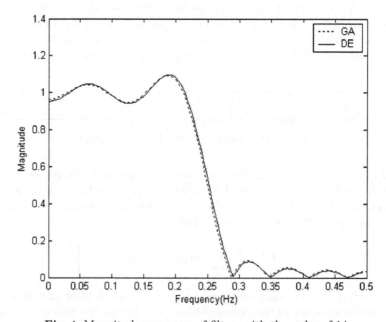

Fig. 4. Magnitude responses of filters with the order of 14

As seen from the Fig.4., the filters designed by DE and GA algorithms have similar magnitude responses for all the frequency regions. In order to compare the algorithms in terms of the convergence speed, Fig. 5. shows the evolution of best solutions obtained when GA and DE are employed. From the figures drawn for filter, it is seen that DE is significantly faster than GA for finding the optimum filter.

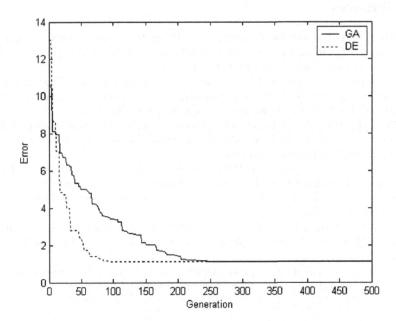

Fig. 5. Evolution of DE and GA for the filter with the order of 14

In Table 2, the LMS error values obtained are given. From the table it is clear that the performance of DE and GA is similar to each other in terms of LMS error.

Table 2. LMS error values for different filter orders

Algorithms	LMS error value
DE	1.1100
GA	1.1150

6   Conclusion

Differential evolution and genetic algorithms has been applied to the design of digital FIR filters. Although DE algorithm has more simple structure than

GA, for the same population size and generation number, DE algorithm demonstrates the similar performance in terms of magnitude response and hence LMS error. Consequently, DE algorithm has successfully designed FIR filters with desired magnitude responses and also found optimal filters much quicker than GA. Therefore, DE can be successfully used in digital FIR filter design.

References

1. Chen, S.: IIR Model Identification Using Batch-Recursive Adaptive Simulated Annealing Algorithm. In Proceedings of 6th Annual Chinese Automation and Computer Science Conference. (2000) 151–155.
2. Mastorakis, N.E., Gonos, I.F., Swamy, M.N.S.: Design of Two Dimensional Recursive Filters Using Genetic Algorithms.IEEE Transaction on Circuits and Systems I-Fundamental Theory and Applications. 50 (2003) 634–639.
3. Storn, R., Price, K.: Differential Evolution - A simple and Efficient Adaptive Scheme for Global Optimization over Continious Spaces. Technical Report TR - 95 - 012, ICSI. (1995) ftp.icsi.berkeley.edu.
4. Karaboga, N., Cetinkaya, B.: Performance Comparison of Genetic Algorithm based Design Methods of Digital Filters with Optimal Magnitude Response and Minimum Phase. The 46th IEEE Midwest Symposium on Circuits and Systems. (2003) (Accepted, In Press).
5. Lee, A., Ahmadi, M., Jullien, G.A., Miller, W.C., Lashkari, R.S.: Design of 1-D FIR Filters with Genetic Algorithms. IEEE Int. Symp. on Circ. and Syst. (1999) 295–298.
6. Xiaomin, M., Yixian, Y.: Optimal Design of FIR Digital Filter using Genetic Algorithm. The J. China Univ. Posts Telecom. 5 (1998) 12–16.

Kidney Allocation Expert System with Case-Based Reasoning

Tatyana Yakhno[1], Can Yilmaz[1], Sevinc Gulsecen[2], and Erkan Yilmaz[3]

[1] Dokuz Eylul University, Computer Engineering Department,
Bornova, Izmir, Turkey
yakhno@cs.deu.edu.tr; can.yilmaz@deu.edu.tr
[2] Istanbul University, Science Faculty Informatics Department,
Istanbul, Turkey
gulsecen@istanbul.edu.tr
[3] Istanbul University, Cerrahpasa Faculty of Medicine,
Istanbul, Turkey
eryilmazkan@superonline.com

Abstract. Experts in fields of organ transplantation have to make crucial decisions based on medical, social, moral and ethical factors. The paper describes the kidney allocation expert system KARES-CBR. Our system consists of two main components. Traditional expert system part uses rule-based knowledge. These rules contain general medical knowledge, such as blood group and antigens matching rules. Another group of rules contains decision making rules related to social and ethical information about organ transplantation. After decision making, the expert system component generates the list of medically suitable patients for the transplantation of an available organ.

Another part of the system collects the archive of previous successful organ transplantation cases. This historical data are used in case-based reasoning part of the system. Using different metrics, the system calculates the similarity values for kidney transplantation of selected patients relative to the previous successful transplantations. As a result, it selects the best suitable patient for organ transplantation. The system is implemented as an expert system shell and the different criteria and parameters can be easily modified. The system was tested on real data in the University hospital.

1 Introduction

Although allocating donor kidneys to patients seems simple, it is a quite complex phenomenon depending on many factors and interactions. A donation is the result of a chain of events, the final result of which will depend upon its weakest link. Even when the individual links have been strengthened, each element of the process of donation must be integrated into the operational policies developed in tune with national, moral and cultural values [1].

T. Yakhno (Ed.): ADVIS 2004, LNCS 3261, pp. 489–498, 2004.
© Springer-Verlag Berlin Heidelberg 2004

There are some allocation systems which are used regionally or nationally. Most of these systems use priority sorting algorithms that prioritize patient's attributes like age, waiting time, destination etc. or point scoring systems that point patients according to their specifications. Eurotransplant and United Network of Organ sharing (UNOS) are two leading examples of such kind computerized systems [1, 2].

The Eurotransplant International Foundation is responsible for the mediation and allocation of organ donation procedures in Austria, Belgium, Germany, Luxemburg, the Netherlands and Slovenia. As a mediator between donor and recipient, Eurotransplant plays a key role in the acquisition and distribution of donor organs for transplantations. The data of all potential recipients, such as blood group, tissue characteristics (HLA groups), cause of the disease, clinical urgency and the hospital where the patient is to be transplanted, are passed on to Eurotransplant. This information is stored in a central computer database. Subsequently, the patient is put on the (inter)national waiting list. At that point, the waiting time starts. The waiting time for kidney patients starts on the date of the first dialysis. As soon as a donor becomes available somewhere within the Eurotransplant area, the regional tissue-typing laboratory determines the donor's blood group and tissue characteristics. All relevant (medical) information about the donor is then transferred on to Eurotransplant's database. Subsequently, the Eurotransplant staff enters the donor information into a computer program especially developed for this purpose. After the data entry, the program selects the patient most suitable to receive the organ of this donor. It is crucial that the donor organ matches as good as possible with the patient. The selection criteria for the most suitable patient vary for different donor organs [1].

The United Network for Organ Sharing (UNOS) is a non-profit, scientific and educational organization that collects and manages data about every transplant event occurring in the United States. The system facilitates the organ matching and placement process using UNOS-developed data technology and the UNOS Organ Center. It brings together medical professionals, transplant recipients and donor families to develop organ transplantation policy. The UNOS Kidney Allocation Model (UKAM) is a software tool for the simulation and analysis of national cadaveric kidney and kidney-pancreas allocation policies for transplantation. UKAM is modular and is designed to enable easy updating of the various components as new data become available. UKAM's flexibility gives the user the ability to create and evaluate an almost infinite number of detailed allocation policies. This will enable the United Network for Organ Sharing (UNOS) to make decisions based on quantitative data when considering changes in organ allocation policies [2].

In transplantation process, decision is made by an expert (physician) who finds the most suitable patient for particular kidneys by scoring or prioritizing. This method can be useful for small number of recipients. But in the case of large number of recipients, the expert can make unfair and inconsistent decisions including emotional biases. Under this circumstance physician's decision may not be consistent regarding his/her personal influenced opinions. To keep decision making as valid as possible and to help physician to choose the most suitable patient is reason why expert systems are necessary in organ transplantation area [3, 4].

The main goal of our research is to integrate and use in one system different types of information and knowledge, such as medical, social, moral as well as statistical information about previous successful transplantation cases. To be able to do this we design and implement a system which integrates expert system properties with case-based reasoning - Kidney Allocation Ranked Expert System with Case-Based Reasoning (KARES-CBR).

The idea to use case-based reasoning (CBR) comes from the success of CBR technique in medical diagnosis systems [5, 6]. The main idea of case-based reasoning is based on the concept that situations recur with regularity and what is successfully done in one situation is likely to be applicable in similar ones. Case-based reasoning allows to propose solutions based on the previous cases and it does not require extensive analysis of domain knowledge. In KARES-CBR the information about all successful previous cases of kidney transplantations is stored in the database and similarity factors are used in final decision making.

The paper has the following structure. The architecture and components of our system are described in Section 2. Section 3 contains a brief description of the case study and the application of the system.

2   System Design and Architecture

KARES-CBR consists of two main components: Expert System and Case-Based Reasoning (CBR) component. The architecture of the system is given in Fig.1.

Expert System component has the properties common to traditional expert systems with rule-based knowledge base [7, 8]. It includes patients database that holds patients medical and social information, a donor database that holds donor's medical and social information, a General Match Process which is used to match a new kidney to patients according to rules. Case-Based Reasoning component includes cases database which has case vectors that show information about the history of successfully transplanted cases and a Similarity Matching Process that constructs a new case from patient and donor information and calculates a similarity value for each patient using similarity functions. Below we describe these components in more details.

2.1 Expert System Component of KARES-CBR

The main problem for Expert System (ES) component is to find the most suitable patient from database for a new available transplant. The solution has to be made on the base of two types of knowledge: medical matching and social factors.

The ES component consists of incoming donor information, patient database, donor database and general match process. When a new donor is available, information is stored into the donor database. Then, general match process takes turn and begins to compare patient and donor records from corresponding databases to construct a suitable patient list, according to knowledge base.

Patient Database. Patient database consists of patients' information stored in the system. In addition to social information, each patient has some medical properties such as ABO Blood Type, HLAs, Waiting Time, Medical Urgency and Prior Transplantation. Patient Database can be considered as a waiting list. If a patient is added to this database, allocation process is said to be started because waiting time attribute value increases everyday while the patient on the list.

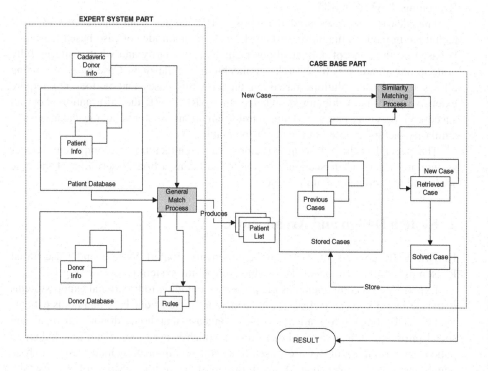

Fig. 1. System architecture of KARES-CBR

Donor Database. Donor Database consists of donors' attributes like ABO Blood Type, HLAs, Age, Race, Location and Gender which are required in the decision of transplantation. These attributes aggregate with patient' attributes considering the predefined rules in the system for selection process and the attribute values set by an expert for constructing feature vectors for each case.

General Match Process. General Match Process is a process of finding convenient patients for related donor. The process compares the donor attributes to all patient attributes according to rules defined in the ES component. Medical rules of the ES component are built–in and can not be changed in the system. Importance of the social factors (attributes) can be corrected by experts, using different weights. For example, an old patient with the medical urgency can get the highest priority even if his tissue matching is not the best one.

After applying the rules, medically suitable patients are selected for transplantation. Patients from this list are ranked according the expert system rules and this list is used as input by Case-Based Reasoning component.

2.2 Case-Based Reasoning Component

Having a list of patient as an output from Expert System part, expert still has more than one choice to decide which patient is the best candidate for available organ transplantation. To facilitate the expert's decision, case-based reasoning component is integrated to the system. This component takes a list of patients selected by ES component and evaluates the similarity of each patient to the successful transplantations done before. The output of the system will still be a list of patients but now, each patient has a rank value and a similarity value.

Patient List. The ES component of the KARES generates a list of patients which are medically suitable for available donor. This list is the input for Case–Based Reasoning part which will rank the patients according to attribute values and similarity functions. In the system, this list is formed dynamically in run time, and holds ID's of selected patients.

Previous Cases. Cases of successful transplantations represent the knowledge base of the CBR component of our system. The definition of case can be formulated as follows: a case is a contextualized piece of knowledge representing an experience that teaches a lesson fundamental to achieve the goals of the reasoner [9].

KARES designed to use a history of successful transplantations done before. If transplantation is done successfully, the system store the information of it by constructing a case vector from donor' and patient' attribute values. This vector then should be stored in the case database to be used for the evaluation of the next transplantations. So reliability of case base part depends on the size of previous cases database.

Similarity Matching Process. KARES constructs a case vector for each patient in the patients list. Case vectors are constituted from donor and patient attributes which should be in a standard form to make an adequate comparison between cases in the database and new case. Similarity Matching Process takes these constructed case vectors and finds a similarity value for each of these vectors comparing them to historical data by using similarity functions. Calculation of distance values and similarity values will be explained in the following section.

2.3 Case Construction and Similarity Measurement

In KARES-CBR every transplantation possibility is called a case. Therefore each case is constructed according to donor and patient attributes. For every case we will create a case vector, which will contain the differences between patient and donor values of attributes. A case vector that is used in KARES-CBR system has 9 attributes:

$$X = (x_1, x_2, x_3, x_4, x_5, x_6, x_7, x_8, x_9)$$

where x_1 is 'age difference ', x_2 is 'medical urgency', x_3 is 'waiting time', x_4 is 'distance of locations', x_5 is 'HLA matching difference ', x_6 is 'ABO matching difference', x_7 is 'prior transplant', x_8 is 'race difference ' and x_9 is 'difference in gender'. All attributes must have values from the interval [0, 1]. These numerical values are calculated from the table which is set by the expert before matching process. Example of difference calculation is given in the Table 1.

Table 1. Attribute condition values

Blood Group		Race		Gender		Prior Transplant	
X_to_X	0.1	Same	1	Same	1	Yes	0.5
O_to_X	0.8	Different	0.9	Different	0.9	No	1
X_to_AB	0.8						
HLA		Age (Years)		Distance (Km)		Waiting Time (Months)	
2A,2B,2DR	1	O-5	1	O-50	1	O-1	0.1
1A,2B,2DR	1	5-10	0.9	50-100	0.9	1-2	0.2
1A,1B,1DR	0.9	1O-15	0.8	100-150	0.8	2-3	0.3
-,2B,2DR	0.9	15-20	0.7	150-200	0.7	3-6	0.4
-,2B,1DR	0.8	2O-25	0.6	200-300	0.6	6-9	0.5
-,1B,2DR	0.7	25-30	0.5	300-400	0.2	9-12	0.6
-,1B,1DR	0.6	30-35	0.2	400-500	0.2	12-18	0.7
-,-,2DR	0.5	35-40	0.1	500-750	0.1	18-24	0.8
-,-,1DR	0.4	40-50	0.1	750-1000	0.1	24-36	0.9
		50+	0.1	1000+	0.1	36+	1

If the patient is 25 years old and the donor is 37 years old, the difference will be 12 and 'age difference ' value of the case vector will be 0.8 according to Table 1.

Like attribute 'age difference' in the above example, the other values of the case vector take the values between 0 and 1 according to the attribute values set by an expert. A sample vector is shown in Table 2 as having the age value $x_1 = 0.8$.

Table 2. Sample case vector

x_1	x_2	x_3	x_4	x_5	x_6	x_7	x_8	x_9
0.8	1	0.5	0.5	0.5	0.5	0.3	0.8	0.7

If the transplantation occurs and was successful, the case will be stored in the case database to be used in future transplantation decisions.

The system provides advices by giving similarity values and ranks to each patient using some distance metrics and ranking formula. Distance metrics normally measure the distance between points in the multi-dimensional feature space [9]. The following distance metrics are used to find the similarity value between two case vectors, one of which is a new case and the other is stored case in the system.

Mean Character Difference (MCD): The distance is defined as follows:

$$d(X,Y) = \frac{1}{n}\sum_{i=1}^{n}|x_i - y_i| \tag{1}$$

Minkowski Metrics: General form of this metric is defined as follows.

$$d(X,Y) = \left(\sum_{i=1}^{n}|x_i - y_i|^r\right)^{1/r} \quad where \ r \geq 1 \tag{2}$$

Here $X = (x_1, x_2 \dots x_n)$ is a new case vector, $Y = (y_1, y_2 \dots y_n)$ is a stored case vector, n - number of attributes.

In addition to having similarity value for each new case to the cases of successful transplantations, the expert can rank all new cases according to weights assigned to each patient attribute. These weights are specified by an expert before matching starts and reflect the expert's confidence how important different attributes are. Example of weights setting is given on Fig. 2. Using these weights the rank of the new case $R(X)$ is calculated by the following formula.

$$R(X) = (\sum_{i=1}^{n} w_i * x_i) / \sum_{i=1}^{n} w_i \tag{3}$$

where $X = (x_1, x_2 \dots x_n)$ is a patient case vector, $w = (w_1, w_2 \dots w_n)$ is weight values vector.

After having the similarity values and ranks for each selected patient, the physician can make more adequate transplantation decisions.

3 A Case Study

Expert system component of KARES includes three main headings: patient characteristics, donor characteristics and decision rules. Patient-Donor characteristics and their rules are shown in Table 3.

ABO compatibility checking is described in the form of if-then rules. The first selection of patients is made on this stage. Blood type compatibility is a must in transplantation process.

The second group of rules contains preordered tissue compatibility, more technically speaking the criteria of HLA match. The last group of rules is called dynamic rules and can be changed through interface of the system.

Dynamic decision rules include race, gender, age, location, medical urgency, prior transplantation and waiting time. The importance of these values can vary from one expert to another. For example, for one expert, the difference of 10 years for age attribute may be reasonable. But the other expert may not accept that difference and he may prefer up to 3 years at most. KARES-CBR system allows the experts to choose their acceptable differences and makes them select the matching scores for age, gender, race and location attributes. In addition, each expert can set his/her own rules in KARES-CBR system.

Table 3. Knowledge base of KARES

Patient Characteristics	Donor Characteristics	Decision Rules
ABO Blood Group	ABO Blood Group	ABO Blood Group Rules
Human Leukocyte Antigen	Human Leukocyte Antigen	HLA Matching Rules
Race	Race	Dynamic Rules (Race)
Gender	Gender	Dynamic Rules (Gender)
Age	Age	Dynamic Rules (Age)
Location	Location	Dynamic Rules (Location)
Waiting Time		Dynamic Rules (W. Time)
Medical Urgency		Dynamic Rules (M. Urgen.)
Prior Transplant		Dynamic Rules (P. Trans.)

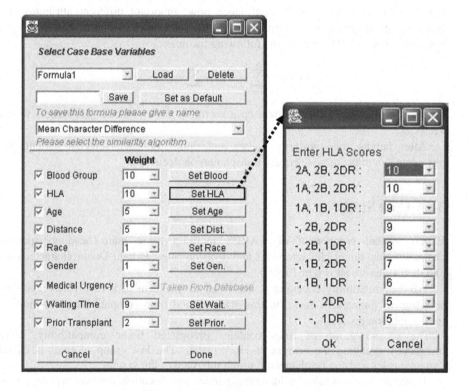

Fig. 2. Setting weights to the attributes

In Fig.2, case attribute values have to be entered and selected by the expert before the use of matching operation. User can select which parameters (criteria) will be considered and which similarity matching algorithm will be used. Weight values are also entered within this window. "Set Blood", "Set HLA", "Set Age", "Set Dist"., "Set Race", "Set Gen", "Set Wait." and "Set Prior" buttons are used to open related criteria menu to set the condition values of that attribute. User can save and load the information entered in this window to use it later. So, each physician is free to set and use his/her own values and functions.

Patient, Donor and Clinic information have to be entered into the system to be able to get reliable result from the KARES system. Case values are used to find distance values, similarity values and construct the case vector. Before the system begins matching, attribute values with their weights must be set, similarity function and attributes to be considered must be selected by an expert.

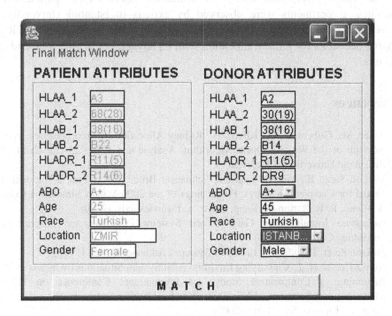

Fig. 3. Final match window

If transplantation occurs, final match operation should be completed by using final match window as seen in Fig.3. This operation constructs a new case and adds it to case base for future use.

4   Conclusion

This study describes the design, implementation and evaluation of the kidney allocation ranked expert system (KARES-CBR) with case-based reasoning (CBR) techniques. Like other allocation systems, KARES gives a rank value to each patient calculating it by using the attribute values that the expert previously set. Beside this feature, KARES-CBR uses CBR techniques by applying similarity matching functions to previously successfully matched results to make the experts decision easy and quick. This extra feature leads us to re-use the history of data that are composed from previous transplantations.

The main idea of the system is to guide the physicians in transplantation process by making their mind clear and obvious. The system achieves this by selecting suitable patients according to pre-defined rules in expert system part and similarity functions which are defined in case base part. At last, system produces prioritized patient list with a similarity and a rank value attached to the each patient. Physicians are free to set their attribute values and select a similarity function that is suitable for them.

The system has been tested for matching twenty-eight patients with nine attributes. Experiments were observed by experts in Istanbul University Medical School and were evaluated as successful. Results show that KARES-CBR provides reliable decisions for kidney allocation with its advantages of rule base and case base features.

References

1. Ahlert M., Gubernatis G., Kliemt H.: Kidney Allocation in Eurotransplant. A Systematic Account of the Wujciak-Opelz Algorithm. Analyse and Critic 23 (2), (2001), Research, ZiF, at the Univeristy of Bielefeld
2. Taranto Sarah E., Murphy Dan and Schmeiser Bruce: Developing a National Allocation Model for Cadaveric Kidneys, Proceedings of the 2000 Winter Simulation Conference, J. A. Joines, R. R. Barton, K. Kang, nad P. A. Fishwick, eds. (2000)
3. Giarratano Joseph, Riley Gary: Expert Systems Principles and Programming, PWS Publishing Company (1994)
4. Jackson Peter: Introduction to Expert Systems, Addison-Wesley (1999)
5. Nunez Hector et al.: Classifying Environmental System Situations by means of Case-Based Reasoning: a Comparative Study, 1st International Conference on Environmental Modelling and Software (iENSs2002), Vol.3, 450-455, Andrea E. Rizzoli & Anthony J. Jakeman (Lugano, Suiza) eds. (2002)
6. Sheng Li and Qiang Yang: ActiveCBR: An Agent System That Integrates Case-Based Reasoning and Active Databases, International Journal of Knowledge and Information Systems, Springer-Verlag London Ltd, Vol. 3, pp. 225-251. (2001)
7. Durkin John: Expert Systems: design and development, New York: Maxwell Macmillan International, Toronto: Maxwell Macmillan Canada (1994)
8. Awad Elias M, Building expert system: principles, procedures and applications, New York: West publishing (1996)
9. Kolodner Janet L.: Case-based Reasoning, Morgan Kaufmann Publishers, Inc. (1993)

Integrating AI and OR: An Industrial Engineering Perspective

Invited Talk

Irem Ozkarahan, Seyda Topaloglu, Ceyhun Araz, Bilge Bilgen, and Hasan Selim

Industrial Engineering Department, Dokuz Eylul University, 35100 Izmir, Turkey
irem.ozkarahan@deu.edu.tr

Abstract. Many researchers have spent significant effort in developing techniques for solving hard combinatorial optimization problems. We see that both the Operations Research (OR) and the Artificial Intelligence (AI) communities are interested in solving these types of problems. OR focuses on tractable representations, such as linear programming whereas AI techniques provide richer and more flexible representations of real world problems. In this paper, we attempt to demonstrate the impressive impact of OR and AI integration. First we discuss opportunities for integration of OR and AI. Then three applications are presented to demonstrate how OR and AI are integrated.

1 Introduction

Operations Research (OR) may be defined as a scientific approach to decision making. It aims to support solving real world problems in a wide variety of application areas, using mathematical and computer modeling [1]. The future of OR is clearly tied to its ability to use the computer technology effectively while devising methods and techniques that will enable organizations to improve productivity and quality. The relationship between OR and advances in computing technology, and the changing role of technology in the work place is an important subject that requires investigation.

In order for OR to prosper, utilizing the computer to provide faster, more powerful and versatile solution algorithms and methods is a necessary but not a sufficient condition. The developments of OR must be linked to organizational improvement since the lifeblood of the profession is its impact on practice. The OR analysts and practitioners find most organizations facing pressures to compete on the basis of cost, flexibility, quality and customer satisfaction.

OR based techniques have demonstrated the ability to identify optimal and locally optimal solutions for well-defined problem spaces. In general, however, OR solutions are restricted to rigid models with limited expressive power. The difficulty with this situation is that a real-world problem cannot be always adapted to a pre-specified

T. Yakhno (Ed.): ADVIS 2004, LNCS 3261, pp. 499–511, 2004.

form. Even if it were forced into a most suitable form, it would not be an accurate representation.

Artificial Intelligence (AI) is the application of methods of heuristic search to the solution of complex problems that defy the mathematics of optimization, contain non-quantifiable components, involve large knowledge basis, incorporate the design of alternative choice, and admit ill-specified goals and constraints. The characterization of AI does not set very definite boundaries. It emphasizes the aspiration of AI to deal with all the aspects of decision making that stretch beyond the limits of classical OR.

AI techniques provide richer and more flexible representation of real world problems. The problem with such rich representations is that in general they lead to intractable problems, and therefore are not capable of handling realistic size problems. AI supports efficient constraint-based reasoning mechanism, as well as mixed initiative framework, which allow the human expertise to be in the loop.

Simon [2] urges us not to take a traditional discipline-oriented approach to problem solving and notes that we must let the problem that we are trying to solve determine the methods we apply to it, instead of letting our techniques determine what we are willing and able to tackle.

A careful integration of OR and AI to problem solving shows significant promise for improving the capability and notably the acceptability of problem solving systems [3]. In other words, this integration provides representations that are expressive enough to describe real-world problems and at the same time guarantees good and fast solutions.

This paper is further organized as follows. Section 2 is devoted to discuss opportunities for integration of AI and OR. In sections 3, 4 and 5, three industrial engineering applications are presented respectively. Final section gives concluding remarks.

2   Opportunities for Integration of AI/OR

The OR community traditionally focused on solving optimization problems. OR from its roots in linear Programming (LP) which is most often used. Integer Programming (IP) and Mixed-Integer Programming (MIP) are the most important extensions of LP to deal with integrality constraints. The first algorithm to solve linear programs is the simplex method invented by Dantzig in 1947. The simplex method generally performs very efficiently in practice, however, Klee and Minty [4] showed that this method can require exponential time for some instances. Other types of algorithms have been proposed to solve linear programs, including the ellipsoid method [5], the interior point method of Karmarkar [6], and the Newton barrier algorithm [7]. Although these algorithms all have a polynomial time complexity, they are no more efficient than the simplex.

The combinatorially complex problem such as the traveling salesman problem, the machine sequencing problem, and the graph coloring problem have always been a challenge to operations researchers, since many OR combinatorial optimization problems can be formulated as integer linear programming problems. Ever since the development of the simplex algorithm, which provided an impetus and foundation for vigorous research in optimization, researchers continue work at developing more efficient and robust techniques for solving problems of this class.

The challenge of the combinatorial optimization problem also exists in AI. In AI techniques, after defining a solution space for a problem, a search strategy is used to move through the solution space in order to find the solution states. In this fashion, the search process becomes one of the most essential parts of the problem solving. Since the search process is the key to many intelligence processes, most AI techniques mimic human intelligence by performing the search process.

In recent years we have seen an increasing dialog between the AI and OR communities, in particular in the area of combinatorial problems. AI techniques can extend the capabilities of OR by facilitating the creation of models, automating model building and analysis, evaluating results, and applying proper model. Thus, the capabilities of OR can be made more accessible to decision makers. AI techniques can be invoked by OR models. This entails an extension to the traditional thinking of OR, in that an algorithm may include steps that carry out inferences, and may interact with users in the course of its execution.

The problem structure is an important theme in OR. Transshipment and network flow problems are notable examples of the importance of exploiting structure. Many combinatorial problems can be efficiently formulated as network flow problems. If a problem cannot be fitted into an LP or a network flow type structure, one uses a more general formulation such as IP. The standard OR approach for solving the IP problem is the branch-and-bound technique which solves several LP relaxations of the original IP model. The most influential strategic choices for the branch-and-bound technique are the selections of which variable to branch on next and which node to branch on next. The variable choice and the order in which nodes are explored in the search tree are extremely important for the sake of efficiency. Today, modern IP solvers such as ILOG-CPLEX [8], include built-in variable and node choice strategies such as "maximum integer feasibility" and "maximum cost evaluation" for variable choice strategies, and "minimum deterioration value in objective function" and "minimum number non-integer variables" for node choice strategies.

As it is mentioned in Gomes [9], when solving IP problems, the derivation of "cutting planes" is very important to eliminate parts of the search space that are guaranteed not to contain the optimal solution. The OR community has developed several techniques for the generation of cuts, but, in general, it is not clear how to construct such cuts. Vossen [10] indicates that a direction of research in the emergence of IP and AI techniques is the creation of methods that can automatically derive cutting planes at each node of the branch and bound tree in order to increase the effectiveness of IP techniques. Furthermore, Gomes [9] emphasized that the combination of cuts with constraint satisfaction techniques leads to more efficient solutions.

Constraint satisfaction techniques mainly rely on domain reduction techniques for inference during search. Researchers in AI usually adopt a constraint satisfaction approach for solving combinatorial optimization problems. Brailsford et al. [11] draws the attention of operations researchers on using these techniques as well. CP on the other hand, is the result of research in the area of logic programming and constraint satisfaction [12,13], which has become a powerful tool as an alternative method to mathematical programming techniques in OR. Recently, there has been a significant effort in developing models and methods that combine IP and CP. In all these efforts, it is aimed at developing integrated models and methods, which use the complementary strengths of IP and CP for solving problems that are otherwise intractable with either of these two methods. IP benefits the LP solver for providing a global view of the problem. Thus, LP could be useful to CP as it is useful to IP in the search process of certain problems. The early example to this approach is the work of Beringer and De Backer [14] that proposes a mixed search that uses constraint propagation on all the constraints, and an LP solver is used with all the linear constraints. Constraint propagation deduces new bounds on the domains of the variables, which are subsequently added to the LP relaxation. Meanwhile, the LP solver can detect whether the LP relaxation is consistent. It can also compute a lower bound in the case of minimization.

Local search methods or metaheuristics are often used to solve challenging combinatorial problems. There is a great deal of overlap in research on local search by the AI and OR communities, namely in simulated annealing [15], tabu search [16], and genetic algorithms [17]. They can be applied to a problem without having to know much about the structural properties of the problem. They exploit the problem specific knowledge to find fairly good solutions, but the amount of computation time needed to provide such a good solution sometimes may be too long. These algorithms need to be adapted specifically to individual problems.

Leading developers of software solutions for managing human resources, accounting, material management, distribution and manufacturing, across different industries, combine different optimization techniques such as constraint programming, mathematical programming and local search methods. Algorithmic innovations during the past 10 years have improved solution times by more than a factor of 100. Together with advances in computers, this dramatic improvement means that problems considered unapproachable only a few years ago are now readily solved - many in real time. For example ILOG's optimization software is now being used in actual applications. The description of how it was used in some of our example applications will be given later in next sections.

These new developments have created a unique opportunity to investigate the integration of AI, constraint satisfaction methods and OR techniques. Gomes [9] outlined the key issues as hybrid solvers, duality, problem structure, local search, randomization, cutting planes and constraint propagation, coupling and column generation with constraint satisfaction problem, and robustness.

In this paper, two of the three examples are based on service systems scheduling activities. There are two reasons for this. First, service sector related research is important since the employment impact of technological change in industrialized countries is great, reflecting an explosive rise in services over the past century. With at least two-thirds of labor force of industrialized economies employed in services, this sector accounts for the majority of their gross national products [18]. Second, many service management problems are fuzzy and unstructured; are multidimensional and complex; less conducive to normalize, analytical modeling, less conventional conceptual and mathematical mindsets. Therefore, they are more suitable for AI applications.

In our examples hybrid solver and local search techniques are used. As can be seen later, these very challenging OR problems become not so challenging anymore with the help of AI.

3 Application 1: Medical Resident Scheduling Problem

Persistent calls come from within the graduate medical education community and from external sources for regulating the resident duty hours in order to meet the obligations about the quality of resident education, the well-being of resident themselves, and the quality of patient care services. A recently released report of the Accreditation Council for Graduate Medical Education (ACGME) proposes common program requirements for resident hours. Today in many hospitals, the chief residents spend very long hours to manually prepare schedules by trial and error. In spite of the effort, the quality of the resulting schedule is not at an optimal level due to the human limitations in dealing with the combinatorial aspects of the problem. There is a great need for modeling the resident scheduling problem and automating the process of preparing resident schedules. We see that in literature there is little work done for solving this problem. The first attempt came from Ozkarahan [19] in which a goal programming model was developed incorporating the requirements of the residency program as well as the desires of residents as to days off, weekends off and on-duty nights for a planning horizon of one week. Sherali et al. [20] addressed the night allocation problem of residents while considering departmental staffing and skill requirements as well as residents' preferences. Their problem has been modeled as a mixed integer program and heuristic solution procedures have also been developed for different scheduling scenarios. Apart from the modeling attempts of residents' scheduling, Seitman [21] has developed a recursive computer program that calculates the daily on-call schedules for faculty, residents, and other personnel. However, the program is not efficient when the number of scheduling constraints and requests for duty hours and off-days increases.

In this study, the resident scheduling problem is considered, which assigns residents to work shifts over a monthly period considering the ACGME requirements, such as limiting the number of monthly duty hours, scheduling one day off out of 7 work days, assigning residents to night shifts no often than a specified frequency, and providing a minimum rest period between consecutive shifts. It also incorporates constraints such as keeping the number of weekly duty hours at an acceptable level, assigning residents to a minimum number of consecutive work days before an off-day, limiting the maximum number of consecutive work days, satisfying the day and night period resident needs, allocating the required number of residents from different seniorities, and distributing the over-assigned and under-assigned residents fairly to the day and night periods. Since constraints related with staffing levels are defined as goal constraints, the model can be fitted to any scheduling environment. A two-phase solution approach has been proposed that consists of solving a CP and a mixed integer goal programming (MIGP) model sequentially instead of one big formulation of the problem, which we will refer to as the (MIGP_1) model for comparison from now on. The proposed approach solves the resident scheduling problem optimally in a reasonable computing time whereas the MIGP_1 model is incapable of producing optimum solutions.

3.1 The Proposed Solution Approach

In the two-phase sequential solution approach (SSA), the first phase uses a CP model to find all feasible monthly schedules that abide the duty hour restrictions only whereas the second phase requires a simplified mixed integer goal program (MIGP_2) that assigns residents optimally to monthly schedules in view of the staffing requirements considering all the alternative schedules obtained from the CP model.

Phase 1: Generation of Monthly Schedules by the CP Model

In the tree search process of the CP model, a solution to the model is constructed by sequentially assigning values to the variables of the problem. In developing the search tree, a search procedure should be specified that consists of choosing which variable to consider for value assignment next (variable ordering) and which value to assign to the selected variable next (value ordering). This process is repeated until all variables are assigned values. Here, the key to success is to find efficient variable and value orderings that exploit problem specific features and complement the underlying constraint solver's own searching techniques. These decisions determine the size and shape of the search tree. Our proposed search procedure implements the so-called first-fail principle [22] that consists of selecting the variable with the fewest possible values in its domain and assigns a value to this variable from its domain in the given order.

Phase 2: In the second phase of SSA, the proposed MIGP_2 model assigns residents to monthly schedules optimally and the assignments are performed according to a specified objective function. Since the MIGP_2 model uses deviational variables in its constraint sets, it gives the scheduler the flexibility of obtaining different schedules for residents by minimizing the appropriate deviational variables in the preferred order.

The MIGP_1 and SSA models have been compared in terms of their solution time for scheduling different number of residents. The minimum and maximum number of residents is 6 and 18 respectively. Residents can be assigned to 3 types of shifts which are 12-h day and night shifts, and a 24-h shift. The objective function minimizes the negative deviation from the night-shift resident requirements as the first priority goal, and as the second priority goal it tries to allocate residents to day shifts as preferred.

All the models were solved with ILOG OPL Studio 3.5 [23] on a microcomputer with a Pentium III processor and 128 MB RAM. The models were coded by the optimization programming language (OPL), which is the core of OPL Studio and provides access to ILOG CPLEX 7.1 and ILOG Solver 5.1 for MIP and CP solvers respectively.

The execution of the original MIGP_1 model was limited to 500000 iterations for all the test problems. The model found an optimum solution for only 6 residents within the specified iteration limit. No optimum solution could be found for the rest of the problems. The SSA approach was implemented using ILOG OPLScript [24], which is a script language for composing and controlling OPL models. In our resident scheduling application, it is used for solving the CP problem, transferring the CP solutions to the MIGP_2 problem and solving the MIGP_2 model. The SSA could find an optimum solution in reasonable time for all the test problems. Since night duty and off-day regulations vary with respect to the seniorities of residents, separate CP models were developed for first-year, second-year and third-year residents. The maximum solution time required by these models was 47.48 CPU seconds and the input transfer to the MIGP_2 model took only 4.12 CPU seconds. The maximum solution time for the MIGP_2 model was 74.48 CPU seconds for optimizing the second priority goal for 18 residents.

As can be seen from the foregoing results, the SSA approach which uses CP in combination with MIGP leads much better results.

4 Application 2: Single Machine Total Tardiness Problem

This section deals with the well-known Single Machine Total Tardiness Problem (SMTTP). The SMTTP is one of the most widely studied scheduling problems. This problem is a special case of the single machine total weighted tardiness problem. SMTTP considers each job to be equally important. Due to the fact that priority factors attached to jobs are not considered, the SMTTP is less complex, so it is easier to solve compared to the weighted tardiness problem. Total tardiness is a regular performance measure [25].

Let us define the SMTTP. Consider n jobs which are simultaneously available at time zero that need to be processed on a single machine. The static representation of the sequencing problem is described by a fixed number of jobs in a queue. Each job has a sequence independent processing time p_i and a nominal due date d_i. Starting at time zero, we seek to minimize total tardiness, T. The machine is available to continuously process the jobs. Once a job begins processing, it is completed without interruption (no preemption). The problem is to determine a processing sequence that minimizes total tardiness [26].

This problem has received an enormous attention in the literature. Many algorithms have been developed for this problem. Most of these algorithms either employ exhaustive search or construct solutions according to a dispatching policy. Only few applications of metaheuristics to this problem have been reported in the literature.

The complexity of the SMTTP remained open for many years. When this problem is examined in terms of complexity, these problems are NP-hard [27]. Optimal solutions to this type of problems can be obtained via either a dynamic programming algorithm or a branch and bound algorithm. However, these methods may take a prohibitive amount of computation even for medium size problems and become intractable for large problems. These lead to the development of heuristic procedures that have a more modest computation requirement but do not guarantee optimality. Many heuristic algorithms were developed in order to cope with the complexity of a great variety of combinatorial optimization problems. But the main deficiency of such an algorithm is inability to continue the search upon becoming trapped in local optimum [26]. Metaheuristics have been developed to overcome this main deficiency. Metaheuristics can be classified into four categories: Tabu Search (TS), Simulated Annealing (SA), Genetic Algorithm (GA) and Ant Colony Optimization (ACO). TS has gained wide attention in recent years in solving many combinatorial optimization problems, especially solving in scheduling problems. In this study, TS technique is compared with the most successful two heuristics in the literature for solving the SMTTP. The algorithm takes the following form when applied to the total tardiness problem. Solution values are obtained by means of PARSIFAL software package [26].

Initial Solution: In PARSIFAL software package, various quick sequences are investigated as starting solutions for the TS algorithm. Earliest Due Date (EDD) sequencing rule is selected as an initial sequence.

Neighborhood Structure: Only swap move mechanism is used to generate a neighborhood, and General Pairwise Interchange (GPI) method is selected as a neighborhood search method.

Selecting the Best Neighbor in the Candidate List: The objective is to minimize total tardiness. The best neighbor in the candidate list is the sequence that yields the smallest total tardiness subject to not creating a tabu move. A critical part involved in finding the best move value is the evaluation of the move values for all candidate moves. PARSIFAL considers evaluation of all candidate moves at each iteration.

Identify the Tabu Restriction and Construct a Tabu List: The tabu list size of seven was selected, as suggested by Glover [16], who had introduced TS algorithm.

Introduce an aspiration level criterion allowing a move to override its tabu status when this move gives a considerable improvement: In order to override the tabu list when there is a good tabu move, aspiration criterion concept is introduced. To afford flexibility, the simplest form of aspiration level criteria has been introduced, which is stated as follows: A tabu move is accepted if it produces a solution better than the obtained so far.

Termination Criterion: The procedure can be terminated after the stated number of iterations. The procedure asks the maximum number of moves which is one hundred.

Implementation Characteristics: In this study, TS algorithm is compared with the most successful two heuristics in the literature. These two heuristics are Adjacent Pairwise Interchange (API) [28] and Panwalkar, Smith, Kouloumas (PSK) [29]. The two heuristics are programmed in Q-Basic [28], and TS technique results are obtained by using PARSIFAL software package. The input set used in this study can be characterized as follows: 800 problems have been generated by using the method suggested by Potts and Van Wassenhove [30]. Instances of varying degrees of difficulty are generated by means of two factors which are the tardiness factor (TF) and range of due dates (RDD). Both the *TF* and the *RDD* are selected from the set {0.2, 0.4, 0.6, 0.8} to give sixteen combinations for each problem size. In our implementation the problem size is taken to be N= 20,40,60,80, and 100. Ten problems are generated for each of the sixteen pairs of *RDD* and *TF*. If we compare the TS with the other heuristics for the problem size N=100, TS algorithm found the best solution for all ten problems in a set for six sets out of sixteen sets generated. The API found the best solution for all ten problems in a set for only three sets and the PSK heuristic did the same for only five sets. It has been seen that for three cases of *TF*, *RDD* pairs which are *TF*=0.2, *RDD*=0.4, 0.6 and 0.8 respectively, the solution value can be immediately found. On the other hand it has been observed that the problem is harder for the cases with a small range of due dates.

In this section, TS approach for solving the SMTTP was tested and compared against two best known heuristics in the literature. All algorithms were tested on the same data set generated. The results indicate that the TS provide better results than the two well-known heuristics.

5 Application 3: A Fuzzy Multi-Objective Covering-Based Vehicle Location Model for Emergency Services

The emergency service vehicle location problem is to determine the best base locations for vehicles so that some service level objectives are optimized. Timeliness is one of the most important objectives that reflect the quality of emergency service systems and can be measured in many ways such as minimization of the total or average time to serve all emergency calls, minimization of the maximum travel time to any single call, maximization of area coverage (ensures that as many zones in the area as possible is covered within S minutes of travel) and maximization of call coverage [31].

The Maximal Covering Location Problem (MCLP) has been a subject of considerable interest in the literature since its debut and has proved to be one of the most useful facility location models from both theoretical and practical points of view. The reader is referred to Goldberg [31] for a review of literature related to deployment and planning analysis pertaining to emergency medical services and fire departments, and to Marianov and ReVelle [32] for a discussion on the problem and applications.

In this paper, a multi-objective maximal covering-based vehicle location model for emergency services is proposed. In order to incorporate the decision maker's imprecise aspiration levels for the goals Fuzzy Goal Programming (FGP) [33] approach is used. As all MCLP models, the proposed model is NP-hard in nature. The model was solved using CPLEX 8.0 optimization software which has ability to drive cutting planes automatically for mixed integer problems.

5.1 Proposed Model

A new model, formed by considering Hogan and ReVelle [34]'s Maximal Backup Coverage Model and Pirkul and Schilling [35]'s Capacitated Maximal Covering Model as the base, is introduced in this paper. The model formulation is stated to allocate a fixed number of emergency service vehicles to previously defined locations so that three important service level objectives can be achieved. These objectives are; maximization of the population covered by at least one vehicle, maximization of the population with backup coverage and increasing the level of service to the uncovered demand zones by minimizing the average travel distance to these zones.

The proposed model distinguishes itself from the previous maximal covering emergency service vehicle location models in the solution approach, FGP, used.

5.2 Fuzzy Goal Programming

Zadeh [36] introduced fuzzy set theory (FST) that is a generalization of conventional set theory as a mathematical way to represent vagueness in everyday life. A fuzzy set A can be characterized by a membership function, usually denoted by μ, which assigns to each object of a domain its grade of membership in A. The nearer the value of membership function to unity, the higher the grade of membership of element or object in a fuzzy set A. Grades of membership may convey different meanings, such as *similarity*, *preference*, *uncertainty*, or even permission. Various types of membership functions can be used to represent the fuzzy set.

Goal programming [37] is one of the most powerful, multi objective decision making approaches in practical decision making. This method requires the decision maker (DM) to set goals for each objective that he/she wishes to attain. GP solution technique focuses on the minimization of the deviations from each goal, subject to the goal constraints and system constraints. In a standard GP formulation, goals and constraints are defined precisely. However, one of the major drawbacks for a DM in using GP is to determine precisely the goal value of each objective function. Applying FST into GP has the advantage of allowing for the vague aspirations of a DM, which can then be qualified by some natural language terms. When vague information related to the objectives are present then the problem can be formulated as a fuzzy goal programming (FGP) problem (see Narasimhan [33], Hannan [38], and Tiwari et al. [39,40]).

5.3 Implementation of the Model

Since target values obtained from the DM may not be crisp and described precisely, the problem is modeled by using FGP approach in order to incorporate the vague aspirations of the DMs into the formulation. In the model, all objectives are wanted to be satisfied simultaneously, and there are no priorities and also no relative importance assigned to the objectives. Then, the resulting linear programming formulation which uses maximin-operator (see Zimmerman [41]) for aggregating goals to determine the fuzzy decision is written. In our experiments, four problem instances with different number of zones, 30, 50, 60 and 70, are randomly generated.

To obtain solutions, ILOG CPLEX 8.0 optimization software is used. The CPLEX Mixed Integer Optimizer contains a number of features that speed up the solution of MIPs, including mixed integer rounding cuts, disjunctive cuts, flow path cuts, gomory fractional cuts, etc. It offers a control mechanism that allows users to specify the branching strategy, node selection strategy and other MIP control features. Indeed, it can automatically drive cutting planes. In the solution stage, default settings of CPLEX 8.0 are used. All problems are run on Pentium IV computer, with 1.6 Ghz CPU and 128 MB RAM.

In the light of the solutions, it can be concluded that backup coverage can be provided without substantial first coverage loss by using FGP approach. It should also be noted that the proposed model has computational efficiency for moderately sized problems in terms of the CPU times.

There are currently several companies packaging commercial solvers. As the capabilities of these solvers continue to grow by incorporating AI techniques, the Integer Programming models may become more and more attractive as in our case.

6 Conclusion

Most of the problems faced in the real world today are very complicated and combinatorial in nature, making their solution almost impossible. AI and OR communities have shown great interest in solving this type of problems on their own. While OR provides efficient solution techniques for rigid models that are well-structured and quantitative, these models may not be capable of representing the real-world problems accurately. On the other hand, while AI is more suitable for ill-structured and qualitative problems by providing richer and more flexible representations, these representations may lead to intractable solutions. In a typical OR problem, the DM is outside of the solution process. AI, on the other hand, allows for the decision maker to navigate the solution process. Recently, it has been realized that the integration of AI and OR shows significant promise for improving the capability and the acceptability of problem-solving systems. In other words, this integration provides representations that are expressive enough to describe real world problems and at the same time guaranteeing good and fast solutions.

In this study, three industrial engineering applications, which are combinatorially complex, have been presented using the integrative ideas of AI and OR. The first application combines CP and MIGP approaches for solving the medical resident scheduling problem. The second application applies tabu search for the single machine total tardiness problem and the last application uses fuzzy goal programming to model the maximal covering-based vehicle location problem for emergency services. The results of the applications indicate that these combinatorial problems can be expressed easily and solved in reasonable time using AI and OR techniques together.

References

1. Luss, H., Rosenwein MB.: Operations Research Applications: Opportunities and Accomplishments, European Journal of Operational Research, 97, (1997) 220-244
2. Simon, H.A.: Two heads are Better than One: The Collaboration between AI and OR. Interface 17 (1987) 8-15
3. CONDOR Committee On the Next Decade in Operations Research: Operations Research: The Next Decade,Anonymous. Operations Research 36 (1988) 619-637
4. Klee, V., Minty, G.: How Good is the Simplex Algoritm. In: Shisha, O. (ed.): Inequalities –III. Academic Press, New York (1972) 159-175

5. Khachiyan, L.G.: A Polynomial Time Algorithm for Linear Programming. Math Doklady 20 (1979) 191-194
6. Karmarkar, N.: A New Polynomial Time Algorithm for Linear Programming. Combinatorica 4 (1984) 373-395
7. Lustig, I.J., Marsten, R.E., Shannon, D.F.: Interior-point Methods for Linear Programming: Computational State of the Art. ORSA Journal on Computing (1994) 1-4
8. ILOG: ILOG CPLEX 8.0 User's Manual. Gentilly France (2002)
9. Gomes, C.P.: Artificial Intelligence and Operations Research: Challenges and Oppurtunities in Planning and Scheduling. The Knowledge Engineering Review 15 (2000) 1-10
10. Vossen, T., Michael, B., Lotem, A., Nau, D.: On the Use of Integer Programming Models in AI Planning. Proceedings of Sixteenth International Joint Conf. Artificial Intelligence (IJCAI-99), Stockholm, Sweden
11. Brailsford, S.C., Potts, C.N., Smith, B.M.: Constraint Satisfaction Problems: Algorithms and Applications. EJOR 119 (1999) 557-581
12. Van Hentenryck, P.: Constraint Satisfaction in Logic Programming. MIT Press, Cambridge MA (1989)
13. Tsang, E.: Foundations of Constraint Satisfaction. Academic Press, London San Diego (1993)
14. Beringer, H., De Backer, B.: Logic Programming: Formal Methods and Practical Applications, Studies in Computer Science and Artificial Intelligence. In Beirle, C., Plumer, L. (eds.): Combinatorial Problem Solving in Constraint Logic Programming with Cooperating Solvers. Elsevier Inc (1995)
15. Kirkpatrick, S., Gelatt, J.r., C.D., Vecchi, M.P.: Optimization by Simulated Annealing. Science 220 (1983) 671-680
16. Glover, F.: Tabu Search-Part I. ORSA Journal on Computing 1 (1989) 190-206
17. Holland, J.H.: Adaptation in natural and artificial systems. The University of Michigan Press, Ann Arbor (1975)
18. Sampson, S.: October Newsletter On-Line Posting, Newsgroup SOMA.byu.edu (1997) October 1
19. Ozkarahan, I.: A Scheduling Model for Hospital Residents. Journal of Medical Systems 18 (1994) 261-265
20. Sherali, H.D., Ramahi, M.H., Saifee, Q.J.: Hospital Resident Scheduling Problem. Production Planning and Control 13 (2002) 220-233
21. Seitman, D.T.: A Recursive Computer Program to Compute the Daily on-call Assignments for a Medical Department. Proceedings of the Annual Conference on Engineering in Medicine and Biology (1990) 1269-1270
22. Haralick, R.M., Elliot, G.L.: Increasing the Efficiency for Constraint Satisfaction Problems. Artificial Intelligence 14 (1989) 263-313
23. ILOG.: ILOG OPL Studio 3.5 Language Manual. Gentilly France (2001)
24. Van Hentenryck, P., Michel, L.: OPL Script: Composing and Controlling Models. Lecture Notes in Artificial Intelligence 1865 (2000)
25. Baker, K. R.: Introduction to Sequencing and Scheduling. New York: John Wiley (1974)
26. Morton, T.E., Pentico D.W. (ed.): Heuristic Scheduling Systems: With Applications to Applications to Production Systems and Project Management. John Wiley &Sons Inc, Canada (1993)
27. Du, J. Leung, J. Y. T.: Minimizing Total Tardiness On One Machine Is NP-Hard. Mathematics of Operations Research. 15 (1990) 483-495

28. Fry, T. D., Vicens, L., Macleod, K., Fernandez, S.: A Heuristic Solution Procedure to Minimize T on A Single Machine. Journal of the Operational Research Society. 40 (1989) 293-297

29. Panwalkar, S.S., Smith, M. L. Koulamas, C.P.: A Heuristic for the Single Machine Tardiness Problem. European Journal of Operational Research, 70 (1993) 304-310

30. Potts, C. N. Van Wassenhove, L. N.: A Decomposition Algorithms for the Single Machine Total Tardiness Problem. Operations Research Letters, 11 (1982) 177-181

31. Goldberg, J.B.: Operations Research Models for the Deployment of Emergency Services Vehicles. EMS Management Journal. 1(1) (2004) 20–39

32. Marianov, V., ReVelle, C.: Siting Emergency Services. In: Drezner, Z. (ed.): Facility location. Springer, Berlin (1995) 199–223

33. Narasimhan, R.: Goal Programming in a Fuzzy Environment. Decision Science. 11 (1980) 325–336

34. Hogan, K., ReVelle, C.: Concepts and Applications of Backup Coverage. Management Science. 32 (1986) 1434–1444

35. Pirkul, H., Schilling, DA.: The Maximal Covering Location Problem with Capacities on Total Workload. Management Science.37 (1991) 233–248

36. Zadeh, L.A.: Fuzzy Sets. Information and Control. 8 (1965) 338–353

37. Charnes. A., Cooper, W.W.: Goal Programming and Multiple Objective Optimizations. European Journal of Operational Research. 1 (1977) 39–54

38. Hannan, E.L.: Some Further Comments on Fuzzy Priorities. Decision Science. 13 (1981) 337–339

39. Tiwari, R.N., Dharmar, S., Rao, JR.: Priority Structure in Fuzzy Goal Programming. Fuzzy Sets and Systems. 19 (1986) 251–259

40. Tiwari, R.N., Dharmar. S, Rao, JR.: Fuzzy Goal Programming-an Additive Method. Fuzzy Sets and Systems. 24 (1987) 27–34

41. Zimmermann, H-J.: Fuzzy programming and linear programming with several objective function. Fuzzy Sets and Systems. 1 (1978) 45-55

Framework for Knowledge-Based IS Engineering

Saulius Gudas[1,2], Tomas Skersys[1], and Audrius Lopata[1,2]

[1]Kaunas University of Technology, Information Systems Department,
Studentu 50, Kaunas, Lithuania
[2]Kaunas Faculty of Humanities of Vilnius University, Muitines 8, Kaunas, Lithuania
{Saulius.Gudas, Tomas.Skersys, Audrius.Lopata}@ktu.lt

Abstract. The approach for Enterprise modelling extended by the management point of view is presented. The enterprise processes, management functions, and their interactions are considered as the critical components of the domain knowledge accumulated for the IS engineering purposes. The resulting framework for knowledge-based IS engineering – Enterprise meta-model (EMM) is developed and presented in this paper. The architecture of the advanced CASE system is also discussed.

1 Introduction

Enterprise model is a source of structured knowledge about the real world (business domain) for business process reengineering and information systems engineering.

There is a great number of Enterprise modelling methods and approaches (such as CIMOSA, GERAM, IDEF suite, GRAI) [4, 9], standards (ISO 14258, ISO 15704, PSL, ISO TR 10314, CEN EN 12204, CEN 40003) [1, 2] and supporting Enterprise modelling tools [12]. Moreover, CASE tools, that appear in contemporary market and are intended for the development of information systems, include graphical editors for Enterprise modelling and analysis techniques. Business process modelling as an integral part of Enterprise modelling has become an essential part of any information system development process. However, the integration of Enterprise modelling techniques into the information systems development process is still not sufficient.

The key point to the solution of this problem it is the development of a normalized definition of the Enterprise meta-model that would be a generalized structure of integrated core constructs from different Enterprise modelling approaches and methodologies [9]. Such meta-model could then be integrated into CASE tool's repository and used as a basic structure for storing business domain knowledge. Moreover, the meta-model would bridge the gap between the Enterprise modelling and information systems engineering techniques.

Some definite results in this area are developed by the IFAC-IFIP Task Force, which works on the Architecture for Enterprise Integration. The goal of this Task Force is the development of the Unified Enterprise Modelling Language [14].

Object Management Group (OMG) has also proposed principles for the standardization of a model-driven process of IS engineering that could potentially incorporate Enterprise modelling constructs [10]. The implementation of MDA

T. Yakhno (Ed.): ADVIS 2004, LNCS 3261, pp. 512–522, 2004.
© Springer-Verlag Berlin Heidelberg 2004

technology in UML-based approaches, that are capable to process Enterprise modelling activities, is highly desirable. However, the UML itself does not satisfy the needs and requirements for the domain knowledge modelling in the area of IS engineering. IS engineering requires business-specific constructs and the Enterprise meta-model (accepted by users as business domain experts and IS developers) from which the particular models of specific business domain could be mapped.

Both MDA approach and the UEML constructs are aimed at the integration of the Enterprise modelling and the processes of information systems engineering. Nevertheless, we will concentrate more on the UEML as it is particularly aimed at the unification of the Enterprise modelling approaches and is unambiguously important to the enhancement of IS engineering methods and tools.

From the perspective of IT and IS, the unified framework for the Enterprise modelling and IS development is a background which makes sure the technology solutions delivered to the business are relevant [8]. The paper deals with a formal framework aimed at the development of the Enterprise Knowledge Base for business process reengineering and information systems engineering. This formal structure is called an Enterprise meta-model (EMM).

2 The UEML Constructs

One of the attempts to integrate approaches of Enterprise modelling is Unified Enterprise Modelling Language (UEML). Figure 1 depicts basic constructs of the UEML core [14]. The UEML core assumes the CEN ENV 12204 [1], CEN ENV 40003 [2], also enterprise-modelling standards and languages such as IDEF, OMT, UML, CIMOSA, ARIS [15], [14], [7]. Constructs of the UEML core [14] are as follows: *Agent, Function, Process, Activity, Event, Time, Input object, Output Object.*

New development of the Unified Enterprise Modelling Language is UEML1.0. The UEML1.0 includes a wider set of the constructs [11], though it must be pointed out that this version of UEML specifies only two essential constructs for enterprise process-oriented modelling, namely, *Activity* and *Flow*. There are no *Process* and *Function* constructs identified in the UEML 1.0 core [11]. We can only assume that those two Enterprise modelling constructs are hidden under the construct *Activity*. The construct *Event* is also omitted in the UEML 1.0 core, nevertheless it was presented in the earlier version of the UEML.

It is also not clear which constructs of UEML support decision-making mechanism, if there is such a mechanism supposed at all in the UEML core. Though, it could be assumed that such decision-making mechanism should be modelled because a control flow *(ControlFlow)* – the output of decision-making is declared as the construct of the UEML 1.0 core.

Both UEML versions are comprised of only two types of modelling constructs – objects (or entities), and relationships between objects (semantic relationships). And that is why only the static structure of the Enterprise is concerned. The dynamic aspects of the Enterprise are still left out of consideration. The sequence of transactions among Enterprise constructs is not included either.

3 Enterprise Modelling Principles

The basic principles of Enterprise modelling are as follows [15]: 1) an Enterprise modelling language is defined as a finite set of constructs; 2) business processes and resources must be separated as two distinct parts of business entity with no fixed coupling; 3) enterprise functionality (the things to be done) and enterprise behaviour (the order in which things are done) must be separated; 4) organisation units (locations) and resources (the doers) should not be confused.

There is one more principle that must be taken into account, and it comes from the Systems and Control Theory. Systems and Control Theory claims that a system can be controlled effectively only if some feedback loops (also called control loops) are implemented [6]. As a consequence of this, the components of the control loop, as well as the control system itself, should be included into the Enterprise meta-model. Consequently, one more aspect can be introduced to the Enterprise modelling, namely, *the management point of view*. The scope of management process modelling is the internal structure of management information (enterprise knowledge, data, objectives) and the management information processing as well.

The Control Theory defines the typical structure of a *System* – a Real World System with internal "mechanism" of control. A *System* comprises of the mandatory (complex) constructs as follows: a real world *Process*, a *Control System*, and a *Feedback Loop* which creates *an information flow (control flow)* between a *Process* and a *Control System* [6]. A *Control System* performs a definite set of activities (*Functions*, related to a definite *criterion*) aimed to control a *Process*. Any *Function* takes (makes measurements of) a *Process state attributes*, calculates a *Process control attributes* and in that way influences the state of a *Process*.

Let us define that any item (structural unit) of a *System* is named *an object*. An *object* could be conceptualised as *an entity* or *a class* (of the UML), or in some other way in accordance with particular modelling methodology. Therefore, any *System* is a set of interdependent objects that interact regularly in order to perform a task. A *System* can be conceptualised in accordance with the above stated considerations (principles) from *the* management *point of view*. A model *of a System* (Figure 1) includes the subsets of constructs as follows: *a Process, a Function, a Control System*, and *a Feedback Loop*. A *Process* consists of a partially ordered set of steps – *sub-processes* (or *stages*). Any *Function* comprises of two constructs– *a Control System* and a *Feedback Loop*. *System* transforms a set of *Process State Attributes* to a set of *Process Control Attributes*, and in that way influences the flow of a *Process*. Any management *Function* is defined as a mandatory sequence of steps - *interactions* between the structural elements of *a Control System* and *Feedback Loop*. An *interaction* of any two constructs of *a Function* is an information transferring process.

Summarising this, a management *Function* is one of the complex constructs of an Enterprise model comprising objects of a *Control System* and *Feedback Loop* and an ordered sequence of *interactions* between these objects.

There are few Enterprise models that contain some enumerated elements of a *System*. One of these models is a Value Chain model that declares *business enterprise* as the mandatory interaction of the primary activities (enterprise processes*)* and secondary activities (management functions) [13]. The process management model of the Framework for Managing Process Improvement [3] should also be mentioned, as it strongly separates the concepts *"function"* and *"process"*. *A process* here is defined as a unit of workflow through an enterprise, and a *function* is a specified type of work applied to a product or service moving within a process. A *function* sets the rules and controls the resources assigned to the process (activity).

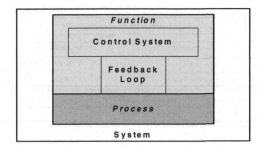

Fig. 1. Interaction of *Function* and *Process* in a *System*

The analysis of the Enterprise modelling from *the management point of view* gives some new aspects for the Enterprise modelling itself:

- The matter under investigation is a content of information, information processing and decision-making activities in the organizational system.
- It is aimed at the enhancement of the Enterprise model that can be used as a source of domain knowledge for business process analysis and IS development.
- A set of EMM core constructs and their relation types should be revised *from the management point of view* (EMM core constructs are the necessary elements of the meta-model in order to support computer-aided modelling of the Enterprise). These constructs should include a definite set of structural elements and relations for the modelling of management functions.

4   Modelling of Function and Process Interaction

The interaction of Enterprise elements *Process* and management *Function* is formally assumed as a control process. It is defined as a feedback loop between *a Process P(j)* and *a Function F(i)*. The analysis of the *Function/Process* interaction is a background of the formalized model of the Enterprise described in [5].

From the management point of view a Process P(j) is defined by two sets of attributes: a set of a Process state attributes, and a set of a Process control attributes. A set of Process state attributes includes the Process Input (material flow) attributes, Process Output (material flow) attributes, and the attributes of the Process P(j).

A management *Function F(i)* is comprised of the predefined sequence of mandatory steps of information transformation (*Interpretation, Information*

Processing, Realization); these steps compose a management cycle (a feedback loop in the Figure 2). Each management step forms and transmits a definite set of attributes (a set of information items). A *Function F(i)* should be initiated by some *Event* – a fact or a message associated with some internal or external (environmental) object.

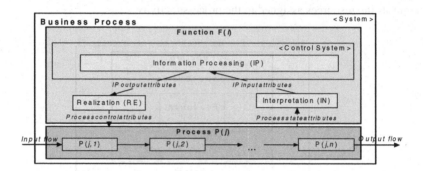

Fig. 2. The structured model of the *Function/Process* interaction

Figure 2 presents the structured model of the *Function/Process* interaction. The concept *Process* is assumed as "a black box". The concept *Process* (dark grey box in the Figure 2) is characterized by a set of *Process state attributes* (this set comprises subsets of *Input flow attributes, Output flow attributes* and *Process attributes*), and is influenced by a management *Function output* - a set of *Process control attributes*.

All other constructs of *Function/Process* interaction in the structured model (except constructs *Process, Input flow,* and *Output flow*) are assumed to be the components of the construct "*Function*" – an Enterprise management function.

It is supposed, that a *Process* (as well as management *Function*) is activated by some *Event*. A definite set of *state attributes* of an activated *Process* is the information flow defined as an input of (one or more) specific management *Function* that should also be activated by some particular *Event*.

It should be pointed out, that the set of attributes of a management *Function* is closely related to the description of a function presented by CIM-OSA [2]. The CIMOSA specification of function includes the structural part (the list of sub-functions is used), the functional part (goals, limitations, functional description, necessary equipment, input, output) and the part of attitude (goals, limitations, procedural rules, events, end state).

The EMM core constructs are shown in Figure 3 (UML Class model notation). The components of the operative part of the construct *Function* are information processes *Interpretation (IN), Realization (RE)* and *Information Processing (IP)*. The *IN, IP* and *RE* are the mandatory steps of a management *Function. Interpretation* transforms *a Process state attributes* (the input of the *IN*) in accordance with the requirements of the next step of the management cycle – *Information Processing*.

The result of *IN* is a control flow *IP input* that is consumed by the next step in the management cycle, namely, *Information Processing*. The management step *Information Processing* includes data processing and decision-making procedures. The output of the information process *IP* is a control flow *IP output*. *Realization (RE)* is the last step in the management cycle. The *RE* is the information process concerning the implementation of decision *IP output*, developed by the management step *IP*. The result of *RE* is *a Process control attributes* – a set of attributes, aimed to influence the state of *a Process*.

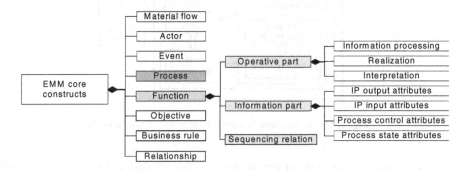

Fig. 3. Composition of the EMM core

The constructs *Event, Actor, Business rule* and *Objective* have their definite roles at *Function/Process* interaction. Construct *Event* depicts a change in the system's state and initiates or triggers *a Process* or/and some *Function*. Construct *Actor* is an active resource (human, application, machine with control device) used to support the execution of *Process* or/and *Function*. Construct *Business rule* defines a set of conditions, constraints, and calculations to be associated with particular *Function* (its information activities). Construct *Objective* defines a set of business enterprise goals. The content of the *Objective* influences the definition of *Business Rules* hence the execution of a *Function* as well. The construct *Environment* represents a business enterprise environment. *An Environment* refers to the outside objects or entities that can influence Enterprise *Objectives* and raises definite *Events*.

5   The Architecture of Knowledge-Based CASE System

Figure 4 depicts the architecture of the CASE system enhanced by the Knowledge Base. The Knowledge Base of the CASE system consists of two parts: an Enterprise meta-model (EMM) and Enterprise model (EM). An Enterprise meta-model is the generic level model; an Enterprise model includes the partial and particular level models in accordance with GERAM [4].

The Knowledge Base of the CASE system is supposed to be the third active source of Enterprise knowledge (next to Analyst and User) for information systems engineering. Enterprise meta-model (EMM) in this enhanced environment of information system development is a source of pre-defined knowledge, and is used to control the process of business domain knowledge acquisition and analysis. It is also used to control the construction of an Enterprise model (EM) for particular business domain

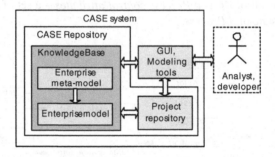

Fig. 4. The architecture of CASE system with Knowledge Base

Knowledge-based IS development supposes that all stages of IS development life cycle are supported by the CASE system's Knowledge Base. The Knowledge Base of the CASE system in conjunction with appropriate algorithms assures the consistency among the IS analysis and design models, gives new possibilities for verification and validation of IS development life cycle steps. Moreover, it can be used to simulate and improve business processes within the enterprise. Enterprise model (EM) is used as an alternative source of knowledge (next to IS developer knowledge) during the IS development process.

The Knowledge Base of the CASE system can be also used to verify business domain knowledge, which was captured by analysts and used to construct particular EM – it is done by verifying constructed EM against the predefined knowledge structure of the EMM.

6   The Enterprise Meta-model

The Knowledge Base of the CASE system (Figure 4) includes the Enterprise meta-model (EMM) as the major part of the whole system. The EMM is used as a "normalized" knowledge structure to control the process of construction of an Enterprise model (EM) for particular business domain.

The Enterprise meta-model (Figure 5) is supposed to be the basic formal structure for domain knowledge. The class diagram of the EMM is presented in Figure 5. The EMM comprises basic constructs for the Enterprise modelling identified from the management point of view: *Business Process, Function, Process, Actor, Business Rule, Event, Objective*. Next we will shortly discuss these constructs and present their formal definitions. The constructs of the EMM are presented in the same formal way as a set of UEML core constructs in [15].

Process. A process is a partially ordered set of steps, which can be executed to achieve some desired material end-result. Process consumes material resources (it is an input of the process) and produces some material output – production. Processes are triggered by one or more event occurrences. Formal definition of *Process*: *Process* = *<ProcID, {ProcStep}, {Expression}, {relatedEMelement}>*, where *ProcID* is a process identifier; {*ProcStep*} is a set of process steps; {*Expression*} is a set of triggering events that need to be true to start the process; {*relatedEMelement*} is a set of Enterprise model elements related to the *Process* (this feature is common to all constructs of the EMM, and therefore its description will not be repeated below). Figure clauses in the formal definition denote a set of elements.

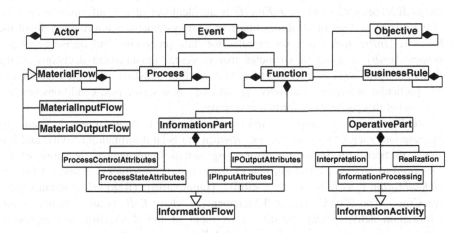

Fig. 5. The Enterprise meta-model (EMM) (presented as UML Class diagram)

Function. A *Function* is a complex construct. The structure of the *Function* is defined in accordance with the formal definition of management function (Figure 2). It can be formally defined as follows: *Function* = *<FuncID, {InformationPart}, {OperativePart}, {relatedEMelement}>*, where *FuncID* is a function identifier; {*InformationPart*} is a set of mandatory attribute types important to the *Function*; {*OperativePart*} is a set of mandatory information processing method types.

InformationPart is formally defined as a set of mandatory attribute types: InformationPart=<ProcessStateAttributes, IPInputAttributes, IPOutputAttributes, ProcessControlAttributes>.

OperativePart is formally defined as a mandatory set of information processing methods: Operative Part=<Interpretation, InformationProcessing, Realization>.

Interpretation is a step of information feedback loop directed from the *Process* to the *InformationProcessing* of the *Function*. *Interpretation* is an information activity, and it is aimed to transform and transfer *ProcessStateAttributes*. Formal definition of *Interpretation* is as follows: IN = <IntID, {InputAttrib}, {IntRule}, {OutputAttrib}, {preCond}, {postCond}, {relatedEMelement}>, where *IntID* is an identifier of this information activity; {*InputAttrib*} is a set of process state attributes

(*ProcessStateAttributes*) related to the identified interaction of the *Function* and the *Process*; {*IntRule*} is a set of rules for identification, capturing and interpretation of the inputted process state attributes; {*OutputAttrib*} is a set of interpreted attributes that are required by the information processing activities of the *Function*; {*preCond*} is a set of pre-conditions that have to be satisfied to enable execution of this particular information activity; {*postCond*} is a set of post-conditions (ending statuses) of this particular information activity.

InformationProcessing is an information activity, and it is aimed to transform systematized actual data about process under control to management decisions. Formal definition of *InformationProcessing* is as follows: IP = <InProcID, {InputAttrib}, {InProcRule}, {OutputAttrib}, {preCond}, {postCond}, {relatedEMelement}>, where *InProcID* is an identifier of this information activity; {*InputAttrib*} is a set of attributes that represent systematized information about the *Process*; {*InProcRule*} is a set of rules for data processing and decision-making; {*OutputAttrib*} is a set of attributes that represent management decisions of the *Function*; {*preCond*} is a set of pre-conditions to be satisfied to enable execution of this particular information activity; {*postCond*} is a set of post-conditions (ending statuses) of this particular information activity.

Realization is a step of information feedback loop directed from the *InformationProcessing* to the *Process*. *Realization* is an information activity, and it is aimed to transform *InformationProcessing* output (management decisions of the *Function*) to process control attributes (*ProcessControlAttributes*). Formal definition of *Realization* is as follows: RE = <ReID, {InputAttrib}, {ReRule}, {OutputAttrib}, {preCond}, {postCond}, {relatedEMelement}>, where *ReID* is an identifier of this information activity; {*InputAttrib*} is an input of the Realization and represents management decisions of the *Function*; {*ReRule*} is a set of rules for realization of management decisions, in other words for transformation of *InformationProcessing* output (*IPOutputAttributes*) into a set of process control attributes (*ProcessControlAttributes*) aimed to influence the *Process*. {*OutputAttrib*} is an output of the *Realization* and represents the *Process* control attributes (*ProcessControlAttributes*); {*preCond*} is a set of pre-conditions to be satisfied to enable execution of the *Realization*; {*postCond*} is a set of post-conditions (ending statuses) of this particular information activity.

Business Rule. A business rule, as a construct of the Enterprise model, is considered as some condition, constraint or calculation related to some enterprise element defined in the Enterprise meta-model. Construct *BusinessRule* can be formally defined as follows: BusinessRule = <BRuleID, BRuleBody, {preCond}, {postCond}, {relatedEMelement}>, where *BRuleID* is an identifier of the business rule, *BRuleBody* is a formal expression of the rule; {*preCond*} is a set of pre-conditions to be satisfied to enable business rule execution; {*postCond*} is a set of post-conditions (ending statuses) of the business rule.

Definitions of the EMM constructs *Event*, *Actor*, *Objective* correspond to the definitions of the corresponding constructs of the UEML core [15].

It should be noted that this minimal set of constructs (core elements of the EMM) complies with the basic principles stated in the section 3 with the emphasis on the implementation of the *Function/Process* interaction principles from the management point of view.

7 Conclusions

The Enterprise modelling is considered as the major source of knowledge in business process reengineering and information systems engineering.

The Enterprise modelling is analysed from the new perspective, namely *the management point of view*. The peculiarity of this approach to Enterprise modelling is the identification of two different types of enterprise activities, defined as *Function* and *Process*. The absence of the constructs *Function* and *Process* in other Enterprise modelling approaches makes it impossible to define the feedback loop, and, consequently, refine the information flow of enterprise management.

The definition of the *Function* in the Enterprise model presented in this paper differs from the definition of this particular construct used in other Enterprise modelling approaches. The definition of the construct *Function* is formalized, because it is based on the principles found in Systems and Control Theory and therefore has a strong theoretical background.

The formalized analysis and modelling of the *Function/Process interaction* refines a set of new constructs of the Enterprise modelling. As a result a new framework – the Enterprise meta-model (EMM) – has been constructed and discussed in this paper. The EMM is intended to be a formal structure aimed to integrate the domain knowledge for the IS engineering needs.

References

1. ENV 12 204. Advanced Manufacturing Technology Systems Architecture - Constructs for Enterprise Modelling. CEN TC 310/WG1 (1996).
2. ENV 40 003. Computer Integrated Manufacturing Systems Architecture - Framework for Enterprise Modelling, CEN/CENELEC (1990).
3. Department of Defence Technical Architecture Framework for Information Management. Version 3.0. Defence Information Systems Agency, Center of Standards (1996).
4. GERAM: Generalised Enterprise Reference Architecture and Methodology, Version 1.6.3. IFIP–IFAC Task Force on Architectures for Enterprise Integration (1999).
5. Gudas, S.: Organisational System as a Hierarchy of Information Processes. Applications of Artificial Intelligence in Engineering VI (AIENG 91). Computational Mechanics Publications, Southampton Boston (1991) 1037 –1050.
6. Gupta, M.M., Sinha, N.K.: Intelligent Control Systems: Theory and Applications. The Institute of Electrical and Electronic Engineers Inc., New York (1996).
7. Lopata, A.: The Analysis of Enterprise modelling standards (in Lithuanian). Information technologies'02. Kaunas, Technologija (2002) 377 – 381.
8. Popkin Software. Building an Enterprise Architecture: The Popkin Process, Version 1.0 (2002). http://www.popkin.com.
9. Schekkerman, J.: How to Survive in the Jungle of Enterprise Architecture Frameworks. Trafford, Canada (2003).

10. Stephen, J., Kendall, S., Uhl, A., Weise, D.: MDA Distilled: Principles of Model-driven Architecture. Addison-Wesley Pub. Co. (2004).
11. The UEML 1.0 Core Class Diagram. UEML Portal, http://rtd.computas.com.
12. Totland, T.: Enterprise Modelling as a Means to Support Human Sense-Making and Communication in Organizations. Norwegian University of Science and Technology (NTNU), Trondheim IDI-raport 1997:8 (1997).
13. Turban, E., McLean, E., Wetherbe, J.: Information Technology for Strategic Advantage, 2nd Edition. John Wiley & Sons, London (1999).
14. Universal Enterprise Modelling Language. IFAC-IFIP Task Force, UEML Group (1999). http://www.cit.gu.edu.au/ ~bernus/taskforce/archive/UEML-TF-IG.ppt.
15. Vernadat, F.: UEML: Towards a Unified Enterprise modelling language. International Conference on Industrial Systems Design, Analysis and Management (MOSIM'01), Troyes, France (2001).

Modelling Variability in Requirements with Maps

Sondes Bennasri, Carine Souveyet, and Colette Rolland

Centre de Recherche en Informatique,
90, rue de Tolbiac, 75013 Paris, France
{bennasri, souveyet, rolland}@univ-paris1.fr

Abstract. Software Customisation also known as Software Variability is a central concept in the development of different kinds of software such as product families or software for disabled people. The solutions proposed in the literature to deal with the variability address design and implementation aspects like the mechanisms that can be used to implement the variability in a software architecture. The representation of the variability at a requirements level is neglected. Our contribution in this paper is to propose a goal driven approach that captures the variability at requirements level.

1 Introduction

Today software companies are faced to the challenge of producing software systems that meet the needs of different kinds of users and at the same time they must decrease their costs. Thus, software should be sufficiently generic to cover a wide range of customer needs, easily adaptable to the requirements of a particular user and based on existing software assets to reduce costs. This fact leads to the emergence of software customisation (also called software variability) which is defined as the ability of a software system to be changed, customised or configured to a specific context [11]. Users of this kind of software play a key role as the success of the software depends on its ability to meet the user specific needs. Thus, user requirements should be considered at the first place during the process of software customisation and also when designing the customisable software.

In the first case, the customer is faced to a multitude of variants, he needs a global view of what each variant does and its dependencies with other variants without being lost in technical details. A representation of the variants at the requirements level facilitates the matching between his requirements and the product functionality.

In the second case, identifying the variability at the requirements level, assures that the designer is building a product satisfying all user needs and provides a systematic way to document design alternatives.

Unfortunately, as mentioned in [4], the representation of the variability at the requirements level is neglected. In general, the exiting approaches such as [1, 2, 10] study the variability as a design problem and concentrate on implementation aspects of system variability.

T. Yakhno (Ed.): ADVIS 2004, LNCS 3261, pp. 523–532, 2004.
© Springer-Verlag Berlin Heidelberg 2004

We propose an approach that treats the variability from a requirements perspective. In this paper, we limit ourselves to variability in functionality. To identify the functionality variants, we propose to use a goal-driven modelling formalism called Map [9] to capture the variability through requirements analysis. The identified variants are then mapped to modules. A conceptual architecture is also proposed to control the selection of the appropriated variants at run time or at design time.

The remainder of this paper is structured as follows. Section 2 introduces the Map formalism and shows how to use it to represent variability in functionality. The use of the Map formalism is illustrated with an example of customisable system in section 3. Section 4 describes the proposed architecture to deal with the variants implementation and the control of their selection. Finally, we summarise our work and conclude with future work.

2   The MAP Representation System

Our work is an extension of previous research results for matching ERP functionality to customer requirements [9]. We use the map to capture the variability at the requirements level and to model it.

A map is a process model expressed in a goal driven perspective. It provides a system representation based on a non-deterministic ordering of goals and strategies.

The map is represented as a labelled directed graph (see an example in Fig.6) with goals as nodes and strategies as edges between goals. The directed nature of the graph shows which goals can follow which one.

A *Goal* can be achieved by the performance of a process. Each map has two special goals, *Start* and *Stop* to start and end the process respectively.

A *Strategy* is an approach, a manner to achieve a goal. A strategy S_{ij} between the couple of goals G_i and G_j represents the way G_j can be achieved once G_i has been satisfied.

A *Section* is a triplet $<G_i, G_j, S_{ij}>$ and represents a way to achieve the target goal G_j from the source goal G_i following the strategy S_{ij}. Each section of the map captures the situation needed to achieve a goal and a specific manner in which the process associated with the target goal can be performed.

For the sake of conciseness, we also use a textual notation in which a section named ab_i designates a way to achieve a target goal b from a source one a following a strategy i. Thus, the section $<G_i, G_j, S_{ij}>$ is named ab_i where a is the code of the goal G_i, b is the code of the goal G_j and I is the code of the strategy S_{ij} (see Fig. 1).

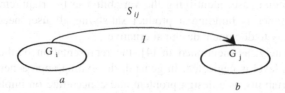

Fig. 1. A section

In order to express variability in functionality at the requirements level, we advocate that sections are a useful abstraction for doing so. We consider a section as an important product characteristic that stakeholders (customers, developers…) want the system to provide and also an abstraction of a product functionality. In other words, a section is a feature. In FODA [7], a feature is defined as " *A prominent or distinctive user-visible aspect, quality or characteristic of a software system or systems* ". In [2], a feature is also *"a logical unit of behaviour that is specified by a set of functional and quality requirements"*. The point of view taken in this paper is that a feature is a representation of a visible product characteristic and an abstraction of a functionality expressed in a requirements driven manner.

The features represented in a map are related to each others by four kinds of relationships namely *multi-thread*, *bundle*, *path* and *multi-path* relationships. The relationships show the possible combination of features from which the user can select the appropriate ones according to her needs.

In the reminder of this subsection, we introduce the relationships and show how they are used to express variability in functionality.

The Multi-thread Relationship: when there are various ways to achieve the same goal starting from a source one, the features are then related by a multi-thread relationship. A multi-thread relationship is represented in a map by several strategies between a couple of goals as represented in Fig.2. It shows through the strategies the different functionality provided to obtain the same result.

A multi-thread relationship expresses a feature variability by grouping optional features from which one or many features can be selected.

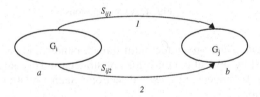

Fig. 2. A multi-thread relationship

The Bundle Relationship: In the case where the several ways to satisfy the same goal are exclusive, we relate them with a bundle relationship. It implies that only one way can be selected to achieve the target goal. Fig. 3 shows an example of a bundle relationship represented with the Map formalism.

The bundle relationship expresses a feature variability by grouping alternative features that are mutually exclusive.

The Path Relationship: when the achievement of a target goal b from a source one a requires the satisfaction of intermediary goals, we introduce a path relationship. It establishes a precedence/succession relationship between features expressing that in order to trigger a functionality, some other functionality must be executed first. In general, a path relationship is a composition of features, features related by multi-thread or bundle relationships or other paths. Some paths can be iterative.

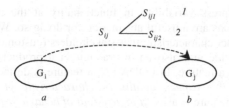

Fig. 3. A bundle relationship

Fig. 4 represents a path relationship between the goals G_i and G_k denoted respectively a and c which is composed of the multi-thread relationship containing the features ab1, ab2, ab3 and the feature denoted bc1. It expresses that in order to achieve the goal G_k , we must first select and execute one or many features among ab1, ab2 or ab3 then execute the feature bc1.

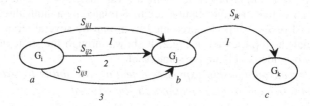

Fig. 4. A path relationship

Multi-path Relationship: given the multi-thread, bundle and path relationships, a goal can be achieved by several combinations of strategies. This is represented in the map by a pair of goals connected by several sections. Such a relationship is called a multi-path relationship.

For example, we show in Fig. 5 two alternative paths to satisfy the goal G_k (denoted c) starting from the goal G_i (denoted a). The first path achieves G_k through the intermediary goal G_j whereas the second path achieves G_k directly from G_i.

A multi-path relationship identifies the several combination of functionality (represented by paths of sections) that can be executed to satisfy the same goal. Thus, *a multi-path relationship is a means to express feature variability by grouping the alternative paths satisfying the same goal.*

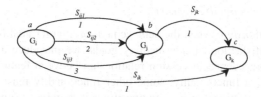

Fig. 5. A multi-path relationship

In general, a map from its *Start* to its *Stop* goals represents all possible combinations of features expressed by multi-thread, multi-path and bundle relationships. Each particular combination of features, from the *Start* goal to the *Stop* one, is a path. It describes a way to reach the final goal *Stop*.

We shall notice that the bundle and multi-thread relationships are easily visible in the map. However it is more difficult to identify all the combinations of features in a map (the multi-path and the path relationships). We apply the algorithm of MacNaughton and Yamada [8] in order to discover systematically all the paths in the map. The algorithm is based on the two following formula :

Let s and t be the source and target goals, Q the set of intermediary goals including s and t and P the set of intermediary goals excluding s and t.

The initial formula $Y_{s,Q,t}$ used to discover the set of all possible paths using the three operators that are the union ("$\cup$"), the composition operator (".") and the iteration operator ("*") is :

$$Y_{s,Q,t} = (X_{s,Q\setminus\{s\},s})^* . X_{s,Q\setminus\{s,t\},t} . X^*_{t,Q\setminus\{s,t\},t} \ (1)$$

And given a particular goal q of P, the formula $X_{s,P,t}$ applied to discover the set of possible paths is :

$$X_{s,P,t} = X_{s,P\setminus\{q\},t} \cup X_{s,P\setminus\{q\},q} . (X_{q,P\setminus\{q\},q})^* . X_{q,P\setminus\{q\},t} \ (2)$$

In this paper we specialise the $X_{s,P,t}$ into paths, multi-paths, multi-threads and bundle relationships that we note as follows :

Multi-thread relationship between two goals k and l is denoted : $MT_{kl} = \{kl_1 \vee kl_2 \vee ... kl_n\}$ where the kl_i are the features related by the multi-thread relationship. Thus, the multi-thread represented in Fig.2 is : $MT_{ab} = \{ab_1 \vee ab_2\}$

Bundle relationship between two goals k and l is denoted : $B_{kl} = \{kl_1 \otimes kl_2 \otimes ... kl_n\}$ where the kl_i are the exclusive features related by the bundle relationship. In Fig.3, the bundle relationship is : $B_{ab} = \{ab_1 \otimes ab_2\}$

Path relationship between two goals k and l is denoted $P_{k,Q,l}$ where Q designates the set of intermediary goals used to achieve the target goal l from the source one k. A path relationship is based on the sequential composition operator "." between features and relationships of any kind. As an example, the path relationship of Fig.4 is denoted: $P_{a,\{b\},c} = MT_{ab} . bc1$

Multi-path relationship between two goals k and l is denoted $MP_{k,Q,l}$ where Q designates the set of intermediary goals used to achieve the target goal l from the source one k. A Multi-path relationship is based on the union operator "$\cup$" between alternative paths. Thus, the multi-path of Fig. 5 is denoted: $MP_{a,\{b\},c} = P_{ac} \cup MT_{ab} . P_{bc}$

Section 3 presents an example of the application of the MacNaughton-Yamada's algorithm. However, due to paper length limit, we present only the results obtained after applying the algorithm.

3 An Example

To illustrate our approach, we consider a case tool supporting use case modelling. The map of Fig. 6 represents the functional requirements that the system must fulfil to

528   S. Bennasri et al.

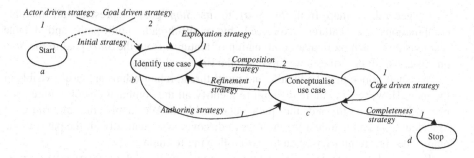

Fig. 6. A map sample

model use cases at a high level by goals and strategies. Each section in the map represents a feature that the system can provide.

The map is composed of two goals *"Identify use case"* and *"Conceptualise use case"* that correspond to the two goals to be achieved to define use cases. Besides, as the conceptualisation of the use case can be made only if it has been identified first, there is an ordering between the two goals as shown in the map.

We shall notice that there are several strategies from one goal to another representing different manners to fulfil a given goal.

For example, the identification of a use case from scratch can be done either driven by actors as suggested in [6] (the *"Actor driven strategy"*) or by the identification of the goal that the use case must fulfil *(the "Goal driven strategy")*.

We may also identify new use cases from existing ones following one of the given strategies: the *"refinement strategy"* that discovers lower level use cases, the *"Composition strategy"* to identify complementary use cases and the *"Case driven strategy"* to discover the alternative scenarios.

This example demonstrates the variability in requirements that is captured by the map. We distinguish two kinds of variability that are:

(i)   a variability in strategies provided to satisfy the same goal and,
(ii) a variability in the combinations of strategies to fulfil the same goal.

The first kind (i) is expressed by the multi-thread or the bundle relationship. In our example, we depict a bundle relationship between the couple of goals "Start" and "Identify use case" respectively denoted *a* and *b* and composed of the two exclusive features *ab1* and *ab2* corresponding to the sections <Start, Identify use case, by actor driven strategy> and <Start, Identify use case, by goal driven strategy>. We also identify a multi-thread relationship composed of the features cb1 and cb2 corresponding to the sections <Conceptualise use case, Identify use case, by refinement strategy> and <Conceptualise use case, Identify use case, by composition strategy>.

The second kind (ii) is expressed by the multi-path relationship. It shows the different combinations of functionality that can be executed to satisfy the same goal. For example, given a conceptualised use case obtained after achieving the goal *"Conceptualise use case"*, we can follow two alternative paths to achieve the goal again. We can either identify alternative scenarios by applying the *"Case driven strategy"* or we can identify other use cases of a lower level or complementary ones by choosing the strategies *"Refinement strategy"* or *"Composition strategy"* then conceptualise them by the *"Authoring strategy"*.

In order to identify all the combinations of features, we apply the algorithm of MacNaughton-Yamada introduced in Sect.2. The initial formula generating all the paths between the goals a and d is :

$$Y_{a\{a,\,b,\,a,\,d\},d} = (X_{a,\,\{b,c,d\},\,a})^* . \ X_{a,\{b,c\},d} . \ X^*_{d,\{b,c\},dt}$$

The identified paths are summarised in Table 1.

Table 1. List of relationships

Relationship kind	Identified relationship
Path	$P_{a,\{b,c\},d} = P_{a,\{b\},c} . \ MP^*_{c\{b\}c} . \ P_{cd}$ where $P_{a,\{b\},c} = B_{ab} . P^*_{bb} . P_{bc}$ $P_{cd} = cd_1$
Multi-Path	$MP_{c\{b\}c} = P_{cc} \cup MT_{cb} . P^*_{bb} . \ P_{bc}$ where $P_{cc} = cc_1$ $P_{bb} = bb_1$ and $P_{bc} = bc_1$
Bundle	$B_{ab} = ab_1 \otimes ab_2$
Multi-thread	$MT_{cb} = cb_1 \vee cb_2$

4 Conceptual Architecture

This section describes how the different combinations of features identified by the map formalism are mapped to a conceptual architecture that serves as a starting point during design. The section also introduces the process by which one can arrive to a particular customisation of the system either at design time or at run-time.

4.1 Presentation of the Architecture

To bring the alternative combinations of features to the design level, we propose an architecture inspired from the Presentation-Abstraction-Control (PAC) architectural pattern [3]. This pattern gives a basic outline for the software architecture of flexible systems.

Similarly to the PAC pattern, we build a hierarchy of agents implementing the features and managing their relationships.

The hierarchy is composed of two kinds of agents: the control agents and the executor agents.

- *An executor agent* is a self contained unit that implements a feature
- *A control agent* controls the selection and the execution of a given path in a map (executors or/and other control agents). We distinguish four kinds of control agents namely the multi-path, the path, the multi-thread and the bundle control agent.

They respectively control the selection and execution of the paths related by multi-path relationships, path relationships, multi-thread relationships and bundle relationships.

To build the hierarchy, we introduce one executor for each feature identified in the map. Fig.7 shows a one-to-one correspondence between the features of the map and the executors. For example, the feature ab_i is mapped to an executor having the same name.

After the feature-executor association, we cast the relationships identified from the map to elements of control flow that are the control agents. The kind of the control agent depends on the kind of the related relationship. For example, in Fig.7, the multi-thread relationship MT_{cb} (see Table 1) is associated to a multi-thread control agent having the same name.

We begin the identification of the control agents by a one-to-one correspondence between the relationships and the control agents. Then, we make some simplifications, for example, a path relationship composed of one feature in not mapped to a control agent.

The executor and control agents are organised into three levels that are a top level, an intermediary one and a bottom level. The top level controls the hierarchy of agents in order to satisfy the global goal of the map (corresponding to the *Stop* goal). The top level is composed of a single control agent which is the root of the hierarchy. The bottom level contains the executor agents. The intermediate level co-ordinates the bottom level agents and compose lower level agents into a single unit at a higher level. This level is composed of several control agents satisfying intermediary goals and participating in the achievement of control agents goals belonging to higher levels. Fig. 7 shows the hierarchy of agents obtained from the map of Fig. 6.

Which children agents are actually co-ordinated by parent ones depend on customisation parameters set at design time or at run-time.

According to the PAC rules, we structure the control and executor agents into three components: Presentation, Abstraction and Control components.

The *presentation component* provides the user interface of the application logic of the agent. Its is the means by which the agent interacts with the external world to get data or provide results.

The *abstraction component* encapsulates the business logic of the agent.

The *control component* is the connection point to the other agents and the only access to the content of the abstraction and presentation components. The implementation of the agents is not discussed in this paper.

4.2   The Customisation Process

Defining the customisation information (the children actually controlled) into the control agents can be done in two different ways:

(a) *Design Time Configuration* : given a customised map representing specific needs of a user, developers select the appropriate executor agents and generate the customised application.

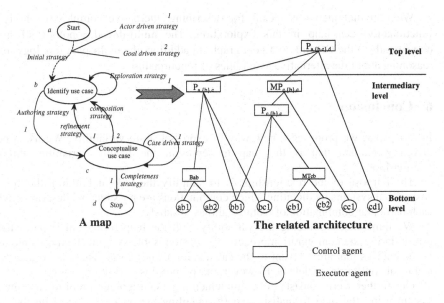

Fig. 7. The agent hierarchy

(b) *Run Time Configuration*: the user runs a configuration procedure that asks her for the desired features during the software installation or before starting the application.

It is important to note that the user does not deal with technical details during the configuration process. The map simplifies the configuration process by showing only the alternatives that are relevant to satisfy her goals in an easy understandable formalism and invites her to select the suitable features.

5 Related Works

Variability modelling is closely related with feature modelling as feature modelling concentrates on representing the relevant characteristics of systems, variable parts as well as common ones.

The well known feature modelling method is FODA [7] where features are captured into a hierarchical graph and classified as mandatory, optional and alternatives. Another approach that directly couples feature and variability is presented in [11] where features are modelled in a UML-like graph and classified into mandatory, optional, variant and external.

The originality of our work consists of dealing with variability from a requirements perspective. However, our approach is a work in progress.

In the literature, there are few works addressing the variability from a requirements perspective. We distinguish the proposal of [5] where the variability is captured through goal analysis using the AND/OR decompositions. The alternative goals (expressed by the OR links) help reasoning about the alternative functionality to achieve a parent goal. However, the exploration of the alternative combinations of functionality across the entire AND/OR goal graph is more difficult.

We find that maps, as means for describing alternative complex assembly of functionality, can help in this exploration. The multi-thread topology of maps corresponds to the OR link in a goal graph. In addition, the multi-path topology helps reasoning about the alternative assemblies of functionality.

6 Conclusion

In this paper, we proposed a new way to express feature variability. We use a goal driven formalism that is the map to represent the feature variability through relationships.

The purpose of the relationships is to simplify the task of building the correct customised systems by dictating which combinations are possible and describing what each particular combination of features allows to satisfy.

We think that expressing the variability with the map formalism is particularly useful during the configuration process of a customisable system. It exposes the user to the choices that are relevant to the satisfaction of her goals. There is no deal with technical configuration details. However, our proposal is a work in progress.

Our further work consists of (a) implementing a configuration tool to customise a system using the map formalism and (b) detailing the approach based on the map formalism to model feature variability.

References

1. Bachmann et al.: Managing variability in software architecture. ACM Press, NY, USA, 2001
2. Bosch et al.: Variability issues in Software Product Lines. 4th International Workshop on Product Family Engineering (PEE-4), Bilbao, Spain, 2001
3. Buschmann et al. : A system of patterns. Pattern-oriented software architecture. Wiley, 1996
4. Halmans et al.: Communicating the variability of a software product family to customers. Software and System Modeling, Springer-Verlag 2003
5. Hui B, Liakos L., Mylopoulos J.: Requirements Analysis for Customizable software : A Goal-Skills-Preferences Framework.. 11th International Requirement Engineering Conference, 2003
6. Jacobson I. : Object-Oriented Software Engineering : A Use Case Driven Approach : Addison Wesley, 1992
7. Kang K.et al. : Feature-Oriented Domain analysis (FODA) Feasibility Study. Technical report CMU/SEI-90-TR-21, Pittsburgh, PA, Software Engineering Institute, Carnegie Mellon University, 1990
8. MacNaugthon R., Yamada : Regular expressions and state graphs for automata. IEEE transactions on electronic computers, EC-9, p39-47, 1960
9. Rolland C.: Bridging the gap between Organizational needs and ERP functionality. Requirements Engineering journal, 2000
10. Svahnberg et al.: On the notion of variability in Software Product Lines. Proceedings of the Working IEEE/IFIP Conference on Software architecture, 2001
11. Van Gurp J.: Variability in Software Systems, the key to Software Reuse. Licentiate Thesis, University of Groningen, Sweden, 2000

Kaliphimos: A Community-Based Peer-to-Peer Group Management Scheme

Hoh Peter In[1†], Konstantinos A. Meintanis[2], Ming Zhang[2], and Eul Gyu Im[3]

[1] Dept. of Computer Sci. & Eng. at Korea University,
136-701 Seoul, Korea
hoh_in@korea.ac.kr
[2] Dept of Computer Science at Texas A&M University,
College Station, TX 77843-3112, USA
meinkos@tamu.edu, mingz@cs.tamu.edu
[3] National Security Research Institute,
Dae Jeon 305-718, Korea
imeg@etri.re.kr

Abstract. Emerging peer-to-peer services such as Freenet, Gnutella, Kazaa, and Napster provide an easy and efficient way to share resources and information. However, misuse or unfair exploitation of resources by users that cannot be trusted has been reported. Trustworthy schemes of peer-to-peer systems are greatly needed. In this paper, a new group management approach to improve trustworthy in peer-to-peer systems, called "Kaliphimos" is proposed. Kaliphimos is an overlay, multidimensional reputation infrastructure for peer-to-peer systems. This trustworthy group management scheme includes algorithms for group member insertion, deletion, merging, and splitting based on community-like reputation model.

1 Introduction

Peer-to-peer (P2P) systems are emerging as a new trend of the computing technology. The P2P applications such as Freenet, Gnutella, Kazaa and Napster are offering an easy-to-use and efficient way to share files and perform on-line commercial transactions. Among the users of the P2P systems, however, one may take advantage of or even exploit other's resources. It is a challenging problem to avoid the misuse of the resources or harmful transactions with other users since the interaction among the peers is not controlled in a systematical way.

Existing approaches to solve this problem rely on single-level reputation models based on "credibility." Successful (or unsuccessful) transactions increase (or decrease) the credibility of the peers. Based on the credibility, every peer determines whether a transaction is accepted or rejected. It is not appropriate to apply these approaches for monitoring peer group behaviors.

[†] Hoh Peter In is the corresponding author.

T. Yakhno (Ed.): ADVIS 2004, LNCS 3261, pp. 533–542, 2004.
© Springer-Verlag Berlin Heidelberg 2004

In this paper, our multi-level reputation model called *Kaliphimos* is proposed. Kaliphimos is an overlay reputation infrastructure which observes peer group behaviors and manage their credibility. Through this way, trust of individuals and groups can be maintained using peer "pressure". Good or bad behaviors of a peer node influence its group reputation, by providing group members strong incentive or penalty so that they can police each other. A peer that behaves badly all the time is gradually restricted and finally expelled by the group. The group imposes "social justice" to its members by not approving and hence by preventing the transactions requested by the malicious users. In other words the system discourages the selfish behavior by making it unprofitable.

The paper presents an overview of Kaliphimos in section 2, the major group management operations (e.g., insertion, splitting, and merging) of the architecture in section 3, a short discussion about the performance of the proposed scheme in section4, the related work in section 5, and conclusion and future work in section 6.

2 Overview of Kaliphimos

For the simplicity, we assume the following conditions:

- Group membership data are always available and can be accessible immediately from the network. These data cannot be faked or distorted.
- Individual and group reputation data are always available in the network. These data cannot be faked or distorted.
- A member must belong to a group to perform any transactions.
- A minimum and maximum number of group members are defined per group.

Kaliphimos is a multi-level reputation model. In Kaliphimos, a set of members is organized as a group. Inside a group, every member p is monitored by all the other members. The group members maintain a profile of p, which contains the recent transaction history associated with p, such as the number of its successful transactions, the type of the transactions, the file types usually used for the transactions, and the average amount of information that p uploads or downloads. Based on the profile, the majority of its groupmates approve or disapprove a transaction requested by p or other party who wants to do a transactions with p. A member who has bad credibility (i.e., worse than a threshold) may be expelled. In this way, individual members should behave well in order to maintain good credibility in their group. In addition, that scheme helps users who want to interact with users of other groups to extract valid information about these users by only "asking" and not "keeping" information. Hence, the nodes of the groups do not maintain information about the profile of the members of other groups.

To perform punishment and monitoring mechanisms *efficiently* in Kaliphimos, it is necessary to maintain the right size of the groups. If the size is very large, the complexity of making a decision on approval or disapproval increases dramatically. If it is very small, the group becomes not trustable since the group reputation is identical to the reputation of only a few members (e.g. one or two) that cannot police each-other. The size can be changed dynamically depending on the P2P applications and the number of the users. In order to maintain a proper group size the following sections describe a series of fundamental group management operations.

3 Kaliphimos Group Management Operations

There are many operations that are relevant to the group management. In this paper, however, we investigate the major group management operations including the insertion (section 3.1), the splitting (section 3.2) and the merging (section 3.3).

3.1 Insertion

The insertion is used for the addition of new users into groups. Two algorithms are presented here: the candidate member insertion algorithm (section 3.1.1) and the candidate group insertion algorithm (section 3.1.2).

3.1.1 The Candidate Member Insertion Algorithm

The main idea is to initially assign low creditability to a new node for a certain period of time and then increase the creditability as the new node accumulates trust through reliable transactions (interactions with other nodes). The credibility of the node is measured based on the proper use of the system resources (e.g. network bandwidth, disk storage, number of files that downloaded / uploaded etc.).

When a new user requests to join a group, or an existing user requests to switch its group membership, the user has to stay in the target group as a candidate member for a specific period of time. During that period, the other nodes of the group monitor the candidate member. The new node is restricted in the way it acquires (downloads) the system resources but not limited to share (uploads) the resources that "holds" (e.g. in a file sharing system, a peer may only download 5MB/day, but can upload as much as it requested). When a candidate member p requests to acquire resources from a site, it sends a request to the other party. The other party checks with the group-mates of p if p is trustable and what kind of access privileges has. The other party then accepts or rejects the transaction with p (Figure 1).

The other members in p's group evaluate the behaviors of the candidate member whenever a transaction is performed (e.g. how many bytes it downloads / uploads). After the "testing period," the group decides by voting about the promotion of the candidate member into a "regular" member. The decision is based on the recent behaviors during the testing period. Since the new peer p is monitored by the other members of the same group, and all members have the right to vote in favor or against p, p should behave well at least for the "testing period."

The disadvantage of this solution is its computation overhead. All the group-mates of the candidate member must keep an "eye" on the newcomer and evaluate its behavior. If there is a great number of candidate members, monitoring activities becomes a high burden for the existing group members.

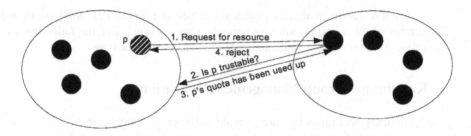

Fig. 1. Candidate Member Insertion algorithm

3.1.2 The Candidate Group Algorithm

The basic idea of the candidate group is to add all the new users into a special group (candidate group). Each member in this group has restricted access to the system resources. For every group, e.g., C (including the candidate group), there is a Group Membership Data Keeper, denoted with $GMDK_c$. $GMDK_c$ records the resource quotas of all members. When a peer p requests resources, the related co-actor (the other party) checks the group membership of p with the $GMDK_c$. The $GMDK_c$ identifies the group and returns the access rights of the node. The co-actor now by knowing that the peer p belongs to a candidate group does not ask p's group members for the evaluation of p's reputation (previous behavior). Hence, decides directly whether the transaction with p is safe or not based on the information provided by the $GMDK_c$ (See Figure 2).

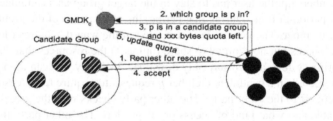

Fig. 2. Candidate Group Insertion algorithm

When the group becomes large enough, it stops adopting new members. After the testing period, the candidate group is transformed into a new, regular self-policing group.

The advantage of this approach is that the existing groups are not affected by the insertion of the new peers. Group members can quit from their group, but they cannot switch their group membership unsolicited. That means that the group size, after it reaches a specific limit, cannot be expanded further. It stays unchanged or decreases monotonically during the time.

However, this solution has also drawbacks. On of them is that new peers are not able to select group. All the new peers are assigned to candidate groups with unknown partners. It is possible that a good user can be in the same group with malicious nodes. As the switching of the group is prohibited, the good user has to wait until the self policing mechanism will force the bad-behaved users to conform. Another drawback is that the insertion operation does not replenish groups who have lost members. In that case, merging groups and switching peers between groups are the only ways to keep the size of the groups in a balance. Merging conditions (e.g., why and when), effectiveness and computation overhead of monitoring group members should be considered to keep the model functional and effective.

3.2 Splitting

As the size of the groups increase (by inserting new nodes, switching group identity or merging groups) the computational cost and the network traffic overhead for authorization increases too. A splitting operation is necessary to reduce the cost and the traffic overhead. A group splits when the following conditions occur:

- If the authorization traffic to a member in the group is higher than a specific threshold, the member can request the splitting of the group into two new groups
- If the group size exceeds a threshold, then group splitting can also be initiated by the GMDK

Since GMDK manages group membership data, the management cost can be a high burden for very large groups (Figure 3a and 3b). Note that one GMDK may work for several groups since we assume that replicated membership data recorded in different GMDKs for availability (robustness) and consistency.

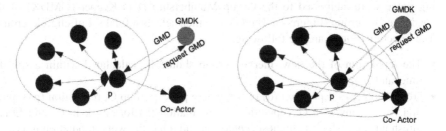

Fig. 3. Splitting algorithm

When a group splits, each of the new groups has approximately the same number of members. The peers with higher reputations are all placed in one group and the peers with lower reputations form the other new group.

With this policy, peers are encouraged to behave well. If all members in the group behave properly and have good reputation, the group splits into two high-reputation subgroups. However, when the group consists of a mix of good and bad peers, it may have several different strategies to split the group. One is to randomly select the members of each subgroup. Another is to sort the reputation of the members and create subgroups with high reputation and other with low reputation. However it may be difficult for the low-reputation group to raise its reputation given a short period of time.

3.3 Merging

In general, the large group size is important for psychological, sociological and practical reasons. A small-size group makes possible to plot or falsely evaluate the reputation of other members on purpose. If the group size is large, it is much more difficult to trick the majority of the group members. Additionally, large size means low communication overhead between peers. The intra-group communication is much more efficient than the inter-group communication since there is not redundant information-traffic between groups (e.g., inquiry of group reputation) and unnecessary communication with the Group Membership Data Keeper (GMDK). Hence, the merging operation reduces the communication overhead when we have to evaluate teammates.

The merging operation is applied either when a group intents to adopts more members or when a four-member group (called also "endangered" group) faces the danger to loose one of its members. The latter case may occur when a node is willing to switch the team or when the group decides to dismiss a bad-behaved member. A special search mechanism is used for the searching of appropriate candidate groups based on specific criteria (e.g. finds groups with less than eight members, or groups that wish to adopt new peers). Candidate groups can be either groups in the same "unsafe" state or volunteer groups that need new members. The results of the searching process are addressed to the Group Membership Data Keeper (GMDK) of the "endangered" group (Figure 4). The GMDK then selects a final set of eligible groups. The selection criteria are the following:

- The reputation of the new, merged group should be calculated within a specific time, and
- | reputation (p) - reputation (q) | $\leq \Theta$, where p, k, q group G, reputation (p) reputation (k) for any k in G, reputation (q) reputation (k) for any k in G, and Θ is a threshold (i.e., p has the highest *reputation* and q has the worst reputation in G).

A voting process is used to select the best one among eligible groups. As shown in Figure 5, each eligible group vote for deciding whether the "endangered" group, D, is joined or not. One of the main decision factors is the group and member reputation of the "endangered" group. The members of the "endangered" group also vote in order to decide which group they want to join. They begin to vote one by one from the group of having the high favor on their join to one of having the least favor until there exists a group which has more than half of their votes. If there does not exist such a group, GMDK selects a group that has the least number of the members. If there are more than one groups of the same size, then the GMDK picks the one that voted by the most "endangered" members. For the calculation of the reputation R of the new group we use the following function:

$$R_{new} = \sum R_i * W_i \,,$$

where, R_{new} = Reputation of new group,

R_i = Reputation of group I,

$\qquad W_i$ = weight of group i (= # of members of group i)

$\qquad \sum$ (members of all groups to be merged)

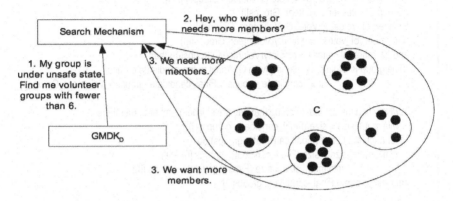

Fig. 4. Merging algorithm, searching eligible groups

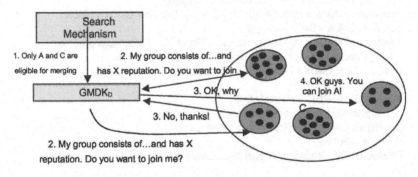

Fig. 5. Merging algorithm, voting process

To minimize traffic and computations, the merging procedure is activated only if it is necessary. A group has to be under the "unsafe" state or to ask for new members in order to initiate the merging process through the GMDK. In addition, the search algorithm uses specific criteria (such as group size and reputation) to minimize the number of the eligible groups and to maximize the satisfaction of the "endangered" group members.

Algorithm Merge

```
// GMDKG – Group Membership Data Keeper of group G. This routine runs in the GMDKG
if (group G is under unsafe state) or (group members of G request more peers to join them) then
{       //Send request to the search mechanism to search volunteer
 //groups based on specific criteria e.g. groups of five members
Volunteer_groups = Search (Criteria);
        If Volunteer groups = Ø then EXIT;
for each i=1 to size(Volunteer_Groups) do
{         //Volunteer group votes for G
          Number_of_votes1 = Vote (Volunteer_Groups[i], G);
   //Group G votes for Volunteer_Groups[i]
   Number_of_votes2 = Vote (G, Volunteer_Groups[i]);
   If (Number_of_votes1 = majority(Volunteer_Groups[i]))
   and (Number_of_votes1 = majority(Volunteer_Groups[i])) then
   //The group is eligible for merging with G. Add it to the candidate groups
                   Final_candidate_groups = Final_candidate_groups + Volunteer_Groups[i];
   }
   //Now find the candidate group that has the smaller number of members
   minimum_size = size (Final_candidate_groups[1]);
   for each i=2 to size(Final_candidate_groups) do
   if minimum_size > size (Final_candidate_groups [i])  then
   {             minimum_size = size (Final_candidate_groups [i]);
   smallest_group = Final_candidate_groups [i];
   }
/* The smallest_group is the group that should be merged with G. Now, choose reputation and
      group information keepers for the new merged group. Update the information about
      the synthesis and the reputation of the new group */
If resources(GMDKG) > resources (GMDKsmallest_group) then New_GMDK = GMDKG ;
else  New_GMDK = GMDKsmallest_group
If resources(Reputation_KeeperG) > resources (Reputation_Keepersmallest_group) then
   New_ Reputation_Keeper = Reputation_KeeperG  ;
else       New_GMDK = Reputation_Keepersmallest_group
//Update reputation
w1 = size(G) / size(G) + size(smallest_group);
w2 = size(smallest_group)/ size(G) + size(smallest_group);
R1 = Reputation(G);   R2 = Reputation(smallest_group)
R = R1* w1 + R2* w2 ;
Release (GMDK, Reputation_Keeper) //Release old keepers
}
```

4   Performance Consideration

When a user in a group sends a request to the other party, the other party sends two inquiries: one to the group that the requesting user belongs to, and the other to GMDK to check credibility of the group. This mechanism may cause traffic overheads as well as delays in the recipient of requests. In addition, GMDK may become a bottleneck of this mechanism.

However, the mechanism expressed in this paper is one way of implementing the main ideas of our peer-to-peer group management scheme. These overheads and problems can be easily alleviated by adopting other techniques, like group key managements [7] and public key algorithms.

5 Related Work

Most of the research that has been done is related to theoretical protocols for calculating the individual "credibility" of the peers. There are also some studies about the management of the reputation data and how these data can be stored efficiently in the system with a secure way. Cryptographic and fragmentation methods have been proposed but a few implementations of reputation management protocols (e.g. Xrep and EigenRep) are still in experimental level. However, research on developing commercial reputation models for peer-to-peer systems has not been focused yet in the research community. In our best knowledge, research on multidimensional reputation of peer groups has not been conducted yet. The idea of assigning individuals in self-policing groups is our innovation and is introduced for first time in Kaliphimos. The uniqueness is due to the fact that there is not existing work or implementation that uses similar reputation scheme. This section presents some of the existing reputation models providing an idea of the general trend in the area of the reputation protocols for peer-to-peer applications.

Ganesh et al. [1] propose a gossip, peer-to-peer membership protocol called SCAMP (SCAlable Membership Protocol). Gossip-based protocols use randomization to reliably broadcast messages in a group. Damiani et al. [2] propose a self regulated system where the P2P network is used to implement a robust reputation system. The problem with this kind of protocols is that they assume that each group member has full knowledge (list of identities of other group members) of the global membership.

Kamvar et al. [3] propose a reputation algorithm (EigenRep) for P2P file sharing systems. EigenRep is a distributed and secure method for the computation of the global reputation of a node. The advantage of the algorithm is that takes into consideration the "history" of each node into the system. What distinguishes that method from the others is the fact that the system rewards peers with highly reputation values (e.g. bandwidth or connectivity increase).

Xiong and Liu [4] have recently developed a new coherent trust model called PeerTrust. PeerTrust determines the credibility of a node based on an enhanced transacttion-based feedback mechanism. Despotovic et al. [5] have developed an interesting protocol for reputation assessment and decision-making. Abdul-Rahman and Hailes [6] propose an interesting model that allows agent to decide which other agents' opinions they trust more and allows agents to "progressively tune their understanding of another agent's subjective recommendations".

6 Conclusions

The main group-management operations for the community based peer-to-peer system, Kaliphimos, are introduced, including four algorithms such as candidate member and the candidate group insertion algorithms, a splitting algorithm, and a merging algorithm. We analyzed why they are important and how their use helps to build efficient punishment mechanism for preventing harmful behaviors.

Issues in the group management area are still open. Our algorithms have not been tested in the real environment of a commercial P2P platform while parameters have to be specified. Questions such as when the network traffic and the computational cost are intolerable or what is the duration of the testing period for a candidate node / group have not been answered yet. Similarly, we haven't decided what the maximum size of a group should be or what other information a Group Manager Data Keeper (GMDK) needs to maintain in order to be able to monitor the members of its group. We are also planning to extend the existing simulation platform of Kaliphimos to test the validity, fairness, robustness and performance of our algorithms.

Acknowledgement. This project was supported by the Ubiquitous Fronteer Project of Ministry of Science & Technology in the Korea Government. We appreciate Ryan Saunders and Hong Lu for discussing this topic.

References

1. Ayalvadi J. Ganesh, Anne-Marie Kermarrec, and Laurent Massoulie. Peer-to-peer membership management for gossip-based protocols, IEEE Transactions on Computers, 52(2), February 2003
2. Damiani et.al. A Reputation-Based Approach for Choosing Reliable Resources in Peer-to-Peer Networks, Proceedings of the 9th ACM conference on Computer and communications security 2002, Washington, DC, USA
3. Kamvar, Scholsser, Garcia-Molina. EigenRep: Reputation Management in P2P Networks, to appear at WWW2003, May, 2003
4. Li Xiong, and Ling Liu. A Reputation-Based Trust Model for Peer-to-Peer eCommerce Communities, In Proceedings of the 2003 IEEE Conference on E-Commerce (CEC'03).
5. Zoran Despodovic, Karl Aberer, and Manfred Hauswirth. Trust Aware Cooperation, 22nd International Conference on Distributed Computing Systems Workshops (ICDCSW '02), July 02 - 05, 2002 Vienna, Austria
6. Alfarez Abdul-Rahman, and Stephen Hailes. Supporting Trust in Virtual Communities, In Proceedings of the Hawaii International Conference on System Sciences, Jan 4-7, 2000, Maui, Hawaii
7. Yair Amir, Yongdae Kim, Cristina Nita-Rotaru, and Gene Tsudik. On the Performance of Group Key Agreement Protocols, In Proceedings of the 22nd International Conference on Distributed Computing Systems, 2002

On the Application of WF-Nets for Checking Hybrid IDEF0-IDEF3 Business Process Models

Costin Bădică[1] and Chris Fox[2]

[1] University of Craiova, Software Engineering Department,
Lapus 5, Craiova, RO–1100, Romania
c_badica@hotmail.com
[2] University of Essex, Department of Computer Science,
Colchester CO4 3SQ, United Kingdom
foxcj@essex.ac.uk

Abstract. In many practical business process modelling scenarios using Petri nets, the resultant model does not have a single input place and a single output place. In particular, this happens when the Petri net model is derived by mapping from an Hybrid IDEF0-IDEF3 model. Therefore, the correctness of the model cannot be assessed with existing techniques, which are devised for WF-nets — a special class of Petri nets with a single input place and a single output place. Moreover, the existing approaches for tackling this problem are rather simplistic and fail to work even for some simple cases. We show that, by an appropriate reduction of a multiple input/multiple output Petri net, existing techniques can be used to check the correctness of the original process. The approach is demonstrated with a suitable example.

1 Introduction

Usually, the mapping between business processes and IT applications is defined in an ad-hoc way. This hinders the process of creating and maintaining the fit between businesses and their supporting IT systems. We believe that one factor causing this situation is the semantic gap between the languages "spoken" by business analysts and those of IT people. Providing bindings between the two could help to improve the current situation. Techniques from formal methods in computer science can be used to achieve this desideratum. Therefore, formal modelling should be an essential activity on the agenda of business process management research.

Business processes are very complex discrete-event dynamic systems involving active and passive participants, activities and goals. Because it has been claimed that any discrete-event system can be modelled using a Petri net, it follows that Petri nets are suitable for modelling business processes. This subject has received much attention, with arguments being given both for and against the use of Petri nets for business and workflow process modelling ([2, 11, 6, 13]).

The seminal paper [1] introduced WF-nets — a class of Petri nets for workflow modelling. WF-nets take into account an essential feature of workflows; namely,

T. Yakhno (Ed.): ADVIS 2004, LNCS 3261, pp. 543–553, 2004.

that they are case-based. Therefore, the WF-net for a particular workflow has a unique input place (i.e. a place with no in-coming arcs) and a unique output place (i.e. a place with no out-going arcs). The assignment of a token to the input place indicates that the case may start, and the assignment of a token to the output place indicates that the case has ended. WF-nets have proven to be a useful tool for workflow analysis. Special properties have been devised for them in order to assess the correctness of the underlying workflows ([1, 7, 12]).

However, modelling business processes with a Petri net frequently results in a model which does not have a single input place and a single output place. Such situations occur naturally when modelling business processes that are driven by some input data or objects. The modelling can be done either directly with Petri nets or by way of a high level formalism like EPC ([3, 7]) or Hybrid IDEF0-IDEF3 ([5]) (HI0-I3) that is then mapped into a Petri net.

Typical examples of this problem are the business processes of the service industry. A case starts when a client submits a request for a service to be delivered. Usually the request is input via a form that asks the client to fill-in the request attributes. For example, a request for a holiday package reservation might ask the client to fill-in a hotel reservation, a car reservation, a train ticket etc. The client does not have to fill-in all these attributes in order for the service to be delivered, but filling in some attributes triggers some corresponding process activities. Moreover, some attributes of the request might be exclusive. Examples are the values of the delivery option for a book purchased from an e-shop.

A common practice when modelling with Petri nets is to interpret tokens as process objects that are consumed or produced by the process ([15]). From this it follows that multiple input and multiple output (MIMO) Petri nets naturally occur when modelling processes that are driven by the presence of the input data. Inputs correspond to places with an empty set of input transitions and outputs correspond to places with an empty set of output transitions.

MIMO processes are also obtained when the modelling is done with EPC ([7]) or HI0-I3 ([5]). In [7] it is shown that an EPC business process model may have MIMO events. Moreover, [8] shows that there is no simple and general way to transform a MIMO Petri net obtained from an EPC model into a WF-net. A similar situation occurs when translating a HI0-I3 model into a Petri net ([5]).

Last but not least we would like to mention the recent results reported in [13] about the formal foundation of what is considered there to be "the most natural interpretation of workflow languages" according to the Workflow Management Coalition[1] — Standard Workflow Models (SWM). There are two points to make: (1) it can be shown that HI0-I3 and SWM have the same expressiveness ([4]); (2) even if SWM is MIMO in the sense of our paper, in defining terminating and deadlock-free SWM models, [13] assumes by default that all the inputs are provided. The case considered in this paper, where not all inputs need be provided, is not covered.

---

[1] http://www.wfmc.org

Below, we will define Generalized Workflow Nets (GWF-nets), a generalization of WF-nets to the MIMO case. Then we show that it is possible to extract one or more WF-nets from a GWF-net. The idea is to consider the original Petri net model as describing a superposition of process definitions, instead of a single process definition. Then, given a pattern of input data availability, we extract a sub-net of the original GWF-net such that it can then be easily translated into a WF-net by adding a unique input place and a unique output place. One advantage of this approach is that the resultant WF-net is useful for checking the correctness of the underlying process definition using existing techniques.

The paper is structured as follows. In Section 2, HI0-I3 business process modelling notation is introduced by way of a motivating example. In Section 3 we show that the motivating example cannot be handled satisfactory using existing techniques. In Section 4 we define GWF-nets, and show that defining the correctness of GWF-nets can be reduced to the case of ordinary WF-nets. Section 5 concludes, and points to future work. We assume familiarity with the Place/Transition nets (P/T nets) class of Petri nets (e.g. see [9, Chapter 2]).

2   Hybrid IDEF0-IDEF3: Syntax and Semantics

IDEF0 and IDEF3 bring complementary features to business process modelling ([6]). Traditionally, IDEF0 is used for producing a function model of a new or existing system or subject area ([10]), while IDEF3 is used for producing a dynamic model of the system ([14]). Some frequently cited strengths of IDEF0 and IDEF3 include: the simplicity of the notation; its ease of use for non-IT specialists; that it has sufficient modularity to aid the production of (syntactically) consistent and compositional modules; its support for top-down development; its wide acceptance. Weaknesses include: the high complexity of the models, which may lead to their rejection by reviewers and users; the lack of formal semantics; the ambiguity of some constructs, such as bundled flows.

IDEF0 and IDEF3 have been proposed for use either independently or together. Clearly, their combination brings the advantage of modelling the process from different perspectives, an important requirement that has been set for process modelling. Originally, their integration has been defined in an ad-hoc way, by referencing IDEF0 activities from within an IDEF3 model ([14, page 145]).

In devising HI0-I3 we started with a functional modelling component, constraining the aspects of IDEF0 that we considered problematic. Then we extended it to include dynamic modelling facilities of IDEF3. The basic modelling component is the labelled black box. It models an activity with inputs and outputs. Unlabelled black boxes, that model "do-nothing" activities (labelled with *null* or λ), are allowed. A glass box view, modelling the logic of inputs selection and outputs production, is attached to each black box. It has three components: (1) an input tree of connectors; (2) an output tree of connectors; (3) a unit of behaviour. There are one-to-one mappings from the sets of inputs and outputs of a black box to the set of leaves of its input tree (output tree, respectively).

Additional facilities of this notation are: that the process model can be presented at different levels of detail using activity decompositions (as in IDEF0); and that the assignment of resources (humans and/or machines needed to execute activities) to activities takes place via resource flows that have a compositional semantics.

Consider a hypothetical business process for material acquisition. This process takes material requests and produces purchase orders and payment authorizations. It contains a sub-process for handling the material requests that takes material requests and produces validated requests (see Fig. 1). The company has a list of authorized suppliers, but it must be prepared to find and handle new potential suppliers. Thus, there is an additional input to model new supplier requirements and an additional output to produce new supplier packages.

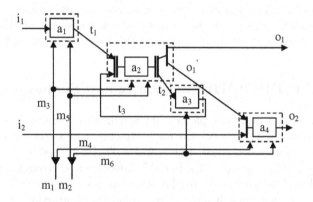

Fig. 1. A business process for handling material requests modelled using HIO-I3

Fig. 1 displays black boxes with dotted line. Double vertical lines indicate OR connectors and single vertical lines indicate AND connectors. Small triangles indicate resource inclusion (i.e. if $ResAtt(m)$ are the resources attached to the resource flow m then $ResAtt(m_3) \subseteq ResAtt(m_1)$ and $ResAtt(m_4) \subseteq ResAtt(m_1)$) and small circles indicate resource reuse (i.e. m_6 is used by both a_3 and a_4). The activities and flows of this example are described in Tables 1 and 2.

Table 1. Activities of the process from Fig. 1

Name	Description
a_1	Log Material Request
a_2	Validate Material Request
a_3	Resolve Request Problems
a_4	Develop New Supplier Specification

An important result established in [5] is that each level of detail is a decomposition of the top-level activity. The semantics of a process model corresponding

Table 2. Data flows (left) and resource flows (right) of the process from Fig. 1

Name	Description	Name	Description
i_1	Material Request	m_1	Data Systems
i_2	New Supplier Requirement	m_2	Materials Staff
o_1, o'_1	Validated Request	m_3	Material Tracking System
o_2	New Supplier Package	m_4	Product Data System
t_1	Logged Request	m_5	Material Clerk
t_2	Request Errors	m_6	Material Supervisor
t_3	Request Updates		

to a level of detail can be defined by mapping to P/T nets. The mapping is
described in [5] by means of an algorithm for translating a level of detail of a
process model to a labelled P/T net ([13]). The algorithm translates flows into
places and activities into transitions labelled with activity names. The translation of input trees and output trees may produce additional places and *null*
transitions (transitions without a label; sometimes the *null* or λ label is used).
The result of mapping the process from Fig. 1 to a P/T net is shown in Figure
2. The mapping of connectors produced the additional places l_1, l_2, l_3 and l_4,
and *null* transitions tr_1, tr_2, tr_3, tr_4, tr_5 and tr_6. The remaining places and
transitions correspond to flows and activities in the original model.

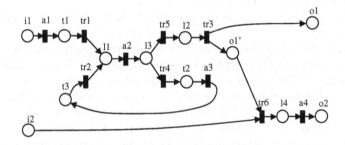

Fig. 2. The P/T net for the process shown in Fig. 1

More details both about the example shown in Fig. 1 and about the HI0-I3
modelling language can be found in [5].

3   A Motivating Example

Intuitively, the process for handling material requests should be executed in
two circumstances: when both inputs are provided or when only the material
request input is provided. In the first case, the process ends by producing both
a validated request and a new supplier package, while in the second case it ends
by producing just a validated request. Note that according to these intuitions,
the process behaves correctly in both cases.

In what follows, let us see what happens when we are checking the correctness of this process by applying the soundness theory of WF-nets. In order to make the presentation self-contained, we first provide the definitions of WF-nets, and the appropriate soundness property.

Definition 1 (WF-Net). *A Petri net $N = (P, T, F)$ is a WF-net or workflow net if and only if: (1) there is one source place $i \in P$ with no in-coming arcs, i.e. $\bullet i = \emptyset$; (2) There is one sink place $o \in P$ with no out-going arcs, i.e. $o\bullet = \emptyset$; (3) each node $n \in P \cup T$ is on a path from i to o.*

Paper [1] defines the soundness property as a minimal correctness requirement for a workflow modelled as a WF-net. Intuitively, a workflow is sound if and only if: (a) it always has the option to complete a case; (b) there are no residual tokens; (c) there are neither deadlocks or livelocks; and (d) there are no dead transitions.

Definition 2 (Soundness of a WF-Net). *A process modelled by a WF-net $N = (P, T, F)$ is sound if and only if: (1) for each state M reachable from the initial state i there exists a firing sequence leading from state M to state o, i.e. $\forall M \ (i \xrightarrow{*} M) \Rightarrow (M \xrightarrow{*} o)$; (2) state o is the only state reachable from state i with at least one token in place o, i.e. $\forall M \ (i \xrightarrow{*} M) \wedge (M \geq o) \Rightarrow (M = o)$; (3) there are no dead transitions in (N, i), i.e. $\forall t \exists M, M'$ such that $i \xrightarrow{*} M \xrightarrow{t} M'$.*

Because the Petri net shown in Fig. 2 is not a WF-net, we cannot check the soundness property in a straightforward way.

In the literature ([3]) it is suggested that such a net can be easily extended with an initialization and/or a termination part such that the first two requirements of Definition 1 are satisfied. However, no explicit indication of how to achieve this is given. This problem is signalled again in [7] and a solution is also outlined there. The author of [7] suggests adding a new start place and a new sink place that are connected to Petri net modules which initialize or clean up the places representing the inputs and the outputs of the original net in the right way. In [8, page 42], the same author states that this connection is not trivial, but depends on the relationship between of the corresponding inputs, and outputs, respectively, in the original net. One way to determine this relationship is to track the paths starting from the different inputs or outputs until they join. The connection of the new place with the primary places would then be a Petri net module that corresponds to the connector complementing the one that was found ([8])[2].

Applying this procedure to the net from Fig. 2, we obtain the sound WF-net from Fig. 3. Note, however, that the behaviour for the case when only input i_1 is provided is not captured by this net, although it was considered correct according to our intuitions. Indeed, in the event the process started and transition ti fired, both i_1 and i_2 will be marked, indicating that both the material request and the new supplier requirement were provided.

---

[2] This construction was originally suggested for modelling with EPC, but it can be naturally extended for modelling with the HI0-I3 notation

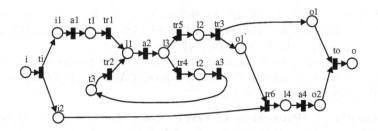

Fig. 3. A WF-net obtained from the Petri net shown in Fig. 2 — first solution

According to [8], the general case may be more difficult because there could be more than two different inputs or outputs with paths possibly meeting in various connectors of different type. Therefore, the suggestion is to link different start places and end places by Petri net modules corresponding to an OR-split or to an OR-join. Using this technique we obtain the WF-net from Fig. 4. However, it is not difficult to see that that this net is not sound. Consider the following sequence of transitions: $i \xrightarrow{ti_1} i_1 \xrightarrow{a_1} t_1 \xrightarrow{tr_1} l_1 \xrightarrow{a_2} l_3 \xrightarrow{tr_5} l_2 \xrightarrow{tr_3} o_1 + o'_1 \xrightarrow{to_1} o + o'_1$. This shows that when o is marked there is a residual token in o'_1.

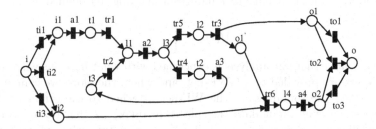

Fig. 4. A WF-net obtained from the Petri net shown in Fig. 2 — second solution

This example highlights that the existing techniques for applying the soundness criteria for WF-nets to the MIMO case are not satisfactory and, therefore, that more investigation is needed. Some new results are now introduced.

4   Generalized WF-Nets

The concept of WF-net can be generalized to the MIMO case as follows.

Definition 3 (GWF-Net). *A Petri net* $N = (P, T, F)$ *is an* (m, n) *GWF-net or generalized workflow net if and only if: (1) there are* m *source places* $i_1, \ldots, i_m \in P$ *with no in-coming arcs, i.e.* $\bullet i_k = \emptyset$ *for all* $1 \le k \le m$; *(2) there are* n *sink places* $o_1, \ldots, o_n \in P$ *with no out-going arcs, i.e.* $o_l \bullet = \emptyset$ *for all* $1 \le l \le n$; *(3) each node* $x \in P \cup T$ *is on a path from* i_k *to* o_l *for some* k *and* l *such that* $1 \le k \le m$ *and* $1 \le l \le n$.

If N is an (m, n) GWF-net, we define $in(N) = \{i_1, \ldots, i_m\}$ and $out(N) = \{o_1, \ldots, o_n\}$. Note that the Petri net from Fig. 2 is a $(2, 2)$ GWF-net with $in(N) = \{i_1, i_2\}$ and $out(N) = \{o_1, o_2\}$.

The following proposition states some syntactic properties of GWF-nets and shows how we can attach a WF-net to a given GWF-net. It follows straightforwardly from Definitions 1 and 3.

Proposition 1 (Properties of GWF-Nets). *Let $N = (P, T, F)$ be a Petri net. There are three cases. (1) If N is a GWF-net then $in(N)$ are the only source places of N. (2) If N is a GWF-net then $out(N)$ are the only sink places of N. (3) If N is a GWF-net then the net $N' = (P', T', F')$, defined by $P' = P \cup \{i, o\}$, $T' = T \cup \{ti, to\}$, $F' = P \cup \{(ti, i_k) | i_k \in in(N)\} \cup \{(i, ti)\} \cup \{(o_p, to) | o_p \in out(N)\} \cup \{(to, o)\}$, is a WF-net. N' is called the* WF-net attached to N.

To define a correctness criterion for a GWF-net we must consider pairs composed of (1) the pattern of the inputs that are provided and (2) the pattern of the outputs that are produced.

Definition 4 (Input/Output Patterns). *Let $N = (P, T, F)$ be a GWF-net. An* input-output pattern *is a pair of sets of places (I, O) such that $I \subseteq in(N)$ and $O \subseteq out(N)$. I is called an* input pattern *and O is called an* output pattern.

Note that an input pattern I induces a marking M_I defined as follows:

$$M_I(p) = \begin{cases} 1, p \in I \\ 0, p \notin I \end{cases}$$

Remember that our analysis is concerned with what happens when not all of the inputs are provided to a GWF-net, and when, therefore, we cannot proceed by checking the soundness of the WF-net attached to the original GWF-net. Moreover, missing input data (i.e. places in $in(N) \setminus I$ that do not contain tokens) will generate dead transitions in (N, M_I) (i.e. transitions of N that are not enabled in any marking reachable from M_I). The intuition behind dead transitions is that they represent work that will never be executed if the inputs in $in(N) \setminus I$ were not provided, and therefore they should be discarded prior to checking soundness.

Fortunately, we can reduce the GWF-net by removing dead transitions in (N, M_I), and other related nodes, resulting either in an empty net or in a smaller GWF-net. The soundness property can then be applied to the WF-net attached to the reduced net. The node reduction policy was devised in order to ensure that the resulted net satisfies the connectivity conditions (3) in Definitions 1 and 3.

Definition 5 (Reducing a GWF-Net). *Let $N = (P, T, F)$ be a GWF-net and let I be an input pattern. Let T_D be the set of all dead transitions of (N, M_I). Let $X = \{x \in P \cup T | x$ is on a path from a node in $in(N)$ to a node in $out(N)$ that does not contain any nodes from $T_D\}$. The net $N' = (P', T', F')$ defined by $P' = P \cap X$, $T' = T \cap X$, $F' = F \cap ((P' \times T') \cup (T' \times P'))$ is called the* reduction *of N with respect to I and it is denoted by $red(N, I)$.*

The net obtained by reducing the original GWF-net plays an important role in our analysis. It has the nice property that it is a GWF-net, and its input places are among the elements of the input pattern that has been used for reduction.

Proposition 2 (Reducing a GWF-Net Yields a GWF-Net). *Let* $N = (P, T, F)$ *be a GWF-net,* I *be an input pattern and let* $N' = red(N, I)$. *If* $P' \cup T' \neq \emptyset$ *then* N' *is a GWF-net with* $in(N') \subseteq I$.

We are now ready to define a correctness criterion for GWF-nets. It is called *MIMO soundness* and its definition is based on the classical soundness property defined for WF-nets.

Definition 6 (MIMO Soundness). *Let* $N = (P, T, F)$ *be a GWF-net,* I *be an input pattern and let* $N' = red(N, I)$ *such that* $P' \cup T' \neq \emptyset$. *The triple* $(in(N'), out(N'), N)$ *is called* MIMO sound *if and only if the WF-net attached to* N' *is sound.*

Let us apply the theory developed in this section to the net N from Fig. 2 and the input pattern $I = \{i_1\}$. The reduction process is detailed in Fig. 5. Transitions marked with an '×' are dead transitions in (N, M_I), nodes marked with a '+' are removed according to Definition 5. The arcs drawn with dotted lines are also removed according to Definition 5. Note that the WF-net attached to $red(N, I)$ is sound. This shows that the triple $(\{i_1\}, \{o_1\}, N)$ is MIMO sound.

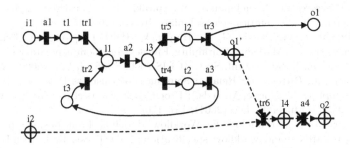

Fig. 5. Reducing the net shown in Fig. 2 with respect to $\{i_1\}$

Finally note that the reduction process outlined here makes the resulting net suitable for checking other soundness-related properties such as *relaxed soundness* for example, as defined in [7]. This increases the applicability of our approach.

5   Conclusions

In this paper we have shown that the soundness theory developed for WF-nets can also be successfully applied to MIMO business processes modelled as GWF-nets. The key point is the reduction of the original GWF-net to an appropriate sub-net that can be checked within the existing soundness framework. Interesting problems for future investigation are: (1) developing algorithms for computing all the input/output patterns for which a MIMO business process has the property of MIMO soundness; and (2) searching for conditions that guarantee the MIMO soundness property. We also intend to experiment with our technique on significantly larger process models, as soon as such models become available.

References

1. Aalst, W.M.P. van der: Verification of Workflow Nets. In: Azéma, P., Balbo, G. (eds.): Application and Theory of Petri Nets, 18th International Conference ICATPN'97, Toulouse, France. Lecture Notes in Comp. Sc., Vol. 1248, Springer-Verlag (1997) 407–426.
2. Aalst, W.M.P. van der: The Application of Petri Nets to Workflow Management. The Journal of Circuits, Systems and Computers 8(1) (1998) 21–66.
3. Aalst, W.M.P. van der: Formalization and Verification of Event-driven Process Chains. Comp.Sc.Rep. 98/01. Eindhoven University of Technology, (1998).
4. Bădică, C., Fox, C.: Hybrid IDEF0/IDEF3 Modelling of Business Processes: Syntax, Semantics and Expressiveness (extended abstract). Presented at the Romanian-Austrian Workshop on Computer-Aided Verification of Information Systems: A Practical Industry-Oriented Approach. Timişoara, Romania, (2004), 20–22.
5. Bădică, C., Bădică, A., Liţoiu, V.: A New Formal IDEF-based Modelling of Business Processes, In: Manolopoulos, Y., Spirakis, P. (eds.): Proc. of the 1st Balkan Conference in Informatics, Thessaloniki, Greece, (2003) 535–549.
6. Bosilj Vuksic, V., Giaglis, G. M., Hlupic. V.: IDEF Diagrams and Petri Nets for Business process Modeling: Suitability, Efficacy, and Complementary Use. In: Proc. Int. Conf. on Enterprise Inf. Syst., ICEIS'2000, Stafford, UK, (2000), 242–247.
7. Dehnert, J., Rittgen, P.: Relaxed Soundness of Business Processes. In: Dittrich, K.; Geppert, A.; Norrie, M. (eds.): Proc.CAISE'01. Lecture Notes in Comp. Sc., Vol. 2068, Springer-Verlag, (2001), 157–170.
8. Dehnert, J.: A Methodology for Workflow Modeling. From business process modeling towards sound workflow specification. PhD Thesis D83, Tech.Univ.Berlin, (2003).
9. Desel, J., Esparza, J.: Free Choice Petri Nets. Cambridge Tracts in Theoretical Computer Science 40. Cambridge University Press (1995).
10. Draft Federal Information Processing Standards Publication 183, Integration Definition for Function Modelling (IDEF0), (1993).
11. Eshuis, R., Wieringa, R.: Comparing Petri net and activity diagram variants for workflow modelling - a quest for reactive Petri nets. In: Ehrig, H., Reisig, W., Rozenberg, G., Weber, H. (eds.): Petri Net Technology for Communication Based Systems. Lecture Notes in Comp. Sc., Vol. 2472, Springer-Verlag, (2002) 321–351.
12. Hee, K.M. van, Sidorova, N., Voorhoeve, M.: Soundness and Separability of Workflow Nets in the Stepwise Refinement Approach. In: Aalst, W.M.P. van der, Best, E. (eds.): Lecture Notes in Comp. Sc., Vol. 2679. Springer-Verlag (2003) 337–356.

13. Kiepuszewski, B., Hofstede, A.H.M. ter, and Aalst, W.M.P. van der: Fundamentals of Control Flow in Workflows. *Acta Informatica*, 39(3) (2003) 143–209.
14. Mayer, R. et al: Information Integration for Concurrent Engineering (IICE): IDEF3 Process Description Capture Method Report, (1993).
15. Uthman, C.V.: Improving the Use of Petri Nets for Business Process Modeling, (Draft Status Paper 99/09/22), (1999).

Practical Investigation into
the Maintainability of Object-Oriented Systems for
Mission Critical Business

Joa Sang Lim[1], Seung Ryul Jeong[2], Min Cheol Whang[1], and Yongjoo Cho[1]

[1] Division of Media Technology,
Sangmyung University,
7 Hongji-dong, Jongro-gu, Seoul, Korea
{jslim, whang, ycho}@smu.ac.kr
[2] The Graduate School of Business IT,
Kookmin University,
861-1 Chongnung-dong, Songbuk-gu, Seoul, Korea
srjeong@kookmin.ac.kr

Abstract. Empirical evidence on the maintainability of object-oriented systems is far from conclusive, partly due to lack of representativeness of the subjects and systems used in the study. This research empirically examined this issue for the systems that are mission-critical, currently operational and maintained by professionals. It was found that the OO group appeared to consume less time while maintaining more amount of software artifacts than the NOO counterpart. This economical utilization of time appeared evident regardless of software development life cycle. This was due to the usefulness of UML for impact analysis which contributed to effective comprehension and communication. Insufficient design specifications led to ambiguity and costly defects in transferring design solutions to development. Also the encapsulation of OO seemed to reduce mental loads at maintenance tasks and improved code reuse. However, the number of files to manage increased and thus, dependency management is required for the OO systems.

1 Introduction

Software is no doubt mortal like any other commodities. It was reported to live for 9.4 years in the 1990s longer than it used to be in the 1980s [33]. Over this lifespan, software maintenance is inevitable to adapt to any changes in requirements, which surprisingly accounts for more than 60% of resource and effort [25]. This overwhelming expenditure in maintenance appears to be persistent despite many of new technological advancements advocated to bring in order of magnitude improvements in productivity and quality of software development [13]. Object-orientation has long been put forward for such claimed payoffs as better quality, code reuse and maintainability among others [20]. However, these claimed benefits are yet to be validated and there exist skeptical views on object-oriented technology for its difficulty to learn,

T. Yakhno (Ed.): ADVIS 2004, LNCS 3261, pp. 554–563, 2004.

and poorer run-time performance. Given the widespread use of object-oriented technology, it may be the right time for us to question if object-orientation is certainly worth investment. There have been a number of empirical studies to address this issue and their results are inconclusive [21]. Due to much variation in research methods among these studies, a cross-comparison would certainly be a challenging task. With respect to the maintainability of object-oriented systems, most of the studies have been conducted in a well controlled laboratory setting with the systems developed by the authors for their studies and thus, may not provide adequate insight into the operational real world systems. This raises an important question as to the benefits of object-orientation that may possibly bear out only when carefully designed [4]. This study was designed to address this issue and examined the maintainability of object oriented systems with practitioners in a field setting. This would certainly help both academics and practitioners to answer what contributes to the prolonged life span of object-oriented systems.

2 Related Research

IEEE [16] defines maintenance as "the process of modifying a software system or component after delivery to correct faults, improve performance or other attributes, or adapt to a changed environment." As such, maintenance activities are classified into three types [31] and a classic survey study in 1978 by Lientz and Swanson [25] found that 17.4% was of corrective, 18.2% of adaptive and 60.3% of perfective maintenance. After a quarter century later, Schach *et al.* [30] doubted if the mangers as respondents of Lientz and Swanson [25] could possibly remember the details and showed somewhat different results with far greater corrective maintenance. A similar term maintainability of interest to this study is defined as "the ease with which a software system or component can be modified to correct faults, improve performance or other attributes, or adapt to a changed environment." This is often operationalised as understandability, modifiability and testability as suggested by Boehm [3].

Empirical evidence to support superior maintainability of object-oriented technology is lacking [19] and thus, research in this area has been urged [1]. Many empirical studies have focused mainly on the issues of what contributes to maintainability (e.g., inheritance) and how to validate the maintainability model. A good example of the former is Chaumun *et al.* [8] who proposed Change Impact Model and suggested WMC as an indicator of changeability for the C++ programs. Likewise, inheritance has been of interest to many empirical studies [9, 15, 28]. The claimed benefits of object-oriented technology have been more directly challenged by a number of so called empirical software engineers [4, 5].

However, maintenance is a very complicated process consisting of numerous factors which may potentially influence maintainability of the systems. Kitchenham *et al.* [23] proposed four ontological factors that may constitute maintenance such as activity types, product, people and process. This view is useful in reviewing the prior empirical studies. There exist a number of experimental studies which have investigated the relationship of structural attributes of object-oriented systems with maintainability and reported conflicting results. One of the earlier studies that questioned this issue is Daly *et al.* [9] who showed that there appeared to be a seemingly optimal level of inheritance (i.e., three levels). A few years later, Harrison *et al.* [15] in a replication study of Daly *et al.* [9] found a contrasting result that inheritance should be avoided to a minimum level. They made use of data oriented University personnel systems written in C++ ranged from 360 to 1200 lines of code. 48 computer science students were asked to perform an impact analysis in response to additional functional requirements. It was shown that the flat systems appeared to be significantly easier to understand and modify than those with deeper inheritance of levels three and five. More recently, Prechelt *et al.* [28] challenged the previous studies by examining the effect of inheritance from a wider perspective. Systems used in their study were made more practical by increasing the size and complexity. The lines of code were ranged from 1187 to 2470 and the number of classes varied between 20 and 28. The experience level of the participants was controlled to see its possible interaction effect with inheritance on maintainability. The results of their study appeared to corroborate Harrison *et al.* [15] that programs with smaller depth of inheritance were easier to maintain. However, further investigation using a linear regression analysis showed that inheritance depth did not contribute to predicting code maintenance effort. The number of relevant methods was found to be more correlated with code maintenance effort.

Briand *et al.* [3] examined a more fundamental issue as to the benefits of object-oriented method over structured counterpart. Requirement and design documents of each method were provided to 13 computer science students. The participants were required to perform impact analysis to locate correctly the parts of design documents to be modified. The good object-oriented design was found to be easier to maintain than the good structured one. It should be, however, noted that the significance level was lowered to 0.2 to test the hypotheses. Interestingly enough, the good design principles (e.g., coupling, cohesion) added to easier maintainability of the object-oriented design whereas they did not to the structured design. These results highlighted the importance of design principles to improve maintainability of the object-oriented method. This study was extended and upheld by Briand *et al.* [5] with its focus shifted toward object-orientation itself as is the case in most studies conducted more recently in the 2000s [10, 11, 27]. These studies commonly argued that application of design principles could result in quality improvements of the object-oriented method. This highlights that the benefits of object-orientation could not be claimed unless well designed.

A careful examination of these foregoing studies appears to prompt some pertinent issues. The subjects used in these studies were often students as surrogates of professional engineers. The experimental systems were also small, ranging from a few hundreds to a few thousands at most. Thus this study is designed to examine the way professionals maintain the systems operational in practice. Given scarce and conflicting empirical evidence, the null hypotheses are formulated in this study as follows:

H1: There is no difference in the maintainability between the object-oriented (OO) and the non object-oriented (NOO) systems over the pre-implementation phases (requirement, analysis & design).

H2: There is no difference in the maintainability between the OO and the NOO systems over the post-design phases (implementation, testing & deployment).

3 Experiment

3.1 Experiment Design

This study was conducted in a field setting at a major credit card company in Korea on a mission-critical credit approval system currently operational and maintained by professionals. Despite its limitation in controlling experimental variables, a field study is useful in observing any causal relationships more practically in real context. This field experiment was made feasible owing to the availability of two versions of the object-oriented (developed in C++) and structured (developed in C) systems operational in parallel over the course of migrating the legacy systems. In order to test the hypotheses set forth in the previous section, we designed two experimental OO and NOO groups in this study.

3.2 Maintenance Task

An experimental task used was of a maintenance scenario, selected from a pool of change requests (CR). The number of CRs amounted to 1,376 in 2002 and decreased by one third to 488 in the following year. Such decline was due to postponing any aggressive marketing operations in response to increased credit risks of customers. All CRs were subject to examination of the IT planning department for their feasibility and validity. Then CRs were awarded appropriate levels in the range between 1 and 9 which served as a baseline for the allocation of required resources. Higher levels of 1-2 were related to the changes in government policy or external environment and thus, often required a few man-months to implement. The next levels 3-5 usually required about one man-month on average. The lower levels 6-7 were usually concerned with enhancing a couple of user interface displays. The bottom levels of 8-9 were relatively very simple in need of several man-days to maintain. Most CRs appeared to be smaller and levels 8-9 amounted to about 50%. The higher CRs above level 4 accounted for about 10 to 20%.

A scenario used in this study was Credit Limit Integration (CLI) that was not artificially made up but actual and randomly selected from the CR level 4. The CLI scenario was to put into effect a 'single' credit limit for each customer that used to be awarded for each credit service (e.g., credit sales, cash service).

3.3 Participants

A total of 12 IS professionals has participated in this experiment. Of them, six participants were assigned to the NOO group. Those in the NOO group were IS staff of the card company and have been maintaining current legacy systems for the last several years and thus, are all well aware of CLI-related activities and processes. The six remnants were allocated to the OO group. Having involved in the whole process of rebuilding the old system in C++, those in the OO group may well be regarded as possessing expertise in the CLI as equivalently as those of the NOO group.

3.4 Procedures

Participants were initially briefed on the maintenance task. They were asked to keep record of their itinerary of time spent, tasks performed and artifacts changed as detailed as possible over the course of all maintenance cycles. Given that the task was performed on the operational systems, the IS manger of those participants volunteered to explain the importance of the task and to ask both groups to record their activities in a correct, honest manner. Participants were not told that the task was of an experiment, so they considered such recording and reporting as part of usual maintenance activities. Then both groups performed the experimental task as their routine.

3.5 Dependent Variables

Collected were two metrics on the maintainability of the OO and the NOO groups [5]. The first metric was the total man-minutes (i.e., minutes spent per person) as required to comprehend, modify and test any artifacts in related to CLI. The other metric was the volume of change made to the artifacts. So the volume was represented by the total number of pages for any documents, by lines of code (NBNC LOC, no comments and no blank lines of code, [18]) modified for programs, number of test cases or number of files to compile and deploy. As this task was real, both groups were required to complete the CLI task successfully, that is free of any defects. Both metrics were collected throughout the full life cycle of system development: requirement, analysis, design, implementation, test, and deployment.

3.6 Data Validation

On completion of the task, the collected records of man-minutes were carefully examined and then interviews were followed to clarify any under or over-statements and possible difference in requirements as they were allowed to contact with users over the experiment. In addition, we had another couple of group meetings with all stakeholders to examine any potential differences at the task. Further adjustments were made to the records in consideration of any differences in the consultation time, additional requirements and acceptance tests.

The change volume was also ensured by walkthrough and inspection where all the participants and administrative staff were called in to discuss the presence of any measurement errors. For example, carriage returns as found in long SQL statements were compared to ensure validity of collected data.

4 Results

The maintenance process and artifacts between two groups were varied largely due to the difference in technologies employed as part of the experiment. That is, the NOO group was required to program in C and structured methods and relevant tools were used accordingly. In contrast, the OO group developed the system in C++ which introduced UML (Unified Modeling Language), UP (Unified Process) and CASE tools.

Over the earlier phase of system analysis and design, the OO group was heavily dependent on UML, while the NOO preferred the direct communication between system analysts and developers. This affected the way impact analysis was performed between two groups. The NOO group had to comprehend the CLI task by reading the existing programs. On the other hand, the OO group examined a variety of UML diagrams including use case diagrams, class diagrams and sequence diagrams.

Noticeable variations were also found in the implementation and test phases of maintenance. The maintainers in the OO group seemed to refer to the design documents to find any modification required to the systems. They also examined operation specification which contained sufficient business logic. The developers of the NOO system, however, had to rely on systems analysts who conveyed verbally aftermath of their impact analysis. Unfortunately, the direct communication rather increased overheads in transferring design solutions back and forth between analysts and developers. Having completed modification, both groups produced test cases in common. However, the technologies employed were different. The NOO group developed a simulator which fed the test case saved in data base to the system and saved the result into the test result log. On the other hand, the OO group employed testing scripts (e.g., CUnit) and saved the test results in the log.

Table 1. The metrics collected over the requirement, analysis and design phases

Phases	Metrics	NOO	OO
Require-ment	Man-Minutes	240	260
	Change vol.	None	2 pages of activity diagram 2 pages of use case spec.
Analysis & Design	Man-Minutes	1,020	310
	Change vol.	2 pages of design spec.	1 page of class diagram a few pages of operation specifications 1 page of program traceability

The first hypothesis was to examine the maintainability of the first three phases (requirement, analysis, and design phases) for each group. The upper section of the Table 1 indicates that the total man-minutes over the earlier three phases as reported by the NOO group were found to be about twice as many as those of the OO group (1,260 vs. 570). In particular, the NOO group took approximately triple the time taken for analysis and design than the OO group (1,020 vs. 310). These results indicate that the NOO system required more efforts to perform the maintenance task than the OO system. Table 1 also shows that the change volume of the analysis and design artifacts of the OO group was more than that of the NOO system. This is not surprising in that the OO group had more artifacts to maintain whereas the NOO only a few mandatory documents. It is rather unexpected that the OO group spent less time to be discussed later. In summary, the OO system needs less efforts (i.e., man-minutes) but slightly more changes on documents than the NOO system. This leads us to reject the first null hypothesis.

Testing the second hypothesis requires the maintainability of the later three phases (implementation, test and deployment). Table 2 reveals that the man-minutes of the

NOO group were about three times more than those of the OO group during the implementation phase (660 vs. 215). In addition, the NOO group surprisingly invested about six times more effort in the test phase than the OO group (1,103 vs. 182). The dominance of OO was persistent in the deployment phase, that is, the NOO group spent more time than the OO group (30 vs. 17). These results seem to corroborate the result obtained earlier for the first hypothesis that the OO system could reduce maintenance efforts.

Table 2. The metrics collected over the implementation, test and deployment phases (The numbers in each bracket are for the credit sales and the cash service respectively)

Phases	Metrics	NOO	OO
Implementation	Man-Minutes	660	215
	LOC changed	182 (51, 131)	277 (268, 9)
	Files changed	5 (2, 3)	11 (6, 5)
Test	Man-Minutes	1,103	182
	Test cases	15 (8, 7)	39
	Files tested	1	4
	LOC test scripts	n/a	283 (278, 5)
Deployment	Man-Minutes	30	17
	Files compiled	2	6 (5, 1)
	Files deployed	2	6 (5, 1)

Moving onto the change volume section in Table 2, the OO group modified more LOC (277) in the implementation phase than did the NOO counterpart (182). Detailed examination by the subsystems of credit sales and cash service, the results were surprising. For the credit sales, 268 LOC were modified for the OO system, which was in contrast to 51 lines for the NOO system. Focusing on the cash sales, however, this tendency was reversed. The LOC updated for the 'cash service' of the OO system was only 9 whereas that of the NOO system, 151. This was attributable mainly to the code reuse of the OO system where the business logic written for the one system (i.e., credit sales) was utilized for the other system (i.e., cash service) with little modification. On the other hand, the NOO systems appeared to duplicate the business logic alike each other. For the test phase the OO group created considerable test programs (CUnit, LOC 283) that interestingly reduced time taken for testing as earlier discussed. As in Table 2, the OO systems increased the number of files to compile and deploy due to fine granularity of classes. Taken together, the additional programs and files, the OO system appeared to offer advantage of requiring less effort and thus, the second null hypothesis is rejected.

5 Discussion and Conclusions

This study found that overall the OO group appeared to consume less time but to maintain more software artifacts than the NOO counterpart. This economical utilization of time was evident regardless of software development life cycle. This finding is rather surprising in that the difficulties associated with the object-oriented methods have been reported in the prior literature. Vessey and Conger [32] found that the OO was more difficult to learn than data-oriented methods. It should be, however, noted that the subjects used in their study were students and somewhat positive results with professionals as in this study were reported that the OO designs were of higher quality and took less time than procedural ones to provide designs and write pseudo-code [2, 26].

The superiority of the OO may be due to the usefulness of UML for impact analysis as employed in the OO group. For example, Hadar and Hazzan [14] did not find any preference of developers among UML diagrams. Purchase *et al.* [29] argued that of semantically equivalent notations, not intuitive notations made people more alert to find the errors embedded in the class diagrams. However, the research on this issue is now emerging and any conclusion is yet to be made.

Software design is a problem solving process and its solution has to be translated into a product where effective communication is essential [7]. In the OO group, operation specifications were written sufficiently enough to include business logic for developers. On the other hand, the software analysts of the NOO group tended to rely on verbal communication to convey their designs to developers. This reliance on the natural language communication of the NOO group appeared to lead to significant possible errors such as ambiguity and missing requirements which necessitated more frequent communication. Such ambiguity embedded in the design documents led to arbitrary coding of developers which in turn contributed to some defects. It has been pointed out that 'the most difficult, time-intensive, and error-prone part of systems development is in analysis and design, rather than programming' [6] and costs to remove any defects found in the later stages of implementation and test accelerate steeply.

The easier maintainability of the OO observed in software design has been also manifested over the later stages of development and test. This study found that the source codes were reused less in the NOO group than the OO group. That is, the NOO group tended to copy a template and modify it. The problem of this heuristic was that much of the logic became duplicated to a large extent across similar modules. This strategy taken by the NOO group was 'comprehension avoidance' [12] where people tended to minimize their mental efforts when faced with complex tasks as often reported in cognitive psychology. Thus, this heuristic would also have been evident in object-oriented paradigm [22]. This heuristic was, however, lessened to a large extent in the OO group since the OO systems were modularized with outbound interfaces and the developers did not need to understand inside the software components. This black-box reuse of interface and components seemed to reduce the mental load and possibly made the maintenance task easier.

To the contrary, the NOO groups seemed to rely on global variables so heavily declared and saved in a separate file for each team, to which any developers could access. Any maintenance task required thorough comprehension of the global file and a small mistake in its updating would bring about detrimental consequences. This certainly affected the maintenance task of the NOO group. On the other hand, any variables were localized and independently encapsulated within classes and closed architectural layers of the OO systems. Also regression testing tools available to the OO systems contributed to the reuse of test case and scripts over the iterative unit and integration tests.

It is often argued that the granularity of decomposition becomes so detailed in OO and thus, the number of files to manage and deploy increases dramatically. The OO group indicated that the increased number of files certainly increased their maintenance efforts. Also a clear separation of roles between designers and developers of the OO group appeared to add to dissatisfaction in that learning different technologies was deprived. Despite its difficulty and possible confounding factors in a real setting, this field study raised many interesting research issues and thus, further research is required with different tasks in a similar context. This study also uphold the notion that the maintainability is not necessarily affected only by the structural attributes of the systems, but the contextual factors such as methods, processes and tools of system design and development should also be taken into maintainability research.

References

1. Basili, V. R. & Lanubile, F., 1999, "Building Knowledge through Families of Experiments," IEEE Transactions on Software Engineering, 25, 4, pp.456 – 473.
2. Boehm-Davis, D. & Ross, 1992, L., 1992, "Program Design Methodologies and the Software Development Process," International Journal of Man-Machine Studies, 36, pp.1-19.
3. Bohem, B. W., 1981, Software Engineering Economics, Prentice-Hall, Inc., NJ.: p.767.
4. Briand, L. C., Bunse, C., Daly, J. W., Differding, C., 1997, "An Experimental Comparison of the Maintainability of Object-Oriented and Structured Design Documents," Empirical Software Engineering, 2, pp.291-312.
5. Briand, L. C., Bunse, C. & Daly, J., 2001, "A Controlled Experiment for Evaluating Quality Guidelines on the Maintainability of Object-Oriented Designs," IEEE Transactions on Software Engineering, 27, 6, pp. 513 - 529.
6. Brooks, F. P., 1987, "No Silver Bullet: Essence and Accidents of Software Engineering," IEEE Computer, 20, 4, pp.10-19.
7. Budgen, D., 2003, Software Design, 2nd Ed., Addison-Wesley, NY.
8. Chaumun, M. A. Kabaili, H., Keller, R. K. & Lustman, F., 2002, "A Change Impact Model for Changeability Assessment in Object-Oriented Software Systems," Science of Computer Programming, 45, pp.155-174.
9. Daly, J., Brooks. A., Miller, J., Roper, M. & Wood, M., 1996, "Evaluating Inheritance Depth on the Maintainability of Object-Oriented Software," Empirical Software Engineering, 1, 2, pp.109-132.
10. Deligiannis, I., Shepperd, M., Roumeliotis, M. & Stamelos, I., 2003a, "An Empirical Investigation of an Object-Oriented Design Heuristic for Maintainability," The Journal of Systems and Software, 65, 127-139.
11. Deligiannis, I., Stamelos, I., Angelis, L., Roumeliotis, M. & Shepperd, M., 2003b, "A Controlled Experiment Investigation of an Object-Oriented Design Heuristic for Maintainability," The Journal of Systems and Software, To appear.
12. Detienne, F., 1997, "Assessing the Cognitive Consequences of the Object-Oriented Approach: A Survey of Empirical Research on Object-Oriented Design by Individuals and Teams," Interacting with Computers, 9, 1, pp.47-72.

13. Glass, R. L., 1999, "The Realities of Software Technology Payoffs," Comms of the ACM, 42, 2, pp.74-79.
14. Hadar, I & Hazzan, O., 2004, "On the Contribution of UML Diagrams to Software System Comprehension," Journal of Object Technology, 3, 1, pp.143 – 156.
15. Harrison, R., Counsell, S. & Nithi, R., 2000, "Experimental Assessment of the Effect of Inheritance on the Maintainability of Object-Oriented Systems," The Journal of Systems and Software, 52, pp.173-179.
16. IEEE, 1993, IEEE Software Engineering Standards Collection, IEEE.
17. ISO 9126, Software Product Quality Characteristics, http://www.cse.dcu.ie/essiscope.
18. Jones, C., 1986, Programming Productivity, New York: McGraw‒Hill.
19. Jones, C., 1994, "Gaps in the Object-Oriented Paradigm," IEEE Computer, 27, 6, pp.90 – 91.
20. Johnson, R. A., 2000, "The Up's and Down's of Object-Oriented Systems Development, Comms of the ACM, 43, 10, pp. 69 - 73.
21. Johnson, R. A., 2002, "Object-Oriented Analysis and Design – What Does the Research Say?," Journal of Computer Information Systems, Spring, pp. 12 – 15.
22. Kim, M., Bergman, L., Lau, T. & Notkin, D., 2004, "Ethnographic Study of Copy and Paste Programming Practice in OOPL," Submitted to International Symposium on Empirical Software Engineering (ISESE04), August, USA.
23. Kitchenham, B. A., Travassos, G. H., Von A. Mayrhauser, A., Niessink, F., Schniedewind, N. F., Singer, J., Takado, S., Vehvilainen, R. & Yang, H., 1999, "Towards an Ontology of Software Maintenance," J Software Maintenance: Research and Practice, 11, pp.365-389.
24. Lientz, B. P. & Swanson, E. B., 1978, "Discovering Issues in Software Maintenance," Data Manage., 16, pp. 15-18.
25. Lientz, B. P., Swanson, E. B. & Tompkins, G.. E., 1978, "Characteristics of Application Software Maintenance," Comms of the ACM, 21, 6, pp.466-471.
26. Pennington, N., Lee, A., Re, Lee & Rehder, B., 1995, "Cognitive Activities and Levels of Abstraction in Procedural and Object-Oriented Design," Human-Computer Interaction, 10, 2-3, pp.171-226.
27. Prechelt, L. & Tichy, W. F., 2001, "A Controlled Experiment in Maintenance Comparing Design Patterns to Simpler Solutions," IEEE Transactions on Software Engineering, 27, 12, pp.1134-1144.
28. Prechelt, L., Unger, B., Philippsen, M. & Tichy, W., 2003, "A Controlled Experiment on Inheritance Depth as a Cost Factor for Code Maintenance," The Journal of Systems and Software, 65, pp.115 - 126.
29. Purchase, H. C., Colpoys, L., McGill, M., Carrington, D., Britton, C., 2001, "UML Class Diagram Syntax: An Empirical Study of Comprehension," Australian Symposium on Information Visualization, Dec., Sydney.
30. Schach S.R., Jin, B., Yu, L. G., Heller, G. Z. & Offutt, J., 2003, "Determining the distribution of maintenance categories: Survey versus measurement," Empirical Software Engineering, 8, 4, pp. 351-365.
31. Swanson, E. B., 1976, "The Dimensions of Maintenance, Proceedings, 2nd International Conference on Software Engineering," San Francisco, Oct. 13 – 15, pp.492 – 497.
32. Vessey, I. & Conger, S., 1994, "Requirement Specification: Learning Object, Process and Data Methodologies," Comms of the ACM, 37, 5, pp.102-113.
33. Zvegintzov, N., 1998, "Software Should Live Longer," IEEE Software, 15, 4, pp. 19 - 21.

A New MAC Protocol Design for WATM Networks

Celal Ceken, Ismail Erturk, and Cuneyt Bayilmis

Kocaeli University, Technical Education Faculty,
Electronics and Computer Education Department,
41300 Kocaeli, Turkey
Telephone: 0 262 3249910, Fax: 0 262 3313909
{cceken,erturk,bayilmis}@kou.edu.tr

Abstract. Traditional wireless networking solutions are almost all unsuitable
for multimedia applications whose QoS requirements may differ from each
other diversely. Main inspiration of WATM, promising ideal transmission of
different traffics such as voice, data and video together over wireless medium,
is to implement high bit rate and QoS guaranteed data transfer, which is already
well realized by ATM technology over wired infrastructure. An effective MAC
protocol must be employed to provide multimedia applications with QoS guaranteed data transfer over the shared wireless medium that naturally is error-
prone and has low bandwidth capacity. In this paper, we propose a new MAC
protocol with a QoS guarantee based scheduling algorithm for WATM networks. It fairly maintains QoS requirements of all real-time wireless multimedia applications. Computer modeling and simulation of a WATM network with
the proposed approach to provide CBR, VBR, ABR and UBR ATM services
are also realized using a commercially available tool named OPNET Modeler.
Preliminary simulation results obtained are presented, including comparisons
with those of a WATM counterpart employing a well-known MAC protocol.

1 Introduction

For the last decade wireless/mobile networking has gained an increasing importance along
with the developments in the cellular communication technologies. Several wireless networking systems have been developed to provide different types of services to various wireless user applications. Current wireless networking infrastructures are not suitable for most
of the multimedia applications each requiring a different Quality of Service (QoS) support.

ATM (Asynchronous Transfer Mode) is a transmission technology considered as a
standard for B-ISDN with guaranteed QoS to all possible traffic types in wired medium.
The success of ATM technology in the wired network has also initiated many researches
about WATM (Wireless ATM) concept [1, 2]. WATM has been proposed to transport
different type of traffics such as voice, data and video in wireless environment. Using
WATM, it is principally intended to support QoS guaranteed data traffics for high bit
rate broadband multimedia applications [3].

To avoid the problems resulting from the wireless medium characteristics
(e.g. error-prone with low bandwidth), new layers must be added to standard ATM layers.

T. Yakhno (Ed.): ADVIS 2004, LNCS 3261, pp. 564–574, 2004.

These are namely a MAC (Medium Access Control) layer providing effective allocation of medium resources shared by many different users, and a DLC (Data Link Control) layer used for flow and error control [2]. They together establish the basis for QoS supported application traffic transfer using WATM.

In this paper, a novel MAC model based on TDMA/FDD (Time Division Multiple Access/Frequency Division Duplexing) technique, which offers QoS guarantees to multimedia application traffics, is proposed. Using this new protocol, it is intended to provide different multimedia applications with QoS support through ATM service categories in wireless medium.

The paper is organized as follows. Section 2 provides an overview of PRMA/DA (Packet Reservation Multiple Access/Dynamic Allocation) MAC protocol which is used for performance comparison. Overall properties and design stages of the proposed MAC protocol together with related algorithms are explained in detail in Section 3. Section 4 includes an example WATM network utilizing the proposed MAC technique, which has been modeled and simulated under different traffic loads using a commercially available program called OPNET Modeler with Radio Module. The simulation results obtained are compared with those of a WATM network utilizing the PRMA/DA MAC protocol, which are also obtained under the same networking conditions as the proposed WATM network, followed by performance evaluation of both networks. Finally, the last Section gives our summary about the proposed TDMA/FDD based MAC protocol with final remarks.

2 Previous Works

To support multimedia traffics, a wireless MAC protocol must be able to provide bandwidth on demand. Several MAC protocols have been defined for WATM such as; DQRUMA [4], E–PRMA [4], MASCARA [4], MDR–TDMA [4], DSA++ [4], PRMA/DA [4, 5] etc. in literature. PRMA/DA, which is proposed in [5], operates on a frame basis. Time on the uplink channel is divided into a contiguous sequence of PRMA/DA frames, and each frame consists of Available slots, CBR reservation slots, VBR reservation slots, and ABR reservation slots as illustrated in Figure 1.

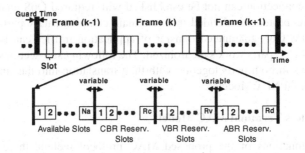

Fig. 1. The PRMA/DA frame format

The number of available slots depends on the intensity of demand to access the network among the mobile stations. In contrast, the number of reservation slots assigned to each reserving station is primarily dependent on the statistical properties of traffic a MS intends to transmit. The BS is responsible for determining the number of slots allotted to each type, as well as the number of slots assigned to each reserving terminal (MT). The DL frame works in the contention-free TDM format, under the total control of the BS in broadcast mode.

3 A New Approach to Support Wireless Multimedia Applications Using TDMA / FDD MAC Protocol Based WATM

A MAC protocol in wireless communication should be used to allocate the limited bandwidth to WTs efficiently. Several MAC schemes have been proposed in the literature for managing multimedia traffics in WATM systems [6]. WATM technology promises to provide QoS guarantees for multimedia applications together with traditional services [7–9]. A demand assignment MAC technique for WATM should be considered to maintain the bursty traffic natures of such applications. In this technique a user terminal needs a control channel in uplink direction to request access channel from a BS and then the BS assigns bandwidth for this request if there is enough resource which can support required level of QoS [10].

Here in this work, a demand assignment scheme is employed to realize the proposed WATM MAC protocol [11]. As a multiplexing technique, TDMA is preferred due to its superiority and suitability for real-time multimedia traffics. In the proposed MAC protocol, radio spectrum is divided into time slots which are assigned to different connections where a user application can send data only in its own dedicated slots. Due to the FDD duplexing technique utilized in the proposed MAC protocol, two distinct carrier frequencies are used for the uplink and downlink channels. When a WT needs to communicate with any other, initially it asks for a transmission channel from the BS. According to the QoS requirements of this connection request, the BS assigns adequate number of time slots for this connection using a dynamic Slot Allocation Table (SAT) that is scheduled with an algorithm based on ATM service classes, explained in the following sub-sections. If there are not enough slots for the request, a connection can not be established with required QoS guarantees. The proposed MAC protocol is divided into two main complementary parts operating at the WT and BS. QoS guaranteed transfer of application traffics can be provided when these two MAC parts work synchronized. The following sub-sections explain in detail all functions in both parts together with their translation into the simulation environment in the OPNET Modeler.

3.1 Wireless Terminal MAC Model

The WT functions of the proposed MAC protocol include three main processes. These are namely requesting a connection establishment/termination from the BS, getting its own time slots from the BS and sending data in the allocated time slots. Since WATM is connection-oriented, for a connection establishment, any WT to inform the BS about its bandwidth requirement creates a control packet called *cc_con_req*. The *cc_con_req* also contains QoS parameters (SLSx) of the wireless application (Figure 2-a). It is then sent to the BS in the first available empty slot. After the connection establishment, the wireless application traffic in WATM cells illustrated in Figure 2-b is sent in the time slots allocated to this connection. WT creates a control packet called *cc_con_end* to terminate the connection and sends it to the BS in the first available empty slot again (Figure 2-c).

a)

TermAdress	ServiceClass	AppNum	SLS1	SLS2	SLS3	SLS4	CRC
(4 bits)	(4 bits)	(4 bits)	(16 bits)	(16 bits)	(16 bits)	(16 bits)	(16 bits)

b)

GFC	VPI	VCI	PT	CLP	HEC	CRC
(4 bits)	(8 bits)	(16 bits)	(3 bits)	(1 bit)	(8 bits)	(16 bits)
PAYLOAD						
(384 bits)						

c)

TermAdress	ServiceClass	CRC
(4 bits)	(4 bits)	(16 bits)

Fig. 2. *a*) Connection request packet   *b*) WATM cell   *c*) Connection terminate packet

WT node model designed using OPNET Modeler is shown in Figure 3-a. The SOURCE module used in the WT is responsible for packet generation according to the packet size and arrival time parameters defined. The SINK module collects statistics of the arrived packets and then destroys them. AAL (ATM Adaptation Layer) and ATM modules have the same functions as defined in the standard ATM. DLC module detects bit errors resulting typically from the physical characteristics of the wireless medium and corrects them while MAC module efficiently manages the allocation of existing bandwidth shared by all WTs. Finally, physical layer (rx, tx) is the interface between the node module and air (Figure 3-a).

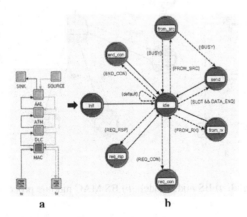

Fig. 3. *a*) WT node model   *b*) WT MAC module process model

In Figure 3-b, the process model of the MAC module used in WT node model is illustrated. The *con_req* state machine creates connection request packets containing

QoS parameters and sends them to the BS. Using the *from_src* state machine, data cells received from the ATM layer are sent to destination in the connection time slots allocated. The *req_resp* state machine obtains connection time slots that are assigned by the BS using its SAT scheduling algorithm. The *con_end* state machine creates connection termination packet and sends it to the BS. The *from_rx* state machine delivers any arrived packets destined to the WT to its ATM layer.

3.2 Base Station MAC Model

The BS functions of the proposed MAC protocol include three main processes. These are namely, assigning adequate number of slots for a connection using the SAT scheduling algorithm considering QoS requirements of the requesting WT, forwarding any arrived data packets to their destinations and terminating any active connection. The core function of the proposed MAC protocol is efficient management of the SAT of the BS. Figure 4-a shows the BS node model realized using OPNET Modeler. The MAC module functions in the BS node are used to allocate the available bandwidth for WT applications and to realize actual data packet transfer to destined WTs. The BS MAC module process model designed is also shown in Figure 4-b.

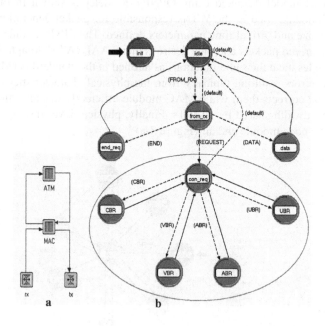

Fig. 4. *a*) BS node model   *b*) BS MAC module process model

The *from_rx* state machine delivers arriving packets to the next state machine according to the packet formats. The *con_req* state machine executes a fair scheduling algorithm that manages the SAT considering QoS requirements of the connection requests. The *end_req* and *data* state machines handle connection termination requests and data packet deliveries, respectively.

Slot Num	1	2	3	4	5	6	7		N-1	N
Term Num	-1	1	3	3	3	3	3		5	5
Appl Num	-1	1	1	1	1	1	2		1	1
Guarantee	-1	1	1	2	2	2	1		2	1
Service Class	-1	0	0	2	2	3	3		3	2

Fig. 5. Structure of the Slot Allocation Table (SAT)

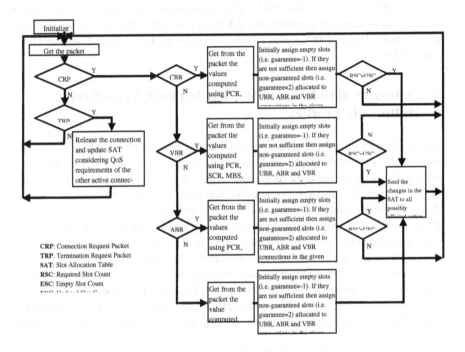

Fig. 6. The SAT scheduling algorithm outline

The SAT and its scheduling algorithm in the BS are the most vital parts of the proposed MAC protocol. Supporting QoS guaranteed services for bursty traffics such as multimedia applications depends on effective and efficient management of the SAT. The structure of SAT is shown in Figure 5. Slot Num, Term Num, Appl Num, Guarantee and Service Class rows of the table represent slot number, terminal address (-1: idle) using the slot, application number (-1: idle), guarantee situation of the slot (-1: idle, 1: guaranteed, 2: non-guaranteed) and service class of connection (-1: idle, 0: CBR, 1: VBR, 2: ABR, 3: UBR), respectively. Outline of the fair scheduling algorithm executed in the BS to manage the SAT is presented in Figure 6.

For a new connection request, to determine the required number of slots and their guarantee situation, QoS parameters and traffic descriptors are used as in the standard ATM connections. According to the Peak Cell Rate (PCR), Sustainable Cell Rate (SCR) and Minimum Cell Rate (MCR) of CBR, VBR and ABR traffics respectively, enough number of slots' guarantee field are set to 1. Using the other QoS parameters and traffic descriptors, the guarantee field of empty slots is set to 2 for VBR, ABR and UBR service classes respectively. Any slot whose guarantee field is 2 may be reassigned for a new connection whose slot guarantee fields must be 1. Guarantee field of UBR slots are always set to 2 and these slots can be used by any guaranteed CBR, VBR or ABR connection if necessary since UBR service does not provide any QoS guarantees (i.e. best effort service). Furthermore, a certain number of slots (i.e. 1, 100, 200......N-100) in the SAT called control slots are reserved for connection request and connection termination packets in case all of the time slots are used for data transfer. When a WT wants to send a control packet, it uses first empty data or control slot.

4 Computer Simulation of WATM Network Transferring Multimedia Traffics

The WTs in the example scenario implemented using OPNET Modeler (Figure 7), employ the proposed TDMA/FDD based MAC protocol explained in the previous section to communicate with each other in the same wireless environment. Diameter of the cell which constructs the network topology is chosen 100 meters. Because of the connection-oriented structure of WATM, before actual data transmission takes place, considering QoS requirements of its application traffic, a WT initially sends a connection request to the BS. If there is enough number of slots available, the BS assigns them for this connection and informs the WT about which slots it can use for data transfer. As soon as the application running on a WT ends, a connection termination request is sent to the BS. The BS then evaluates it and updates the SAT using the proposed scheduling algorithm, considering fair reallocation of the released slots according to the QoS requirements of any ongoing data transfer of other WT applications.

In the example scenario, there are 20 WTs on which four different applications operate to generate and receive data traffics. There is only one type of application running at the same time on each WT. The data traffic introduced to the network by any WT is randomly destined to another WT. One of these applications is set to create voice transfer traffic requiring ATM CBR service, one for compressed video traffic requiring ATM VBR service, eight of them for critical data application traffic carried with ATM ABR service support while the other applications are set to create data transfer traffic requiring ATM UBR service. For instance, a voice application traffic originated from the WT1 is transferred to the WT5 over a connection providing a CBR service which is sensitive to delay and delay variation (jitter). Similarly a data application traffic originated from the WT16 is transferred to the WT20 over a connection providing a UBR service with no QoS guarantees. It should be noted that in a real-life situation every WT will not generate data or video sources at a given time.

Another WATM model analogous to the one above except for that PRMA/DA [5] MAC protocol is utilized instead of the proposed MAC is also simulated using OPNET Modeler for consistent performance comparisons. Working conditions of both models are chosen to be same.

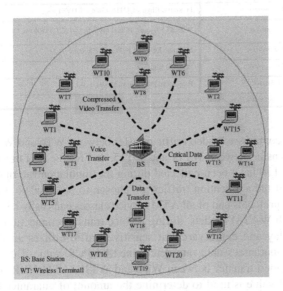

Fig. 7. WATM scenario using the proposed TDMA/FDD based MAC protocol

4.1 Simulation Results and Performance Analysis

Preliminary simulation results of the both WATM models described above are presented under varying network load conditions, followed by performance comparisons and analysis. To focus on the performance of the proposed MAC model, the channel is assumed to be ideal such that there is no distortion, noise, or other interference for packet transmissions resulting in low BER, and it is assumed that the CRC bits added to the packets avoids the bit errors resulting from the physical characteristics of the wireless environment. The simulation parameters used are given in Table 1.

The performance metrics concerned in this research work are average cell transfer delay and cell transfer delay variation, which also reflect the system utilization effect on different real-time multimedia application traffics. The cell loss ratio metric is not considered here since the buffers are assumed to have enough capacity so that no data cell is lost due to buffer overflow.

For both MAC protocols used in WATM, a slot length of 200 μseconds which has been determined considering 25 Mb/s data rate is chosen. With a total number of 1000 slots/frame, each time slot contains 5 WATM cells.

Varying the message size of all WT application traffics, average end-to-end delay (EED) and delay variation (jitter) results for the voice traffic transfer between WT1 and

Table 1. Simulation parameters

Traffic Sources	30,000–100,000*(Bytes/s)
Uplink/Downlink Bit Rate	25 Mb/s
Modulation Schema	QPSK
CBR Parameters	PCR=100 Kbytes/s, CTD=150 ms, CDV=1 ms
VBR Parameters	SCR=85 Kbytes/s, PCR = 110 Kbytes/s, CTD=100 ms, CDV=1 ms
ABR Parameters	MCR=50 Kbytes/s, PCR=100 Kbytes/s
UBR Parameters	PCR=50 Kbytes/s
Channel Model	Free Space Propagation Model (LoS)
*Generated using Exponential Distribution Function, Exp(Mean).	

WT5, for the compressed video traffic transfer between WT6 and WT10, for the critical data traffic transfer between WT11 and WT15, and for the data traffic transfer between WT16 and WT20 have been collected during the simulation run time for both WATM models. All of the application traffics are chosen to be equal so that the performance of both MAC protocols and of all ATM service classes can easily be compared together.

In the both WATM models, during a voice transfer connection between WT1 and WT5, the delay and delay variation sensitive traffic utilizes an ATM CBR service support that guarantees data rate determined by PCR value. During a bursty nature compressed video transfer between WT6 and WT10, ATM VBR service class is utilized and SCR value is used to determine the amount of guaranteed bandwidth. Critical data transfer application between WT11 and WT15 is supported by ATM ABR service and the data rate indicated by MCR value is guaranteed for this connection. Finally, during a data traffic transfer between WT16 and WT20, any available bandwidth unused or remaining from other service classes is utilized over an ATM UBR connection with no QoS guarantees. The PCR parameter of the UBR service class represents the maximum data rate that can be supported in such a given connection.

Figure 8 shows the average EED results for the proposed MAC based WATM model, normalized with those of the PRMA/DA MAC based WATM counterparts, as a function of the offered load per wireless application. The voice application traffic (i.e. between WT1 and WT5) with CBR service support experiences 3 to 5 times, the compressed video application traffic (i.e. between WT6 and WT10) with VBR service support experiences 3 to 5 times, and the critical data application traffic (i.e. between WT11 and WT15) with ABR service support experiences 2 to 3 times lower average message delays in the proposed MAC based WATM model compared to the same traffic carried with the PRMA/DA MAC based WATM model. However, the non-critical data application traffic (i.e. between WT16 and WT20) with UBR service support supplies 3 to 8 times better results than those of the WATM model using the proposed MAC method. This is because, in the proposed MAC based WATM model the slots assigned to the UBR connections can be utilized by other services such as CBR, VBR or ABR whereas in the PRMA/DA reserved slots of any type are used by the applications until the end of the connection time.

Figure 9 illustrates the EED variation results for the proposed MAC based WATM model, normalized with those of the PRMA/DA MAC based WATM counterparts, as a function of the offered load per wireless application. Considering the delay variation sensitive voice and compressed video traffics, the proposed MAC based WATM model has a better EED variation results than those of PRMA/DA based WATM model. Lower message delay and delay variation results are expected as the proposed MAC protocol, unlike PRMA/DA MAC protocol, distributes the allocated slots according to required CDV parameter of the connection.

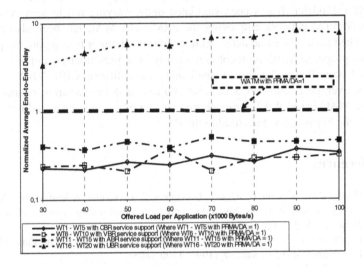

Fig. 8. Normalized average EED results for the proposed WATM model

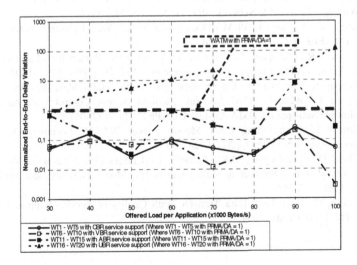

Fig. 9. Normalized EED variation results for the proposed WATM model

5 Conclusions

A new TDMA/FDD based MAC protocol for multimedia communications in WATM networks is proposed. Its design stages are also outlined. The WATM designed promises to provide a QoS guarantee based transmission of different real-time multimedia application traffics. QoS guaranteed data transfer in such an error-prone wireless medium with scarce resources requires a MAC protocol allowing efficient and fair bandwidth allocation and utilization for different end user applications.

A WATM network with the proposed MAC protocol has been modeled using OPNET Modeler. It has been simulated under varying traffic load conditions. Another WATM network employing the PRMA/DA MAC has been also modeled and simulated under the same networking conditions in order to compare the performance of the proposed MAC protocol consistently. The preliminary simulation results presented show that especially for the connections utilizing CBR, VBR, and ABR services, average end-to-end delay and end-to-end delay variation results of the proposed MAC based WATM model are considerably improved as a direct result of the new scheduling algorithms used in the BS.

References

1. Houdt, V.B., Blondia, C., Casals, O., Garcia, J.: Performance Analysis of a MAC protocol for Broadband Wireless Networks with QoS Provisioning. Journal of Interconnection Networks, Vol. 2. (2001) 103-130
2. Raychaudhuri, D.: Wireless ATM Networks Technology Status and Future Directions. In Proceedings of IEEE, Vol. 87. (1999) 1790-1805
3. Ayanoglu, E.: Wireless Broadband and ATM Systems. Computer Networks, Vol. 31. (1999) 395-409
4. Sanchez, J., Martinez, R., Marcellin, M.V.: A Survey of MAC Protocols Proposed for Wireless ATM. IEEE Network, Vol. 11. No. 6. (1997) 52–62
5. Kim, J.G., Widjaja, I.: PRMA/DA: A New Media Access Control Protocol for Wireless ATM. IEEE ICC. (1996) 240-244
6. Fantacci, R., Giambene, G., Nistico, G.: A QoS-aware Policer for a Fair Resource Sharing in Wireless ATM. Computer Communications, Vol. 26. (2003) 1392–1404
7. Rappaport, T.S.: Wireless Communications. Prentice Hall (1996) 395-438
8. Hyon, T.: Wireless ATM Network Medium Access Control with Adaptive Parallel Multiple Substream CDMA Air-interface. Ph.D Thesis (2001)
9. Erturk, I.: Transporting CAN Messages over WATM. Lecture Notes in Artificial Intelligence, LNAI 2639. (2003) 724-729
10. Chen, J.C., Sivalingam, M.K., Acharya, R.: Comparative Analysis of Wireless Channel Access Protocols Supporting Multimedia Traffic. Mobile Networks and Applications, Vol. 3. (1998) 293-306
11. Ceken, C.: Real Time Data Transfer With Quality of Service Support Using Wireless ATM. Ph.D Thesis (2004)

Fuzzy Logic Based Congestion Avoidance
in TCP/AQM Networks

Mahdi Jalili-Kharaajoo

Young Researchers Club, Islamic Azad University, Tehran, IRAN
P.O. Box: 14395/1355, Tehran, Iran
mahdijalili@ece.ut.ac.ir

Abstract. Active Queue management (AQM) takes a trade-off between link utilization and delay experienced by data packets. From the viewpoint of control theory, it is rational to regard AQM as a typical regulation system. Although PI controller for AQM outperforms RED algorithm, the mismatches in simplified TCP flow model inevitably degrades the performance of controller designed with classic control theory. In this paper, a novel fuzzy logic based sliding mode controller is designed for Active Queue Management (AQM) in TCP/AQM networks. This type of controller is insensitive to noise and variance of the parameters, thus it is suitable to time varying network systems. Recently many AQM algorithms have been proposed to address performance degradations of end-to-end congestion control. However, these AQM algorithms show weaknesses to detect and control congestion under dynamically changing network situations. A simulation study over a wide range of IP traffic conditions shows the effectiveness of the proposed controller in terms of the queue length dynamics, the packet loss rates, and the link utilization.

1 Introduction

TCP congestion control mechanism, while necessary and powerful, are not sufficient to provide good service in all circumstances, specially with the rapid growth in size and the strong requirements to Quality of Service (QoS) support, because there is a limit to how much control can be accomplished at end system. It is needed to implement some measures in the intermediate nodes to complement the end system congestion avoidance mechanisms. Active Queue Management (AQM), as one class of packet dropping/marking mechanism in the router queue, has been recently proposed to support the end-to-end congestion control in the Internet [1–5]. It has been a very active research area in the Internet community. The goals of AQM are (1) reduce the average length of queue in routers and thereby decrease the end-to-end delay experimented by packets, and (2) ensure the network resources to be used efficiently by reducing the packet loss that occurs when queues overflow. AQM highlights the tradeoff between delay and throughput. By keeping the average queue size small, AQM will have the ability to provide greater capacity to accommodate nature-occurring burst without dropping packets, at the same time, reduce the delays

T. Yakhno (Ed.): ADVIS 2004, LNCS 3261, pp. 575–584, 2004.
© Springer-Verlag Berlin Heidelberg 2004

seen by flow, this is very particularly important for real-time interactive applications. RED [6, 7] was originally proposed to achieve fairness among sources with different burst attributes and to control queue length, which just meets the requirements of AQM. However, many subsequent studies verified that RED is unstable and too sensitive to parameter configuration, and tuning of RED has been proved to be a difficult job [8–10].

Fuzzy logic controllers have been developed and applied to nonlinear system for the last two decades [11]. The most attractive feature of fuzzy logic control is that the expert knowledge can be easily incorporated into the control laws [12].

The intuition and heuristic design is not always scientific and reasonable under any conditions. Of course, since Internet is a rather complex huge system, it is very difficult to have a full-scale and systematic comprehension, but importance has been considerably noted. The mathematical modeling of the Internet is the first step to have an in-depth understanding, and the algorithms designed based on the rational model should be more reliable than one original from intuition. In some of the references, the nonlinear dynamic model for TCP flow control has been utilized and some controllers like PI and Adaptive Virtual Queue Algorithm have been designed for that [13–17].

Although PI controller successfully related some limitations of RED, for instance, the queue length and dropping/marking probability are decoupled, whenever the queue length can be easily controlled to the desired value; the system has relatively high stability margin. The shortcomings of PI controller are also obvious. The modification of probability excessively depends on buffer size. As a result, for small buffer the system exhibits sluggishness. Secondly, for small reference queue length, the system tends to performance poorly, which is unfavorable to achieve the goal of AQM because small queue length implies small queue waiting delay. Thirdly, the status of actual network is rapidly changeable, so we believe that it is problematic and unrealistic, at least inaccurate, to take the network as a linear and constant system just like the designing of PI controller. Affirmatively, the algorithm based on this assumption should have limited validity, such as inability against disturbance or noise. We need more robust controller to adapt complex and mutable network environment, which will be our motivation and aim in this study. In the research, we will apply a fuzzy controller to design the AQM system for congestion avoidance. The simulation results show the superior performance of the proposed controller in comparison with classic PI controller.

2 TCP Flow Control Model

In [13], a nonlinear dynamic model for TCP flow control has been developed based on fluid-flow theory. This model can be stated as follows

$$
\begin{cases}
\dfrac{dW(t)}{dt} = \dfrac{1}{R(t)} - \dfrac{W(t)W(t-R(t))}{2R(t)} p(t-R(t)) \\
\dfrac{dq(t)}{dt} = \dfrac{N(t)}{R(t)} W(t) - C(t)
\end{cases}
\tag{1}
$$

The above nonlinear and time-varying system was approximated as a linear constant system by small-signal linearization about an operating point [12, 13] (Fig. 1). In the block diagram, $C(s)$ and $G(s)$ are the controller and the plant, respectively. The meaning of parameters presented in Fig. 1 are as following

$$K(t) = \frac{[R(t)C(t)]^3}{[2N(t)]^2}, \quad T_1(t) = R(t), \quad T_2(t) = \frac{R^2(t)C(t)}{2N(t)} \tag{2}$$

where

$C(t)$: Link capacity (packets/sec)

q_o : Queue reference value

$N(t)$: Load factor, i.e., number of active sessions

$R(t)$: Round-trip time (RTT), $R(t) = 2(q(t)/C(t) + T_p)$, T_p is the fixed propagation delay

$p(t)$: Dropping/marking probability

$q(t)$: Instantaneous queue

We believe that the AQM controller designed with the simplified and inaccurate linear constant model should not be optimal, because the actual network is very changeful; the state parameters are hardly kept at a constant value for a long time [2, 5]. Moreover, the equations (1) only take consideration into the fast retransmission and fast recovery, but ignore the timeout mechanism caused by lacking of enough duplicated ACK, which is very usual in burst and short-lived services. In addition to, there are many non-respective UDP flows besides TCP connections in networks; they are also not included in equations (1). These mismatches in model will have negative impact on the performance of controller designed with the approach depending with the accurate model. For the changeable network, the robust control should be an appropriate choice to design controller for AQM.

To describe the system in state space form, suppose that $x_1 = e$, $x_2 = de/dt$, so the plant depicted in Fig. 1 is described by a second order system as

$$\begin{cases} \dfrac{dx_1}{dt} = x_2 \\ \dfrac{dx_2}{dt} = -a_1(t)x_1 - a_2(t)x_2 - b(t) + F(t) \end{cases} \quad \begin{aligned} & a_{1\min} \le a_1 \le a_{1\max}, \\ & ; \; a_{2\min} \le a_2 \le a_{2\max}, \\ & 0 < b_{\min} \le b \le b_{\max} \end{aligned} \tag{3}$$

where

$$a_1(t) = \frac{1}{T_1(t)T_2(t)}, a_2(t) = \frac{T_1(t) + T_2(t)}{T_1(t)T_2(t)}, b(t) = \frac{K(t)}{T_1(t)T_2(t)}$$

$$F(t) = \frac{d^2}{dt^2}q_o + \frac{T_1(t) + T_2(t)}{T_1(t)T_2(t)}\frac{d}{dt}q_o + \frac{1}{T_1(t)T_2(t)}q_o \tag{4}$$

$F(t)$ is regarded as the system disturbance.

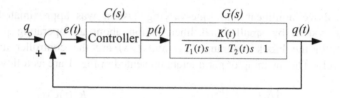

Fig. 1. Block diagram of AQM control system

3   Design of Fuzzy Sliding Mode Controller

3.1   Sliding Mode Controller

A Sliding Mode Controller is a Variable Structure Controller(VSC). Basically, a VSC includes several different continuous functions that map plant state to a control surface, and the switching among different functions is determined by plant state that is represented by a switching function. Without lost of generality, consider the design of a sliding mode controller for the following second order system:

$$\ddot{x} = f(x, \dot{x}, t) + bu(t)$$

Here we assume $b > 0$. $u(t)$ is the input to the system. The following is a possible choice of the structure of a sliding mode controller [18]:

$$u = -k \, \text{sgn}(s) + u_{eq} \tag{5}$$

where u_{eq} is called equivalent control which is used when the system state is in the sliding mode [18]. k is a constant, representing the maximum controller output. s is called switching function because the control action switches its sign on the two sides of the switching surface $s = 0$. s is defined as:

$$s = e + \lambda e \tag{6}$$

where $e = x - x_d$ and x_d is the desired state. λ is a constant. The definition of e here requires that k in (5) be positive. $\text{sgn}(s)$ is a sign function, which is defined as:

$$\text{sgn}(s) = \begin{cases} -1 & \text{if } s < 0 \\ 1 & \text{if } s > 0 \end{cases}$$

The control strategy adopted here will guarantee a system trajectory move toward and stay on the sliding surface $s = 0$ from any initial condition if the following condition meets:

$$ss \le -\eta|s|$$

where η is a positive constant that guarantees the system trajectories hit the sliding surface in finite time.

Using a sign function often causes chattering in practice. One solution is to introduce a boundary layer around the switch surface [18]:

$$u = -ksat(\frac{s}{\phi}) + u_{eq} \tag{7}$$

where constant factor ϕ defines the thickness of the boundary layer. $sat(\frac{s}{\phi})$ is a saturation function that is defined as:

$$sat(\frac{s}{\phi}) = \begin{cases} \frac{s}{\phi} & if \quad \left|\frac{s}{\phi}\right| \le 1 \\[2mm] sgn(\frac{s}{\phi}) & if \quad \left|\frac{s}{\phi}\right| > 1 \end{cases}$$

This controller is actually a continuous approximation of the ideal relay control. The consequence of this control scheme is that invariance property of sliding mode control is lost. The system robustness is a function of the width of the boundary layer. A variation of the above controller structures is to use a hyperbolic tangent function instead of a saturation function [19]:

$$u = k\tanh(\frac{s}{\phi}) + u_{eq} \tag{8}$$

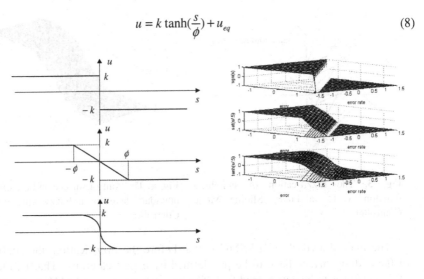

Fig. 2. Various Sliding Mode Controllers and control surfaces

It is proven that if k is large enough, the sliding model controllers of (1), (3) and (4) are guaranteed to be asymptotically stable [18]. For a 2-dimensional system, the controller structure and the corresponding control surface are illustrated in Fig. 2.

3.2 Fuzzy Sliding Mode Control (FSMC)

In the case of 2-dimensional systems, the sliding surface will be just a line without any width. Control action then alternatively changes its sign when the system state switches from one side of the line to the other side of the line as the line has no width. A boundary layer can alleviate the chattering problem. The majority research effort of combining fuzzy logic control and sliding mode control has been spent on how to use fuzzy logic to approximate the control command u as a nonlinear function of s within the boundary layer [19–24]. The resulting Fuzzy Sliding Mode Controller (FSMC) is actually a Single-Input-Single-Output fuzzy logic controller. The input to the controller is the switching function s. The output from the controller is the control command u. The number of rules in the rule base depends on the fuzzification level of s and u however it is generally much fewer than a typical fuzzy logic controller for the same system. A typical rule of a FSMC has the following format:

If s is PB (and $\dot{s}$ is PB), then u is PB or a constant.

How the switching function s is fuzzified is illustrated in Fig 3. This kind of rule format effectively adds a boundary layer to the system. This boundary layer is illustrated in Fig 4.

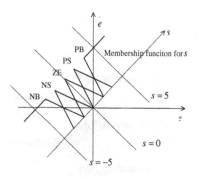 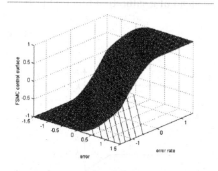

Fig. 3. The fuzzification of switching function s for a Fuzzy Sliding Mode Controller

Fig. 4. The control surface and the effective boundary layer of a Fuzzy Sliding Mode Controller

The main drawback of a FSMC is that before the fuzzification, the coefficients of the sliding surface have to be pre-defined by expert carefully. That is, the value of λ in (6) has to be determined first. The only advantage of a FSMC compared with a typical SMC is that in the former case, the boundary layer is nonlinear whereas in the latter case the boundary layer is linear. A nonlinear boundary does not add much control performance since it is the width of the boundary layer that influence the controller performance, not the form of the boundary layer. From authors' point of view, FSMC has little practical value, if not totally useless.

4 Simulation Results

The network topology used for simulation, is depicted in Fig. 5 [2, 5]. The only bottleneck link lies between node A and node B. the buffer size of node A is 200 packets, and default size of the packet is 350 bytes. All sources are classed into three groups. The first one includes N_1 greedy sustained FTP application sources, the second one is composed of N_2 burst HTTP connections, each connection has 10 sessions, and the number of pages per session is 3. The thirds one has N_3 UDP sources, which follow the exponential service model, the idle and burst time are 10000msec and 1000msec, respectively, and the sending rate during "on" duration is 40kbps. We introduced short-lived HTTP flows and non-responsive UDP services into the router in order to generate a more realistic scenario, because it is very important for a perfect AQM scheme to achieve full bandwidth utilization in the presence of noise and disturbance introduced by these flows. The links between node A and all sources have the same capacity and propagation delay pair (L_1, τ_1). The pair (L_2, τ_2) and (L_3, τ_3) define the parameter of links AB and BC, respectively.

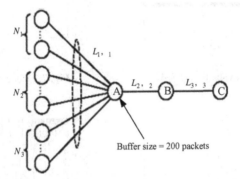

Fig. 5. The simulation network topology

In the first study, we will use the most general network configuration to testify whether the proposed Adaptive Fuzzy Logic Controller (FLC) can reach the goals of AQM, and freely control the queue length to stabilize at the arbitrary expected value. Therefore, given that $(L_1, \tau_1) = (10Mbps, 15ms)$, $(L_2, \tau_2) = (15Mbps, 15ms)$, $(L_3, \tau_3) = (45Mbps, 15ms)$. $N_1 = 270$, $N_2 = N_3 = 0$. Let the expected queue length equal to 75 packets.

The instantaneous queue length using the proposed FSMC is depicted in Fig. 6. After a very short regulating process, the queue settles down its stable operating point. RED algorithm is unable to accurately control the queue length to the desired value [7,9]. The queue length varies with network loads. The load is heavier the queue length is longer. Attempting to control queue length through decreasing the interval between high and law thresholds, then it is likely to lead queue oscillation.

To investigate the performance of the proposed FLC, we will consider a classic PI controller as

$$p(k) = (a-b)(q(k)-q_o) + b(q(k)-q(k-1)) + p(k-1) \tag{9}$$

The coefficients a and b are fixed at $1.822e^{-5}$ and $1.816e^{-5}$, respectively, the sampling frequency is 500Hz, the control variable p is accumulative [5]. Because the parameter b is very small, and the sample interval is very short, the negative contribution to p made by the second item in the right can be omitted in initial process, then the positive contribution mainly come from the first item. The queue evaluation using PI controller is shown in Fig. 7. As it can be seen FSMC acts much better that PI one.

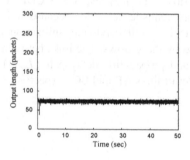

Fig. 6. Queue evaluation (FSMC)

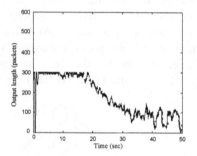

Fig. 7. Queue evluation (PI)

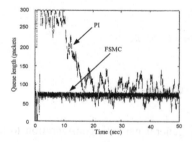

Fig. 8. Queue evaluation (FTP+HTTP)

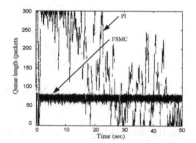

Fig. 9. Queue evaluation (FTP+UDP)

In this section, firstly, let $N_1 = 270, N_2 = 400, N_3 = 0,$ the evaluation of queue size is shown in Fig. 8. As it can be seen, the proposed FSMC has better performance than that of PI one. Next, given that $N_1 = 270, N_2 = 0, N_3 = 50,$ we further investigate performance against the disturbance caused by the non-responsive UDP flows. Fig. 9 shows the results, obviously, PI is very sensitive to this disturbance, while FSMC operates in a relatively stable state. The queue fluctuation increases with introducing the UDP flows, but the variance is too much smaller comparing with PI controller.

Finally, we evaluate the integrated performance of the FSMC using one relatively real scenario, i.e., the number of active flows is changeable, which has 270 FTP flows, 400 HTTP connections and 30 UDP flows. Figs. 10 and 11 show the evaluation of queue controlled by FSMC and PI controllers, respectively. It is clear that the integrated performance of FSMC controller, namely transient and steady state responses is superior to that of PI controller. FSMC is always keeping the queue length at the reference value, even if the network loads abruptly change, but PI controller has the inferior adaptability. In other words, the former is more powerful, robust and adaptive than the later one, which is in the favor of achievement to the objectives of the AQM policy.

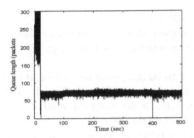   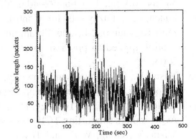

Fig. 10. Queue evaluation (FSMC)   **Fig. 11.** Queue evaluation (PI)

5 Conclusion

In this paper, a fuzzy logic based sliding mode controller was applied to TCP/AQM networks for the objective of queue management and congestion avoidance. For this purpose, a linearized model of the TCP flow was considered. We took a complete comparison between performance of the proposed FSMC and classical PI controller under various scenarios. The conclusion was that the integrated performance of FSMC was superior to that of PI one.

References

1. Barden, B. et al., Recommendation on queue management and congestion avoidance in the internet, REC2309, April 1998.
2. Jalili-Kharaajoo, M., Application of robust fuzzy adaptive second-order sliding-mode control to active queue management, LNCS, 2957, pp.109-119, 2004.
3. S. Ryu, C. Rump and C. Qiao, A Predictive and Robust Active Queue Management for Internet Congestion Control, in Proc. Eighth IEEE International Symposium on Computers and Communication (ISCC'03), Antalya, Turkey, 2003.
4. S. Ryu, C. Rump, and C. Qiao. Advances in Internet congestion control. IEEE Communication Survey and Tutorial, 2002.

5. R. Fengyuan, L. Chuang, Y. Xunhe, S. Xiuming, and W. Fubao, A Robust Active Queue Management algorithm based on Sliding Mode Variable Structure Control. in Proc. INFOCOM'2002, 21, pp.13–20, 2002.

6. Floyd, S. and Jacobson, V., Random early detection gateway for congestion avoidance, IEEE/ACM Trans. Networking, August 1993.

7. V. Hollot, V. Misra, D. Towsley, and W. Gong. A control theoretic analysis of RED. In Proc. of INFOCOM'2001, pages 1510–1519, April 2001.

8. Firoiu, V. and Borden, M., A study of active queue management for congestion control, in Proc. INFOCOM, March 2000.

9. May, M., Bonald, T. and Bolot, T., Analytic evaluation of RED performance, in Proc. INFOCOM, March 2000.

10. S. Floyd and V. Paxson. Difficulties in simulating the Internet, IEEE/ACM Transactions on Networking, 9(4), pp.392–403, 2001.

11. Zadeh, L.A., Fuzzy sets, Inf. Control (1965), 338-353.

12. Jalili-Kharaajoo, M., and Ebrahimirad, H., Improvement of second order sliding mode control applied to position control of induction motors using fuzzy logic, LNAI, 2715, 2003.

13. Misra, V., Gong, W.B. and Towsley, D., Fluid-based analysis of network of AQM routers supporting TCP flows with an application to RED, in Proc. ACM/SIGCOMM, 2000.

14. Hollot, C., Misra, V., Towsley, D. and Gong, W.B., On designing improved controllers for AQM routers supporting TCP flows, in Proc. INFOCOM, 2001.

15. Misra, V., Gong, W.B. and Towsley, D., Analysis and design an adaptive virtual queue (AVQ) algorithm for active queue management, in Proc. ACM/SIGCOMM, 2001.

16. Kelly, F.P., Maulloo, A. and Tan, D., Rate control in communication networks, Journal of the Operation research Society, 49, pp.237-252, 1998.

17. Athuraliya, S., Lapsley, D.E. and Low, S.H., Random early marking for Internet congestion control, in Proc. Globecom, 1999.

18. J.J. Slotine and W. Li, Applied Nonlinear Control, *Englewood Cliffs, NJ: Prentice-Hall,* 1991.

19. J.S. Glower and J. Munighan, Designing Fuzzy Controllers from a Variable Structures Standpoint, *IEEE Transactions on Fuzzy Systems,* vol.5, no.1, pp.138-144, 1997.

20. Tzuu-Hseng S. Li and Chin-Yin Tsai, Parallel Fuzzy Sliding Mode Control of the Cart-Pole System, *IEEE Int. Conference on Industrial Electronics, Control, and Instrumentation,* pp.1468-1473, 1995.

21. H. Allamehzadeh and J.Y. Cheung, Design of a Stable and Robust Fuzzy Controller for a Class of Nonlinear System, *IEEE International Conference on Fuzzy Systems,* pp.2150-2154, 1996.

22. Guang-Chyan Hwang and Shih-Chang Lin, A Stability Approach to Fuzzy Control Design for Nonlinear System, *Fuzzy Sets and Systems,* vol.48, pp.279-287, 1992.

23. Yean-Ren Hwang and M. Tomizuka, Fuzzy Smoothing Algorithm for Variable Structure Systems, *IEEE Transactions on Fuzzy Systems,* vol.2, no.4, pp.277-284, 1994.

24. H. Lee, H. Son, E. Kim and M. Park, Variable Structure Control of Nonlinear System Using Fuzzy Variable Boundary Layer, *IEEE International Conference on Fuzzy Systems,* pp.348-353, 1998.

Distributed Group Access Control Architecture for Secure Multicast

John Felix C and Valli S

Anna University, College of Engineering, Guindy, Chennai 600 025, TN, India
johnfelix@cs.annauniv.edu, valli@annauniv.edu

Abstract. Multicast technology has become significant due to its support for collaborative applications such as distance learning, multiparty conferencing etc. Commercial deployment of multicast is hindered due to its security vulnerabilities such as denial of service, theft of service, masquerading and eavesdropping. The proposed group access control architecture is overlaid on a distributed routing scheme, which reduces the rekeying frequency through a distributed approach. Three major modules developed for this distributed group access control architecture are the group access control system, the group policy management system and group key management. The core of the architecture namely, the group access control system obtains a mutual support from group policy and group key management systems. Analysis is done, by observing the message and computational overhead due to the implementation of this architecture.

1 Introduction

Services in todays Internet are experiencing increasing demand for one-to-many and many-to-many communication so as to support collaborative communications, which requires a mechanism, which is efficient, scalable and promisingly secure [2]. The primary technology available for this requirement is multicast. This work addresses the most significant consideration namely security. There are security problems in the existing multicast models such as denial of service, theft of service, eavesdropping and masquerading [3]. Multicast security problems start right from routing in a multicast transmission. Different routing protocols exist, but, when security mechanisms are implemented in them, they become complex [4] due to high rekeying frequency. This work is an extension of distributed multicast routing to support security mechanisms [1].

2 Existing Work

Extensive work on group access control system have been done, but none of these systems provide a complete solution for both sender as well as receiver access control. Initial work on secure group management protocol was lolus [5], which raised many issues regarding multicast security.

T. Yakhno (Ed.): ADVIS 2004, LNCS 3261, pp. 585–594, 2004.

GOTHIC In [6], Judge and Ammar proposed GOTHIC, a comprehensive architecture for providing group access control. A host first requests a capability from the access control server and forwards it to the router along with the join request. The capabilities are identity-based and time-limited. The router host authenticates the host and verifies the capability before allowing the host to join the group. The authors discuss leveraging the state maintained by a group key management system by using the group encryption key as the access token. The authors also propose group access control aware group key management (GACA-GKM) that leverages the trust built into a group access control system to reduce the requirements of GKM and obtain substantial overhead reductions.

3   Distributed Multicast Routing

The group access control architecture is overlaid on a distributed routing scheme [1]. The distributed routing uses a two-dimensional approach. The key design concern of this routing scheme is to decrease the rekeying frequency by segregating nodes into different domains.

3.1   First Dimension

The first dimension of this routing scheme is implemented over a partially complete bi-directional graph. This graph is formed by different Multicast Access Controllers (MAC) nodes, which are responsible for managing and maintaining the graph. Each MAC in the graph is functionally independent of every other MAC in the graph. The MACs uses a minimum diameter approach to generate the graph such that every MAC is connected to the neighbor MACs through a shortest path. These MAC nodes form the multicast routing backbone for the proposed architecture. All MACs maintain a spanning tree that covers all the MACs in the multicast routing backbone. Each MAC will provide multicast service to a subset of nodes in the multicast group and form a domain of that particular MAC. The domain of a MAC may contain Non-MAC nodes and hosts. All MACs domains form the multicast service network of the multicast group. The shortest path between MACs ensures a low latency. The number of MACs in the routing backbone is inversely proportional to the induced latency.

3.2   Second Dimension

The second dimension of this routing scheme consists of security and management nodes. In this dimension, there are number of GMACs (Gateway Multicast Access Controllers) which are MACs that are capable of supporting security mechanisms. The proposed group access control architecture is implemented in this dimension at every GMAC. These GMACs are connected to the multicast routing backbone and form a secure backbone for the multicast group. Similar to MAC, GMAC controls a domain containing MAC nodes and their respective domains. Every node in the multicast group should be controlled by a GMAC.

Each GMAC is responsible for its domain and functions independently from every other GMAC.

4   Overview

In the existing model any host can send a request to IGMP and join the multicast group. After the join operation the new host can send or receive packets to the multicast without any restriction. This kind of open network interface for multicast leads to security threats. Typically in unicast, Eavesdropping and masquerading are commonly defended using encryption techniques. In a multicast scenario, unicast encryption schemes will also fail due to the fact that all members of the group are treated similarly and distinguishing between a legal and a malicious user of the group is impossible [7].

This work addresses the solution to existing multicast security issues by implementing a distributed access control system supported by group policy management and group key management. Access control [8] provides good network management principles in any kind of network. Since network management is also another important multicast deployment issue [9], access control implementation will provide a good solution to both network management and security issues of multicast transmission. This proposed model defines a comprehensive architecture for group access control supported by group policy and key management. The design goals are to maintain security while providing a scalable system that involves low computation overhead at the routers, low message overhead and low support infrastructure requirements.

The proposed architecture of GMAC has three major systems, namely, Group Access Control, Group Policy Management, Group Key Management. Each of the modules is mutually dependent on the other two modules in the architecture. This architecture is designed to function in a GMAC.

5   Group Access Control System

The generic functions of the group access control architecture are the authentication as in figure 1a and authorization module as shown in figure 1b. These modules provide access control through a secure protocol, which manages node join operation to the multicast graph. Authentication module is responsible for a node to join the multicast graph with only receiver functionality. Authorization module deals with how a sender joins to the multicast group under secure and policy based system.

5.1   Authentication Module

This module gives the joining entity receiver functionality on successful authentication. In this architecture, the trusted server for group access control is not a third party system. But instead, control servers are active nodes in the multicast graph, which are responsible for providing routing and security for the multicast group. All messages between GMAC and the joining entity may or may not pass through a MAC, but the confirmation of the authentication to the host is strictly routed through a MAC that is closest to the joining entity. This property will ease the overhead by updating the MAC routing table on receipt of authentication confirm message by the joining entity.

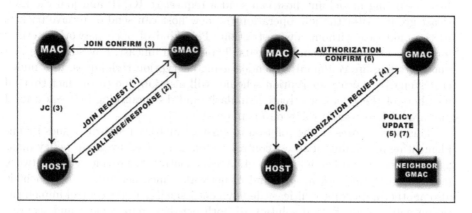

Fig. 1. *a*) Authentication procedure   *b*) Authorization procedure

This approach focuses on a generic join procedure that can be applied for both GMAC and also for a host authentication. The host and GMACs have the public keys denoted by K_{PH} and K_{PGMAC} and the corresponding private keys K_{RH} and K_{RGMAC}. Since public key infrastructure is optional in this model, classical symmetric schemes can also be used. In this case the shared key is used for both authentication and encryption. The shared key is obtained from the password that is used for authentication and authorization. This password is maintained by the host and also at the policy management system of hosts GMAC.

Authentication Procedure

$$NewNode \Rightarrow GMAC : JoinRequest : ID_N \parallel [ID_G \parallel K_{PH} \parallel N_1]K_{P_{GMAC}} \quad (1)$$

This module implements a receiver initiated join operation. Therefore, the host sends a Join Request (JR) to the GMAC along with the identifier of the host (ID_N), as in (1). Join request contains identifier of the group (ID_G), shared key or public key (K_{PH}) of the host which is optional and nonce (N_1). The contents are encrypted using public key of the GMAC or if symmetric encryption is employed the shared key is used as in (1). The public key or shared key specified by the host in the join request should match the key defined for it in the policy table. On receiving a join request, all senders of the group are requested a policy update. If receivers policing is used, only receivers who are policy definers in the domain of the GMAC define policies for the authentication module. This property reduces total message overhead at the multicast security backbone. All senders policies are given high priority and it is mandatory that all senders agree upon a new node to join the multicast group.

$$NewNode \Longleftrightarrow GMAC : Challenge \backslash Response : N_2 \backslash F_K(N_2) \qquad (2)$$

The GMAC authenticates a host by initiating a challenge response sequence as in (2). A Nonce is sent to the host by the GMAC. The host encrypts the nonce using its password as a key for the group join operation and sends the response to the GMAC. The nodes password is defined in the policy table stated for each node local to a domain. Verification of the response is done at the GMAC by comparing the response with the expected response.

$$GMAC \Rightarrow N : Token : [ID_N \parallel ID_G \parallel [K_S]K_{PH} \parallel Time \parallel R.V.T]K_{RGMAC} \qquad (3)$$

The Join Confirm (JC) contains a token, as given in (3) which is used for reauthorization. Join confirm is strictly routed through a MAC neighbor to the joining node. If the joining node is a GMAC then the neighbor MAC transacts routing information regarding the current multicast graph. JC message contains identifier of the node (ID_N), identifier of the group the node belongs to (ID_G), session key (K_S) encrypted using hosts public or shared key, time (T) at which the token was issued and revocation period (R.V.T). The token is encrypted by GMAC using its private or shared key. On confirmation the new node is spanned to the current multicast routing backbone.

5.2   Authorization Module

Sender capability privilege is granted by the authorization module to the new node on successful authorization procedure. A node requesting a sender authorization should first undergo a successful authentication procedure sequence. The token obtained by the node in the join confirm of the authentication procedure is used for initiating the authorization request of the authorization procedure. The entities requesting for authorization can be of two types namely, host and GMAC.

If the joining entity is a host, it receives a shared key from the GMAC for encrypting the data on successful authorization procedure. The host then in return replies to the GMAC with the policy definition. The policy statement defined by the host is propagated to all GMACs in the multicast security backbone. This is done by group policy management system that exists in every GMAC. When the joining entity is a GMAC, the GMAC gets a shared key, which is common only among GMACs, which form the multicast security backbone. Then the authorizing GMAC transacts existing policies to the new GMAC. The newly joined GMAC also gives its policy definitions to its neighbor GMACs that will in turn be propagated to all GMACs in the multicast security backbone. The authorization procedure is a generic sequence and is applicable for both GMAC and a host.

Authorization Procedure

$$N \Rightarrow GMAC : Token \parallel ID_N \parallel N_1 \tag{4}$$

The authorization request given in (4) should contain the token received at the join confirm (JC) through the authentication module. To avoid replay attacks and to provide second level of authentication, the identifier of the new node (ID_N) and a nonce (N_1) is also sent in an authorization request.

$$GMAC \Rightarrow NeighborGMACs : RequestPolicyupdates \parallel ID_N \tag{5}$$

Similar to authentication procedure, the GMAC request a policy update and sends the identifier of new node wishing to join as a sender this is given in (5). This is done only if the new nodes policy definition is not found in the current policy table. Policy definers in the multicast group whose policy definitions have changed since last policy update respond. These policies may or may not contain a policy definition supporting the new sender join operation.

$$GMAC \Rightarrow N : [ID_G \parallel ID_N \parallel [K_S]K_{PH} \parallel Time \parallel N_2 \parallel R.V.T]K_{RGMAC} \tag{6}$$

The GMAC authorizes the new node by issuing a token as given in (6). The token is very similar to the token issued by the authentication module expect that the session key (K_S) differs.

$$GMAC \Longleftrightarrow N : Policyupdate \tag{7}$$

Depending upon which type of entity initiated the join operation the authorization module initiates the policy update sequence. GMAC includes a two-way policy update sequence with the authorizing GMAC, whereas host includes a one-way policy update between itself and the authorizing GMAC as given in (7).

6   Group Policy Management System

Policy management deals with managing the policies from policy definers in the multicast graph. It is responsible for accepting or rejecting a join or authorization request depending upon policies defined in its database. Every policy definition contains a list of new authorized senders and receivers of the group. A nodes policy contains identifier of the node, identifier of its group and its password. Nodes send the policy definition to their respective GMACs. On receiving the policy definition the GMAC will add the list of policies for nodes local to their domain and forward the rest to neighbor GMACs. The new list of policies will be added to the policy management database that handles the policies of the domain controlled by the particular GMAC. The core function of this system is to manage policies in distributed environment.

Three levels of security are incorporated namely basic level security, high-level security and threshold scheme. In basic level security, only senders in the multicast graph define policies. In high-level security scheme all nodes including receivers in the multicast group are allowed to define policies. Allowing receivers to define policies will increase message overhead. To overcome this problem, the threshold scheme is used in decision making for a join or authorization operation. In this threshold scheme, a value N is defined which states the number of policies required to approve a join or authorization request. If in case where the number of nodes in the GMAC domain is less than N, then threshold scheme will be switched to high-level security scheme. The N value for a GMAC is fixed depending upon the security requirement for a domain. Only M receivers define policies, which are formed by adding receivers that are policy definers in every GMAC domain.

The Group policy management is mainly responsible for distributing the policies to the different GMACs so that they maintain only policies for nodes located only to the specific domain. Distributing policies is impossible using nave techniques. Therefore, this work addresses an innovative approach to this problem. A tree traversing technique is used in this approach. The GMAC at which a new policy is defined becomes the root of the spanning tree. The spanning tree has all the GMACs of the multicast graph as nodes. A GMAC receiving a policy definition filters the policies that belong to its domain and forwards to its child nodes the remaining policy definitions.

When all the nodes in the spanning tree have been traversed, the leaf nodes of the tree will have policy definitions for nodes, which are not currently present in the multicast group. Therefore, the remaining policies have to be sent to all the GMACs since the new node may join at any of the GMACs domain in the multicast graph. The remaining policy list then back-trace from the leaf nodes to their parent nodes and propagates until it reaches the root of the spanning tree. The parent nodes check the back-tracing policy list of its child nodes and forward only policies, which are common in all back-traced policy lists of its child nodes. This will prevent policies to be duplicated due to the presence of branches in the spanning tree. The policy definitions are done periodically through policy update sequence in order to segregate policies to their respective GMAC domain.

7 Group Key Management System

The Group Key Management System manages the session keys and public-private keys if public key infrastructure [12] is implemented. This approach uses encryption schemes implemented in unicast scenario, such as RSA-512 for the optional public key infrastructure and 2 Key 3DES 112 bits [12] for symmetric key encryption schemes.

Another major consideration for this system is rekeying. The session keys have to be changed during a join or leave operation of a host. This is done in order to maintain security so that future messages are not read by node that have left the group and past messages are not read by newly joined node of the multicast group. This architecture uses a rekeying strategy discussed by Wong [11], which uses key graphs. This work doesnt focus on efficient group key

management schemes, which are suitable for multicast transmission, and this
area is left for future work.

8   Results

Analysis of this model is performed using a discrete event simulator. The events,
which can be expected in a multicast scenario, are ranged over random distributions. Join / Leave operations of a host is ranged over normal distribution.
The N value in the policy threshold scheme for a domain is ranged over uniform
distribution. The goal of the analysis is to calculate the message and computational overhead incurred at the node of the multicast graph due to the group
access control schemes. Results of the simulation are represented in the graphs
by obtaining discrete values of the different specifications during the simulation time. Computation overhead is obtained by probing the total operations
executed during the simulation time by a GMAC.

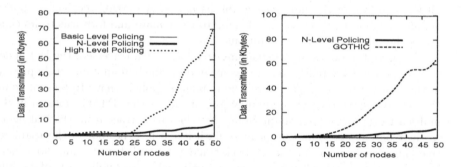

Fig. 2. *a*) Message overhead at GMAC   *b*) Gothic vs N-level policing

8.1   Message Overhead

Message overhead is calculated by the total data cumulatively transmitted by
a GMAC during the simulation time. The total cumulative data calculated includes the traffic due to authentication, authorization procedures and also the
traffic due to policy management schemes. In basic security level, Figure 2a,
where only senders define policies the message overhead is very low. Since the
policy maintained by the nodes is very less in this scheme the overhead due to
policy maintenance is also low. N-Threshold scheme increases the message overhead as shown in Figure 2a. This is due to increase in number of policy definers
since the policies increase as N receivers in a domain can define there policies. In
maximum security level policing where all nodes specify policies, the nodes experience a high message overhead due to the increased number of policies handled
by the nodes. When N is 36, the result is as in figure 2a, which is very optimal
for achieving both low overhead and fair security schemes. The total complexity is high when compared to gothic, but distributed. On the contrary, when a

single GMAC is considered, the message overhead is low compared to gothic as shown in figure 2b. The results from the analysis show that the N-Threshold can be used with an explicitly chosen N-value, which acts as tradeoff point between security and overhead.

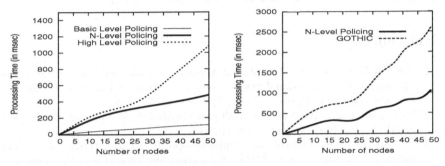

Fig. 3. *a*) Computational overhead at GMAC   *b*) Gothic vs N-level POlicing

8.2   Computational Overhead

The computations comprise host authentication, authorization, verification and encryptions. Number of operations to actual overhead experienced by a node is found by calculating the processing time. Processing overhead is dependent on the policy decision-making scheme. Similar to message overhead the computational overhead experienced increases as the number of policy definers in the group increases. As shown in the Figure 3a, the basic level policing incurs the minimum computational overhead whereas the N-threshold scheme, Figure 3a, increases the overhead depending upon the N value of the GMAC. Maximum overhead is experienced when high level security policing is used, Figure 3a that is when all nodes define policies. The performance of this architecture is dependent on number of GMACs in the multicast group. If the multicast group contains only one GMAC then the architecture is much similar to that of gothic as shown in figure 3b. As the number of GMACs increase the complexity and overhead becomes distributed. In this case, the processing overhead increases rapidly due to the number of nodes participating in decision making for a new node. All of the schemes aggregate the required processing time for each node joined to the multicast group.

9   Conclusion

In this work, group access control schemes were implemented to provide control access to a group. These schemes are mutually supported by two systems namely, group policy and group key management systems. This architecture uses a distributed approach with the help of GMACs, which form the security backbone for the multicast group. GMACs are responsible for providing all security system features to the multicast group. GMACs, which are the trusted servers for the multicast group, are not third party systems but active nodes in the multicast graph. Different policing schemes are defined, which provide security level for the multicast group ranging from a basic level to high-level security implementation. This implemented model also shows how all these three systems integrate to form a complex security system for the multicast group.

References

1. John Felix C, Valli S, "Distributed Multicast routing for Efficient Group Key Management", International Symposium on Computer Information Science 2003, Lecture Notes in Computer Science, Springer, pp 738-746.
2. Hans Eriksson, "MBONE: The Multicast Backbone", in Communications of the ACM, August 1994, Vol. 37, No.8, pp. 54-60.
3. A. Ballardie and J. Crowcroft, "Multicast-specific security threats and counter-measures", in Proceedings of ISOC Symposium on Network and Distributed System Security, San Diego, California, Feb. 1995, pp. 216.
4. D. Wallner, E. Harder, and R. Agee, "Key management for multicast: Issues and architectures", RFC 2627, IETF, June 1999.
5. S. Mittra. Iolus: A Framework for Scalable Secure Multicasting, In Proc. ACM SIGCOMM, pp 277-288, Cannes, France, September 1997.
6. Paul Judge and Mostafa Ammar, "Gothic: A Group Access Control Architecture for Secure Multicast and Anycast", IEEE INFOCOM, June 2002, pp. 1547-1556.
7. Laxman H. Sahasrabuddhe, Biswanath Mukherjee, "Multicast routing algorithms and protocols: A tutorial", IEEE Network, no. 1, January/February 2000 pp. 90-102
8. L. Gong and N. Shacham, "Elements of trusted multicasting", in Proceedings of the 2nd ACM Conference on Computer and Communications Security, Fairfax, Virginia, 1994, pp. 176183.
9. R. Rivest and B. Lampson, "SDSI a simple distributed security infrastructure", Technical report, M.I.T., Apr. 1996
10. Denis Trcek, "Security policy management for networked information systems", NOMS 2000 - IEEE/IFIP Network Operations and Management Symposium, no. 1, September 2000 pp. 817-830
11. Chung Kei Wong, Mohamed Gouda and Simon S. Lam, "Secure group communication using key graphs", IEEE/ACM Transactions on Networking, Vol. 8 No. 1, Feburary 2000 pp 16-30.
12. W. Stallings, Network and Internetwork Security. Prentice Hall Inc. 1995.

Virtual-IP Zone Algorithm in IP Micro Mobility Environments

Taehyoun Kim, Bongjun Choi, Hyunho Lee, Hyosoon Park, and Jaiyong Lee

Department of Electrical & Electronic Engineering, Yonsei University,
134 Shinchon-dong Seodaemun-gu Seoul, Korea
{tuskkim, jyl}@nasla.yonsei.ac.kr

Abstract. Since a cell size will be smaller and Mobile IP users are expected to grow in the next mobile network, micro mobility occurs more frequently. In IP micro mobility environments, the wireless link has far less available bandwidth resources and limited scalability compared to the wired network. Therefore, the signaling overhead associated with mobility management has a severe effect on the wireless link. In this paper, we propose the Virtual-IP (VIP) Zone algorithm. In the proposed algorithm, Access Routers (ARs) with a large rate of handoff are allocated into a VIP Zone. The signaling overhead in the wireless link can be greatly reduced as the current Care-of Address (CoA) of Mobile Node (MNs) is not changed whenever the handoffs occur between ARs within the same VIP Zone. We present the performance evaluation for VIP Zone algorithm and HMIPv6. As a result, we present various simulation results in different environments.

1 Introduction

In Internet environments, when a Mobile Node (MN) moves and attaches itself to another network, it needs to obtain a new IP address. With this change of IP address, all existing connections to the MN as the IP routing mechanisms cannot deliver the data to the correct end-point. Mobile IPv6 (MIPv6) [5] allows a MN to change its location without the need to restart its applications or terminal any ongoing communication based on IP packets. However, MIPv6 suffers from a large signaling load for frequent binding updates on the IP core network and the access network. To overcome this problem, Hierarchical Mobile IPv6 (HMIPv6) [1, 2] uses a local anchor point called Mobility Anchor Point (MAP) to allow the MN to send binding update messages only up to the MAP when it moves within the same MAP domain. This reduces additional signaling cost in the wired network link between the MAP and the CN that exists in MIPv6. But, HMIPv6 cannot reduce the binding update messages in the wireless link. In addition, IETF proposed the fast handoff over HMIPv6 [3, 4, 11] that integrates HMIPv6 and the fast handoff mechanism to reduce the handoff latency by address pre-configuration. Since the fast handoff over HMIPv6 inherits the basic signaling structure of HMIPv6, the signaling cost in the wireless link is unchanged from HMIPv6.

T. Yakhno (Ed.): ADVIS 2004, LNCS 3261, pp. 595–604, 2004.

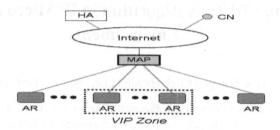

Fig. 1. Network architecture of VIP Zone algorithm

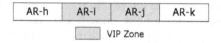

Fig. 2. Definition of VIP Zone

In IP micro mobility environments, the wireless link has far less available bandwidth resources and limited scalability compared to the wired network link [3]. Therefore, the signaling overhead associated with mobility management has a severe effect on the wireless link. Moreover, each cell becomes smaller [6, 8] and this increases handoff rates yielding more signaling overhead in the wireless link.

In this paper, we propose the Virtual-IP(VIP) Zone algorithm to reduce the wireless signaling overhead in areas with a large rate of handoff. The Access Routers (ARs) create dynamically VIP Zone by using the measured handoff rate derived from the history of the handoff contained in ARs. Within the same VIP Zone, even if the handoff of MNs occurs between ARs, the current Care of Address (CoA) of MNs is not changed. As a result, local binding updates are not generated and thus the signaling overhead in the wireless link is greatly reduced. Therefore, VIP Zone algorithm has benefits since MNs within the VIP Zone does not need the registration procedure. First of all, wireless network resource is saved. Second, power consumption of the MN is reduced. Third, interferences in the wireless link are reduced and a better communication quality can be achieved.

The rest of the paper is organized as follows. Section 2 provides the definition of VIP Zone and Section 3 presents the detailed design of VIP Zone algorithm. Section 4 present the simulation results. Finally, we summarize the paper in Section 5.

2   The Definition of VIP Zone

Virtual-IP(VIP) Zone algorithm is based on the hierarchical structure as shown in Fig.1. AR monitors the Movement Status(MS) that has a trace of handoff history. ARs count the number of handoffs to its neighboring ARs. In this framework, ARs create the VIP Zone by using the measured handoff rate derived from the history of the handoff in ARs. For example, we assume the linear AR topology as shown in Fig. 2 and if the condition in (1) is met, AR-i send a request to the MAP to create VIP

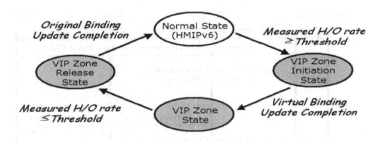

Fig. 3. State diagram of VIP Zone algorithm

Zone with AR-j, and the MAP commands AR-i and AR-j to create a VIP Zone. Therefore a VIP Zone is formed at AR-i and AR-j.

$$rateHO(i, j) \geq Th(HO) \tag{1}$$

where *rateHO(i, j)* is the number of handoff from AR-i to AR-j during a certain period of time, and *Th(HO)* is the threshold value of handoff in AR-i.

Also, if the condition in (2) is met, AR-i sends a request to the MAP to release a VIP Zone with AR-j, and the MAP commands AR-i and AR-j to release a VIP Zone. Therefore a VIP Zone is released at AR-i and AR-j.

$$rateHO(i, j) \leq Th(HO) \tag{2}$$

Here, *Th(HO)* to create and *Th(HO)* to release a VIP have different value from some hysteresis. (i.e., ensure that the trigger condition for the creation of a VIP Zone is sufficiently different from the trigger condition for the release of a VIP Zone to avoid oscillation in stable condition)

3   The Design of VIP Zone Algorithm

As shown in Fig. 3, VIP Zone algorithm operates in four states. First, the Normal State operates as the HMIPv6 until the measured handoff rate of the AR (calculated from the rate of handoffs to its neighboring ARs) exceeds the threshold value and it switches to the VIP Zone Initiate State when the measured handoff rate of the AR exceeds the threshold value. Second, in the VIP Zone Initiate State, the ARs involved in VIP Zone algorithm send the virtual network prefixes to MNs in their area and switches to VIP Zone State. Third, in the VIP Zone State, a VIP Zone is created with ARs with the same virtual network prefix. When the MN moves to a new AR within the same VIP Zone, the handoff occurs through L2 Source Trigger without the current CoA being changed. As a result, local binding updates are not generated and it greatly reduces the signaling cost in the wireless links. Also, when the measured handoff rate of the AR within the VIP Zone drops below the threshold value, the VIP Zone State switches to the VIP Zone Release State. Finally, the VIP Zone Release State switches to the Normal State by sending different original network prefixes in each AR of the VIP Zone.

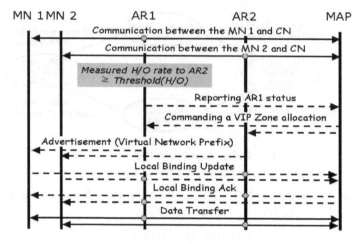

Fig. 4. Message flow in VIP Zone Initiation State

More detailed description of operations of each state is as follows. Note that for simplicity, the paper explains VIP Zone algorithm of only one out of many MNs under each AR and also VIP Zone adapted just two ARs out of many ARs. There are actually many MNs and ARs operating simultaneously by VIP Zone algorithm.

3.1 Normal State (HMIPv6)

In the Normal state, it operates as HMIPv6 proposed by IETF. An MN entering a MAP domain will receive Router Advertisements containing information on one or more local MAPs. The MN can binding its current CoA(LCoA) with an CoA on the subnet of the MAP(RCoA). Acting as a local HA, the MAP receives all packets on behalf of the MN. And then, the MAP encapsulates and forwards them directly to the LCoA of the MN. If the MN changes its current address within a local MAP domain, it only need to register the new address with the MAP. Hence, only the RCoA needs to be registered with the CNs and the HA. The RCoA does not change as long as the MN moves within the same MAP domain. This makes the MN mobility transparent to the CNs it is communicating with. The boundaries of the MAP domain are defined by means of the ARs advertising the MAP information to the attached MNs.

3.2 VIP Zone Initiation State

Fig. 4 shows the message flow in VIP Zone Initiation State. MN1 and MN2 are communicating with AR1 and AR2 respectively in Normal State (binding cache of MN1 – Regional CoA1(RCoA1) : On-link CoA1(LCoA1), binding cache of MN2 – RCoA2 : LCoA2, binding cache of MAP – RCoA1 : LCoA1, RCoA2 : LCoA2). When AR1 detects that the measured handoff rate exceeds the threshold value of HO, AR1 sends its status and IP address of AR2 to the MAP. Then, the MAP commands to AR1 and AR2 to create a VIP Zone.

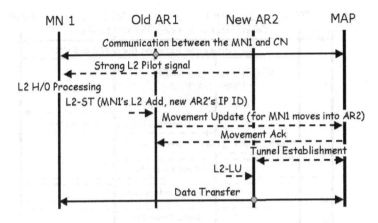

Fig. 5. Message flow of handoff in VIP Zone State

Following the procedure, AR1 and AR2 send a virtual network prefix using Router Advertisement instead of the original network prefix. MN1 and MN2 receive this network prefix and compare to its original network prefix [9]. They each recognize an arrival of a new network prefix and generate new Virtual CoA1(VCoA1) and VCoA2 by auto-configuration [10]. This mechanism causes MN1 and MN2 to perceive as if they are separately being handed over to a new AR, and causes them to change their current CoA. MN1 and MN2 register newly acquired VCoA1 and VCoA2 to the MAP. The MAP updates its binding cache (as MN1 - RCoA1 : VCoA1 : AR1, MN2 - RCoA2 : VCoA2 : AR2). Through this procedure, VIP Zone is performed on AR1 and AR2 and the state then switches to VIP Zone state.

3.3 VIP Zone State

In VIP Zone State, the packet data sent from CN to a MN1 and a MN2 are encapsulated with the new VCoA1 and VCoA2 by the MAP and forwarded to MN1 and MN2 respectively. Fig. 5 shows the message flow of handoff in VIP Zone State. MN1 is communicating with AR1 (binding cache of MN1 and MAP - RCoA1: VCoA1: AR1). When MN1 approaches new AR2, it receives a strong L2 pilot signal and performs L2 handoff. Here, old AR1 determines the IP address of new AR2 using L2 Source Trigger(L2-ST) [4]. L2-ST includes the information such as the L2 ID of the MN1 and the IP ID of new AR2 (it is transferred using the L2 message of L2 handoff. Therefore, it is not the newly generated message from the MN). Through this procedure, old AR1 detects MN1 moving towards new AR2 and sends a Movement Update message to the MAP. Then, the MAP updates its binding cache (as RCoA1: VCoA1: AR2), and establishes a tunnel to new AR2. And new AR2 sets up a host route for VCoA1 of MN1. After that, MN1 moves to new AR2 and sets up a L2 link after completing a L2 handoff. At the same time, since MN1 receives same virtual network prefix as old AR1 from new AR2, it does not perform a binding update.

600   T. Kim et al.

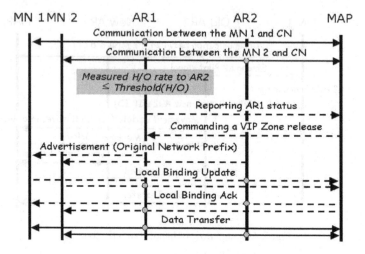

Fig. 6. Message flow in VIP Zone Release State

From this point on, the packet data sent from CN to MN1 is encapsulated with
VCoA1 and forward to MN1 through new AR2 by MAP. Hence, even if MN1 is
handed over to new AR2 in VIP Zone, binding update requests and acknowledges
need not to be sent over the wireless network link. Therefore, the signaling overhead
in the wireless link is greatly reduced. If a MN in VIP Zone state moves to AR out of
VIP Zone or if a MN in outside VIP Zone moves into AR in VIP Zone, in both cases,
MN receives a different network prefix. Hence, it acquires new CoA and performs a
binding update the MAP.

3.4 VIP Zone Release State

Fig. 6 shows the message flow in VIP Zone Release State. MN1 and MN2 are communicating with AR1 and AR2 respectively in VIP Zone State (binding cache of
MN1 – RCoA1 : VCoA1, binding cache of MN2 – RCoA2 : VCoA2, binding cache
of MAP – RCoA1 : VCoA1 : AR1, RCoA2 : VCoA2 : AR2). When AR1 detects that
the measured handoff rate drops below the threshold value of handoff, AR1 sends its
status and the IP address of the AR2 to the MAP. Then the MAP commands AR1 and
AR2 to release a VIP Zone.

Following the procedure, AR1 and AR2 independently send different original
network prefix instead of the virtual network prefix. MN1 and MN2 each receive this
network prefix and compare to its virtual network prefix. And MN1 and MN2 sepa-
rately recognize the arrival of a new network prefix and generate new LCoA1 and
LCoA2 by auto-configuration. MN1 and MN2 register newly acquired LCoA1 and
LCoA2 to the MAP. The MAP updates its binding cache (as RCoA1 : LCoA1,
RCoA2 : LCoA2). Through this procedure, VIP Zone Release State is finished at
AR1 and AR2 and the state switches to Normal State.

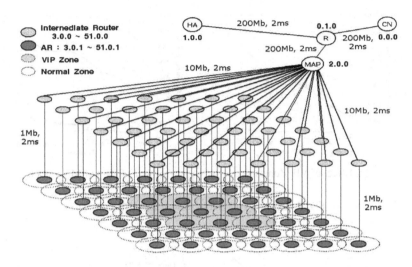

Fig. 7. Simulation network topology

4 Performance Evaluation

4.1 Simulation Environment

We now study the performance of VIP Zone algorithm using our ns simulation environment. This allows us to validate our proposed algorithm. We have used the ns-2.1b7a with wireless extension for our VIP Zone simulation [7]. Fig. 7 shows the network topology used for the simulation. The link characteristics, namely the bandwidth (megabits/sec) and the delay (milliseconds) is also shown. Constant bit rate (CBR) sources are used as traffic sources. A source agent is attached to the CN and sink agents are attached at MNs. The duration of each simulation experiment is 180s. The total number of cells in the MAP area is 49 and the VIP Zone size is varied between 4, 9, 16, 25, and 36 cells. Also, the diameter of each cell is 70 units in the simulation environment and it represents 500m in the real world. If we assume the simulation duration of 180s is equivalent to one hour in the real world, the maximum velocity of 100 km/h then translates to 9 units/s in the simulation. 78 MNs are distributed in 49 cells and cells are attached to a MAP. There is 2 MNs within each cell that belongs to the VIP Zone and rests of the MNs are randomly distributed in the Normal Zone. That is, as the size of the VIP Zone increases, the density of MNs in the cells of VIP Zone is maintained as 2 but the density varies from 1.56 to 0.5 in the Normal Zone. This is because the threshold value to form the VIP Zone is set as 2 MNs per cell. And movement of MN is generated randomly. Also we investigate the impact of the continuous movement and the discrete movement of MNs.

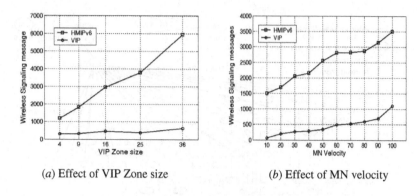

(a) Effect of VIP Zone size   (b) Effect of MN velocity

Fig. 8. Effect of continuous movement (VIP Zone case)

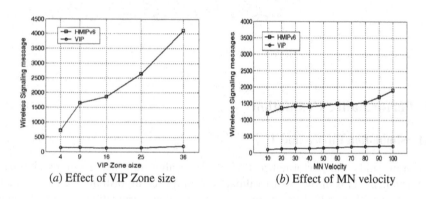

(a) Effect of VIP Zone size   (b) Effect of MN velocity

Fig.9. Effect of discrete movement (VIP Zone case)

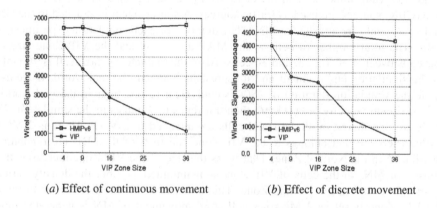

(a) Effect of continuous movement   (b) Effect of discrete movement

Fig. 10. Effect of continuous movement (MAP Area case)

4.2 Simulation Results

We record the wireless signaling counts for VIP Zone and MAP Area.

4.2.1 Wireless Signaling Cost in the VIP Zone

4.2.1.1 VIP Zone Size and MN Velocity with Continuous Movement

All MNs operate with a pause time of 0, supporting continuous movement. This movement pattern has similarity to the fluid flow model which all MNs constantly move. The simulation results for continuous movement are shown in Fig.8. Simulation results imply that the performance of the VIP Zone algorithm is closely related to the size of the VIP Zone and the velocity of the MNs.

4.2.1.2 VIP Zone Size and MN Velocity with Discrete Movement

We also investigate the impact of the discrete movement of mobile nodes that cannot be observed by using the fluid flow model. All MNs are now set to operate with a pause time of 30, supporting discrete movement. In contrast to the continuous movement discussed above, MNs move to a destination, stay there for certain period of time and then move again. The results shown in Fig.9 show that VIP Zone algorithm can reduce the wireless signaling cost for MNs that move infrequently. Besides, the wireless signaling cost savings are little less than the continuous movement. This is because the number of cell boundary crossings is reduced as the MNs move less frequently.

4.2.2 Wireless Signaling Cost in the MAP Area

In this section, we investigate the effect of VIP Zone algorithm within MAP area with 49 ARs. Fig. 10a shows the result in case of continuous movement. In this figure, we can observe that the wireless signaling cost of HMIPv6 maintains constantly in MAP area regardless of the change in the VIP Zone size. In contrast, the overall wireless cost gradually decrease within the MAP area as the VIP Zone size increases in VIP Zone algorithm since binding updates do not occur within the VIP Zone. In addition, Fig. 10b shows the result in case of discrete movement. We can see that the wireless signaling cost savings are similar with those of continuous movement. As a result, VIP Zone algorithm reduces wireless signaling cost within the VIP Zone and thus can reduce significant amount of signaling cost in the MAP area.

5 Conclusion

In this paper, we proposed VIP Zone algorithm that can reduce the wireless signaling overhead in the wireless link. The proposed algorithm establishes the VIP Zone by using the measured handoff rate derived from the history of the handoff in ARs. Simulation results show that the wireless signaling cost in VIP Zone algorithm is much lower than that of the HMIPv6 as the MN velocity and the VIP Zone size increase respectively. Furthermore, if VIP Zone persists for several hours, it will reduce several tens of thousands of binding update message in the wireless link than the

HMIPv6. As VIP Zone algorithm is deployed to reduce the wireless signaling cost in the with a large rate of handoff, we expect that mobile users will be offered with more reliable service in IP micro mobility environments.

References

1. C. Castelluccia, and L. Bellier : Hierarchical Mobile IPv6. Internet Draft, draft-ietf-mobileip-hmipv6-08.txt, work in progress, (2003)
2. Sangheon. Park and Yanghee Choi : Performance Analysis of Hierarchical Mobile IPv6 in IP-based Cellular networks. IPCN, Conference, (2003)
3. Robert Hsieh, Zhe Guang Zhou, Aruna Seneviratne : SMIP : A Seamless Handoff Architecture for Mobile IP. Infocom, (2003)
4. Rajeev Koodli : Fast Handoffs for Mobile IPv6. Internet Draft, draft-ieft-mobileip-fast-mipv6-06.txt, work in progress, (2003)
5. D. Johnson, and C. Perkins : Mobility Support in IPv6. Internet Draft, draft-ietf-mobileip-ipv6-24.txt, work in progress, (2003)
6. R. Berezdivin, R. Breinig, and R. Topp.: Next-Generation Wireless Communication Concepts and Technologies. IEEE Communication Magazine, (2002) 108-116
7. ns2 simulator, version 2.1b7a : http://www.isi.edu/nanam/ns
8. G. Evans, K. Baughan : Visions of 4G. IEEE, Electronics & Communications, Vol.12, No.6. (2000), 293-303
9. T. Narten et al : Neighbor Discovery for IP Version 6. RFC 2461, (1998)
10. S. Thomson and T. Narten : IPv6 stateless address autoconfiguration. RFC2462, IETF, (1998)
11. R. Hsieh and A. Seneviratne : Performance Analysis on Hierarchical Mobile IPv6 with Fast-handoff over TCP, GLOBECOM, Taipei, Taiwan, (2002)

A Network Management Approach for QoS Evaluation of IP Multimedia Services

Yong-Hoon Choi[1], Beomjoon Kim[2], and Jaesung Park[3]

[1] RAN S/W Group, System S/W Dept.,
System Research Lab., LG Electronics Inc.,
LG R&D Complex, 533 Hogye-dong, Dongan-gu,
Anyang-City, Kyongki-do, 431-749, Korea
[2] Standardiztion & System Research Group (SSRG),
Mobile Communication Technology Research Lab., LG Electronics Inc.,
LG R&D Complex, 533 Hogye-dong, Dongan-gu,
Anyang-city, Kyongki-do, 431-749, Korea
[3] Architecture Group, System Lab., LG Electronics Inc.,
LG R&D Complex, 533 Hogye-dong, Dongan-gu,
Anyang-City, Kyongki-do, 431-749, Korea
{dearyonghoon, beom, 4better}@lge.com

Abstract. Since the traditional periodic polling based network management framework is not suitable to understand network-wide behavior of a large-scale Internet, dedicated measurement tools have been required for the precise service evaluation. This paper proposes a measurement scheme to monitor the quality of service (QoS) of IP multimedia services. The proposed scheme gives users the ability to evalaute their services within the current Internet engineering task force (IETF) management framework. We dispatch an Internet control message protocol (ICMP) based test packet to a remote server repeatedly and gather the performance information using the proposed service monitoring management information base (SM MIB). The experiments conducted on the real networks show that the SM MIB is useful for end-to-end QoS monitoring.

1 Introduction

Current network management system uses simple network management protocol (SNMP) [1] for handling managed objects of IP networks. However, SNMP-based management platforms basically can't handle the end-to-end management of Internet. This typical approach suffers from lack of scalability and scope restriction. If an end-to-end user flow traverses multiple Internet service provider (ISP) domains, then the private network management system (NMS) could obtain information from multiple agents to retrieve the customer's end-to-end view of their service. For example, a private NMS can obtain end-to-end performance information through local management interface and inter-carrier management interfaces. This typical approach may cause management traffic and data retrieval time to increase because of querying the various hops and manager-to-manager interactions.

T. Yakhno (Ed.): ADVIS 2004, LNCS 3261, pp. 605–614, 2004.

The problems associated with centralized management architecture, the lack of extensibility and poor support for end-to-end management have been identified and addressed by many researchers. Recently, several mechanisms have been proposed for end-to-end monitoring and control in the literature. Over the last few years, mobile agent/code approach [2] has achieved a widespread interest to decentralize network management tasks. Autonomous delegated agent, which moves network element dynamically, makes an end-to-end management feasible. It gives much flexibility and scalability to a network management system by relieving it from periodic polling. Performance management using management by delegation (MbD) has been studied by Cherkaoui et al. [3], and Bohoris et al. [4]. Work on comparing monitoring cost of MbD and periodic polling was investigated by Liotta et al. [5].

The concept of MbD influences the IETF Distributed Management (DIS-MAN) working group to integrate this concept to its management framework. The IETF efforts to standardize distributed management have focused on SNMP compliant MIB's and Agent. Currently, two types of developments in the Internet community with respect to distributed management can be observed. One is agent extensibility protocol (AgentX) [6], [7] and the other is distributed Internet management with functional MIB's [8, 9, 10, 11, 12, 13]. The goal of AgentX technology is to distribute agent functions to sub-agents. In this approach, however, relatively complex operations on the master agent side are required in order to realize SNMP lexicographic ordering and access control efficiently. The common goal of the functional MIB's is to delegate functionality to network elements, still assuming that the control and coordination of a management task resides within a centralized management system. The Script MIB [13] is one of the good tools for function delegation. It assumes that management functions are defined in the form of executable code/scripts that can be installed on network elements. The Script MIB approach for building distributed management applications has been studied and developed by Schonwalder and Quitteck [14].

RMON (Remote Network Monitoring) [15] is a major step towards decentralization of monitoring statistical analysis functions. It provides an effective and efficient way to monitor subnetwork-wide behavior while reducing the burden on other agents and on management stations. It can monitor the total traffic within a local area network (LAN) segment such as the number of collisions and the number of packets delivered per second. RMON2 [16] has the capability of seeing above the media access control (MAC) layer by reading the header of the enclosed network-layer protocol. This enables the agent to determine the ultimate source and destination and allows a network manager to monitor traffic in great detail. Although RMON MIB provides network-wide information, the data collection is quite a CPU and memory intensive task because RMON operates in *promiscuous* mode, viewing every packet on a subnetwork. It also doesn't handle delay-related information.

Active measurement approach is one of the most promising schemes in terms of end-to-end QoS monitoring. The examples of active measurement architecture in practice today include [17, 18, 19]. Besides, the IETF IP Performance

Metrics (IPPM) working group has proposed measurement architecture and protocols [20, 21, 22]. A drawback is that they need special devices or protocol implementations at both sides of measurement point. Some ICMP extensions such as [23, 24] are useful for performance monitoring. They can give monitoring information to both operators and end-users without any additional protocol implementations unless intermediate routers discard ICMP packets.

Our approach is to utilize dynamic packet rather than dynamic agent (e.g., MbD and AgentX) or passive packet probe (e.g., RMON). For the purpose of management, we designed and implemented a *test packet* and service monitoring (SM) MIB. The test packet is a measurement packet (ICMP extensions in our case) and it is an integral part of the SM MIB. Instead of using our proposed ICMP extensions, different work such as [24] is a good substitute as a test packet. The SM MIB provides a network manager with dynamic end-to-end management information, in particular, QoS information by utilizing *test packets*, which move through network elements. The MIB gives a network manager the ability to obtain end-to-end information, reduces the need to distribute MIB's throughout the network, and cuts the amount of management-related traffic.

2 MIB Design for Service Quality Monitoring

2.1 Test Packet Design and Implementation

In order to extend ICMP message to sophisticated QoS monitoring tool, we developed *test packet*. It gives capabilities for an IP router or a host to measure the quality of service metrics of user flows by dispatching test packets periodically. The test packets are generated periodically and circulate on a user flow. They are interspersed with user traffic at regular intervals to collect the information such as network throughput, packet loss, delay, and delay variation from the routers along user flow. They have the same packet length, type of service (TOS) value (differentiated services (Diffserv) codepoint field for IPv4 and Traffic Class field for IPv6), and followed the same route - They experience the same QoS as user packets. The following information is included in the test packet.

- MPSN: Test packet sequence number.
- TOS value: Type of Service value of a test packet.
- Time Stamp: The time at which a test packet was inserted.

As the packets are received at the destination endpoint, the test packets are replied. They can measure the following QoS metrics.

- RTT (Round Trip Time): A test packet is able to calculate the round-trip time (RTT) by storing the time at which it sends the echo request in the data portion of the message.
- Loss, the end-to-end packet loss of a flow: The end-to-end packet loss ratio can be estimated as the total number of replied test packets over the total number of requested test packets.

```
smControlEntry ::=
    INDEX {smControlIndex}


smControlIndex            ←              INTEGER
smControlDataSource                      INTEGER
smControlSourceAddressType               InetAddressType
smControlSourceAddress                   InetAddress
smControlDestAddressType                 InetAddressType
smControlDestAddress                     InetAddress
smControlAdminStatus                     INTEGER
smControlOperStatus                      INTEGER
smControlDSField                         Unsigned32
smControlTimeOut                         Unsigned32
smControlProbeInterval                   Unsigned32
smControlTotalProbe                      Unsigned32
smControlMaxRows                         Unsigned32
smControlDataSize                        Unsinged32
smControlRowStatus                       RowStatus
```

```
smRequestEntry ::=
    INDEX {smControlIndex, smRequestIndex}


smRequestIndex         ←               INTEGER
smRequestSeqNumber                     INTEGER
smRequestTimeStamp                     Unsigned32
```

```
smReplyEntry ::=
    INDEX {smControlIndex, smReplyIndex}


smReplyIndex          ←                INTEGER
smReplySeqNumber                       INTEGER
smReplyTimeStamp                       Unsigned32
```

Fig. 1. Logical structure of the SM MIB. The entries represent the three tables of the MIB. Table index components used to identify entries are indicated by an arrow

– Jitter, the variation of latency between packets: The end-to-end packet delay variation can be estimated as test packet delay variation.

We implemented the test packet that works with both IPv4 and IPv6 based on the publicly available ping program source.

2.2 Service Monitoring MIB Design and Implementation

The SM MIB is an SNMP-compliant MIB for the delegation of dynamic packets to a destination endpoint and for gathering end-to-end QoS management information. Fig. 1 shows the logical structure of the SM MIB. It consists of three tables: one control table (named smControlTable) which specifies the destination and the details of sampling function, and two data tables (named smRequestTable and smReplyTable), which record the data.

For each of the K rows of smControlTable, there is a set of rows of smRequestTable and smReplyTable. For information of activated test flow specified by the row in the smControlTable, the data tables contain one row for each QoS information delivered by one test packet. Thus, as long as the control table information is not changed, one row is added to the smReplyTable each time a test packet arrives to the agent. The data tables are indexed by smRequestIndex (or smReplyIndex) and smRequestSeqNum (or smReplySeqNum).

smControlMaxRows, one of the control table objects limits the size of the data table. The number of rows in the data table can be expressed as

$$\sum_{i=0}^{N} \text{smControlMaxRows}(i)$$

where, smControlMaxRows(i) is value of smControlMaxRows for row i of the smControlTable, and N is the number of rows in the smControlTable.

After a new row is defined in the smControlTable, a new test flow starts. In other words, the network manager starts a test flow by writing an smControlEntry. Whenever a new test packet is captured by local network element, a new row is added to the data table. Once the number of rows for a data table becomes equal to smControlMaxRows, the set of rows for that test flow functions as a circular buffer. As each new row is added to the set, the oldest row associated with this test flow is deleted. The object is to prevent resource abuse; however, if a network manager sets smControlMaxRows too small, it may cause problems such that management information might be deleted before the manager obtains the information using Get/GetBulk request message. Each instances of the data table associated with smControlRowStatus will be deleted (associated test flow is deactivated) by the agent if this smControlRowStatus is *destroy (6)*.

A prototype of the SNMP agent including SM MIB was built using ucd-snmp-4.2.6 package [25]. If the SM MIB is deployed in DiffServ platform, the TOS field is interpreted in conformance with the definition given in [26].

3   Results and Discussions

We have performed a number of measurement experiments on Internet. We varied the multimedia sources (Live TV sites, voice over IP (VoIP) services, video conferencing, and VoD/AoD), the time of day, and the day of the week. We evaluate service quality in terms of RTT, jitter, and packet loss rate.

3.1   In-Service Monitoring

We sent test packets with 36-byte payload (which is the same to the user datagram protocol (UDP) payload size of user packets) at 2 s regular intervals to Internet telephony site, www.dialpad.co.kr during call holding time, 60 minutes. Fig. 2 and 3 show the value of data table instances of SM MIB as graphs. For RTT, jitter and packet loss, the measured data are sampled with rate of 30/m

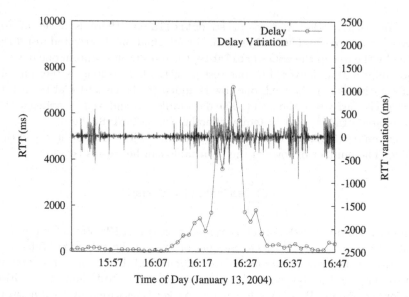

Fig. 2. RTT and RTT variation between site at Yonsei University in Seoul, Korea and IP Telephony site (www.dialpad.co.kr) in Korea. In-service Monitoring during 15:47 (PM) January 13, 2004 - 16:47 (PM) January 13, 2004

during call holding time 60 m. We obtained 1800 samples for this flow. During the experimentation, from 16:10pm to 16:31pm, we offered high background load to simulate delay and packet loss.

RTT and Jitter. The circled line of Fig. 2 shows the RTT versus each monitoring time. The RTT values fluctuate from 12 ms to 7789 ms and the average RTT and standard deviation are 837.951 ms and 1501.671 ms, respectively. As shown in Fig. 2, RTT values increase when we offered high background load. The solid line of Fig. 2 shows the jitter versus monitoring time. The jitter fluctuates from -1007 ms to 1073 ms and the average jitter and standard deviation are 0.907 ms and 157.184 ms, respectively.

Data Accuracy. For end-to-end delay variation, the measured data are sampled with the rate of λ_i (test packet generation rate) during call holding time $1/\beta_i$. We can get λ_i/β_i samples for user flow i. Suppose that $X_1, \cdots, X_n$ is a sample from a normal population having unknown real traffic mean end-to-end delay variation μ and variance σ^2. It is clear that $\sum_{i=1}^{n} X_i/n$ is the maximum likelihood estimator for μ. Since the sample mean $\overline{X}$ does not exactly equal μ, we specify an interval for which we have a certain degree of confidence that μ lies within. To obtain such an interval we make use of probability distribution of the point estimator. For example, 95% confidence interval for μ are:

$$\left(\overline{X} - 1.96\sigma/\sqrt{\lambda_i/\beta_i}, \quad \overline{X} + 1.96\sigma/\sqrt{\lambda_i/\beta_i} \right) \tag{1}$$

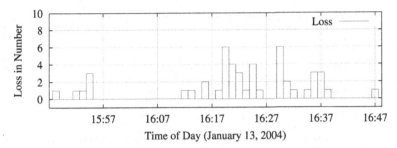

Fig. 3. Number of test packet losses between site at Yonsei University in Seoul, Korea and IP Telephony site (www.dialpad.co.kr) in Korea. In-Service Monitoring during 15:47 (PM) January 13, 2004–16:47 (PM) January 13, 2004

assuming that the delay variation samples have normal distribution. The confidence interval of the average jitter is (0.906993 ms, 0.907007 ms) with 95% confidence level.

Packet Loss. We have monitored 48 test packet losses from 1800 samples during 60 m. By the results, we can get 2.67% packet loss ratio for this application. We monitored small number of packet drops under the low background load. In this experiment, we observed that the packet loss behavior is affected by delay or delay variation.

3.2 Long Time Scale Service Estimation

Every hour, we sent 11 test packets with 1000-byte payload to Live TV site, www.kbs.co.kr at 2 s intervals. This is repeated for a week. This site is located at a distance of 9 hops from our workstation. In order to experience the same QoS as the user packets, the test packet size set to 1,000 bytes, which is the same to the UDP payload size of user packets. The RTT, jitter, and the number of test packet losses are recorded at SM MIB.

Fig. 4 shows the round trip time (RTT) and jitter versus each monitoring time. After control table entry being created, the first `smRequestTable` row is created right away, and the first `smReplyTable` row is created at t = 135 ms. The average time gap between the creation of request table row and relevant reply table row is 717.594 ms for this flow. For RTT, jitter and packet loss, the measured data are sampled with rate of 10/h [1] during a week. We obtained 1710 samples for this flow.

RTT and Jitter. Fig. 4(a) shows the RTT versus each monitoring time. The RTT values fluctuate from 11 ms to 10366 ms and the average RTT and standard deviation are 717.594 ms and 1887.739 ms, respectively. As shown in Fig. 4(a), RTT values decrease during the weekend. Fig. 4(b) shows the jitter versus each

---

[1] The first test packet is discarded because it is assumed that it is slow due to priming address resolution protocol (ARP) cache.

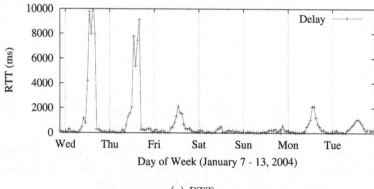

(a) RTT

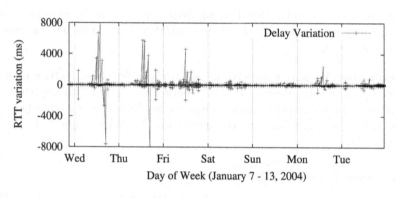

(b) Jitter

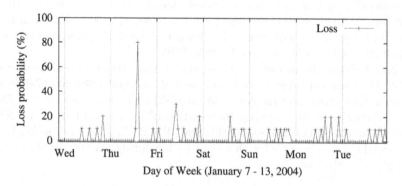

(c) Packet loss ratio

Fig. 4. RTT, jitter, and packet loss ratio between site at Yonsei University in Seoul, Korea and Live TV site (www.kbs.co.kr) in Korea. Weekly plots during 22:16 (PM) January 7, 2004–21:24 (PM) January 13, 2004

monitoring time. The jitter fluctuates from -10776 ms to 8255 ms and the average jitter and standard deviation are -0.00058 ms 618.944 ms, respectively. If we assume that the delay variation follow normal distribution, the confidence interval of the average jitter is (-0.00055 ms, 0.00061 ms) with 95% confidence level.

Packet Loss. Fig. 4(c) shows the packet loss versus every monitoring time. We have monitored 54 test packet drops from 1710 samples for a week. By the results, we can get 3.158% packet loss ratio.

We collected samples at periodic intervals. Currently our SM MIB does not support other sampling methods such as Poisson and Geometric sampling. Periodic sampling is particularly attractive because of its simplicity, but it may suffer from potential problem: If the metric being measured itself exhibits periodic behavior, then there is a possibility that the sampling will observe only part of the periodic behavior if the period happen to agree.

4   Conclusions

Our goal is to suggest a practical solution for end-to-end management, still maintaining typical manager-agent paradigm. This paper proposed a new MIB approach, called SM MIB. It offers a convenient solution for end-to-end QoS management. It provides a network manager with dynamic end-to-end management information by utilizing special test packets, which move through network elements dynamically. The MIB gives the network manager the ability to obtain end-to-end information, reduces the need to distribute MIB's throughout the network, and cuts the amount of management-related traffic. The implementation and maintenance of the MIB are simple because the method requires no special management functions at every intermediate router in the network, but just requires us to implement the SM MIB at edge routers/end hosts only.

The real examples showed that the SM MIB is useful for a real-time in-service monitoring tool as well as a long time scale load analysis tool. The accuracy of obtained data depends on the number of samples. We specified an interval for which we have 95% degree of confidence that measured RTT and jitter lies within.

Finally, we address the weakness of our work. SM MIB does not guarantee 100% accuracy due to the unavoidable errors of periodic sampling method and the limitations of test packet capabilities. The inaccuracy of the proposed test packet can be overcome by improving functionality of the packet, such as in [21] and [24]. We expect that the SM MIB will be useful for end-to-end service evaluation, as well as QoS monitoring.

References

1. J. Case et al.: A Simple Network Management Protocol (SNMP). RFC 1157, (1990).
2. G. Goldszmidt: Distributed Management by Delegation. Ph. D. Dissertation, Columbia University (1996).

3. O. Cherkaoui et al.: QOS Metrics tool using management by delegation. IEEE Network Operation and Management Symposium (NOMS'98) New Orleans LA, USA, (1998) 836-839.
4. C. Bohoris et al.: Using Mobile Agents for Network Performance Management. IEEE Network Operation and Management Symposium (NOMS'2000), Honolulu Hawaii, USA, (2000) 637-652.
5. A. Liotta et al.: Modeling Network and System Monitoring over the Internet with Mobile Agents. IEEE Network Operation and Management Symposium (NOMS'98) New Orleans LA, USA, (1998) 303-312.
6. M. Daniele et al: Agent Extensibility (AgentX) Protocol Version 1. RFC 2741, (2000).
7. L. Heintz et al: Definitions of Managed Objects for Extensible SNMP Agents. RFC 2742, (2000).
8. R. Kavasseri and B. Stewart: Distributed Management Expression MIB. RFC 2982, (2000).
9. R. Kavasseri and B. Stewart: Event MIB. RFC2981, (2000).
10. D. Levi and J. Schonwalder: Definitions of Managed Objects for Scheduling Management Operations. RFC 3231, (2002).
11. K. White: Definitions of Managed Objects for Remote Ping, Traceroute, and Lookup Operations. RFC 2925, (2000).
12. R. Kavasseri: Notification Log MIB. RFC 3014, (2000).
13. D. Levi and J. Schonwalder: Definitions of Managed Objects for the Delegation of Management Scripts. RFC 3165, (2001).
14. J. Schonwalder et al.: Building Distributed Management Applications with the IETF Script MIB. IEEE J. on Selected Areas in Comm., 18 (5) (2000), 702-714.
15. S. Waldbusser: Remote Network Monitoring Management Information Base. RFC 2819, (2000).
16. S. Waldbusser: Remote Network Monitoring Management Information Base Version 2 using SMIv2. RFC 2021, (1997).
17. The Skitter Project, Online: http://www.caida.org/tools/measurement/skitter/
18. The Surveyor Project, Online: http://www.advanced.org/surveyor and http://betelgeuse.advanced.org/csg-ippm/
19. V. Paxson et al: An Architecture for Large-Scale Internet Measurement. IEEE Comm. Mgz., 36 (8) (1998), 48-54.
20. V. Paxson et al.: Framework for IP Performance Metrics. RFC 2330, (1998).
21. G. Almes et al.: A One-way Delay Metric for IPPM. RFC 2679, (1999).
22. G. Almes et al.: A One-way Packet Loss Metric for IPPM. RFC 2680, (1999).
23. W. Matthews and L. Cottrell: The PingER Project: Active Internet Performance Monitoring for the HENP Community. IEEE Comm. Mgz., (2000) 130-136.
24. A. Elwalid: ICMP Extensions for One-Way Performance Metrics. Internet Draft: draft-elwalid-icmp-ext-01.txt, (2000)
25. UCD-SNMP-4.2.6, Online: http://sourceforge.net/project/showfiles.php, (2002).
26. S. Blake et al.: An Architecture for Differentiated Services. RFC 2475, (1998).

Author Index